Solutions Manual

SAXON MATH™

8/7

with **Prealgebra**

Stephen Hake

John Saxon

SAXON™
PUBLISHERS

Printed in the United States of America

ISBN: 1-59141-276-5

Manufacturing Code: 01S0403

Lesson 1, Lesson Practice

a. **\$0.45 per glass; 45¢ per glass**

b. **0**

c. Product of 4 and 4 = 16
Sum of 4 and 4 = 8

$$\begin{array}{r} \mathbf{2} \\ 8\overline{)16} \\ \underline{16} \\ 0 \end{array}$$

d.
$$\begin{array}{r} \overset{1}{\$1}.75 \\ \$0.60 \\ +\ \$3.00 \\ \hline \mathbf{\$5.35} \end{array}$$

e.
$$\begin{array}{r} \$\ \overset{1}{\not 2}.\ \overset{9}{\not 0}{}^{1}0 \\ -\ \$\ 0.\ 4\ 7 \\ \hline \mathbf{\$\ 1.\ 5\ 3} \end{array}$$

f.
$$\begin{array}{r} \$0.65 \\ \times\quad 5 \\ \hline \mathbf{\$3.25} \end{array}$$

g.
$$\begin{array}{r} 250 \\ \times\ 24 \\ \hline 1000 \\ 500 \\ \hline \mathbf{6000} \end{array}$$

h.
$$\begin{array}{r} \mathbf{\$4.80} \\ 5\overline{)\$24.00} \\ \underline{20} \\ 4\,0 \\ \underline{4\,0} \\ 0 \end{array}$$

i.
$$\begin{array}{r} \mathbf{13} \\ 18\overline{)234} \\ \underline{18} \\ 54 \\ \underline{54} \\ 0 \end{array}$$

j.
$$\begin{array}{r} 20 \\ +\ \ 4 \\ \hline \mathbf{24} \end{array}$$

k.
$$\begin{array}{r} 20 \\ -\ \ 4 \\ \hline \mathbf{16} \end{array}$$

l.
$$\begin{array}{r} 20 \\ \times\ \ 4 \\ \hline \mathbf{80} \end{array}$$

m.
$$\begin{array}{r} \mathbf{5} \\ 4\overline{)20} \end{array}$$

Lesson 1, Mixed Practice

1. Product of 5 and 6 = 30
Sum of 5 and 6 = 11
30 − 11 = **19**

2.
$$\begin{array}{r} 8 \\ +\ 9 \\ \hline \mathbf{17} \end{array}$$

3. $\begin{array}{r} 8 \\ 4\overline{)\text{dividend}} \end{array}$; the dividend is **32**

4. Product of 6 and 6 = 36
Sum of 6 and 6 = 12

$$\begin{array}{r} \mathbf{3} \\ 12\overline{)36} \\ \underline{36} \\ 0 \end{array}$$

5. **Addition, subtraction, multiplication, and division**

6. (a) 12 + 4 = **16**

(b) 12 − 4 = **8**

(c) 12 · 4 = **48**

(d) $\frac{12}{4}$ = **3**

7.
$$\begin{array}{r} \$\ \overset{3}{\not 4}{}^{1}3.\ \overset{6}{\not 7}{}^{1}4 \\ -\ \$\ 1\ 6.\ 5\ 9 \\ \hline \mathbf{\$\ 2\ 7.\ 1\ 5} \end{array}$$

8.
$$\begin{array}{r} 64 \\ \times\ 37 \\ \hline 448 \\ 192 \\ \hline \mathbf{2368} \end{array}$$

9.
$$\begin{array}{r} 7 \\ 8 \\ 4 \\ 6 \\ 9 \\ 3 \\ 5 \\ +\ 7 \\ \hline \mathbf{49} \end{array}$$

10.
$$\begin{array}{r} \overset{1\,2}{364} \\ 52 \\ 867 \\ +\quad 9 \\ \hline \mathbf{1292} \end{array}$$

11.
$$\begin{array}{r} \overset{3}{\cancel{4}}\,\overset{9}{\cancel{0}}\,\overset{9}{\cancel{0}}{}^{1}0 \\ -\ 3\,6\,2\,5 \\ \hline \mathbf{3\,7\,5} \end{array}$$

12.
$$\begin{array}{r} 316 \\ \times\quad 18 \\ \hline 2528 \\ 316 \\ \hline \mathbf{5688} \end{array}$$

13.
$$\begin{array}{r} \mathbf{\$2.18} \\ 20\overline{)\$43.60} \\ \underline{40} \\ 3\,6 \\ \underline{2\,0} \\ 160 \\ \underline{160} \\ 0 \end{array}$$

14.
$$\begin{array}{r} 300 \\ \times\quad 40 \\ \hline \mathbf{12{,}000} \end{array}$$

15.
$$\begin{array}{r} 12 \\ \times\ 8 \\ \hline 96 \end{array} \qquad \begin{array}{r} 96 \\ \times\ 0 \\ \hline \mathbf{0} \end{array}$$

16.
$$\begin{array}{r} \mathbf{309} \\ 12\overline{)3708} \\ \underline{36} \\ 108 \\ \underline{108} \\ 0 \end{array}$$

17.
$$\begin{array}{r} 365 \\ \times\quad 20 \\ \hline \mathbf{7300} \end{array}$$

18.
$$\begin{array}{r} \mathbf{30\ R\,17} \\ 25\overline{)767} \\ \underline{75} \\ 17 \\ \underline{0} \\ 17 \end{array}$$

19.
$$\begin{array}{r} 30 \\ \times\quad 40 \\ \hline \mathbf{1200} \end{array}$$

20.
$$\begin{array}{r} \$\,\overset{0}{\cancel{1}}\,\overset{9}{\cancel{0}}.\,\overset{9}{\cancel{0}}{}^{1}0 \\ -\quad \$\,2.\,3\,4 \\ \hline \mathbf{\$\,7.\,6\,6} \end{array}$$

21.
$$\begin{array}{r} \overset{3}{\cancel{4}}\,\overset{9}{\cancel{0}}{}^{1}1\,7 \\ -\ 3\,9\,5\,2 \\ \hline \mathbf{6\,5} \end{array}$$

22.
$$\begin{array}{r} \$2.50 \\ \times\qquad 80 \\ \hline \mathbf{\$200.00} \end{array}$$

23.
$$\begin{array}{r} \$2.50 \\ \times\qquad 20 \\ \hline \mathbf{\$50.00} \end{array}$$

24.
$$\begin{array}{r} \mathbf{40} \\ 14\overline{)560} \\ \underline{56} \\ 0 \\ \underline{0} \\ 0 \end{array}$$

25.
$$\begin{array}{r} \$1.25 \\ 8\overline{)\$10.00} \\ \underline{8} \\ 2\,0 \\ \underline{1\,6} \\ 40 \\ \underline{40} \\ 0 \end{array}$$

26. **Natural numbers**

27. **$0.25; 25¢**

28. **All counting numbers are whole numbers.**

29. **Quotient**

30. **Minuend − subtrahend = difference**

Lesson 2, Lesson Practice

a. **The additive identity is zero. The multiplicative identity is 1.**

b. **Division**

c. $(x + y) + z = x + (y + z)$
Numerical answers may vary.

d. **Commutative property of multiplication**

e. $(5 + 4) + 3 = (9) + 3 = \mathbf{12}$

f. $5 + (4 + 3) = 5 + (7) = \mathbf{12}$

g. $(10 - 5) - 3 = (5) - 3 = \mathbf{2}$

h. $10 - (5 - 3) = 10 - (2) = \mathbf{8}$

i. $(6 \cdot 2) \cdot 5 = (12) \cdot 5 = \mathbf{60}$

j. $6 \cdot (2 \cdot 5) = 6 \cdot (10) = \mathbf{60}$

k. $(12 \div 6) \div 2 = (2) \div 2 = \mathbf{1}$

l. $12 \div (6 \div 2) = 12 \div (3) = \mathbf{4}$

m. $k = n \cdot n$
Eighth term: $k = 8 \cdot 8 = \mathbf{64}$
Ninth term: $k = 9 \cdot 9 = \mathbf{81}$
Tenth term: $k = 10 \cdot 10 = \mathbf{100}$

n. **Each term in the sequence can be found by doubling the preceding term; 16, 32, 64.**

o. $k = (2n) - 1$
$k = (2 \cdot 1) - 1 = (2) - 1 = 1$
$k = (2 \cdot 2) - 1 = (4) - 1 = 3$
$k = (2 \cdot 3) - 1 = (6) - 1 = 5$
$k = (2 \cdot 4) - 1 = (8) - 1 = 7$
First four terms: **1, 3, 5, 7**

Lesson 2, Mixed Practice

1. Product of 2 and 3 = 6
Sum of 4 and 5 = 9
$9 - 6 = \mathbf{3}$

2. **$0.04; 4¢**

3. **75¢ per glass; $0.75 per glass**

4. **Subtraction**

5.
$$\begin{array}{r} \mathbf{15} \\ 4\overline{)60} \\ \underline{4} \\ 20 \\ \underline{20} \\ 0 \end{array}$$

6. **3 × 5 = 15   15 ÷ 5 = 3**
5 × 3 = 15   15 ÷ 3 = 5

7. **Each term in the sequence can be found by multiplying the preceding term by ten.**
$100(10) = \mathbf{1000}$
$1000(10) = \mathbf{10{,}000}$

8.
$$\begin{array}{r} \$\,\overset{1}{\cancel{2}}\,\overset{9}{\cancel{0}}.\,\overset{9}{\cancel{0}}{}^{1}0 \\ -\ \$\,1\,4.\,7\,9 \\ \hline \mathbf{\$\ 5.\,2\,1} \end{array}$$

9.
$$\begin{array}{r} \$1.54 \\ \times\quad 7 \\ \hline \mathbf{\$10.78} \end{array}$$

10. $\begin{array}{r} \textbf{\$3.75} \\ 8\overline{)\$30.00} \\ \underline{24} \\ 6\,0 \\ \underline{5\,6} \\ 40 \\ \underline{40} \\ 0 \end{array}$

11. $\begin{array}{r} \$4.36 \\ \$0.75 \\ \$12.00 \\ +\ \$0.06 \\ \hline \textbf{\$17.17} \end{array}$

12. $\begin{array}{r} \$4.89 \\ +\ \$0.74 \\ \hline \$5.63 \end{array}$ $\begin{array}{r} \$10.00 \\ -\ \$5.63 \\ \hline \textbf{\$4.37} \end{array}$

13. $\begin{array}{r} 8 \\ 5 \\ 4 \\ 6 \\ 5 \\ 4 \\ 3 \\ 7 \\ 2 \\ 4 \\ 1 \\ +\ 8 \\ \hline \textbf{57} \end{array}$

14. $\begin{array}{r} \textbf{207} \\ 15\overline{)3105} \\ \underline{30} \\ 10 \\ \underline{0} \\ 105 \\ \underline{105} \\ 0 \end{array}$

15. $\begin{array}{r} \textbf{40 R 30} \\ 40\overline{)1630} \\ \underline{160} \\ 30 \\ \underline{0} \\ 30 \end{array}$

16. $9 \div 3 = 3$ $\begin{array}{r} \textbf{27} \\ 3\overline{)81} \\ \underline{6} \\ 21 \\ \underline{21} \\ 0 \end{array}$

17. $\begin{array}{r} 9 \\ 9\overline{)81} \\ \underline{81} \\ 0 \end{array}$ $9 \div 3 = \mathbf{3}$

18. $\begin{array}{r} \$3.75 \\ \times\ \ 10 \\ \hline \textbf{\$37.50} \end{array}$

19. $\begin{array}{r} 450 \\ -\ 78 \\ \hline 372 \end{array}$ $\begin{array}{r} 3167 \\ -\ 372 \\ \hline \textbf{2795} \end{array}$

20. $\begin{array}{r} 3167 \\ -\ 450 \\ \hline 2717 \end{array}$ $\begin{array}{r} 2717 \\ -\ 78 \\ \hline \textbf{2639} \end{array}$

21. $\begin{array}{r} \textbf{\$1.25} \\ 16\overline{)\$20.00} \\ \underline{16} \\ 4\,0 \\ \underline{3\,2} \\ 80 \\ \underline{80} \\ 0 \end{array}$

22. $\begin{array}{r} 70 \\ \times\ 800 \\ \hline \textbf{56,000} \end{array}$

23. $\begin{array}{r} 3714 \\ 268 \\ 47 \\ +\ \ 9 \\ \hline \textbf{4038} \end{array}$

24. $\begin{array}{r} 5 \\ \times\ 4 \\ \hline 20 \end{array}$ $\begin{array}{r} 20 \\ \times\ 3 \\ \hline 60 \end{array}$ $\begin{array}{r} 60 \\ \times\ 2 \\ \hline 120 \end{array}$ $\begin{array}{r} 120 \\ \times\ \ 1 \\ \hline \textbf{120} \end{array}$

25.
$$\begin{array}{r} \$1.47 \\ +\ \$8.00 \\ \hline \$9.47 \end{array} \qquad \begin{array}{r} \$\,\overset{1}{\cancel{2}}\,\overset{9}{\cancel{0}}.\,\overset{9}{\cancel{0}}{}^{1}0 \\ -\ \ \$\,9.\,4\,7 \\ \hline \mathbf{\$\,1\,0.\,5\,3} \end{array}$$

26.
$$\begin{array}{r} \$0.45 \\ \times \quad 30 \\ \hline \mathbf{\$13.50} \end{array}$$

27. (a) **Property of zero for multiplication**

(b) **Identity property of multiplication**

28. (a) $18 - 3 = \mathbf{15}$

(b)
$$\begin{array}{r} 18 \\ \times \ \ 3 \\ \hline \mathbf{54} \end{array}$$

(c) $\frac{18}{3} = \mathbf{6}$

(d) $18 + 3 = \mathbf{21}$

29. Zero is called the additive identity because when zero is added to another number, the sum is identical to that number.

30. Dividend ÷ divisor = quotient

Lesson 3, Lesson Practice

a.
$$\begin{array}{r} \overset{2}{\cancel{3}}{}^{1}1 \\ -\ 1\,2 \\ \hline \mathbf{1\,9} \end{array}$$

b.
$$\begin{array}{r} 15 \\ +\ 24 \\ \hline \mathbf{39} \end{array}$$

c.
$$\begin{array}{r} \mathbf{12} \\ 15\overline{)180} \\ \underline{15} \\ 30 \\ \underline{30} \\ 0 \end{array}$$

d.
$$\begin{array}{r} 12 \\ \times \ \ 8 \\ \hline \mathbf{96} \end{array}$$

e.
$$\begin{array}{r} \mathbf{30} \\ 14\overline{)420} \\ \underline{42} \\ 00 \\ \underline{0} \\ 0 \end{array}$$

f.
$$\begin{array}{r} \overset{3}{\cancel{4}}{}^{1}3 \\ -\ 2\,6 \\ \hline \mathbf{1\,7} \end{array}$$

g.
$$\begin{array}{r} 51 \\ -\ 20 \\ \hline \mathbf{31} \end{array}$$

h.
$$\begin{array}{r} \mathbf{52} \\ 7\overline{)364} \\ \underline{35} \\ 14 \\ \underline{14} \\ 0 \end{array}$$

i.
$$\begin{array}{r} \mathbf{2} \\ 12\overline{)24} \\ \underline{24} \\ 0 \end{array}$$

j. $3 + 6 + 12 + 5 = 26$
$30 - 26 = \mathbf{4}$

Lesson 3, Mixed Practice

1. Product of 4 and 4 = 16
Sum of 4 and 4 = 8
$\frac{16}{8} = \mathbf{2}$

2. Add the subtrahend and the difference to find the minuend.

3. Associative property of addition

4.
$$\begin{array}{r} \overset{1}{\cancel{2}}{}^{1}1 \\ -\ \ \ 7 \\ \hline \mathbf{1\,4} \end{array}$$

5. $\mathbf{3 \cdot 4 = 4 \cdot 3}$

6. (1) $k = 3(1) = 3$

(2) $k = 3(2) = 6$

(3) $k = 3(3) = 9$

(4) $k = 3(4) = 12$

3, 6, 9, 12

7.
$$\begin{array}{r} {}^{0}\ {}^{10} \\ \not{1}\,\not{1}{}^{1}2 \\ -\ \ 8\ 3 \\ \hline 2\ 9 \end{array}$$

$x =$ **29**

8.
$$\begin{array}{r} {}^{8} \\ \not{9}{}^{1}6 \\ -\ 2\ 7 \\ \hline 6\ 9 \end{array}$$

$r =$ **69**

9.
$$\begin{array}{r} 17 \\ 7\overline{)119} \\ 7 \\ \hline 49 \\ 49 \\ \hline 0 \end{array}$$

$k =$ **17**

10.
$$\begin{array}{r} {}^{2}\ {}^{9} \\ \not{3}\,\not{0}{}^{1}0 \\ -\ 1\ 2\ 7 \\ \hline 1\ 7\ 3 \end{array}$$

$z =$ **173**

11.
$$\begin{array}{r} 731 \\ +\ 137 \\ \hline 868 \end{array}$$

$m =$ **868**

12.
$$\begin{array}{r} 16 \\ 25\overline{)400} \\ 25 \\ \hline 150 \\ 150 \\ \hline 0 \end{array}$$

$n =$ **16**

13.
$$\begin{array}{r} 25 \\ 25\overline{)625} \\ 50 \\ \hline 125 \\ 125 \\ \hline 0 \end{array}$$

$w =$ **25**

14.
$$\begin{array}{r} 700 \\ \times\ \ \ 60 \\ \hline 42{,}000 \end{array}$$

$x =$ **42,000**

15. (a) $\frac{20}{5} =$ **4**

(b) $20 - 5 =$ **15**

(c) $20(5) =$ **100**

(d) $20 + 5 =$ **25**

16. $16 \div 2 = 8$
$$\begin{array}{r} \mathbf{12} \\ 8\overline{)96} \\ 8 \\ \hline 16 \\ 16 \\ \hline 0 \end{array}$$

17.
$$\begin{array}{r} 6 \\ 16\overline{)96} \\ 96 \\ \hline 0 \end{array}$$
$6 \div 2 =$ **3**

18.
$$\begin{array}{r} {}^{1\,1\ \ 1} \\ \$16.47 \\ \$15.00 \\ +\ \ \$0.63 \\ \hline \mathbf{\$32.10} \end{array}$$

19.
$$\begin{array}{r} {}^{1\ 1} \\ \$31.75 \\ +\ \ \$6.48 \\ \hline \$38.23 \end{array} \qquad \begin{array}{r} {}^{4\ \ 9\ \ 9} \\ \$\,\not{5}\,\not{0}.\,\not{0}{}^{1}0 \\ -\ \$\,3\,8.\,2\,3 \\ \hline \mathbf{\$\,1\,1.\,7\,7} \end{array}$$

20.
$$\begin{array}{r} 47 \\ \times\ 39 \\ \hline 423 \\ 141\ \ \\ \hline \mathbf{1833} \end{array}$$

21.
$$\begin{array}{r} \$8.79 \\ \times\ \ \ \ \ 80 \\ \hline \mathbf{\$703.20} \end{array}$$

22.
$$\begin{array}{r} \mathbf{158} \\ 30\overline{)4740} \\ 30\ \ \\ \hline 174\ \\ 150\ \\ \hline 240 \\ 240 \\ \hline 0 \end{array}$$

23.
$$\begin{array}{r} {}^{2\ \ 16} \\ \not{3}\,\not{7}{}^{1}4 \\ -\ \ \ 8\ 7 \\ \hline 2\ 8\ 7 \end{array} \qquad \begin{array}{r} {}^{0\ \,10\ \,9} \\ \not{1}\,\not{1}\,\not{0}{}^{1}0 \\ -\ \ 2\ 8\ 7 \\ \hline \mathbf{8\ 1\ 3} \end{array}$$

24.

$$\begin{array}{r} 1100 \\ -\ 374 \\ \hline 726 \end{array} \qquad \begin{array}{r} 726 \\ -\ 87 \\ \hline \mathbf{639} \end{array}$$

25.

$$\begin{array}{r} 4736 \\ 271 \\ 9 \\ +\ 88 \\ \hline \mathbf{5104} \end{array}$$

26.

$$\begin{array}{r} 30,145 \\ -\ 4\,299 \\ \hline \mathbf{25,846} \end{array}$$

27.

$$\begin{array}{r} \mathbf{60\ R\ 4} \\ 35\overline{)2104} \\ \underline{210} \\ 04 \\ \underline{0} \\ 4 \end{array}$$

28.

$$\begin{array}{r} \mathbf{\$1.25} \\ 32\overline{)\$40.00} \\ \underline{32} \\ 8\,0 \\ \underline{6\,4} \\ 1\,60 \\ \underline{1\,60} \\ 0 \end{array}$$

29.

$$\begin{array}{r} \$0.48 \\ \times\ \ 40 \\ \hline \mathbf{\$19.20} \end{array}$$

30. **One is the multiplicative identity because when any given number is multiplied by 1, the product is identical to the given number.**

Lesson 4, Lesson Practice

a.

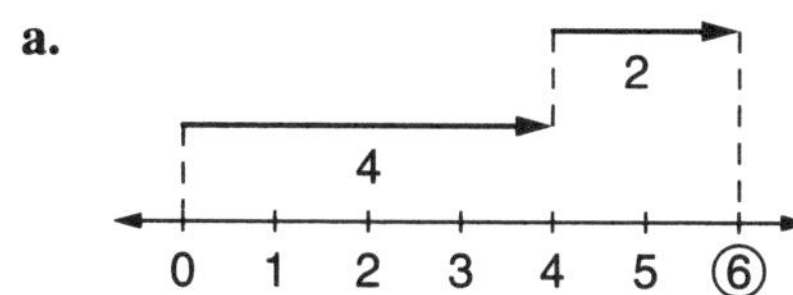

b.

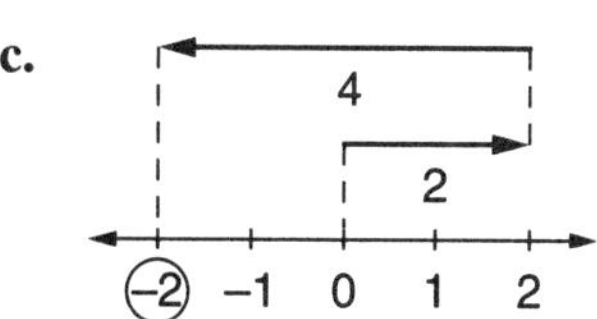

c.

4
2
−2 −1 0 1 2

d. **−3, −2, −1, 0**

e. **$2 + 3 < 2 \times 3$**

f. $3 - 4 < 4 - 3$

g. $2 \cdot 2 = 2 + 2$

h. **0**

i.

$$\begin{array}{r} 630 \\ -\ 436 \\ \hline 194 \end{array} \qquad \mathbf{-194}$$

j. **−2, −3, −4**

Lesson 4, Mixed Practice

1.

Sum of 5 and 4 = 9
Product of 3 and 3 = 9
9 − 9 = **0**

2. $27 - 9 =$ **18**

3. **Positive numbers**

4. (a) $24 - 6 =$ **18**

(b) $6 - 24 =$ **−18**

(c) $\frac{24}{6} =$ **4**

(d)

$$\begin{array}{r} 24 \\ \times\ \ 6 \\ \hline \mathbf{144} \end{array}$$

5. $\mathbf{5 \cdot 2 > 5 + 2}$

6. $\mathbf{-2, -1, 0, 1}$

7. (a) $3 \cdot 4 = 2(6)$
(b) $-3 < -2$
(c) $3 - 5 < 5 - 3$
(d) $xy = yx$

8. **Multiply the divisor by the quotient to find the dividend.**

9. 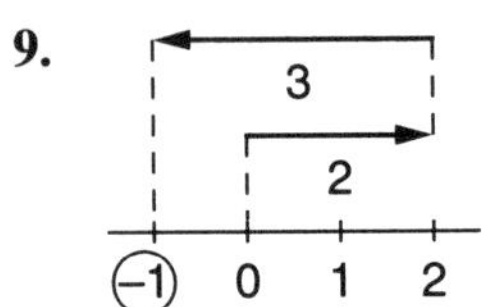

10. $\dfrac{12}{12} = 1$
$k = \mathbf{1}$

11. $\begin{array}{r} 4 \\ 8 \\ +\ 6 \\ \hline 18 \end{array}$ $\quad \begin{array}{r} \overset{2}{\not 3}{}^{1}0 \\ -\ 1\ 8 \\ \hline 1\ 2 \end{array}$
$n = \mathbf{12}$

12. $\begin{array}{r} 654 \\ +\ 123 \\ \hline 777 \end{array}$
$z = \mathbf{777}$

13. $\begin{array}{r} \overset{0}{\not 1}\overset{9}{\not 0}\overset{9}{\not 0}{}^{1}0 \\ -\ 1\ 0\ 1 \\ \hline 8\ 9\ 9 \end{array}$
$m = \mathbf{899}$

14. $\begin{array}{r} \$4.95 \\ -\ \$1.45 \\ \hline \$3.50 \end{array}$
$p = \mathbf{\$3.50}$

15. $\begin{array}{r} 7 \\ 32\overline{)224} \\ 224 \\ \hline 0 \end{array}$
$k = \mathbf{7}$

16. $\begin{array}{r} 24 \\ \times\ 8 \\ \hline 192 \end{array}$
$r = \mathbf{192}$

17. $\begin{array}{r} \$3.\overset{1}{6}\overset{1}{7} \\ \$0.14 \\ +\ \$52.75 \\ \hline \mathbf{\$56.56} \end{array}$

18. $\begin{array}{r} \$\,\overset{0}{\not 1}\overset{9}{\not 0}\overset{9}{\not 0}.\overset{9}{\not 0}{}^{1}0 \\ -\ \$36.49 \\ \hline \mathbf{\$63.51} \end{array}$

19. $\begin{array}{r} \$0.36 \\ \times\ 48 \\ \hline 288 \\ 144\ \\ \hline \mathbf{\$17.28} \end{array}$

20. $5 \cdot 6 = 30$ $\quad \begin{array}{r} 30 \\ \times\ 7 \\ \hline \mathbf{210} \end{array}$

21. $\begin{array}{r} \mathbf{550} \\ 18\overline{)9900} \\ 90\ \ \\ \hline 90\ \\ 90\ \\ \hline 00 \\ 0 \\ \hline 0 \end{array}$

22. $\begin{array}{r} 30 \\ \times\ 20 \\ \hline 600 \end{array}$ $\quad \begin{array}{r} 600 \\ \times\ 40 \\ \hline \mathbf{24{,}000} \end{array}$

23. $\begin{array}{r} \overset{0}{\not 1}\overset{12}{\not 3}{}^{1}0 \\ -\ 5\ 7 \\ \hline 7\ 3 \end{array}$ $\quad \begin{array}{r} \overset{1}{7}3 \\ +\ 9 \\ \hline \mathbf{82} \end{array}$

24. $\begin{array}{r} \overset{1}{\not 2}\overset{9}{\not 0}\overset{10}{\not 1}{}^{1}4 \\ -\ 1\ 9\ 8\ 7 \\ \hline 2\ 7 \end{array}$ $\quad \mathbf{-27}$

25. $\begin{array}{r} \mathbf{\$9.80} \\ 7\overline{)\$68.60} \\ 63\ \ \ \ \\ \hline 5\,6\ \ \\ 5\,6\ \ \\ \hline 00 \\ 0 \\ \hline 0 \end{array}$

26.
$$\begin{array}{r} \overset{1\,1}{\$0.46} \\ +\ \$0.64 \\ \hline \mathbf{\$1.10} \end{array}$$

27.
$$\begin{array}{r} \mathbf{58} \\ 80\overline{)4640} \\ \underline{400} \\ 640 \\ \underline{640} \\ 0 \end{array}$$

28.
$$\begin{array}{r} \$3.75 \\ \times\ \ 30 \\ \hline \mathbf{\$112.50} \end{array}$$

29. **Answers may vary. One answer is** $(2 \times 3) \times 6 = 2 \times (3 \times 6)$.

30. $10 + 20 = 30 \quad 30 - 20 = 10$
$20 + 10 = 30 \quad 30 - 10 = 20$

Lesson 5, Lesson Practice

a. **3**

b. **Billions**

c. $(2 \times 1000) + (5 \times 100)$

d. **Thirty-six million, four hundred twenty-seven thousand, five hundred eighty**

e. **Forty million, three hundred two thousand, ten**

f. **25,206,040**

g. **50,402,100,000**

h. **$15,000,000,000**

Lesson 5, Mixed Practice

1.
$$\begin{array}{r} \overset{1\,1}{{}_1607} \\ +\ 2393 \\ \hline \mathbf{3000} \end{array}$$

2. **101,000 > 1100**

3. **Fifty million, five hundred seventy-four thousand, six**

4. **2**

5. **250,005,070**

6. $-12 > -15$
Negative twelve is greater than negative fifteen

7. $-7, -1, 0, 4, 5, 7$

8. **Draw a number line. Start at the origin and draw an arrow 5 units long to the right. From this point draw an arrow 4 units long to the left. The second arrow ends at 1, showing that** $5 - 4 = 1$. **Circle the number 1.**

9. **7 units**

10. $2 \cdot 3 = 6 \qquad 6 \cdot 5 = 30$
$$\begin{array}{r} 32 \\ 30\overline{)960} \\ \underline{90} \\ 60 \\ \underline{60} \\ 0 \end{array}$$
$n = \mathbf{32}$

11.
$$\begin{array}{r} 2500 \\ +\ 1367 \\ \hline 3867 \end{array}$$
$a = \mathbf{3867}$

12. $17 + 5 = 22$
$$\begin{array}{r} \overset{4}{\cancel{5}}{}^{1}0 \\ -\ 2\,2 \\ \hline 2\,8 \end{array}$$
$b = \mathbf{28}$

13.
$$\begin{array}{r} \$\,\overset{1}{\cancel{2}}\,\overset{14}{\cancel{5}}.{}^{1}0\,0 \\ -\ \$\,1\,8.\,7\,0 \\ \hline \$\,6.\,3\,0 \end{array}$$
$k = \mathbf{\$6.30}$

14.
$$\begin{array}{r} \overset{0}{\cancel{1}}\,\overset{9}{\cancel{0}},{}^{1}0\,0\,0 \\ -\ \ 6\,4\,0\,0 \\ \hline 3\,6\,0\,0 \end{array}$$
$d = \mathbf{3600}$

15.
$$\begin{array}{r} 18 \\ 8\overline{)144} \\ \underline{8} \\ 64 \\ \underline{64} \\ 0 \end{array}$$
$f = \mathbf{18}$

16. **(7 × 100,000) + (5 × 10,000)**

17.
$$\begin{array}{r} {}^{11\,11} \\ 37{,}428 \\ +\ 59{,}775 \\ \hline \mathbf{97{,}203} \end{array}$$

18.
$$\begin{array}{r} 3\ 1,\ 0\ 1\ 4 \\ -\ 2\ 4,\ 7\ 6\ 7 \\ \hline \mathbf{6\ 2\ 4\ 7} \end{array}$$

19.
$$\begin{array}{r} 45 \\ 362 \\ 7 \\ +\ 4319 \\ \hline \mathbf{4733} \end{array}$$

20.
$$\begin{array}{r} \$64.59 \\ \$124.00 \\ \$6.30 \\ +\quad \$0.37 \\ \hline \mathbf{\$195.26} \end{array}$$

21. 12 ÷ 3 = 4
$$\begin{array}{r} \mathbf{36} \\ 4\overline{)144} \\ \underline{12} \\ 24 \\ \underline{24} \\ 0 \end{array}$$

22.
$$\begin{array}{r} 12 \\ 12\overline{)144} \\ \underline{12} \\ 24 \\ \underline{24} \\ 0 \end{array}$$
12 ÷ 3 = **4**

23.
$$\begin{array}{r} 40 \\ \times\ 500 \\ \hline \mathbf{20{,}000} \end{array}$$

24.
$$\begin{array}{r} \mathbf{405} \\ 21\overline{)8505} \\ \underline{84} \\ 10 \\ \underline{0} \\ 105 \\ \underline{105} \\ 0 \end{array}$$

25.
$$\begin{array}{r} \$\,4.\,6\,0 \\ -\ \$\,0.\,3\,9 \\ \hline \mathbf{\$\,4.\,2\,1} \end{array} \qquad \begin{array}{r} \$\,1\,0.\,0\,0 \\ -\quad \$\,4.\,2\,1 \\ \hline \mathbf{\$\,5.\,7\,9} \end{array}$$

26.
$$\begin{array}{r} \$0.29 \\ \times\quad 36 \\ \hline 174 \\ 87\ \\ \hline \mathbf{\$10.44} \end{array}$$

27. (a) **Identity property of multiplication**

(b) **Commutative property of multiplication**

28. **Each term in the sequence can be found by subtracting two from the preceding term.**

2 − 2 = **0**
0 − 2 = **−2**
−2 − 2 = **−4**

29. (a) **Counting numbers or natural numbers**

(b) **Whole numbers**

(c) **Integers**

30. **{. . . , −6, −4, −2}**

Lesson 6, Lesson Practice

a. **1, 5, 25**

b. **1, 2, 3, 4, 6, 8, 12, 24**

c. **1, 23**

d. 1 + 2 + 6 + 0 = 9
1, 2, 3, 4, 5, 6, 7, 9, 10

$$\begin{array}{r} 180 \\ 7\overline{)1260} \\ \underline{7} \\ 56 \\ \underline{56} \\ 00 \\ \underline{0} \\ 0 \end{array}$$

e. 7 + 3 + 5 + 0 + 0 = 15
1, 2, 3, 4, 5, 6, 7, 10

$$\begin{array}{r} 10{,}500 \\ 7\overline{)73{,}500} \\ \underline{7} \\ 03 \\ \underline{0} \\ 35 \\ \underline{35} \\ 00 \\ \underline{0} \\ 00 \\ \underline{0} \\ 0 \end{array}$$

f. 3 + 6 + 0 + 0 = 9
1, 2, 3, 4, 5, 6, 8, 9, 10

$$\begin{array}{r} 514 \text{ R } 2 \\ 7\overline{)3600} \\ \underline{35} \\ 10 \\ \underline{7} \\ 30 \\ \underline{28} \\ 2 \end{array}$$

g. 1 + 3 + 5 + 6 = 15
1, 2, 3, 4, 6

$$\begin{array}{r} 193 \text{ R } 5 \\ 7\overline{)1356} \\ \underline{7} \\ 65 \\ \underline{63} \\ 26 \\ \underline{21} \\ 5 \end{array}$$

h. **1, 2, 4, 5, 7, 8**

i. Factors of 12: 1, 2, 3, 4, 6, 12
Factors of 20: 1, 2, 4, 5, 10, 20
1, 2, 4

j. Factors of 24: 1, 2, 3, 4, 6, 8, 12, 24
Factors of 40: 1, 2, 4, 5, 8, 10, 20, 40
8

Lesson 6, Mixed Practice

1. Product of 10 and 20 = 200
Sum of 20 and 30 = 50

$$\frac{200}{50} = \mathbf{4}$$

2. (a) Factors of 30: 1, 2, 3, 5, 6, 10, 15, 30
Factors of 40: 1, 2, 4, 5, 8, 10, 20, 40
1, 2, 5, 10

(b) **10**

3. **{. . . , −5, −3, −1}**

4. **407,006,962**

5. 1 + 2 + 3 + 0 + 0 = 6
1, 2, 3, 4, 5, 6, 10

$$\begin{array}{r} 1\,757 \text{ R } 1 \\ 7\overline{)12{,}300} \\ \underline{7} \\ 53 \\ \underline{49} \\ 40 \\ \underline{35} \\ 50 \\ \underline{49} \\ 1 \end{array}$$

6. −7 > −11
Negative seven is greater than negative eleven.

7.

$$\begin{array}{r} 14 \\ 4\overline{)56} \\ \underline{4} \\ 16 \\ \underline{16} \\ 0 \end{array} \qquad \begin{array}{r} 57 \\ 8\overline{)456} \\ \underline{40} \\ 56 \\ \underline{56} \\ 0 \end{array} \qquad \begin{array}{r} 493 \text{ R } 5 \\ 7\overline{)3456} \\ \underline{28} \\ 65 \\ \underline{63} \\ 26 \\ \underline{21} \\ 5 \end{array}$$

3 + 4 + 5 + 6 = 18
1, 2, 3, 4, 6, 8, 9

8.

5
2
(−3) −2 −1 0 1 2

9. **(6 × 1000) + (4 × 100)**

10.
$$\begin{array}{r} \$10.00 \\ - \ \$4.60 \\ \hline \$5.40 \end{array}$$
$x = \mathbf{\$5.40}$

11.
$$\begin{array}{r} 4500 \\ + \ 3850 \\ \hline 8350 \end{array}$$
$p = \mathbf{8350}$

12.
$$\begin{array}{r} \$6.25 \\ 8\overline{)\$50.00} \\ 48 \\ \hline 2\,0 \\ 1\,6 \\ \hline 40 \\ 40 \\ \hline 0 \end{array}$$
$z = \mathbf{\$6.25}$

13.
$$\begin{array}{r} 7 \\ 4 \\ 8 \\ 6 \\ 2 \\ 1 \\ 6 \\ 8 \\ + \ 9 \\ \hline 51 \end{array} \qquad \begin{array}{r} 60 \\ - \ 51 \\ \hline 9 \end{array}$$
$n = \mathbf{9}$

14.
$$\begin{array}{r} 1426 \\ - \ 87 \\ \hline 1339 \end{array}$$
$k = \mathbf{1339}$

15.
$$\begin{array}{r} 22 \\ 45\overline{)990} \\ 90 \\ \hline 90 \\ 90 \\ \hline 0 \end{array}$$
$p = \mathbf{22}$

16.
$$\begin{array}{r} 32 \\ \times \ 8 \\ \hline 256 \end{array}$$
$z = \mathbf{256}$

17.
$$\begin{array}{r} \mathbf{35} \\ 35\overline{)1225} \\ 105 \\ \hline 175 \\ 175 \\ \hline 0 \end{array}$$

18.
$$\begin{array}{r} 800 \\ \times \ 50 \\ \hline \mathbf{40,000} \end{array}$$

19.
$$\begin{array}{r} \$100.00 \\ - \ \$48.37 \\ \hline \mathbf{\$51.63} \end{array}$$

20.
$$\begin{array}{r} 46,302 \\ + \ 49,998 \\ \hline \mathbf{96,300} \end{array}$$

21.
$$\begin{array}{r} \mathbf{\$2.25} \\ 20\overline{)\$45.00} \\ 40 \\ \hline 5\,0 \\ 4\,0 \\ \hline 1\,00 \\ 1\,00 \\ \hline 0 \end{array}$$

22.
$$\begin{array}{r} 11 \\ \times \ 7 \\ \hline 77 \end{array} \qquad \begin{array}{r} 77 \\ \times \ 13 \\ \hline 231 \\ 77 \\ \hline \mathbf{1001} \end{array}$$

23.
$$\begin{array}{r} \mathbf{4\,807} \ \mathbf{R\,8} \\ 9\overline{)43,271} \\ 36 \\ \hline 7\,2 \\ 7\,2 \\ \hline 07 \\ 0 \\ \hline 71 \\ 63 \\ \hline 8 \\ 0 \\ \hline 8 \end{array}$$

24.
$$\begin{array}{r} 3625 \\ 59 \\ 570 \\ + \ 8 \\ \hline \mathbf{4262} \end{array}$$

25.
$$\begin{array}{r} \$0.48 \\ \$8.49 \\ +\ \$14.00 \\ \hline \mathbf{\$22.97} \end{array}$$

26.
$$\begin{array}{r} 430 \\ -\ \ 58 \\ \hline 372 \end{array} \qquad \begin{array}{r} 1000 \\ -\ \ 372 \\ \hline \mathbf{628} \end{array}$$

27.
$$\begin{array}{r} 140 \\ \times\ \ 16 \\ \hline 840 \\ 140\ \ \\ \hline \mathbf{2240} \end{array}$$

28.
$$\begin{array}{r} \$0.25 \\ \times\ \ \ \ 24 \\ \hline 1\ 00 \\ 5\ 0\ \ \\ \hline \mathbf{\$6.00} \end{array}$$

29.
$$\begin{array}{r} \mathbf{\$4.35} \\ 10\overline{)\$43.50} \\ 40\ \ \ \ \ \\ \hline 3\ 5\ \ \ \\ 3\ 0\ \ \ \\ \hline 50 \\ 50 \\ \hline 0 \end{array}$$

30. **Commutative property of multiplication; the order of the factors can be changed without changing the product.**

Lesson 7, Lesson Practice

a. **Point** ***A***

b. $XY = XZ - YZ$
$XY = 10 - 6$
$XY = \mathbf{4\ cm}$

c.

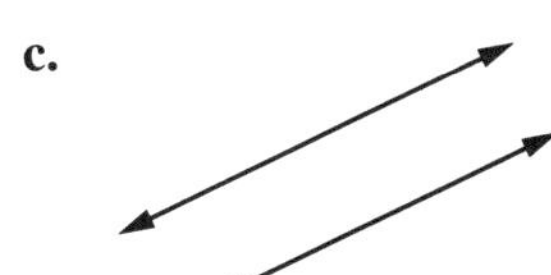

d.

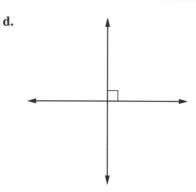

e.

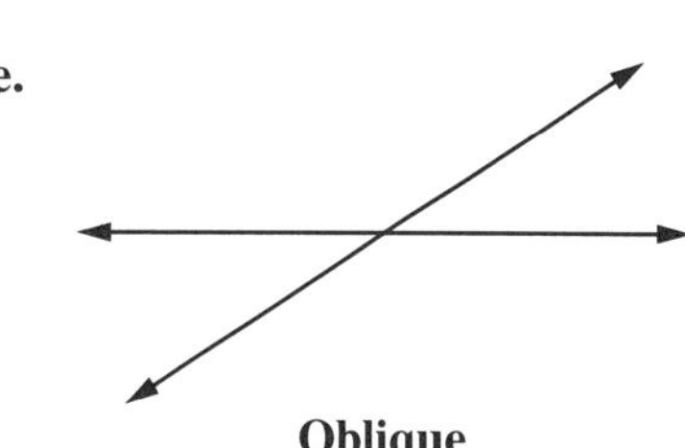

Oblique

f.

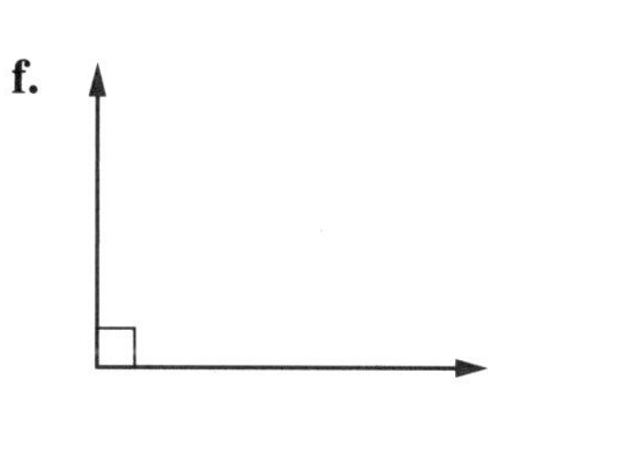

g.

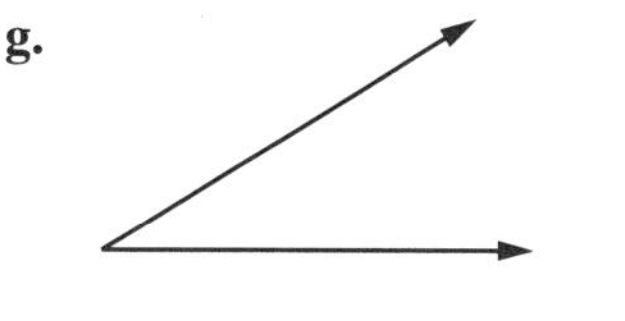

h.

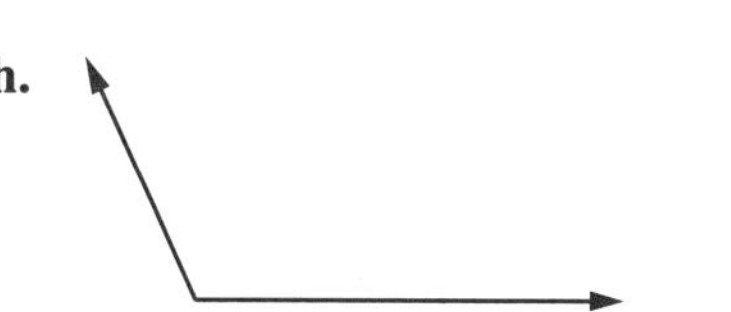

i. **Perpendicular**

Lesson 7, Mixed Practice

1. $7 + 5 = \mathbf{12}$

2. **Identity property of multiplication**

3. **1, 2, 5, 10, 25, 50**

4. $\mathbf{2 - 5 = -3}$

5. **90,000,000**

6.
```
   115 R 4        132
 8)924         7)924
   8             7
   12            22
    8            21
    44            14
    40            14
     4             0
```
9 + 2 + 4 = 15
1, 2, 3, 4, 5, 6, 7

7. **−10, −7, −2, 0, 5, 8**

8. **This is a sequence of perfect squares.**
11 · 11 = **121**
12 · 12 = **144**
13 · 13 = **169**

9. **Posts**

10. (a) Factors of 24: 1, 2, 3, 4, 6, 8, 12, 24
Factors of 32: 1, 2, 4, 8, 16, 32
1, 2, 4, 8

(b) **8**

11. **7 units**

12. 6 · 6 = 36
```
      34
 36)1224
    108
     144
     144
       0
```
z = **34**

13.
```
   $100.00
 −  $17.54
    $82.46
```
k = **$82.46**

14.
```
   432
 +  98
   530
```
w = **530**

15.
```
      $1.80
 20)$36.00
     20
     16 0
     16 0
        00
         0
         0
```
x = **$1.80**

16.
```
    200
 ×   20
   4000
```
w = **4000**

17.
```
     10
 30)300
    30
     00
      0
      0
```
x = **10**

18. **The quotient does not have a remainder (the remainder is zero). A number is divisible by 9 if the sum of its digits is divisible by 9. The sum of the digits in 4554 is 18, which is divisible by 9.**

19.
```
   36,475
 + 55,984
   92,459
```
(**92,459**)

20.
```
    476
 ×   38
   3 808
  14 28
  18,088
```
(**18,088**)

21.
```
   $80.00
 − $72.45
    $7.55
```
(**$7.55**)

22.
```
     49
    387
   1579
 +   98
   2113
```
(**2113**)

23. $\$1.70$
$40\overline{)\$68.00}$
40
28 0
28 0
00
0
0

24. $8 \cdot 7 = 56$ $\quad 56 \times 5 = \mathbf{280}$

25. $200 \div 10 = 20$ $\quad 20\overline{)4000}$ = 200
40
00
0
00
0
0

$200\overline{)4000}$ = 20 $\quad 20 \div 10 = 2$
400
00
0
0

$200 > 2$

26. (a) $200(400) = \mathbf{80,000}$

(b) $200 - 400 = \mathbf{-200}$

(c) $\frac{400}{200} = \mathbf{2}$

27. (a) $\angle BMC$ **or** $\angle CMB$

(b) $\angle AMC$ **or** $\angle CMA$

28. **Right angle**

29. $\overline{XY}$ (or $\overline{YX}$), $\overline{YZ}$ (or $\overline{ZY}$), $\overline{XZ}$ (or $\overline{ZX}$)

30. **Add m$\overline{XY}$ and m$\overline{YZ}$ to find m$\overline{XZ}$.**

Lesson 8, Lesson Practice

a. $\mathbf{\frac{3}{5}}$

b. $100\% \div 5 = 20\%$
$20\% \times 3 = \mathbf{60\%}$

c. $100\% \div 2 = \mathbf{50\%}$

d.

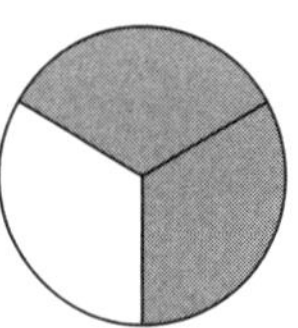

e.

f.

g. $\mathbf{4\frac{2}{3}}$

h. $\mathbf{13\frac{1}{4}}$

i. $\mathbf{3\frac{5}{16}}$ **in.**

j. $\frac{1}{2}$ of $\frac{1}{8} = \mathbf{\frac{1}{16}}$ **inch**

Lesson 8, Mixed Practice

1. $\mathbf{1\frac{3}{4} > 1\frac{3}{5}}$

2. $XY = 2\frac{4}{16} = \mathbf{2\frac{1}{4}}$ **in.**

$YZ = \mathbf{1\frac{1}{16}}$ **in.**

3. Product of 20 and 20 = 400
Sum of 10 and 10 = 20

$$\begin{array}{r} \mathbf{20} \\ 20\overline{)400} \\ \underline{40} \\ 00 \\ \underline{0} \\ 0 \end{array}$$

4.
$$\begin{array}{r} 85 \\ 8\overline{)680} \\ \underline{64} \\ 40 \\ \underline{40} \\ 0 \end{array} \qquad \begin{array}{r} 240 \\ 7\overline{)1680} \\ \underline{14} \\ 28 \\ \underline{28} \\ 00 \\ \underline{0} \\ 0 \end{array}$$

1 + 6 + 8 + 0 = 15
1, 2, 3, 4, 5, 6, 7, 8

5. $\mathbf{3\frac{4}{5}}$

6. (a) 3 + 2 **=** 2 + 3
(b) **Commutative property of addition**

7. **Thirty-two billion, five hundred million**

8. (a) $\mathbf{\frac{3}{8}}$
(b) $\mathbf{\frac{5}{8}}$

9. (a) 100% ÷ 5 = 20%
20% × 1 = **20%**
(b) 20% × 4 = **80%**

10. **Denominator**

11.
$$\begin{array}{r} \$2.35 \\ +\ \$4.70 \\ \hline \$7.05 \end{array}$$
a = **$7.05**

12.
$$\begin{array}{r} \$60.00 \\ -\ \$25.48 \\ \hline \mathbf{\$34.52} \end{array}$$
b = **$34.52**

13.
$$\begin{array}{r} \$7.50 \\ 8\overline{)\$60.00} \\ \underline{56} \\ 4\,0 \\ \underline{4\,0} \\ 00 \\ \underline{0} \\ 0 \end{array}$$
c = **$7.50**

14.
$$\begin{array}{r} 10{,}000 \\ -\ 5\,420 \\ \hline 4\,580 \end{array}$$
d = **4580**

15.
$$\begin{array}{r} 15 \\ \times\ 15 \\ \hline 75 \\ 15 \\ \hline 225 \end{array}$$
e = **225**

16.
$$\begin{array}{r} 14 \\ 14\overline{)196} \\ \underline{14} \\ 56 \\ \underline{56} \\ 0 \end{array}$$
f = **14**

17.
$$\begin{array}{r} 8 \\ 9 \\ 8 \\ 8 \\ 9 \\ +\ 8 \\ \hline 50 \end{array} \qquad \begin{array}{r} 60 \\ -\ 50 \\ \hline 10 \end{array}$$
n = **10**

18.
$$\begin{array}{r} 400 \\ \times\ \ 500 \\ \hline \mathbf{200{,}000} \end{array}$$

19.
$$\begin{array}{r} \$0.79 \\ \times\ \ 30 \\ \hline \mathbf{\$23.70} \end{array}$$

20.
$$\begin{array}{r} {}^{1\,1\,1} \\ 3625 \\ 431 \\ +\ 687 \\ \hline \mathbf{4743} \end{array}$$

21.
$$\begin{array}{r} \mathbf{120} \\ 50\overline{)6000} \\ \underline{50} \\ 100 \\ \underline{100} \\ 00 \\ \underline{0} \\ 0 \end{array}$$

22.
$$\begin{array}{r} 20 \\ \times\ 10 \\ \hline 200 \end{array} \qquad \begin{array}{r} 200 \\ \times\ \ 5 \\ \hline \mathbf{1000} \end{array}$$

23.
$$\begin{array}{r} \mathbf{\$1.50} \\ 18\overline{)\$27.00} \\ \underline{18} \\ 9\,0 \\ \underline{9\,0} \\ 00 \\ \underline{0} \\ 0 \end{array}$$

24.
$$\begin{array}{r} \mathbf{576} \\ 6\overline{)3456} \\ \underline{30} \\ 45 \\ \underline{42} \\ 36 \\ \underline{36} \\ 0 \end{array}$$

25. (a)
$$\begin{array}{r} 1000 \\ -\ \ \ 11 \\ \hline \mathbf{989} \end{array}$$

(b) $\mathbf{-989}$

26.
$$k = 3(10) - 1$$
$$k = 30 - 1$$
$$k = \mathbf{29}$$

27.
$$\begin{array}{r} 86 \\ +\ 119 \\ \hline 205 \end{array} \qquad \begin{array}{r} 416 \\ -\ 205 \\ \hline 211 \end{array}$$

$$\begin{array}{r} \overset{3}{\cancel{4}}\,{}^{1}1\ 6 \\ -\ \ \ 8\ 6 \\ \hline 3\ 3\ 0 \end{array} \qquad \begin{array}{r} 330 \\ +\ 119 \\ \hline 449 \end{array}$$

$211 < 449$

28. Acute: **∠CBA** (or **∠ABC**)
Obtuse: **∠DAB** (or **∠BAD**)
Right: **∠CDA** (or **∠ADC**)
and **∠DCB** (or **∠BCD**)

29. (a) $\overline{CB}$ (or $\overline{BC}$)

(b) $\overline{DC}$ (or $\overline{CD}$)

30. **$\overline{QR}$ identifies the segment QR, while QR refers to the distance from Q to R. So $\overline{QR}$ is a segment and QR is a length.**

Lesson 9, Lesson Practice

a. $\frac{5}{6} + \frac{1}{6} = \frac{6}{6} = \mathbf{1}$

b. $\mathbf{\frac{1}{5}}$

c. $\frac{3}{5} \times \frac{1}{2} = \frac{3}{10} \qquad \frac{3}{10} \times \frac{3}{4} = \mathbf{\frac{9}{40}}$

d. $\mathbf{\frac{8}{3}}$

e. $\mathbf{\frac{8}{21}}$

f. $\frac{5}{8} - \frac{5}{8} = \frac{0}{8} = \mathbf{0}$

g. $\mathbf{28\frac{4}{7}\%}$

h. **75%**

i. $\mathbf{\frac{5}{4}}$

j. $\mathbf{\frac{7}{8}}$

k. $\mathbf{\frac{1}{5}}$

l. $\mathbf{\frac{8}{5}}$

m. $\mathbf{\frac{1}{6}}$

n. **$\frac{1}{20}$ of an inch, because $\frac{1}{2}$ of $\frac{1}{10}$ is $\frac{1}{20}$.**

o. $\mathbf{\frac{3}{2}}$

p. $\mathbf{\frac{1}{4}}$

Lesson 9, Mixed Practice

1. $1 + 2 + 3 = 6$ $\quad \frac{6}{6} = \mathbf{1}$
   $1 \cdot 2 \cdot 3 = 6$

2. **45¢ per pound; $0.45 per pound**

3. (a) $\frac{1}{2} > \frac{1}{2} \cdot \frac{1}{2}$ **One half is greater than one half times one half.**

   (b) $-2 > -4$ **Negative two is greater than negative four.**

4. **(2 × 10,000) + (6 × 1000)**

5. (a) $\frac{10}{100} = \mathbf{\frac{1}{10}}$

   (b) 100% ÷ 10 = **10%**

6. (a) $\mathbf{\frac{5}{9}}$

   (b) $\mathbf{\frac{4}{9}}$

7. **It is a segment because it has two endpoints.**

8. $LM = \mathbf{1\frac{1}{4}}$ **in.**

   $MN = \mathbf{1\frac{1}{4}}$ **in.**

   $LN = \mathbf{2\frac{1}{2}}$ **in.**

9. (a) **1, 2, 3, 6, 9, 18**

   (b) **1, 2, 3, 4, 6, 8, 12, 24**

   (c) **1, 2, 3, 6**

   (d) **6**

10. (a) $\frac{2}{5} + \frac{2}{5} = \mathbf{\frac{4}{5}}$

    (b) $\frac{2}{5} - \frac{2}{5} = \frac{0}{5} = \mathbf{0}$

11. $$\begin{array}{r} 200{,}000 \\ -\ 85{,}000 \\ \hline 115{,}000 \end{array}$$
    $b = \mathbf{115{,}000}$

12. $$\begin{array}{r} 15 \\ 60\overline{)900} \\ 60 \\ \hline 300 \\ 300 \\ \hline 0 \end{array}$$
    $c = \mathbf{15}$

13. $$\begin{array}{r} \$20.00 \\ -\ \$5.60 \\ \hline \$14.40 \end{array}$$
    $d = \mathbf{\$14.40}$

14. $$\begin{array}{r} \$2.50 \\ 12\overline{)\$30.00} \\ 24 \\ \hline 6\,0 \\ 6\,0 \\ \hline 00 \\ 0 \\ \hline 0 \end{array}$$
    $e = \mathbf{\$2.50}$

15. $$\begin{array}{r} \$12.47 \\ +\ \$98.03 \\ \hline \$110.50 \end{array}$$
    $f = \mathbf{\$110.50}$

16. $$\begin{array}{r} 5 \\ 7 \\ 5 \\ 7 \\ 6 \\ 1 \\ 2 \\ 3 \\ +\ 4 \\ \hline 40 \end{array} \qquad \begin{array}{r} 40 \\ -\ 40 \\ \hline 0 \end{array}$$
    $n = \mathbf{0}$

17. $2\frac{8}{15}$

18. $2\frac{7}{8}$

19. $\frac{3}{16}$

20.
```
     106
17)1802
   17
    10
     0
   102
   102
     0
```

21.
```
     $8.97
   $110.00
+    $0.53
   $119.50
```

22.
```
  $60.00
− $49.49
  $10.51
```

23.
```
   607
×   78
  4856
 4249
47,346
```

24.
```
  $0.09
×    56
     54
    45
  $5.04
```

25.
```
  50        3000
× 60     ×    70
3000     210,000
```

26. $\frac{4}{5} \times \frac{2}{3} = \frac{8}{15}$ $\quad \frac{8}{15} \times \frac{1}{3} = \mathbf{\frac{8}{45}}$

27. $\frac{7}{9}$

28. (a) $\angle A$ and $\angle B$

(b) $\overline{AC}$ or $\overline{CA}$

29. **Each term is half of the preceding term.**

$\frac{1}{8} \times \frac{1}{2} = \mathbf{\frac{1}{16}}$

30. $\frac{5}{2}$

Lesson 10, Lesson Practice

a.
```
   8
4)35
  32
   3
```
$8\frac{3}{4}$ **inches**

b.
```
   14
7)100%
  7
  30
  28
   2
```
$14\frac{2}{7}\%$

c.
```
   2
5)12
  10
   2
```
$2\frac{2}{5}$

d.
```
   2
6)12
```
2

e. $2\frac{12}{7} = \frac{7 \times 2 + 12}{7} = \frac{26}{7}$

```
   3
7)26
  21
   5
```
$3\frac{5}{7}$

f.

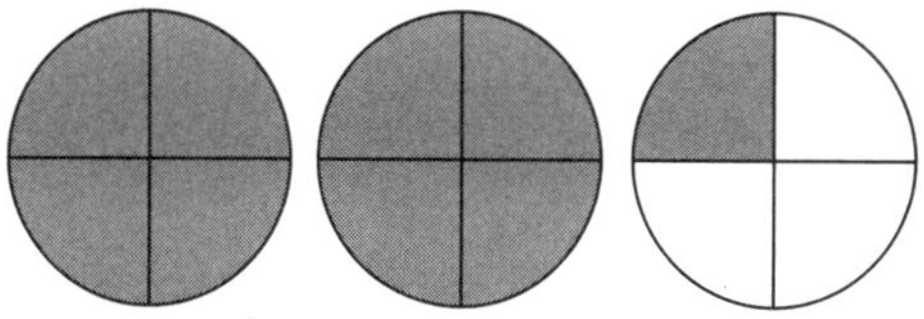

g. $\frac{2}{3} + \frac{2}{3} + \frac{2}{3} = \frac{6}{3} = \mathbf{2}$

h. $\frac{7}{3} \times \frac{2}{3} = \frac{14}{9}$

$$\begin{array}{r} 1 \\ 9\overline{)14} \\ \underline{9} \\ 5 \end{array} \longrightarrow \mathbf{1\frac{5}{9}}$$

i. $1\frac{2}{3} + 1\frac{2}{3} = 2\frac{4}{3} = \mathbf{3\frac{1}{3}}$

j. $1\frac{2}{3} = \frac{3 \times 1 + 2}{3} = \mathbf{\frac{5}{3}}$

k. $3\frac{5}{6} = \frac{6 \times 3 + 5}{6} = \mathbf{\frac{23}{6}}$

l. $4\frac{3}{4} = \frac{4 \times 4 + 3}{4} = \mathbf{\frac{19}{4}}$

m. $5\frac{1}{2} = \frac{2 \times 5 + 1}{2} = \mathbf{\frac{11}{2}}$

n. $6\frac{3}{4} = \frac{4 \times 6 + 3}{4} = \mathbf{\frac{27}{4}}$

o. $10\frac{2}{5} = \frac{5 \times 10 + 2}{5} = \mathbf{\frac{52}{5}}$

Lesson 10, Mixed Practice

1. **Answers will vary. One answer is** $\left(\frac{1}{2} \cdot \frac{1}{3}\right) \cdot \frac{1}{6} = \frac{1}{2} \cdot \left(\frac{1}{3} \cdot \frac{1}{6}\right)$.

2. (a) **Parallel**

   (b) **Perpendicular**

3. $2 + 3 + 4 = 9$
   $2 \times 3 \times 4 = 24$
   $24 - 9 = \mathbf{15}$

4. (a) $100\% \div 10 = 10\%$
   $10\% \times 3 = \mathbf{30\%}$

   (b) **70%**

5. $3\frac{2}{3} = \frac{3 \times 3 + 2}{3} = \mathbf{\frac{11}{3}}$

6. (a) $2 - 2 \mathbf{<} 2 \div 2$

   (b) $\frac{1}{2} + \frac{1}{2} \mathbf{>} \frac{1}{2} \times \frac{1}{2}$

7. $\mathbf{9\frac{5}{6}}$

8. 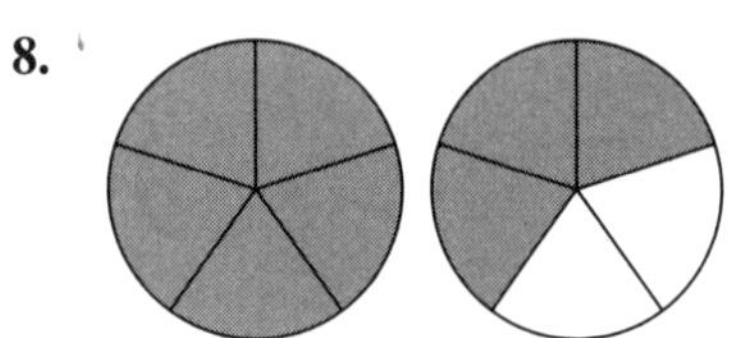

9. $$\begin{array}{r} 52 \\ 8\overline{)420} \\ \underline{40} \\ 20 \\ \underline{16} \\ 4 \end{array} \qquad \begin{array}{r} 60 \\ 7\overline{)420} \\ \underline{42} \\ 00 \\ \underline{0} \\ 0 \end{array}$$
   $4 + 2 + 0 = 6$
   1, 2, 3, 4, 5, 6, 7

10. $$\begin{array}{r} 36{,}275 \\ -\ 12{,}500 \\ \hline 23{,}775 \end{array}$$
    $x = \mathbf{23{,}775}$

11. $$\begin{array}{r} 22 \\ 18\overline{)396} \\ \underline{36} \\ 36 \\ \underline{36} \\ 0 \end{array}$$
    $y = \mathbf{22}$

12. $$\begin{array}{r} 77{,}000 \\ -\ 39{,}400 \\ \hline \mathbf{37{,}600} \end{array}$$
    $z = \mathbf{37{,}600}$

13. $$\begin{array}{r} \$1.25 \\ \times\ \ \ \ 8 \\ \hline \$10.00 \end{array}$$
    $a = \mathbf{\$10.00}$

14. $$\begin{array}{r} \$8.75 \\ +\ \$16.25 \\ \hline \$25.00 \end{array}$$
    $b = \mathbf{\$25.00}$

15. $$\begin{array}{r} \$75.00 \\ -\ \$37.50 \\ \hline \$37.50 \end{array}$$
$c = \mathbf{\$37.50}$

16. $$\begin{array}{r} 8 \\ 7 \\ 5 \\ 6 \\ 4 \\ 3 \\ +\ 7 \\ \hline 40 \end{array} \qquad \begin{array}{r} 50 \\ -\ 40 \\ \hline 10 \end{array}$$
$n = \mathbf{10}$

17. $\frac{5}{2} \times \frac{5}{4} = \frac{25}{8}$ $\quad$ $8\overline{)25}$ = 3 R 1 (24, 1) $\quad$ $\mathbf{3\frac{1}{8}}$

18. $\frac{5}{8} - \frac{5}{8} = \frac{0}{8} = \mathbf{0}$

19. $\frac{11}{20} + \frac{18}{20} = \frac{29}{20} = \frac{20}{20} + \frac{9}{20} = \mathbf{1\frac{9}{20}}$

20. $$\begin{array}{r} 680 \\ -\ 59 \\ \hline 621 \end{array} \qquad \begin{array}{r} 2000 \\ -\ 621 \\ \hline \mathbf{1379} \end{array}$$

21. $9\overline{)100\%}$ = 11 (9, 10, 9, 1) $\quad$ $\mathbf{11\frac{1}{9}\%}$

22. $$\begin{array}{r} \$0.89 \\ \$0.57 \\ +\ \$15.74 \\ \hline \mathbf{\$17.20} \end{array}$$

23. $$\begin{array}{r} 800 \\ \times\ 300 \\ \hline \mathbf{240{,}000} \end{array}$$

24. $2\frac{2}{3} + 2\frac{2}{3} = 4\frac{4}{3} = 4\frac{1}{3} + \frac{3}{3}$
$= 4\frac{1}{3} + 1 = \mathbf{5\frac{1}{3}}$

25. $\mathbf{\frac{8}{27}}$

26. (a) **Ray;** $\overrightarrow{MC}$
(b) **Line;** $\overleftrightarrow{PM}$ or $\overleftrightarrow{MP}$
(c) **Segment;** $\overline{FH}$ or $\overline{HF}$

27. $\mathbf{\frac{9}{5}}$

28. $\frac{1}{2}$ of $2 = \mathbf{1}$
$\frac{1}{2}$ of $1 = \mathbf{\frac{1}{2}}$
$\frac{1}{2}$ of $\frac{1}{2} = \mathbf{\frac{1}{4}}$

29. **C.** $\mathbf{\frac{1}{2}}$

30. (a) $\mathbf{-5}$
(b) $\mathbf{\frac{1}{3}}$

Lesson 11, Lesson Practice

a. $\mathbf{118 + N = 230}$
$$\begin{array}{r} 230 \\ -\ 118 \\ \hline 112 \end{array} \rightarrow \begin{array}{r} 118 \text{ pounds} \\ +\ 112 \text{ pounds} \\ \hline 230 \text{ pounds} \end{array} \quad \text{check}$$
112 pounds

b. $\mathbf{T + 216 = 400}$
$$\begin{array}{r} 400 \\ -\ 216 \\ \hline 184 \end{array} \rightarrow \begin{array}{r} 216 \text{ turns} \\ +\ 184 \text{ turns} \\ \hline 400 \text{ turns} \end{array} \quad \text{check}$$
184 turns

c. $\mathbf{254 - H = 126}$
$$\begin{array}{r} 254 \\ -\ 126 \\ \hline 128 \end{array} \rightarrow \begin{array}{r} 126 \text{ horses} \\ +\ 128 \text{ horses} \\ \hline 254 \text{ horses} \end{array} \quad \text{check}$$
128 horses

d. $\mathbf{P - 36 = 164}$
$$\begin{array}{r} 164 \\ +\ 36 \\ \hline 200 \end{array} \rightarrow \begin{array}{r} 200 \text{ sheets} \\ -\ 36 \text{ sheets} \\ \hline 164 \text{ sheets} \end{array} \quad \text{check}$$
200 sheets

e. **Answers will vary. See student work. Sample answer: The price on the tag was \$15.00, but after tax the total was \$16.13. How much was the tax?**

f. **Answers will vary. See student work. Sample answer: There were 32 students in the class. When some students left for band practice, 25 students remained. How many students left for band practice?**

Lesson 11, Mixed Practice

1. **85,000 + *V* = 200,000**

$$\begin{array}{r} 200{,}000 \\ -\ 85{,}000 \\ \hline 115{,}000 \end{array} \;\rightarrow\; \begin{array}{r} 85{,}000 \text{ people} \\ +\ 115{,}000 \text{ people} \\ \hline 200{,}000 \text{ people} \end{array} \quad \text{check}$$

115,000 visitors

2. **M − \$98.03 = \$12.47**

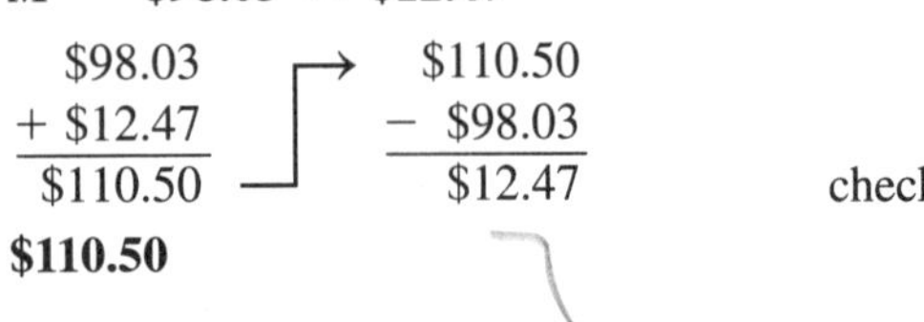

$$\begin{array}{r} \$98.03 \\ +\ \$12.47 \\ \hline \$110.50 \end{array} \;\rightarrow\; \begin{array}{r} \$110.50 \\ -\ \$98.03 \\ \hline \$12.47 \end{array} \quad \text{check}$$

\$110.50

3. **10,000 − *D* = 5420**

$$\begin{array}{r} 10{,}000 \\ -\ 5420 \\ \hline 4580 \end{array} \;\rightarrow\; \begin{array}{r} 5420 \text{ runners} \\ +\ 4580 \text{ runners} \\ \hline 10{,}000 \text{ runners} \end{array} \quad \text{check}$$

4580 runners

4. (a) $\mathbf{\frac{7}{8}}$

(b) $\mathbf{\frac{1}{8}}$

(c) $100\% \div 8 = 12\frac{1}{2}\%$

$12\frac{1}{2}\% \times 1 = \mathbf{12\frac{1}{2}\%}$

5. (a) $\mathbf{-2, 0, \frac{1}{2}, 1}$

(b) $\mathbf{\frac{1}{2}}$

6. $\begin{array}{r} 4 \\ 8\overline{)35} \\ \underline{32} \\ 3 \end{array}$ inches $\mathbf{4\frac{3}{8}}$ **inches**

7. $\mathbf{1 \cdot 2 < 1 + 2}$

8. $\begin{array}{r} 100 \text{ million} \\ -\ 89 \text{ million} \\ \hline 11 \text{ million} \end{array}$

Eleven million

9. (a) **1, 2, 4, 8, 16**

(b) **1, 2, 3, 4, 6, 8, 12, 24**

(c) **1, 2, 4, 8**

(d) **8**

10. $\begin{array}{r} 8000 \\ -\ 5340 \\ \hline 2660 \end{array}$

$k = \mathbf{2660}$

11. $\begin{array}{r} 1760 \\ -\ 1320 \\ \hline 440 \end{array}$

$m = \mathbf{440}$

12. $4 \cdot 9 = 36$ $\begin{array}{r} 20 \\ 36\overline{)720} \\ \underline{72} \\ 00 \\ \underline{0} \\ 0 \end{array}$

$n = \mathbf{20}$

13. $\begin{array}{r} \$375 \\ -\ \$126 \\ \hline \$249 \end{array}$

$r = \mathbf{\$249}$

14. $\begin{array}{r} 13 \\ 13\overline{)169} \\ \underline{13} \\ 39 \\ \underline{39} \\ 0 \end{array}$

$s = \mathbf{13}$

15. $\begin{array}{r} \$25.00 \\ \times\ 40 \\ \hline \$1000.00 \end{array}$

$t = \mathbf{\$1000.00}$

16. $5 \times 20 = 100 \qquad 100 - 100 = 0$

$100 - 5 = 95 \qquad \begin{array}{r} 95 \\ \times\ 20 \\ \hline 1900 \end{array}$

$0 < 1900$

$100 - (5 \times 20) < (100 - 5) \times 20$

17. $1\frac{5}{9} + 1\frac{5}{9} = 2\frac{10}{9} = 2\frac{1}{9} + \frac{9}{9}$

$= 2\frac{1}{9} + 1 = \mathbf{3\frac{1}{9}}$

18. $\frac{5}{3} \times \frac{2}{3} = \frac{10}{9} = \frac{9}{9} + \frac{1}{9} = \mathbf{1\frac{1}{9}}$

19. $\begin{array}{r} 135 \\ \times\ 72 \\ \hline 270 \\ 945 \\ \hline \mathbf{9720} \end{array}$

20. $\begin{array}{r} \mathbf{25} \\ 40\overline{)1000} \\ 80 \\ \hline 200 \\ 200 \\ \hline 0 \end{array}$

21. $\begin{array}{r} \$1.49 \\ \times\ \ 30 \\ \hline \mathbf{\$44.70} \end{array}$

22. $\begin{array}{r} \mathbf{\$4.02} \\ 35\overline{)\$140.70} \\ 140 \\ \hline 0\,7 \\ 0 \\ \hline 70 \\ 70 \\ \hline 0 \end{array}$

23. $\mathbf{\frac{5}{54}}$

24. $\frac{5}{8} + \left(\frac{3}{8} - \frac{1}{8}\right) = \frac{5}{8} + \left(\frac{2}{8}\right) = \mathbf{\frac{7}{8}}$

25. $3\frac{3}{4} = \frac{4 \times 3 + 3}{4} = \mathbf{\frac{15}{4}}$

26. **C. 40%**

27. $\frac{1}{2} + \frac{1}{8} = \frac{4}{8} + \frac{1}{8} = \frac{5}{8}$

$\frac{5}{8} + \frac{1}{8} = \frac{6}{8} = \frac{3}{4}$

$\frac{6}{8} + \frac{1}{8} = \frac{7}{8}$

$\frac{7}{8} + \frac{1}{8} = \frac{8}{8} = 1$

$\mathbf{\frac{5}{8}, \frac{3}{4}, \frac{7}{8}, 1}$

28. (a) **∠1, ∠3**
(b) **∠2, ∠4**

29. $AB = \mathbf{1\frac{7}{8}}$ **inches**

$BC = \mathbf{1\frac{5}{8}}$ **inches**

A B C

30. $\mathbf{\frac{8}{7}}$

Lesson 12, Lesson Practice

a. **1,000,000,000 − 25,000,000 =** ***G***

$\begin{array}{r} 1{,}000{,}000{,}000 \\ -\quad 25{,}000{,}000 \\ \hline 975{,}000{,}000 \end{array}$

975,000,000

b. **1791 − 1215 =** ***Y***

$\begin{array}{r} 1791 \\ -\ 1215 \\ \hline 576 \end{array}$

576 years

c. **1963 −** ***B*** **= 46**

$\begin{array}{r} 1963 \\ -\quad 46 \\ \hline 1917 \end{array}$

John F. Kennedy was born in **1917.**

d. **Answers will vary. See student work. Sample answer: Todd is 58 in. tall and Glenda is 55 in. tall. Todd is how many inches taller than Glenda?**

e. **Answers will vary. See student work. Sample answer: Rosalie turned 14 in 2003. In what year was she born?**

Lesson 12, Mixed Practice

1. **77,000 − L = 39,400**

$$\begin{array}{r} 77{,}000 \\ -\ 39{,}400 \\ \hline 37{,}600 \end{array} \quad \begin{array}{r} 39{,}400 \text{ fans} \\ +\ 37{,}600 \text{ fans} \\ \hline 77{,}000 \text{ fans} \end{array} \quad \text{check}$$

37,600 fans

2. **B + 18 = 31**

$$\begin{array}{r} 31 \\ -\ 18 \\ \hline 13 \end{array} \quad \begin{array}{r} 18 \text{ bananas} \\ +\ 13 \text{ bananas} \\ \hline 31 \text{ bananas} \end{array} \quad \text{check}$$

13 bananas

3. **1215 − 1066 = Y**

$$\begin{array}{r} 1215 \\ -\ 1066 \\ \hline 149 \end{array}$$

149 years

4. **77,000 − 49,600 = F**

$$\begin{array}{r} 77{,}000 \text{ fans} \\ -\ 49{,}600 \text{ fans} \\ \hline 27{,}400 \text{ fans} \end{array}$$

27,400 fans

5. **Answers will vary. See student work. Sample answer: Marla gave the clerk \$20.00 to purchase a CD. Marla got back \$7.13. How much did the CD cost?**

6. **Identity property of multiplication**

7. **1,000,000 − 23,000 = D**

$$\begin{array}{r} 1{,}000{,}000 \\ -\ 23{,}000 \\ \hline 977{,}000 \end{array}$$

Nine hundred seventy-seven thousand

8. (a) $2 - 3 = -1$

(b) $\frac{1}{2} > \frac{1}{3}$

9. $\overline{PQ}$ (or $\overline{QP}$), $\overline{QR}$ (or $\overline{RQ}$), $\overline{PR}$ (or $\overline{RP}$)

10.

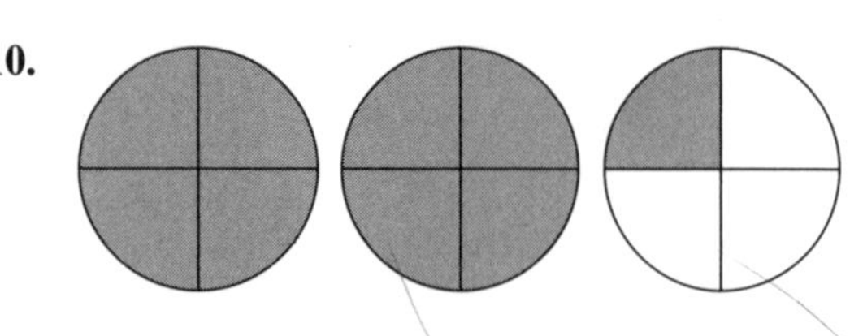

11. (a) $\mathbf{\frac{3}{4}}$

(b) $100\% \div 4 = 25\%$
$25\% \times 1 = \mathbf{25\%}$

12. **1, 2, 4, 5, 10, 20, 25, 50, 100**

13.

$$\begin{array}{r} 42 \\ 15\overline{)630} \\ 60 \\ \hline 30 \\ 30 \\ \hline 0 \end{array}$$

$x = \mathbf{42}$

14.

$$\begin{array}{r} 3601 \\ +\ 2714 \\ \hline 6315 \end{array}$$

$y = \mathbf{6315}$

15.

$$\begin{array}{r} 2900 \\ -\ \ \ 64 \\ \hline 2836 \end{array}$$

$p = \mathbf{2836}$

16.

$$\begin{array}{r} \$5.00 \\ -\ \$1.53 \\ \hline \$3.47 \end{array}$$

$q = \mathbf{\$3.47}$

17.

$$\begin{array}{r} 60 \\ 20\overline{)1200} \\ 120 \\ \hline 00 \\ 0 \\ \hline 0 \end{array}$$

$r = \mathbf{60}$

18.

$$\begin{array}{r} 16 \\ \times\ 14 \\ \hline 64 \\ 160 \\ \hline 224 \end{array}$$

$m = \mathbf{224}$

19.

$$\begin{array}{r} 72{,}112 \\ -\ 64{,}309 \\ \hline \mathbf{7\,803} \end{array}$$

20.
$$\begin{array}{r} 453{,}978 \\ +\ 386{,}864 \\ \hline \mathbf{840{,}842} \end{array}$$

21. $\frac{8}{9} - \left(\frac{3}{9} + \frac{5}{9}\right) = \frac{8}{9} - \left(\frac{8}{9}\right) = \mathbf{0}$

22. $\left(\frac{8}{9} - \frac{3}{9}\right) + \frac{5}{9} = \left(\frac{5}{9}\right) + \frac{5}{9} = \frac{10}{9}$

$= \mathbf{1\frac{1}{9}}$

23. $\frac{9}{2} \times \frac{3}{5} = \frac{27}{10} = \mathbf{2\frac{7}{10}}$

24.
$$\begin{array}{r} \mathbf{\$2.48} \\ 15\overline{)\$37.20} \\ \underline{30} \\ 7\,2 \\ \underline{6\,0} \\ 1\,20 \\ \underline{1\,20} \\ 0 \end{array}$$

25.
$$\begin{array}{r} 4760 \\ 9\overline{)42{,}847} \\ \underline{36} \\ 6\,8 \\ \underline{6\,3} \\ 54 \\ \underline{54} \\ 07 \\ \underline{0} \\ 7 \end{array}$$

$\mathbf{4760\frac{7}{9}}$

26.
$$\begin{array}{r} \$4.36 \\ \$15.96 \\ \$0.76 \\ +\ \$35.00 \\ \hline \mathbf{\$56.08} \end{array}$$

27. $\frac{3}{4} + \frac{1}{4} = \frac{4}{4} = 1$

$\frac{4}{4} + \frac{1}{4} = \frac{5}{4} = 1\frac{1}{4}$

$\frac{5}{4} + \frac{1}{4} = \frac{6}{4} = \frac{3}{2}$

$\mathbf{1,\ 1\frac{1}{4},\ \frac{3}{2}}$

28. $\mathbf{\frac{3}{2}}$

29. $1\frac{2}{3} = \frac{3 \times 1 + 2}{3} = \frac{5}{3}$

$\frac{5}{3} \times \frac{1}{2} = \mathbf{\frac{5}{6}}$

30.

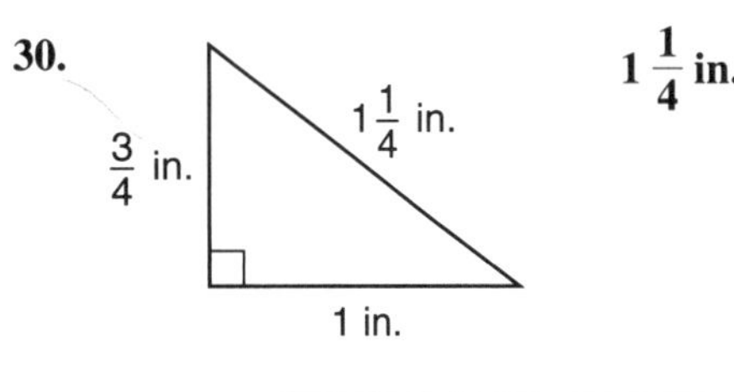

$\mathbf{1\frac{1}{4}}$ **in.**

Lesson 13, Lesson Practice

a. $\mathbf{24 \times 18¢ = M}$

$$\begin{array}{r} \$0.18 \\ \times\quad 24 \\ \hline 72 \\ \underline{36} \\ \$4.32 \end{array}$$

$4.32

b. $\mathbf{R \times 25 = 375}$

$$\begin{array}{r} 15 \\ 25\overline{)375} \\ \underline{25} \\ 125 \\ \underline{125} \\ 0 \end{array}$$

15 × 25 = 375 check

15 rows

c. $\mathbf{7P = 1225}$

$$\begin{array}{r} 175 \\ 7\overline{)1225} \\ \underline{7} \\ 52 \\ \underline{49} \\ 35 \\ \underline{35} \\ 0 \end{array}$$

7 × 175 = 1225 check

175 push-ups

d. **Answers will vary. See student work. Sample answer: If a dozen doughnuts cost $3.00, what is the cost per doughnut?**

Lesson 13, Mixed Practice

1. $\mathbf{72{,}112 - 64{,}309 = I}$

$$\begin{array}{r} 72{,}112 \\ -\ 64{,}309 \\ \hline \mathbf{7\,803} \end{array}$$

2. **60 − N = 17**

$$\begin{array}{r} \text{60 night crawlers} \\ -\ \text{17 night crawlers} \\ \hline \textbf{43 night crawlers} \end{array}$$

3. **1945 − B = 63**

$$\begin{array}{r} 1945 \\ -\ \ 63 \\ \hline \mathbf{1882} \end{array}$$

4. **75 × 12 = B**

$$\begin{array}{r} 75 \\ \times\ 12 \\ \hline 150 \\ 75\ \\ \hline 900 \end{array}$$

900 beach balls

5. **T × 8 = 120**

$$8\overline{)120} = 15$$

$$\begin{array}{r} 8 \\ \hline 40 \\ 40 \\ \hline 0 \end{array}$$

$15 \times 8 = 120$ check

15 truckloads

6. **Answers will vary. See student work. Sample answer: Five tickets for the show cost $63.75. If all the tickets were the same price, then what was the cost per ticket?**

$$5\overline{)\$63.75} = \$12.75$$

$$\begin{array}{r} 5 \\ \hline 13 \\ 10 \\ \hline 37 \\ 35 \\ \hline 25 \\ 25 \\ \hline 0 \end{array}$$

$5(\$12.75) = \$63.75$ check

$12.75

7. $(5 \times 8) - (5 + 8) = 40 - 13 = \mathbf{27}$

8. (a) $\dfrac{\text{3 quarters}}{\text{4 quarters}} = \mathbf{\dfrac{3}{4}}$

(b) $\dfrac{75¢}{100¢} = \mathbf{75\%}$

9. **10 units**

10. (a) **Line;** $\overleftrightarrow{BR}$ (or $\overleftrightarrow{RB}$)

(b) **Segment;** $\overline{TV}$ (or $\overline{VT}$)

(c) **Ray;** $\overrightarrow{MW}$

11. (a) Factors of 24: 1, 2, 3, 4, 6, 8, 12, 24
Factors of 36: 1, 2, 3, 4, 6, 9, 12, 18, 36
1, 2, 3, 4, 6, 12

(b) **12**

12. (a) A: $\mathbf{\frac{6}{7}}$; B: $\mathbf{1\frac{4}{7}}$

(b) $1\frac{4}{7} - \frac{6}{7} = \frac{7 \times 1 + 4}{7} - \frac{6}{7}$

$= \frac{11}{7} - \frac{6}{7} = \mathbf{\frac{5}{7}}$ **units**

13. $36\overline{)1800} = 50$

$$\begin{array}{r} 180\ \\ \hline 00 \\ 0 \\ \hline 0 \end{array}$$

$c = \mathbf{50}$

14.
$$\begin{array}{r} \$3.77 \\ +\ \$1.64 \\ \hline \$5.41 \end{array}$$

$f = \mathbf{\$5.41}$

15.
$$\begin{array}{r} 28 \\ \times\ \ 7 \\ \hline 196 \end{array}$$

$d = \mathbf{196}$

16. $30\overline{)4500} = 150$

$$\begin{array}{r} 30\ \ \\ \hline 150\ \\ 150\ \\ \hline 00 \\ 0 \\ \hline 0 \end{array}$$

$e = \mathbf{150}$

17.

$$\begin{array}{r} 4 \\ 7 \\ 6 \\ 8 \\ 4 \\ 5 \\ 5 \\ 7 \\ 9 \\ 6 \\ +\ 8 \\ \hline 69 \end{array} \qquad \begin{array}{r} 75 \\ -\ 69 \\ \hline 6 \end{array}$$

$n = \mathbf{6}$

18.

$$\begin{array}{r} 3674 \\ -\ 2159 \\ \hline 1515 \end{array}$$

$a = \mathbf{1515}$

19.

$$\begin{array}{r} 5179 \\ -\ 4610 \\ \hline 569 \end{array}$$

$b = \mathbf{569}$

20.

$$\begin{array}{r} 363 \\ 4579 \\ 86 \\ +\ \ 7 \\ \hline \mathbf{5035} \end{array}$$

21. $(5 \cdot 4) \div (3 + 2) = (20) \div (5) = \mathbf{4}$

22. $\frac{5}{3} \cdot \frac{5}{2} = \frac{25}{6} = \mathbf{4\frac{1}{6}}$

23. $3\frac{4}{5} - \left(\frac{2}{5} + 1\frac{1}{5}\right)$

$= \frac{5 \times 3 + 4}{5} - \left(\frac{2}{5} + \frac{5 \times 1 + 1}{5}\right)$

$= \frac{19}{5} - \left(\frac{2}{5} + \frac{6}{5}\right) = \frac{19}{5} - \left(\frac{8}{5}\right)$

$= \frac{11}{5} = \mathbf{2\frac{1}{5}}$

24.

$$\begin{array}{r} \mathbf{24} \\ 25\overline{)600} \\ \underline{50} \\ 100 \\ \underline{100} \\ 0 \end{array}$$

25.

$$\begin{array}{r} 600 \\ \times\ \ 25 \\ \hline 3000 \\ 1200 \\ \hline \mathbf{15{,}000} \end{array}$$

26.

$100 \div 10 = 10,\ 1000 \div 10 = 100$

$1000 \div 100 = 10,\ 10 \div 10 = 1$

$100 > 1$

$1000 \div (100 \div 10) \mathbf{>} (1000 \div 100) \div 10$

27. $2\frac{1}{2} = \frac{2 \times 2 + 1}{2} = \frac{5}{2}$

$\frac{5}{2} \cdot \frac{1}{3} = \mathbf{\frac{5}{6}}$

28. $\frac{11}{12} \cdot \frac{12}{11} = \mathbf{1}$

29. Obtuse: $\angle \mathbf{D}$
Acute: $\angle \mathbf{A}$
Right: $\angle \mathbf{B}$ and $\angle \mathbf{C}$

30. (a) $\overline{\mathbf{DC}}$ (or $\overline{\mathbf{CD}}$)

(b) $\overline{\mathbf{CB}}$ (or $\overline{\mathbf{BC}}$)

Lesson 14, Lesson Practice

a. $\mathbf{39\% + N = 100\%}$

$100\% - 39\% = 61\%$

$39\% + 61\% = 100\%$ check

61%

b. $\mathbf{\frac{2}{5} + S = \frac{5}{5}}$

$$\begin{array}{r} \frac{5}{5} \\ -\ \frac{2}{5} \\ \hline \frac{3}{5} \end{array} \qquad \begin{array}{rl} \frac{2}{5} & \text{pioneers did not survive} \\ +\ \frac{3}{5} & \text{pioneers survived} \\ \hline \frac{5}{5} & \text{total pioneers} \quad \text{check} \end{array}$$

$\mathbf{\frac{3}{5}}$

c. **Answers will vary. See student work. Sample answer: If 45% of the students were boys, then what percent of the students were girls?**

LESSON 14, MIXED PRACTICE

1. $\mathbf{65 + C = 142}$

```
  142          65 grams
-  65    ┌─→ + 77 grams
   77  ──┘    142 grams        check
```

77 grams

2. $\mathbf{\frac{7}{10} + W = \frac{10}{10}}$

$\frac{10}{10} - \frac{7}{10} = \frac{3}{10}$ → $\frac{3}{10}$ recruits liked haircut + $\frac{7}{10}$ recruits did not like haircut = $\frac{10}{10}$ total recruits check

$\mathbf{\frac{3}{10}}$

3. $\mathbf{1789 - 1776 = Y}$

```
  1789          1776
- 1776   ┌─→ +   13
    13 ──┘     1789        check
```

13 years

4. Answers will vary. See student work. Sample answer: If a dozen flavored icicles cost $2.40, then what is the cost per flavored icicle?

5. $\mathbf{24\% + N_A = 100\%}$

$100\% - 24\% = 76\%$

$24\% + 76\% = 100\%$ check

76%

6.

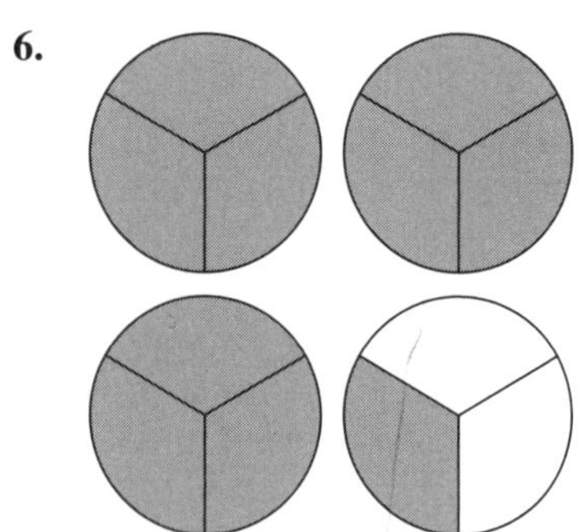

7. 407,042,603

8. Property of zero for multiplication

9. (a) Factors of 40: 1, 2, 4, 5, 8, 10, 20, 40

Factors of 72: 1, 2, 3, 4, 6, 8, 9, 12, 18, 24, 36, 72

1, 2, 4, 8

(b) **8**

10. $\overline{XY}$ (or $\overline{YX}$), $\overline{WX}$ (or $\overline{XW}$), $\overline{WY}$ (or $\overline{YW}$)

11. Count the number in the group, which is 12. Use this as the denominator. Count the number that are shaded, which is 5. Use this as the numerator $\frac{5}{12}$.

12.

```
  623
+ 407
 1030
```

b = **1030**

13.

```
  $20.00
-  $3.47
  $16.53
```

e = **$16.53**

14.

```
     202
35)7070
   70
    07
     0
    70
    70
     0
```

f = **202**

15.

```
   25
×  25
  125
  50
  625
```

m = **625**

16.

```
   5          89
   8        - 83
   7           6
   6
   5
   9
   4
   3
   6
   4
   7
   8
   5
 + 6
  83
```

n = **6**

17.
$$\begin{array}{r} 1000 \\ -\ 295 \\ \hline 705 \end{array}$$
$a = \mathbf{705}$

18. $3\frac{3}{5} + 2\frac{4}{5} = \frac{18}{5} + \frac{14}{5}$
$= \frac{32}{5} = \mathbf{6\frac{2}{5}}$

19. $\frac{5}{2} \cdot \frac{3}{2} = \frac{15}{4} = \mathbf{3\frac{3}{4}}$

20.
$$\begin{array}{r} \$3.63 \\ \$0.87 \\ +\ \$0.96 \\ \hline \mathbf{\$5.46} \end{array}$$

21. $5 \cdot 4 \cdot 3 \cdot 2 \cdot 1 = 20 \cdot 3 \cdot 2 \cdot 1$
$= 60 \cdot 2 \cdot 1 = 120 \cdot 1 = \mathbf{120}$

22. $\mathbf{\frac{8}{27}}$

23.
$$\begin{array}{r} \mathbf{45} \\ 20\overline{)900} \\ \underline{80} \\ 100 \\ \underline{100} \\ 0 \end{array}$$

24.
$$\begin{array}{r} 145 \\ \times\ 74 \\ \hline 580 \\ 1015 \\ \hline \mathbf{10{,}730} \end{array}$$

25.
$$\begin{array}{r} \$0.65 \\ \times\ \ 30 \\ \hline \mathbf{\$19.50} \end{array}$$

26. $(5)(5 + 5) = 5(10) = \mathbf{50}$

27.
$$\begin{array}{r} 13{,}456 \\ -\ 9714 \\ \hline 3742 \end{array}$$
$\mathbf{-3742}$

28. $1000 - 100 = 900,\ 900 - 10 = 890$
$100 - 10 = 90,\ 1000 - 90 = 910$
$890 < 910$
$(1000 - 100) - 10 \mathbf{<} 1000 - (100 - 10)$

29. (a) **Right angle**

(b) **Straight angle**

(c) **Obtuse angle**

30. $\mathbf{\frac{5}{4}}$

Lesson 15, Lesson Practice

a. $\frac{3}{4} \times \frac{5}{5} = \mathbf{\frac{15}{20}}$
$\frac{3}{4} \times \frac{7}{7} = \mathbf{\frac{21}{28}}$
$\frac{3}{4} \times \frac{3}{3} = \mathbf{\frac{9}{12}}$

b. $\frac{3}{4} \times \frac{4}{4} = \mathbf{\frac{12}{16}}$

c. $\frac{4}{5} \times \frac{4}{4} = \frac{\mathbf{16}}{20}$

d. $\frac{3}{8} \times \frac{3}{3} = \frac{9}{\mathbf{24}}$

e.
$$\begin{array}{r} \frac{3}{5} \times \frac{2}{2} = \frac{6}{10} \\ -\ \frac{1}{2} \times \frac{5}{5} = \frac{5}{10} \\ \hline \mathbf{\frac{1}{10}} \end{array}$$

f. $\frac{3}{6} = \frac{3 \div 3}{6 \div 3} = \mathbf{\frac{1}{2}}$

g. $\frac{8}{10} = \frac{8 \div 2}{10 \div 2} = \mathbf{\frac{4}{5}}$

h. $\frac{8}{16} = \frac{8 \div 8}{16 \div 8} = \mathbf{\frac{1}{2}}$

i. $\frac{12}{16} = \frac{12 \div 4}{16 \div 4} = \mathbf{\frac{3}{4}}$

j. $\frac{4}{8} = \frac{4 \div 4}{8 \div 4} = \frac{1}{2},\ 4\frac{4}{8} = \mathbf{4\frac{1}{2}}$

k. $\frac{9}{12} = \frac{9 \div 3}{12 \div 3} = \frac{3}{4}$, $6\frac{9}{12} = \mathbf{6\frac{3}{4}}$

l. $\mathbf{12\frac{8}{15}}$

m. $\frac{16}{24} = \frac{16 \div 8}{24 \div 8} = \frac{2}{3}$, $8\frac{16}{24} = \mathbf{8\frac{2}{3}}$

n. $\frac{5}{12} + \frac{5}{12} = \frac{10}{12} = \frac{10 \div 2}{12 \div 2} = \mathbf{\frac{5}{6}}$

o. $3\frac{7}{10} - 1\frac{1}{10} = 2\frac{6}{10}$

$\frac{6}{10} = \frac{6 \div 2}{10 \div 2} = \frac{3}{5}$, $\mathbf{2\frac{6}{10} = 2\frac{3}{5}}$

p. $\frac{5}{8} \cdot \frac{2}{3} = \frac{10}{24} = \frac{10 \div 2}{24 \div 2} = \mathbf{\frac{5}{12}}$

q. $90\% = \frac{90}{100}$

$\frac{90}{100} \div \frac{10}{10} = \mathbf{\frac{9}{10}}$

r. $75\% = \frac{75}{100}$

$\frac{75}{100} \div \frac{25}{25} = \mathbf{\frac{3}{4}}$

s. $5\% = \frac{5}{100}$

$\frac{5}{100} \div \frac{5}{5} = \mathbf{\frac{1}{20}}$

t. $\frac{2}{3} \cdot \frac{2}{2} = \frac{4}{6}$

$\frac{4}{6} - \frac{1}{6} = \frac{3}{6} = \frac{3 \div 3}{6 \div 3} = \mathbf{\frac{1}{2}}$

Lesson 15, Mixed Practice

1. **1998 − *B* = 75**

$$\begin{array}{r} 1998 \\ -\ \ \ 75 \\ \hline \mathbf{1923} \end{array}$$

2. **27 + 38 + 56 = *T***

$$\begin{array}{r} 27 \text{ geese} \\ 38 \text{ geese} \\ +\ 56 \text{ geese} \\ \hline \mathbf{121 \text{ geese}} \end{array}$$

3. $40\% = \frac{40}{100}$

$\frac{40}{100} \div \frac{20}{20} = \mathbf{\frac{2}{5}}$

4. **60*C* = 9000**

$$\begin{array}{r} 150 \\ 60\overline{)9000} \\ \underline{60} \\ 300 \\ \underline{300} \\ 00 \\ \underline{0} \\ 0 \end{array}$$

150 bushels

5. $2\frac{1}{2}\text{ in.} - 1\frac{7}{8}\text{ in.} = \frac{5}{2}\text{ in.} - \frac{15}{8}\text{ in.}$

$= \frac{20}{8}\text{ in.} - \frac{15}{8}\text{ in.} = \mathbf{\frac{5}{8}\text{ in.}}$

6. **3 · 5 > 3 + 5**

7.
$$\begin{array}{r} 12 \\ 8\overline{)100} \\ \underline{8} \\ 20 \\ \underline{16} \\ 4 \\ \underline{0} \\ 4 \end{array}$$

8. (a) $\frac{6}{8} = \frac{6 \div 2}{8 \div 2} = \mathbf{\frac{3}{4}}$

(b) $\frac{6}{10} = \frac{6 \div 2}{10 \div 2} = \frac{3}{5}$, $2\frac{6}{10} = \mathbf{2\frac{3}{5}}$

9. $\frac{2}{3} \cdot \frac{3}{3} = \mathbf{\frac{6}{9}}$

$\frac{2}{3} \cdot \frac{5}{5} = \mathbf{\frac{10}{15}}$

$\frac{2}{3} \cdot \frac{6}{6} = \mathbf{\frac{12}{18}}$

10. (a) $\frac{3}{5} \cdot \frac{4}{4} = \mathbf{\frac{12}{20}}$

(b) $\frac{1}{2} \cdot \frac{10}{10} = \mathbf{\frac{10}{20}}$

(c) $\frac{3}{4} \cdot \frac{5}{5} = \mathbf{\frac{15}{20}}$

11. (a) $\overleftrightarrow{QS}$ or $\overleftrightarrow{QR}$ or $\overleftrightarrow{RS}$ (or $\overleftrightarrow{SQ}$ or $\overleftrightarrow{RQ}$ or $\overleftrightarrow{SR}$)

(b) $\overrightarrow{RT}$, $\overrightarrow{RQ}$, $\overrightarrow{RS}$

(c) $\angle TRS$ or $\angle SRT$

12. (a) $\mathbf{3\frac{2}{3}}$

(b) $\frac{12}{3} = \frac{12 \div 3}{3 \div 3} = \frac{4}{1} = \mathbf{4}$

(c) $\mathbf{4\frac{1}{3}}$

13.

$$11(6 + 7) = 11(13) = 143$$
$$66 + 77 = 143$$
$$143 = 143$$
$$(11)(6 + 7) \mathbf{=} 66 + 77$$

14.

$$\begin{array}{r} 50 \\ -\ 39 \\ \hline 11 \end{array}$$

$b = \mathbf{11}$

15.

$$\begin{array}{r} 50 \\ 6\overline{)300} \\ 30 \\ \hline 00 \\ 0 \\ \hline 0 \end{array}$$

$a = \mathbf{50}$

16.

$$\begin{array}{r} \$5.00 \\ +\ \$0.05 \\ \hline \$5.05 \end{array}$$

$c = \mathbf{\$5.05}$

17.

$$\begin{array}{r} 35 \\ \times\ 35 \\ \hline 175 \\ 105 \\ \hline 1225 \end{array}$$

$w = \mathbf{1225}$

18.

$$80\% = \frac{80}{100}$$
$$\frac{80}{100} \div \frac{20}{20} = \mathbf{\frac{4}{5}}$$

19.

$$35\% = \frac{35}{100}$$
$$\frac{35}{100} \div \frac{5}{5} = \mathbf{\frac{7}{20}}$$

20. **8**

21. $\frac{2}{5} + \frac{3}{5} + \frac{4}{5} = \frac{9}{5} = \mathbf{1\frac{4}{5}}$

22. $3\frac{5}{8} - 1\frac{3}{8} = 2\frac{2}{8} = \mathbf{2\frac{1}{4}}$

23. $\frac{4}{3} \cdot \frac{3}{4} = \frac{12}{12} = \mathbf{1}$

24. $\frac{3}{4} + \frac{3}{4} = \frac{6}{4} = 1\frac{2}{4} = \mathbf{1\frac{1}{2}}$

25. $\frac{7}{5} + \frac{8}{5} = \frac{15}{5} = \mathbf{3}$

26.

$$\frac{11}{12} - \frac{1}{12} = \frac{10}{12}$$
$$\frac{10 \div 2}{12 \div 2} = \mathbf{\frac{5}{6}}$$

27.

$$\frac{5}{6} \cdot \frac{2}{3} = \frac{10}{18}$$
$$\frac{10 \div 2}{18 \div 2} = \mathbf{\frac{5}{9}}$$

28. (a) $\frac{4}{8} + \frac{4}{8} = \frac{8}{8} = \mathbf{1}$

(b) $\frac{4}{8} - \frac{4}{8} = \frac{0}{8} = \mathbf{0}$

29.

$$\frac{1}{3} \cdot \frac{2}{2} = \frac{2}{6}$$
$$\frac{2}{6} + \frac{1}{6} = \frac{3}{6} = \mathbf{\frac{1}{2}}$$

30.

$$2\frac{2}{3} = \frac{8}{3}$$
$$\frac{8}{3} \cdot \frac{1}{4} = \frac{8}{12}$$
$$\frac{8 \div 4}{12 \div 4} = \mathbf{\frac{2}{3}}$$

Lesson 16, Lesson Practice

a. **2 yards**

b. **2 quarts**

c. **8 lb**

d. $\frac{3}{8}$ in. + $\frac{5}{8}$ in. = $\frac{8}{8}$ in. = **1 in.**

e.
$$\begin{array}{r} 32° \text{ F} \\ +\ 180° \text{ F} \\ \hline \mathbf{212° \text{ F}} \end{array}$$

f. 2(3 ft + 4 ft) = 2(7 ft) = **14 ft**

g. 1 ton = 2000 pounds
$$\begin{array}{r} 2000 \text{ pounds} \\ -\ 1000 \text{ pounds} \\ \hline \mathbf{1000 \text{ pounds}} \end{array}$$

h. $\mathbf{\frac{1}{2}}$ **ounce**

Lesson 16, Mixed Practice

1. **35 +** N_A **= 118**
$$\begin{array}{r} 118 \text{ students} \\ -\ 35 \text{ students} \\ \hline \mathbf{83 \text{ students}} \end{array}$$

2. **18*C* = 4500**
$$\begin{array}{r} 250 \\ 18\overline{)4500} \\ \underline{36} \\ 90 \\ \underline{90} \\ 00 \\ \underline{0} \\ 0 \end{array}$$
250 cartons

3. **324 − *F* = 27**
$$\begin{array}{r} 324 \text{ ducks} \\ -\ 27 \text{ ducks} \\ \hline \mathbf{297 \text{ ducks}} \end{array}$$

4. **(2 × 100) + (5 × 10)**

5. (a) $\frac{8}{10} = \frac{4}{5}$

(b) $\frac{8}{5} = 1\frac{3}{5}$

$\frac{8}{5} > 1\frac{2}{5}$

6. ***AB*** **is** $\mathbf{1\frac{3}{8}}$ **in.;** ***CB*** **is** $\mathbf{1\frac{3}{8}}$ **in.;** ***CA*** **is** $\mathbf{2\frac{3}{4}}$ **in.**

7. (a) $\frac{8}{12} = \frac{8 \div 4}{12 \div 4} = \mathbf{\frac{2}{3}}$

(b) $40\% = \frac{40}{100}$

$\frac{40}{100} \div \frac{20}{20} = \mathbf{\frac{2}{5}}$

(c) $\frac{10}{12} = \frac{10 \div 2}{12 \div 2} = \frac{5}{6}$, $6\frac{10}{12} = \mathbf{6\frac{5}{6}}$

8.

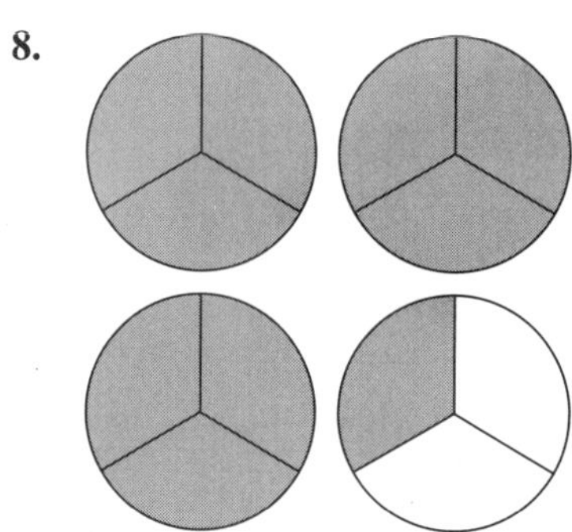

9. (a) $\frac{5}{6} \cdot \frac{4}{4} = \mathbf{\frac{20}{24}}$

(b) $\frac{3}{8} \cdot \frac{3}{3} = \mathbf{\frac{9}{24}}$

(c) $\frac{1}{4} \cdot \frac{6}{6} = \mathbf{\frac{6}{24}}$

10. (a) 100% ÷ 3 = $\mathbf{33\frac{1}{3}}$%

(b) $\frac{1 \text{ quart}}{4 \text{ quarts}} = \mathbf{\frac{1}{4}}$

11.
$$\begin{array}{r} 90 \\ 7\overline{)630} \\ \underline{63} \\ 00 \\ \underline{0} \\ 0 \end{array}$$
1, 2, 3, 5, 6, 7, 9

12. (a) $\mathbf{2\frac{2}{7}}$

(b) $3\frac{16}{8} = 3\frac{2}{1} = \frac{5}{1} = \mathbf{5}$

(c) $2\frac{16}{9} = \frac{34}{9} = \mathbf{3\frac{7}{9}}$

13. **Identity property of multiplication**

14.
$$\begin{array}{r} 1776 \\ +\quad 87 \\ \hline 1863 \end{array}$$
$m = \mathbf{1863}$

15.
$$\begin{array}{r} \$16.25 \\ -\ \$10.15 \\ \hline \$6.10 \end{array}$$
$b = \mathbf{\$6.10}$

16.
$$\begin{array}{r} 77 \\ 13\overline{)1001} \\ \underline{91} \\ 91 \\ \underline{91} \\ 0 \end{array}$$
$n = \mathbf{77}$

17.
$$\begin{array}{r} 42 \\ 42\overline{)1764} \\ \underline{168} \\ 84 \\ \underline{84} \\ 0 \end{array}$$
$d = \mathbf{42}$

18. $3\frac{3}{4} - 1\frac{1}{4} = 2\frac{2}{4} = \mathbf{2\frac{1}{2}}$

19. $\frac{3}{10}$ in. $+ \frac{8}{10}$ in. $= \frac{11}{10}$ in. $= \mathbf{1\frac{1}{10}}$ **in.**

20. $\frac{3}{4} \times \frac{1}{3} = \frac{3}{12} = \frac{3 \div 3}{12 \div 3} = \mathbf{\frac{1}{4}}$

21. $\frac{4}{3} \cdot \frac{3}{2} = \frac{12}{6} = \mathbf{2}$

22.
$$\begin{array}{r} \mathbf{625} \\ 16\overline{)10{,}000} \\ \underline{9\,6} \\ 40 \\ \underline{32} \\ 80 \\ \underline{80} \\ 0 \end{array}$$

23. $\frac{100\%}{8} = \frac{100\% \div 4}{8 \div 4} = \frac{25\%}{2}$

$= \mathbf{12\frac{1}{2}\%}$

24.
$$\begin{array}{r} 7\,777 \\ 9\overline{)70{,}000} \\ \underline{63} \\ 7\,0 \\ \underline{6\,3} \\ 70 \\ \underline{63} \\ 70 \\ \underline{63} \\ 7 \end{array}$$
$\mathbf{7777\frac{7}{9}}$

25.
$$\begin{array}{r} 45 \\ \times\ 45 \\ \hline 225 \\ 180 \\ \hline \mathbf{2025} \end{array}$$

26. **Each term can be found by adding $\frac{1}{16}$ to the preceding term** $\left(\textbf{or } K = \frac{1}{16}n\right)$.

$\frac{3}{16} + \frac{1}{16} = \frac{4}{16} = \frac{1}{4}$

$\frac{4}{16} + \frac{1}{16} = \frac{5}{16}$

$\frac{5}{16} + \frac{1}{16} = \frac{6}{16}, \frac{6 \div 2}{16 \div 2} = \frac{3}{8}$

$\mathbf{\frac{1}{4}, \frac{5}{16}, \frac{3}{8}}$

27. **Acute angle, obtuse angle**

28. $2\frac{1}{2} = \frac{5}{2}, 1\frac{2}{3} = \frac{5}{3}$

$\frac{5}{2} \times \frac{5}{3} = \frac{25}{6}$

$= \mathbf{4\frac{1}{6}}$

29. $\frac{2}{3} \cdot \frac{2}{2} = \frac{4}{6}$

$\frac{4}{6} + \frac{1}{6} = \mathbf{\frac{5}{6}}$

30. $\mathbf{\frac{8}{3}}$

Lesson 17, Lesson Practice

a. **90°**

b. **50°**

c. **115°**

d. **65°**

e. **130°**

f. **23°**

g.

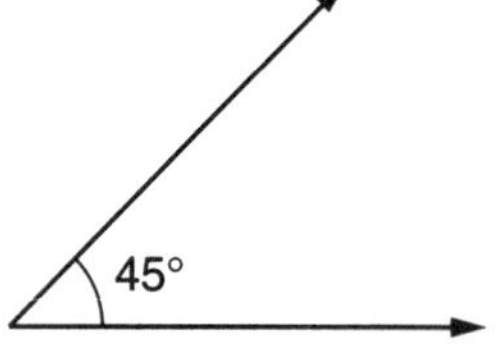

h.

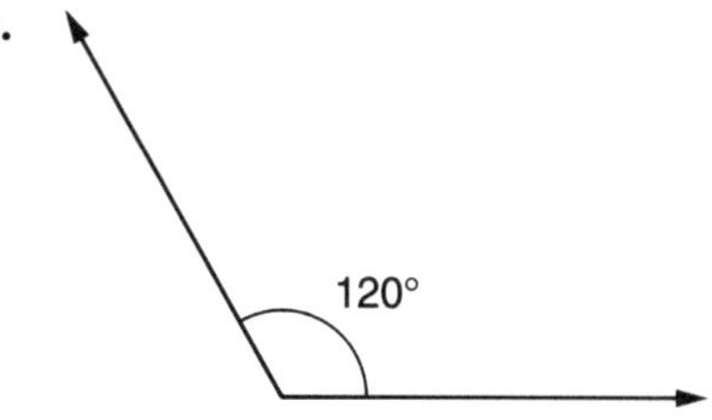

i.

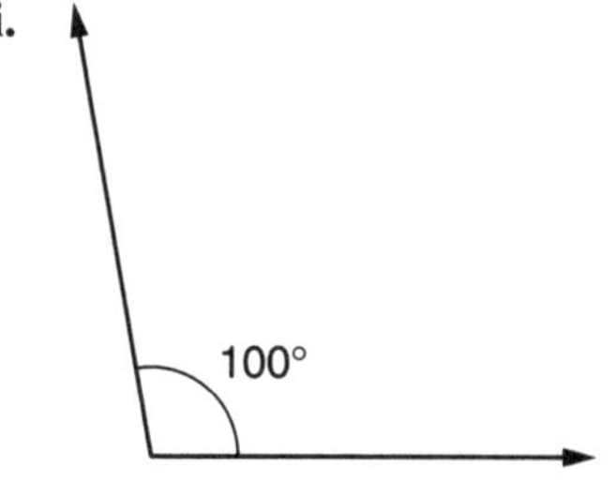

j.

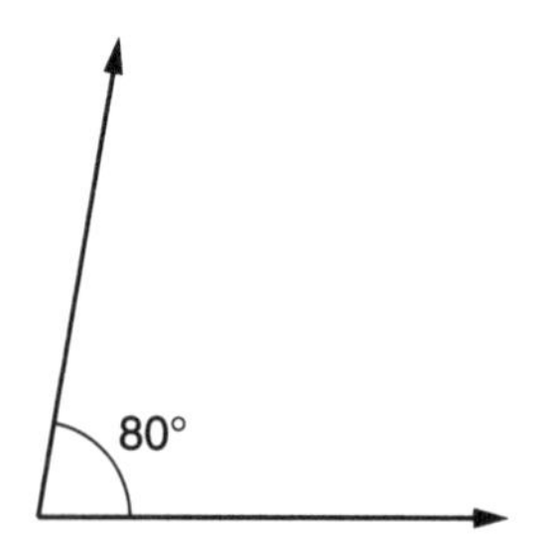

k. $\mathbf{\frac{1}{2}}$ **degree**

Lesson 17, Mixed Practice

1. **2420 + 5090 = *T***

$$\begin{array}{r} 2420 \text{ soldiers} \\ +\ 5090 \text{ soldiers} \\ \hline \mathbf{7510 \text{ soldiers}} \end{array}$$

2. $\mathbf{\frac{3}{20} + F = \frac{20}{20}}$

$$\begin{array}{r} \frac{20}{20} \\ -\ \frac{3}{20} \\ \hline \mathbf{\frac{17}{20}} \end{array}$$

3. **15*S* = 210**

$$\begin{array}{r} 14 \\ 15\overline{)210} \\ 15 \\ \hline 60 \\ 60 \\ \hline 0 \end{array}$$

14 students

4. **1620 − 1492 = *D***

$$\begin{array}{r} 1620 \\ -\ 1492 \\ \hline 128 \end{array}$$

128 years

5. C. $\mathbf{\frac{5}{3}}$

6. (a) $\overleftrightarrow{QR}$ (or $\overleftrightarrow{RQ}$)

(b) $\overleftrightarrow{\mathbf{RT}}$ (or $\overleftrightarrow{\mathbf{TR}}$)

(c) **90°**

7. (a) $\frac{12 \div 4}{16 \div 4} = \mathbf{\frac{3}{4}}$

(b) $\frac{12 \div 6}{18 \div 6} = \frac{2}{3}$, $3\frac{12}{18} = \mathbf{3\frac{2}{3}}$

(c) $\frac{25}{100} \div \frac{25}{25} = \mathbf{\frac{1}{4}}$

8. 2 lb = 2 (16 oz) = 32 oz
32 oz + 8 oz = **40 oz**

9. (a) $\frac{2}{9} \cdot \frac{2}{2} = \mathbf{\frac{4}{18}}$

(b) $\frac{1}{3} \cdot \frac{6}{6} = \mathbf{\frac{6}{18}}$

(c) $\frac{5}{6} \cdot \frac{3}{3} = \mathbf{\frac{15}{18}}$

10.

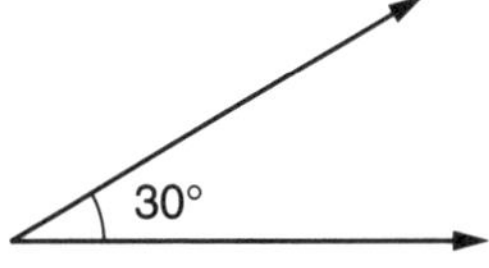

11. (a) Factors of 20: 1, 2, 4, 5, 10, 20
Factors of 50: 1, 2, 5, 10, 25, 50
1, 2, 5, 10

(b) **10**

12.

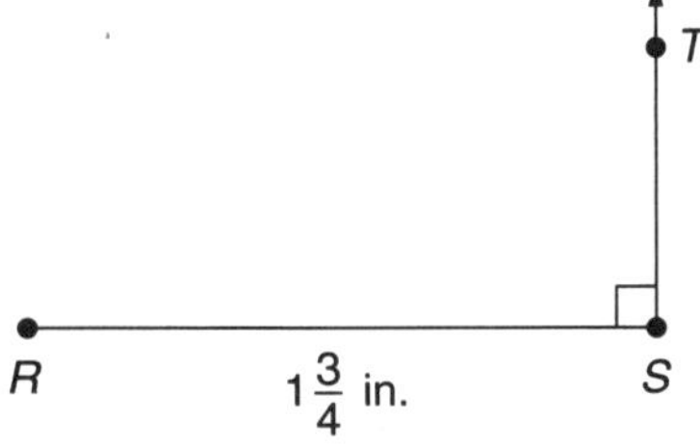

13. (a) $\frac{8}{4} - \frac{4}{8} = \frac{8}{4} - \frac{4 \div 2}{8 \div 2}$

$= \frac{8}{4} - \frac{2}{4} = \frac{6}{4} = \mathbf{\frac{3}{2}}$ or $\mathbf{1\frac{1}{2}}$

(b) $4 - \frac{4}{8} = \frac{4}{1} - \frac{4}{8}$

$= \frac{4}{1} \cdot \frac{8}{8} - \frac{4}{8} = \frac{32}{8} - \frac{4}{8}$

$= \frac{28}{8} = \frac{28 \div 4}{8 \div 4} = \mathbf{\frac{7}{2}}$ or $\mathbf{3\frac{1}{2}}$

14.
$$\begin{array}{r} 141 \\ +\ 231 \\ \hline 372 \end{array}$$
x = **372**

15.
$$\begin{array}{r} \$25.00 \\ -\ \$6.30 \\ \hline \$18.70 \end{array}$$
y = **$18.70**

16.
$$\begin{array}{r} \$3.75 \\ 8\overline{)\$30.00} \\ \underline{24} \\ 60 \\ \underline{56} \\ 40 \\ \underline{40} \\ 0 \end{array}$$
w = **$3.75**

17. 100% ÷ 20% = 5
m = **5**

18. $3\frac{5}{6} - 1\frac{1}{6} = 2\frac{4}{6}$

$\frac{4 \div 2}{6 \div 2} = \frac{2}{3}$

$2\frac{4}{6} = \mathbf{2\frac{2}{3}}$

19. $\frac{1}{2} \cdot \frac{2}{3} = \frac{2}{6} = \mathbf{\frac{1}{3}}$

20.
$$\begin{array}{r} \mathbf{\$2.50} \\ 40\overline{)\$100.00} \\ \underline{80} \\ 200 \\ \underline{200} \\ 00 \\ \underline{0} \\ 0 \end{array}$$

21.
$$\begin{array}{r} 55 \\ \times\ 55 \\ \hline 275 \\ 275 \\ \hline \mathbf{3025} \end{array}$$

22. 2(8 in. + 6 in.) = 2(14 in.)
= **28 in.**

23. $\frac{3}{4}$ in. + $\frac{3}{4}$ in. = $\frac{6}{4}$ in.
= $\frac{3}{2}$ in. = $\mathbf{1\frac{1}{2}}$ **in.**

24. $\frac{15}{16}$ in. − $\frac{3}{16}$ in. = $\frac{12 \div 4}{16 \div 4}$ in.
= $\mathbf{\frac{3}{4}}$ **in.**

25. $\frac{1}{2} \cdot \frac{4}{3} \cdot \frac{9}{2} = \frac{4}{6} \cdot \frac{9}{2}$
$= \frac{36}{12} = \mathbf{3}$

26. $20.25
− $15.17
$5.08
$5 bill, 1 nickel, 3 pennies

27. (a) $\left(\frac{1}{2} \cdot \frac{3}{4}\right) \cdot \frac{2}{3} = \left(\frac{3}{8}\right) \cdot \frac{2}{3}$
$= \frac{6 \div 6}{24 \div 6}$
$= \frac{1}{4}$
$\frac{1}{2} \cdot \left(\frac{3}{4} \cdot \frac{2}{3}\right) = \frac{1}{2} \cdot \left(\frac{6}{12}\right)$
$= \frac{6}{24} = \frac{1}{4}, \frac{1}{4} = \frac{1}{4}$
$\left(\frac{1}{2} \cdot \frac{3}{4}\right) \cdot \frac{2}{3} = \frac{1}{2}\left(\frac{3}{4} \cdot \frac{2}{3}\right)$
(b) **Associative property of multiplication**

28. **Answers will vary. See student work. Sample answer: If 85% of Shyla's answers were correct, then what percent were not correct?**

29. $3\frac{3}{4} = \frac{4 \times 3 + 3}{4} = \mathbf{\frac{15}{4}}$
reciprocal $= \mathbf{\frac{4}{15}}$

30. $\frac{3}{4} \cdot \frac{2}{2} = \frac{6}{8}$
$\frac{6}{8} + \frac{5}{8} = \frac{11}{8} = \mathbf{1\frac{3}{8}}$

Lesson 18, Lesson Practice

a. **Octagon**

b. **Square**

c. **Acute angle**

d. **Yes**

e. **No**

f. **∠B**

g. **Equal in measure; each angle is a right angle with a measure of 90°.**

h. 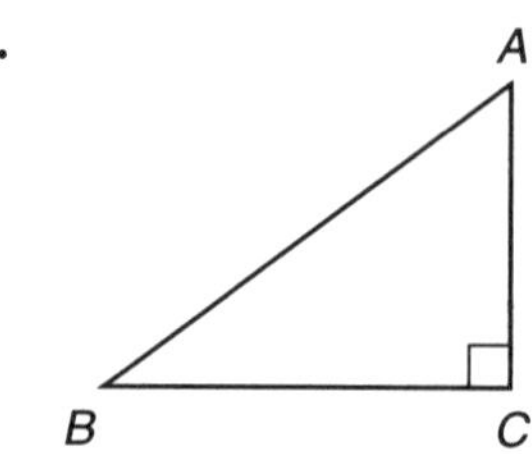

Lesson 18, Mixed Practice

1. **6D = 3300**
```
   550
6)3300      550 miles
  30
   30
   30
    00
     0
     0
```

2. **456 + 517 = T**
456 miles
+ 517 miles
973 miles

3. **3977 + W = 5000**
5000 meters
− 3977 meters
1023 meters

4. **1,000,000,000 − 10,000,000 = D**
1,000,000,000
− 10,000,000
990,000,000
Nine hundred ninety million

5. (a) $\mathbf{-1, 0, \frac{3}{4}, 1, \frac{5}{3}}$
(b) $\mathbf{-1, 0}$

6. **Side *AD*** (or **side *DA***)

7. (a) **−2**

(b) **4**

8. (a) $2\% = \frac{2}{100} = \frac{2}{100} \div \frac{2}{2} = \mathbf{\frac{1}{50}}$

(b) $\frac{12 \div 4}{20 \div 4} = \mathbf{\frac{3}{5}}$

(c) $\frac{15 \div 5}{20 \div 5} = \frac{3}{4},\ 6\frac{15}{20} = \mathbf{6\frac{3}{4}}$

9. (a) $\frac{4}{5} \cdot \frac{6}{6} = \mathbf{\frac{24}{30}}$

(b) $\frac{2}{3} \cdot \frac{10}{10} = \mathbf{\frac{20}{30}}$

(c) $\frac{1}{6} \cdot \frac{5}{5} = \mathbf{\frac{5}{30}}$

10. $8 - 5 = 3$
3 sides

11. (a)

(b) **Acute angles**

12. (a) **25%**

(b) $\mathbf{\frac{6}{8}}$ or $\mathbf{\frac{3}{4}}$

13. **Identity property of multiplication**

14. $\frac{5}{8} + \frac{3}{8} = \frac{8}{8}$

$x = \mathbf{\frac{8}{8}}$ or **1**

15. $\frac{7}{10} - \frac{3}{10} = \frac{4}{10}$

$y = \mathbf{\frac{4}{10}}$ or $\mathbf{\frac{2}{5}}$

16. $\frac{5}{6} - \frac{1}{6} = \frac{4}{6}$

$m = \mathbf{\frac{4}{6}}$ or $\mathbf{\frac{2}{3}}$

17. $\mathbf{\frac{4}{3}}$

18. $5\frac{7}{10} - \frac{3}{10} = 5\frac{4}{10} = \mathbf{5\frac{2}{5}}$

19. $\frac{3}{2} \cdot \frac{2}{4} = \frac{6}{8} = \mathbf{\frac{3}{4}}$

20.
```
     45
45)2025
   180
    225
    225
      0
```

21.
```
   750
×   80
60,000
```

22.
```
   21
×  21
   21
  42
  441
```

23. $2(50 \text{ in.} + 40 \text{ in.}) = 2(90 \text{ in.})$
$= \mathbf{180 \text{ in.}}$

24. $\frac{8}{16} = \frac{1}{2} = \frac{50}{100} = \mathbf{50\%}$

25. (a) $360° \div 4 = \mathbf{90°}$

(b) $360° \div 6 = \mathbf{60°}$

26. (a)

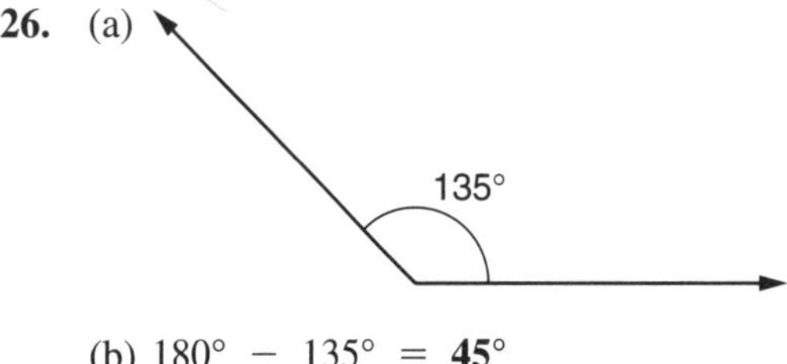

(b) $180° - 135° = \mathbf{45°}$

27. (a) **ΔSQR**

(b) **ΔXYZ**

(c) **∠F**

28. $\frac{1}{2} \cdot \frac{3}{3} = \frac{3}{6}$

$\frac{1}{3} \cdot \frac{2}{2} = \frac{2}{6}$

$\frac{3}{6} + \frac{2}{6} = \mathbf{\frac{5}{6}}$

29. $2\frac{1}{4} = \frac{9}{4}$

$\frac{9}{4} \cdot \frac{4}{3} = \frac{36}{12} = \mathbf{3}$

30.

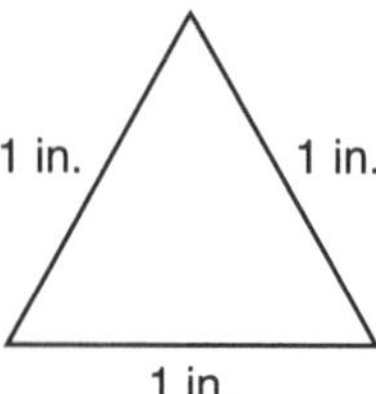

Regular

Lesson 19, Lesson Practice

a. Perimeter $= 3 \text{ in.} + 3 \text{ in.} + 2 \text{ in.} + 5 \text{ in.}$
$= \mathbf{13 \text{ in.}}$

b. Perimeter $= 5(5 \text{ cm}) = \mathbf{25 \text{ cm}}$

c. Perimeter $= 8(12 \text{ in.}) = \mathbf{96 \text{ in.}}$

d. Missing length $= 10 \text{ in.} - 4 \text{ in.} = 6 \text{ in.}$
Missing height $= 5 \text{ in.} - 2 \text{ in.} = 3 \text{ in.}$
Perimeter $= 10 \text{ in.} + 2 \text{ in.} + 6 \text{ in.}$
$+ 3 \text{ in.} + 4 \text{ in.} + 5 \text{ in.}$
$= \mathbf{30 \text{ in.}}$

e. $100 \text{ feet} \div 4 = \mathbf{25 \text{ feet}}$

f.

$\frac{3}{4}$ in.

$\frac{3}{4}$ in.

Perimeter $= 4\left(\frac{3}{4} \text{ in.}\right)$

$= \frac{4}{1} \cdot \frac{3}{4} \text{ in.} = \frac{12}{4} \text{ in.}$

$= \mathbf{3 \text{ in.}}$

Lesson 19, Mixed Practice

1. $\mathbf{\frac{1}{8} + N_L = \frac{8}{8}}$

$$\begin{array}{r} \frac{8}{8} \\ -\ \frac{1}{8} \\ \hline \mathbf{\frac{7}{8}} \end{array}$$

2. $\mathbf{F - 76 = 124}$

$$\begin{array}{r} 124 \text{ people} \\ +\ \ 76 \text{ people} \\ \hline \mathbf{200 \text{ people}} \end{array}$$

3. $\mathbf{84 \times 6 = T}$

$$\begin{array}{r} 84 \\ \times\ \ 6 \\ \hline 504 \end{array}$$

504 slices

4. $4(20 \text{ years}) + 7 \text{ years} = \mathbf{87 \text{ years}}$

5. (a) **Eighteen million, seven hundred thousand**

(b) $\mathbf{(8 \times 100) + (7 \times 10) + (4 \times 1)}$

6. $\mathbf{3 - 7 = -4}$

7. **Water freezes at 32°F. Water boils at 212°F.**

8. Perimeter $= 6 \text{ cm} + 6 \text{ cm} + 8 \text{ cm} + 8 \text{ cm}$
$= \mathbf{28 \text{ cm}}$

9. (a) $3\frac{16}{24} = 3\frac{16 \div 8}{24 \div 8} = \mathbf{3\frac{2}{3}}$

(b) $\frac{15 \div 3}{24 \div 3} = \mathbf{\frac{5}{8}}$

(c) $4\% = \frac{4}{100} = \frac{4 \div 4}{100 \div 4} = \mathbf{\frac{1}{25}}$

10. (a) $\frac{3}{4} \cdot \frac{9}{9} = \mathbf{\frac{27}{36}}$

(b) $\frac{4}{9} \cdot \frac{4}{4} = \mathbf{\frac{16}{36}}$

11.

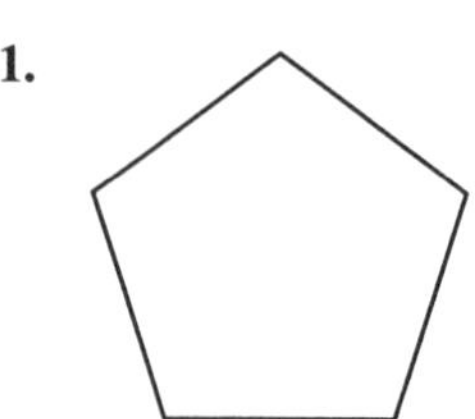

12. **Octagon**

13. (a) **90°**

(b) $4(90°) = \mathbf{360°}$

14. $k = \frac{1}{8} \cdot 8 = \frac{1}{8} \cdot \frac{8}{1} = \frac{8}{8} = \mathbf{1}$

15.
$$\begin{array}{r} 8998 \\ -\ 1547 \\ \hline 7451 \end{array}$$
$a = \mathbf{7451}$

16.
$$\begin{array}{r} \$1.37 \\ 30\overline{)\$41.10} \\ \underline{30} \\ 11\,1 \\ \underline{9\,0} \\ 2\,10 \\ \underline{2\,10} \\ 0 \end{array}$$
$b = \mathbf{\$1.37}$

17.
$$\begin{array}{r} 23 \\ \$0.32\overline{)\$7.36} \\ \underline{6\,4} \\ 96 \\ \underline{96} \\ 0 \end{array}$$
$c = \mathbf{23}$

18.
$$\begin{array}{r} \$30.10 \\ -\ \$26.57 \\ \hline \$3.53 \end{array}$$
$d = \mathbf{\$3.53}$

19. $\frac{2}{3} + \frac{2}{3} + \frac{2}{3} = \frac{6}{3} = \mathbf{2}$

20. $3\frac{7}{8} - \frac{5}{8} = 3\frac{2}{8} = \mathbf{3\frac{1}{4}}$

21. $\frac{2}{3} \cdot \frac{3}{7} = \frac{6}{21} = \mathbf{\frac{2}{7}}$

22. $3\frac{7}{8} + \frac{5}{8} = 3\frac{12}{8} = 4\frac{4}{8} = \mathbf{4\frac{1}{2}}$

23.
$$\begin{array}{r} 50 \\ \times\ 50 \\ \hline \mathbf{2500} \end{array}$$

24.
$$\begin{array}{r} \mathbf{9\,100} \\ 11\overline{)100{,}100} \\ \underline{99} \\ 1\,1 \\ \underline{1\,1} \\ 00 \\ \underline{0} \\ 00 \\ \underline{0} \\ 0 \end{array}$$

25. (a) **2**

(b) $2 \cdot 5 = \mathbf{10}$

26.

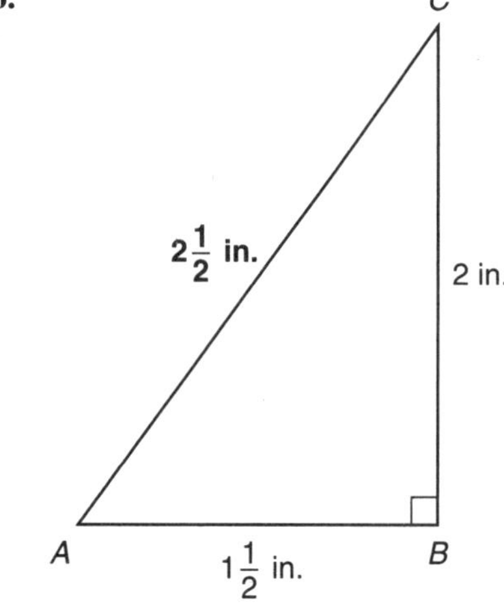

27. $3\frac{1}{3} = \frac{10}{3}$

$\frac{10}{3} \cdot \frac{3}{2} = \frac{30}{6} = \mathbf{5}$

28. $\frac{1}{2} \cdot \frac{5}{5} = \frac{5}{10}$

$\frac{9}{10} - \frac{5}{10} = \frac{4}{10} = \mathbf{\frac{2}{5}}$

29. $100\% \div 3 = \mathbf{33\frac{1}{3}\%}$

30. Missing length = 10 in. − 6 in. = 4 in.
Missing height = 7 in. − 4 in. = 3 in.
Perimeter = 10 in. + 4 in. + 6 in. + 3 in. + 4 in. + 7 in.
= **34 in.**

Lesson 20, Lesson Practice

a. **Four cubed**
$4 \cdot 4 \cdot 4 = \mathbf{64}$

b. **One half squared**
$\frac{1}{2} \cdot \frac{1}{2} = \mathbf{\frac{1}{4}}$

c. **Ten to the sixth power**
$10 \cdot 10 \cdot 10 \cdot 10 \cdot 10 \cdot 10 = \mathbf{1{,}000{,}000}$

d. **Base is 10; exponent is 3**

e. $2^3 \cdot 2^2 = 2 \cdot 2 \cdot 2 \cdot 2 \cdot 2$
$= 2^5$

f. $\frac{2^6}{2^2} = \frac{2 \cdot 2 \cdot 2 \cdot 2 \cdot 2 \cdot 2}{2 \cdot 2}$
$= \frac{64}{4} = 16 = 2 \cdot 2 \cdot 2 \cdot 2 = 2^4$

g. **10**

h. **20**

i. **15**

j. Area $= 15 \text{ m} \times 10 \text{ m}$
$= \mathbf{150 \text{ m}^2}$

k. Area $= 2 \text{ in.} \times 5 \text{ in.}$
$= \mathbf{10 \text{ in.}^2}$

l. Area $= 4 \text{ cm} \times 4 \text{ cm}$
$= \mathbf{16 \text{ cm}^2}$

m. $20 \text{ cm} \div 4 = 5 \text{ cm}$
Area $= 5 \text{ cm} \times 5 \text{ cm} = \mathbf{25 \text{ cm}^2}$

n. Area $= 100$ yards $\times$ 100 yards
$=$ **10,000 square yards**

Lesson 20, Mixed Practice

1. **$4D = 628$**

$$\begin{array}{r} 157 \\ 4\overline{)628} \\ \underline{4} \\ 22 \\ \underline{20} \\ 28 \\ \underline{28} \\ 0 \end{array}$$

157 students

2. **$P - 36 = 46$**
46 parrots
+ 36 parrots
82 parrots

3. **$225 + N_T = 600$**
600 fish
− 225 fish
375 fish

4. **$21{,}050 + 48{,}972 = T$**
21,050
+ 48,972
70,022

5. $k = 2^6 = 2 \cdot 2 \cdot 2 \cdot 2 \cdot 2 \cdot 2$
$= \mathbf{64}$

6. (a) $\mathbf{-2, -\frac{1}{2}, 0, \frac{1}{3}, 1}$

(b) $\mathbf{\frac{1}{3}, -\frac{1}{2}}$

7. **B. $33\frac{1}{3}\%$**

8. **Side *DC*** (or **side *CD***) and **side *AB*** (or **side *BA***)

9. (a) $\left(\frac{1}{3}\right)^3 = \frac{1}{3} \cdot \frac{1}{3} \cdot \frac{1}{3} = \mathbf{\frac{1}{27}}$

(b) $10^4 = 10 \cdot 10 \cdot 10 \cdot 10$
$= \mathbf{10{,}000}$

(c) $\sqrt{12^2} = \sqrt{144} = \mathbf{12}$

10. (a) $\frac{2}{9} \cdot \frac{4}{4} = \mathbf{\frac{8}{36}}$

(b) $\frac{3}{4} \cdot \frac{9}{9} = \mathbf{\frac{27}{36}}$

11. (a) **1, 2, 5, 10**
(b) **1, 7**
(c) **1**

12. 2 feet = 24 inches
24 inches ÷ 4 = **6 inches**

13.
$$\begin{array}{r} 54 \\ -\ 36 \\ \hline 18 \end{array}$$
a = **18**

14.
$$\begin{array}{r} 46 \\ -\ 20 \\ \hline 26 \end{array}$$
w = **26**

15.
$$\begin{array}{r} 12 \\ 5\overline{)60} \\ \underline{5} \\ 10 \\ \underline{10} \\ 0 \end{array}$$
x = **12**

16.
$$\begin{array}{r} 100 \\ -\ 64 \\ \hline 36 \end{array}$$
m = **36**

17. $5^4 \cdot 5^2 = 5 \cdot 5 \cdot 5 \cdot 5 \cdot 5 \cdot 5 = 5^6$
n = **6**

18.
$$\begin{array}{r} 15 \\ 4\overline{)60} \\ \underline{4} \\ 20 \\ \underline{20} \\ 0 \end{array}$$
y = **15**

19. $1\frac{8}{9} + 1\frac{7}{9} = 2\frac{15}{9} = 3\frac{6}{9} = \mathbf{3\frac{2}{3}}$

20. $\frac{5}{2} \cdot \frac{5}{6} = \frac{25}{12} = \mathbf{2\frac{1}{12}}$

21.
$$\begin{array}{r} \mathbf{705} \\ 9\overline{)6345} \\ \underline{63} \\ 04 \\ \underline{0} \\ 45 \\ \underline{45} \\ 0 \end{array}$$

22.
$$\begin{array}{r} 360 \\ \times\ 25 \\ \hline 1800 \\ 720 \\ \hline \mathbf{9000} \end{array}$$

23. $\frac{3}{4} - \left(\frac{1}{4} + \frac{2}{4}\right) = \frac{3}{4} - \left(\frac{3}{4}\right) = \mathbf{0}$

24. $\left(\frac{3}{4} - \frac{1}{4}\right) + \frac{2}{4} = \frac{2}{4} + \frac{2}{4}$
$= \frac{4}{4} = \mathbf{1}$

25. (a) $\frac{3}{10} + \frac{3}{10} = \frac{6}{10} = \mathbf{\frac{3}{5}}$
(b) $\frac{3}{10} \cdot \frac{3}{10} = \mathbf{\frac{9}{100}}$

26. $\frac{1}{2} \cdot \frac{5}{5} = \frac{5}{10}$
$\frac{5}{10} + \frac{3}{10} = \frac{8}{10} = \mathbf{\frac{4}{5}}$

27. $1\frac{4}{5} = \frac{9}{5}$
$\frac{9}{5} \cdot \frac{1}{3} = \frac{9}{15} = \mathbf{\frac{3}{5}}$

28. **Identity property of multiplication**

29. (a) Perimeter = 12 in. + 12 in. + 12 in. + 12 in. = **48 in.** or **4 ft**
(b) Area = 12 in. × 12 in. = **144 in.^{2}** or **1 ft^2**

30. Missing length = 10 in. − 5 in. = 5 in.
Missing height = 8 in. − 4 in. = 4 in.
Perimeter = 10 in. + 4 in. + 5 in. + 4 in. + 5 in. + 8 in.
= **36 in.**

Lesson 21, Lesson Practice

a. **2, 3, 5, 7, 11, 13, 17, 19, 23, 29**

b. **Composite number**

c. 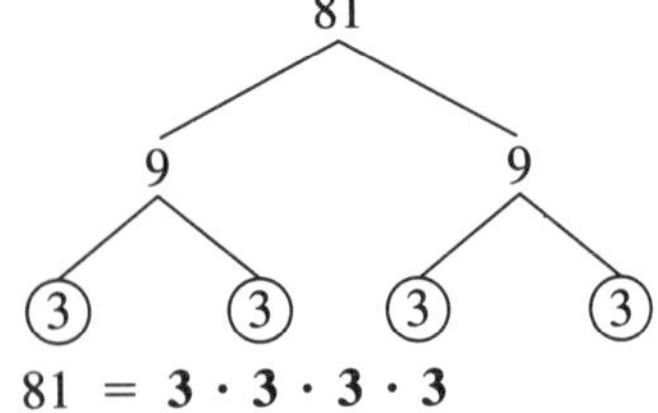

$81 = \mathbf{3 \cdot 3 \cdot 3 \cdot 3}$

d. $360 = \mathbf{2 \cdot 2 \cdot 2 \cdot 3 \cdot 3 \cdot 5}$

$$\begin{array}{r} 1 \\ 5\overline{)5} \\ 3\overline{)15} \\ 3\overline{)45} \\ 2\overline{)90} \\ 2\overline{)180} \\ 2\overline{)360} \end{array}$$

e. 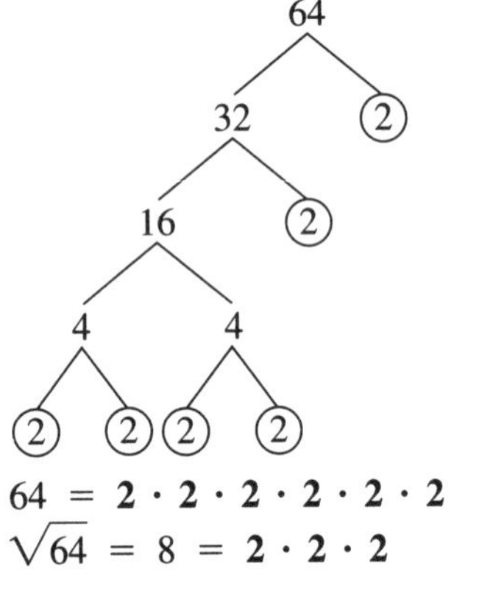

$64 = \mathbf{2 \cdot 2 \cdot 2 \cdot 2 \cdot 2 \cdot 2}$

$\sqrt{64} = 8 = \mathbf{2 \cdot 2 \cdot 2}$

Lesson 21, Mixed Practice

1. $\mathbf{\frac{2}{3} + N_G = \frac{3}{3}}$

$\frac{3}{3} - \frac{2}{3} = \mathbf{\frac{1}{3}}$

2. $\mathbf{7Q = 343}$

$$\begin{array}{r} 49 \\ 7\overline{)343} \\ \underline{28} \\ 63 \\ \underline{63} \\ 0 \end{array}$$

49 quills

3. $\mathbf{2{,}000{,}000{,}000 - 21{,}000{,}000 = D}$

$$\begin{array}{r} 2{,}000{,}000{,}000 \\ -\quad 21{,}000{,}000 \\ \hline 1{,}979{,}000{,}000 \end{array}$$

One billion, nine hundred seventy-nine million

4. **\$14,289 + \$824 =** $\mathbf{N}$

$$\begin{array}{r} \$14{,}289 \\ +\quad \$824 \\ \hline \mathbf{\$15{,}113} \end{array}$$

5. (a) $3\,\frac{12 \div 3}{21 \div 3} = \mathbf{3\frac{4}{7}}$

(b) $\frac{12 \div 12}{48 \div 12} = \mathbf{\frac{1}{4}}$

(c) $12\% = \frac{12}{100} \div \frac{4}{4} = \mathbf{\frac{3}{25}}$

6. **53, 59**

7. (a) $50 = \mathbf{2 \cdot 5 \cdot 5}$

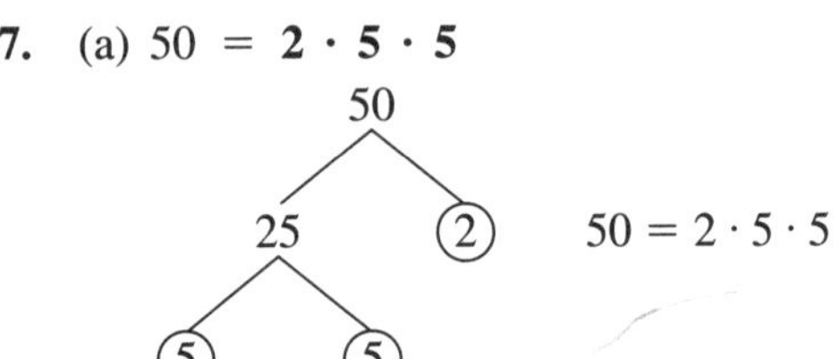

(b) $60 = \mathbf{2 \cdot 2 \cdot 3 \cdot 5}$

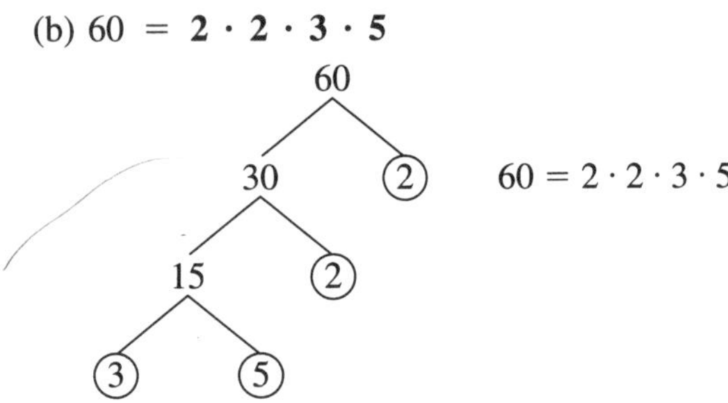

(c) $300 = \mathbf{2 \cdot 2 \cdot 3 \cdot 5 \cdot 5}$

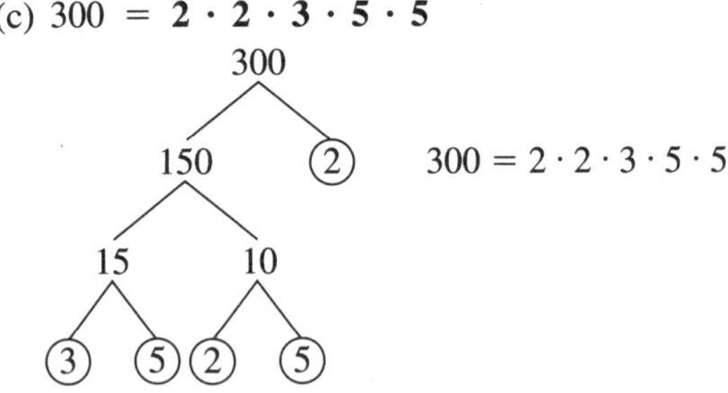

8. **Point *C*; The tick mark between points *B* and *C* is halfway between 1000 and 2000, which is 1500, so points *A* and *B* are eliminated. Point *C* is closer to 1500 than 2000, so *C* is the best choice. Point *D* is too close to 2000 to represent 1610.**

9. (a) $\frac{2}{3} \cdot \frac{5}{5} = \mathbf{\frac{10}{15}}$

(b) $\frac{3}{5} \cdot \frac{3}{3} = \mathbf{\frac{9}{15}}$

(c) $\frac{8 \div 4}{12 \div 4} = \mathbf{\frac{2}{3}}$

10. (a) **3**

(b) **9**

11. 12 inches ÷ 4 = 3 inches
Area = 3 inches × 3 inches
= **9 square inches**

12.

$\frac{3}{4}$ in.

$1\frac{1}{2}$ in.

(a) $2 \times \frac{3}{4}$ in. $= \frac{6}{4}$ in. $= \mathbf{1\frac{1}{2}}$ **in.**

(b) Perimeter $= \frac{3}{4}$ in. $+ \frac{3}{4}$ in. $+ 1\frac{1}{2}$ in.
$+ 1\frac{1}{2}$ in. $= \frac{6}{4}$ in. $+ 2\frac{2}{2}$ in.
$= \frac{6}{4}$ in. $+ \frac{6}{2}$ in. $= \frac{6}{4}$ in.
$+ \frac{12}{4}$ in. $= \frac{18}{4}$ in. $= \mathbf{4\frac{1}{2}}$ **in.**

13. Missing length = 3 in. + 12 in. = 15 in.
Missing height = 8 in. − 5 in. = 3 in.
Perimeter = 8 in. + 15 in. + 5 in.
+ 12 in. + 3 in. + 3 in.
= **46 in.**

14. **Check polygon for five sides; one possibility:**

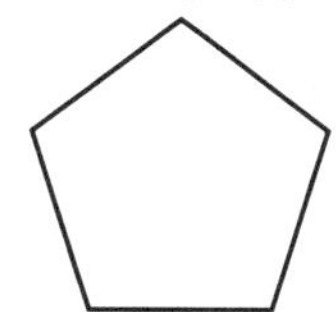

15. $1 - \frac{3}{5} = \frac{5}{5} - \frac{3}{5} = \frac{2}{5}$

$p = \mathbf{\frac{2}{5}}$

16. $1 \cdot \frac{5}{3}$

$q = \mathbf{\frac{5}{3}}$

17.
$$\begin{array}{r} 25 \\ \times\ 50 \\ \hline 1250 \end{array}$$
$w = \mathbf{1250}$

18. $\frac{5}{6} - \frac{1}{6} = \frac{4}{6}$

$f = \mathbf{\frac{4}{6}}$ or $\mathbf{\frac{2}{3}}$

19. $1\frac{2}{3} + 3\frac{2}{3} = 4\frac{4}{3} = 5\frac{1}{3}$

$m = \mathbf{5\frac{1}{3}}$

20.
$$\begin{array}{r} \mathbf{17} \\ 3\overline{)51} \\ \underline{3} \\ 21 \\ \underline{21} \\ 0 \end{array}$$
$c = \mathbf{17}$

21. $\frac{2}{3} + \frac{2}{3} + \frac{2}{3} = \frac{6}{3} = \mathbf{2}$

22. $\left(\frac{2}{3}\right)^3 = \frac{2}{3} \cdot \frac{2}{3} \cdot \frac{2}{3} = \mathbf{\frac{8}{27}}$

23. (a) 225 = **3 · 3 · 5 · 5**

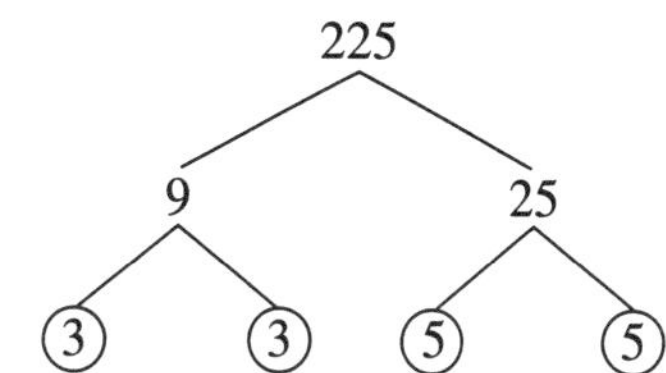

(b) $\sqrt{225} = 15$
15 = **3 · 5**

24. **If we divide the numerator and the denominator of a fraction by their GCF, we reduce the fraction to lowest terms in one step.**

25.

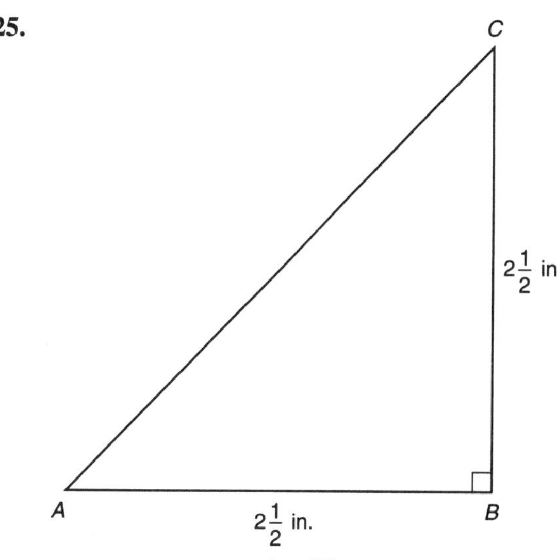

26. $1\frac{3}{4} = \frac{7}{4}$

$\frac{7}{4} \times \frac{3}{2} = \frac{21}{8} = \mathbf{2\frac{5}{8}}$

27. (a) $\overline{CB}$ (or $\overline{BC}$)

(b) $\overline{AB}$ (or $\overline{BA}$)

(c) $\overline{MC}$ and $\overline{MB}$

(d) $\angle ABC$ (or $\angle CBA$)

28. $\frac{1 \text{ ~~quart~~}}{4 \text{ ~~quarts~~}} = \frac{1}{4}, \frac{1}{4} \cdot \frac{25}{25} = \frac{25}{100} = \mathbf{25\%}$

29. (a) $a + b = b + a$

(b) **Commutative property of addition**

30. (a) ΔKLJ

(b) ΔDEF

(c) $\angle S$

Lesson 22, Lesson Practice

a.–b.

	60 pumpkins
$\frac{1}{4}$ were not ripe.	15 pumpkins
$\frac{3}{4}$ were ripe.	15 pumpkins
	15 pumpkins
	15 pumpkins

a. 3×15 pumpkins $=$ **45 pumpkins**

b. **15 pumpkins**

c.–d.

	20 tomatoes
$\frac{3}{5}$ were green.	4 tomatoes
	4 tomatoes
	4 tomatoes
$\frac{2}{5}$ were not green.	4 tomatoes
	4 tomatoes

c. $100\% - 60\% = 40\%$

$40\% = \frac{40}{100} \div \frac{20}{20} = \mathbf{\frac{2}{5}}$

d. 3×4 tomatoes $=$ **12 tomatoes**

e. **See student work.**

Lesson 22, Mixed Practice

1. $\mathbf{28 + 30 + 23 = T}$

28 students
30 students
$+$ 23 students
81 students

2. $\mathbf{3R = 81}$

$$\begin{array}{r} 27 \\ 3\overline{)81} \\ \underline{6} \\ 21 \\ \underline{21} \\ 0 \end{array}$$

27 students

3. $\mathbf{126{,}000 - L = 79{,}000}$

126,000
$-$ 79,000
47,000

4. $\mathbf{10{,}313 - 2700 = D}$

10,313
$-$ 2 700
7 613

Seven thousand, six hundred thirteen

5.

	36 spectators
$\frac{5}{9}$ were happy.	4 spectators
	4 spectators
	4 spectators
	4 spectators
	4 spectators
$\frac{4}{9}$ were not happy.	4 spectators
	4 spectators
	4 spectators
	4 spectators

(a) 5×4 spectators $=$ **20 spectators**

(b) 4×4 spectators $=$ **16 spectators**

6.

36 eggs

$\frac{3}{4}$ were not cracked. { 9 eggs, 9 eggs, 9 eggs

$\frac{1}{4}$ were cracked. { 9 eggs

$$25\% = \frac{25}{100} \div \frac{25}{25}$$
$$= \frac{1}{4}$$

(a) $\frac{4}{4} - \frac{1}{4} = \mathbf{\frac{3}{4}}$

(b) 3×9 eggs $=$ **27 eggs**

7. (a) $\mathbf{\frac{2}{5}}$

(b) $\frac{6}{10} = \frac{6}{10} \times \frac{10}{10} = \frac{60}{100} = \mathbf{60\%}$

8. (a) **4**

(b) $4 \times 3 = \mathbf{12}$

9. (a) **0**

(b) **Property of zero for multiplication**

10. $\frac{3}{3} - \left(\frac{1}{3} \cdot \frac{3}{1}\right) = \frac{3}{3} - \left(\frac{3}{3}\right) = 0$

$\left(\frac{3}{3} - \frac{1}{3}\right) \cdot \frac{3}{1} = \left(\frac{2}{3}\right) \cdot \frac{3}{1} = \frac{6}{3} = 2$

$\mathbf{0 < 2}$

11.

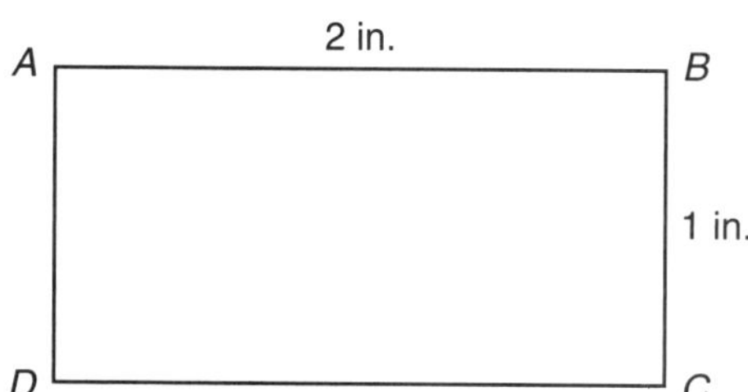

(a) Perimeter $=$ 2 in. $+$ 2 in. $+$ 1 in. $+$ 1 in. $=$ **6 in.**

(b) Area $=$ 2 in. $\times$ 1 in. $=$ **2 in.^{2}**

(c)
$$\begin{array}{r} 90^\circ \\ 90^\circ \\ 90^\circ \\ +\ 90^\circ \\ \hline \mathbf{360^\circ} \end{array}$$

12. (a)

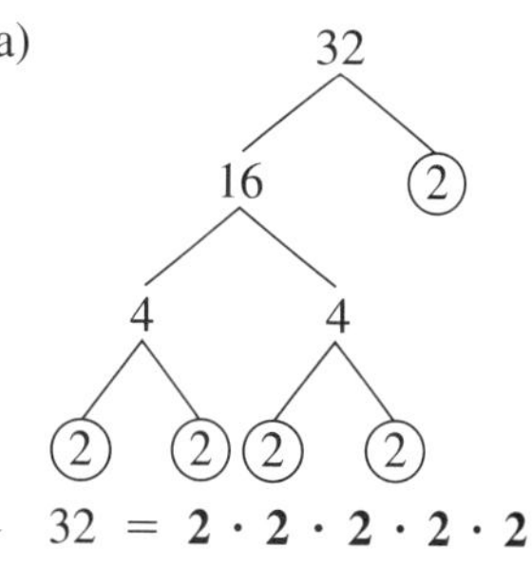

$32 = \mathbf{2 \cdot 2 \cdot 2 \cdot 2 \cdot 2}$

(b)

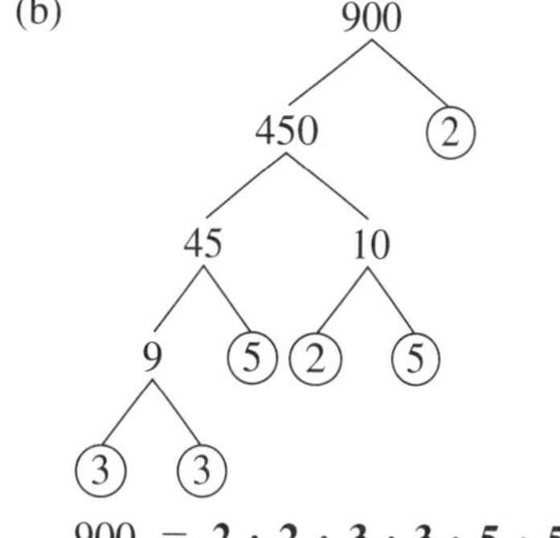

$900 = \mathbf{2 \cdot 2 \cdot 3 \cdot 3 \cdot 5 \cdot 5}$

(c) $\sqrt{900} = 30$

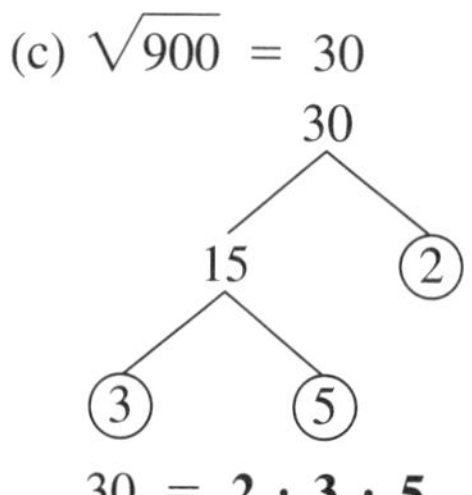

$30 = \mathbf{2 \cdot 3 \cdot 5}$

13. (a) $\frac{5}{6} \cdot \frac{10}{10} = \mathbf{\frac{50}{60}}$

(b) $\frac{3}{5} \cdot \frac{12}{12} = \mathbf{\frac{36}{60}}$

(c) $\frac{7}{12} \cdot \frac{5}{5} = \mathbf{\frac{35}{60}}$

14. $\frac{50}{60} + \frac{36}{60} + \frac{35}{60} = \frac{121}{60} = \mathbf{2\frac{1}{60}}$

15. (a) $\mathbf{-2, -\frac{2}{3}, 0, 1, \frac{3}{2}}$

(b) $\mathbf{1, \frac{3}{2}}$

16. $\frac{11}{12} - \frac{5}{12} = \frac{6}{12}$

$a = \mathbf{\frac{6}{12}}$ or $\mathbf{\frac{1}{2}}$

17. $\begin{array}{r} 10 \\ 90\overline{)900} \\ \underline{90} \\ 00 \\ \underline{0} \\ 0 \end{array}$

$c = \mathbf{10}$

18. $\begin{array}{r} 11 \\ 11\overline{)121} \\ \underline{11} \\ 11 \\ \underline{11} \\ 0 \end{array}$

$x = \mathbf{11}$

19. $2\frac{2}{3} + 1\frac{1}{3} = 3\frac{3}{3} = 4$

$y = \mathbf{4}$

20. $10^2 \cdot 10^5 =$

$10 \cdot 10 \cdot 10 \cdot 10 \cdot 10 \cdot 10 \cdot 10$

$= 10^7$

$n = \mathbf{7}$

21. $\frac{5}{6} + \frac{5}{6} + \frac{5}{6} = \frac{15}{6} = \mathbf{2\frac{1}{2}}$

22. $\frac{15}{2} \cdot \frac{10}{3} = \frac{150}{6} = \mathbf{25}$

23. $\left(\frac{5}{6}\right)^2 = \frac{5}{6} \cdot \frac{5}{6} = \mathbf{\frac{25}{36}}$

24. **30**

25. $\mathbf{\frac{9}{5}}$

26. $1\frac{1}{2} = \frac{3}{2}, 1\frac{2}{3} = \frac{5}{3}$

$\frac{3}{2} \times \frac{5}{3} = \frac{15}{6} = \mathbf{2\frac{1}{2}}$

27. 1 lb = 16 oz

16 oz + 5 oz = **21 oz**

28.

45°

29. $\frac{1}{10} \times \frac{1}{10} = \mathbf{\frac{1}{100}}$

30. **−1**

Lesson 23, Lesson Practice

a. $\begin{array}{r} 7 \\ -\ 2\frac{1}{3} \\ \hline \end{array} \longrightarrow \begin{array}{r} 6\frac{3}{3} \\ -\ 2\frac{1}{3} \\ \hline 4\frac{2}{3} \end{array}$

b. $\begin{array}{r} 6\frac{2}{5} \\ -\ 1\frac{4}{5} \\ \hline \end{array} \xrightarrow{5 + \frac{5}{5} + \frac{2}{5}} \begin{array}{r} 5\frac{7}{5} \\ -\ 1\frac{4}{5} \\ \hline \mathbf{4\frac{3}{5}} \end{array}$

c. $\begin{array}{r} 5\frac{1}{6} \\ -\ 1\frac{5}{6} \\ \hline \end{array} \xrightarrow{4 + \frac{6}{6} + \frac{1}{6}} \begin{array}{r} 4\frac{7}{6} \\ -\ 1\frac{5}{6} \\ \hline 3\frac{2}{6} \end{array}$

$3\frac{2}{6} = \mathbf{3\frac{1}{3}}$

d. $\begin{array}{r} 100\% \\ -\ 12\frac{1}{2}\% \\ \hline \end{array} \longrightarrow \begin{array}{r} 99\frac{2}{2}\% \\ -\ 12\frac{1}{2}\% \\ \hline \mathbf{87\frac{1}{2}\%} \end{array}$

e. $\begin{array}{r} 83\frac{1}{3}\% \\ -\ 16\frac{2}{3}\% \\ \hline \end{array} \xrightarrow{\left(82 + \frac{3}{3} + \frac{1}{3}\right)\%} \begin{array}{r} 82\frac{4}{3}\% \\ -\ 16\frac{2}{3}\% \\ \hline \mathbf{66\frac{2}{3}\%} \end{array}$

Lesson 23, Mixed Practice

1. $18 \times 36 = E$

$$\begin{array}{r} 18 \\ \times\ 36 \\ \hline 108 \\ 54\ \\ \hline 648 \end{array}$$

648 exposures

2. $50{,}000{,}000 - 250{,}000 = D$

$$\begin{array}{r} 50{,}000{,}000 \\ -\ \ 250{,}000 \\ \hline 49{,}750{,}000 \end{array}$$

Forty-nine million, seven hundred fifty thousand

3. $259 + 269 + 307 = T$

259 people
269 people
+ 307 people
835 people

4. $16P = \$14.24$

$$\begin{array}{r} \$0.89 \\ 16)\overline{\$14.24} \\ 12\ 8\ \\ \hline 1\ 44 \\ 1\ 44 \\ \hline 0 \end{array}$$

89¢ per pound

5.

56 restaurants

$\frac{3}{8}$ were closed.	7 restaurants
	7 restaurants
	7 restaurants
$\frac{5}{8}$ were open.	7 restaurants
	7 restaurants
	7 restaurants
	7 restaurants
	7 restaurants

(a) 3×7 restaurants $=$ **21 restaurants**

(b) 5×7 restaurants $=$ **35 restaurants**

6. $40\% = \frac{40}{100} \div \frac{20}{20} = \mathbf{\frac{2}{5}}$

30 students

$\frac{3}{5}$ were girls.	6 students
	6 students
	6 students
$\frac{2}{5}$ were boys.	6 students
	6 students

(a) 2×6 students $=$ 12 students; **12 boys**.

(b) $\frac{5}{5} - \frac{2}{5} = \frac{3}{5}$
3×6 students $=$ 18 students; **18 girls**

7. 1 yard $=$ 36 inches

$$\begin{array}{r} 115 \\ 36)\overline{4140} \\ 36\ \ \\ \hline 54\ \\ 36\ \\ \hline 180 \\ 180 \\ \hline 0 \end{array}$$

115 yards

8. (a) **5**

(b) $5 \times 3 = \mathbf{15}$

9. **Express the mixed number as an improper fraction. Then switch the numerator and the denominator of the improper fraction.**

10. (a) $\frac{2}{3} \cdot \frac{3}{2} \mathbf{=} \frac{5}{5}$

(b) $\frac{12}{36} \mathbf{<} \frac{12}{24}$

11. $2\frac{1}{4} = \frac{9}{4}$, $3\frac{1}{3} = \frac{10}{3}$

$\frac{9}{4} \times \frac{10}{3} = \frac{90}{12} = \frac{15}{2} = \mathbf{7\frac{1}{2}}$

12. (a) $\frac{3}{4} \cdot \frac{10}{10} = \mathbf{\frac{30}{40}}$

(b) $\frac{2}{5} \cdot \frac{8}{8} = \mathbf{\frac{16}{40}}$

(c) $\frac{15 \div 5}{40 \div 5} = \mathbf{\frac{3}{8}}$

13. (a)

400
20 20
10 (2) (2) 10
(2) (5) (2) (5)

$400 = 2 \cdot 2 \cdot 2 \cdot 2 \cdot 5 \cdot 5$
$= \mathbf{2^4 \cdot 5^2}$

(b) $\sqrt{400} = 20$

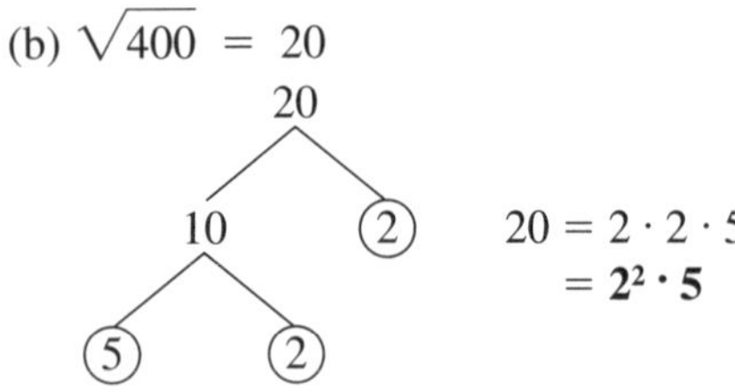

$20 = 2 \cdot 2 \cdot 5$
$= \mathbf{2^2 \cdot 5}$

14. (a) **Acute angle**

(b) **Right angle**

(c) **Obtuse angle**

(d) $\overrightarrow{DC}$

15. **Check polygon for eight sides; one possibility:**

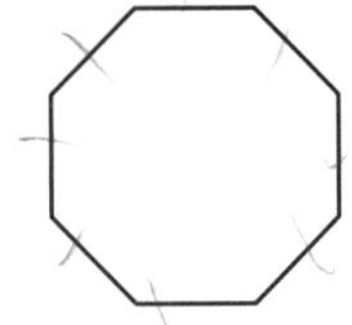

16. $7\overline{)105}$ = 15; 7, 35, 35, 0

$w = \mathbf{15}$

17. $2x = 100, 100 \div 2 = 50$

$x = \mathbf{50}$

18. $6\frac{3}{4} - 1\frac{1}{4} = 5\frac{2}{4}$

$x = \mathbf{5\frac{2}{4}}$ or $\mathbf{5\frac{1}{2}}$

19. $1\frac{5}{8} + 4\frac{1}{8} = 5\frac{6}{8}$

$x = \mathbf{5\frac{6}{8}}$ or $\mathbf{5\frac{3}{4}}$

20. $5 - 3\frac{1}{3} \longrightarrow 4\frac{3}{3} - 3\frac{1}{3} = \mathbf{1\frac{2}{3}}$

21. $83\frac{1}{3}\% - 66\frac{2}{3}\% \xrightarrow{\left(82 + \frac{3}{3} + \frac{1}{3}\right)\%} 82\frac{4}{3}\% - 66\frac{2}{3}\% = \mathbf{16\frac{2}{3}\%}$

22. $\frac{7}{12} + \left(\frac{1}{4} \cdot \frac{1}{3}\right) = \frac{7}{12} + \left(\frac{1}{12}\right)$

$= \frac{8}{12} = \mathbf{\frac{2}{3}}$

23. $\frac{7}{8} - \left(\frac{3}{4} \cdot \frac{1}{2}\right) = \frac{7}{8} - \left(\frac{3}{8}\right) = \frac{4}{8} = \mathbf{\frac{1}{2}}$

24.

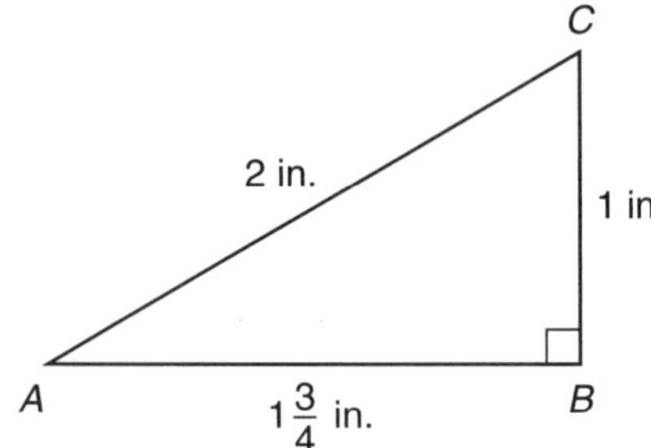

$\overline{AC}$ is about 2 inches long.

Perimeter $= 2 \text{ in.} + 1 \text{ in.} + 1\frac{3}{4} \text{ in.}$

$= 4\frac{3}{4} \text{ in.}$

The perimeter is about $4\frac{3}{4}$ inches.

25. **About 30°**

26. Perimeter $= 14 \text{ ft} + 14 \text{ ft} + 12 \text{ ft} + 12 \text{ ft}$

$= \mathbf{52 \text{ ft}}$

27. $\frac{3}{4} \times \frac{1}{3} = \frac{3}{12} = \mathbf{\frac{1}{4}}$

28. $\frac{3}{4} \cdot \frac{3}{3} = \frac{9}{12}$

$\frac{2}{3} \cdot \frac{4}{4} = \frac{8}{12}$

$\frac{9}{12} - \frac{8}{12} = \mathbf{\frac{1}{12}}$

29. (a) $\mathbf{4^3, 5^3}$

(b) $4^3 = 4 \cdot 4 \cdot 4 = 64$

$5^3 = 5 \cdot 5 \cdot 5 = 125$

64, 125

30. (a) $\overline{AB}$ (or $\overline{BA}$)

(b) $\angle CMB$ (or $\angle BMC$)

(c) $\angle ACB$ (or $\angle BCA$)

Lesson 24, Lesson Practice

a. $\frac{48}{144} = \frac{\cancel{2}^1 \cdot \cancel{2}^1 \cdot \cancel{2}^1 \cdot \cancel{2}^1 \cdot \cancel{3}^1}{\cancel{2}_1 \cdot \cancel{2}_1 \cdot \cancel{2}_1 \cdot \cancel{2}_1 \cdot \cancel{3}_1 \cdot 3} = \mathbf{\frac{1}{3}}$

b. $\frac{90}{324} = \frac{\cancel{2}^1 \cdot \cancel{3}^1 \cdot \cancel{3}^1 \cdot 5}{\cancel{2}_1 \cdot 2 \cdot \cancel{3}_1 \cdot \cancel{3}_1 \cdot 3 \cdot 3} = \mathbf{\frac{5}{18}}$

c.
$90 = 2 \cdot 3 \cdot 3 \cdot 5$
$324 = 2 \cdot 2 \cdot 3 \cdot 3 \cdot 3 \cdot 3$
$\text{GCF} = 2 \cdot 3 \cdot 3 = \mathbf{18}$

d. $\frac{\cancel{5}^1}{8} \cdot \frac{3}{\cancel{10}_2} = \mathbf{\frac{3}{16}}$

e. $\frac{\cancel{8}^{\cancel{2}^1}}{\cancel{15}_{\cancel{3}_1}} \cdot \frac{\cancel{5}^1}{\cancel{12}_{\cancel{3}_1}} \cdot \frac{\cancel{9}^{\cancel{3}^1}}{\cancel{10}_5} = \mathbf{\frac{1}{5}}$

f. $\frac{\cancel{8}^1}{\cancel{3}_1} \cdot \frac{\cancel{6}^{\cancel{2}^1}}{7} \cdot \frac{5}{\cancel{16}_{\cancel{2}_1}} = \mathbf{\frac{5}{7}}$

g. $\frac{\cancel{2}^1 \cdot \cancel{2}^1 \cdot \cancel{3}^1 \cdot \cancel{3}^1}{\cancel{3}_1 \cdot \cancel{3}_1 \cdot \cancel{5}_1} \cdot \frac{\cancel{5}^1 \cdot 5}{\cancel{2}_1 \cdot \cancel{2}_1 \cdot 2 \cdot 3} = \mathbf{\frac{5}{6}}$

Lesson 24, Mixed Practice

1. **3026 − 2895 = *D***
```
  3026 miles
− 2895 miles
   131 miles
```
131 miles

2. **15 × 24 = *M***
```
   15
×  24
   60
  30
  360
```
360 microprocessors

3. $75\% = \frac{75}{100} \div \frac{25}{25} = \frac{3}{4}$

	$30.00
$\frac{1}{4}$ not spent	$ 7.50
$\frac{3}{4}$ spent	$ 7.50
	$ 7.50
	$ 7.50

(a) $\mathbf{\frac{3}{4}}$

(b)
```
  $7.50
×     3
 $22.50
```
$22.50

4.
Diameter = 2 × radius
1 yard = 36 inches
36 inches = 2 × radius
Radius = 36 inches ÷ 2 = **18 inches**

5.
30 steps ÷ 3 = 10 steps
10 steps × 2 = **20 steps**

6. (a) **8**

(b) 8 × 3 = **24**

7. (a) $\mathbf{\frac{1}{3}}$

(b) $\mathbf{\frac{1}{3}}$

8. (a) $\frac{540}{600} = \frac{\cancel{2}^1 \cdot \cancel{2}^1 \cdot \cancel{3}^1 \cdot 3 \cdot 3 \cdot \cancel{5}^1}{\cancel{2}_1 \cdot \cancel{2}_1 \cdot 2 \cdot \cancel{3}_1 \cdot \cancel{5}_1 \cdot 5} = \mathbf{\frac{9}{10}}$

(b) 2 · 2 · 3 · 5 = **60**

9. (a) **Acute angle**

(b) **Right angle**

(c) **Obtuse angle**

10. **Equivalent fractions are formed by multiplying or dividing a fraction by a fraction equal to 1. To change from fifths to thirtieths, multiply $\frac{3}{5}$ by $\frac{6}{6}$.**

11. (a)
$$\begin{aligned} 10{,}000 &= 1000 \cdot 10 \\ 1000 &= 2 \cdot 2 \cdot 2 \cdot 5 \cdot 5 \cdot 5 \\ 10 &= 2 \cdot 5 \\ 1000 \cdot 10 &= 2 \cdot 2 \cdot 2 \cdot 5 \cdot 5 \cdot 5 \cdot 2 \cdot 5 \\ &= \mathbf{2^4 \cdot 5^4} \end{aligned}$$

(b) $\sqrt{10{,}000} = 100$
$$100 = 2 \cdot 2 \cdot 5 \cdot 5 = \mathbf{2^2 \cdot 5^2}$$

12. (a)

(b) **Right angles**

13. (a)
$$\begin{aligned} 1 \text{ yard} &= 36 \text{ inches} \\ 36 \text{ inches} \div 4 &= \textbf{9 inches} \end{aligned}$$

(b)
$$\begin{aligned} \text{Area} &= 9 \text{ inches} \times 9 \text{ inches} \\ &= \textbf{81 square inches} \end{aligned}$$

14. **Commutative property**

15. $4\frac{7}{12} - 1\frac{1}{12} = 3\frac{6}{12} = 3\frac{1}{2}$

$x = \mathbf{3\frac{1}{2}}$

16. $2\frac{3}{4} + 3\frac{3}{4} = 5\frac{6}{4} = 6\frac{1}{2}$

$w = \mathbf{6\frac{1}{2}}$

17.
$$\begin{array}{r} 12 \\ 8\overline{)100} \\ \underline{8} \\ 20 \\ \underline{16} \\ 4 \\ \underline{0} \\ 4 \end{array}$$

$12\frac{4}{8} = 12\frac{1}{2}$

$m = \mathbf{12\frac{1}{2}}$

18.
$$\begin{array}{r} \$0.28 \\ \times \quad 12 \\ \hline 56 \\ \underline{28} \\ \$3.36 \end{array}$$

$n = \mathbf{\$3.36}$

19.
$$\frac{10^5}{10^2} = \frac{\overset{1}{\cancel{10}} \cdot \overset{1}{\cancel{10}} \cdot 10 \cdot 10 \cdot 10}{\underset{1}{\cancel{10}} \cdot \underset{1}{\cancel{10}}}$$
$$= 10 \cdot 10 \cdot 10 = \mathbf{10^3} \text{ or } \mathbf{1000}$$

20. $\sqrt{9} - \sqrt{4^2} = 3 - 4 = \mathbf{-1}$

21.
$$\begin{array}{r} 100\% \\ -\ 66\frac{2}{3}\% \\ \hline \end{array} \longrightarrow \begin{array}{r} 99\frac{3}{3}\% \\ -\ 66\frac{2}{3}\% \\ \hline \mathbf{33\frac{1}{3}\%} \end{array}$$

22.
$$\begin{array}{r} 5\frac{1}{8} \\ -\ 1\frac{7}{8} \\ \hline \end{array} \xrightarrow{4 + \frac{8}{8} + \frac{1}{8}} \begin{array}{r} 4\frac{9}{8} \\ -\ 1\frac{7}{8} \\ \hline 3\frac{2}{8} \end{array}$$

$3\frac{2}{8} = \mathbf{3\frac{1}{4}}$

23. $\left(\frac{5}{6}\right)^2 = \frac{5}{6} \cdot \frac{5}{6} = \mathbf{\frac{25}{36}}$

24. $\frac{\overset{1}{\cancel{3}}}{\underset{1}{\cancel{4}}} \cdot \frac{1}{\underset{1}{\cancel{2}}} \cdot \frac{\overset{\overset{1}{\cancel{2}}}{\cancel{8}}}{\underset{3}{\cancel{9}}} = \mathbf{\frac{1}{3}}$

25. **Heptagon**

26. (a) $10 \cdot 100 = \mathbf{1000}$

(b) $10 - 100 = \mathbf{-90}$

(c) $\frac{10}{100} = \mathbf{\frac{1}{10}}$

27.
$$\begin{aligned} \text{Missing length} &= 10 \text{ yards} + 10 \text{ yards} \\ &= 20 \text{ yards} \\ \text{Missing height} &= 25 \text{ yards} - 20 \text{ yards} \\ &= 5 \text{ yards} \end{aligned}$$
$$\begin{aligned} \text{Perimeter} &= 25 \text{ yards} + 10 \text{ yards} + 5 \text{ yards} \\ &\quad + 10 \text{ yards} + 20 \text{ yards} + 20 \text{ yards} \\ &= \textbf{90 yards} \end{aligned}$$

28. $\frac{1}{4} \cdot \frac{3}{3} = \frac{3}{12}, \frac{1}{6} \cdot \frac{2}{2} = \frac{2}{12}$

$\frac{3}{12} + \frac{2}{12} = \mathbf{\frac{5}{12}}$

29. $\angle \boldsymbol{DAC}$ and $\angle \boldsymbol{BCA}$ (or $\angle \boldsymbol{CAD}$ and $\angle \boldsymbol{ACB}$);
$\angle \boldsymbol{DCA}$ and $\angle \boldsymbol{BAC}$ (or $\angle \boldsymbol{ACD}$ and $\angle \boldsymbol{CAB}$)

30. (a) $\mathbf{-1, -\frac{1}{2}, 0, \frac{1}{2}, 1}$

(b) $1 + \frac{1}{2} = 1\frac{1}{2}$

$1\frac{1}{2} + \frac{1}{2} = 1\frac{2}{2} = 2$

$2 + \frac{1}{2} = 2\frac{1}{2}$

$\mathbf{1\frac{1}{2}, 2, 2\frac{1}{2}}$

Lesson 25, Lesson Practice

a. $1 \div \frac{2}{3} = \frac{3}{2}$

$\frac{3}{4} \div \frac{2}{3} = \frac{3}{4} \times \frac{3}{2} = \frac{9}{8} = \mathbf{1\frac{9}{8}}$

b. $1 \div \frac{3}{4} = \frac{4}{3}$

$3 \div \frac{3}{4} = 3 \times \frac{4}{3} = \frac{12}{3} = \mathbf{4}$

c. **Instead of dividing by the divisor, multiply by the reciprocal of the divisor.**

d. **Pressing this key changes the number previously entered to its reciprocal (in decimal form).**

e. $1 \div \frac{2}{3} = \frac{3}{2}$

$\frac{3}{5} \div \frac{2}{3} = \frac{3}{5} \times \frac{3}{2} = \mathbf{\frac{9}{10}}$

f. $1 \div \frac{1}{4} = \mathbf{\frac{4}{1}}$

$\frac{7}{8} \div \frac{1}{4} = \frac{7}{\cancel{8}_2} \times \frac{\cancel{4}^1}{1} = \frac{7}{2} = \mathbf{3\frac{1}{2}}$

g. $1 \div \frac{2}{3} = \frac{3}{2}$

$\frac{5}{6} \div \frac{2}{3} = \frac{5}{\cancel{6}_2} \times \frac{\cancel{3}^1}{2} = \frac{5}{4} = \mathbf{1\frac{1}{4}}$

Lesson 25, Mixed Practice

1. $\mathbf{6B = 324}$

```
   54
6)324      54 boxes
  30
   24
   24
    0
```

2.

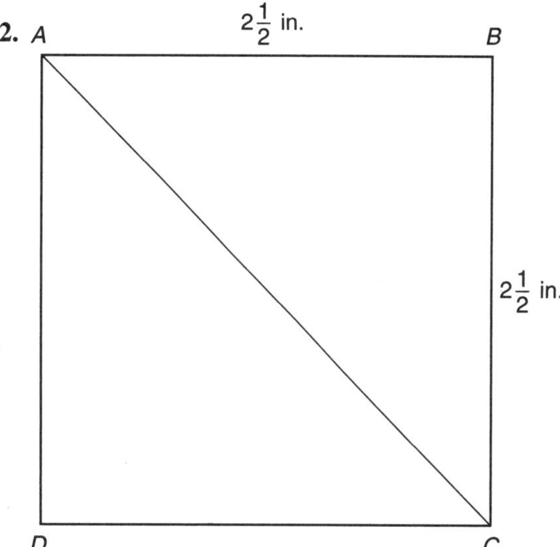

(a) Perimeter $= 2\frac{1}{2}$ in. $+ 2\frac{1}{2}$ in. $+ 2\frac{1}{2}$ in. $+ 2\frac{1}{2}$ in.

$= 8\frac{4}{2}$ in. $=$ **10 in.**

(b) **90°**

(c) $180° - 90° = 90°$
$90° \div 2 =$ **45°**

(d) $90° + 45° + 45° =$ **180°**

3. 56 relatives ÷ 2 = **28 relatives**

4.
$$\begin{array}{r} 28 \text{ players} \\ -\ \ 7 \text{ players} \\ \hline \mathbf{21\ players} \end{array}$$

5. 28 players ÷ 2 = **14 players**

6. $70\% = \frac{70}{100} \div \frac{10}{10} = \frac{7}{10}$

310 pages

$\frac{7}{10}$ have been read.	31 pages
	31 pages
	31 pages
	31 pages
	31 pages
	31 pages
	31 pages
$\frac{3}{10}$ have not been read.	31 pages
	31 pages
	31 pages

(a) 7 × 31 pages = **217 pages**

(b) 3 × 31 pages = **93 pages**

7. (a) $1 \div \frac{3}{4} = \mathbf{\frac{4}{3}}$

(b) $\frac{7}{8} \div \frac{3}{4} = \frac{7}{\cancel{8}_2} \times \frac{\cancel{4}^1}{3} = \frac{7}{6} = \mathbf{1\frac{1}{6}}$

8. **C.** $\mathbf{\frac{2}{5}}$

A little less than half is shaded. We eliminate $\frac{2}{3}$, which is more than $\frac{1}{2}$. Since $\frac{2}{4}$ equals $\frac{1}{2}$, and $\frac{2}{5}$ is a little less than $\frac{1}{2}$, we choose $\frac{2}{5}$.

9. $84 = 2 \cdot 2 \cdot 3 \cdot 7$
$210 = 2 \cdot 3 \cdot 5 \cdot 7$
$$\frac{\cancel{2}^1 \cdot 2 \cdot \cancel{3}^1 \cdot \cancel{7}^1}{\cancel{2}_1 \cdot \cancel{3}_1 \cdot 5 \cdot \cancel{7}_1} = \mathbf{\frac{2}{5}}$$

10. (a) $\mathbf{\frac{10}{9}}$

(b) $\mathbf{\frac{1}{8}}$

(c) $2\frac{3}{8} = \frac{19}{8}, \mathbf{\frac{8}{19}}$

11. $\frac{3}{4} \cdot \frac{5}{5} = \frac{15}{20}, \frac{4}{5} \cdot \frac{4}{4} = \frac{16}{20}$
$$\frac{15}{20} + \frac{16}{20} = \frac{31}{20} = \mathbf{1\frac{11}{20}}$$

12. $640 = 40 \cdot 16 = 2^3 \cdot 5 \cdot 16$
$= 2 \cdot 2 \cdot 2 \cdot 5 \cdot 2 \cdot 2 \cdot 2 \cdot 2$
$= \mathbf{2^7 \cdot 5}$

13. $2\frac{2}{3} = \frac{8}{3}, 2\frac{1}{4} = \frac{9}{4}$
$$\frac{\cancel{8}^2}{\cancel{3}_1} \times \frac{\cancel{9}^3}{\cancel{4}_1} = \mathbf{6}$$

14. (a) A: $4\frac{4}{6} = \mathbf{4\frac{2}{3}}$

B: $5\frac{3}{6} = \mathbf{5\frac{1}{2}}$

(b) $5\frac{3}{6} \xrightarrow{4 + \frac{6}{6} + \frac{3}{6}} 4\frac{9}{6}$

$$\begin{array}{r} 5\frac{3}{6} \\ -\ 4\frac{4}{6} \\ \hline \end{array} \qquad \begin{array}{r} 4\frac{9}{6} \\ -\ 4\frac{4}{6} \\ \hline \mathbf{\frac{5}{6}} \end{array}$$

15. (a)

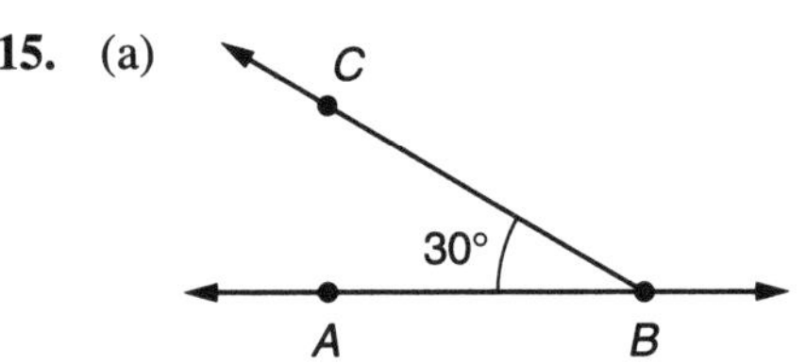

(b) **Acute angle**

16. $3 \longrightarrow 2\frac{12}{12}$
$$\begin{array}{r} 3 \\ -\ 1\frac{7}{12} \\ \hline \end{array} \qquad \begin{array}{r} 2\frac{12}{12} \\ -\ 1\frac{7}{12} \\ \hline y = \mathbf{1\frac{5}{12}} \end{array}$$

17. $5\frac{7}{8} + 4\frac{5}{8} = 9\frac{12}{8} = 10\frac{4}{8} = 10\frac{1}{2}$
$$x = \mathbf{10\frac{1}{2}}$$

18. $\begin{array}{r} 45° \\ 8\overline{)360°} \\ \underline{32} \\ 40 \\ \underline{40} \\ 0 \end{array}$

$n = \mathbf{45°}$

19. $1^3 = 1 \cdot 1 \cdot 1 = 1, \frac{3}{4}$

$m = \mathbf{\frac{3}{4}}$

20. $6\frac{1}{6} + 1\frac{5}{6} = 7\frac{6}{6} = \mathbf{8}$

21. $\frac{\overset{1}{\cancel{3}}}{\underset{1}{\cancel{4}}} \cdot \frac{\overset{1}{\cancel{5}}}{\underset{3}{\cancel{9}}} \cdot \frac{\overset{2}{\cancel{8}}}{\underset{3}{\cancel{15}}} = \mathbf{\frac{2}{9}}$

22. $1 \div \frac{2}{1} = \frac{1}{2}$

$\frac{4}{5} \div \frac{2}{1} = \frac{\overset{2}{\cancel{4}}}{5} \times \frac{1}{\underset{1}{\cancel{2}}} = \mathbf{\frac{2}{5}}$

23. $1 \div \frac{6}{5} = \frac{5}{6}$

$\frac{8}{5} \div \frac{6}{5} = \frac{\overset{4}{\cancel{8}}}{\underset{1}{\cancel{5}}} \times \frac{\overset{1}{\cancel{5}}}{\underset{3}{\cancel{6}}} = \frac{4}{3} = \mathbf{1\frac{1}{3}}$

24. $1 \div \frac{5}{6} = \frac{6}{5}$

$\frac{3}{7} \div \frac{5}{6} = \frac{3}{7} \times \frac{6}{5} = \mathbf{\frac{18}{35}}$

25. $\begin{array}{r} 12 \\ 8\overline{)100} \\ \underline{8} \\ 20 \\ \underline{16} \\ 4 \\ \underline{0} \\ 4 \end{array}$

$12\frac{4}{8}\% = \mathbf{12\frac{1}{2}}\%$

26. $\mathbf{\frac{5}{3}}$

27. (a) $2^2 \cdot 2^3 = 4 \cdot 8$

$\mathbf{4 \cdot 8 = 8 \cdot 4}$ or

$\mathbf{32 = 32}$

(b) **2**

28. Perimeter = 6 inches + 6 inches + 6 inches + 6 inches + 6 inches + 6 inches = 36 inches

36 inches ÷ 12 = **3 feet**

29. Perimeter = 4 in. + 2 in. + 2 in. + 2 in. + 2 in. + 4 in. = **16 in.**

30. Third prime number = 5, **−5**

Lesson 26, Lesson Practice

a.

$\text{Area} = 2 \text{ in.}^2 + \frac{3}{2} \text{ in.}^2 + \frac{1}{4} \text{ in.}^2$

$= 2 \text{ in.}^2 + \frac{6}{4} \text{ in.}^2 + \frac{1}{4} \text{ in.}^2$

$= 2\frac{7}{4} \text{ in.}^2 = \mathbf{3\frac{3}{4} \text{ in.}^2}$

check: $1\frac{1}{2} \text{ in.} \times 2\frac{1}{2} \text{ in.}$

$= \frac{3}{2} \text{ in.} \times \frac{5}{2} \text{ in.} = \frac{15}{4} \text{ in.}^2$

$= 3\frac{3}{4} \text{ in.}^2$

b. $6\frac{2}{3} \times \frac{3}{5} = \frac{\overset{4}{\cancel{20}}}{\underset{1}{\cancel{3}}} \times \frac{\overset{1}{\cancel{3}}}{\underset{1}{\cancel{5}}} = \mathbf{4}$

c. $2\frac{1}{3} \times 3\frac{1}{2} = \frac{7}{3} \times \frac{7}{2} = \frac{49}{6} = \mathbf{8\frac{1}{6}}$

d. $3 \times 3\frac{3}{4} = \frac{3}{1} \times \frac{15}{4} = \frac{45}{4} = \mathbf{11\frac{1}{4}}$

e. $1\frac{2}{3} \div 3 = 1\frac{2}{3} \times \frac{1}{3} = \frac{5}{3} \times \frac{1}{3} = \mathbf{\frac{5}{9}}$

f. $2\frac{1}{2} \div 3\frac{1}{3} = \frac{5}{2} \div \frac{10}{3}$

$= \frac{\overset{1}{\cancel{5}}}{2} \times \frac{3}{\underset{2}{\cancel{10}}} = \mathbf{\frac{3}{4}}$

g. $5 \div \frac{2}{3} = \frac{5}{1} \times \frac{3}{2} = \frac{15}{2} = \mathbf{7\frac{1}{2}}$

h. $2\frac{2}{3} \div 1\frac{1}{3} = \frac{8}{3} \div \frac{4}{3}$

$= \frac{\overset{2}{\cancel{8}}}{\underset{1}{\cancel{3}}} \times \frac{\overset{1}{\cancel{3}}}{\underset{1}{\cancel{4}}} = \mathbf{2}$

i. $1\frac{1}{3} \div 2\frac{2}{3} = \frac{4}{3} \div \frac{8}{3} = \frac{\overset{1}{\cancel{4}}}{\underset{1}{\cancel{3}}} \times \frac{\overset{1}{\cancel{3}}}{\underset{2}{\cancel{8}}} = \mathbf{\frac{1}{2}}$

j. $4\frac{1}{2} \times 1\frac{2}{3} = \frac{\overset{3}{\cancel{9}}}{2} \times \frac{5}{\underset{1}{\cancel{3}}} = \frac{15}{2} = \mathbf{7\frac{1}{2}}$

Lesson 26, Mixed Practice

1. **23 + *M* = 61**

$$\begin{array}{r} 61 \text{ millimeters} \\ -\ 23 \text{ millimeters} \\ \hline \mathbf{38 \text{ millimeters}} \end{array}$$

2. **26 × 85¢ = *T***

$$\begin{array}{r} \$0.85 \\ \times\quad 26 \\ \hline 510 \\ 170 \\ \hline \mathbf{\$22.10} \end{array}$$

3. **1453 − 330 = *B***

$$\begin{array}{r} 1453 \\ -\ 330 \\ \hline 1123 \end{array}$$

1123 years

4. **\$20.00 − *S* = \$11.25**

$$\begin{array}{r} \$20.00 \\ -\ \$11.25 \\ \hline \mathbf{\$8.75} \end{array}$$

5. **12 × 12 = *P***

$$\begin{array}{r} 12 \\ \times\ 12 \\ \hline 24 \\ 12 \\ \hline 144 \end{array}$$

144 pencils

6.

60 marbles

$\frac{2}{5}$ were blue.	12 marbles
	12 marbles
$\frac{3}{5}$ were not blue.	12 marbles
	12 marbles
	12 marbles

$40\% = \frac{40}{100} \div \frac{20}{20} = \mathbf{\frac{2}{5}}$

(a) 2 × 12 marbles = **24 marbles**

(b) 3 × 12 marbles = **36 marbles**

7. 1 ton = 2000 pounds

$\frac{\overset{500}{\cancel{2000}} \text{ pounds}}{\underset{1}{\cancel{4}}} =$ **500 pounds**

8. (a) $\mathbf{\frac{3}{100}}$

(b) $\frac{97}{100} =$ **97%**

9. (a) $210 = 2 \cdot 3 \cdot 5 \cdot 7$

$252 = 2 \cdot 2 \cdot 3 \cdot 3 \cdot 7$

$\frac{\overset{1}{\cancel{2}} \cdot \overset{1}{\cancel{3}} \cdot 5 \cdot \overset{1}{\cancel{7}}}{\underset{1}{\cancel{2}} \cdot 2 \cdot \underset{1}{\cancel{3}} \cdot 3 \cdot \underset{1}{\cancel{7}}} = \mathbf{\frac{5}{6}}$

(b) GCF = $2 \cdot 3 \cdot 7 =$ **42**

10. (a) $\mathbf{\frac{9}{5}}$

(b) $\mathbf{\frac{4}{23}}$

(c) $\mathbf{\frac{1}{7}}$

11. (a) $\frac{5}{8} \cdot \frac{3}{3} = \mathbf{\frac{15}{24}}$

(b) $\frac{5}{12} \cdot \frac{2}{2} = \mathbf{\frac{10}{24}}$

(c) $\frac{15}{24} + \frac{10}{24} = \frac{25}{24} = \mathbf{1\frac{1}{24}}$

12. **Check polygon for 7 sides; one possibility:**

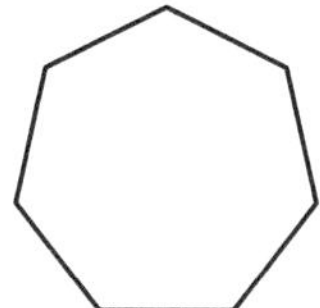

13.

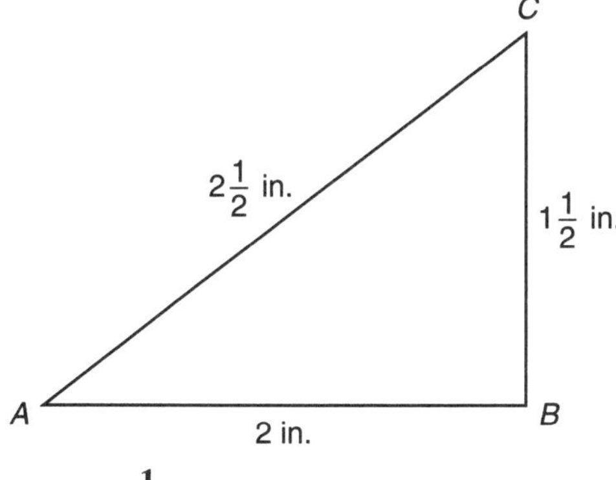

$AC = \mathbf{2\frac{1}{2}\ in.}$

14. (a) $\mathbf{-3,\ 0,\ \frac{5}{6},\ 1,\ \frac{4}{3}}$

(b) **0, 1**

15. $6\frac{5}{12} + 8\frac{11}{12} = 14\frac{16}{12} = 15\frac{4}{12}$

$x = \mathbf{15\frac{1}{3}}$

16.

$$\begin{array}{r} 180 \\ -\ 75 \\ \hline 105 \end{array}$$

$y = \mathbf{105}$

17.

$$\begin{array}{r} 30° \\ 12\overline{)360°} \\ \underline{36} \\ 00 \\ \underline{0} \\ 0 \end{array}$$

$w = \mathbf{30°}$

18.

$$\begin{array}{r} 100 \\ -\ 58\frac{1}{3} \\ \hline \end{array} \longrightarrow \begin{array}{r} 99\frac{3}{3} \\ -\ 58\frac{1}{3} \\ \hline \end{array}$$

$w = \mathbf{41\frac{2}{3}}$

19. (a) Area $= 10\text{ in.} \times 10\text{ in.}$

$= \mathbf{100\ in.^2}$

(b) $\frac{100\text{ in.}^2}{2} = \mathbf{50\ in.^2}$

20.

$$\begin{array}{r} 9\frac{1}{9} \\ -\ 4\frac{4}{9} \\ \hline \end{array} \xrightarrow{8 + \frac{9}{9} + \frac{1}{9}} \begin{array}{r} 8\frac{10}{9} \\ -\ 4\frac{4}{9} \\ \hline 4\frac{6}{9} \end{array}$$

$4\frac{6}{9} = \mathbf{4\frac{2}{3}}$

21. $\frac{\overset{1}{\cancel{5}}}{8} \cdot \frac{\overset{1}{\cancel{3}}}{\underset{2}{\cancel{10}}} \cdot \frac{1}{\underset{2}{\cancel{6}}} = \mathbf{\frac{1}{32}}$

22. $\left(2\frac{1}{2}\right)^2 = 2\frac{1}{2} \times 2\frac{1}{2}$

$= \frac{5}{2} \times \frac{5}{2} = \frac{25}{4} = \mathbf{6\frac{1}{4}}$

23. $1\frac{3}{5} \div 2\frac{2}{3}$

$= \frac{8}{5} \div \frac{8}{3} = \frac{\overset{1}{\cancel{8}}}{5} \times \frac{3}{\underset{1}{\cancel{8}}} = \mathbf{\frac{3}{5}}$

24. $3\frac{1}{3} \div 4 = \frac{10}{3} \div \frac{4}{1}$

$= \frac{\overset{5}{\cancel{10}}}{3} \times \frac{1}{\underset{2}{\cancel{4}}} = \mathbf{\frac{5}{6}}$

25. $5 \cdot 1\frac{3}{4} = \frac{5}{1} \times \frac{7}{4} = \frac{35}{4}$

$= \mathbf{8\frac{3}{4}}$

26. $\sqrt{10^2 \cdot 10^4}$
$= \sqrt{10 \cdot 10 \cdot 10 \cdot 10 \cdot 10 \cdot 10}$
$= \sqrt{1{,}000{,}000} = \mathbf{1000}$ **or** $\mathbf{10^3}$

27.
$$\begin{array}{r} \mathbf{459} \\ 36\overline{)16{,}524} \\ \underline{14\,4} \\ 2\,12 \\ \underline{1\,80} \\ 324 \\ \underline{324} \\ 0 \end{array}$$

28. (a) $3 - \frac{6}{3} = 3 - 2 = \mathbf{1}$

(b) $\frac{3 \cdot \cancel{6}^{1}}{\cancel{6}_{1}} = \mathbf{3}$

(c) $\frac{\cancel{3}^{1}}{\cancel{6}_{1}} \cdot \frac{\cancel{6}^{1}}{\cancel{3}_{1}} = \mathbf{1}$

29. $k = 3(9) - 2 = 27 - 2 = \mathbf{25}$

30. $\frac{1}{2} \times 90° = \frac{90°}{2} = \mathbf{45°}$

Lesson 27, Lesson Practice

a. 8, 16, 24, 32, (40), 48, . . .
10, 20, 30, (40), 50, . . .
LCM (8, 10) = **40**

b.
$4 = 2 \cdot 2$
$6 = 2 \cdot 3$
$10 = 2 \cdot 5$
LCM $(4, 6, 10) = 2 \cdot 2 \cdot 3 \cdot 5 = 4 \cdot 15$
$= \mathbf{60}$

c.
$24 = 2 \cdot 2 \cdot 2 \cdot 3$
$40 = 2 \cdot 2 \cdot 2 \cdot 5$
LCM $(24, 40) = 2 \cdot 2 \cdot 2 \cdot 3 \cdot 5$
$= 24 \cdot 5 = \mathbf{120}$

d.
$30 = 2 \cdot 3 \cdot 5$
$75 = 3 \cdot 5 \cdot 5$
LCM $(30, 75) = 2 \cdot 3 \cdot 5 \cdot 5$
$= \mathbf{150}$

e. $\left(7\frac{1}{2}\right)2 = 15; \left(1\frac{1}{2}\right)2 = 3$
$15 \div 3 = \mathbf{5}$

f.–h. See student work. Sample answers:

f. $240 \div 4 = \mathbf{60}$

g. $\frac{\$6.00 \div 6}{12 \div 6} = \frac{\$1.00}{2} = \mathbf{50¢}$

h. $280 \div 10 = \mathbf{28}$

Lesson 27, Mixed Practice

1. **11,460 + 9420 + 8916 = *P***
$$\begin{array}{r} 11{,}460 \\ 9420 \\ +\ \ 8916 \\ \hline \mathbf{29{,}796} \end{array}$$

2. **6 · 12 = *I***
$$\begin{array}{r} 12 \\ \times\ \ 6 \\ \hline 72 \end{array}$$
72 inches

3. **$0.15 per egg; Some equivalent division problems:**
$0.90 ÷ 6 = $0.15
$0.60 ÷ 4 = $0.15
$0.45 ÷ 3 = $0.15
$0.30 ÷ 2 = $0.15

4. **C.** $\mathbf{10^9}$

5.

	712 students
$\frac{3}{8}$ bought their lunch.	89 students
	89 students
	89 students
$\frac{5}{8}$ did not buy their lunch.	89 students
	89 students
	89 students
	89 students
	89 students

(a) 3 × 89 students = **267 students**

(b) 5 × 89 students = **445 students**

6. (a) $30\text{ in.} - 6\text{ in.} - 6\text{ in.} = 18\text{ in.}$

$18\text{ in.} \div 2 = \mathbf{9\text{ in.}}$

(b) $\text{Area} = 6\text{ in.} \times 9\text{ in.} = \mathbf{54\text{ in.}^2}$

7.

$$\begin{aligned} 25 &= 5 \cdot 5 \\ 45 &= 3 \cdot 3 \cdot 5 \\ \text{LCM}(25, 45) &= 3 \cdot 3 \cdot 5 \cdot 5 \\ &= \mathbf{225} \end{aligned}$$

8. **3500**

9. (a) $\frac{24}{100} \div \frac{4}{4} = \mathbf{\frac{6}{25}}$

(b)

$$\begin{aligned} 36 &= 2 \cdot 2 \cdot 3 \cdot 3 \\ 180 &= 2 \cdot 2 \cdot 3 \cdot 3 \cdot 5 \end{aligned}$$

$$\frac{\overset{1}{\cancel{2}} \cdot \overset{1}{\cancel{2}} \cdot \overset{1}{\cancel{3}} \cdot \overset{1}{\cancel{3}}}{\underset{1}{\cancel{2}} \cdot \underset{1}{\cancel{2}} \cdot \underset{1}{\cancel{3}} \cdot \underset{1}{\cancel{3}} \cdot 5} = \mathbf{\frac{1}{5}}$$

10. (a)

$$\begin{array}{r} 102°\text{ F} \\ -\ 32°\text{ F} \\ \hline \mathbf{70°\text{ F}} \end{array}$$

(b)

$$\begin{array}{r} 212°\text{ F} \\ -\ 102°\text{ F} \\ \hline \mathbf{110°\text{ F}} \end{array}$$

11. (a) $\frac{5}{12} \cdot \frac{3}{3} = \mathbf{\frac{15}{36}}$

(b) $\frac{1}{6} \cdot \frac{6}{6} = \mathbf{\frac{6}{36}}$

(c) $\frac{7}{9} \cdot \frac{4}{4} = \mathbf{\frac{28}{36}}$

(d) **Identity property of multiplication**

12. (a)

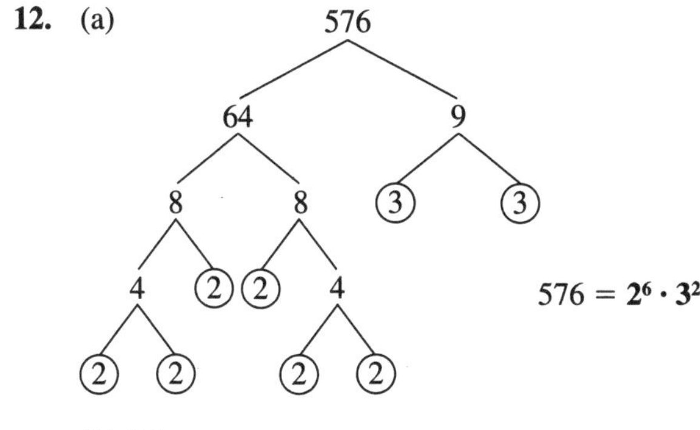

$576 = \mathbf{2^6 \cdot 3^2}$

(b) **24**

13. $5\frac{5}{6} \times 6\frac{6}{7} = \frac{\overset{5}{\cancel{35}}}{\underset{1}{\cancel{6}}} \times \frac{\overset{8}{\cancel{48}}}{\underset{1}{\cancel{7}}} = \mathbf{40}$

14. (a) **Obtuse angle**

(b) $\overline{AB}$ (or $\overline{BA}$) and $\overline{ED}$ (or $\overline{DE}$)

15. (a) $\mathbf{\frac{1}{2}}$

(b) $\mathbf{\frac{1}{2}}$

(c) $\mathbf{\frac{1}{2}}$

16. (a) $\text{Perimeter} = 3\text{ ft} + 3\text{ ft} + 6\text{ ft} + 6\text{ ft} = \mathbf{18\text{ ft}}$

(b) $\text{Area} = 3\text{ ft} \times 6\text{ ft} = \mathbf{18\text{ ft}^2}$

17.

$$\begin{array}{r} 36° \\ 10\overline{)360°} \\ \underline{30} \\ 60 \\ \underline{60} \\ 0 \end{array}$$

$y = \mathbf{36°}$

18. $12^2 - 2^4 = 144 - 16 = 128$

$p = \mathbf{128}$

19.

$$\begin{array}{r} 5\frac{1}{8} \\ -\ 1\frac{3}{8} \\ \hline \end{array} \xrightarrow{4 + \frac{8}{8} + \frac{1}{8}} \begin{array}{r} 4\frac{9}{8} \\ -\ 1\frac{3}{8} \\ \hline 3\frac{6}{8} \end{array}$$

$n = 3\frac{6}{8} = \mathbf{3\frac{3}{4}}$

20. $4\frac{1}{3} + 6\frac{2}{3} = 10\frac{3}{3} = 11$

$m = \mathbf{11}$

21.

$$\begin{array}{r} 10 \\ -\ 1\frac{3}{5} \\ \hline \end{array} \longrightarrow \begin{array}{r} 9\frac{5}{5} \\ -\ 1\frac{3}{5} \\ \hline \mathbf{8\frac{2}{5}} \end{array}$$

22. $5\frac{1}{3} \cdot 1\frac{1}{2} = \frac{\overset{8}{\cancel{16}}}{\underset{1}{\cancel{3}}} \cdot \frac{\overset{1}{\cancel{3}}}{\underset{1}{\cancel{2}}} = \mathbf{8}$

23. $3\frac{1}{3} \div \frac{5}{6} = \frac{10}{3} \div \frac{5}{6}$

$= \frac{\overset{2}{\cancel{10}}}{\underset{1}{\cancel{3}}} \times \frac{\overset{2}{\cancel{6}}}{\underset{1}{\cancel{5}}} = \mathbf{4}$

24. $5\frac{1}{4} \div 3 = \frac{21}{4} \div \frac{3}{1}$

$= \frac{\overset{7}{\cancel{21}}}{4} \times \frac{1}{\underset{1}{\cancel{3}}} = \frac{7}{4} = \mathbf{1\frac{3}{4}}$

25. $\frac{\overset{1}{\cancel{5}}}{\underset{2}{\cancel{6}}} \cdot \frac{\overset{\overset{1}{\cancel{3}}}{\cancel{9}}}{\underset{2}{\cancel{8}}} \cdot \frac{\overset{1}{\cancel{4}}}{\underset{\underset{1}{\cancel{3}}}{\cancel{15}}} = \mathbf{\frac{1}{4}}$

26. $\frac{8}{9} - \left(\frac{7}{9} - \frac{5}{9}\right) = \frac{8}{9} - \left(\frac{2}{9}\right) = \frac{6}{9} = \mathbf{\frac{2}{3}}$

27. 1 yard = 36 inches

$\frac{36 \text{ inches}}{2} = 18 \text{ inches}$

$\text{radius} = \frac{18 \text{ inches}}{2} = \mathbf{9 \text{ inches}}$

28. Example: $1.50 ÷ 2 = **75¢**

29. (a) Missing length = 5 in. − 3 in.
= 2 in.
Missing height = 5 in. − 3 in.
= 2 in.
Perimeter = 5 in. + 5 in.
+ 2 in.
+ 3 in. + 3 in. + 2 in.
= **20 in.**

(b) Area = 25 in.^{2} − 9 in.^{2} = **16 in.^{2}**

30. (a) $\overline{CB}$ (or $\overline{BC}$)

(b) $\overline{AB}$ (or $\overline{BA}$)

(c) $\angle AMC$ (or $\angle CMA$)

(d) $\angle ABC$ (or $\angle CBA$ or $\angle ABM$ or $\angle MBA$) and $\angle BAM$ (or $\angle MAB$)

(e) $\overline{MA}$ (or $\overline{AM}$) and $\overline{MB}$ (or $\overline{BM}$)

Lesson 28, Lesson Practice

a.
```
   $20.00
 −  $5.36
   $14.64

    $4.88
 3)$14.64
    12
     2 6
     2 4
       24
       24
        0
```
$4.88

b. 32 students ÷ 8 = 4 students
5 × 4 students = 20 students
20 boys

c.
```
   28 students
   29 students
   30 students
 + 25 students
  112 students

   28
 4)112
    8
   32
   32
    0
```
28 students

d.
```
   46        33
   37      6)201
   34        18
   31         21
   29         18
 + 24          3
  201
```
$33\frac{3}{6} = \mathbf{33\frac{1}{2}}$

e.
```
   40        55
 + 70      2)110
  110        10
              10
              10
               0
```
55; 55

f. **B. 84; The average score must fall between the highest and lowest scores.**

Lesson 28, Mixed Practice

1.
$$\begin{array}{r} 242 \text{ pounds} \\ 236 \text{ pounds} \\ 248 \text{ pounds} \\ 268 \text{ pounds} \\ +\ 226 \text{ pounds} \\ \hline 1220 \text{ pounds} \end{array} \qquad \begin{array}{r} 244 \\ 5\overline{)1220} \\ \underline{10} \\ 22 \\ \underline{20} \\ 20 \\ \underline{20} \\ 0 \end{array}$$

244 pounds

2. 5 minutes = 5 × 60 seconds
= 300 seconds

$$\begin{array}{r} 300 \text{ seconds} \\ +\ 14 \text{ seconds} \\ \hline \mathbf{314 \text{ seconds}} \end{array}$$

3.
$$\begin{array}{r} \$15.99 \\ \times\quad 3 \\ \hline \$47.97 \end{array}$$

$$\begin{array}{r} \$47.97 \\ +\ \$24.95 \\ \hline \mathbf{\$72.92} \end{array}$$

4.
$$\begin{array}{r} 1492 \\ -\quad 41 \\ \hline \mathbf{1451} \end{array}$$

5. $75\% = \frac{75}{100} = \frac{3}{4}$

	5000 meters
Salma led $\frac{3}{4}$.	1250 meters
	1250 meters
	1250 meters
Salma did not lead $\frac{1}{4}$.	1250 meters

(a)
$$\begin{array}{r} 1250 \\ \times\quad 3 \\ \hline 3750 \end{array}$$
3750 meters

(b) **1250 meters**

6. (a) Perimeter = 4 in. + 4 in. + 8 in. + 8 in. = **24 in.**

(b) Area = 4 in. × 8 in. = **32 in.^{2}**

7. (a) **3, 6, 9, 12, 15, 18**

(b) **4, 8, 12, 16, 20, 24**

(c) **12**

(d)
$$\begin{aligned} 27 &= 3 \cdot 3 \cdot 3 \\ 36 &= 2 \cdot 2 \cdot 3 \cdot 3 \\ \text{LCM}\,(27, 36) &= 2 \cdot 2 \cdot 3 \cdot 3 \cdot 3 \\ &= \mathbf{108} \end{aligned}$$

8. (a) **280**

(b) **300**

9.
$$\begin{aligned} 56 &= 2 \cdot 2 \cdot 2 \cdot 7 \\ 240 &= 2 \cdot 2 \cdot 2 \cdot 2 \cdot 3 \cdot 5 \end{aligned}$$
$$\frac{\overset{1}{\cancel{2}} \cdot \overset{1}{\cancel{2}} \cdot \overset{1}{\cancel{2}} \cdot 7}{\underset{1}{\cancel{2}} \cdot \underset{1}{\cancel{2}} \cdot \underset{1}{\cancel{2}} \cdot 2 \cdot 3 \cdot 5} = \mathbf{\frac{7}{30}}$$

10.
$$\begin{array}{r} 1760 \\ 3\overline{)5280} \\ \underline{3} \\ 22 \\ \underline{21} \\ 18 \\ \underline{18} \\ 00 \\ \underline{0} \\ 0 \end{array}$$
1760 yards

11. (a) $\frac{7}{8} \cdot \frac{3}{3} = \mathbf{\frac{21}{24}}$

(b) $\frac{11}{12} \cdot \frac{2}{2} = \mathbf{\frac{22}{24}}$

(c) $\frac{21}{24} + \frac{22}{24} = \frac{43}{24} = \mathbf{1\frac{19}{24}}$

12. (a)

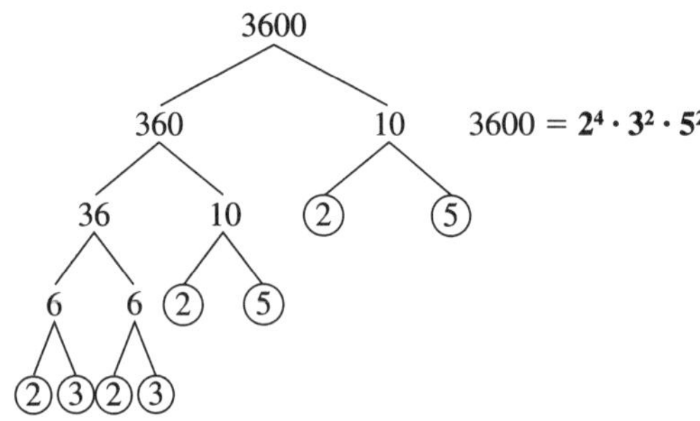

(b) $\sqrt{3600} = \sqrt{60^2} = \mathbf{60}$

13. **Add the six numbers. Then divide the sum by 6.**

14. (a)

D A

1 in.

C B

Area = 1 in. × 1 in.
= **1 square inch**

(b)–(c)

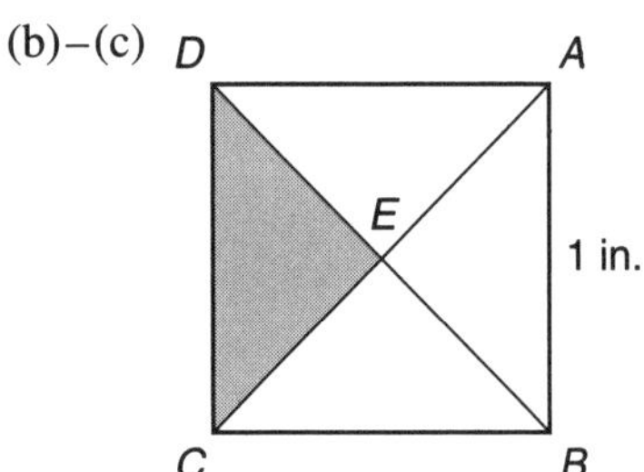

(d) **25%**

15. (a) $\mathbf{-1,\ 0,\ \frac{1}{10},\ 1,\ \frac{11}{10}}$

(b) $\mathbf{-1,\ 1}$

16.
$$12\overline{)360°} = 30°$$
36
00
0
0

$y = \mathbf{30°}$

17. $10^2 - 8^2 = 100 - 64 = 36$
$m = \mathbf{36}$

18.
$$60\overline{)180} = 3$$
180
0

$w = \mathbf{3}$

19. $4\frac{5}{12} - 1\frac{1}{12} = 3\frac{4}{12} = \mathbf{3\frac{1}{3}}$

20. $8\frac{7}{8} + 3\frac{3}{8} = 11\frac{10}{8} = 12\frac{2}{8} = \mathbf{12\frac{1}{4}}$

21.
$$12 - 8\frac{1}{8} \longrightarrow 11\frac{8}{8} - 8\frac{1}{8} = \mathbf{3\frac{7}{8}}$$

22. $6\frac{2}{3} \cdot 1\frac{1}{5} = \frac{\overset{4}{\cancel{20}}}{\underset{1}{\cancel{3}}} \cdot \frac{\overset{2}{\cancel{6}}}{\underset{1}{\cancel{5}}} = \mathbf{8}$

23.
$$\left(1\frac{1}{2}\right)^2 \div 7\frac{1}{2} = \left(\frac{3}{2}\right)^2 \div \frac{15}{2}$$
$$= \left(\frac{3}{2} \cdot \frac{3}{2}\right) \div \frac{15}{2} = \frac{9}{4} \div \frac{15}{2}$$
$$= \frac{\overset{3}{\cancel{9}}}{\underset{2}{\cancel{4}}} \times \frac{\overset{1}{\cancel{2}}}{\underset{5}{\cancel{15}}} = \mathbf{\frac{3}{10}}$$

24. $8 \div 2\frac{2}{3} = \frac{8}{1} \div \frac{8}{3} = \frac{\overset{1}{\cancel{8}}}{1} \times \frac{3}{\underset{1}{\cancel{8}}} = \mathbf{3}$

25.
$$80\overline{)10{,}000} = \mathbf{125}$$
8 0
2 00
1 60
400
400
0

26. $\frac{3}{4} - \left(\frac{1}{2} \div \frac{2}{3}\right)$

$= \frac{3}{4} - \left(\frac{1}{2} \times \frac{3}{2}\right) = \frac{3}{4} - \left(\frac{3}{4}\right) = \mathbf{0}$

27. (a) $3^4 = 3 \cdot 3 \cdot 3 \cdot 3 = 9 \cdot 9 = \mathbf{81}$

(b) $3^2 + 4^2 = 9 + 16 = \mathbf{25}$

28. Check polygon for ten sides; one possibility:

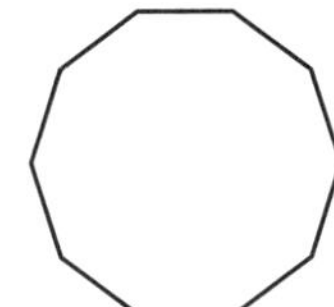

29. (a) $\angle ACD$

(b) $\overline{CB}$

(c) Area $= 2\left(7\frac{1}{2}\text{ in.}^2\right)$

$= 2 \times \frac{15}{2}\text{ in.}^2 = \mathbf{15\text{ in.}^2}$

30.

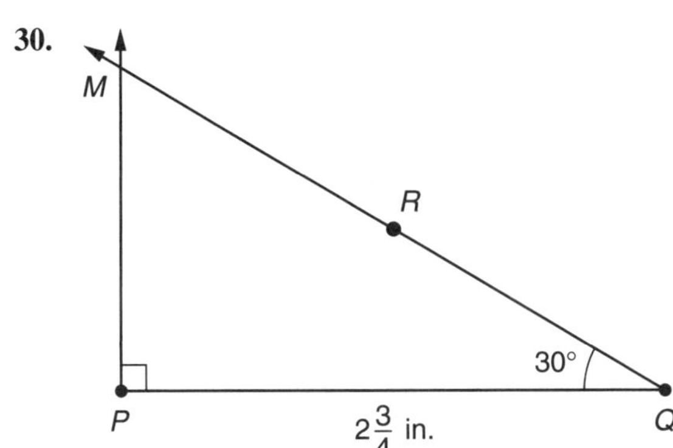

$\angle PMQ$ measures 60°.

Lesson 29, Lesson Practice

a. 17⑥0 ⟶ **1800**

b. 5④89 ⟶ **5000**

c. 186,②82 ⟶ **186,000**

d. 7986 − 3074

↓ ↓

8000 − 3000 = **5000**

e.
$$\begin{array}{r} 300 \\ \times\ \ 30 \\ \hline \mathbf{9000} \end{array}$$

f. $\frac{5860}{19} \longrightarrow \frac{6000}{20} = \mathbf{300}$

g. $12\frac{1}{4} \div 3\frac{7}{8}$

↓ ↓

$12 \div 4 = \mathbf{3}$

h. Area $= 1\frac{7}{8}\text{ in.} \times 1\frac{1}{8}\text{ in.}$

$= \frac{15}{8}\text{ in.} \times \frac{9}{8}\text{ in.} = \frac{135}{64}\text{ in.}^2$

$= \mathbf{2\frac{7}{64}\text{ in.}^2}$

The answer is reasonable because the estimated area is 2 in. × 1 in. = 2 in.².

Lesson 29, Mixed Practice

1. 16 feet = 16 (12 inches)

$$\begin{array}{r} 16 \\ \times\ 12 \\ \hline 32 \\ 16\ \ \\ \hline 192 \end{array}$$ inches

192 inches + 8 inches = **200 inches**

2. The cost per pound means the cost for each pound. We divide \$3.68, which is the cost for 8 pounds, by 8.

3.

$$\begin{array}{r} 75 \\ 70 \\ 80 \\ 80 \\ 85 \\ +\ 90 \\ \hline 480 \end{array} \qquad \begin{array}{r} \mathbf{80} \\ 6\overline{)480} \\ \underline{48} \\ 00 \\ \underline{0} \\ 0 \end{array}$$

4.

$$\begin{array}{r} 1{,}000{,}000{,}000{,}000 \\ \underline{219{,}800{,}000{,}000} \\ 780{,}200{,}000{,}000 \end{array}$$

Seven hundred eighty billion, two hundred million

5. $40\% = \frac{40}{100} \div \frac{20}{20} = \frac{2}{5}$

	80 chips
$\frac{2}{5}$ were blue.	16 chips
	16 chips
$\frac{3}{5}$ were not blue.	16 chips
	16 chips
	16 chips

(a) 2×16 chips $=$ **32 chips**

(b) 3×16 chips $=$ **48 chips**

6. (a)

$$\begin{aligned} 4 &= 2 \cdot 2 \\ 6 &= 2 \cdot 3 \\ 8 &= 2 \cdot 2 \cdot 2 \\ \text{LCM}(4, 6, 8) &= 2 \cdot 2 \cdot 2 \cdot 3 = \mathbf{24} \end{aligned}$$

(b)

$$\begin{aligned} 16 &= 2 \cdot 2 \cdot 2 \cdot 2 \\ 36 &= 2 \cdot 2 \cdot 3 \cdot 3 \\ \text{LCM}(16, 36) &= 2 \cdot 2 \cdot 2 \cdot 2 \cdot 3 \cdot 3 \\ &= \mathbf{144} \end{aligned}$$

7. (a) Perimeter $= \frac{3}{4}\text{ in.} + \frac{3}{4}\text{ in.} + \frac{3}{4}\text{ in.} + \frac{3}{4}\text{ in.} = \frac{12}{4}\text{ in.} = \mathbf{3\ in.}$

(b) Area $= \frac{3}{4}\text{ in.} \times \frac{3}{4}\text{ in.} = \mathbf{\frac{9}{16}\ in.^2}$

8. (a) $3\underline{}$⑥$6 \longrightarrow$ **400**

(b) $36$⑥ $\longrightarrow$ **370**

9.

$$\begin{array}{ccccc} 6143 & + & 4952 & & \\ \downarrow & & \downarrow & & \\ 6000 & + & 5000 & = & \mathbf{11{,}000} \end{array}$$

10. (a)

$$\begin{array}{ccccccc} \frac{3}{4} & \cdot & 5\frac{1}{3} & \cdot & 1\frac{1}{8} & & \\ \downarrow & & \downarrow & & \downarrow & & \\ 1 & \cdot & 5 & \cdot & 1 & = & \mathbf{5} \end{array}$$

(b) $\frac{3}{4} \cdot 5\frac{1}{3} \cdot 1\frac{1}{8}$

$$= \frac{\overset{1}{\cancel{3}}}{\underset{2}{\cancel{4}}} \cdot \frac{\overset{\overset{1}{\cancel{2}}}{\cancel{16}}}{\underset{1}{\cancel{3}}} \cdot \frac{9}{\underset{1}{\cancel{8}}} = \frac{9}{2} = \mathbf{4\frac{1}{2}}$$

11. (a) $\frac{2}{3} \cdot \frac{10}{10} = \mathbf{\frac{20}{30}}$

(b) $\frac{25 \div 5}{30 \div 5} = \mathbf{\frac{5}{6}}$

12. $1{,}000{,}000{,}000 =$
$1{,}000{,}000 \cdot 1000 =$
$1000 \cdot 1000 \cdot 1000 =$
$2 \cdot 2 \cdot 2 \cdot 5 \cdot 5 \cdot 5 \cdot 2 \cdot 2 \cdot 2 \cdot 5 \cdot 5 \cdot 5$
$\cdot\ 2 \cdot 2 \cdot 2 \cdot 5 \cdot 5 \cdot 5$
$= \mathbf{2^9 \cdot 5^9}$

13. (a) **50%**

(b) **50%**

(c) **50%**

14. $BC = 2\text{ in.} + 2\text{ in.} = 4\text{ in.}$
$AC = 2\text{ in.} + 4\text{ in.} = 6\text{ in.}$
$AF + CD = AC = 6\text{ in.}$
$AF = 3\text{ in.}$
$CD = 3\text{ in.}$

(a) Perimeter $= 3\text{ in.} + 3\text{ in.} + 2\text{ in.} + 2\text{ in.} = \mathbf{10\ in.}$

(b) Area $= 4\text{ in.} \times 3\text{ in.} = \mathbf{12\ in.^2}$

15. (a) $\angle \mathbf{AFB}$

(b) **90°**

16. $8^2 = 64$

$$\begin{array}{r} 16 \\ 4\overline{)64} \\ \underline{4} \\ 24 \\ \underline{24} \\ 0 \end{array}$$

$m =$ **16**

17. $$\begin{array}{r} 15 \\ -\ 4\frac{4}{9} \\ \hline \end{array} \longrightarrow \begin{array}{r} 14\frac{9}{9} \\ -\ 4\frac{4}{9} \\ \hline x = \mathbf{10\frac{5}{9}} \end{array}$$

18. $3\frac{5}{9} + 4\frac{7}{9} = 7\frac{12}{9} = 8\frac{3}{9} = 8\frac{1}{3}$

$n = \mathbf{8\frac{1}{3}}$

19. $$\begin{array}{r} 6\frac{1}{3} \\ -\ 5\frac{2}{3} \\ \hline \end{array} \xrightarrow{5 + \frac{3}{3} + \frac{1}{3}} \begin{array}{r} 5\frac{4}{3} \\ -\ 5\frac{2}{3} \\ \hline \mathbf{\frac{2}{3}} \end{array}$$

20. $\frac{\overset{4}{\cancel{20}}}{3} \times \frac{1}{\underset{1}{\cancel{5}}} = \frac{4}{3} = \mathbf{1\frac{1}{3}}$

21. $1\frac{2}{3} \div 3\frac{1}{2} = \frac{5}{3} \div \frac{7}{2} =$

$\frac{5}{3} \times \frac{2}{7} = \mathbf{\frac{10}{21}}$

22. $$\begin{array}{r} \$7.49 \\ \times\ \ 24 \\ \hline 2996 \\ 1498\ \ \\ \hline \mathbf{\$179.76} \end{array}$$

23. **Round $5\frac{1}{3}$ to 5 and round $4\frac{7}{8}$ to 5. Then multiply the rounded numbers. The product of the mixed numbers is about 25.**

24. (a) $10^3 \cdot 10^3 = 10 \cdot 10 \cdot 10 \cdot 10 \cdot 10 \cdot 10$

$= 10^6$

$m = \mathbf{6}$

(b) $\frac{10^6}{10^3} = \frac{\overset{1}{\cancel{10}} \cdot \overset{1}{\cancel{10}} \cdot \overset{1}{\cancel{10}} \cdot 10 \cdot 10 \cdot 10}{\underset{1}{\cancel{10}} \cdot \underset{1}{\cancel{10}} \cdot \underset{1}{\cancel{10}}}$

$= 10 \cdot 10 \cdot 10 = 10^3$

$n = \mathbf{3}$

25. $k = 2^5 + 1 = 2 \cdot 2 \cdot 2 \cdot 2 \cdot 2 + 1$

$= 32 + 1 = \mathbf{33}$

26. (a) Diameter = 2 (1 inch)
= **2 inches**

(b) Perimeter = 6 (1 inch)
= **6 inches**

27. $\frac{2}{3} \cdot \frac{2}{2} = \frac{4}{6}; \frac{1}{2} \cdot \frac{3}{3} = \frac{3}{6}$

$\frac{4}{6} - \frac{3}{6} = \mathbf{\frac{1}{6}}$

28. (a) **Acute angle**

(b) **Obtuse angle**

(c) **Straight angle**

29. 1 quart = 4 cups = 32 ounces
2 cups = 16 ounces
32 ounces − 16 ounces = **16 ounces**

30. Missing height = 6 in. − 4 in.
= 2 in.
Missing length = 8 in. + 3 in.
= 11 in.
Perimeter = 4 in. + 8 in. + 2 in.
+ 3 in. + 6 in. + 11 in.
= **34 in.**

Lesson 30, Lesson Practice

a. $\frac{3}{5} \cdot \frac{2}{2} = \frac{6}{10}$

$\mathbf{\frac{6}{10} < \frac{7}{10}}$

b. $\frac{5}{12} \cdot \frac{5}{5} = \frac{25}{60}, \frac{7}{15} \cdot \frac{4}{4} = \frac{28}{60}$

$\mathbf{\frac{25}{60} < \frac{28}{60}}$

c.
$$\frac{3}{4}\cdot\frac{6}{6}=\frac{18}{24}$$
$$\frac{5}{6}\cdot\frac{4}{4}=\frac{20}{24}$$
$$+\ \frac{3}{8}\cdot\frac{3}{3}=\frac{9}{24}$$
$$\frac{47}{24}$$
$$\frac{47}{24}=\mathbf{1\frac{23}{24}}$$

d.
$$7\frac{5}{6}=7\frac{5}{6}$$
$$-\ 2\frac{1}{2}=2\frac{3}{6}$$
$$5\frac{2}{6}=\mathbf{5\frac{1}{3}}$$

e.
$$4\frac{3}{4}=4\frac{6}{8}$$
$$+\ 5\frac{5}{8}=5\frac{5}{8}$$
$$9\frac{11}{8}=\mathbf{10\frac{3}{8}}$$

f.
$$4\frac{1}{6}\cdot\frac{3}{3}=4\frac{3}{18}$$
$$2\frac{5}{9}\cdot\frac{2}{2}=2\frac{10}{18}$$

$$4\frac{3}{18} - 2\frac{10}{18} \xrightarrow{3+\frac{18}{18}+\frac{3}{18}} 3\frac{21}{18} - 2\frac{10}{18} = \mathbf{1\frac{11}{18}}$$

g.
$$\frac{3}{25}=\frac{3}{5\cdot5},\quad\frac{2}{45}=\frac{2}{3\cdot3\cdot5}$$
$$3\cdot3\cdot5\cdot5=225$$
$$\frac{3}{25}\cdot\frac{9}{9}=\frac{27}{225}$$
$$-\ \frac{2}{45}\cdot\frac{5}{5}=\frac{10}{225}$$
$$\mathbf{\frac{17}{225}}$$

Lesson 30, Mixed Practice

1.
76 inches
77 inches
77 inches
78 inches
+ 82 inches
390 inches

$$5\overline{)390} = 78$$
35
40
40
0

78 inches

2.
$0.87 × 6 = $5.22

$10.00 − $5.22 = **$4.78**

3. **Barney is correct. By estimating, we know the total is closer to 12,000 pounds than 120,000 pounds.**

4.
260 − 140 = 120
$$\frac{120\div10}{260\div10}=\frac{12}{26}=\mathbf{\frac{6}{13}}$$

5.
$$30\%=\frac{30}{100}\div\frac{10}{10}=\frac{3}{10}$$

2140 miles

$\frac{3}{10}$ completed	214 miles
	214 miles
	214 miles
$\frac{7}{10}$ not completed	214 miles
	214 miles
	214 miles
	214 miles
	214 miles
	214 miles
	214 miles

(a) 3 × 214 miles = **642 miles**

(b) 7 × 214 miles = **1498 miles**

6. 5 feet = 5(12 inches) = 60 inches
60 inches ÷ 4 = **15 inches**

7.
$$18 = 2 \cdot 3 \cdot 3$$
$$30 = 2 \cdot 3 \cdot 5$$
$$2 \cdot 3 \cdot 3 \cdot 5 = 90$$
$$\frac{1}{18} \cdot \frac{5}{5} = \frac{5}{90}$$
$$-\frac{1}{30} \cdot \frac{3}{3} = \frac{3}{90}$$
$$\frac{2}{90} = \mathbf{\frac{1}{45}}$$

8. (a) 36,④67 ⟶ **36,000**

(b) 36,4⑥7 ⟶ **36,500**

9.
$$50\overline{)30{,}000} = \mathbf{600}$$
30 0
00
0
00
0
0

10. (a) $\frac{32}{100} \div \frac{4}{4} = \mathbf{\frac{8}{25}}$

(b) $\frac{48}{72} = \frac{\cancel{2} \cdot \cancel{2} \cdot \cancel{2} \cdot 2 \cdot \cancel{3}}{\cancel{2} \cdot \cancel{2} \cdot \cancel{2} \cdot \cancel{3} \cdot 3}$
$= \mathbf{\frac{2}{3}}$

11. $\frac{5}{6} \cdot \frac{4}{4} = \frac{20}{24}, \frac{7}{8} \cdot \frac{3}{3} = \frac{21}{24}$

$\mathbf{\frac{20}{24} < \frac{21}{24}}$

12. (a) Area = 3 in. × 3 in. = **9 in.²**

(b) Area = 4 in. × 4 in. = **16 in.²**

(c) 16 in.² + 9 in.² = **25 in.²**

13. (a) Perimeter = 3 in. + 3 in.
+ 1 in. + 4 in. + 4 in.
+ 4 in. + 3 in. = **22 in.**

(b) **The perimeter of the hexagon is 6 in. less than the combined perimeter of the squares because a 3 in. side of the smaller square and the adjoining 3 in. portion of a side of the larger square are not part of the perimeter of the hexagon.**

14. (a)

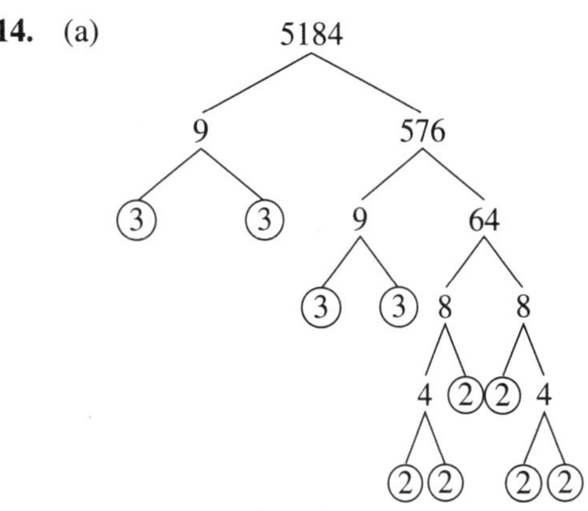

$5184 = \mathbf{2^6 \cdot 3^4}$

(b) $\sqrt{5184} = \sqrt{2^6 \cdot 2^4}$
$= 2^3 \cdot 2^2 = \mathbf{72}$

15.
5
7
9
11
12
13
24
25
26
\+ 28
160

$$10\overline{)160} = \mathbf{16}$$
10
60
60
0

16. **1, 2, 3, 5, 6, 7, 9**

17. $6^3 = 6 \cdot 6 \cdot 6 = 36 \cdot 6 = 216$

$$6\overline{)216} = 36$$
18
36
36
0

$w = \mathbf{36}$

18.
$$90° + 30° = 120°$$
$$180° - 120° = 60°$$
$$a = \mathbf{60°}$$

19.
$$\begin{array}{r} \$1.25 \\ 36\overline{)\$45.00} \\ \underline{36} \\ 9\,0 \\ \underline{7\,2} \\ 1\,80 \\ \underline{1\,80} \\ 0 \end{array}$$
$p = \mathbf{\$1.25}$

20.
$$\begin{array}{r} \$3.75 \\ \times \quad 32 \\ \hline 750 \\ 1125 \\ \hline \$120.00 \end{array}$$
$t = \mathbf{\$120.00}$

21.
$$\begin{array}{r} \frac{1}{2} \cdot \frac{3}{3} = \frac{3}{6} \\ + \frac{1}{3} \cdot \frac{2}{2} = \frac{2}{6} \\ \hline \mathbf{\frac{5}{6}} \end{array}$$

22.
$$\begin{array}{r} \frac{3}{4} \cdot \frac{3}{3} = \frac{9}{12} \\ - \frac{1}{3} \cdot \frac{4}{4} = \frac{4}{12} \\ \hline \mathbf{\frac{5}{12}} \end{array}$$

23.
$$\begin{array}{r} 2\frac{5}{6} = 2\frac{5}{6} \\ - 1\frac{1}{2} = 1\frac{3}{6} \\ \hline 1\frac{2}{6} \end{array}$$
$1\frac{2}{6} = \mathbf{1\frac{1}{3}}$

24. $\frac{4}{5} \cdot 1\frac{2}{3} \cdot 1\frac{1}{8}$
$$= \frac{\overset{1}{\cancel{4}}}{\underset{1}{\cancel{5}}} \cdot \frac{\overset{1}{\cancel{5}}}{\underset{1}{\cancel{3}}} \cdot \frac{\overset{3}{\cancel{9}}}{\underset{2}{\cancel{8}}} = \frac{3}{2} = \mathbf{1\frac{1}{2}}$$

25. $1\frac{3}{4} \div 2\frac{2}{3} = \frac{7}{4} \div \frac{8}{3}$
$$= \frac{7}{4} \times \frac{3}{8} = \mathbf{\frac{21}{32}}$$

26. $3 \div 1\frac{7}{8} = \frac{3}{1} \div \frac{15}{8}$
$$= \frac{\overset{1}{\cancel{3}}}{1} \times \frac{8}{\underset{5}{\cancel{15}}} = \frac{8}{5} = \mathbf{1\frac{3}{5}}$$

27. $3\frac{2}{3} + 1\frac{5}{6}$
$$\downarrow \qquad \downarrow$$
$$4 + 2 = \mathbf{6}$$
$$\begin{array}{r} 3\frac{2}{3} = 3\frac{4}{6} \\ + 1\frac{5}{6} = 1\frac{5}{6} \\ \hline 4\frac{9}{6} = \mathbf{5\frac{1}{2}} \end{array}$$

28. $5\frac{1}{8} - 1\frac{3}{4}$
$$\downarrow \qquad \downarrow$$
$$5 - 2 = \mathbf{3}$$
$$1\frac{3}{4} \cdot \frac{2}{2} = 1\frac{6}{8}$$
$$\begin{array}{r} 5\frac{1}{8} \\ - 1\frac{6}{8} \\ \hline \end{array} \xrightarrow{4 + \frac{8}{8} + \frac{1}{8}} \begin{array}{r} 4\frac{9}{8} \\ - 1\frac{6}{8} \\ \hline \mathbf{3\frac{3}{8}} \end{array}$$

29.
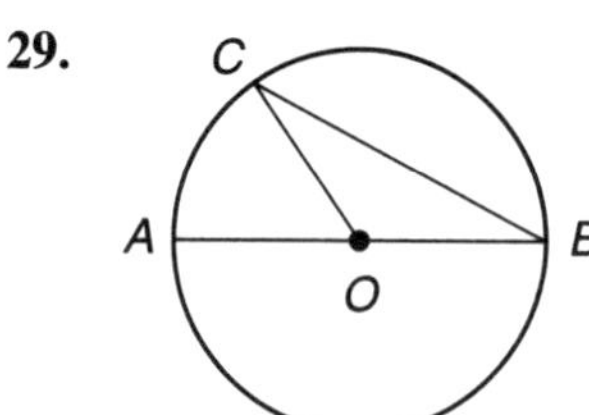

See student work. One possibility is shown.

30. (a) $\overline{AB}$ (or $\overline{BA}$)

(b) $\overline{OA}, \overline{OB}, \overline{OC}$

(c) $\angle BOC$ (or $\angle COB$)

Lesson 31, Lesson Practice

a. $\mathbf{\frac{3}{100}}$; **0.03**

b. $\mathbf{\frac{3}{10}}$; **0.3**

c. **3**

d. **4**

e. **Twenty-five and one hundred thirty-four thousandths**

f. **One hundred and one hundredth**

g. **102.3**

h. **0.0125**

i. **300.075**

Lesson 31, Mixed Practice

1.
$$\begin{array}{r} \$26.47 \\ +\ \$32.54 \\ \hline \$59.01 \end{array} \qquad \begin{array}{r} \$89.89 \\ -\ \$59.01 \\ \hline \mathbf{\$30.88} \end{array}$$

2.
$$\begin{array}{rl} 326 & \text{pages} \\ 288 & \text{pages} \\ 349 & \text{pages} \\ +\ 401 & \text{pages} \\ \hline 1364 & \text{pages} \end{array}$$

$$4\overline{)1364} = \mathbf{341 \text{ pages}}$$

3.
$$\begin{array}{r} \mathbf{\$1.33} \\ 12\overline{)\$15.96} \\ 12 \\ \hline 3\,9 \\ 3\,6 \\ \hline 36 \\ 36 \\ \hline 0 \end{array}$$

4.
$$\begin{array}{r} 1607 \\ -\ 1492 \\ \hline \mathbf{115 \text{ years}} \end{array}$$

5. **Divide the perimeter of the square by 4 to find the length of a side. Then multiply the length of a side by 6 to find the perimeter of the hexagon.**

6. $80\% = \frac{80}{100} = \mathbf{\frac{4}{5}}$

20 questions

$\frac{4}{5}$ were correct.
- 4 questions
- 4 questions
- 4 questions
- 4 questions

$\frac{1}{5}$ were incorrect.
- 4 questions

(a) 4×4 questions $=$ **16 questions**

(b) **4 questions**

7. (a) **500,000**

(b) **481,000**

8. $50{,}000 - 20{,}000 =$ **30,000**

9. (a) $\mathbf{\frac{7}{100}}$

(b) **0.07**

(c) $\frac{7}{100} =$ **7%**

10. **7**

11. (a) $\frac{3}{10} \mathbf{=} 0.3$

(b) $\frac{3}{100} \mathbf{<} 0.3$

12.

(–3, 3)
(3, 3)
(–3, –3)
(3, –3)

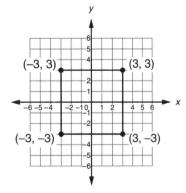

(a) Perimeter $= 4(6 \text{ units}) =$ **24 units**

(b) Area $= (6 \text{ units})(6 \text{ units})$
$=$ **36 units²**

13. (a) $\dfrac{15 \div 3}{24 \div 3} = \dfrac{5}{\mathbf{8}}$

(b) $\dfrac{7}{12} \cdot \dfrac{2}{2} = \dfrac{\mathbf{14}}{24}$

(c) $\dfrac{4 \div 4}{24 \div 4} = \dfrac{\mathbf{1}}{6}$

14.  (a)

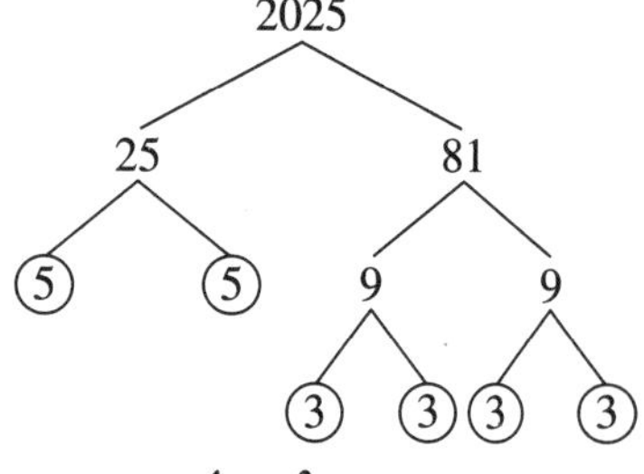

$2025 = \mathbf{3^4 \cdot 5^2}$

(b) $\sqrt{2025} = \sqrt{3^4 \cdot 5^2}$
$= 3^2 \cdot 5 = \mathbf{45}$

15. **One possibility:**

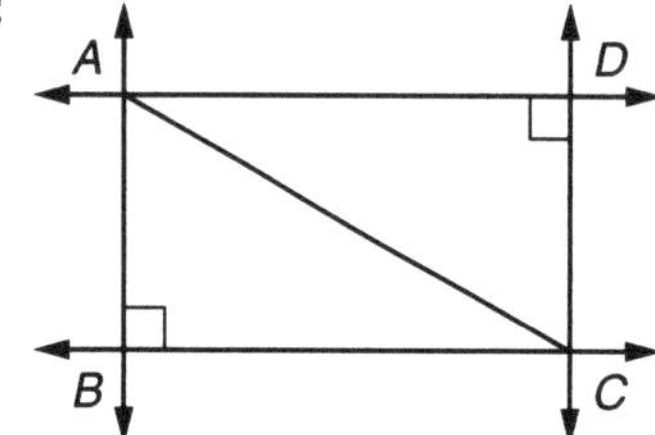

(a) **Rectangle**

(b) $\angle \boldsymbol{BCA}$ (or $\angle \boldsymbol{ACB}$)

16. $\dfrac{\overset{2}{\cancel{6}} \cdot \overset{4}{\cancel{12}}}{\underset{1}{\cancel{\underset{\cancel{3}}{\cancel{9}}}}} = 8 \qquad n = \mathbf{8}$

17.
$$\begin{array}{r} 90° \\ +\ 45° \\ \hline 135° \end{array} \qquad \begin{array}{r} 180° \\ -\ 135° \\ \hline 45° \end{array}$$
$b = \mathbf{45°}$

18.
$$\begin{array}{r} \$220.15 \\ -\ \$98.75 \\ \hline \$121.40 \end{array}$$
$w = \mathbf{\$121.40}$

19.
$$\begin{array}{r} \$4.65 \\ \times\ \ 48 \\ \hline 37\ 20 \\ 186\ 0 \\ \hline \$223.20 \end{array}$$
$m = \mathbf{\$223.20}$

20.
$$\begin{array}{rcl} \dfrac{1}{2} \cdot \dfrac{3}{3} & = & \dfrac{3}{6} \\ +\ \dfrac{2}{3} \cdot \dfrac{2}{2} & = & \dfrac{4}{6} \\ \hline & & \dfrac{7}{6} = \mathbf{1\dfrac{1}{6}} \end{array}$$

21. $\dfrac{\overset{1}{\cancel{3}}}{\underset{2}{\cancel{4}}} \cdot \dfrac{\overset{1}{\cancel{2}}}{\underset{1}{\cancel{3}}} = \dfrac{1}{2}$

$\dfrac{1}{2} - \dfrac{1}{2} = \mathbf{0}$

22.
$$\begin{array}{rcl} 3\dfrac{5}{6} & = & 3\dfrac{5}{6} \\ -\ \dfrac{1}{3} \cdot \dfrac{2}{2} & = & \dfrac{2}{6} \\ \hline & & 3\dfrac{3}{6} = \mathbf{3\dfrac{1}{2}} \end{array}$$

23. $\dfrac{5}{8} \cdot 2\dfrac{2}{5} \cdot \dfrac{4}{9}$

$= \dfrac{\overset{1}{\cancel{5}}}{\underset{2}{\cancel{8}}} \cdot \dfrac{\overset{1}{\cancel{\overset{3}{\cancel{12}}}}}{\underset{1}{\cancel{5}}} \cdot \dfrac{4}{\underset{3}{\cancel{9}}} = \dfrac{4}{6} = \mathbf{\dfrac{2}{3}}$

24. $2\dfrac{2}{3} \div 1\dfrac{3}{4}$

$= \dfrac{8}{3} \div \dfrac{7}{4} = \dfrac{8}{3} \times \dfrac{4}{7}$

$= \dfrac{32}{21} = \mathbf{1\dfrac{11}{21}}$

25. $1\dfrac{7}{8} \div 3 = \dfrac{15}{8} \div \dfrac{3}{1}$

$= \dfrac{\overset{5}{\cancel{15}}}{8} \times \dfrac{1}{\underset{1}{\cancel{3}}} = \mathbf{\dfrac{5}{8}}$

26.
$$\begin{array}{rcl} 3\dfrac{1}{2} & = & 3\dfrac{3}{6} \\ +\ 1\dfrac{5}{6} & = & 1\dfrac{5}{6} \\ \hline & & 4\dfrac{8}{6} = 5\dfrac{2}{6} = \mathbf{5\dfrac{1}{3}} \end{array}$$

27.
$$\begin{array}{rcl} 5\dfrac{1}{4} & = & 5\dfrac{2}{8} \\ -\ 1\dfrac{5}{8} & = & 1\dfrac{5}{8} \\ \hline \end{array} \longrightarrow \begin{array}{r} 4\dfrac{10}{8} \\ -\ 1\dfrac{5}{8} \\ \hline \mathbf{3\dfrac{5}{8}} \end{array}$$

28. $\frac{4}{3} = \frac{16}{12}$
$+\ \frac{3}{4} = \frac{9}{12}$
$\frac{25}{12} = \mathbf{2\frac{1}{12}}$

29. $k = 10^6 = 10 \cdot 10 \cdot 10 \cdot 10 \cdot 10 \cdot 10$
$= 1{,}000{,}000$
One million

30. (a) **180°**
(b) **90°**
(c) **45°**

Lesson 32, Lesson Practice

a. 2 meters = 2(100 centimeters)
= **200 centimeters**

b. **A 1-gallon jug can hold a little less than four liters. (Have students check the label on a gallon bottle; 3.78 liters.)**

c. **1000 × 2.2 pounds is about 2200 pounds.**

d. A 100°C difference is equivalent to a difference of 180°F. Divide both by 10°. A 10°C difference is equivalent to a difference of 18°F.
18°F

e. 3 kilometers = 3000 meters
3000 meters
− 800 meters
2200 meters

f. 30 cm = 300 mm
300 mm
− 120 mm
180 mm

Lesson 32, Mixed Practice

1. 4248 + 3584 + 9418 = 17,250
$3\overline{)17250}$ = **5750**
15
22
21
15
15
00
00
0

2. $60\overline{)206}$ = 3 R 26
3 hours 26 minutes

3. $\frac{440}{1760}$ mile $= \frac{22}{88}$ mile $= \mathbf{\frac{1}{4}}$ **mile**

4. 20 cm ÷ 4 = 5 cm
Perimeter = (5)(5 cm) = **25 cm**

5. (a) 3,000,000
(b) 3,200,000

6. 300
× 500
150,000

7. 200 songs

25 songs
25 songs
25 songs
25 songs
25 songs
25 songs
25 songs
25 songs

$\frac{5}{8}$ were about love and chivalry.
$\frac{3}{8}$ were not about love and chivalry.

(a) 5(25 songs) = **125 songs**
(b) 3(25 songs) = **75 songs**

8. (a) $\mathbf{\frac{9}{10}}$
(b) **0.9**
(c) $\frac{9}{10} = \frac{90}{100} = \mathbf{90\%}$

9. **Three and twenty-five thousandths**

10. **76.05**

11. **$30.00 ÷ 5 = $6.00**

12. (a) **(2 × 1000) + (5 × 100)**

(b)

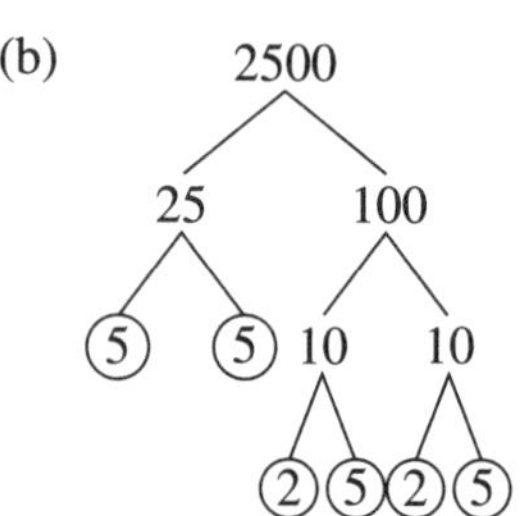

$2500 = \mathbf{2^2 \cdot 5^4}$

(c) $\sqrt{2500} = \sqrt{2^2 \cdot 5^4}$
$= 2 \cdot 5^2 = \mathbf{50}$

13. $35\overline{)\$21.00}$ = **$0.60 per liter**

14.

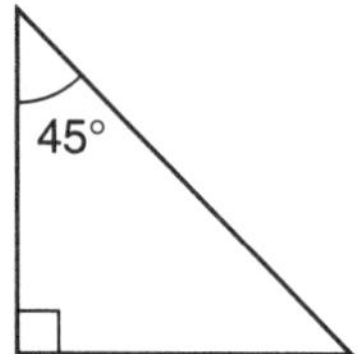

15. (a) Area = (6 cm)(6 cm) = **36 cm²**

(b) Area = (8 cm)(8 cm) = **64 cm²**

(c) Area = 36 cm² + 64 cm² = **100 cm²**

16. Perimeter = 6 cm + 6 cm + 6 cm
+ 2 cm + 8 cm + 8 cm + 8 cm
= **44 cm**

17. $\frac{\overset{5}{\cancel{10}} \cdot \overset{3}{\cancel{6}}}{\underset{1}{\cancel{\cancel{4}}}} = 15 \qquad w = \mathbf{15}$

18. $180° - 65° = 115°$

$s = \mathbf{115°}$

19. $\frac{1}{4} = \frac{2}{8}$

$\frac{3}{8} = \frac{3}{8}$

$+\ \frac{1}{2} = \frac{4}{8}$

$\frac{9}{8} = \mathbf{1\frac{1}{8}}$

20. $\frac{5}{6} = \frac{10}{12}$

$-\ \frac{3}{4} = \frac{9}{12}$

$\mathbf{\frac{1}{12}}$

21. $\frac{5}{16} = \frac{25}{80}$

$-\ \frac{3}{20} = \frac{12}{80}$

$\mathbf{\frac{13}{80}}$

22. $\frac{8}{9} \cdot 1\frac{1}{5} \cdot 10 = \frac{8}{\underset{3}{\cancel{9}}} \cdot \frac{\overset{2}{\cancel{6}}}{\underset{1}{\cancel{5}}} \cdot \frac{\overset{2}{\cancel{10}}}{1}$

$= \frac{32}{3} = \mathbf{10\frac{2}{3}}$

23. $6\frac{1}{6} = 6\frac{1}{6} \longrightarrow 5\frac{7}{6}$

$-\ 2\frac{1}{2} = 2\frac{3}{6} \qquad -\ 2\frac{3}{6}$

$3\frac{4}{6}$

$3\frac{4}{6} = \mathbf{3\frac{2}{3}}$

24. $4\frac{5}{8} = 4\frac{5}{8}$

$+\ 1\frac{1}{2} = 1\frac{4}{8}$

$5\frac{9}{8} = \mathbf{6\frac{1}{8}}$

25. $\frac{2}{3} \div \frac{1}{2} = \frac{2}{3} \cdot \frac{2}{1} = \frac{4}{3}$

$\frac{2}{3} + \frac{4}{3} = \frac{6}{3} = \mathbf{2}$

26. $\frac{\overset{1}{\cancel{\overset{5}{\cancel{25}}}}}{\underset{1}{\cancel{\underset{4}{\cancel{36}}}}} \cdot \frac{\overset{1}{\cancel{9}}}{\underset{1}{\cancel{\underset{2}{\cancel{10}}}}} \cdot \frac{\overset{1}{\cancel{\overset{2}{\cancel{8}}}}}{\underset{3}{\cancel{15}}} = \mathbf{\frac{1}{3}}$

27. $5\frac{2}{5} \div \frac{9}{10}$

$\downarrow \quad \downarrow$

$5 \div 1 = \mathbf{5}$

$5\frac{2}{5} \div \frac{9}{10} = \frac{\overset{3}{\cancel{27}}}{\underset{1}{\cancel{5}}} \times \frac{\overset{2}{\cancel{10}}}{\underset{1}{\cancel{9}}} = \mathbf{6}$

28. $7\frac{3}{4} + 1\frac{7}{8}$

$\downarrow \quad \downarrow$

$8 + 2 = \mathbf{10}$

$$\begin{array}{r} 7\frac{3}{4} = 7\frac{6}{8} \\ + 1\frac{7}{8} = 1\frac{7}{8} \\ \hline 8\frac{13}{8} = \mathbf{9\frac{5}{8}} \end{array}$$

29.

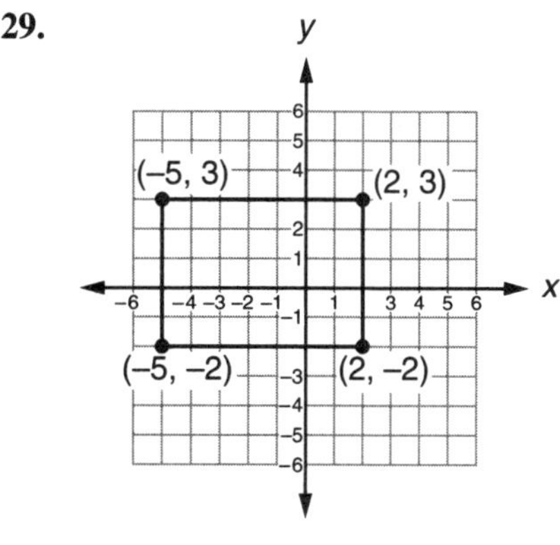

(a) **(2, 3)**

(b) Area = (5 units)(7 units) = **35 units²**

30. (a) $\overline{BC}$ (or $\overline{CB}$)

(b) **∠AOC** (or **∠COA**) or **∠BOC** (or **∠COB**)

(c) **∠ABC** (or **∠CBA**) or **∠BCO** (or **∠OCB**)

Lesson 33, Lesson Practice

a. 10.30 **=** 10.3

b. 5.06 **<** 5.60

c. 1.1 **>** 1.099

d. 3.1415⑨ → **3.1416**

e. 3⑥5.2418 ⟶ 400.~~0000~~ ⟶ **400**

f. 57.④32 ⟶ 57.~~000~~ ⟶ **57**

g. 10.2~~000~~ ⟶ **10.2**

h. 8.⑥5 ⟶ 9
21.⑦ ⟶ 22
11.⓪38 ⟶ 11

$$\begin{array}{r} 9 \\ 22 \\ +\ 11 \\ \hline \mathbf{42} \end{array}$$

Lesson 33, Mixed Practice

1. Multiply 12 inches by 5 to find the number of inches in 5 feet. Then add 8 inches to find the total number of inches in 5 feet 8 inches.

2.

$$\begin{array}{r} 42°F \\ 43°F \\ 38°F \\ 47°F \\ 51°F \\ 52°F \\ +\ 49°F \\ \hline 322°F \end{array} \qquad \begin{array}{r} \mathbf{46°F} \\ 7\overline{)322°F} \end{array}$$

3.

$$\begin{array}{r} 120{,}310 \text{ people} \\ -\ 87{,}196 \text{ people} \\ \hline \mathbf{33{,}114 \text{ people}} \end{array}$$

4. 75 − 15 = 60; 60 − 15 = 45
60, 45

5. 24 cm ÷ 6 = 4 cm
Perimeter = (4 cm) 8 = **32 cm**

6.

	60 questions
$\frac{2}{3}$ were not T–F.	20 questions
	20 questions
$\frac{1}{3}$ were T–F.	20 questions

(a) **20 questions**

(b) 2×20 questions
$= \mathbf{40}$ **questions**

(c) $\frac{100\%}{3} = \mathbf{33\frac{1}{3}}\%$

7.

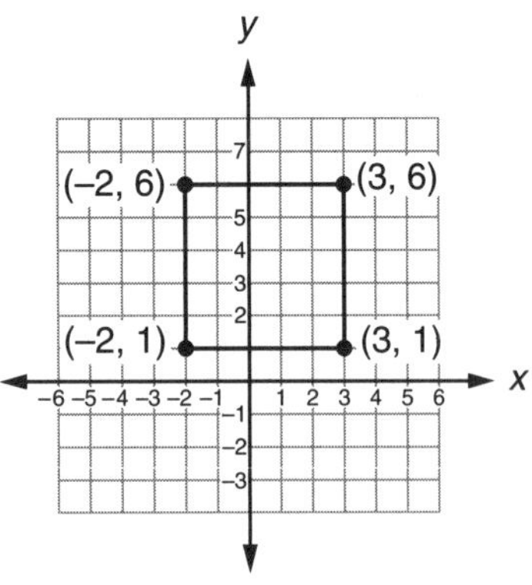

Area = (5 units)(5 units) = **25 units²**

8. (a) 15.73⑤91 ⟶ **15.74**

(b) 15.⑦3591 ⟶ 16
3.①4 ⟶ 3
$16 \times 3 = \mathbf{48}$

9. (a) **One hundred fifty and thirty-five thousandths**

(b) **Fifteen ten-thousandths**

10. (a) **0.125**

(b) **100.025**

11. (a) $0.128 < 0.14$

(b) $0.03 > 0.0015$

12. (a) **4 cm**

(b) **40 mm**

13.

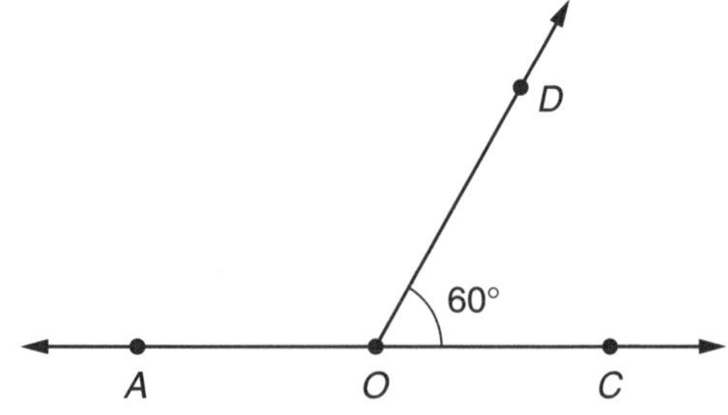

14. $n \cdot 0 = \mathbf{0}$

15.

$$63 = 3 \cdot 3 \cdot 7$$
$$49 = 7 \cdot 7$$
$$3 \cdot 3 \cdot 7 \cdot 7 = \mathbf{441}$$

16. $\frac{\overset{1}{\cancel{4}} \cdot \overset{9}{\cancel{18}}}{\underset{\underset{1}{\cancel{2}}}{\cancel{8}}} = 9$

$m = \mathbf{9}$

17.

$$\begin{array}{r} 180^\circ \\ -\ 135^\circ \\ \hline 45^\circ \end{array}$$

$a = \mathbf{45^\circ}$

18.

$$\begin{array}{rcl} \frac{3}{4} & = & \frac{6}{8} \\ \frac{5}{8} & = & \frac{5}{8} \\ +\ \frac{1}{2} & = & \frac{4}{8} \\ \hline & & \frac{15}{8} = \mathbf{1\frac{7}{8}} \end{array}$$

19.

$$\begin{array}{rcl} \frac{3}{4} & = & \frac{9}{12} \\ -\ \frac{1}{6} & = & \frac{2}{12} \\ \hline & & \mathbf{\frac{7}{12}} \end{array}$$

20.

$$\begin{array}{rcl} 4\frac{1}{2} & = & 4\frac{4}{8} \\ -\ \frac{3}{8} & = & \frac{3}{8} \\ \hline & & \mathbf{4\frac{1}{8}} \end{array}$$

21. $\frac{3}{8} \cdot 2\frac{2}{5} \cdot 3\frac{1}{3}$

$$= \frac{\overset{1}{\cancel{3}}}{\underset{\underset{1}{\cancel{2}}}{\cancel{8}}} \cdot \frac{\overset{3}{\cancel{12}}}{\underset{1}{\cancel{5}}} \cdot \frac{\overset{\overset{1}{\cancel{2}}}{\cancel{10}}}{\underset{1}{\cancel{3}}} = \mathbf{3}$$

22. $2\frac{7}{10} \div 5\frac{2}{5} = \frac{27}{10} \div \frac{27}{5}$

$$= \frac{\overset{1}{\cancel{27}}}{\underset{2}{\cancel{10}}} \times \frac{\overset{1}{\cancel{5}}}{\underset{1}{\cancel{27}}} = \mathbf{\frac{1}{2}}$$

23. $5 \div 4\frac{1}{6} = \frac{5}{1} \div \frac{25}{6}$

$$= \frac{\overset{1}{\cancel{5}}}{1} \times \frac{6}{\underset{5}{\cancel{25}}} = \frac{6}{5} = \mathbf{1\frac{1}{5}}$$

24.

$$\begin{array}{r} 6\frac{1}{2} = 6\frac{3}{6} \\ -\ 2\frac{5}{6} = 2\frac{5}{6} \\ \hline \end{array} \longrightarrow \begin{array}{r} 5\frac{9}{6} \\ -\ 2\frac{5}{6} \\ \hline 3\frac{4}{6} \end{array}$$

$$3\frac{4}{6} = \mathbf{3\frac{2}{3}}$$

25. $\frac{1}{2} \div \frac{2}{3} = \frac{1}{2} \times \frac{3}{2} = \frac{3}{4}$

$$\frac{3}{4} + \frac{3}{4} = \frac{6}{4} = \mathbf{1\frac{1}{2}}$$

26.

$$\begin{array}{r} \mathbf{\$2.50} \\ 16\overline{)\$40.00} \\ \underline{32} \\ 8\,0 \\ \underline{8\,0} \\ 00 \\ \underline{00} \\ 0 \end{array}$$

27. (a) $54 - 54 = 0$

$y = \mathbf{0}$

(b) **Identity property of addition**

28. **The quotient will be greater than 1 because a larger number is divided by a smaller number.**

29. **The mixed numbers are greater than 8 and 5, so the sum is greater than 13. The mixed numbers are less than 9 and 6, so the sum is less than 15.**

30.

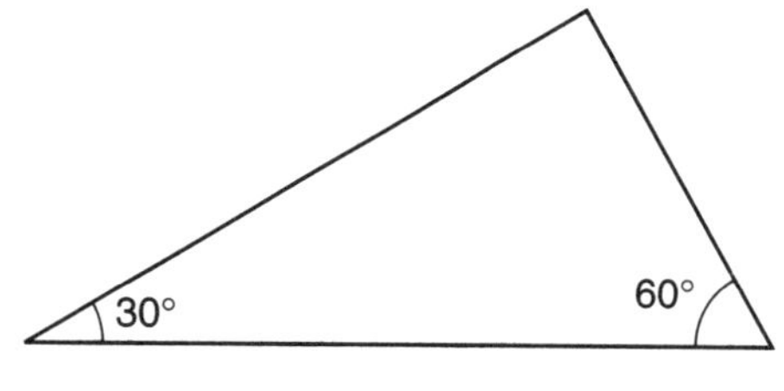

Lesson 34, Lesson Practice

a. **1.6 cm**

b. **16 mm**

c. $\mathbf{\frac{1}{2}}$ **mm** or **0.5 mm**

d. **0.75 meter**

e. **157 centimeters**

f. **2.65**

g. **10.01**

h. **5 cm**

i. 3.5 cm + 1.2 cm = **4.7 cm**

j. 40 mm − 12 mm = **28 mm**

Lesson 34, Mixed Practice

1.

$$\begin{array}{r} 188 \text{ raisins} \\ 212 \text{ raisins} \\ +\ 203 \text{ raisins} \\ \hline 603 \text{ raisins} \end{array} \qquad \begin{array}{r} \mathbf{201 \text{ raisins}} \\ 3\overline{)603} \end{array}$$

2.

$$\begin{array}{r} 1032 \text{ parts per million} \\ -\ 497 \text{ parts per million} \\ \hline \mathbf{535 \text{ parts per million}} \end{array}$$

3.

$$\begin{array}{r} \$12.55 \\ +\ \$3.95 \\ \hline \mathbf{\$16.50} \end{array}$$

4.

$$\begin{array}{r} 1903 \\ +\ 66 \\ \hline \mathbf{1969} \end{array}$$

5. $\text{Perimeter} = 6(6 \text{ inches})$
$= 36 \text{ inches}$

$\frac{36 \text{ inches}}{4} = \mathbf{9\ inches}$

6. $40\% = \frac{40}{100} = \mathbf{\frac{2}{5}}$

	$4.00
$\frac{2}{5}$ is saved.	$0.80
	$0.80
$\frac{3}{5}$ is not saved.	$0.80
	$0.80
	$0.80

(a) $\begin{array}{r} \$0.80 \\ \times \quad 2 \\ \hline \mathbf{\$1.60} \end{array}$

(b) $\begin{array}{r} \$0.80 \\ \times \quad 3 \\ \hline \mathbf{\$2.40} \end{array}$

7. **First round 396 to 400 and 71 to 70. Then multiply 400 by 70.**

8. $7.49\underline{3}⑥2 \longrightarrow \mathbf{7.494}$

9. (a) **Two hundred and two hundredths**

(b) **One thousand, six hundred twenty-five millionths**

10. (a) **0.000175**

(b) **3030.03**

11. (a) $6.174 < 6.17401$

(b) $14.276 > 1.4276$

12. (a) **2.7 cm**

(b) **27 mm**

13. **8.25**

14.

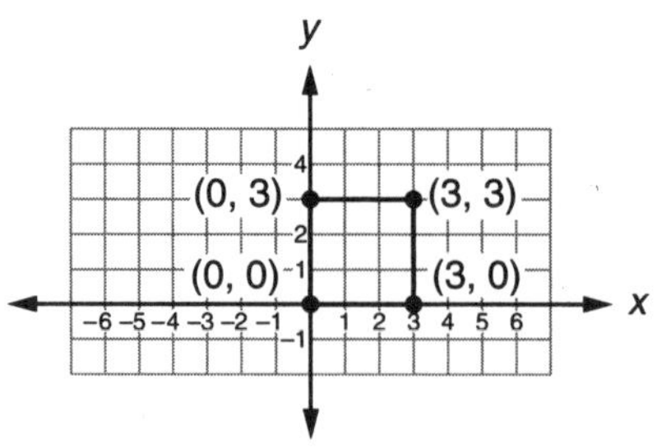

(a) **(3, 0)**

(b) $\text{Area} = (3 \text{ units})(3 \text{ units})$
$= \mathbf{9\ units^2}$

15. (a) **7.5**

(b) **0.75**

16. $\frac{\overset{5}{\cancel{15}} \cdot \overset{\overset{5}{\cancel{10}}}{\cancel{20}}}{\underset{\underset{\underset{1}{\cancel{2}}}{\cancel{6}}}{\cancel{12}}} = 25$

$y = \mathbf{25}$

17. $\begin{array}{r} 180° \\ -\ \ 74° \\ \hline 106° \end{array}$

$c = \mathbf{106°}$

18. $\begin{array}{rcl} \frac{5}{6} & = & \frac{5}{6} \\ \frac{2}{3} & = & \frac{4}{6} \\ +\ \frac{1}{2} & = & \frac{3}{6} \\ \hline & & \frac{12}{6} = \mathbf{2} \end{array}$

19. $\begin{array}{rcl} \frac{5}{36} & = & \frac{10}{72} \\ -\ \frac{1}{24} & = & \frac{3}{72} \\ \hline & & \mathbf{\frac{7}{72}} \end{array}$

20. $\begin{array}{rcl} 5\frac{1}{6} & = & 5\frac{1}{6} \\ -\ 1\frac{2}{3} & = & 1\frac{4}{6} \\ \hline \end{array} \longrightarrow \begin{array}{r} 4\frac{7}{6} \\ -\ 1\frac{4}{6} \\ \hline 3\frac{3}{6} \end{array}$

$3\frac{3}{6} = \mathbf{3\frac{1}{2}}$

21. $\frac{1}{10} \cdot 2\frac{2}{3} \cdot 3\frac{3}{4}$

$$= \frac{1}{\underset{\underset{1}{\cancel{5}}}{\cancel{10}}} \cdot \frac{\overset{\overset{1}{\cancel{2}}}{\cancel{8}}}{\underset{1}{\cancel{3}}} \cdot \frac{\overset{\overset{1}{\cancel{5}}}{\cancel{15}}}{\underset{1}{\cancel{4}}} = \mathbf{1}$$

22. $5\frac{1}{4} \div 1\frac{2}{3} = \frac{21}{4} \div \frac{5}{3}$

$$= \frac{21}{4} \times \frac{3}{5} = \frac{63}{20} = \mathbf{3\frac{3}{20}}$$

23. $3\frac{1}{5} \div 4 = \frac{16}{5} \div \frac{4}{1}$

$$= \frac{\overset{4}{\cancel{16}}}{5} \times \frac{1}{\underset{1}{\cancel{4}}} = \mathbf{\frac{4}{5}}$$

24.

$$\begin{array}{rcl} 6\frac{7}{8} & = & 6\frac{7}{8} \\ +\ 4\frac{1}{4} & = & 4\frac{2}{8} \\ \hline & & 10\frac{9}{8} = \mathbf{11\frac{1}{8}} \end{array}$$

25. $\frac{5}{\underset{2}{\cancel{6}}} \cdot \frac{\overset{1}{\cancel{3}}}{4} = \frac{5}{8}$

$$\frac{1}{8} + \frac{5}{8} = \frac{6}{8} = \mathbf{\frac{3}{4}}$$

26. (a) 3.6 cm − 2.4 cm = **1.2 cm**

(b) 36 mm − 24 mm = **12 mm**

27. **A. 2^5**

28. **0.3575, 0.36, 0.365**

29. $\frac{10}{5} - 5 = 2 - 5 = \mathbf{-3}$

30. *Note:* Not actual size. See student work.

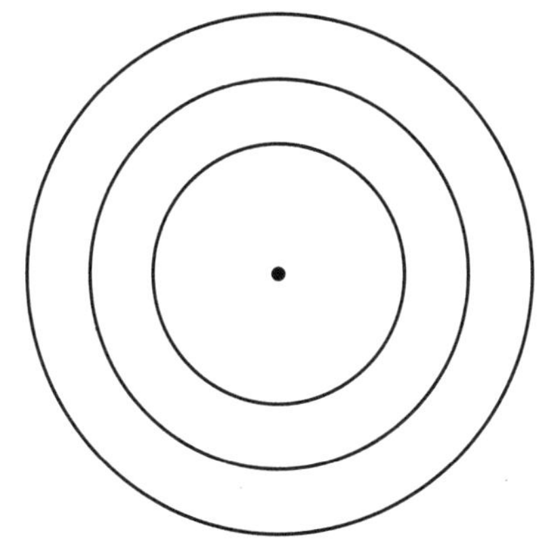

Lesson 35, Lesson Practice

a.

$$\begin{array}{r} \overset{1}{1}.2 \\ 3.45 \\ +\ 23.6 \\ \hline \mathbf{28.25} \end{array}$$

b.

$$\begin{array}{r} \overset{1}{4}.5 \\ 0.51 \\ {}_{1}6 \\ +\ 12.4 \\ \hline \mathbf{23.41} \end{array}$$

c.

$$\begin{array}{r} \overset{2}{0}.2 \\ 0.4 \\ 0.6 \\ +\ 0.8 \\ \hline 2.0 \end{array} = \mathbf{2}$$

d.

$$\begin{array}{r} 3\,\overset{5}{\cancel{6}}.\,\overset{11}{\cancel{2}}\,{}^{1}\cancel{7}\,4 \\ -\ 5.\,3\,9 \\ \hline \mathbf{3\,0.\,8\,8\,4} \end{array}$$

e.

$$\begin{array}{r} 1\,\overset{5}{\cancel{6}}.\,\overset{16}{\cancel{7}}\,\overset{9}{\cancel{0}}\,{}^{1}0 \\ -\ 1.\,9\,3\,4 \\ \hline \mathbf{1\,4.\,7\,6\,6} \end{array}$$

f.

$$\begin{array}{r} 1\,\overset{1}{\cancel{2}}.\,\overset{9}{\cancel{0}}\,\overset{9}{\cancel{0}}\,{}^{1}0 \\ -\ 0.\,8\,7\,5 \\ \hline \mathbf{1\,1.\,1\,2\,5} \end{array}$$

g.

$$\begin{array}{r} 4.20 \\ \times\ 0.24 \\ \hline 1680 \\ 840 \\ \hline 1.0080 \end{array} = \mathbf{1.008}$$

h.

$$\begin{array}{r} 0.12 \\ \times\ 0.06 \\ \hline \mathbf{0.0072} \end{array}$$

i.

$$\begin{array}{r} 5.4 \\ \times\ \ 7 \\ \hline \mathbf{37.8} \end{array}$$

j. $3 \times 2 \times 1 = 6$

$0.\_\,\_\,6 \longrightarrow \mathbf{0.006}$

k.
$$\begin{array}{r} 0.04 \\ \times\ \ 10 \\ \hline 00 \\ 04\ \\ \hline 0.40 \end{array} \longrightarrow \mathbf{0.4}$$

l.
$$\begin{array}{r} 0.045 \\ \times\ \ 0.6 \\ \hline 0270 \\ 000\ \\ \hline 0.0270 \end{array} \longrightarrow \mathbf{0.027}$$

m.
$$\begin{array}{r} \mathbf{2.4} \\ 6\overline{)14.4} \\ 12\ \ \\ \hline 2\,4 \\ 2\,4 \\ \hline 0 \end{array}$$

n.
$$\begin{array}{r} \mathbf{0.006} \\ 8\overline{)0.048} \\ 48 \\ \hline 0 \end{array}$$

o.
$$\begin{array}{r} \mathbf{0.68} \\ 5\overline{)3.40} \\ 3\,0\ \\ \hline 40 \\ 40 \\ \hline 0 \end{array}$$

p.
$$\begin{array}{r} \mathbf{0.05} \\ 6\overline{)0.30} \\ 30 \\ \hline 0 \end{array}$$

Lesson 35, Mixed Practice

1. Add all the bills together and divide by 6.

2.
$$\begin{array}{r} 2\frac{1}{2} = 2\frac{2}{4} \\ -\ 1\frac{3}{4} = 1\frac{3}{4} \\ \hline \end{array} \longrightarrow \begin{array}{r} 1\frac{6}{4} \\ -\ 1\frac{3}{4} \\ \hline \mathbf{\frac{3}{4}} \end{array} \textbf{ gallon}$$

3.
$$\begin{array}{r} \$1.30 \\ 12\overline{)\$15.60} \\ 12\ \ \ \ \\ \hline 3\,6\ \ \\ 3\,6\ \ \\ \hline 00 \\ 00 \\ \hline 0 \end{array} \qquad \begin{array}{r} \$1.75 \\ -\ \$1.30 \\ \hline \mathbf{\$0.45} \end{array}$$

4. 1 minute = 60 seconds
60 seconds + 3 seconds = 63 seconds
63 seconds − 5 seconds = **58 seconds**

5. Perimeter = 5(16 cm) = 80 cm
$$\frac{80 \text{ cm}}{4} = \mathbf{20\ cm}$$

6.

54 fish	
$\frac{2}{9}$ were guppies.	6 fish
	6 fish
$\frac{7}{9}$ were not guppies.	6 fish
	6 fish
	6 fish
	6 fish
	6 fish
	6 fish
	6 fish

(a) 2(6 fish) = **12 fish**

(b) 7(6 fish) = **42 fish**

7. (a) Area = (10 cm)(10 cm) = $\mathbf{100\ cm^2}$

(b) Area = (6 cm)(6 cm) = $\mathbf{36\ cm^2}$

(c) Area = $100\ \text{cm}^2 - 36\ \text{cm}^2$
= $\mathbf{64\ cm^2}$

8. (a) $\mathbf{\frac{99}{100}}$

(b) **0.99**

(c) $\frac{99}{100} =$ **99%**

9. 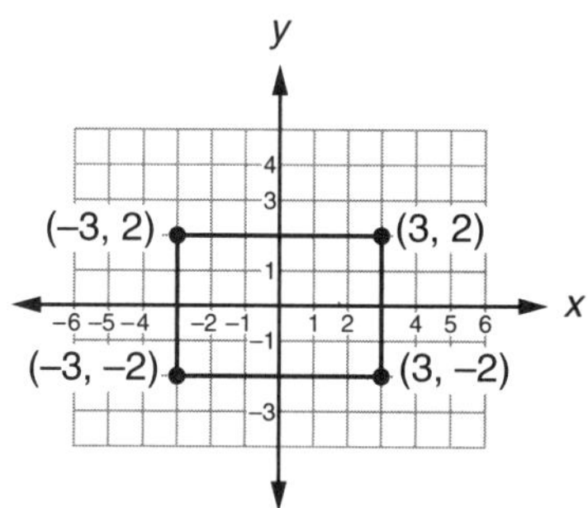

(a) **(3, 2)**

(b) Area = (4 units)(6 units)
= **24 units²**

10. (a) **One hundred and seventy-five thousandths**

(b) **0.00025**

11. (a) **3.5 centimeters**

(b) **35 millimeters**

12.
$$\begin{array}{r} \$1.50 \\ \times\quad 12 \\ \hline 3\,00 \\ 15\,0 \\ \hline \mathbf{\$18.00} \end{array}$$

13. **3.37**

14. **0.5 × 0.7 = 0.35**

15. **1.25**

16. $\frac{\overset{3}{\cancel{9}} \cdot \overset{2}{\cancel{10}}}{\underset{\underset{1}{\cancel{3}}}{\cancel{15}}} = 6 \qquad x = \mathbf{6}$

17.
$$\begin{array}{r} 5.83 \\ -\ 4.6 \\ \hline 1.23 \end{array}$$
$f = \mathbf{1.23}$

18.
$$\begin{array}{r} 5.8 \\ 8\overline{)46.4} \\ 40 \\ \hline 6\,4 \\ 6\,4 \\ \hline 0 \end{array}$$
$y = \mathbf{5.8}$

19.
$$\begin{array}{r} 12 \\ +\ 3.4 \\ \hline 15.4 \end{array}$$
$w = \mathbf{15.4}$

20.
$$\begin{array}{r} \overset{1}{3}.65 \\ 0.9 \\ {}_1 8 \\ +\ 15.23 \\ \hline \mathbf{27.78} \end{array}$$

21.
$$\begin{array}{rcl} 1\frac{1}{2} & = & 1\frac{6}{12} \\ 2\frac{2}{3} & = & 2\frac{8}{12} \\ +\ 3\frac{3}{4} & = & 3\frac{9}{12} \\ \hline & & 6\frac{23}{12} = \mathbf{7\frac{11}{12}} \end{array}$$

22. $1\frac{1}{2} \cdot 2\frac{2}{3} \cdot 3\frac{3}{4} = \frac{\overset{1}{\cancel{3}}}{\underset{1}{\cancel{2}}} \cdot \frac{\overset{\overset{1}{\cancel{2}}}{\cancel{8}}}{\underset{1}{\cancel{3}}} \cdot \frac{15}{\underset{1}{\cancel{4}}} = \mathbf{15}$

23.
$$\begin{array}{rcl} \frac{1}{2} & = & \frac{3}{6} \\ +\ \frac{1}{3} & = & \frac{2}{6} \\ \hline & & \frac{5}{6} \end{array}$$

$$\begin{array}{r} 1\frac{1}{6} \\ -\ \frac{5}{6} \\ \hline \end{array} \longrightarrow \begin{array}{r} \frac{7}{6} \\ -\ \frac{5}{6} \\ \hline \frac{2}{6} \end{array} = \mathbf{\frac{1}{3}}$$

24.
$$\begin{array}{rcl} 3\frac{1}{12} & = & 3\frac{1}{12} \\ -\ 1\frac{3}{4} & = & 1\frac{9}{12} \\ \hline \end{array} \longrightarrow \begin{array}{r} 2\frac{13}{12} \\ -\ 1\frac{9}{12} \\ \hline 1\frac{4}{12} \end{array}$$

$1\frac{4}{12} = \mathbf{1\frac{1}{3}}$

25.
$$\begin{array}{r} \mathbf{0.12} \\ 10\overline{)1.20} \\ 1\,0 \\ \hline 20 \\ 20 \\ \hline 0 \end{array}$$

26. $3 \times 4 \times 5 = 60$

$0.60 \longrightarrow \mathbf{0.06}$

27.
$$
\begin{array}{r}
3\frac{1}{2} = 3\frac{2}{4} \\
+\ 1\frac{3}{4} = 1\frac{3}{4} \\
\hline
4\frac{5}{4} = 5\frac{1}{4}
\end{array}
$$

$$
\begin{array}{r}
4 \\
-\ 3\frac{1}{8} \\
\hline
\end{array}
\longrightarrow
\begin{array}{r}
3\frac{8}{8} \\
-\ 3\frac{1}{8} \\
\hline
\frac{7}{8}
\end{array}
$$

$$5\frac{1}{4} \div \frac{7}{8} = \frac{21}{4} \div \frac{7}{8} = \frac{\overset{3}{\cancel{21}}}{\underset{1}{\cancel{4}}} \times \frac{\overset{2}{\cancel{8}}}{\underset{1}{\cancel{7}}} = \mathbf{6}$$

28. $36.45 - 4.912$

$\downarrow \qquad \downarrow$

$36 - 5 = \mathbf{31}$

$$
\begin{array}{r}
3\overset{5}{\cancel{6}}.{}^{1}4\,\overset{4}{\cancel{5}}{}^{1}0 \\
-\ \ 4.\,9\,1\,2 \\
\hline
\mathbf{31.538}
\end{array}
$$

29. 4.2×0.9

$\downarrow \qquad \downarrow$

$4 \times 1 = \mathbf{4}$

$$
\begin{array}{r}
4.2 \\
\times\ 0.9 \\
\hline
\mathbf{3.78}
\end{array}
$$

30.

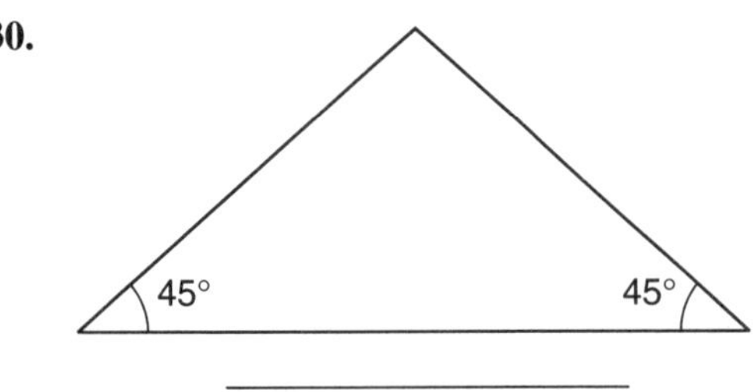

Lesson 36, Lesson Practice

a. $\dfrac{\text{big fish}}{\text{little fish}} = \dfrac{90}{240} = \mathbf{\dfrac{3}{8}}$

b.
$$
\begin{array}{r}
14 \text{ girls} \\
+\ \ ?\text{ boys} \\
\hline
30 \text{ total}
\end{array}
\longrightarrow
\begin{array}{r}
14 \text{ girls} \\
+\ 16 \text{ boys} \\
\hline
30 \text{ total}
\end{array}
$$

$\dfrac{\text{boys}}{\text{girls}} = \dfrac{16}{14} = \mathbf{\dfrac{8}{7}}$

c.
$$
\begin{array}{r}
3 \text{ won} \\
+\ \ ?\text{ lost} \\
\hline
8 \text{ total}
\end{array}
\longrightarrow
\begin{array}{r}
3 \text{ won} \\
+\ 5 \text{ lost} \\
\hline
8 \text{ total}
\end{array}
$$

$\dfrac{\text{won}}{\text{lost}} = \mathbf{\dfrac{3}{5}}$

d.
$$
\begin{array}{r}
5 \text{ red marbles} \\
+\ 3 \text{ blue marbles} \\
\hline
8 \text{ total}
\end{array}
$$

$\dfrac{\text{blue marbles}}{\text{total marbles}} = \mathbf{\dfrac{3}{8}}$

e. $\dfrac{3}{6} = \mathbf{\dfrac{1}{2}}$

f. $\mathbf{\dfrac{1}{4}}$

g. $\dfrac{0}{4} = \mathbf{0}$

h. $\dfrac{4}{4} = \mathbf{1}$

i. $\dfrac{2}{4} = \mathbf{\dfrac{1}{2}}$

j. $\mathbf{\dfrac{3}{4}}$

Lesson 36, Mixed Practice

1.
$$
\begin{array}{r}
14 \text{ girls} \\
+\ \ ?\text{ boys} \\
\hline
32 \text{ total}
\end{array}
\longrightarrow
\begin{array}{r}
14 \text{ girls} \\
+\ 18 \text{ boys} \\
\hline
32 \text{ total}
\end{array}
$$

$\dfrac{\text{boys}}{\text{girls}} = \dfrac{18}{14} = \mathbf{\dfrac{9}{7}}$

2.
$$
\begin{array}{r}
23 \text{ inches} \\
21 \text{ inches} \\
+\ 16 \text{ inches} \\
\hline
60 \text{ inches}
\end{array}
$$

$$3\overline{)60 \text{ inches}} \quad \mathbf{20 \text{ inches}}$$

3.
$$
\begin{array}{r}
35 \text{ pages} \\
\times\ \ 7 \\
\hline
\mathbf{245 \text{ pages}}
\end{array}
$$

4.
$$\begin{array}{r} 59.48 \text{ seconds} \\ -\ 56.24 \text{ seconds} \\ \hline \mathbf{3.24 \text{ seconds}} \end{array}$$

5. $40\% = \frac{40}{100} = \mathbf{\frac{2}{5}}$

	30 players
$\frac{2}{5}$ had never played rugby.	6 players
	6 players
$\frac{3}{5}$ had played rugby.	6 players
	6 players
	6 players

(a) 2×6 players $=$ **12 players**

(b) $\frac{\text{had played}}{\text{had not played}} = \mathbf{\frac{3}{2}}$

6. **One way to find *BC* in millimeters is to first convert *AB* to 40 mm and *AC* to 95 mm. Then subtract 40 mm from 95 mm.**

7. (a) Area $= (8 \text{ cm})(13 \text{ cm}) = \mathbf{104 \text{ cm}^2}$

(b) Perimeter $= 8 \text{ cm} + 8 \text{ cm} + 13 \text{ cm} + 13 \text{ cm} = \mathbf{42 \text{ cm}}$

8.
$$\begin{array}{r} 3600 \\ 2900 \\ +\ 900 \\ \hline \mathbf{7400} \end{array}$$

9. (a) $6.857\underline{1}42 \longrightarrow \mathbf{6.857}$ (the 1 circled)

(b) $6.8571420 \longrightarrow 7$
$1.9870 \longrightarrow 2$
$7 \times 2 = \mathbf{14}$

10. (a) **12,000,000**

(b) **0.000012**

11.
$$\begin{array}{r} 3 \text{ red marbles} \\ 4 \text{ white marbles} \\ +\ 5 \text{ blue marbles} \\ \hline 12 \text{ total} \end{array}$$

(a) $\frac{\text{red marbles}}{\text{total marbles}} = \frac{3}{12} = \mathbf{\frac{1}{4}}$

(b) $\frac{\text{white marbles}}{\text{total marbles}} = \frac{4}{12} = \mathbf{\frac{1}{3}}$

(c) $\frac{\text{blue marbles}}{\text{total marbles}} = \mathbf{\frac{5}{12}}$

(d) $\frac{\text{green marbles}}{\text{total marbles}} = \frac{0}{12} = \mathbf{0}$

12. (a) **4.2 cm**

(b) **42 mm**

13. **13.56**

14. (a) $85\% = \frac{85}{100} = \mathbf{\frac{17}{20}}$

(b) $\frac{144}{600} = \frac{\cancel{2}^1 \cdot \cancel{2}^1 \cdot \cancel{2}^1 \cdot 2 \cdot \cancel{3}^1 \cdot 3}{\cancel{2}_1 \cdot \cancel{2}_1 \cdot \cancel{2}_1 \cdot \cancel{3}_1 \cdot 5 \cdot 5} = \mathbf{\frac{6}{25}}$

15. Estimate: $\mathbf{6\frac{3}{4}}$ **hr** or **7 hr**
\$8 per hour
\$8 × 7 hr = \$56
She earned a little less than \$56.

16. (a) **∠*MPN*** (or **∠*NPM***)

(b) **∠*LPM*** (or **∠*MPL***)

(c) **∠*LPN*** (or **∠*NPL***)

17. $8y = 12^2$
$8y = 144$

$$\begin{array}{r} 18 \\ 8\overline{)144} \\ \underline{8} \\ 64 \\ \underline{64} \\ 0 \end{array}$$

$y = \mathbf{18}$

18.
$$\begin{array}{r} 1.2 \\ \times\ 4 \\ \hline 4.8 \end{array}$$

$w = \mathbf{4.8}$

19. $4.27 + 16.3 + 10$
$\downarrow \quad \downarrow \quad \downarrow$
$4 + 16 + 10 = \mathbf{30}$

$$\begin{array}{r} {}^1 4.27 \\ 16.3 \\ +\ 10. \\ \hline \mathbf{30.57} \end{array}$$

20. $4.2 - 0.42$
$\downarrow \quad \downarrow$
$4 - 0 = \mathbf{4}$

$$\begin{array}{r} \overset{3}{\cancel{4}}.\overset{1}{\cancel{2}}{}^1 0 \\ -\ 0.4\,2 \\ \hline \mathbf{3.7\,8} \end{array}$$

21.
$$3\frac{1}{2} = 3\frac{6}{12}$$
$$1\frac{1}{3} = 1\frac{4}{12}$$
$$+\ 2\frac{1}{4} = 2\frac{3}{12}$$
$$6\frac{13}{12} = \mathbf{7\frac{1}{12}}$$

22. $3\frac{1}{2} \cdot 1\frac{1}{3} \cdot 2\frac{1}{4}$

$$= \frac{7}{2} \cdot \frac{\overset{1}{\cancel{4}}}{\underset{1}{\cancel{3}}} \cdot \frac{\overset{3}{\cancel{9}}}{\underset{1}{\cancel{4}}} = \frac{21}{2} = \mathbf{10\frac{1}{2}}$$

23.
$$\frac{2}{3} = \frac{4}{6}$$
$$-\ \frac{1}{2} = \frac{3}{6}$$
$$\frac{1}{6}$$

$$3\frac{5}{6} - \frac{1}{6} = 3\frac{4}{6} = \mathbf{3\frac{2}{3}}$$

24.
$$8\frac{5}{12} = 8\frac{5}{12} \longrightarrow 7\frac{17}{12}$$
$$-\ 3\frac{2}{3} = 3\frac{8}{12} \qquad -\ 3\frac{8}{12}$$
$$4\frac{9}{12} = \mathbf{4\frac{3}{4}}$$

25. $2\frac{3}{4} \div 4\frac{1}{2} = \frac{11}{4} \div \frac{9}{2}$

$$= \frac{11}{\underset{2}{\cancel{4}}} \times \frac{\overset{1}{\cancel{2}}}{9} = \mathbf{\frac{11}{18}}$$

26. $\frac{2}{3} \div \frac{1}{2} = \frac{2}{3} \times \frac{2}{1} = \frac{4}{3} = 1\frac{1}{3}$

$$5 \longrightarrow 4\frac{3}{3}$$
$$-\ 1\frac{1}{3} \qquad -\ 1\frac{1}{3}$$
$$\mathbf{3\frac{2}{3}}$$

27.
$$8\overline{)1.400} = \mathbf{0.175}$$
8
60
56
40
40
0

28. $2 \times 3 \times 4 = 24$
0.24 ⟶ **0.024**

29. (a)
$$12.25 \times 10 = 122.50 = \mathbf{122.5}$$

(b)
$$10\overline{)12.250} = \mathbf{1.225}$$
10
22
20
25
20
50
50
0

30. Answers may vary. See student work.
Sample answer:

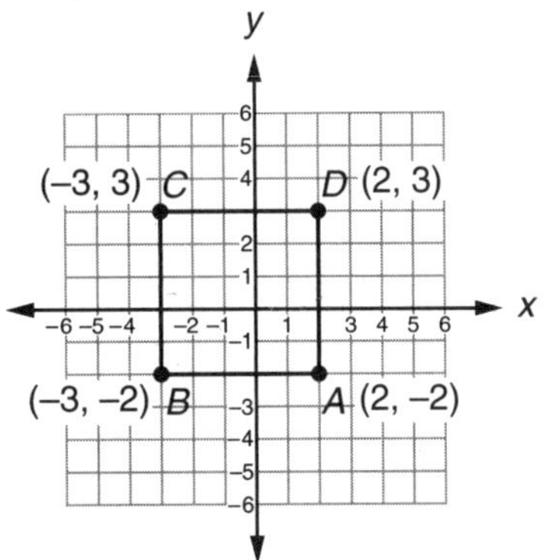

Coordinates: ***A* (2, −2), *B* (−3, −2), *C* (−3, 3), *D* (2, 3)**

Lesson 37, Lesson Practice

a. $\text{Area} = \frac{5\text{ cm} \cdot 12\text{ cm}}{2} = \frac{60\text{ cm}^2}{2}$
$= \mathbf{30\ cm^2}$

b. $\text{Area} = \frac{12\text{ cm} \cdot 8\text{ cm}}{2} = \frac{96\text{ cm}^2}{2}$
$= \mathbf{48\ cm^2}$

c. $\text{Area} = \frac{6\text{ cm} \cdot 6\text{ cm}}{2} = \frac{36\text{ cm}^2}{2}$
$= \mathbf{18\ cm^2}$

d.

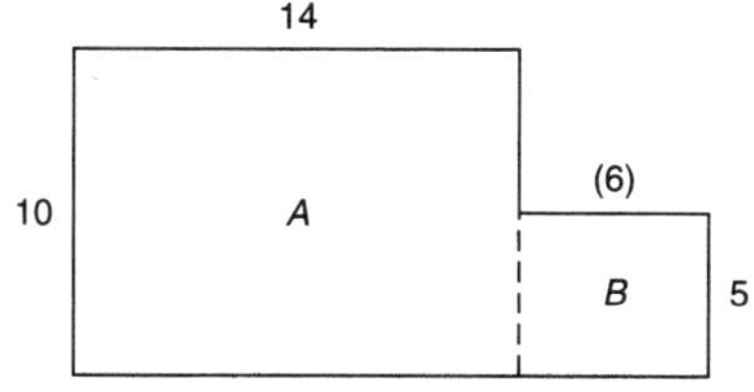

$$\begin{array}{rrcrcr} \text{Area } A & = 14 \text{ m} & \times & 10 \text{ m} & = & 140 \text{ m}^2 \\ + \text{ Area } B & = 6 \text{ m} & \times & 5 \text{ m} & = & 30 \text{ m}^2 \\ \hline & & & \text{Total} & = & \mathbf{170 \text{ m}^2} \end{array}$$

or

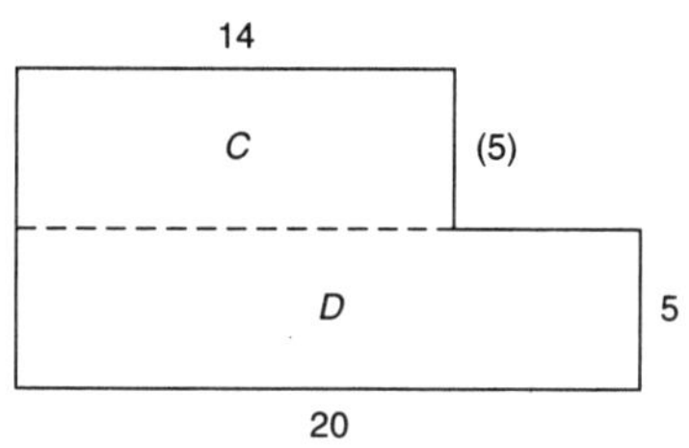

$$\begin{array}{rrcrcr} \text{Area } C & = 14 \text{ m} & \times & 5 \text{ m} & = & 70 \text{ m}^2 \\ + \text{ Area } D & = 20 \text{ m} & \times & 5 \text{ m} & = & 100 \text{ m}^2 \\ \hline & & & \text{Total} & = & \mathbf{170 \text{ m}^2} \end{array}$$

e.

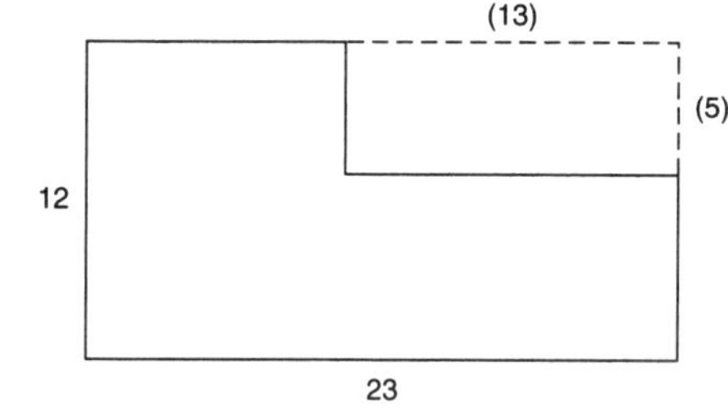

$$\begin{array}{rrcrcr} \text{Area of large} & = 12 \text{ cm} & \times & 23 \text{ cm} & = & 276 \text{ cm}^2 \\ - \text{ Area of small} & = 13 \text{ cm} & \times & 5 \text{ cm} & = & 65 \text{ cm}^2 \\ \hline & & & \text{Total} & = & \mathbf{211 \text{ cm}^2} \end{array}$$

f.

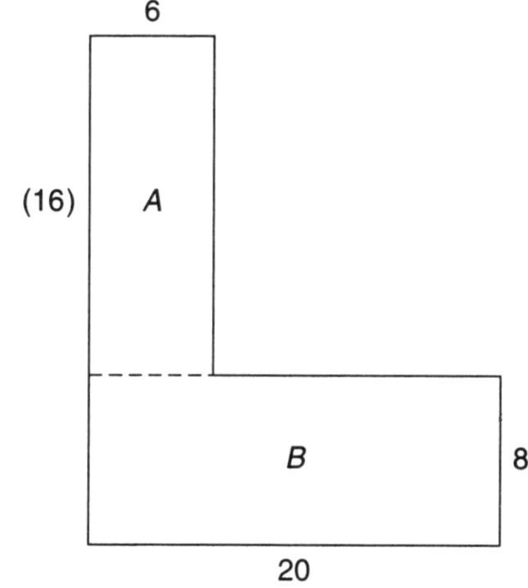

$$\begin{array}{rrcrcr} \text{Area } A & = 16 \text{ in.} & \times & 6 \text{ in.} & = & 96 \text{ in.}^2 \\ + \text{ Area } B & = 20 \text{ in.} & \times & 8 \text{ in.} & = & 160 \text{ in.}^2 \\ \hline & & & \text{Total} & = & \mathbf{256 \text{ in.}^2} \end{array}$$

or

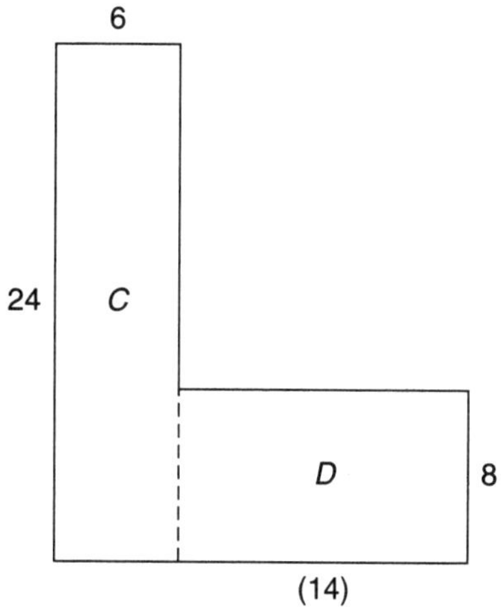

$$\begin{array}{rrcrcr} \text{Area } C & = 24 \text{ in.} & \times & 6 \text{ in.} & = & 144 \text{ in.}^2 \\ + \text{ Area } D & = 14 \text{ in.} & \times & 8 \text{ in.} & = & 112 \text{ in.}^2 \\ \hline & & & \text{Total} & = & \mathbf{256 \text{ in.}^2} \end{array}$$

g. $\boldsymbol{A = \frac{1}{2}bh;\ A = \frac{bh}{2}}$

LESSON 37, MIXED PRACTICE

1.

$$\begin{array}{r} 2 \text{ won} \\ + \ ? \text{ lost} \\ \hline 3 \text{ total} \end{array} \longrightarrow \begin{array}{r} 2 \text{ won} \\ + \ 1 \text{ lost} \\ \hline 3 \text{ total} \end{array}$$

$$\frac{\text{won}}{\text{lost}} = \mathbf{\frac{2}{1}}$$

2.

$$\begin{array}{r} 47 \\ 53 \\ 62 \\ 56 \\ 46 \\ + \ 48 \\ \hline 312 \text{ cars} \end{array} \qquad \begin{array}{r} \mathbf{52 \text{ cars}} \\ 6\overline{)312 \text{ cars}} \\ \underline{30} \\ 12 \\ \underline{12} \\ 0 \end{array}$$

3.

$$\begin{array}{r} \overset{2}{1}1.6 \text{ seconds} \\ 11.3 \text{ seconds} \\ 11.2 \text{ seconds} \\ + \ 10.9 \text{ seconds} \\ \hline 45.0 \text{ seconds} \end{array} = \mathbf{45 \text{ seconds}}$$

4. **Subtract $1.30 from $10 to find how much the 3 gallons of milk cost. Then divide that number by 3 to find how much each gallon cost.**

5.

18 holes

$\frac{2}{3}$ were par holes. { 6 holes | 6 holes }

$\frac{1}{3}$ were not par holes. { 6 holes }

(a) 2×6 holes $=$ **12 holes**

(b) **6 holes**

6.

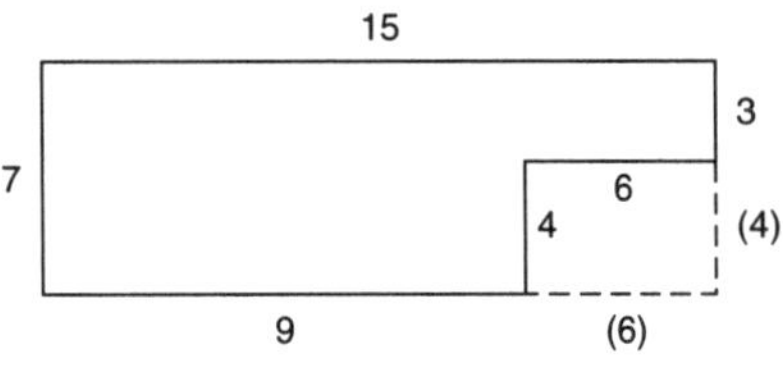

$$\text{Perimeter} = 15 \text{ in.} + 7 \text{ in.} + 9 \text{ in.} + 4 \text{ in.} + 6 \text{ in.} + 3 \text{ in.} = \mathbf{44\ in.}$$

7.

$$\begin{aligned} \text{Area of large rectangle} &= 7 \text{ in.} \times 15 \text{ in.} \\ &= 105 \text{ in.}^2 \\ - \text{ Area of small rectangle} &= 6 \text{ in.} \times 4 \text{ in.} \\ &= 24 \text{ in.}^2 \\ \hline \text{Area of figure} &= \mathbf{81\ in.^2} \end{aligned}$$

8. (a) $\frac{5}{6} \cdot \frac{3}{3} = \mathbf{\frac{15}{18}}$

(b) $\frac{9 \div 3}{24 \div 3} = \mathbf{\frac{3}{8}}$

(c) $\frac{3}{4} \cdot \frac{5}{5} = \frac{15}{\mathbf{20}}$

9. (a) **0.49**

(b) **0.51**

(c) $\frac{51}{100} =$ **51%**

10. (a) 3184.56④1 ⟶
3184.56

(b) 31⑧4.5641 ⟶
3200.~~0000~~
⟶ **3200**

11. (a) **Twenty-five hundred-thousandths**

(b) **60.07**

12. (a) $2\% = \frac{2}{100} = \mathbf{\frac{1}{50}}$

(b) $\frac{720}{1080} = \frac{\overset{1}{\cancel{2}} \cdot \overset{1}{\cancel{2}} \cdot \overset{1}{\cancel{2}} \cdot 2 \cdot \overset{1}{\cancel{3}} \cdot \overset{1}{\cancel{3}} \cdot \overset{1}{\cancel{5}}}{\underset{1}{\cancel{2}} \cdot \underset{1}{\cancel{2}} \cdot \underset{1}{\cancel{2}} \cdot \underset{1}{\cancel{3}} \cdot \underset{1}{\cancel{3}} \cdot 3 \cdot \underset{1}{\cancel{5}}} = \mathbf{\frac{2}{3}}$

13. $\mathbf{1\frac{1}{8}}$ **in.**

14. **One possibility:**

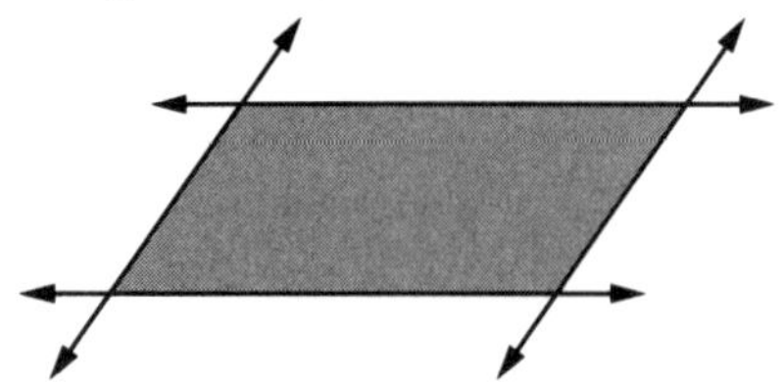

15. (a) Perimeter $= 15 \text{ cm} + 15 \text{ cm} + 18 \text{ cm} = \mathbf{48\ cm}$

(b) Area $= \frac{18 \text{ cm} \cdot 12 \text{ cm}}{2} = \mathbf{108\ cm^2}$

16.

$$\begin{array}{r} 0.2 \\ + \ 0.3 \\ \hline 0.5 \end{array} \qquad \begin{array}{r} 0.2 \\ \times \ 0.3 \\ \hline 0.06 \end{array}$$

0.5 > 0.06

17.

$$\begin{array}{r} 1 \text{ heads} \\ + \ 1 \text{ tails} \\ \hline 2 \text{ total} \end{array} \qquad \frac{\text{heads}}{\text{total}} = \mathbf{\frac{1}{2}}$$

18. $\frac{7 \cdot \overset{2}{\cancel{8}}}{\underset{1}{\cancel{4}}} = 14 \qquad x = \mathbf{14}$

19.

$$\begin{array}{r} \overset{3}{\cancel{4}}.{}^{1}2 \\ - \ 1.\ 7 \\ \hline \mathbf{2.\ 5} \end{array}$$

20.

$$\begin{array}{r} 0.45 \\ + \ 3.6 \\ \hline \mathbf{4.05} \end{array}$$

21.

$$\begin{array}{r} \mathbf{1.5} \\ 3\overline{)4.5} \\ 3 \\ \hline 1\,5 \\ 1\,5 \\ \hline 0 \end{array}$$

22. $\frac{3}{5} \cdot 12 \cdot 4\frac{1}{6} = \frac{3}{\underset{1}{\cancel{5}}} \cdot \frac{\overset{2}{\cancel{12}}}{1} \cdot \frac{\overset{5}{\cancel{25}}}{\underset{1}{\cancel{6}}}$

$= \mathbf{30}$

23.
$$\begin{array}{rcl} \frac{5}{6} & = & \frac{10}{12} \\ 1\frac{3}{4} & = & 1\frac{9}{12} \\ +\ 2\frac{1}{2} & = & 2\frac{6}{12} \\ \hline & & 3\frac{25}{12} = \mathbf{5\frac{1}{12}} \end{array}$$

24.
$$\begin{array}{rcl} \frac{5}{8} & = & \frac{5}{8} \\ \frac{1}{2} & = & \frac{4}{8} \\ +\ \frac{3}{8} & = & \frac{3}{8} \\ \hline & & \frac{12}{8} = \mathbf{1\frac{1}{2}} \end{array}$$

25.
$$\begin{array}{rcl} 3\frac{9}{20} & = & 3\frac{27}{60} \\ -\ 1\frac{5}{12} & = & 1\frac{25}{60} \\ \hline & & 2\frac{2}{60} = \mathbf{2\frac{1}{30}} \end{array}$$

26. $\frac{a}{b} = a \div b = 3\frac{1}{3} \div 5$

$= \frac{10}{3} \div \frac{5}{1} = \frac{\overset{2}{\cancel{10}}}{3} \times \frac{1}{\underset{1}{\cancel{5}}} = \mathbf{\frac{2}{3}}$

27. $2 \cdot 2 \cdot 2 \cdot 2 \cdot 2 \cdot 2 = 2^6$

28. (a)
$$\begin{array}{r} 0.25 \\ \times \quad 10 \\ \hline 2.50 \end{array} = \mathbf{2.5}$$

(b)
$$\begin{array}{r} \mathbf{0.025} \\ 10\overline{)0.250} \\ \underline{20} \\ 50 \\ \underline{50} \\ 0 \end{array}$$

29.

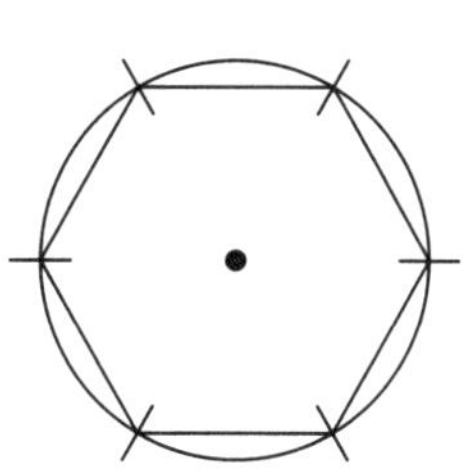

30. **Fourth quadrant**

LESSON 38, LESSON PRACTICE

a. January: 4 × 10,000 doughnuts
= 40,000 doughnuts
February: 6 × 10,000 doughnuts
= 60,000 doughnuts

$$\begin{array}{r} 60{,}000 \text{ doughnuts} \\ -\ 40{,}000 \text{ doughnuts} \\ \hline \mathbf{20{,}000 \text{ doughnuts}} \end{array}$$

b.
$$\begin{array}{r} 5000 \text{ cans} \\ 8000 \text{ cans} \\ 9000 \text{ cans} \\ +\ 4000 \text{ cans} \\ \hline \mathbf{26{,}000 \text{ cans}} \end{array}$$

c. **Test 4**

d. $\frac{4}{24} = \mathbf{\frac{1}{6}}$

LESSON 38, MIXED PRACTICE

1.
$$\begin{array}{r} 7 \text{ civilians} \\ +\ 3 \text{ soldiers} \\ \hline 10 \text{ total} \end{array}$$

$\frac{\text{soldiers}}{\text{total}} = \mathbf{\frac{3}{10}}$

2.
$$\begin{array}{r} \mathbf{115 \text{ pages}} \\ 3\overline{)345} \text{ pages} \\ \underline{3} \\ 04 \\ \underline{3} \\ 15 \\ \underline{15} \\ 0 \end{array}$$

3. 5 minutes = 5(60 seconds) = 300 seconds

$$\begin{array}{r} 300 \text{ seconds} \\ +\ 52 \text{ seconds} \\ \hline \mathbf{352 \text{ seconds}} \end{array}$$

4.
$$\begin{array}{r} 9000 \text{ cans} \\ -\ 4000 \text{ cans} \\ \hline \mathbf{5000 \text{ cans}} \end{array}$$

5.
```
  60        75
  70     7)525
  75
  70
  80
  85
+ 85
 525
```

6. **Answers will vary. See student work.**

7.

384 pages

Mira read $\frac{3}{8}$.	48 pages
	48 pages
	48 pages
Mira did not read $\frac{5}{8}$.	48 pages
	48 pages
	48 pages
	48 pages
	48 pages

(a) 3×48 pages $=$ **144 pages**

(b) $\frac{3}{8} + \frac{1}{8} = \frac{4}{8} = \frac{1}{2}$ **48 pages**

8.

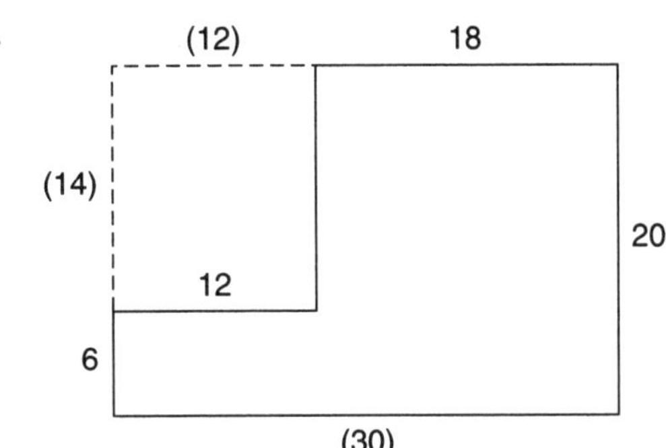

(a) Area of large rectangle $= 30 \text{ in.} \times 20 \text{ in.}$
$= 600 \text{ in.}^2$

Area of small rectangle $= 12 \text{ in.} \times 14 \text{ in.}$
$= 168 \text{ in.}^2$

Area of figure $= 600 \text{ in.}^2 - 168 \text{ in.}^2$
$=$ **432 in.²**

(b) Perimeter $= 18 \text{ in.} + 20 \text{ in.} + 30 \text{ in.} + 6 \text{ in.} + 12 \text{ in.} + 14 \text{ in.}$
$=$ **100 in.**

9. (a) $\frac{7}{9} \cdot \frac{2}{2} = \mathbf{\frac{14}{18}}$

(b) $\frac{20}{36} \div \frac{4}{4} = \mathbf{\frac{5}{9}}$

(c) $\frac{4}{5} \cdot \frac{6}{6} = \frac{24}{\mathbf{30}}$

10. (a) 2⑨86.34157 ⟶ 3000.~~00000~~ ⟶ **3000**

(b) 2986.341⑤7 ⟶ **2986.342**

11. Probability of stopping on

$1 = \frac{3}{8}$

$2 = \frac{2}{8} = \frac{1}{4}$

$3 = \frac{2}{8} = \frac{1}{4}$

$4 = \frac{1}{8}$

(a) **1**

(b) **4**

12. (a) **1.2 cm**

(b) **12 mm**

13. Perimeter $= 1.2 \text{ cm} + 1 \text{ cm} + 1.2 \text{ cm} + 1 \text{ cm} =$ **4.4 cm**

14. **The number 3.4 is about halfway between 3 and 4. Point *B* is too close to 3 to represent 3.4. So the best choice is *C*.**

15. (a) $\overline{AC}$ (or $\overline{CA}$)

(b) $\overline{BC}$ (or $\overline{CB}$)

16. (a) Area $= \frac{6 \text{ cm} \cdot 6 \text{ cm}}{2} =$ **18 cm²**

(b) Area $= \frac{6 \text{ cm} \cdot 6 \text{ cm}}{2} =$ **18 cm²**

(c) Area $= 18 \text{ cm}^2 + 18 \text{ cm}^2 =$ **36 cm²**

17.
```
  6.7
- 4.3
  2.4
```
$a =$ **2.4**

18.
```
  ¹
  4.7
+ 3.6
  8.3
```
$m =$ **8.3**

19.
$$\begin{array}{r} 0.45 \\ 10\overline{)4.50} \\ \underline{4\,0} \\ 50 \\ \underline{50} \\ 0 \end{array}$$
$w = \mathbf{0.45}$

20.
$$\begin{array}{r} 2.5 \\ \times\ 2.5 \\ \hline 125 \\ \underline{50\ } \\ 6.25 \end{array}$$
$x = \mathbf{6.25}$

21.
$$\begin{array}{r} \overset{1}{{}_{1}5}.37 \\ 27.7 \\ +\ \ 4. \\ \hline \mathbf{37.07} \end{array}$$

22.
$$\begin{array}{r} \mathbf{0.25} \\ 5\overline{)1.25} \\ \underline{1\,0} \\ 25 \\ \underline{25} \\ 0 \end{array}$$

23. $\frac{5}{9} \cdot 6 \cdot 2\frac{1}{10}$

$\frac{\overset{1}{\cancel{5}}}{\underset{\underset{1}{\cancel{3}}}{\cancel{9}}} \cdot \frac{\overset{\overset{1}{\cancel{2}}}{\cancel{6}}}{1} \cdot \frac{\overset{7}{\cancel{21}}}{\underset{\underset{1}{\cancel{2}}}{\cancel{10}}} = \mathbf{7}$

24.
$$\begin{aligned} \frac{5}{8} &= \frac{5}{8} \\ \frac{3}{4} &= \frac{6}{8} \\ +\ \frac{1}{2} &= \frac{4}{8} \\ \hline & \frac{15}{8} = \mathbf{1\frac{7}{8}} \end{aligned}$$

25. $5 \div 3\frac{1}{3} = \frac{5}{1} \div \frac{10}{3} = \frac{\overset{1}{\cancel{5}}}{1} \times \frac{3}{\underset{2}{\cancel{10}}}$

$= \frac{3}{2} = \mathbf{1\frac{1}{2}}$

26.
$$\begin{aligned} \frac{1}{2} &= \frac{5}{10} \\ -\ \frac{1}{5} &= \frac{2}{10} \\ \hline & \frac{3}{10} \end{aligned}$$
$\frac{3}{10} - \frac{3}{10} = \mathbf{0}$

27. **A. $4 \cdot 4^2$**

28. (a) **125 mL**

(b)
$$\begin{array}{r} 1000\text{ mL} \\ -\ \ 125\text{ mL} \\ \hline \mathbf{875\ mL} \end{array}$$

29. **Switch 916.42 and 916.37**

30.

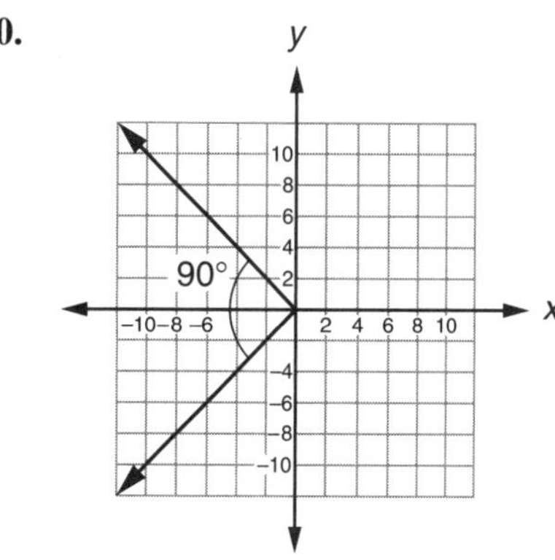

Lesson 39, Lesson Practice

a.
$$\begin{aligned} \frac{a}{12} &= \frac{6}{8} \\ 8 \cdot a &= 12 \cdot 6 \\ 8a &= 72 \\ a &= \frac{72}{8} \\ a &= \mathbf{9} \\ \frac{9}{12} &= \frac{6}{8} \end{aligned}$$

b.
$$\begin{aligned} \frac{30}{b} &= \frac{20}{16} \\ 20 \cdot b &= 30 \cdot 16 \\ 20b &= 480 \\ b &= \frac{480}{20} \\ b &= \mathbf{24} \\ \frac{30}{24} &= \frac{20}{16} \end{aligned}$$

c. $\frac{14}{21} = \frac{c}{15}$
$$21 \cdot c = 15 \cdot 14$$
$$21c = 210$$
$$c = \frac{210}{21}$$
$$c = \mathbf{10}$$
$$\frac{14}{21} = \frac{10}{15}$$

d. $\frac{30}{25} = \frac{24}{d}$
$$30 \cdot d = 24 \cdot 25$$
$$30d = 600$$
$$d = \mathbf{20}$$
$$\frac{30}{25} = \frac{24}{20}$$

e. $\frac{30}{100} = \frac{n}{40}$
$$100 \cdot n = 40 \cdot 30$$
$$100n = 1200$$
$$n = \frac{1200}{100}$$
$$n = \mathbf{12}$$
$$\frac{30}{100} = \frac{12}{40}$$

f. $\frac{m}{100} = \frac{9}{12}$
$$12 \cdot m = 100 \cdot 9$$
$$12m = 900$$
$$m = \frac{900}{12}$$
$$m = \mathbf{75}$$
$$\frac{75}{100} = \frac{9}{12}$$

Lesson 39, Mixed Practice

1. 64 inches − 61 inches = **3 inches**

2. **Between his thirteenth and fourteenth birthdays**

3. $\frac{\text{princes}}{\text{princesses}} = \frac{12}{16} = \mathbf{\frac{3}{4}}$

4. 497 + 513 + 436 + 410 = 1856 miles

1856 ÷ 4 = **464 miles**
(4)1856: 16, 25, 24, 16, 16, 0

5. $4.50 × 52: 900, 2250, **$234.00**

6. 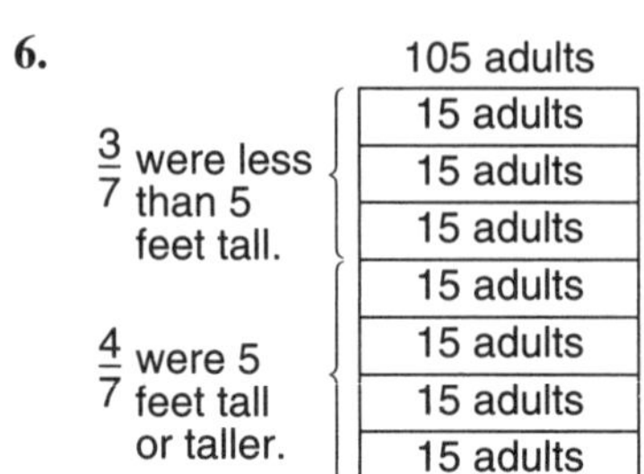

(a) 3 × 15 adults = **45 adults**

(b) 4 × 15 adults = **60 adults**

7. 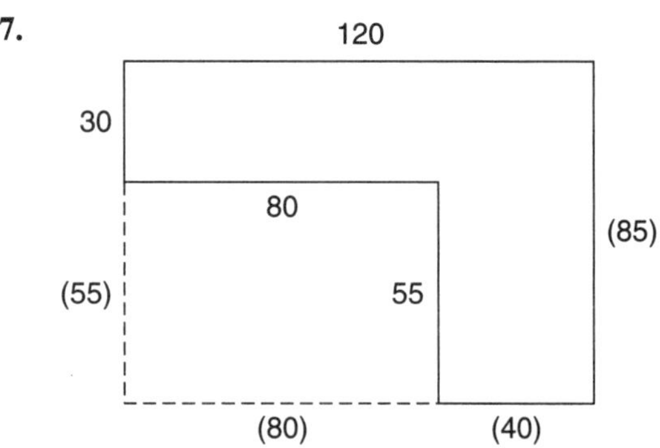

Area of large rectangle = 85 mm × 120 mm = 10,200 mm^2

Area of small rectangle = 55 mm × 80 mm = 4400 mm^2

Area of figure = 10,200 mm^2 − 4400 mm^2 = **5800 mm^2**

8. Perimeter = 120 mm + 85 mm + 40 mm + 55 mm + 80 mm + 30 mm = **410 mm**

9. (a) **2.5**

(b) $2\frac{5}{10} = \mathbf{2\frac{1}{2}}$

10. (a) 0.91⑥6666 ⟶ **0.92**

(b) 0.91666⑥6 ⟶ **0.91667**

11. 9.16 ⟶ 9

$\$1.39\frac{9}{10} \longrightarrow \$1.40$

$$\begin{array}{r} \$1.40 \\ \times \quad 9 \\ \hline \mathbf{\$12.60} \end{array}$$

12. (a) **100.075**

(b) **0.175**

13. (a) **∠*RPS*** (or **∠*SPR***)

(b) **∠*QPR*** (or **∠*RPQ***)

(c) **∠*QPS*** (or **∠*SPQ***)

14. **Each term can be found by dividing the previous term by 10.**

0.1 ÷ 10 = 0.01
0.01 ÷ 10 = 0.001
0.001 ÷ 10 = 0.0001
0.01, 0.001, 0.0001

15.
$$\begin{aligned} \frac{8}{12} &= \frac{6}{x} \\ 8 \cdot x &= 6 \cdot 12 \\ 8x &= 72 \\ x &= \frac{72}{8} \\ x &= \mathbf{9} \end{aligned}$$

16.
$$\begin{aligned} \frac{16}{y} &= \frac{2}{3} \\ 2 \cdot y &= 16 \cdot 3 \\ 2y &= 48 \\ y &= \frac{48}{2} \\ y &= \mathbf{24} \end{aligned}$$

17.
$$\begin{aligned} \frac{21}{14} &= \frac{n}{4} \\ 14 \cdot n &= 4 \cdot 21 \\ 14n &= 84 \\ n &= \frac{84}{14} \\ n &= \mathbf{6} \end{aligned}$$

18.
$$\begin{array}{r} 0.\,\overset{6}{\not 7}{}^{1}5 \\ -\ 0.\,3\,6 \\ \hline 0.\,3\,9 \end{array}$$
$m = \mathbf{0.39}$

19.
$$\begin{array}{r} \overset{0}{\not 1}.{}^{1}4 \\ -\ 0.\,8 \\ \hline 0.\,6 \end{array}$$
$w = \mathbf{0.6}$

20.
$$\begin{array}{r} 0.9 \\ 8\overline{)7.2} \\ 7\,2 \\ \hline 0 \end{array}$$
$x = \mathbf{0.9}$

21.
$$\begin{array}{r} 1.2 \\ \times\ 0.4 \\ \hline 0.48 \end{array}$$
$y = \mathbf{0.48}$

22. 9.6 + 12 + 8.59
↓ ↓ ↓
10 + 12 + 9 = **31**

$$\begin{array}{r} {}_{2}\overset{1}{9}.6 \\ 12. \\ +\ 8.59 \\ \hline \mathbf{30.19} \end{array}$$

23. 3.15 − (2.1 − 0.06)
↓ ↓ ↓
3 − (2 − 0) = **1**

$$\begin{array}{r} 2.{}^{0}\not 1{}^{1}0 \\ -\ 0.\,0\,6 \\ \hline 2.\,0\,4 \end{array} \qquad \begin{array}{r} 3.15 \\ -\ 2.04 \\ \hline \mathbf{1.11} \end{array}$$

24.
$$\begin{array}{rcl} 4\frac{5}{12} &=& 4\frac{10}{24} \\ +\ 6\frac{5}{8} &=& 6\frac{15}{24} \\ \hline && 10\frac{25}{24} = \mathbf{11\frac{1}{24}} \end{array}$$

25.
$$\begin{array}{rcl} 4\frac{1}{4} &=& 4\frac{5}{20} \longrightarrow \\ -\ 1\frac{3}{5} &=& 1\frac{12}{20} \\ \hline \end{array} \qquad \begin{array}{r} 3\frac{25}{20} \\ -\ 1\frac{12}{20} \\ \hline \mathbf{2\frac{13}{20}} \end{array}$$

26. $8\frac{1}{3} \cdot 1\frac{4}{5} = \frac{\overset{5}{\cancel{25}}}{\underset{1}{\cancel{3}}} \cdot \frac{\overset{3}{\cancel{9}}}{\underset{1}{\cancel{5}}} = \mathbf{15}$

27. $5\frac{5}{6} \div 7 = \frac{35}{6} \div \frac{7}{1}$

$= \frac{\overset{5}{\cancel{35}}}{6} \times \frac{1}{\underset{1}{\cancel{7}}} = \mathbf{\frac{5}{6}}$

28. (a) Perimeter = 15 mm + 15 mm + 18 mm = **48 mm**

(b) Area $= \frac{18 \text{ mm} \cdot 12 \text{ mm}}{2} = \mathbf{108\ mm^2}$

29. Odd primes: 3, 5

$\frac{2}{6} = \mathbf{\frac{1}{3}}$

30. $\frac{2}{3} = \frac{8}{12}$

$\frac{1}{2} = \frac{6}{12}$

$\frac{5}{6} = \frac{10}{12}$

$\mathbf{\frac{1}{2}, \frac{7}{12}, \frac{2}{3}, \frac{5}{6}}$

Lesson 40, Lesson Practice

a. **Each angle measures 60° because the angles equally share 180°.**

$\frac{180°}{3} = 60°$

b. **20°. Angle *ACB* and ∠*ACD* are complementary:**

90° − 70° = 20°

c. **Angle *CAB* measures 70° because it is the third angle of a triangle whose other angles measure 90° and 20°:**

180° − (90° + 20°) = 180° − 110° = 70°

d. **They are not vertical angles. Their angles are equal in measure, but they are not nonadjacent angles formed by two intersecting lines.**

e. Angle x is the third angle of a triangle:

m∠x = 180° − (40° + 80°) = 180° − 120° = 60°

Angle x and ∠y are supplementary angles:

m∠y = 180° − 60° = 120°

Angles z and x are vertical angles:

m∠z = 60°

Lesson 40, Mixed Practice

1. (a)
3 red marbles
+ 2 white marbles
5 total marbles

$\frac{\text{white marbles}}{\text{total marbles}} = \mathbf{\frac{2}{5}}$

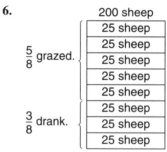

(b) $\mathbf{\frac{2}{5}}$

2. (a) 6 minutes = 6(60 seconds) = 360 seconds

6 minutes + 20 seconds = **380 seconds**

(b) $\frac{380 \text{ seconds}}{4}$ = **95 seconds**

3.
```
   18
× 24 miles
   72
  36
 432 miles
```
432 miles

4.
```
  103.4°F
−  98.6°F
    4.8°F
```
4.8°F

5. (a) Perimeter = 35 mm + 35 mm + 70 mm + 70 mm = **210 mm**

(b) Area = 35 mm × 70 mm = $\mathbf{2450\ mm^2}$

6.

200 sheep	
$\frac{5}{8}$ grazed.	25 sheep
	25 sheep
	25 sheep
	25 sheep
	25 sheep
$\frac{3}{8}$ drank.	25 sheep
	25 sheep
	25 sheep

(a) 5 · 25 sheep = **125 sheep**

(b) 3 · 25 sheep = **75 sheep**

7. BC = 100 mm − (30 mm + 45 mm) = 100 mm − 75 mm = 25 mm

25 mm = **2.5 cm**

8. (a) 0.083③33 ⟶ **0.083**

(b) 0.0⑧3333 ⟶ **0.1**

9. (a) **Twelve and fifty-four thousandths**

(b) **Ten and eleven hundredths**

10.

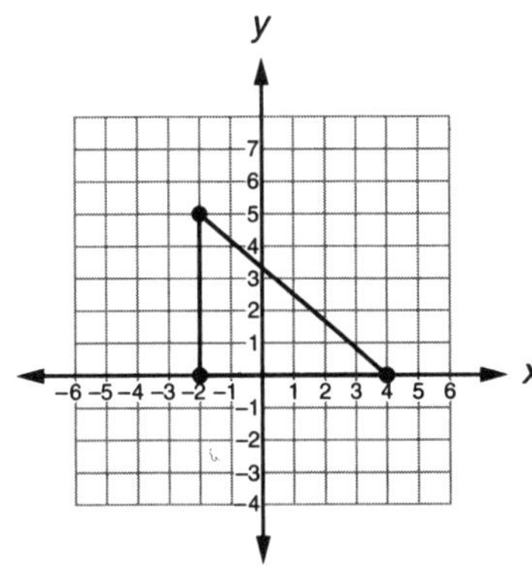

$$\text{Area} = \frac{6 \text{ units} \cdot 5 \text{ units}}{2} = \mathbf{15\ units^2}$$

11. **0.76**

12. (a) $\angle ACB = 180° - (70° + 75°)$
$= 180° - 145° = \mathbf{35°}$

(b) $\angle ACD = 180° - 35° = \mathbf{145°}$

(c) $\angle DCE = \mathbf{35°}$

13. $\boldsymbol{\angle BCE}$ (or $\boldsymbol{\angle ECB}$)

14. (a) **Identity property of multiplication**

(b) $5\overline{)120}$ = **24**

15. $10w = 25 \cdot 8$

$w = \frac{25 \cdot 8}{10}$

$w = \mathbf{20}$

16. $9n = 1.5 \cdot 6$

$n = \frac{(1.5)(6)}{9}$

$n = \mathbf{1}$

17. $9m = 12 \cdot 15$

$m = \frac{12 \cdot 15}{9}$

$m = \mathbf{20}$

18. $4.0 - 1.8 = 2.2$

$a = \mathbf{2.2}$

19. $3.9 + 0.39 = 4.29$

$t = \mathbf{4.29}$

20. 12 cm = 0.12 m

1.20 m − 0.12 m = **1.08 m**

21. $0.15 \times 0.05 = \mathbf{0.0075}$

22. 15×1.5: 75 + 150 = **22.5**

23. $12\overline{)14.4}$ = **1.2**

12
24
24
0

24. $4.00 - 1.25 = 2.75$ $\qquad$ $5.60 - 2.75 = \mathbf{2.85}$

25. $3.14 + 1.20 = 4.34$ $\qquad$ $5.00 - 4.34 = \mathbf{0.66}$

26. $6\frac{1}{4} \cdot 1\frac{3}{5} = \frac{\overset{5}{\cancel{25}}}{\underset{1}{\cancel{4}}} \cdot \frac{\overset{2}{\cancel{8}}}{\underset{1}{\cancel{5}}} = \frac{10}{1} = \mathbf{10}$

27. $7 \div 5\frac{5}{6} = \frac{7}{1} \div \frac{35}{6} = \frac{\overset{1}{\cancel{7}}}{1} \cdot \frac{6}{\underset{5}{\cancel{35}}}$

$= \frac{6}{5} = \mathbf{1\frac{1}{5}}$

28.
$$\begin{array}{r} \frac{8}{15} = \frac{40}{75} \\ + \frac{12}{25} = \frac{36}{75} \\ \hline \frac{76}{75} = \mathbf{1\frac{1}{75}} \end{array}$$

29.
$$\begin{array}{rrr} 4\frac{2}{5} = & 4\frac{8}{20} \longrightarrow & 3\frac{28}{20} \\ -1\frac{3}{4} = & -1\frac{15}{20} & -1\frac{15}{20} \\ \hline & & \mathbf{2\frac{13}{20}} \end{array}$$

30. 31.⑨75 ⟶ 32

$$\frac{1}{4} \times 32 = \frac{1}{\cancel{4}_1} \times \frac{\cancel{32}^8}{1} = \mathbf{8}$$

Lesson 41, Lesson Practice

a. $A = (15 \text{ in.})(8 \text{ in.}) = \mathbf{120\ in.^2}$

b. $\frac{(6 \text{ ft})(8 \text{ ft})}{2} = \mathbf{24\ ft^2}$

c. **One possibility:** $x(y + z) = xy + xz$

d. $\mathbf{6(15) = 90}$
$\mathbf{(6 \cdot 20) - (6 \cdot 5) = 120 - 30 = 90}$

e. $p = 2(l + w)$
$p = 2l + 2w$

f. **One way is to add 6 and 4. Then multiply the sum by 2. Another way is to multiply 6 by 2 and 4 by 2. Then add the products.**

Lesson 41, Mixed Practice

1. $\frac{\text{gazelles}}{\text{wildebeests}} = \frac{150}{200} = \mathbf{\frac{3}{4}}$

2.
$$\begin{array}{r} 105 \text{ points} \\ 112 \text{ points} \\ 98 \text{ points} \\ 113 \text{ points} \\ + 107 \text{ points} \\ \hline 535 \text{ points} \end{array}$$

$535 \text{ points} \div 5 = \mathbf{107\ points}$

3. 19 feet 6 inches = 19 (12 inches) + 6 inches = **234 inches**

4. (a) **Associative property of addition**

(b) **Associative property of multiplication**

(c) **Distributive property**

5.

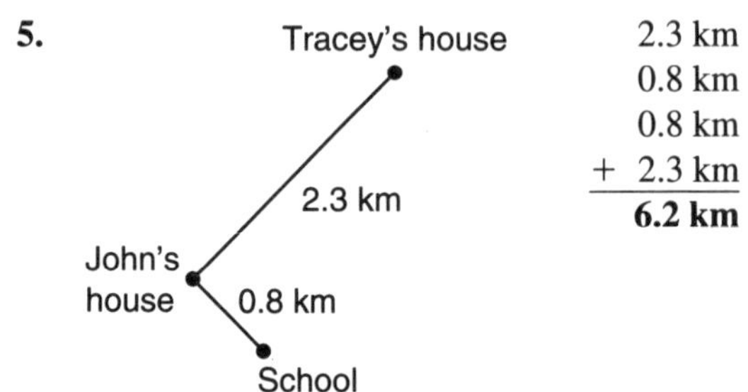

$$\begin{array}{r} 2.3 \text{ km} \\ 0.8 \text{ km} \\ 0.8 \text{ km} \\ + 2.3 \text{ km} \\ \hline \mathbf{6.2\ km} \end{array}$$

6. (a) $100\% - 70\% = 30\%$

$30\% = \frac{30}{100} = \mathbf{\frac{3}{10}}$

(b) $\frac{\text{water area}}{\text{land area}} = \mathbf{\frac{7}{3}}$

7. (a) **30 correct answers**

(b) **26 correct answers**

(c) **34 correct answers**

(d) **11 correct answers**

8.

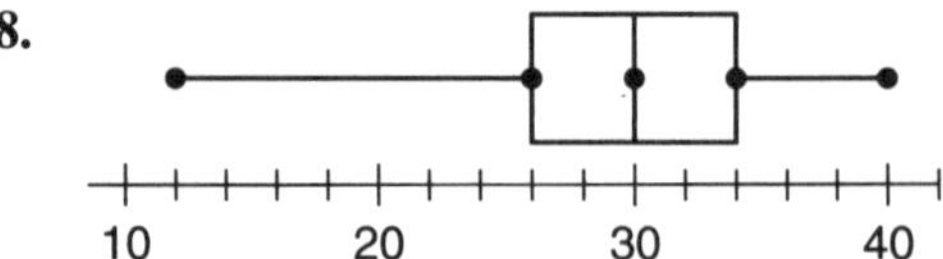

9.

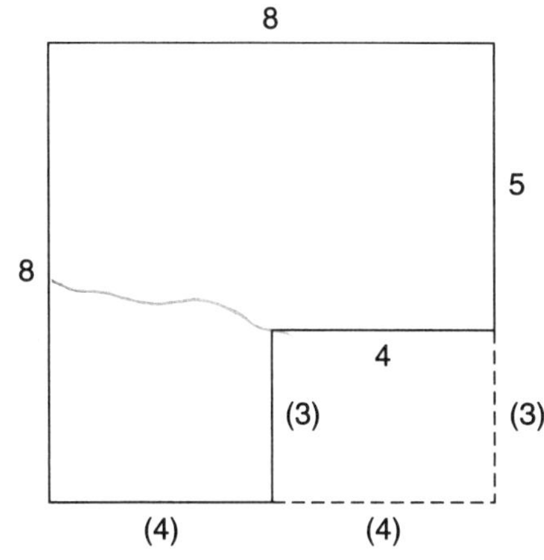

(a) Area of large rectangle $= (8 \text{ ft})(8 \text{ ft})$
$= 64 \text{ ft}^2$
Area of small rectangle $= (3 \text{ ft})(4 \text{ ft})$
$= 12 \text{ ft}^2$
Area of figure $= 64 \text{ ft}^2 - 12 \text{ ft}^2$
$= \mathbf{52\ ft^2}$

(b) Perimeter $= 8 \text{ ft} + 5 \text{ ft} + 4 \text{ ft} + 3 \text{ ft} + 4 \text{ ft} + 8 \text{ ft} =$ **32 ft**

10. (a) **3.6**

(b) $3\frac{6}{10} = \mathbf{3\frac{3}{5}}$

11. $2 + 3 + 5 + 7 =$ **17**

12. (a) Perimeter $= 13 \text{ mm} + 15 \text{ mm} + 14 \text{ mm} =$ **42 mm**

(b) Area $= \dfrac{(14 \text{ mm})(12 \text{ mm})}{2} = \mathbf{84\ mm^2}$

13. (a) **0.00067**

(b) **100.023**

14. $2\pi r = 2(3.14)(10)$
$= 2(31.4) =$ **62.8**

15. $\frac{3}{5} \cdot \frac{14}{14} = \frac{42}{70}$
$\frac{1}{2} \cdot \frac{35}{35} = \frac{35}{70}$
$\frac{5}{7} \cdot \frac{10}{10} = \frac{50}{70}$
$\mathbf{\frac{35}{70}, \frac{42}{70}, \frac{50}{70}}$

16. Area $= (5.6 \text{ cm})(3.4 \text{ cm}) = \mathbf{19.04\ cm^2}$

17. $\frac{x}{2.4} = \frac{10}{16}$
$16x = 2.4(10)$
$x = \frac{24}{16}$
$x = 1\frac{8}{16} = 1\frac{1}{2} =$ **1.5**

18. $\frac{18}{8} = \frac{m}{20}$
$8m = 18 \cdot 20$
$m = \frac{360}{8}$
$m =$ **45**

19.
```
     5
  7. 6¹0
- 3. 4 5
--------
  4. 1 5
```
$a =$ **4.15**

20.
```
  0.048
3)0.144
   12
    24
    24
     0
```
$y =$ **0.048**

21.
```
  0.925
8)7.400
  7 2
    20
    16
     40
     40
      0
```

22.
```
   0.4        0.24
 × 0.6      × 0.02
  0.24      0.0048
```
0.0048

23.
```
  0.863
5)4.315
  4 0
    31
    30
     15
     15
      0
```

24. $$\begin{array}{r} 0.065 \\ 100\overline{)6.500} \\ \underline{6\ 00} \\ 500 \\ \underline{500} \\ 0 \end{array}$$

25. $$\begin{aligned} 3\frac{1}{3} &= 3\frac{4}{12} \\ 1\frac{5}{6} &= 1\frac{10}{12} \\ +\ \frac{7}{12} &= \frac{7}{12} \\ \hline 4\frac{21}{12} &= 5\frac{9}{12} = \mathbf{5\frac{3}{4}} \end{aligned}$$

26. $$4 \longrightarrow 3\frac{4}{4}$$
$$-\ 1\frac{1}{4} \qquad -\ 1\frac{1}{4}$$
$$2\frac{3}{4}$$

$$4\frac{1}{6} = 4\frac{2}{12} \longrightarrow 3\frac{14}{12}$$
$$-\ 2\frac{3}{4} = 2\frac{9}{12} \qquad -\ 2\frac{9}{12}$$
$$\mathbf{1\frac{5}{12}}$$

27. $$3\frac{1}{5} \cdot 2\frac{5}{8} \cdot 1\frac{3}{7}$$
$$= \frac{\overset{2}{\cancel{16}}}{\underset{1}{\cancel{5}}} \cdot \frac{\overset{3}{\cancel{21}}}{\underset{1}{\cancel{8}}} \cdot \frac{\overset{2}{\cancel{10}}}{\underset{1}{\cancel{7}}} = \mathbf{12}$$

28. $$4\frac{1}{2} \div 6 = \frac{9}{2} \div \frac{6}{1} = \frac{\overset{3}{\cancel{9}}}{2} \times \frac{1}{\underset{2}{\cancel{6}}} = \mathbf{\frac{3}{4}}$$

29. (a) $(12 \cdot 7) + (12 \cdot 13)$
$= 84 + 156 = 240$
or
$12(7 + 13) = 12 \cdot 20 = 240$
$(12 \cdot 7) + (12 \cdot 13) \mathbf{=} 12(7 + 13)$

(b) **Distributive property**

30. $m\angle x = 180° - (90° + 42°)$
$= 180° - 132° = \mathbf{48°}$
$m\angle y = 180° - 48° = \mathbf{132°}$
$m\angle z = m\angle x = \mathbf{48°}$

LESSON 42, LESSON PRACTICE

a. $\mathbf{2.\overline{72}}$

b. $\mathbf{0.81\overline{6}}$

c. $0.\overline{6} = 0.6666\ldots$
$0.66\underline{6}⑥\ldots \longrightarrow \mathbf{0.667}$

d. $5.3\overline{81} = 5.38181\ldots$
$5.38\underline{1}⑧1\ldots \longrightarrow \mathbf{5.382}$

e. $$\begin{array}{r} 0.141666\ldots \\ 12\overline{)1.7000000\ldots} \\ \underline{1\ 2} \\ 50 \\ \underline{48} \\ 20 \\ \underline{12} \\ 80 \\ \underline{72} \\ 80 \\ \underline{72} \\ 80 \end{array}$$

$\mathbf{0.141\overline{6}}$

f. $0.141\underline{6}⑥6\ldots \longrightarrow \mathbf{0.1417}$

LESSON 42, MIXED PRACTICE

1. $$\begin{array}{r} 2 \text{ boys} \\ +\ ?\text{ girls} \\ \hline 5 \text{ total} \end{array} \longrightarrow \begin{array}{r} 2 \text{ boys} \\ +\ 3\text{ girls} \\ \hline 5 \text{ total} \end{array}$$
$$\frac{\text{boys}}{\text{girls}} = \mathbf{\frac{2}{3}}$$

2. $$\begin{array}{r} \mathbf{27\ students} \\ 16\overline{)432} \\ \underline{32} \\ 112 \\ \underline{112} \\ 0 \end{array}$$

3. $$\begin{array}{r} 23 \text{ miles} \\ \underline{\times\ \ 7} \\ \mathbf{161\ miles} \end{array}$$

4.

450 students

$\frac{7}{9}$ were enthralled.	50 students
	50 students
	50 students
	50 students
	50 students
	50 students
	50 students
$\frac{2}{9}$ were not enthralled.	50 students
	50 students

(a) 7(50 students) = **350 students**

(b) 2(50 students) = **100 students**

5. (a) $5.1\overline{6} = 5.16666\ldots$
$5.166\underline{6}⑥\ldots \longrightarrow$ **5.1667**

(b) $5.\overline{27} = 5.272727\ldots$
$5.272\underline{7}②7\ldots \longrightarrow$ **5.2727**

6. (a)

$$\begin{array}{r} 19 \text{ students} \\ -\ 11 \text{ students} \\ \hline \mathbf{8\ students} \end{array}$$

(b) $\frac{9}{30} = \mathbf{\frac{3}{10}}$

7. $\text{Area} = \frac{(6\text{ units})(6\text{ units})}{2} = \mathbf{18\ units^2}$

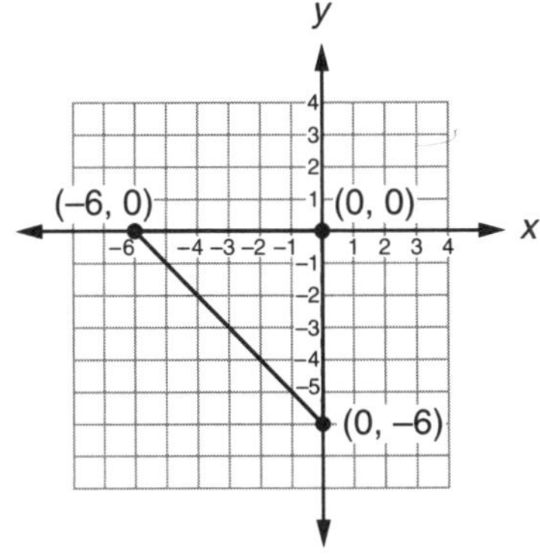

8. (a) Perimeter = 10 in. + 8 in. + 10 in.
+ 20 in. + 20 in. + 12 in.
= **80 in.**

(b)

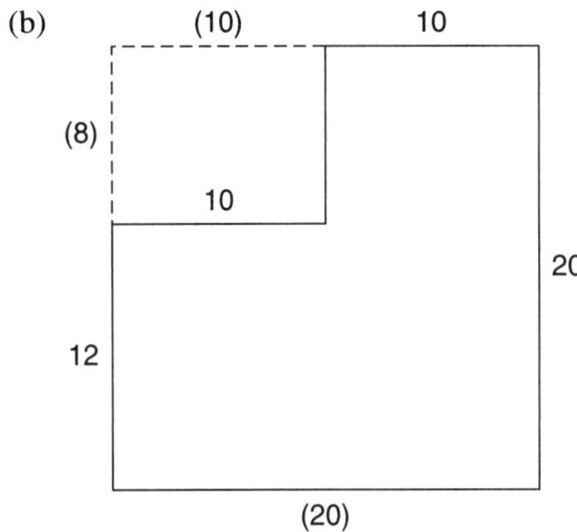

Area of large rectangle = 20 in. × 20 in.
= 400 in.^{2}

Area of small rectangle = 10 in. × 8 in.
= 80 in.^{2}

Area of figure = 400 in.^{2} − 80 in.^{2}
= **320 in.^{2}**

9.

$$\begin{array}{r} 0.15454\ldots \\ 11\overline{)1.700000}\ldots \\ \underline{1\,1} \\ 60 \\ \underline{55} \\ 50 \\ \underline{44} \\ 60 \\ \underline{55} \\ 50 \\ \underline{44} \\ 60 \end{array}$$

(a) $\mathbf{0.1\overline{54}}$

(b) $0.15\underline{4}⑤4\ldots \longrightarrow$ **0.155**

10.

$$\begin{array}{r} \overset{1}{0.027} \\ +\ 0.58 \\ \hline \mathbf{0.607} \end{array}$$

11. $\frac{2}{6} = \mathbf{\frac{1}{3}}$

12. (a) **One possibility:**

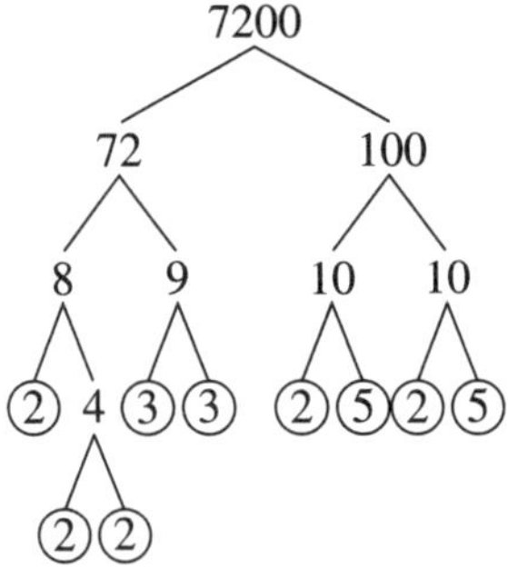

(b) $\mathbf{2^5 \cdot 3^2 \cdot 5^2}$

13.

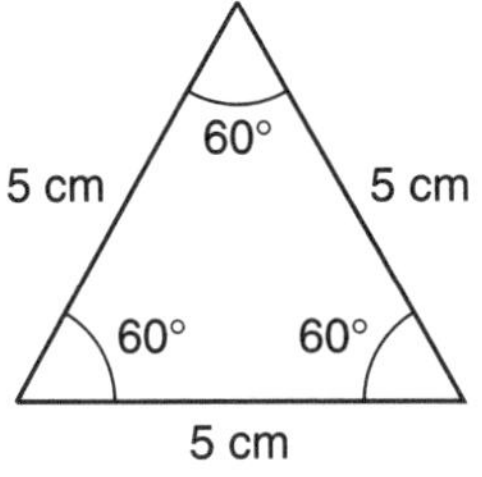

14. $12 = 2 \cdot 2 \cdot 3$
$15 = 3 \cdot 5$
$\text{LCM}(12, 15) = 2 \cdot 2 \cdot 3 \cdot 5 = \mathbf{60}$

15. $\frac{21}{24} = \frac{w}{40}$
$24w = 21 \cdot 40$
$w = \frac{840}{24}$
$w = \mathbf{35}$

16. $\frac{1.2}{x} = \frac{9}{6}$
$9x = (1.2)6$
$x = \frac{7.2}{9}$
$x = \mathbf{0.8}$

17.
$$\begin{array}{r} \overset{0}{\cancel{1}}\,\overset{13}{\cancel{4}}.{}^{1}0 \\ -\quad 9.\,6 \\ \hline 4.\,4 \end{array}$$
$m = \mathbf{4.4}$

18.
$$\begin{array}{r} 1.63 \\ +\ 4.2 \\ \hline 5.83 \end{array}$$
$n = \mathbf{5.83}$

19. $\frac{1}{2}(12)(10) = \frac{1}{2}(120) = \mathbf{60}$

20. $\mathbf{4(11) = 44}$
or
$\mathbf{(4 \cdot 5) + (4 \cdot 6) = 20 + 24 = 44}$

21. **343**

22.
$$\begin{array}{r} \$4.56 \\ \times\ 0.08 \\ \hline \$0.3648 \end{array} \longrightarrow \mathbf{\$0.36}$$

23. $\mathbf{24 \div 6 = 4}$

24. (a) **Diameter**

(b) **Radius**

25.
$$\begin{array}{r} \mathbf{1.775} \\ 4\overline{)7.100} \\ \underline{4} \\ 3\,1 \\ \underline{2\,8} \\ 30 \\ \underline{28} \\ 20 \\ \underline{20} \\ 0 \end{array}$$

26.
$$\begin{array}{rcl} 6\frac{1}{4} & = & 6\frac{3}{12} \\ 5\frac{5}{12} & = & 5\frac{5}{12} \\ +\ \frac{2}{3} & = & \frac{8}{12} \\ \hline & & 11\frac{16}{12} = 12\frac{4}{12} = \mathbf{12\frac{1}{3}} \end{array}$$

27.
$$\begin{array}{rcl} 4\frac{1}{6} & = & 4\frac{2}{12} \longrightarrow 3\frac{14}{12} \\ -\ 1\frac{1}{4} & = & 1\frac{3}{12} \qquad -\ 1\frac{3}{12} \\ \hline & & \qquad\qquad 2\frac{11}{12} \end{array}$$

$$\begin{array}{rcl} 4 & \longrightarrow & 3\frac{12}{12} \\ -\ 2\frac{11}{12} & & -\ 2\frac{11}{12} \\ \hline & & \mathbf{1\frac{1}{12}} \end{array}$$

28. $6\frac{2}{5} \cdot 2\frac{5}{8} \cdot 2\frac{6}{7} =$

$\frac{\overset{4}{\cancel{32}}}{\underset{1}{\cancel{5}}} \cdot \frac{\overset{3}{\cancel{21}}}{\underset{1}{\cancel{8}}} \cdot \frac{\overset{4}{\cancel{20}}}{\underset{1}{\cancel{7}}} = \mathbf{48}$

29. The quotient is greater than 1 because the dividend is greater than the divisor.

$6 \div 4\frac{1}{2} = \frac{6}{1} \div \frac{9}{2} = \frac{\overset{2}{\cancel{6}}}{1} \times \frac{2}{\underset{3}{\cancel{9}}} = \frac{4}{3}$

$= \mathbf{1\frac{1}{3}}$

30. $m\angle a = 180° - 40° = \mathbf{140°}$
$m\angle b = 180° - (90° + 40°)$
$= 180° - 130° = \mathbf{50°}$
$m\angle c = 180° - 50° = \mathbf{130°}$

LESSON 43, LESSON PRACTICE

a. $0.24 = \frac{24}{100} = \mathbf{\frac{6}{25}}$

b. $45.6 = 45\frac{6}{10} = \mathbf{45\frac{3}{5}}$

c. $2.375 = 2\frac{375}{1000} = \mathbf{2\frac{3}{8}}$

d.
```
    5.75
 4)23.00
   20
    3 0
    2 8
      20
      20
       0
```
(quotient **5.75**)

e. $4\frac{3}{5} = \frac{23}{5}$
```
   4.6
 5)23.0
   20
    3 0
    3 0
      0
```
(quotient **4.6**)

f.
```
   0.625
 8)5.000
   4 8
     20
     16
      40
      40
       0
```
(quotient **0.625**)

g.
```
  0.8333 . . .
 6)5.0000 . . .
   4 8
     20
     18
      20
      18
       20
```
$\mathbf{0.8\overline{3}}$

h. $8\% = \frac{8}{100} = \mathbf{0.08}$

i. $12.5\% = \frac{12.5}{100} = \mathbf{0.125}$

j. $150\% = \frac{150}{100} = \mathbf{1.50}$

k. $6\frac{1}{2}\% = 6.5\% = \frac{6.5}{100} = \mathbf{0.065}$

LESSON 43, MIXED PRACTICE

1. $\frac{\text{Celtic soldiers}}{\text{total soldiers}} = \mathbf{\frac{2}{7}}$

2. (a) 11 minutes 44 seconds =
11(60 seconds) + 44 seconds =
704 seconds

(b)
```
  88 seconds
8)704 seconds
  64
   64
   64
    0
```
(quotient **88 seconds**)

3.
```
    1 10
    2̸ 1̸.¹0 gallons
 −  1 3. 3 gallons
      7. 7 gallons
```
7.7 gallons

4.
$$\begin{array}{r} 1{,}000{,}200{,}000 \text{ people} \\ -\ 725{,}000{,}000 \text{ people} \\ \hline \mathbf{275{,}200{,}000 \text{ people}} \end{array}$$

5.

15 games

$\frac{2}{3}$ won.	5 games
	5 games
$\frac{1}{3}$ lost.	5 games

(a) $2(5 \text{ games}) = \mathbf{10 \text{ games}}$

(b) $\frac{\text{won}}{\text{lost}} = \mathbf{\frac{2}{1}}$

6. (a) **13.5 seconds**

(b) **12.8 seconds**

(c) **14.7 seconds**

7.

11 12 13 14 15 16

8. $\frac{120 \text{ mm}}{6} = 20 \text{ mm}$

$\text{Perimeter} = (4)(20 \text{ mm}) = \mathbf{80 \text{ mm}}$

9. (a) $0.375 = \frac{375}{1000} = \mathbf{\frac{3}{8}}$

(b) $5.55 = 5\frac{55}{100} = \mathbf{5\frac{11}{20}}$

10. (a) $2\frac{2}{5} = \frac{12}{5}$

$$\begin{array}{r} \mathbf{2.4} \\ 5\overline{)12.0} \\ \underline{10} \\ 2\ 0 \\ \underline{2\ 0} \\ 0 \end{array}$$

(b)
$$\begin{array}{r} \mathbf{0.125} \\ 8\overline{)1.000} \\ \underline{8} \\ 20 \\ \underline{16} \\ 40 \\ \underline{40} \\ 0 \end{array}$$

11. (a) $0.\overline{45} = 0.4545\ldots$

$0.45\underline{4}⑤\ldots \longrightarrow \mathbf{0.455}$

(b) $3.\overline{142857} =$

$3.142857142857\ldots$

$3.14\underline{2}⑧57142857 \longrightarrow \mathbf{3.143}$

12.
$$\begin{array}{r} 0.15833\ldots \\ 12\overline{)1.90000\ldots} \\ \underline{1\ 2} \\ 70 \\ \underline{60} \\ 100 \\ \underline{96} \\ 40 \\ \underline{36} \\ 40 \\ \underline{36} \\ 40 \end{array}$$

(a) $\mathbf{0.158\overline{3}}$

(b) $0.15\underline{8}③\ldots \longrightarrow \mathbf{0.158}$

13.
$$\begin{array}{r} \overset{3}{\not{4}}.\ \overset{9}{\not{0}}\ \overset{14}{\not{5}}\ {}^{1}0 \\ -\ 0.\ 1\ 6\ 7 \\ \hline \mathbf{3.\ 8\ 8\ 3} \end{array}$$

14.

C

$\frac{3}{4}$ in. $1\frac{1}{4}$ in.

A 1 in. B

$BC = \mathbf{1\frac{1}{4} \text{ inches}}$

15. $\frac{26}{52} = \mathbf{\frac{1}{2}}$

16. (a) **One possibility:**

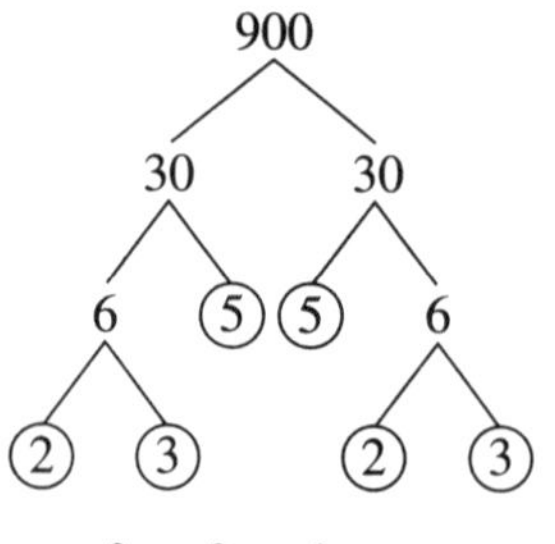

(b) $2^2 \cdot 3^2 \cdot 5^2$

(c) $\sqrt{900} = 30 = \mathbf{2 \cdot 3 \cdot 5}$

17. 1 liter = 1000 milliliters

$$\frac{1000 \text{ milliliters}}{2 \text{ milliliters}} = 500$$

500 eyedroppers

18. (a) $8\% = \frac{8}{100} = \mathbf{0.08}$

(b)
$$\begin{array}{r} \$8.90 \\ \times\ 0.08 \\ \hline \$0.7120 \end{array} \longrightarrow \mathbf{\$0.71}$$

19. (a) Perimeter = 0.6 m + 1 m + 0.8 m = **2.4 m**

(b) $\text{Area} = \frac{(0.8 \text{ m})(0.6 \text{ m})}{2} = \mathbf{0.24\ m^2}$

20. $\frac{32}{2} = \frac{320}{20}$

The division problems are equivalent problems because the quotients are equal.

21. $2(3 + 4) = 2(7) = \mathbf{14}$

22.
$$\frac{10}{18} = \frac{c}{4.5}$$
$$18c = 10 \cdot 4.5$$
$$c = \frac{45}{18}$$
$$c = 2\frac{1}{2} \text{ or } \mathbf{2.5}$$

23.
$$\begin{array}{r} 1.\ \overset{8}{\cancel{9}}{}^{1}0 \\ -\ 0.\ 4\ 2 \\ \hline 1.\ 4\ 8 \end{array}$$
$w = \mathbf{1.48}$

24.
$$\begin{array}{r} \mathbf{1.625} \\ 4\overline{)6.500} \\ \underline{4} \\ 2\,5 \\ \underline{2\,4} \\ 10 \\ \underline{8} \\ 20 \\ \underline{20} \\ 0 \end{array}$$

25.
$$\begin{array}{rcl} 3\frac{3}{10} & = & 3\frac{9}{30} \\ -\ 1\frac{11}{15} & = & 1\frac{22}{30} \\ \hline \end{array} \longrightarrow \begin{array}{r} 2\frac{39}{30} \\ -\ 1\frac{22}{30} \\ \hline \mathbf{1\frac{17}{30}} \end{array}$$

26.
$$\begin{array}{rcl} 5\frac{1}{2} & = & 5\frac{5}{10} \\ 6\frac{3}{10} & = & 6\frac{3}{10} \\ +\ \frac{4}{5} & = & \frac{8}{10} \\ \hline & & 11\frac{16}{10} = 12\frac{6}{10} = \mathbf{12\frac{3}{5}} \end{array}$$

27. $7\frac{1}{2} \cdot 3\frac{1}{3} \cdot \frac{4}{5} = \frac{\overset{5}{\cancel{15}}}{\underset{1}{\cancel{2}}} \cdot \frac{\overset{\overset{1}{\cancel{2}}}{\cancel{10}}}{\underset{1}{\cancel{3}}} \cdot \frac{4}{\underset{1}{\cancel{5}}} = 20$

$20 \div 5 = \mathbf{4}$

28. **(5, 10)**

29.
$$\begin{aligned} m\angle a &= 180° - 110° = \mathbf{70°} \\ m\angle b &= 180° - (70° + 50°) \\ &= 180° - 120° = \mathbf{60°} \\ m\angle c &= 180° - 60° = \mathbf{120°} \end{aligned}$$

30. (a) **180°**

(b) **90°**

(c) **45°**

Lesson 44, Lesson Practice

a.
$$\begin{array}{r} \mathbf{13\ R\ 3} \\ 4\overline{)55} \\ \underline{4} \\ 15 \\ \underline{12} \\ 3 \end{array}$$

b.
$$\begin{array}{r} \mathbf{13\frac{3}{4}} \\ 4\overline{)55} \\ \underline{4} \\ 15 \\ \underline{12} \\ 3 \end{array}$$

c. $$\begin{array}{r} 13.75 \\ 4\overline{)55.00} \\ \underline{4} \\ 15 \\ \underline{12} \\ 3\,0 \\ \underline{2\,8} \\ 20 \\ \underline{20} \\ 0 \end{array}$$

d. $$\begin{array}{l} 1.8333\ldots \\ 3\overline{)5.5000\ldots} \\ \underline{3} \\ 2\,5 \\ \underline{2\,4} \\ 10 \\ \underline{9} \\ 10 \\ \underline{9} \\ 10 \end{array}$$

1.833③ . . . ⟶ **1.833**

e. $$\begin{array}{l} 23 \text{ R } 1 \\ 4\overline{)93} \\ \underline{8} \\ 13 \\ \underline{12} \\ 1 \end{array}$$

23 students are in three classrooms, and 24 students are in the fourth classroom.
23, 23, 23, and 24 students

LESSON 44, MIXED PRACTICE

1. $\dfrac{\text{length}}{\text{width}} = \dfrac{24}{18} = \mathbf{\dfrac{4}{3}}$

2. $$\begin{array}{r} 90 \\ 95 \\ 90 \\ 85 \\ 80 \\ 85 \\ 90 \\ 80 \\ 95 \\ +\ 100 \\ \hline 890 \end{array} \qquad \begin{array}{r} \mathbf{89} \\ 10\overline{)890} \end{array}$$

3. $\dfrac{\text{able to find a job}}{\text{total}} = \mathbf{\dfrac{3}{5}}$

4. $$\begin{array}{r} \$0.34 \\ \times \quad 50 \\ \hline \$17.00 \end{array} \qquad \begin{array}{r} \$20.00 \\ -\ \$17.00 \\ \hline \mathbf{\$3.00} \end{array}$$

5. $$\begin{array}{r} 2.\,\overset{8}{\not 9}\,\overset{17}{\not 8}\,{}^{1}0 \\ -\ 0.\,0\,9\,7 \\ \hline 2.\,8\,8\,3 \end{array}$$

Two and eight hundred eighty-three thousandths

6. 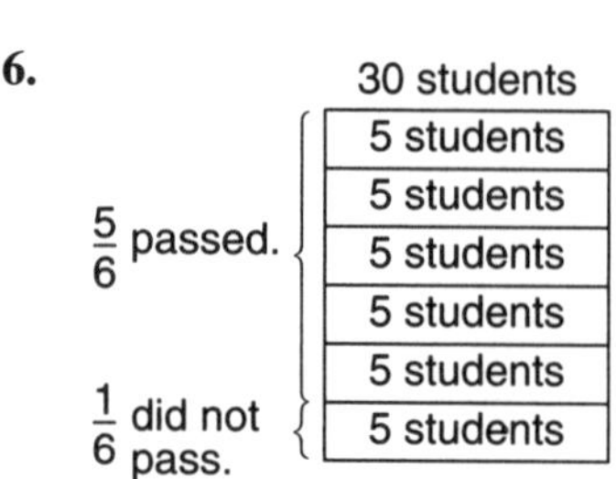

(a) **5 students**

(b) $\dfrac{\text{passed}}{\text{did not pass}} = \dfrac{25}{5} = \mathbf{\dfrac{5}{1}}$

7. 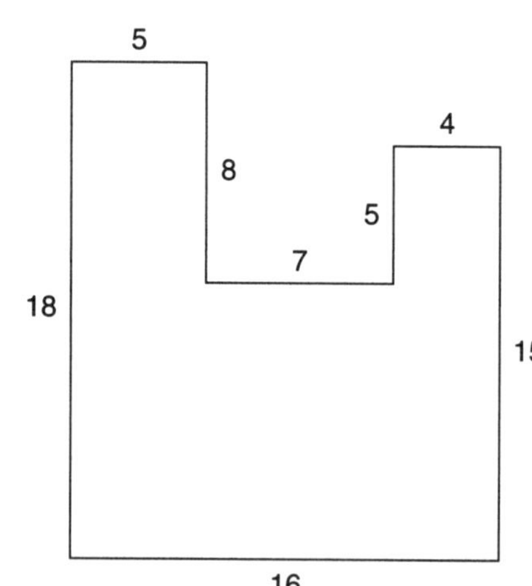

Perimeter = 18m + 5m + 8m + 7m + 5m + 4m + 15m + 16m = **78 m**

8. (a) $0.75 = \dfrac{75}{100} = \mathbf{\dfrac{3}{4}}$

(b) $$\begin{array}{r} \mathbf{0.625} \\ 8\overline{)5.000} \\ \underline{4\,8} \\ 20 \\ \underline{16} \\ 40 \\ \underline{40} \\ 0 \end{array}$$

(c) $125\% = \dfrac{125}{100} = \mathbf{1.25}$

9. $\dfrac{\text{hearts}}{\text{total cards}} = \dfrac{13}{52} = \mathbf{\dfrac{1}{4}}$

10. **B. (2 · 3) + (2 · 4)**

11. $10 + 5 = 15$
$15 + 6 = 21$
$21 + 7 = 28$
15, 21, 28

12.
$$\begin{array}{r} 0.49090\ldots \\ 11\overline{)5.40000\ldots} \\ \underline{4\,4} \\ 1\,00 \\ \underline{99} \\ 10 \\ \underline{0} \\ 100 \\ \underline{99} \\ 10 \\ \underline{0} \\ 10 \end{array}$$

(a) $\mathbf{0.4\overline{90}}$

(b) $0.49\underline{0}⑨0\ldots \longrightarrow$ **0.491**

13. $2 \times 3 \times 5 \times 7 = \mathbf{210}$

14. (a) $\mathbf{-12, 0, 0.12, \frac{1}{2}, 1.2}$

(b) $\mathbf{-12, 0}$

15. (a) $12\left(1\frac{1}{2} \text{ inches}\right)$

$= 12\left(\frac{3}{2} \text{ inches}\right) = 6 \times 3 \text{ inches}$

$=$ **18 inches**

(b) 1 yard = 36 inches

$36 \text{ inches} \div 1\frac{1}{2} = \frac{36}{1} \div \frac{3}{2}$

$= \frac{\overset{12}{\cancel{36}}}{1} \times \frac{2}{\underset{1}{\cancel{3}}} =$ **24 books**

16.
$$\begin{array}{r} \overset{1\,1}{2.46} \\ +\ 2.54 \\ \hline 5.00 \end{array} = \mathbf{5}$$

17. $3 \times 10 \text{ meters} =$ **30 meters**

18. **Answers will vary. See student work.**

(a) Area = (2.5 cm)(2.5 cm) = $\mathbf{6.25\ cm^2}$

(b) Perimeter = 4(2.5 cm) = **10 cm**

19.

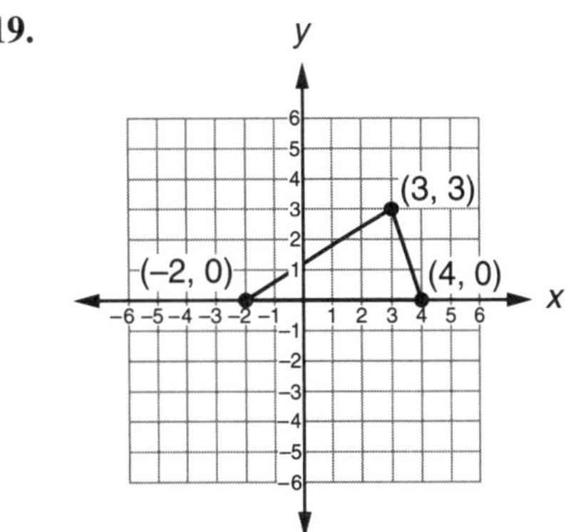

$\text{Area} = \dfrac{(6 \text{ units})(3 \text{ units})}{2} = \mathbf{9\ units^2}$

20. $\dfrac{25}{15} = \dfrac{n}{1.2}$
$15n = 25 \cdot 1.2$
$n = \dfrac{30}{15}$
$n = \mathbf{2}$

21. $\dfrac{p}{90} = \dfrac{4}{18}$
$18p = 90 \cdot 4$
$p = \dfrac{360}{18}$
$p = \mathbf{20}$

22.
$$\begin{array}{r} \overset{3}{\cancel{4}}.\overset{9}{\cancel{^1 0}}{}^1 0 \\ -\ 3.\,1\,4 \\ \hline 0.\,8\,6 \end{array}$$
$x = \mathbf{0.86}$

23.
$$\begin{array}{r} \overset{0}{\cancel{1}}.{}^1 0 \\ -\ 0.\,1 \\ \hline 0.\,9 \end{array}$$
$z = \mathbf{0.9}$

24.
$$\begin{array}{r} \mathbf{2.0525} \\ 8\overline{)16.4200} \\ \underline{16} \\ 0\,4 \\ \underline{0} \\ 42 \\ \underline{40} \\ 20 \\ \underline{16} \\ 40 \\ \underline{40} \\ 0 \end{array}$$

25.
$$\begin{array}{r} \mathbf{0.017} \\ 9\overline{)0.153} \\ \underline{9} \\ 63 \\ \underline{63} \\ 0 \end{array}$$

26.
$$\begin{array}{rcl} 5\frac{3}{4} & = & 5\frac{9}{12} \\ \frac{5}{6} & = & \frac{10}{12} \\ +\ 2\frac{1}{2} & = & 2\frac{6}{12} \\ \hline & & 7\frac{25}{12} = \mathbf{9\frac{1}{12}} \end{array}$$

27.
$$\begin{array}{r} 5 \\ -\ 1\frac{5}{6} \\ \hline \end{array} \longrightarrow \begin{array}{r} 4\frac{6}{6} \\ -\ 1\frac{5}{6} \\ \hline 3\frac{1}{6} \end{array} \qquad \begin{array}{rcl} 3\frac{1}{3} & = & 3\frac{2}{6} \\ -\ 3\frac{1}{6} & = & 3\frac{1}{6} \\ \hline & & \mathbf{\frac{1}{6}} \end{array}$$

28. $3\frac{3}{4} \cdot 3\frac{1}{3} \cdot 8 = \frac{\overset{5}{\cancel{15}}}{\underset{1}{\cancel{4}}} \cdot \frac{10}{\underset{1}{\cancel{3}}} \cdot \frac{\overset{2}{\cancel{8}}}{1} = \mathbf{100}$

29. $7 \div 10\frac{1}{2} = \frac{7}{1} \div \frac{21}{2} = \frac{\overset{1}{\cancel{7}}}{1} \times \frac{2}{\underset{3}{\cancel{21}}} = \mathbf{\frac{2}{3}}$

30. (a) $m\angle ABD = 180° - (35° + 90°)$
$= 180° - 125° = \mathbf{55°}$

(b) $m\angle CBD = 90° - 55° = \mathbf{35°}$

(c) $m\angle BDC = 90° - 35° = \mathbf{55°}$

(a) The other two angles of ΔABD measure 35° and 90°. For the sum to be 180°, m$\angle ABD$ must be 55°.

(b) Since the figure is a rectangle, m$\angle ABC$ is 90°. We found that m$\angle ABC$ is 55°; $\angle CBD$ is the complement of $\angle ABD$, so m$\angle CBD$ is 35°.

(c) Angle BDC is the complement of a 35° angle. Also, $\angle BCD$ is the third angle of a triangle whose other two angles measure 35° and 90°.

Lesson 45, Lesson Practice

a.
$$\begin{array}{r} \mathbf{8.6} \\ 06.\overline{)51.6} \\ \underline{48} \\ 36 \\ \underline{36} \\ 0 \end{array}$$

b.
$$\begin{array}{r} \mathbf{1.6} \\ 009.\overline{)14.4} \\ \underline{9} \\ 54 \\ \underline{54} \\ 0 \end{array}$$

c.
$$\begin{array}{r} \mathbf{340.} \\ 007.\overline{)2380.} \\ \underline{21} \\ 28 \\ \underline{28} \\ 00 \\ \underline{0} \\ 0 \end{array}$$

d.
$$\begin{array}{r} \mathbf{300.} \\ 008.\overline{)2400.} \\ \underline{24} \\ 00 \\ \underline{0} \\ 00 \\ \underline{0} \\ 0 \end{array}$$

e.
$$\begin{array}{r} \mathbf{16}\text{ pens} \\ \$075.\overline{)\$1200.} \\ \underline{75} \\ 450 \\ \underline{450} \\ 0 \end{array}$$

f. **If we multiply $\frac{0.25}{0.5}$ by $\frac{10}{10}$, the result is $\frac{2.5}{5}$. Since $\frac{10}{10}$ equals 1, we have not changed the value by multiplying—we have only changed the form.**

Lesson 45, Mixed Practice

1. $\frac{\text{raisins}}{\text{nuts}} = \mathbf{\frac{3}{5}}$

2. $\$1 + \$0.40(8)$
$= \$1 + \$3.20 = \mathbf{\$4.20}$

3.
$$\begin{array}{r} 54.05 \\ -\ 50.04 \\ \hline 4.01 \end{array}$$
Four and one-hundredth

4. (a)
$$\begin{array}{r} 22 \text{ votes} \\ -\ 18 \text{ votes} \\ \hline \mathbf{4 \text{ votes}} \end{array}$$

(b) $\frac{\text{Carlos's votes}}{\text{total votes}} = \frac{14}{70} = \mathbf{\frac{1}{5}}$

5.

Riders on
the Giant Gyro

$\frac{4}{7}$ were euphoric.
- $\frac{1}{7}$ of riders
- $\frac{1}{7}$ of riders
- $\frac{1}{7}$ of riders
- $\frac{1}{7}$ of riders

$\frac{3}{7}$ were vertiginous.
- $\frac{1}{7}$ of riders
- $\frac{1}{7}$ of riders
- $\frac{1}{7}$ of riders

(a) $\mathbf{\frac{3}{7}}$

(b) $\frac{\text{euphoric riders}}{\text{vertiginous riders}} = \mathbf{\frac{4}{3}}$

6. $10 = 2 \cdot 5$
$16 = 2 \cdot 2 \cdot 2 \cdot 2$
$\text{LCM}(10, 16) = 2 \cdot 2 \cdot 2 \cdot 2 \cdot 5 = \mathbf{80}$

7. $5^2 \times 10^2 = 5 \cdot 5 \cdot 10 \cdot 10$
$= 25 \cdot 100 = \mathbf{2500}$

8. (a) $56 \text{ cm} - 20 \text{ cm} = 36 \text{ cm}$
$\frac{36 \text{ cm}}{2} = \mathbf{18 \text{ cm}}$

(b) $\text{Area} = (10 \text{ cm})(18 \text{ cm})$
$= \mathbf{180 \text{ cm}^2}$

9. (a) $\mathbf{62\frac{1}{2}}$

(b) **0.09**

(c) $7.5\% = \frac{7.5}{100} = \mathbf{0.075}$

10. (a) 23.54545④5 . . . ⟶ **23.54545**

(b) 0.91666⑥ . . . ⟶ **0.91667**

11. $2 \text{ kilograms} = 2(1000 \text{ grams})$
$= \mathbf{2000 \text{ grams}}$

12.
$$\begin{array}{r} 0.065 \\ \times\ \$5.00 \\ \hline \$0.32500 \end{array} \longrightarrow \mathbf{\$0.33}$$

13.
$$\begin{array}{r} 0.566\ldots \\ 9\overline{)5.100\ldots} \\ \underline{4\,5} \\ 60 \\ \underline{54} \\ 60 \\ \underline{54} \\ 6 \end{array}$$

(a) 0.566⑥ . . . ⟶ **0.567**

(b) $\mathbf{0.5\overline{6}}$

14. $\frac{\text{aces}}{\text{total cards}} = \frac{4}{52} = \mathbf{\frac{1}{13}}$

15.

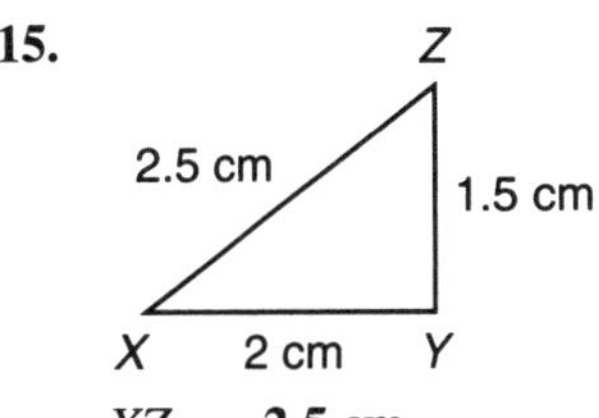

$XZ = \mathbf{2.5 \text{ cm}}$

16. (a) $\text{Perimeter} = 2.5 \text{ cm} + 1.5 \text{ cm} + 2 \text{ cm}$
$= \mathbf{6 \text{ cm}}$

(b) $\text{Area} = \frac{(1.5 \text{ cm})(2 \text{ cm})}{2}$
$= \mathbf{1.5 \text{ cm}^2}$

17. $\dfrac{3}{w} = \dfrac{25}{100}$
$25w = 3 \cdot 100$
$w = \dfrac{300}{25}$
$w = \mathbf{12}$

18. $\dfrac{1.2}{4.4} = \dfrac{3}{a}$
$1.2a = 3 \cdot 4.4$
$a = \dfrac{13.2}{1.2}$
$a = \mathbf{11}$

19.
```
  0 1
  1.2 1 0
− 0. 2 3
  0. 9 7
```
$m = \mathbf{0.97}$

20.
```
  1 1
  0.65
+ 1.97
  2.62
```
$r = \mathbf{2.62}$

21.
```
    0.15
  × 0.15
      75
     15
  0.0225
```
0.0225

22.
```
   1.2
 × 2.5
   6 0
  2 4
  3.00 = 3
```
$3 \times 4 = \mathbf{12}$

23.
```
   2.828
5)14.140
  10
   4 1
   4 0
     14
     10
      40
      40
       0
```
2.828

24.
```
      0.8
0.12)0.09.6
        96
         0
```
0.8

25. $\dfrac{5}{8} = \dfrac{15}{24}$
$\dfrac{5}{6} = \dfrac{20}{24}$
$+\ \dfrac{5}{12} = \dfrac{10}{24}$
$\dfrac{45}{24} = 1\dfrac{21}{24} = \mathbf{1\dfrac{7}{8}}$

26. $2\dfrac{1}{3} = 2\dfrac{4}{12}$
$-\ 1\dfrac{1}{4} = 1\dfrac{3}{12}$
$1\dfrac{1}{12}$

$4\dfrac{1}{2} = 4\dfrac{6}{12}$
$-\ 1\dfrac{1}{12} = 1\dfrac{1}{12}$
$\mathbf{3\dfrac{5}{12}}$

27. $\dfrac{7}{15} \cdot 10 \cdot 2\dfrac{1}{7} = \dfrac{\cancel{7}^{1}}{\cancel{15}_{1}} \cdot \dfrac{10}{1} \cdot \dfrac{\cancel{15}^{1}}{\cancel{7}_{1}} = \mathbf{10}$

28. $6\dfrac{3}{5} \div 1\dfrac{1}{10} = \dfrac{33}{5} \div \dfrac{11}{10}$
$= \dfrac{\cancel{33}^{3}}{\cancel{5}_{1}} \times \dfrac{\cancel{10}^{2}}{\cancel{11}_{1}} = \mathbf{6}$

29.
```
          33 1/3
$0.21)$7.00
        63
         70
         63
          7
```
33 pencils

30. (a) **Answers will vary. See student work.**
(b) **The sum of the angle measures of a triangle is 180°.**

Lesson 46, Lesson Practice

a. $\frac{\$1.12}{28 \text{ ounces}} = \frac{\$0.04}{1 \text{ ounce}}$

4¢ per ounce

b. $\frac{\$0.55}{11 \text{ ounces}} = \frac{\$0.05}{1 \text{ ounce}}$

5¢ per ounce

c. $\frac{\$1.98}{18 \text{ ounces}} = \frac{\$0.11}{1 \text{ ounce}}$

$\frac{\$2.28}{24 \text{ ounces}} = \frac{\$0.095}{1 \text{ ounce}}$

The 24-ounce jar is the better buy because 9.5¢ per ounce is less than 11¢ per ounce.

d. $\frac{416 \text{ mi}}{8 \text{ hr}} = 52 \frac{\text{mi}}{\text{hr}}$

52 mi/hr or **52 mph**

e. $\frac{322 \text{ mi}}{14 \text{ gal}} = 23 \frac{\text{mi}}{\text{gal}}$

23 mi/gal or **23 mpg**

f. (a) $\frac{44 \text{ euros}}{40 \text{ dollars}} = \frac{11 \text{ euros}}{10 \text{ dollars}}$

11 euros per 10 dollars

(b) $\frac{40 \text{ dollars}}{44 \text{ euros}} = \frac{10 \text{ dollars}}{11 \text{ euros}}$

10 dollars per 11 euros

g.
$$\begin{array}{r} \$36.89 \\ \times \quad .07 \\ \hline \$2.5823 \end{array} \longrightarrow \mathbf{\$2.58}$$

h.
$$\begin{array}{r} \$36.89 \\ + \ \$2.58 \\ \hline \mathbf{\$39.47} \end{array}$$

i.
$$\begin{array}{r} \$6.95 \\ \$0.95 \\ + \ \$2.45 \\ \hline \$10.35 \end{array}$$

$$\begin{array}{r} \$10.35 \\ \times \quad .06 \\ \hline \$0.6210 \end{array} \longrightarrow \$0.62$$

$$\begin{array}{r} \$10.35 \\ + \ \$0.62 \\ \hline \mathbf{\$10.97} \end{array}$$

j.
$$\begin{array}{r} \$15 \\ \times \ 0.15 \\ \hline 75 \\ 15 \\ \hline \$2.25 \end{array}$$

About $2.25

k.
$$\begin{array}{r} 0.15 \\ \times \ 12 \\ \hline 30 \\ 15 \\ \hline \mathbf{\$1.80} \end{array}$$

l. **One way is to think of 10% of the bill and then double that number.**

Lesson 46, Mixed Practice

1. $\frac{\$2.40}{16 \text{ ounces}} = \frac{\$0.15}{1 \text{ ounce}}$

$\frac{\$1.92}{12 \text{ ounces}} = \frac{\$0.16}{1 \text{ ounce}}$

Brand X = $0.15/ounce
Brand Y = $0.16/ounce
Brand X is the better buy.

2. $\frac{702 \text{ kilometers}}{6 \text{ hours}} = 117 \frac{\text{kilometers}}{\text{hour}}$

117 kilometers per hour

3. $\frac{\text{sheep}}{\text{cows}} = \frac{48}{36} = \mathbf{\frac{4}{3}}$

4.

$$\begin{array}{r} \$2.86 \\ \$2.83 \\ \$2.98 \\ +\ \$3.09 \\ \hline \$11.76 \end{array} \qquad \begin{array}{r} \mathbf{\$2.94} \\ 4\overline{)\$11.76} \\ \underline{8} \\ 3\,7 \\ \underline{3\,6} \\ 16 \\ \underline{16} \\ 0 \end{array}$$

5.

$$\begin{array}{r} 3.\ \overset{1}{\cancel{2}}{}^{1}0 \\ -\ 2.\ 0\ 3 \\ \hline 1.\ 1\ 7 \end{array}$$

One and seventeen hundredths

6.

$$2 \text{ feet} = 24 \text{ inches}$$

$$24 \text{ inches} \div 1\frac{1}{2} = \frac{24 \text{ inches}}{1} \div \frac{3}{2}$$

$$= \frac{\overset{8}{\cancel{24}}}{1} \times \frac{2}{\underset{1}{\cancel{3}}}$$

$$= \mathbf{16\ books}$$

7.

48 roses	
$\frac{3}{8}$ were red.	6 roses
	6 roses
	6 roses
$\frac{5}{8}$ were not red.	6 roses
	6 roses
	6 roses
	6 roses
	6 roses

(a) $3(6 \text{ roses}) = \mathbf{18\ roses}$

(b) $5(6 \text{ roses}) = \mathbf{30\ roses}$

(c) $\dfrac{\text{not red roses}}{\text{total roses}} = \dfrac{30}{48} = \mathbf{\dfrac{5}{8}}$

8. (a) $3.0303 < 3.303$

(b) $0.6 = 0.600$

9. $100 \text{ yards} = 100(3 \text{ feet})$
$= \mathbf{300\ feet}$

10. (a) $0.080 = \dfrac{8}{100} = \mathbf{\dfrac{2}{25}}$

(b) $37\frac{1}{2}\% = 37.5\%$

$$= \frac{37.5}{100} = \mathbf{0.375}$$

(c)

$$\begin{array}{r} 0.0909\ldots \\ 11\overline{)1.0000\ldots} \\ \underline{99} \\ 10 \\ \underline{0} \\ 100 \\ \underline{99} \\ 1 \end{array}$$

$\mathbf{0.\overline{09}}$

11. (a)

$$\begin{array}{r} \$14.95 \\ \times\ \ 0.07 \\ \hline \$1.0465 \end{array} \longrightarrow \mathbf{\$1.05}$$

(b)

$$\begin{array}{r} \$14.95 \\ +\ \ \$1.05 \\ \hline \mathbf{\$16.00} \end{array}$$

12.

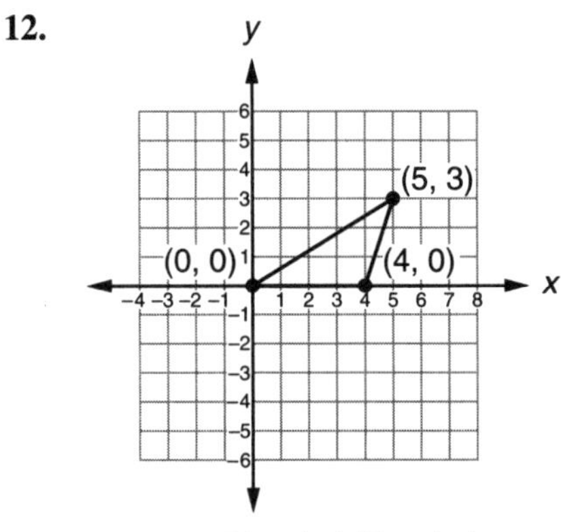

$$\text{Area} = \frac{(4 \text{ units})(3 \text{ units})}{2}$$

$$= \mathbf{6\ units^2}$$

13. $\dfrac{\text{face cards}}{\text{total cards}} = \dfrac{12}{52} = \mathbf{\dfrac{3}{13}}$

14.

$$\begin{array}{r} 2 \\ 3 \\ 5 \\ 7 \\ +\ 11 \\ \hline 28 \end{array} \qquad \begin{array}{r} \mathbf{5.6} \\ 5\overline{)28.0} \\ \underline{25} \\ 3\,0 \\ \underline{3\,0} \\ 0 \end{array}$$

15. $\mathbf{0.3(0.4 + 0.5) = 0.3(0.9) = 0.27}$
or
$\mathbf{0.3(0.4 + 0.5) = 0.12 + 0.15 = 0.27}$

16. (a) Perimeter = 3 in. + 5 in. + 4 in. + 3 in. + 11 in. + 3 in. + 4 in. + 5 in. = **38 in.**

(b)

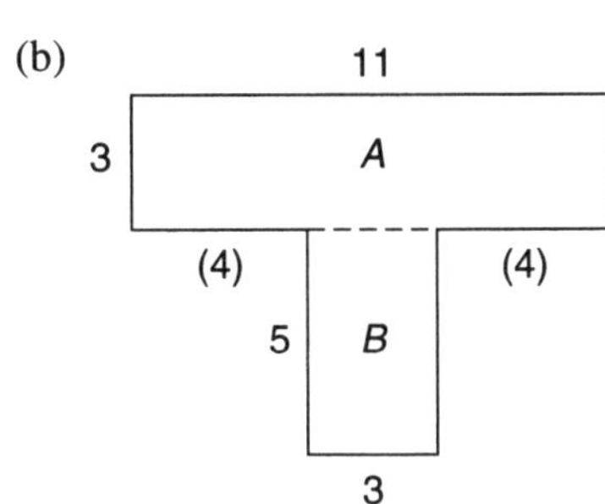

$$\begin{aligned} \text{Area } A &= (11 \text{ in.})(3 \text{ in.}) = 33 \text{ in.}^2 \\ + \text{ Area } B &= (5 \text{ in.})(3 \text{ in.}) = 15 \text{ in.}^2 \\ \hline \text{Area of figure} &= \mathbf{48 \text{ in.}^2} \end{aligned}$$

17. (a) **180°**

(b) $\frac{360°}{3} = \mathbf{120°}$

(c) $\frac{360°}{6} = \mathbf{60°}$

18.
$$\frac{10}{12} = \frac{2.5}{a}$$
$$10a = 2.5 \cdot 12$$
$$a = \frac{30}{10}$$
$$a = \mathbf{3}$$

19.
$$\frac{6}{8} = \frac{b}{100}$$
$$8b = 100 \cdot 6$$
$$b = \frac{600}{8}$$
$$b = \mathbf{75}$$

20.
$$\begin{array}{r} 4.7 \\ -\ 1.2 \\ \hline 3.5 \end{array}$$
$w = \mathbf{3.5}$

21. $\frac{10^2}{10} = \frac{100}{10} = 10$
$x = \mathbf{10}$

22.
$$1\frac{11}{18} + 2\frac{11}{24}$$
$$\downarrow \qquad \downarrow$$
$$2 + 2 = \mathbf{4}$$

$$\begin{array}{rcl} 1\frac{11}{18} &=& 1\frac{44}{72} \\ +\ 2\frac{11}{24} &=& 2\frac{33}{72} \\ \hline && 3\frac{77}{72} = \mathbf{4\frac{5}{72}} \end{array}$$

23.
$$5\frac{5}{6} - \left(3 - 1\frac{1}{3}\right)$$
$$\downarrow \qquad \downarrow \quad \downarrow$$
$$6 - (3 - 1) = 6 - 2 = \mathbf{4}$$

$$\begin{array}{rcl} 3 &=& 2\frac{3}{3} \\ -\ 1\frac{1}{3} &=& 1\frac{1}{3} \\ \hline && 1\frac{2}{3} \end{array}$$

$$\begin{array}{rcl} 5\frac{5}{6} &=& 5\frac{5}{6} \\ -\ 1\frac{2}{3} &=& 1\frac{4}{6} \\ \hline &=& \mathbf{4\frac{1}{6}} \end{array}$$

24. $\frac{2}{3} \times 4 \times 1\frac{1}{8} = \frac{\cancel{2}^{1}}{\cancel{3}_{1}} \times \frac{\cancel{4}^{1}}{1} \times \frac{\cancel{9}^{3}}{\cancel{8}_{\cancel{2}_{1}}} = \mathbf{3}$

25. $6\frac{2}{3} \div 4 = \frac{20}{3} \div \frac{4}{1} = \frac{\cancel{20}^{5}}{3} \times \frac{1}{\cancel{4}_{1}}$
$= \frac{5}{3} = \mathbf{1\frac{2}{3}}$

26.
$$\begin{array}{r} \overset{4}{\cancel{5}}.\overset{1}{\cancel{2}}{}^{1}0 \\ -\ 0.\ 5\ 7 \\ \hline 4.\ 6\ 3 \end{array} \qquad \begin{array}{r} \overset{1}{3}.45 \\ 6 \\ +\ 4.63 \\ \hline \mathbf{14.08} \end{array}$$

27.
$$\begin{array}{r} 150. \\ 0016.\overline{)2400.} \\ \underline{16} \\ 80 \\ \underline{80} \\ 00 \\ \underline{0} \\ 0 \end{array}$$

28. **Round $6\frac{7}{8}$ to 7 and round $5\frac{1}{16}$ to 5. Then multiply 7 by 5.**

29. (a) $\angle CAB$

(b) $\overline{BA}$

30. (a) $m\angle B = m\angle ADC = \mathbf{60°}$

(b) $m\angle CAB = 180° - (60° + 45°)$
$= 180° - 105° = \mathbf{75°}$

(c) $m\angle CAD = m\angle ACB = \mathbf{45°}$

Lesson 47, Lesson Practice

a. $400 + 50 + 6$
$\mathbf{(4 \times 10^2) + (5 \times 10^1) + (6 \times 10^0)}$

b. $1000 + 700 + 60$
$\mathbf{(1 \times 10^3) + (7 \times 10^2) + (6 \times 10^1)}$

c. $100{,}000 + 80{,}000 + 6000$
$\mathbf{(1 \times 10^5) + (8 \times 10^4) + (6 \times 10^3)}$

d. 24.25×10^3
$= 24.25 \times 1000$
$= \mathbf{24{,}250}$

e. $25 \times 10^6 = 25 \times 1{,}000{,}000$
$= \mathbf{25{,}000{,}000}$

f. $12.5 \div 10^3$
$= 12.5 \div 1000$
$= \mathbf{0.0125}$

g. $4.8 \div 10^4 = 4.8 \div 10{,}000$
$= \mathbf{0.00048}$

h. $10^3 \cdot 10^4 = 10^7$

i. $10^8 \div 10^2 = 10^6$

j. **2,500,000**

k. **15,000,000,000**

l. **1,600,000,000,000**

Lesson 47, Mixed Practice

1. (a) **True**

(b) **True**

2. $\dfrac{\text{walk}}{\text{ride in bus}} = \dfrac{10}{12} = \mathbf{\dfrac{5}{6}}$

3. $\dfrac{\text{ride in bus}}{\text{total}} = \dfrac{12}{33} = \mathbf{\dfrac{4}{11}}$

4.
$$\begin{array}{r} ^{1}1.2 \\ 1.4 \\ 1.5 \\ 1.7 \\ \underline{+\ 2} \\ 7.8 \end{array} \qquad \begin{array}{r} \mathbf{1.56} \\ 5\overline{)7.80} \\ \underline{5} \\ 2\,8 \\ \underline{2\,5} \\ 30 \\ \underline{30} \\ 0 \end{array}$$

5. (a) **134,800,000 viewers**

(b) $5000 + 200 + 80$
$\mathbf{(5 \times 10^3) + (2 \times 10^2) + (8 \times 10^1)}$

6.

	40 students
$\frac{1}{8}$ answered correctly.	5 students
$\frac{7}{8}$ did not answer correctly.	5 students
	5 students
	5 students
	5 students
	5 students
	5 students
	5 students

(a) **5 students**

(b) 7(5 students) = **35 students**

7. (a)
$$\begin{array}{r} 10\frac{2}{3} \\ 12\overline{)128} \\ \underline{12} \\ 08 \\ \underline{0} \\ 8 \end{array}$$
10 glasses

(b) **11 glasses**

8. (a) **Answers may vary.**

(b) **Answers may vary.**

9. (a) $0.375 = \frac{375}{1000} = \mathbf{\frac{3}{8}}$

(b) $62\frac{1}{2}\% = 62.5\% = \frac{62.5}{100} = \mathbf{0.625}$

10.
$$\begin{array}{r} \$56.40 \\ \times \quad 0.08 \\ \hline \$4.5120 \end{array} \longrightarrow \mathbf{\$4.51}$$

11. (a) 53,714.54$\underline{5}$④ . . .
⟶ **53,714.545**

(b) 5$\underline{3}$,⑦14.5454 . . .
⟶ **54,000**

12. (a) $10^5 \cdot 10^2 = 10^7$

(b) $10^8 \div 10^4 = 10^4$

13. **3.03**

14. BC = 6 cm, AF = 6 cm
AB = 6 cm, FE = 9 cm
ED = 12 cm
Perimeter = 6 cm + 6 cm + 6 cm
+ 3 cm + 12 cm + 9 cm
= **42 cm**

15.

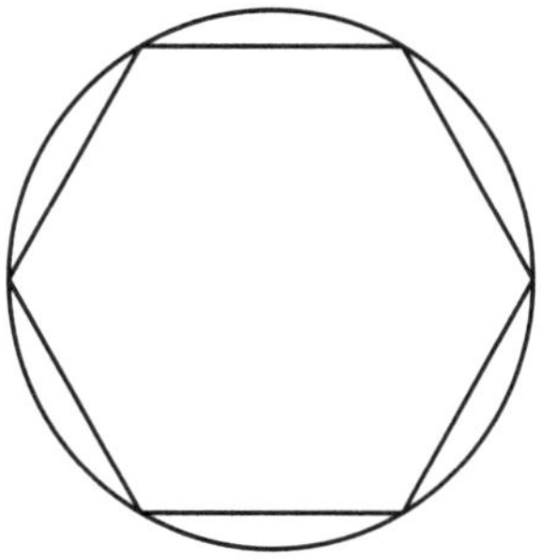

(a) Diameter = 2(1 inch) = **2 inches**

(b) Perimeter = 6(1 inch) = **6 inches**

16.
$$\begin{aligned} \frac{6}{10} &= \frac{w}{100} \\ 10w &= 6 \cdot 100 \\ w &= \frac{600}{10} \\ w &= \mathbf{60} \end{aligned}$$

17.
$$\begin{aligned} \frac{3.6}{x} &= \frac{16}{24} \\ 16x &= (3.6)(24) \\ x &= \frac{86.4}{16} \\ x &= \mathbf{5.4} \end{aligned}$$

18.
$$\begin{array}{r} 1.5 \\ \times \ 1.5 \\ \hline 7\,5 \\ 15 \\ \hline 2.25 \end{array}$$
$a = \mathbf{2.25}$

19.
$$\begin{array}{r} \overset{8}{\cancel{9}}.{}^{1}8 \\ -\ 8.9 \\ \hline 0.9 \end{array}$$
$x = \mathbf{0.9}$

20.
$$4\frac{1}{5} + 5\frac{1}{3} + \frac{1}{2}$$
↓ ↓ ↓
$4 + 5 + 1 = \mathbf{10}$
$$\begin{array}{rcr} 4\frac{1}{5} &=& 4\frac{6}{30} \\ 5\frac{1}{3} &=& 5\frac{10}{30} \\ +\ \frac{1}{2} &=& \frac{15}{30} \\ \hline && 9\frac{31}{30} \end{array} = \mathbf{10\frac{1}{30}}$$

21.
$$6\frac{1}{8} - \left(5 - 1\frac{2}{3}\right)$$
↓ ↓ ↓
$6 - (5 - 2) = 6 - 3 = \mathbf{3}$
$$\begin{array}{r} 5 \\ -\ 1\frac{2}{3} \\ \hline \end{array} \longrightarrow \begin{array}{r} 4\frac{3}{3} \\ -\ 1\frac{2}{3} \\ \hline 3\frac{1}{3} \end{array}$$
$$\begin{array}{rcr} 6\frac{1}{8} &=& 6\frac{3}{24} \\ -\ 3\frac{1}{3} &=& 3\frac{8}{24} \\ \hline \end{array} \longrightarrow \begin{array}{r} 5\frac{27}{24} \\ -\ 3\frac{8}{24} \\ \hline \mathbf{2\frac{19}{24}} \end{array}$$

22. $\sqrt{16 \cdot 25} = \sqrt{400} = \mathbf{20}$

23. 3.6×10^3
$= 3.6 \times 1000$
$= \mathbf{3600}$

24. $8\frac{1}{3} \times 3\frac{3}{5} \times \frac{1}{3}$

$= \frac{\overset{5}{\cancel{25}}}{\underset{1}{\cancel{3}}} \times \frac{\overset{2}{\cancel{\overset{\cancel{6}}{18}}}}{\underset{1}{\cancel{5}}} \times \frac{1}{\underset{1}{\cancel{3}}}$

$= \mathbf{10}$

25. $3\frac{1}{8} \div 6\frac{1}{4} = \frac{25}{8} \div \frac{25}{4}$

$= \frac{\overset{1}{\cancel{25}}}{\underset{2}{\cancel{8}}} \times \frac{\overset{1}{\cancel{4}}}{\underset{1}{\cancel{25}}} = \mathbf{\frac{1}{2}}$

26.
```
   21
   26.7
    3.45
    0.036
   12
 +  8.7
   50.886
```
50.886

27. (a) Perimeter $= 15 \text{ in.} + 13 \text{ in.} + 14 \text{ in.}$
$= \mathbf{42 \text{ in.}}$

(b) Area $= \frac{(14 \text{ in.})(12 \text{ in.})}{2}$
$= \mathbf{84 \text{ in.}^2}$

28. $125 \div 10^2 = 125 \div 100 = 1.25$
$0.125 \times 10^2 = 0.125 \times 100 = 12.5$
$\mathbf{1.25 < 12.5}$

29. $\frac{2}{3} = \frac{8}{12}$
$\frac{1}{2} = \frac{6}{12}$ $\quad \mathbf{\frac{1}{2}, \frac{7}{12}, \frac{2}{3}, \frac{5}{6}}$
$\frac{5}{6} = \frac{10}{12}$

30. (a) $\angle a = 180° - 130° = \mathbf{50°}$

(b) $\angle b = 180° - (65° + 50°)$
$= 180° - 115° = \mathbf{65°}$

(c) **Together, ∠b and ∠c form a straight angle that measures 180°. To find the measure of ∠c, we subtract the measure of ∠b from 180°.**

Lesson 48, Lesson Practice

a. $3\overline{)2.00\ldots}$ quotient $0.66\ldots$; 18, 20, 18, 2 $\quad \mathbf{0.\overline{6}}$

b. $\frac{2}{3} \times 100\% = \frac{200\%}{3} = \mathbf{66\frac{2}{3}\%}$

c. $1.1 = \mathbf{1\frac{1}{10}}$

d. $1.1 \times 100\% = \mathbf{110\%}$

e. $4\% = \frac{4}{100} = \mathbf{\frac{1}{25}}$

f. $4\% = \frac{4}{100} = \mathbf{0.04}$

Lesson 48, Mixed Practice

1. $\frac{80 \text{ kilometers}}{2.5 \text{ hours}} = \mathbf{32 \frac{kilometers}{hour}}$

2. $\frac{1008}{1323} = \frac{2 \cdot 2 \cdot 2 \cdot 2 \cdot \overset{1}{\cancel{3}} \cdot \overset{1}{\cancel{3}} \cdot \overset{1}{\cancel{7}}}{\underset{1}{\cancel{3}} \cdot \underset{1}{\cancel{3}} \cdot 3 \cdot \underset{1}{\cancel{7}} \cdot 7}$
$= \mathbf{\frac{16}{21}}$

3.
```
   1867
 - 1803
   64 years
```
64 years

4. (a) $\frac{\text{blue marbles}}{\text{total marbles}} = \mathbf{\frac{7}{12}}$

(b) $\frac{\text{red marbles}}{\text{blue marbles}} = \mathbf{\frac{5}{7}}$

5. $\frac{\$0.90}{6 \text{ ounces}} = \frac{\$0.15}{1 \text{ ounce}}$

$\frac{\$1.26}{9 \text{ ounces}} = \frac{\$0.14}{1 \text{ ounce}}$

6-ounce can is \$0.15 per ounce; 9-ounce can is \$0.14 per ounce; 9-ounce can is the better buy.

6. $2550 + 2900 = 5450$

$5450 \div 2 = \mathbf{2725}$

$$\begin{array}{r} 4 \\ \hline 14 \\ 14 \\ \hline 5 \\ 4 \\ \hline 10 \\ 10 \\ \hline 0 \end{array}$$

7.

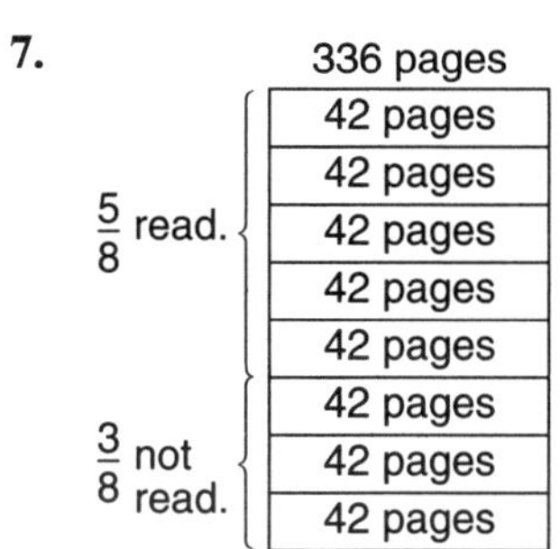

(a) $5(42 \text{ pages}) = \mathbf{210 \text{ pages}}$

(b) $3(42 \text{ pages}) = \mathbf{126 \text{ pages}}$

8. (a) $1.0 \div 2 = \mathbf{0.5}$

(b) $\frac{1}{2} \times 100\% = \frac{100\%}{2} = \mathbf{50\%}$

(c) $0.1 = \mathbf{\frac{1}{10}}$

(d) $0.1 \times 100\% = \mathbf{10\%}$

(e) $25\% = \frac{25}{100} = \mathbf{\frac{1}{4}}$

(f) $25\% = \frac{25}{100} = \mathbf{0.25}$

9. (a) $100\% - (10\% + 12\% + 20\% + 25\% + 20\%) = 100\% - 87\% = \mathbf{13\%}$

(b) $20\% = \frac{20}{100} = \mathbf{\frac{1}{5}}$

(c) $2(\$3200) = \mathbf{\$6400}$

10. $0.545④ \ldots \longrightarrow$ **0.545**

11. (a) **See student answers.**

(b) **5 centimeters**

12. (a) **The exponent is 3 and the base is 5.**

(b) $10^4 \cdot 10^4 = \mathbf{10^8}$

13. $1 \text{ foot} = 12 \text{ inches}$

$\frac{12 \text{ inches}}{6} = \mathbf{2 \text{ inches}}$

14.

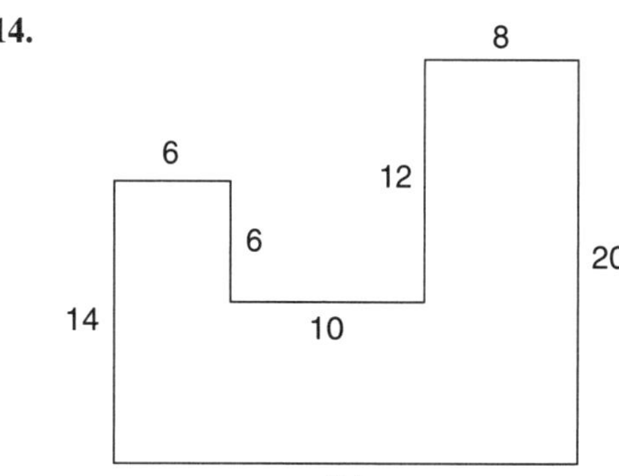

Perimeter $= 24 \text{ cm} + 14 \text{ cm} + 6 \text{ cm} + 6 \text{ cm} + 10 \text{ cm} + 12 \text{ cm} + 8 \text{ cm} + 20 \text{ cm} = \mathbf{100 \text{ cm}}$

15. $\frac{78 \text{ miles}}{1.2 \text{ gallons}} = 65 \frac{\text{miles}}{\text{gallon}}$

65 mpg

16. $\frac{6}{100} = \frac{15}{w}$

$6w = 100 \cdot 15$

$w = \frac{1500}{6}$

$w = \mathbf{250}$

17. $\frac{20}{x} = \frac{15}{12}$

$15x = 20 \cdot 12$

$x = \frac{240}{15}$

$x = \mathbf{16}$

18. $6\overline{)1.44}$ = 0.24
$$\begin{array}{r} 12 \\ \hline 24 \\ 24 \\ \hline 0 \end{array}$$
$m = \mathbf{0.24}$

19.
$$\begin{aligned} \frac{1}{2} &= \frac{3}{6} \\ -\frac{1}{3} &= \frac{2}{6} \\ \hline f &= \mathbf{\frac{1}{6}} \end{aligned}$$

20. $2^5 + 1^4 + 3^3$
$= 2 \cdot 2 \cdot 2 \cdot 2 \cdot 2 + 1 + 3 \cdot 3 \cdot 3$
$= 32 + 1 + 27 = \mathbf{60}$

21. $\sqrt{10^2 \cdot 6^2} = \sqrt{100 \cdot 36} = \sqrt{3600}$
$= \mathbf{60}$

22.
$$\begin{aligned} 1\frac{1}{4} &= 1\frac{3}{12} \\ +\ 1\frac{1}{6} &= 1\frac{2}{12} \\ \hline & \quad 2\frac{5}{12} \end{aligned}$$
$$\begin{aligned} 3\frac{5}{6} &= 3\frac{10}{12} \\ -\ 2\frac{5}{12} &= 2\frac{5}{12} \\ \hline & \quad \mathbf{1\frac{5}{12}} \end{aligned}$$

23.
$$\begin{array}{rcr} 4 & \longrightarrow & 3\frac{3}{3} \\ -\ \frac{2}{3} & & -\ \frac{2}{3} \\ \hline & & 3\frac{1}{3} \end{array}$$
$$\begin{aligned} 8\frac{3}{4} &= 8\frac{9}{12} \\ +\ 3\frac{1}{3} &= 3\frac{4}{12} \\ \hline & \quad 11\frac{13}{12} = \mathbf{12\frac{1}{12}} \end{aligned}$$

24. $\frac{15}{16} \cdot \frac{24}{25} \cdot 1\frac{1}{9}$

$= \frac{\cancel{15}}{\cancel{16}} \cdot \frac{\cancel{24}}{\cancel{25}} \cdot \frac{\cancel{10}}{\cancel{9}} = \mathbf{1}$

25. $2\frac{2}{3} \div 4 = \frac{8}{3} \div \frac{4}{1}$

$= \frac{\cancel{8}}{3} \times \frac{1}{\cancel{4}} = \frac{2}{3}$

$1\frac{1}{3} \div \frac{2}{3} = \frac{4}{3} \div \frac{2}{3} = \frac{\cancel{4}}{\cancel{3}} \times \frac{\cancel{3}}{\cancel{2}}$

$= \mathbf{2}$

26. $\frac{a}{b} = \frac{\$13.93}{0.07}$

$$\begin{array}{r} \mathbf{\$199.} \\ 007.\overline{)\$1393.} \\ 7 \\ \hline 69 \\ 63 \\ \hline 63 \\ 63 \\ \hline 0 \end{array}$$
$199.00

27.

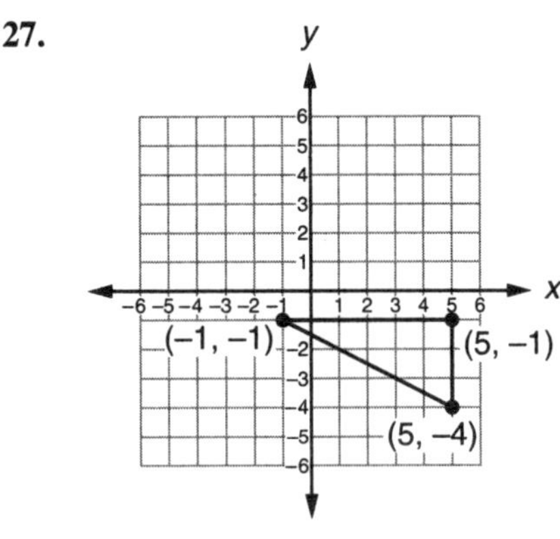

$\text{Area} = \frac{(6 \text{ units})(3 \text{ units})}{2} = \mathbf{9\ sq.\ units}$

28. $\frac{\text{students with more than one sibling}}{\text{total students}}$

$= \frac{8}{20} = \mathbf{\frac{2}{5}}$

29.
$$\begin{array}{r} \$50.00 \\ \times \quad .075 \\ \hline 25000 \\ 35000 \\ \hline \$3.75000 \end{array} \longrightarrow \$3.75$$

$$\begin{array}{r} \$50.00 \\ + \quad \$3.75 \\ \hline \mathbf{\$53.75} \end{array}$$

30. $m\angle a = 180° - (50° + 90°)$
$= 180° - 140° = \mathbf{40°}$
$m\angle b = \mathbf{50°}$
$m\angle c = 180° - 50° = \mathbf{130°}$

Lesson 49, Lesson Practice

a.
$$\begin{array}{r} 5 \\ 12\overline{)70} \\ 60 \\ \hline 10 \end{array}$$
5 feet 10 in.

b. 6 feet = 6(12 inches)
= 72 inches
72 inches + 3 inches
= **75 inches**

c. 20 in. = 1 ft 8 in.
$$\begin{array}{l} \quad 1 \text{ ft } 8 \text{ in.} \\ + \ 5 \text{ ft} \\ \hline \quad \mathbf{6 \text{ ft } 8 \text{ in.}} \end{array}$$

d.
$$\begin{array}{rrr} 2 \text{ yd} & 1 \text{ ft} & 8 \text{ in.} \\ + \ 1 \text{ yd} & 2 \text{ ft} & 9 \text{ in.} \\ \hline 3 \text{ yd} & 3 \text{ ft} & 17 \text{ in.} \end{array}$$

17 in. = 1 ft 5 in.
$$\begin{array}{l} \quad 1 \text{ ft } 5 \text{ in.} \\ + \ 3 \text{ ft} \\ \hline \quad 4 \text{ ft } 5 \text{ in.} \end{array} \longrightarrow 3 \text{ yd } 4 \text{ ft } 5 \text{ in.}$$

4 ft = 1 yd 1 ft
$$\begin{array}{l} \quad 1 \text{ yd} \quad 1 \text{ ft} \\ + \ 3 \text{ yd} \\ \hline \quad 4 \text{ yd} \quad 1 \text{ ft} \end{array} \longrightarrow \mathbf{4 \text{ yd } 1 \text{ ft } 5 \text{ in.}}$$

e.
$$\begin{array}{rrr} 5 \text{ hr} & 42 \text{ min} & 53 \text{ s} \\ + \ 6 \text{ hr} & 17 \text{ min} & 27 \text{ s} \\ \hline 11 \text{ hr} & 59 \text{ min} & 80 \text{ s} \end{array}$$

80 s = 1 min 20 s
$$\begin{array}{l} \quad 1 \text{ min} \quad 20 \text{ s} \\ + \ 59 \text{ min} \\ \hline \quad 60 \text{ min} \quad 20 \text{ s} \end{array} \longrightarrow 11 \text{ hr} \quad 60 \text{ min} \quad 20 \text{ s}$$

60 min = 1 hr
11 hr + 1 hr = 12 hr
12 hr 20 s

Lesson 49, Mixed Practice

1.
$$\begin{array}{r} 0.2 \\ + \ 0.05 \\ \hline 0.25 \end{array} \qquad \begin{array}{r} 0.05 \\ \times \ 0.2 \\ \hline 0.010 \end{array} \longrightarrow 0.01 \qquad \begin{array}{r} \mathbf{25} \\ 001.\overline{)025.} \\ 2 \\ \hline 05 \\ 5 \\ \hline 0 \end{array}$$

2.
$$\begin{array}{r} \mathbf{9.2 \text{ yards}} \\ 20\overline{)184.0} \\ 180 \\ \hline 4\,0 \\ 4\,0 \\ \hline 0 \end{array}$$

3.
$$\begin{array}{r} \$0.25 \\ 24\overline{)\$6.00} \\ 4\,8 \\ \hline 1\,20 \\ 1\,20 \\ \hline 0 \end{array}$$
25¢ per arrow

4. 3(8 sides) + 2(6 sides) + 5 sides
+ 2(4 sides)
= 24 sides + 12 sides + 5 sides + 8 sides
= **49 sides**

5.
$$\begin{array}{r} {}^{2\ 1} \\ 6.21 \\ 4.38 \\ 7.5 \\ 6.3 \\ 5.91 \\ + \ 8.04 \\ \hline 38.34 \end{array} \qquad \begin{array}{r} \mathbf{6.39} \\ 6\overline{)38.34} \\ 36 \\ \hline 2\,3 \\ 1\,8 \\ \hline 54 \\ 54 \\ \hline 0 \end{array}$$

6.

	72 billy goats
$\frac{2}{9}$ were gruff.	8 billy goats
	8 billy goats
$\frac{7}{9}$ were cordial.	8 billy goats
	8 billy goats
	8 billy goats
	8 billy goats
	8 billy goats
	8 billy goats
	8 billy goats

(a) 7(8 billy goats) = **56 billy goats**

(b) $\frac{\text{gruff billy goats}}{\text{cordial billy goats}} = \mathbf{\frac{2}{7}}$

7. $\mathbf{0.5, 0.\overline{54}, 0.\overline{5}}$

8. (a) **Answers may vary.**

(b) $\mathbf{2\frac{5}{8}}$ **inches**

9. (a) $0.9 \times 100\% = \mathbf{90\%}$

(b) $1\frac{3}{5} \times 100\%$

$= \frac{8}{5} \times 100\% = \frac{800\%}{5}$

$= \mathbf{160\%}$

(c) $\frac{5}{6} \times 100\% = \frac{500\%}{6}$

$\frac{250\%}{3} = \mathbf{83\frac{1}{3}\%}$

10. (a) $75\% = \frac{75}{100} = \mathbf{\frac{3}{4}}$

(b) $75\% = \frac{75}{100} = \mathbf{0.75}$

(c) $5\% = \frac{5}{100} = \mathbf{\frac{1}{20}}$

(d) $5\% = \frac{5}{100} = \mathbf{0.05}$

11.
$$\begin{array}{r} 62 \\ \times\ 60 \\ \hline \end{array}$$
3720 times

12. even primes: 2

$\frac{\text{even primes}}{\text{total}} = \mathbf{\frac{1}{6}}$

13. (a) Area $= (1\text{ in.})(1\text{ in.}) = \mathbf{1\ in.^2}$

(b) Area $= \left(\frac{1}{2}\text{ in.}\right)\left(\frac{1}{2}\text{ in.}\right) = \mathbf{\frac{1}{4}\ in.^2}$

(c) Area $= 1\text{ in.}^2 - \frac{1}{4}\text{ in.}^2$

$= \frac{4}{4}\text{ in.}^2 - \frac{1}{4}\text{ in.}^2 = \mathbf{\frac{3}{4}\ in.^2}$

14. Perimeter $= \frac{1}{2}\text{ in.} + 1\text{ in.} + 1\text{ in.}$

$+ \frac{1}{2}\text{ in.} + \frac{1}{2}\text{ in.} + \frac{1}{2}\text{ in.}$

$= 2\text{ in.} + \frac{4}{2}\text{ in.} = 2\text{ in.} + 2\text{ in.}$

$= \mathbf{4\ in.}$

15. (a) **8 cm**

(b) **6 cm**

(c) **4.8 cm**

16.
$$\frac{y}{100} = \frac{18}{45}$$
$$45y = 100 \cdot 18$$
$$y = \frac{1800}{45}$$
$$y = \mathbf{40}$$

17.
$$\frac{35}{40} = \frac{1.4}{m}$$
$$35m = (1.4)(40)$$
$$m = \frac{56}{35}$$
$$m = 1\frac{21}{35} = 1\frac{3}{5} = \mathbf{1.6}$$

18.
$$\begin{array}{rcl} \frac{1}{2} & = & \frac{3}{6} \\ -\ \frac{1}{6} & = & \frac{1}{6} \\ \hline & & \frac{2}{6} = \frac{1}{3} \end{array}$$
$$n = \mathbf{\frac{1}{3}}$$

19.
$$\begin{array}{r} 0.29 \\ 9\overline{)2.61} \\ 1\,8 \\ \hline 81 \\ 81 \\ \hline 0 \end{array}$$
$$d = \mathbf{0.29}$$

20. $\sqrt{100} + 4^3 = 10 + 4 \cdot 4 \cdot 4$
$= 10 + 64 = \mathbf{74}$

21. $3.14 \times 10^4 = 3.14 \times 10{,}000 = \mathbf{31{,}400}$

22.
$$4\frac{1}{6} = 4\frac{1}{6} \longrightarrow 3\frac{7}{6}$$
$$-\ 2\frac{1}{2} = 2\frac{3}{6} \qquad -\ 2\frac{3}{6}$$
$$1\frac{4}{6} = 1\frac{2}{3}$$

$$3\frac{3}{4} = 3\frac{9}{12}$$
$$+\ 1\frac{2}{3} = 1\frac{8}{12}$$
$$4\frac{17}{12} = \mathbf{5\frac{5}{12}}$$

23. $3\frac{3}{4} \div 1\frac{1}{2} = \frac{15}{4} \div \frac{3}{2} = \frac{\cancel{15}^{5}}{\cancel{4}_{2}} \times \frac{\cancel{2}^{1}}{\cancel{3}_{1}} = \frac{5}{2}$

$6\frac{2}{3} \cdot \frac{5}{2} = \frac{\cancel{20}^{10}}{3} \cdot \frac{5}{\cancel{2}_{1}} = \frac{50}{3} = \mathbf{16\frac{2}{3}}$

24.
3 days 8 hr 15 min
+ 2 days 15 hr 45 min
5 days 23 hr 60 min
60 min = 1 hr; 23 hr + 1 hr = 24 hr
24 hr = 1 day
5 days + 1 day = **6 days**

25.
1 yd 2 ft 6 in.
+ 2 yd 1 ft 9 in.
3 yd 3 ft 15 in.

15 in. = 1 ft 3 in.

1 ft 3 in.
+ 3 ft
4 ft 3 in. ⟶ 3 yd 4 ft 3 in.

4 ft = 1 yd 1 ft
1 yd 1 ft
+ 3 yd
4 yd 1 ft ⟶ **4 yd 1 ft 3 in.**

26.
$$\begin{array}{r} \mathbf{\$300.} \\ 006.\overline{)\$1800.} \\ 18 \\ \hline 00 \\ 0 \\ \hline 00 \\ 0 \\ \hline 0 \end{array}$$
$300.00

27. **Round 35.675 to 36. Round $2\frac{7}{8}$ to 3. Then divide 36 by 3.**

28.
$$\begin{array}{r} \$18.50 \\ +\ \$3.50 \\ \hline \$22.00 \end{array}$$
$$\begin{array}{r} \$22.00 \\ \times\ 0.06 \\ \hline \$1.3200 \end{array} \longrightarrow \$1.32$$
$$\begin{array}{r} \$22.00 \\ \$1.32 \\ \hline \mathbf{\$23.32} \end{array}$$

29. $LWH = (0.5)(0.2)(0.1)$
$$\begin{array}{r} 0.5 \\ \times\ 0.2 \\ \hline 0.10 \end{array} \longrightarrow 0.1 \qquad \begin{array}{r} 0.1 \\ \times\ 0.1 \\ \hline \mathbf{0.01} \end{array}$$

30. $m\angle a = \mathbf{32°}$
$m\angle b = 180° - (90° + 32°)$
$= 180° - 122° = \mathbf{58°}$
$m\angle c = 180° - 58° = \mathbf{122°}$

Lesson 50, Lesson Practice

a. $\mathbf{\frac{1\text{ yd}}{36\text{ in.}}}$ and $\mathbf{\frac{36\text{ in.}}{1\text{ yd}}}$

b. $\mathbf{\frac{100\text{ cm}}{1\text{ m}}}$ and $\mathbf{\frac{1\text{ m}}{100\text{ cm}}}$

c. $\mathbf{\frac{16\text{ oz}}{1\text{ lb}}}$ and $\mathbf{\frac{1\text{ lb}}{16\text{ oz}}}$

d. $10\ \cancel{\text{yards}} \cdot \frac{36\text{ inches}}{1\ \cancel{\text{yard}}}$
$= \mathbf{360\ inches}$

e. $24\ \cancel{\text{ft}} \cdot \frac{1\text{ yd}}{3\ \cancel{\text{ft}}}$
$= \mathbf{8\ yd}$

f. $24\ \cancel{\text{shillings}} \cdot \frac{12\text{ pence}}{1\ \cancel{\text{shilling}}}$
$= \mathbf{288\ pence}$

Lesson 50, Mixed Practice

1. $$\begin{array}{r} 3.5 \\ \times\ 0.4 \\ \hline 1.40 \end{array} \longrightarrow 1.4 \qquad \begin{array}{r} 3.5 \\ +\ 0.4 \\ \hline 3.9 \end{array}$$

$$\begin{array}{r} 3.9 \\ -\ 1.4 \\ \hline \mathbf{2.5} \end{array}$$

2. (a) $\dfrac{\text{parts with 1}}{\text{total parts}} = \dfrac{4}{10} = \mathbf{\dfrac{2}{5}}$

(b) $\dfrac{3}{5} \times 100\% = \dfrac{300\%}{5} = \mathbf{60\%}$

(c) $\dfrac{\text{numbers greater than 2}}{\text{total}} = \mathbf{\dfrac{3}{10}}$

3. $\dfrac{\$1.17}{\text{13 ounces}} = \dfrac{\$0.09}{\text{1 ounce}}$

$\dfrac{\$1.44}{\text{18 ounces}} = \dfrac{\$0.08}{\text{1 ounce}}$

13-ounce box = 9¢ per ounce
18-ounce box = 8¢ per ounce
18-ounce box is the better buy.

4. $\dfrac{\text{20 miles}}{\text{2.5 hours}} = \mathbf{8\ \dfrac{miles}{hour}}$

5. $\$2 + \$0.50(5)$
$= \$2 + \$2.50 = \mathbf{\$4.50}$

6. $60\overline{)420}$ with quotient **7 hours**

7.

30 football players

$\frac{2}{5}$ were endomorphic.	6 players
	6 players
$\frac{3}{5}$ were not endomorphic.	6 players
	6 players
	6 players

(a) 2(6 football players)
= **12 football players**

(b) $\dfrac{3}{5} \times 100\% = \dfrac{300\%}{5} = \mathbf{60\%}$

8. **B. 40%**

9. $$\begin{array}{r} 0.8333\ldots \\ 6\overline{)5.0000\ldots} \\ \underline{4\,8} \\ 20 \\ \underline{18} \\ 20 \\ \underline{18} \\ 20 \\ \underline{18} \\ 2 \end{array}$$ **3.8333**

10. 7,500,000
$= 7{,}000{,}000 + 500{,}000$
$= \mathbf{(7 \times 10^6) + (5 \times 10^5)}$

11. (a) $0.6 \times 100\% = \mathbf{60\%}$

(b) $\dfrac{1}{6} \times 100\% = \dfrac{100\%}{6}$
$= \mathbf{16\dfrac{2}{3}\%}$

(c) $1\dfrac{1}{2} \times 100\% = \dfrac{3}{2} \times 100\%$
$= \dfrac{300\%}{2} = \mathbf{150\%}$

12. (a) $30\% = \dfrac{30}{100} = \mathbf{\dfrac{3}{10}}$

(b) $$\begin{array}{r} 0.3 \\ 10\overline{)3.0} \\ \underline{3\,0} \\ 0 \end{array}$$ **0.3**

(c) $250\% = \dfrac{250}{100} = \dfrac{25}{10} = \dfrac{5}{2} = \mathbf{2\dfrac{1}{2}}$

(d) $250\% = 2\dfrac{1}{2} = \mathbf{2.5}$

13. **97**

14. (a) Area $= (8\text{ cm})(12\text{ cm})$
$= \mathbf{96\ cm^2}$

(b) Area $= \dfrac{(6\text{ cm})(8\text{ cm})}{2} = \mathbf{24\ cm^2}$

(c) Area $= 96\text{ cm}^2 + 24\text{ cm}^2$
$= \mathbf{120\ cm^2}$

15.

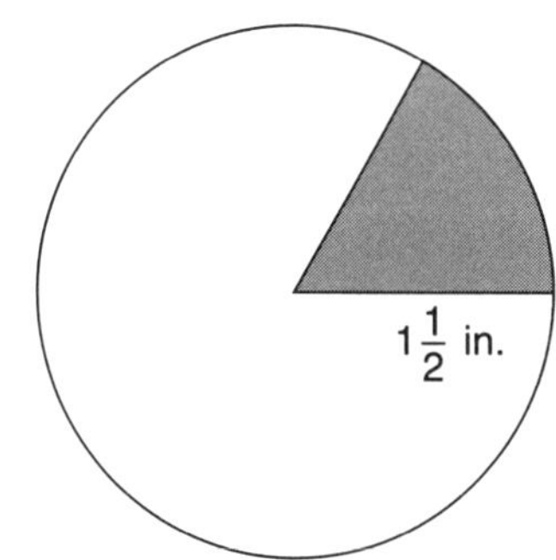

16.
$$\begin{aligned} \frac{10}{x} &= \frac{7}{42} \\ 7x &= 10 \cdot 42 \\ x &= \frac{420}{7} \\ x &= \mathbf{60} \end{aligned}$$

17.
$$\begin{aligned} \frac{1.5}{1} &= \frac{w}{4} \\ 1w &= (1.5)4 \\ w &= \frac{6}{1} \\ w &= \mathbf{6} \end{aligned}$$

18.
$$\begin{array}{r} 5.\overset{5}{\cancel{6}}{}^{1}0 \\ -\ 3.56 \\ \hline 2.04 \end{array}$$
$y = \mathbf{2.04}$

19.
$$\begin{array}{rcl} \frac{3}{20} &=& \frac{9}{60} \\ -\ \frac{1}{15} &=& \frac{4}{60} \\ \hline && \frac{5}{60} = \frac{1}{12} \end{array}$$
$w = \mathbf{\frac{1}{12}}$

20. (a) **Distributive property**

(b) **Commutative property of addition**

(c) **Identity property of multiplication**

21. **B. 10^4**

22.

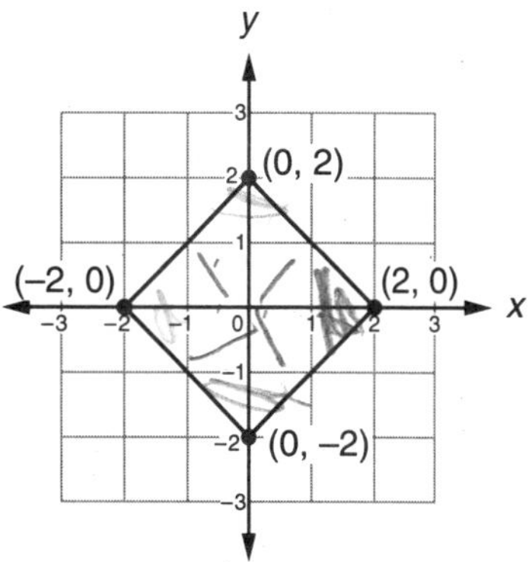

(a) **(0, 2)**

(b) Area $= 4(1 \text{ sq. units}) + 8\left(\frac{1}{2} \text{ sq. units}\right)$

$= 4 \text{ sq. units} + 4 \text{ sq. units}$

$= \mathbf{8 \text{ sq. units}}$

23.
$$\begin{array}{r} \mathbf{2\frac{1}{2}\ cookies} \\ 4\overline{)10} \\ \underline{8} \\ 2 \end{array}$$

24. (a) **14**

(b) **15**

(c) **See student work.**

25. $\mathbf{\frac{10 \text{ mm}}{1 \text{ cm}}, \frac{1 \text{ cm}}{10 \text{ mm}}}$

$\overset{16}{\cancel{160}}\ \cancel{\text{mm}} \cdot \frac{1 \text{ cm}}{\underset{1}{\cancel{10}}\ \cancel{\text{mm}}} = \mathbf{16 \text{ cm}}$

26.
$$\begin{array}{rrr} 4 \text{ yd} & 2 \text{ ft} & 7 \text{ in.} \\ +\ 3 \text{ yd} & & 5 \text{ in.} \\ \hline 7 \text{ yd} & 2 \text{ ft} & 12 \text{ in.} \end{array}$$
12 in. = 1 ft, 1 ft + 2 ft = 3 ft

3 ft = 1 yd, 7 yd + 1 yd = **8 yd**

27.
$$1\frac{3}{4} \div 2\frac{1}{3} = \frac{7}{4} \div \frac{7}{3}$$
$$= \frac{\overset{1}{\cancel{7}}}{4} \times \frac{3}{\underset{1}{\cancel{7}}} = \frac{3}{4}$$

$$\begin{array}{rcl} 5\frac{1}{6} = 5\frac{2}{12} & \longrightarrow & 4\frac{14}{12} \\ -\ \frac{3}{4} = \ \ \frac{9}{12} & & -\ \frac{9}{12} \\ \hline & & \mathbf{4\frac{5}{12}} \end{array}$$

28. $3\frac{1}{8} \cdot 2\frac{2}{5} = \frac{\overset{5}{\cancel{25}}}{\underset{2}{\cancel{8}}} \cdot \frac{\overset{3}{\cancel{12}}}{\underset{1}{\cancel{5}}} = \frac{15}{2}$

$$\begin{array}{rcl} 3\frac{5}{7} & = & 3\frac{10}{14} \\ + \frac{15}{2} & = & \frac{105}{14} \\ \hline & & 3\frac{115}{14} = \mathbf{11\frac{3}{14}} \end{array}$$

29. (a) m$\angle BAC$ = m$\angle CDB$ = **60°**

(b) m$\angle BCA$ = 180° − (70° + 60°) = 180° − 130° = **50°**

(c) m$\angle CBD$ = m$\angle BCA$ = **50°**

30. **4(5 − 3)** or **4(5 − 3)**
4(2) **20 − 12**
8 **8**

LESSON 51, LESSON PRACTICE

a. 1,5000000 ⟶ **1.5 × 10^7**

b. 4,00000000000 ⟶ **4 × 10^{11}**

c. 5,090000 ⟶ **5.09 × 10^6**

d. 2,50000000000 ⟶ **2.5 × 10^{11}**

e. 3400000, ⟶ **3,400,000**

f. 500000000, ⟶ **500,000,000**

g. 100000, ⟶ **100,000**

h. 150000, ⟶ 150,000
1500000, ⟶ 1,500,000
1.5 × 10^5 **<** 1.5 × 10^6

i. 1000000, ⟶ 1,000,000
1,000,000 **=** 1,000,000
one million **=** 1 × 10^6

LESSON 51, MIXED PRACTICE

1. **3 tests**

2.
$$\begin{array}{r} 70 \\ 80 \\ 75 \\ 85 \\ + \ 90 \\ \hline 400 \end{array} \qquad 5\overline{)400} = \mathbf{80}$$

3. $\frac{9 \text{ in.}}{6} = \frac{3}{2}$ in.

$5\left(\frac{3}{2} \text{ in.}\right) = \frac{15}{2}$ in. $= \mathbf{7\frac{1}{2} \text{ in.}}$

4. $\frac{\$1.98}{6 \text{ cans}} = \frac{\$0.33}{1 \text{ can}}$

$$\begin{array}{r} \$0.40 \\ - \ \$0.33 \\ \hline \$0.07 \end{array}$$

7¢ per can

5. (a) $\frac{\text{unconvinced people}}{\text{total people}} = \mathbf{\frac{2}{7}}$

(b) $\frac{\text{convinced people}}{\text{unconvinced people}} = \mathbf{\frac{5}{2}}$

6. (a) 1,2000000 ⟶ **1.2 × 10^7**

(b) 1,7600 ⟶ **1.76 × 10^4**

7. (a) 12000, ⟶ **12,000**

(b) 5000000, ⟶ **5,000,000**

8. (a) $8\overline{)1.000} = \mathbf{0.125}$

$$\begin{array}{r} 8 \\ \hline 20 \\ 16 \\ \hline 40 \\ 40 \\ \hline 0 \end{array}$$

(b) $87\frac{1}{2}\% = \frac{87.5}{100} = \mathbf{0.875}$

9. (a) **30,000**

(b) **5000**

10. (a) $40\% = \frac{40}{100} = \mathbf{\frac{2}{5}}$

(b) $40\% = \frac{40}{100} = \frac{4}{10} = \mathbf{0.4}$

(c) $4\% = \frac{4}{100} = \mathbf{\frac{1}{25}}$

(d) $4\% = \frac{4}{100} = \mathbf{0.04}$

11. (a) $0.5 \times 360° = \mathbf{180°}$

(b) $0.25 \times 360° = \mathbf{90°}$

(c) $0.125 \times 360° = \mathbf{45°}$

(d) $0.125 \times 360° = \mathbf{45°}$

12.
$$\begin{array}{r} \$15.80 \\ \times \quad 0.05 \\ \hline \$0.7900 \end{array} \longrightarrow \$0.79$$
$$\begin{array}{r} \$15.80 \\ + \quad \$0.79 \\ \hline \mathbf{\$16.59} \end{array}$$

13. **0**

14. (a) $\boldsymbol{\angle Z}$

(b) $\boldsymbol{\overline{DC}}$

15. Perimeter = 2 m + 5 m + 4 m + 6 m
+ 8 m + 7 m + 14 m + 18 m
= **64 m**

16.

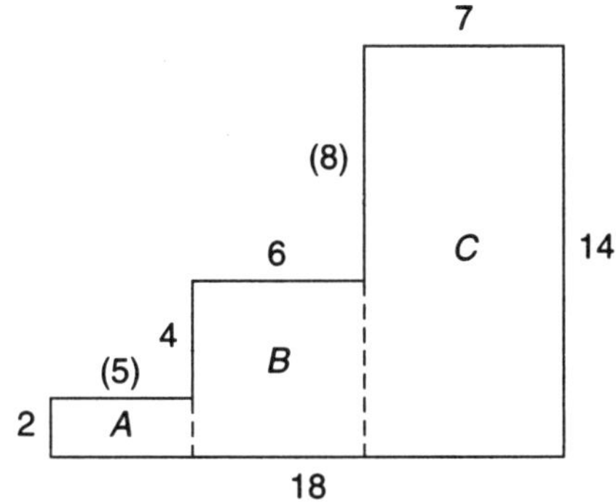

$$\begin{array}{rcrcr} \text{Area } A & = & (2\text{ m})(5\text{ m}) & = & 10\text{ m}^2 \\ \text{Area } B & = & (6\text{ m})(6\text{ m}) & = & 36\text{ m}^2 \\ + \ \text{Area } C & = & (14\text{ m})(7\text{ m}) & = & 98\text{ m}^2 \\ \hline & & \text{Area of figure} & = & \mathbf{144\ m^2} \end{array}$$

17.
$$\frac{24}{x} = \frac{60}{40}$$
$$60x = 24 \cdot 40$$
$$x = \frac{960}{60}$$
$$x = \mathbf{16}$$

18.
$$\frac{6}{4.2} = \frac{n}{7}$$
$$4.2n = 6 \cdot 7$$
$$n = \frac{42}{4.2}$$
$$n = \mathbf{10}$$

19.
$$\begin{array}{r} 1.68 \\ 5\overline{)8.40} \\ \underline{5} \\ 3\,4 \\ \underline{3\,0} \\ 40 \\ \underline{40} \\ 0 \end{array}$$
$m = \mathbf{1.68}$

20.
$$\begin{array}{r} 6.50 \\ -\ 5.06 \\ \hline 1.44 \end{array}$$
$y = \mathbf{1.44}$

21. $5^2 + 3^3 + \sqrt{64}$
$= 25 + 27 + 8 = \mathbf{60}$

22. $16\ \cancel{\text{cm}} \cdot \frac{10\text{ mm}}{1\ \cancel{\text{cm}}} = \mathbf{160\ mm}$

23.

	5 days	18 hr	50 min
+	2 days	8 hr	25 min
	7 days	26 hr	75 min

75 min = 1 hr 15 min

	1 hr	15 min
+	26 hr	
	27 hr	15 min

27 hr = 1 day 3 hr

	1 day	3 hr	15 min
+	7 days		
	8 days	**3 hr**	**15 min**

24.

$$\begin{array}{rrr} 3\text{ yd} & 2\text{ ft} & 5\text{ in.} \\ +\ 1\text{ yd} & & 9\text{ in.} \\ \hline 4\text{ yd} & 2\text{ ft} & 14\text{ in.} \end{array}$$

14 in. = 1 ft 2 in.

$$\begin{array}{rr} 1\text{ ft} & 2\text{ in.} \\ +\ 2\text{ ft} & \\ \hline 3\text{ ft} & 2\text{ in.} \end{array}$$

3 ft = 1 yd; 1 yd + 4 yd = 5 yd

5 yd 2 in.

25.

$$\begin{array}{rcl} 5\frac{1}{4} = 5\frac{2}{8} & \longrightarrow & 4\frac{10}{8} \\ -\ 3\frac{7}{8} = 3\frac{7}{8} & & -\ 3\frac{7}{8} \\ \hline & & 1\frac{3}{8} \end{array}$$

$$\begin{array}{rcl} 6\frac{2}{3} & = & 6\frac{16}{24} \\ +\ 1\frac{3}{8} & = & 1\frac{9}{24} \\ \hline & & 7\frac{25}{24} = \mathbf{8\frac{1}{24}} \end{array}$$

26. $2\frac{2}{3} \div 1\frac{1}{2} = \frac{8}{3} \div \frac{3}{2}$

$= \frac{8}{3} \times \frac{2}{3} = \frac{16}{9}$

$3\frac{1}{3} \times \frac{16}{9} = \frac{10}{3} \times \frac{16}{9} = \frac{160}{27}$

$= \mathbf{5\frac{25}{27}}$

27. **0.5(0.5 + 0.6)**
0.5(1.1)
0.55

or

0.5(0.5 + 0.6)
0.25 + 0.3
0.55

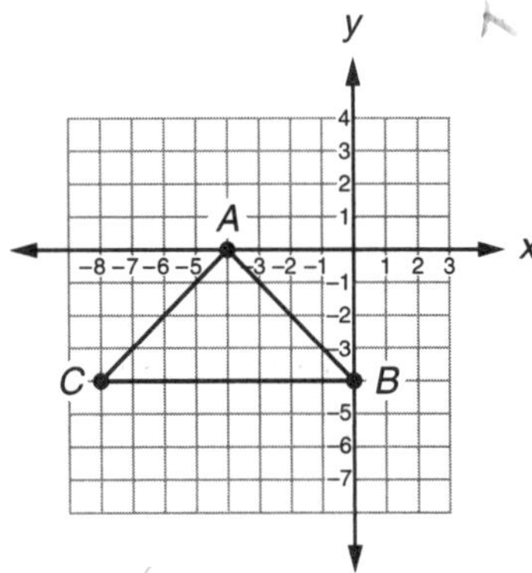

28. m∠*A* = **90°**; m∠*B* = **45°**; m∠*C* = **45°**

29. Area $= \frac{(8\text{ units})(4\text{ units})}{2}$

$= \mathbf{16\ sq.\ units}$

30. **180°F**

Lesson 52, Lesson Practice

a. $5 + 5 \cdot 5 - 5 \div 5$
$5 + 25 - 1$
$30 - 1$
29

b. $50 - 8 \cdot 5 + 6 \div 3$
$50 - 40 + 2$
$10 + 2$
12

c. $24 - 8 - 6 \cdot 2 \div 4$
$24 - 8 - 12 \div 4$
$24 - 8 - 3$
$16 - 3$
13

d. $\frac{2^3 + 3^2 + 2 \cdot 5}{3}$

$\frac{8 + 9 + 2 \cdot 5}{3}$

$\frac{8 + 9 + 10}{3}$

$\frac{17 + 10}{3}$

$\frac{27}{3}$

9

e. $(5)(3) - (3)(4)$
$15 - 12$
3

f. $(6)(4) + \frac{(6)}{(2)}$
$24 + 3$
27

g. $\left(\frac{2}{3}\right) - \left(\frac{2}{3}\right)\left(\frac{3}{4}\right)$

$\frac{2}{3} - \frac{1}{2}$

$\frac{4}{6} - \frac{3}{6}$

$\mathbf{\frac{1}{6}}$

Lesson 52, Mixed Practice

1. $(2 \cdot 3 \cdot 5) \div (2 + 3 + 5)$
$= 30 \div 10 = \mathbf{3}$

2. $100 - 4(7) = 100 - 28 = 72$
$72 \div 9 = 8$
8 nonagons

3.
$$\begin{array}{r} 202.020 \\ -\ \ 25.217 \\ \hline \mathbf{176.803} \end{array}$$

4. (a) $3\overline{)\$5.9500\ldots}$ = \$1.9833 . . .
3
2 9
2 7
25
24
10
9
10
9
1
\$1.98 per tape

(b)
$$\begin{array}{r} \$5.95 \\ \times\ \ 0.07 \\ \hline \$0.4165 \end{array} \longrightarrow \$0.42$$

$$\begin{array}{r} \$5.95 \\ +\ \$0.42 \\ \hline \mathbf{\$6.37} \end{array}$$

5. (a)
$$\begin{array}{r} 35 \\ \times\ \ 4 \\ \hline \mathbf{140\ pages} \end{array}$$

(b)
$$\begin{array}{r} 330\ \text{pages} \\ -\ 140\ \text{pages} \\ \hline \mathbf{190\ pages} \end{array}$$

6. $75\% = \frac{75}{100} = \mathbf{\frac{3}{4}}$

60 passengers
$\frac{3}{4}$ disembarked: 15 passengers, 15 passengers, 15 passengers
$\frac{1}{4}$ did not disembark: 15 passengers

(a) **45 passengers**

(b) **25%**

7. (a) $3\underset{\smile}{,}750000 \longrightarrow \mathbf{3.75 \times 10^6}$

(b) $8\underset{\smile}{,}0000000 \longrightarrow \mathbf{8 \times 10^7}$

8. (a) $2050000. \longrightarrow$ **2,050,000**

(b) $40. \longrightarrow$ **40**

9. (a) $8\overline{)3.000}$ = **0.375**
2 4
60
56
40
40
0

(b) $6.5\% = \frac{6.5}{100} = \mathbf{0.065}$

10. $3.\overline{27} = 3.2727\ldots$
3.273

11. (a) $250\% = \frac{250}{100} = \frac{5}{2} = \mathbf{2\frac{1}{2}}$

(b) $250\% = 2\frac{1}{2} = \mathbf{2.5}$

(c) $25\% = \frac{25}{100} = \mathbf{\frac{1}{4}}$

(d) $25\% = \frac{25}{100} = \mathbf{0.25}$

12. (a) $9\overline{)70}$ = $\mathbf{7\frac{7}{9}}$
63
7

(b) $9\overline{)70.00\ldots}$ = 7.77 . . . $\quad \mathbf{7.\overline{7}}$
63
7 0
6 3
70
63
7

13. **0.99**

14. 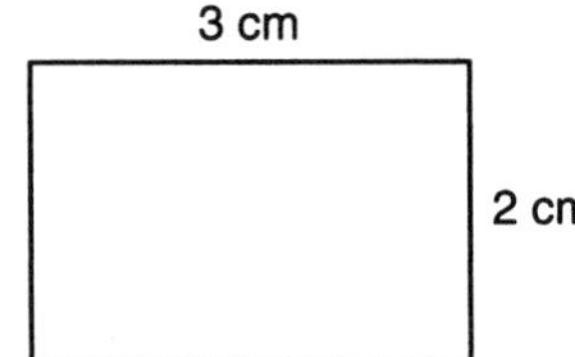

(a) Perimeter $= 2(30\text{ mm}) + 2(20\text{ mm})$
$= 60\text{ mm} + 40\text{ mm} = \mathbf{100\text{ mm}}$

(b) Area $= (2\text{ cm})(3\text{ cm}) = \mathbf{6\text{ cm}^2}$

15. (a) Area $= \dfrac{(12\text{ cm})(6\text{ cm})}{2} = \mathbf{36\text{ cm}^2}$

(b) Area $= \dfrac{(8\text{ cm})(6\text{ cm})}{2} = \mathbf{24\text{ cm}^2}$

(c) Area $= 36\text{ cm}^2 + 24\text{ cm}^2 = \mathbf{60\text{ cm}^2}$

16. $\dfrac{8}{f} = \dfrac{56}{105}$

$56f = 105 \cdot 8$

$f = \dfrac{840}{56}$

$f = \mathbf{15}$

17. $\dfrac{12}{15} = \dfrac{w}{2.5}$

$15w = 12 \cdot 2.5$

$w = \dfrac{30}{15}$

$w = \mathbf{2}$

18.
$$\begin{array}{r} 20.0 \\ -\ 6.8 \\ \hline 13.2 \end{array}$$
$p = \mathbf{13.2}$

19.
$$\begin{array}{r} 6.4 \\ +\ 3.6 \\ \hline 10.0 \end{array} = 10$$
$q = \mathbf{10}$

20. $5^3 - 10^2 - \sqrt{25}$
$= 125 - 100 - 5 = \mathbf{20}$

21. $4 + 4 \cdot 4 - 4 \div 4$
$4 + 16 - 1$
$20 - 1$
$\mathbf{19}$

22. $\dfrac{4.8 - 0.24}{(0.2)(0.6)}$

$= \dfrac{4.8 - 0.24}{0.12}$

$= \dfrac{4.56}{0.12} = \mathbf{38}$

23.
$$\begin{array}{rrr} 5\text{ hr} & 45\text{ min} & 30\text{ s} \\ +\ 2\text{ hr} & 53\text{ min} & 55\text{ s} \\ \hline 7\text{ hr} & 98\text{ min} & 85\text{ s} \end{array}$$
$85\text{ s} = 1\text{ min}\ \ 25\text{ s}$
$$\begin{array}{rr} 1\text{ min} & 25\text{ s} \\ +\ 98\text{ min} & \\ \hline 99\text{ min} & 25\text{ s} \end{array}$$
$99\text{ min} = 1\text{ hr}\ \ 39\text{ min}$
$$\begin{array}{rrr} 1\text{ hr} & 39\text{ min} & 25\text{ s} \\ +\ 7\text{ hr} & & \\ \hline \mathbf{8\text{ hr}} & \mathbf{39\text{ min}} & \mathbf{25\text{ s}} \end{array}$$

24. $5\dfrac{1}{3} \cdot 2\dfrac{1}{2} = \dfrac{\overset{8}{\cancel{16}}}{3} \cdot \dfrac{5}{\underset{1}{\cancel{2}}}$

$= \dfrac{40}{3} = 13\dfrac{1}{3}$

$$\begin{array}{rcl} 6\dfrac{3}{4} & = & 6\dfrac{9}{12} \\ +\ 13\dfrac{1}{3} & = & 13\dfrac{4}{12} \\ \hline & & 19\dfrac{13}{12} = \mathbf{20\dfrac{1}{12}} \end{array}$$

25. $3\dfrac{3}{4} \div 2 = \dfrac{15}{4} \div \dfrac{2}{1}$

$= \dfrac{15}{4} \times \dfrac{1}{2} = \dfrac{15}{8} = 1\dfrac{7}{8}$

$$\begin{array}{rcl} 5\dfrac{1}{2} & = & 5\dfrac{4}{8} \\ -\ 1\dfrac{7}{8} & = & 1\dfrac{7}{8} \\ \hline \end{array} \longrightarrow \begin{array}{r} 4\dfrac{12}{8} \\ -\ 1\dfrac{7}{8} \\ \hline \mathbf{3\dfrac{5}{8}} \end{array}$$

26. $9 + 13 + 8 + 70 = \mathbf{100}$

$$\begin{array}{r} 8.575 \\ 12.625 \\ 8.4 \\ +\ 70.4 \\ \hline 100.000 \end{array} = \mathbf{100}$$

27.
$$\begin{array}{r} 1.25 \\ \times\ \ 0.8 \\ \hline 1.000 \end{array} = 1$$
$1 \times 10^6 = \mathbf{1{,}000{,}000}$

28. $(4)(0.5) + \dfrac{(4)}{(0.5)}$
$2 + 8$
10

29. $1.4 \text{ meters} \cdot \dfrac{100 \text{ centimeters}}{1 \text{ meter}}$
$= \textbf{140 centimeters}$

30. $\dfrac{\text{favorite sport is basketball}}{\text{total}} = \dfrac{10}{30}$
$= \mathbf{\dfrac{1}{3}}$

LESSON 53, LESSON PRACTICE

a. $\mathbf{\dfrac{15 \text{ chairs}}{1 \text{ row}}; \dfrac{1 \text{ row}}{15 \text{ chairs}}}$

b. $18 \text{ rows} \cdot \dfrac{15 \text{ chairs}}{1 \text{ row}} = \textbf{270 chairs}$

c. $\mathbf{\dfrac{24 \text{ miles}}{1 \text{ gallon}}; \dfrac{1 \text{ gallon}}{24 \text{ miles}}}$

d. $\overset{20}{\cancel{160}} \text{ miles} \cdot \dfrac{1 \text{ gallon}}{\underset{3}{\cancel{24}} \text{ miles}}$
$= \dfrac{20}{3} \text{ gallons} = \mathbf{6\dfrac{2}{3} \text{ gallons}}$

LESSON 53, MIXED PRACTICE

1. (a) **16 boys**
(b) **16 girls**

2. $\dfrac{\text{January through June birthdays}}{\text{total birthdays}}$
$= \dfrac{16}{32} = \dfrac{1}{2}$
$\dfrac{1}{2} \times 100\% = \dfrac{100\%}{2} = \mathbf{50\%}$

3. $\dfrac{\text{April through June boys' birthdays}}{\text{total boys' birthdays}} = \mathbf{\dfrac{5}{16}}$

4. (a)
$$\begin{array}{r} \$3.95 \\ \$4.47 \\ \$4.95 \\ \$4.95 \\ \hline \$18.32 \end{array}$$

$4.58 per book
$$\begin{array}{r} 4\overline{)\$18.32} \\ \underline{16} \\ 2\,3 \\ \underline{2\,0} \\ 32 \\ \underline{32} \\ 0 \end{array}$$

(b)
$$\begin{array}{r} \$18.32 \\ \times\ \ \ 0.08 \\ \hline \$1.4656 \end{array} \longrightarrow \$1.47 \text{ tax}$$
$$\begin{array}{r} \$18.32 \\ \underline{\$1.47} \\ \textbf{\$19.79 total} \end{array}$$

5.
840 gerbils

70 gerbils
70 gerbils
70 gerbils
70 gerbils
70 gerbils
70 gerbils
70 gerbils
70 gerbils
70 gerbils
70 gerbils
70 gerbils
70 gerbils

$\frac{7}{12}$ were hiding. (first 7 rows)
$\frac{5}{12}$ were not hiding. (last 5 rows)

(a) $\mathbf{\dfrac{5}{12}}$

(b) **350 gerbils**

6. (a) $1{,}000000000000 \longrightarrow \mathbf{1 \times 10^{12}}$
(b) $4{,}75000 \longrightarrow \mathbf{4.75 \times 10^5}$

7. (a) $700. \longrightarrow \mathbf{700}$
(b) $2500000. \longrightarrow 2{,}500{,}000$
$250000. \longrightarrow 250{,}000$
$2.5 \times 10^6 > 2.5 \times 10^5$

8. (a) $35 \text{ yd} \cdot \dfrac{3 \text{ ft}}{1 \text{ yd}} = \textbf{105 ft}$

(b) $\overset{20}{\cancel{2000}} \text{ cm} \cdot \dfrac{1 \text{ m}}{\underset{1}{\cancel{100}} \text{ cm}} = \textbf{20 m}$

9.
$$\begin{aligned} 54 &= 2 \cdot 3 \cdot 3 \cdot 3 \\ 36 &= 2 \cdot 2 \cdot 3 \cdot 3 \\ \text{LCM}(54, 36) &= 2 \cdot 2 \cdot 3 \cdot 3 \cdot 3 \\ &= \mathbf{108} \end{aligned}$$

10.
$$\begin{array}{r} 20{,}000 \\ -\ 12{,}000 \\ \hline \mathbf{8\ 000} \end{array}$$

11. (a) $150\% = \frac{150}{100} = \frac{3}{2} = \mathbf{1\frac{1}{2}}$

(b) $150\% = \frac{3}{2} = 1\frac{1}{2} = \mathbf{1.5}$

(c) $15\% = \frac{15}{100} = \mathbf{\frac{3}{20}}$

d) $15\% = \frac{15}{100} = \mathbf{0.15}$

12. (a) $\frac{4}{5} \times 100\% = \frac{400\%}{5} = \mathbf{80\%}$

(b) $0.06 = \frac{6}{100} = \mathbf{6\%}$

13. 2 m = 200 cm
$$\begin{array}{r} 200 \text{ cm} \\ -\ 165 \text{ cm} \\ \hline \mathbf{35 \text{ cm}} \end{array}$$

14.

8
7
(11)
A
(4)
B
4
12

(a)
$$\begin{array}{rl} \text{Area } A = (11 \text{ ft})(8 \text{ ft}) = & 88 \text{ ft}^2 \\ +\ \text{Area } B = (4 \text{ ft})(4 \text{ ft}) = & 16 \text{ ft}^2 \\ \hline \text{Area of figure} = & \mathbf{104 \text{ ft}^2} \end{array}$$

(b) Perimeter = 8 ft + 7 ft + 4 ft + 4 ft + 12 ft + 11 ft = **46 ft**

15. (a) $\mathbf{\frac{1.6 \text{ C\$}}{1 \text{ US\$}}; \frac{1 \text{ US\$}}{1.6 \text{ C\$}}}$

(b) $160 \cancel{\text{US\$}} \cdot \frac{1.6 \text{ C\$}}{1 \cancel{\text{US\$}}} = \mathbf{256 \text{ C\$}}$

16.
$$\begin{aligned} \frac{18}{100} &= \frac{90}{p} \\ 18p &= 100 \cdot 90 \\ p &= \frac{9000}{18} \\ p &= \mathbf{500} \end{aligned}$$

17.
$$\begin{aligned} \frac{6}{9} &= \frac{t}{1.5} \\ 9t &= 6 \cdot 1.5 \\ t &= \frac{9}{9} \\ t &= \mathbf{1} \end{aligned}$$

18.
$$\begin{array}{r} 8.00 \\ -\ 7.25 \\ \hline 0.75 \end{array}$$
$m = \mathbf{0.75}$

19. $\frac{1.5}{10} = 0.15$

$n = \mathbf{0.15}$

20. $\sqrt{81} + 9^2 - 2^5$

$= 9 + 81 - 32 = \mathbf{58}$

21. $16 \div 4 \div 2 + 3 \times 4$

$4 \div 2 + 12$

$2 + 12$

14

22.
$$\begin{array}{rrr} 3 \text{ yd} & 1 \text{ ft} & 7\frac{1}{2} \text{ in.} \\ + & 2 \text{ ft} & 6\frac{1}{2} \text{ in.} \\ \hline 3 \text{ yd} & 3 \text{ ft} & 14 \text{ in.} \end{array}$$

14 in. = 1 ft 2 in.

$$\begin{array}{rr} 1 \text{ ft} & 2 \text{ in.} \\ +\ 3 \text{ ft} & \\ \hline 4 \text{ ft} & 2 \text{ in.} \end{array}$$

4 ft = 1 yd 1 ft

$$\begin{array}{rrr} 1 \text{ yd} & 1 \text{ ft} & 2 \text{ in.} \\ +\ 3 \text{ yd} & & \\ \hline \mathbf{4 \text{ yd}} & \mathbf{1 \text{ ft}} & \mathbf{2 \text{ in.}} \end{array}$$

23. $5\frac{5}{6} \div 2\frac{1}{3} = \frac{35}{6} \div \frac{7}{3}$

$= \frac{\overset{5}{\cancel{35}}}{\underset{2}{\cancel{6}}} \times \frac{\overset{1}{\cancel{3}}}{\underset{1}{\cancel{7}}} = \frac{5}{2} = 2\frac{1}{2}$

$$\begin{array}{rcr} 12\frac{2}{3} & = & 12\frac{4}{6} \\ + \quad 2\frac{1}{2} & = & 2\frac{3}{6} \\ \hline & & 14\frac{7}{6} = \mathbf{15\frac{1}{6}} \end{array}$$

24. $1\frac{1}{2} \cdot 3\frac{1}{5} = \frac{3}{\underset{1}{\cancel{2}}} \cdot \frac{\overset{8}{\cancel{16}}}{5} = \frac{24}{5} = 4\frac{4}{5}$

$$\begin{array}{rcr} 8\frac{3}{5} & \longrightarrow & 7\frac{8}{5} \\ -\ 4\frac{4}{5} & & -\ 4\frac{4}{5} \\ \hline & & \mathbf{3\frac{4}{5}} \end{array}$$

25. $3.875 \times 10^1 \longrightarrow 38.75$

$$\begin{array}{r} 10.6 \\ 4.2 \\ 16.4 \\ +\ 38.75 \\ \hline \mathbf{69.95} \end{array}$$

26. $7 \times 4 = \mathbf{28}$

27. $\frac{(6)(0.9)}{(0.9)(5)}$

$\frac{5.4}{4.5}$

1.2

28. $30\overline{)1000}$ = $33\frac{1}{3}$

33 flats

29. $\frac{\text{guessing wrong answer}}{\text{all answers}} = \mathbf{\frac{4}{5}}$

30.
$$\begin{aligned} m\angle a &= 180° - 130° = \mathbf{50°} \\ m\angle b &= 180° - (90° + 50°) \\ &= 180° - 140° = \mathbf{40°} \\ m\angle c &= 180° - (40° + 60°) \\ &= 180° - 100° = \mathbf{80°} \end{aligned}$$

Lesson 54, Lesson Practice

a.

	Ratio	Actual Count
Girls	9	63
Boys	7	B

$$\begin{aligned} \frac{9}{7} &= \frac{63}{B} \\ 9B &= 441 \\ B &= \textbf{49 boys} \end{aligned}$$

b.

	Ratio	Actual Count
Sparrows	5	S
Blue jays	3	15

$$\begin{aligned} \frac{5}{3} &= \frac{S}{15} \\ 3S &= 75 \\ S &= \textbf{25 sparrows} \end{aligned}$$

c.

	Ratio	Actual Count
Tagged fish	2	90
Untagged fish	9	U

$$\begin{aligned} \frac{2}{9} &= \frac{90}{U} \\ 2U &= 810 \\ U &= \textbf{405 untagged fish} \end{aligned}$$

d. **See student work. If desired, have students form other ratios that use the classroom environment (e.g., lefthanders to righthanders, windows to doors, students to computers).**

Lesson 54, Mixed Practice

1. $1776 + 50 = 1826$

$$\begin{array}{r} 1826 \\ -\ 1743 \\ \hline \textbf{83 years} \end{array}$$

2.
$$\begin{array}{r} 190 \text{ cm} \\ 195 \text{ cm} \\ 197 \text{ cm} \\ 201 \text{ cm} \\ +\ 203 \text{ cm} \\ \hline 986 \text{ cm} \end{array}$$

$5\overline{)986}$ = 197.2

197 cm

3.

	Ratio	Actual Count
Winners	5	1200
Losers	4	L

$$\frac{5}{4} = \frac{1200}{L}$$
$$5L = 4800$$
$$L = \textbf{960 losers}$$

4. $2.6 \text{ \sout{pounds}} \frac{\$1.75}{1 \text{ \sout{pound}}}$
$= \mathbf{\$4.55}$

5.
$4 = 2 \cdot 2$
$6 = 2 \cdot 3$
$LCM\ (4, 6) = 2 \cdot 2 \cdot 3 = 12$
$GCF\ (4, 6) = 2$
$\frac{12}{2} = \mathbf{6}$

6.

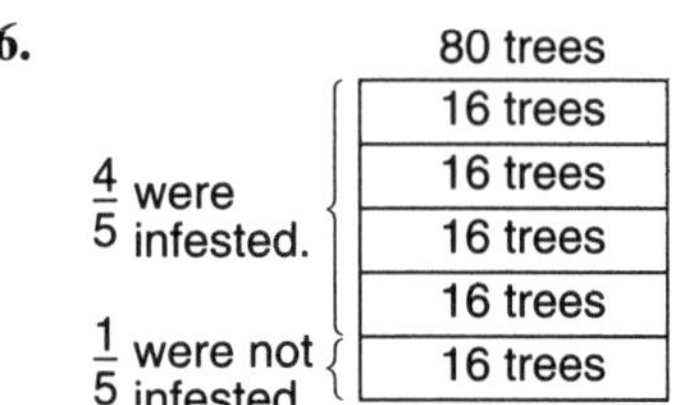

(a) **64 trees**

(b) **16 trees**

7. (a) $4{,}05000 \longrightarrow \mathbf{4.05 \times 10^5}$

(b) $004000. \longrightarrow \mathbf{4000}$

8. (a) 10^8

(b) 10^4

9. (a) $\overset{1760}{5280}\ \text{ft} \cdot \frac{1 \text{ yd}}{\underset{1}{3} \text{ ft}} = \textbf{1760 yd}$

(b) $300 \text{ cm} \cdot \frac{10 \text{ mm}}{1 \text{ cm}} = \textbf{3000 mm}$

10. 3.1416

11. (a) $0.4 \times 360° = \mathbf{144°}$

(b) $0.3 \times 360° = \mathbf{108°}$

(c) $0.2 \times 360° = \mathbf{72°}$

(d) $0.1 \times 360° = \mathbf{36°}$

12. (a) $4 \text{ hours} \cdot \frac{60 \text{ miles}}{1 \text{ hour}} = \textbf{240 miles}$

(b) $\overset{5}{300}\ \text{miles} \cdot \frac{1 \text{ hour}}{\underset{1}{60} \text{ miles}} = \textbf{5 hours}$

13. B. $\mathbf{2^4}$

14. Perimeter $= 5 \text{ cm} + 8 \text{ cm} + 3 \text{ cm} + 5 \text{ cm} + 6 \text{ cm} + 9 \text{ cm} + 2 \text{ cm} + 4 \text{ cm} = \textbf{42 cm}$

15.

5, 3, (4), (4), C, 6, B (3), 5, A, (2), 9, (4)

Area A = (4 cm)(5 cm) = 20 cm²
Area B = (4 cm)(3 cm) = 12 cm²
+ Area C = (5 cm)(6 cm) = 30 cm²
Area of figure = **62 cm²**

16. (a) **Identity property of addition**

(b) **Distributive property**

(c) **Associative property of addition**

17.

0.5 in.
0.5 in.

(a) Perimeter = 4(0.5 in.) = **2 inches**

(b) Area = (0.5 in.)(0.5 in.)
= **0.25 square inch**

18. The average score is likely to be below the median score. The mean "balances" low scores with high scores. The scores above the median are not far enough above the median to allow the balance point for all the scores to be at or above the median.

19.
$$\begin{array}{r} 6.2 \\ -\ 4.1 \\ \hline 2.1 \end{array}$$
$x = \mathbf{2.1}$

20.
$$\begin{array}{r} 1.2 \\ +\ 0.21 \\ \hline 1.41 \end{array}$$
$y = \mathbf{1.41}$

21. $\dfrac{24}{r} = \dfrac{36}{27}$
$36r = 24 \cdot 27$
$r = \dfrac{648}{36}$
$r = \mathbf{18}$

22.
$$\begin{array}{r} 6.25 \\ \times\ 0.16 \\ \hline 3750 \\ 625 \\ \hline 1.0000 \end{array} = 1$$
$w = \mathbf{1}$

23. $11^2 + 1^3 - \sqrt{121}$
$= 121 + 1 - 11 = \mathbf{111}$

24. $24 - 4 \times 5 \div 2 + 5$
$24 - 20 \div 2 + 5$
$24 - 10 + 5$
$14 + 5$
$\mathbf{19}$

25. $\dfrac{(2.5)^2}{2(2.5)} = \dfrac{6.25}{5} = \mathbf{1.25}$

26.

	1 week	5 days	14 hr
+	2 weeks	6 days	10 hr
	3 weeks	11 days	24 hr

24 hr = 1 day
11 days + 1 day = 12 days
12 days = 1 week 5 days

	1 week	5 days
+	3 weeks	
	4 weeks	**5 days**

27.
$$\begin{array}{rcl} 9\frac{1}{2} = 9\frac{3}{6} & \longrightarrow & 8\frac{9}{6} \\ -\ 6\frac{2}{3} = 6\frac{4}{6} & & -\ 6\frac{4}{6} \\ \hline & & 2\frac{5}{6} \end{array}$$

$$\begin{array}{r} 3\frac{5}{10} = 3\frac{15}{30} \\ +\ 2\frac{5}{6} = 2\frac{25}{30} \\ \hline 5\frac{40}{30} \end{array} = 6\frac{10}{30} = \mathbf{6\frac{1}{3}}$$

28. $6 \div 3\frac{2}{3} = \dfrac{6}{1} \div \dfrac{11}{3}$
$= \dfrac{6}{1} \times \dfrac{3}{11} = \dfrac{18}{11}$

$7\frac{1}{3} \cdot \dfrac{18}{11} = \dfrac{\overset{2}{\cancel{22}}}{\underset{1}{\cancel{3}}} \cdot \dfrac{\overset{6}{\cancel{18}}}{\underset{1}{\cancel{11}}}$
$= \mathbf{12}$

29.

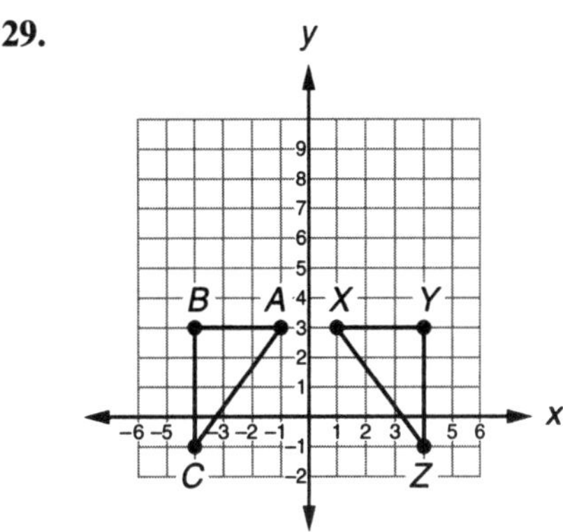

30. (a) **Yes**

(b) **Yes**

(c) $\angle C$

Lesson 55, Lesson Practice

a. $5(18 \text{ points}) = \mathbf{90 \text{ points}}$

b. $4(45) = 180$
$$24 + 36 + 52 + n = 180$$
$$n = \mathbf{68}$$

c. $5(91) = 455$
$6(89) = 534$
$$\begin{array}{r} 534 \\ -\ 455 \\ \hline \mathbf{79} \end{array}$$

Lesson 55, Mixed Practice

1.

	Ratio	Actual Count
Sailboats	7	56
Rowboats	4	R

$$\frac{7}{4} = \frac{56}{R}$$
$$7R = 56 \cdot 4$$
$$R = \mathbf{32 \text{ rowboats}}$$

2. $4(85) = 340$
$$76 + 78 + 81 + n = 340$$
$$n = \mathbf{105}$$

3. $$\begin{array}{r} \$0.72 \\ 12\overline{)\$8.64} \\ 8\,4 \\ \hline 24 \\ 24 \\ \hline 0 \end{array} \qquad \begin{array}{r} \$0.89 \\ -\ \$0.72 \\ \hline \$0.17 \end{array}$$

$0.17 per container

4. $BC - AB = 2\frac{2}{8} \text{ in.} - 1\frac{6}{8} \text{ in.}$

$$\begin{array}{r} 2\frac{2}{8} \text{ in.} \\ -\ 1\frac{6}{8} \text{ in.} \\ \hline \end{array} \longrightarrow \begin{array}{r} 1\frac{10}{8} \text{ in.} \\ -\ 1\frac{6}{8} \text{ in.} \\ \hline \frac{4}{8} \text{ in.} \end{array} = \mathbf{\frac{1}{2} \text{ in.}}$$

5.

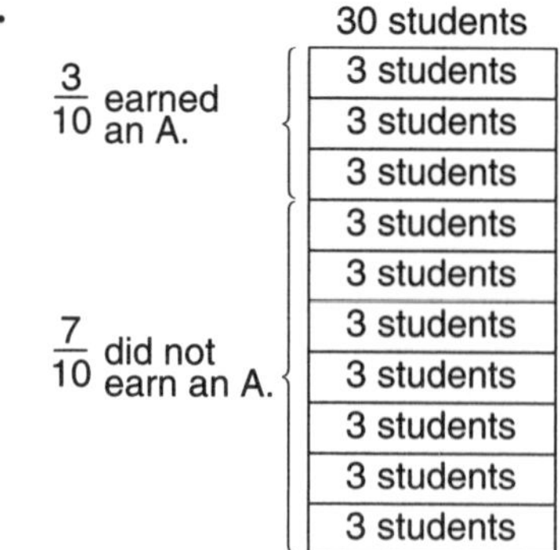

(a) **9 students**

(b) $\frac{3}{10} \times 100\% = \mathbf{30\%}$

6. (a) $6{,}75000000 \longrightarrow \mathbf{6.75 \times 10^8}$

(b) $186000. \longrightarrow \mathbf{186{,}000}$

7. (a) 10^{10}

(b) 10^{6}

8. (a) $24 \text{ feet} \cdot \frac{12 \text{ inches}}{1 \text{ foot}} = \mathbf{288 \text{ inches}}$

(b) $\overset{50}{500} \text{ millimeters} \cdot \frac{1 \text{ centimeter}}{\underset{1}{10} \text{ millimeters}}$

$= \mathbf{50 \text{ centimeters}}$

9. $0.02 \cdot 0.025 = \mathbf{0.0005}$

10. $$\begin{array}{r} \$3.25 \\ +\ \$1.10 \\ \hline \$4.35 \end{array} \qquad \begin{array}{r} \$4.35 \\ \times\ 0.07 \\ \hline \$0.3045 \end{array} \longrightarrow \$0.30$$

$$\begin{array}{r} \$4.35 \\ +\ \$0.30 \\ \hline \mathbf{\$4.65} \end{array}$$

11. (a) $$\begin{array}{r} \mathbf{0.2} \\ 5\overline{)1.0} \end{array}$$

(b) $\frac{1}{5} \times 100\% = \frac{100\%}{5} = \mathbf{20\%}$

(c) $0.1 = \mathbf{\frac{1}{10}}$

(d) $0.1 \times 100\% = \mathbf{10\%}$

(e) $75\% = \frac{75}{100} = \mathbf{\frac{3}{4}}$

(f) $75\% = \frac{75}{100} = \mathbf{0.75}$

12. (a) $\overline{AD}$ (or $\overline{DA}$)
(b) $\overline{DC}$ (or $\overline{CD}$) and $\overline{AH}$ (or $\overline{HA}$)
(c) $\angle DAB$ (or $\angle BAD$)

13. (a) Area $= (6\text{ cm})(8\text{ cm}) = \mathbf{48\text{ cm}^2}$
(b) Area $= \dfrac{(4\text{ cm})(8\text{ cm})}{2} = \mathbf{16\text{ cm}^2}$
(c) Area $= 48\text{ cm}^2 + 16\text{ cm}^2 = \mathbf{64\text{ cm}^2}$

14. 6 feet 2 inches = 6(12 inches) + 2 inches
= 74 inches

$$\begin{array}{r} 74\text{ inches} \\ -\ 68\text{ inches} \\ \hline \mathbf{6\text{ inches}} \end{array}$$

15. (a) $\mathbf{\dfrac{5\text{ laps}}{4\text{ min}}}$; $\mathbf{\dfrac{4\text{ min}}{5\text{ laps}}}$
(b) $\overset{5}{\cancel{20}}\ \cancel{\text{min}} \cdot \dfrac{5\text{ laps}}{\underset{1}{\cancel{4}}\ \cancel{\text{min}}} = \mathbf{25\text{ laps}}$
(c) $\overset{4}{\cancel{20}}\ \cancel{\text{laps}} \cdot \dfrac{4\text{ min}}{\underset{1}{\cancel{5}}\ \cancel{\text{laps}}} = \mathbf{16\text{ minutes}}$

16. $\mathbf{\dfrac{1}{2}\left(\dfrac{1}{4} + \dfrac{1}{2}\right)}$ or $\mathbf{\dfrac{1}{2}\left(\dfrac{1}{4} + \dfrac{1}{2}\right)}$

$\mathbf{\dfrac{1}{2}\left(\dfrac{3}{4}\right)}$ $\qquad$ $\mathbf{\dfrac{1}{8} + \dfrac{1}{4}}$

$\mathbf{\dfrac{3}{8}}$ $\qquad$ $\mathbf{\dfrac{3}{8}}$

17. $\dfrac{30}{70} = \dfrac{21}{x}$
$30x = 21 \cdot 70$
$x = \dfrac{1470}{30}$
$x = \mathbf{49}$

18. $25\overline{)10000}$ with quotient 400
$w = \mathbf{400}$

19. $2 + 7 + 5 = \mathbf{14}$

$$\begin{array}{rcl} 2\dfrac{5}{12} &=& 2\dfrac{10}{24} \\ 6\dfrac{5}{6} &=& 6\dfrac{20}{24} \\ +\ 4\dfrac{7}{8} &=& 4\dfrac{21}{24} \\ \hline && 12\dfrac{51}{24} = 14\dfrac{3}{24} = \mathbf{14\dfrac{1}{8}} \end{array}$$

20. $6 - (7 - 5) = 6 - 2 = \mathbf{4}$

$$\begin{array}{rcl} 7\dfrac{1}{3} &=& 7\dfrac{5}{15} \longrightarrow \\ -\ 4\dfrac{4}{5} &=& 4\dfrac{12}{15} \\ \hline \end{array} \qquad \begin{array}{r} 6\dfrac{20}{15} \\ -\ 4\dfrac{12}{15} \\ \hline 2\dfrac{8}{15} \end{array}$$

$$\begin{array}{r} 6 \\ -\ 2\dfrac{8}{15} \\ \hline \end{array} \longrightarrow \begin{array}{r} 5\dfrac{15}{15} \\ -\ 2\dfrac{8}{15} \\ \hline \mathbf{3\dfrac{7}{15}} \end{array}$$

21. $10\ \cancel{\text{yd}} \cdot \dfrac{36\text{ in.}}{1\ \cancel{\text{yd}}} = \mathbf{360\text{ in.}}$

22.

$$\begin{array}{rrr} 8\text{ yd} & 2\text{ ft} & 7\text{ in.} \\ + & & 5\text{ in.} \\ \hline 8\text{ yd} & 2\text{ ft} & 12\text{ in.} \end{array}$$

12 in. = 1 ft
2 ft + 1 ft = 3 ft
3 ft = 1 yd
8 yd + 1 yd = 9 yd
9 yd

23. $12^2 - 4^3 - 2^4 - \sqrt{144}$
$= 144 - 64 - 16 - 12 = \mathbf{52}$

24. $50 + 30 \div 5 \cdot 2 - 6$
$50 + 6 \cdot 2 - 6$
$50 + 12 - 6$
$62 - 6$
$\mathbf{56}$

25. $6\dfrac{2}{3} \cdot 5\dfrac{1}{4} \cdot 2\dfrac{1}{10}$

$= \dfrac{\overset{\overset{1}{\cancel{2}}}{\cancel{20}}}{\underset{1}{\cancel{3}}} \cdot \dfrac{\overset{7}{\cancel{21}}}{\underset{2}{\cancel{4}}} \cdot \dfrac{21}{\underset{1}{\cancel{10}}} = \dfrac{147}{2} = \mathbf{73\dfrac{1}{2}}$

26. $3\dfrac{1}{3} \div 3 \div 2\dfrac{1}{2}$

$= \dfrac{10}{3} \div \dfrac{3}{1} \div \dfrac{5}{2}$

$= \left(\dfrac{10}{3} \times \dfrac{1}{3}\right) \div \dfrac{5}{2} = \dfrac{10}{9} \div \dfrac{5}{2}$

$= \dfrac{\overset{2}{\cancel{10}}}{9} \times \dfrac{2}{\underset{1}{\cancel{5}}} = \mathbf{\dfrac{4}{9}}$

27.

$$\begin{array}{r} 6.000 \\ -\ 1.359 \\ \hline 4.641 \end{array} \qquad \begin{array}{r} 3.47 \\ +\ 4.641 \\ \hline \mathbf{8.111} \end{array}$$

28.

$$\begin{array}{r} 0.28 \\ \times\ \ 0.6 \\ \hline 0.168 \end{array} \qquad \begin{array}{r} 0.168 \\ \times\ \ 0.01 \\ \hline \mathbf{0.00168} \end{array}$$

29.

$$\begin{array}{r} \mathbf{\$20.00} \\ 75\overline{)\$1500.00} \end{array}$$

30.

$$\begin{aligned} m\angle a &= 180° - (90° + 52°) \\ &= 180° - 142° = \mathbf{38°} \\ m\angle b &= 90° - 38° = \mathbf{52°} \\ m\angle c &= 90° - 52° = \mathbf{38°} \end{aligned}$$

Lesson 56, Lesson Practice

a.

$$\begin{array}{rrr} \overset{2}{\not 3}\text{ hr} \to (60\text{ min}) & & 3\text{ s} \\ -\ 1\text{ hr} & 15\text{ min} & 55\text{ s} \\ \hline \end{array} \longrightarrow$$

$$\begin{array}{rrr} \overset{2}{\not 3}\text{ hr} & \overset{59}{\not 60}\text{ min} & \overset{63}{\not 3}\text{ s} \\ -\ 1\text{ hr} & 15\text{ min} & 55\text{ s} \\ \hline \mathbf{1\ hr} & \mathbf{44\ min} & \mathbf{8\ s} \end{array}$$

b.

$$\begin{array}{rrr} 8\text{ yd} & \overset{0}{\not 1}\text{ ft} \to (12\text{ in.}) & 5\text{ in.} \\ -\ 3\text{ yd} & 2\text{ ft} & 7\text{ in.} \\ \hline \end{array} \longrightarrow$$

$$\begin{array}{rrr} \overset{7}{\not 8}\text{ yd} \to (3\text{ ft}) & \overset{0}{\not 1}\text{ ft} & \overset{17}{\not 5}\text{ in.} \\ -\ 3\text{ yd} & 2\text{ ft} & 7\text{ in.} \\ \hline & & 10\text{ in.} \end{array} \longrightarrow$$

$$\begin{array}{rrr} \overset{7}{\not 8}\text{ yd} & \overset{3}{\not 0}\ \not 1\text{ ft} & \overset{17}{\not 5}\text{ in.} \\ -\ 3\text{ yd} & 2\text{ ft} & 7\text{ in.} \\ \hline \mathbf{4\ yd} & \mathbf{1\ ft} & \mathbf{10\ in.} \end{array}$$

c.

$$\begin{array}{rrr} 2\text{ days} & \overset{2}{\not 3}\text{ hr} \to (60\text{ min}) & 30\text{ min} \\ -\ 1\text{ day} & 8\text{ hr} & 45\text{ min} \\ \hline \end{array} \longrightarrow$$

$$\begin{array}{rrr} \overset{1}{\not 2}\text{ days} \to (24\text{ hr}) & \overset{2}{\not 3}\text{ hr} & \overset{90}{\not 30}\text{ min} \\ -\ 1\text{ day} & 8\text{ hr} & 45\text{ min} \\ \hline & & 45\text{ min} \end{array} \longrightarrow$$

$$\begin{array}{rrr} \overset{1}{\not 2}\text{ days} & \overset{26}{\not 2}\ \not 3\text{ hr} & \overset{90}{\not 30}\text{ min} \\ -\ 1\text{ day} & 8\text{ hr} & 45\text{ min} \\ \hline & \mathbf{18\ hr} & \mathbf{45\ min} \end{array}$$

Lesson 56, Mixed Practice

1.

$$\begin{array}{r} 0.0329 \\ -\ 0.0320 \\ \hline 0.0009 \end{array}$$

Nine ten-thousandths

2.

	Ratio	Actual Count
Length	4	12 feet
Width	3	W

(a)
$$\begin{aligned} \frac{4}{3} &= \frac{12\text{ feet}}{W} \\ 4W &= 3(12\text{ feet}) \\ W &= \mathbf{9\ feet} \end{aligned}$$

(b)
$$\begin{aligned} \text{Perimeter} &= 2(12\text{ feet}) + 2(9\text{ feet}) \\ &= 24\text{ feet} + 18\text{ feet} = \mathbf{42\ feet} \end{aligned}$$

3. $\$2 + \$0.50(4) = \$2 + \$2 = \mathbf{\$4}$

4.

$$\begin{aligned} 4(85) &= 340 \\ 340 + 90 &= 430 \\ \frac{430}{5} &= \mathbf{86} \end{aligned}$$

5.

$$\frac{\$1.50}{12\text{ ounces}} = \frac{\$0.125}{1\text{ ounce}}$$

$$\frac{\$1.92}{16\text{ ounces}} = \frac{\$0.12}{1\text{ ounce}}$$

Brand X = 12.5¢ per ounce
Brand Y = 12¢ per ounce
Brand Y is the better buy.

6. (a) $\dfrac{\text{igneous rocks}}{\text{total rocks}} = \mathbf{\dfrac{3}{8}}$

(b) $\dfrac{\text{igneous rocks}}{\text{metamorphic rocks}} = \mathbf{\dfrac{3}{5}}$

(c) $\dfrac{5}{8} \times 100\% = \dfrac{500\%}{8} = \mathbf{62\dfrac{1}{2}\%}$

7. (a) **∠*QPR* and ∠*TPS*** (or **∠*RPQ* and ∠*SPT***)
∠*RPS* and ∠*QPT* (or **∠*SPR* and ∠*TPQ***)

(b) **∠*RPQ*** (or **∠*QPR***) and **∠*SPT*** (or **∠*TPS***)

8. (a) 6,10000 ⟶ $\mathbf{6.1 \times 10^5}$

(b) 15000. ⟶ **15,000**

9. (a) $\cancel{216}^{9}\ \cancel{\text{hours}} \cdot \dfrac{1 \text{ day}}{\cancel{24}_{1}\ \cancel{\text{hours}}} = \mathbf{9 \text{ days}}$

(b) $5\ \cancel{\text{minutes}} \cdot \dfrac{60 \text{ seconds}}{1\ \cancel{\text{minute}}} = \mathbf{300 \text{ seconds}}$

10. (a)

$$\begin{array}{r} 0.166\ldots \\ 6\overline{)1.000\ldots} \\ \underline{6} \\ 40 \\ \underline{36} \\ 40 \\ \underline{36} \\ 4 \end{array}$$

0.17

(b) $\dfrac{1}{6} \times 100\% = \dfrac{100\%}{6} = \mathbf{16\dfrac{2}{3}\%}$

11. $1{,}000{,}000\ \cancel{\text{dollars}} \cdot \dfrac{100 \text{ pennies}}{1\ \cancel{\text{dollar}}}$
$= 100{,}000{,}000 \text{ pennies} = \mathbf{1 \times 10^8 \text{ pennies}}$

12. 1,1000000 ⟶ $\mathbf{1.1 \times 10^7}$
11 million > 1.1×10^6

13. **70**

14. $\dfrac{100°}{180°} = \dfrac{10°}{\mathbf{F}}$

$\mathbf{F}(100°) = (180°)(10°)$
$= \mathbf{18° \ F}$

15. Perimeter = 20 mm + 30 mm + 10 mm
+ 15 mm + 15 mm + 8 mm
+ 5 mm + 7 mm = **110 mm**

16.

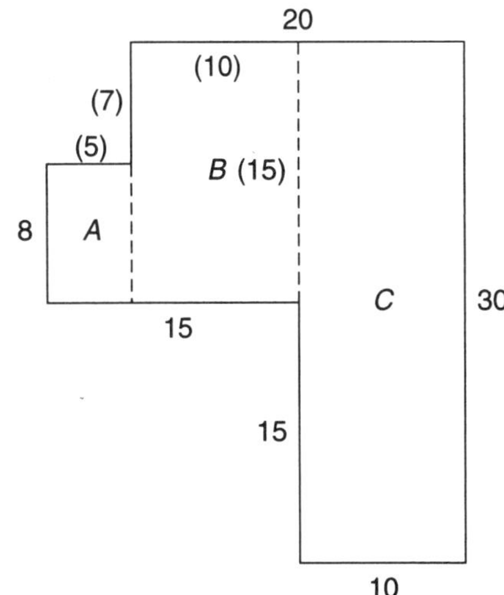

$$\begin{array}{rcrcr} \text{Area } A & = & (5 \text{ mm})(8 \text{ mm}) & = & 40 \text{ mm}^2 \\ \text{Area } B & = & (10 \text{ mm})(15 \text{ mm}) & = & 150 \text{ mm}^2 \\ + \ \text{Area } C & = & (30 \text{ mm})(10 \text{ mm}) & = & 300 \text{ mm}^2 \\ \hline & & \text{Area of figure} & = & \mathbf{490 \text{ mm}^2} \end{array}$$

17. $\dfrac{3}{2.5} = \dfrac{48}{c}$

$3c = 48(2.5)$

$c = \dfrac{120}{3}$

$c = \mathbf{40}$

18.

$$\begin{array}{r} 0.75 \\ +\ 0.75 \\ \hline 1.50 \end{array} = 1.5$$

$k = \mathbf{1.5}$

19. $15^2 - 5^3 - \sqrt{100} = 225 - 125 - 10$
$= 100 - 10 = \mathbf{90}$

20. $6 + 12 \div 3 \cdot 2 - 3 \cdot 4$
$6 + 4 \cdot 2 - 12$
$6 + 8 - 12$
$14 - 12$
$\mathbf{2}$

21.

	5 yd	2 ft	3 in.
+	2 yd	2 ft	9 in.
	7 yd	4 ft	12 in.

12 in. = 1 ft
4 ft + 1 ft = 5 ft
5 ft = 1 yd 2 ft

	1 yd	2 ft
+	7 yd	
	8 yd	**2 ft**

22.
$$\begin{array}{rrr} 5\text{ yd} & \overset{1}{\cancel{2}}\text{ ft} & 3\text{ in.} \\ -\ 2\text{ yd} & 2\text{ ft} & 9\text{ in.} \\ \hline \end{array} \quad (12\text{ in.}) \longrightarrow$$

$$\begin{array}{rrr} \overset{4}{\cancel{5}}\text{ yd} & \overset{1}{\cancel{2}}\text{ ft} & \overset{15}{\cancel{3}}\text{ in.} \\ -\ 2\text{ yd} & 2\text{ ft} & 9\text{ in.} \\ \hline & & 6\text{ in.} \end{array} \quad (3\text{ ft}) \longrightarrow$$

$$\begin{array}{rrr} \overset{4}{\cancel{5}}\text{ yd} & \overset{4}{\cancel{1}}\ \cancel{2}\text{ ft} & \overset{15}{\cancel{3}}\text{ in.} \\ -\ 2\text{ yd} & 2\text{ ft} & 9\text{ in.} \\ \hline \mathbf{2\text{ yd}} & \mathbf{2\text{ ft}} & \mathbf{6\text{ in.}} \end{array}$$

23. $\dfrac{88\text{ km}}{1\cancel{\text{hr}}} \cdot 4\ \cancel{\text{hr}} = \mathbf{352\text{ km}}$

24.
$$\begin{array}{rcl} 5\dfrac{1}{6} & = & 5\dfrac{2}{12} \\ -\ 1\dfrac{1}{4} & = & 1\dfrac{3}{12} \\ \hline \end{array} \longrightarrow \begin{array}{r} 4\dfrac{14}{12} \\ -\ 1\dfrac{3}{12} \\ \hline 3\dfrac{11}{12} \end{array}$$

$$\begin{array}{rcl} 2\dfrac{3}{4} & = & 2\dfrac{9}{12} \\ +\ 3\dfrac{11}{12} & = & 3\dfrac{11}{12} \\ \hline 5\dfrac{20}{12} & = & 6\dfrac{8}{12} = \mathbf{6\dfrac{2}{3}} \end{array}$$

25. $3\dfrac{3}{4} \cdot 2\dfrac{1}{2} \div 3\dfrac{1}{8}$

$= \left(\dfrac{15}{4} \cdot \dfrac{5}{2}\right) \div \dfrac{25}{8}$

$= \dfrac{75}{8} \div \dfrac{25}{8} = \dfrac{\overset{3}{\cancel{75}}}{\underset{1}{\cancel{8}}} \times \dfrac{\overset{1}{\cancel{8}}}{\underset{1}{\cancel{25}}} = \mathbf{3}$

26. $3\dfrac{3}{4} \div 2\dfrac{1}{2} \cdot 3\dfrac{1}{8}$

$= \left(\dfrac{15}{4} \div \dfrac{5}{2}\right) \cdot \dfrac{25}{8} = \left(\dfrac{\overset{3}{\cancel{15}}}{\underset{2}{\cancel{4}}} \times \dfrac{\overset{1}{\cancel{2}}}{\underset{1}{\cancel{5}}}\right) \cdot \dfrac{25}{8}$

$= \dfrac{3}{2} \cdot \dfrac{25}{8} = \dfrac{75}{16} = \mathbf{4\dfrac{11}{16}}$

27. **The first five numbers in the sequence are the squares of the first five counting numbers. So the 99th number in the sequence is 99^2.**

28. **See student work. If the triangle is drawn and measured accurately, the longest side is twice the length of the shortest side.**

29.
$$\begin{aligned} 0.5\text{ meter} &= 50\text{ centimeters} \\ \text{radius} &= \frac{50\text{ centimeters}}{2} \\ &= \mathbf{25\text{ centimeters}} \end{aligned}$$

30.

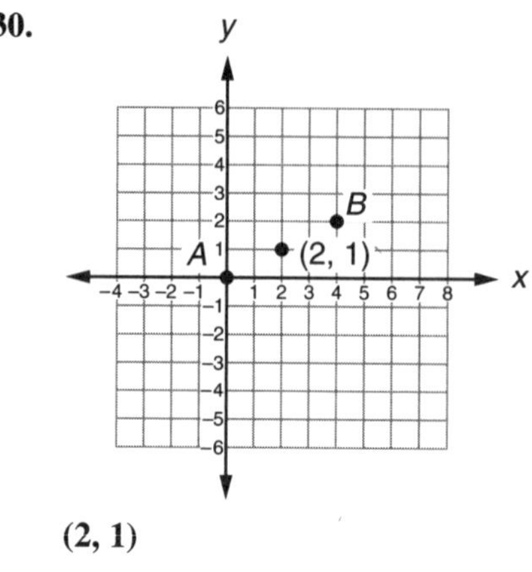

(2, 1)

Lesson 57, Lesson Practice

a. $5^{-2} = \dfrac{1}{5^2} = \mathbf{\dfrac{1}{25}}$

b. $3^0 = \mathbf{1}$

c. $10^{-4} = \dfrac{1}{10^4} = \mathbf{\dfrac{1}{10{,}000}}$ **or 0.0001**

d. 0000002.5 ⟶ $\mathbf{2.5 \times 10^{-7}}$

e. 000000001. ⟶ $\mathbf{1 \times 10^{-9}}$

f. 0001.05 ⟶ $\mathbf{1.05 \times 10^{-4}}$

g. .00000045 ⟶ **0.00000045**

h. .001 ⟶ **0.001**

i. .0000125 ⟶ **0.0000125**

j. $1 \times 10^{-3} = 0.001$
$1 \times 10^2 = 100$
$1 \times 10^{-3} \mathbf{<} 1 \times 10^2$

k. $2.5 \times 10^{-2} = 0.025$
$2.5 \times 10^{-3} = 0.0025$
$2.5 \times 10^{-2} > 2.5 \times 10^{-3}$

Lesson 57, Mixed Practice

1.

	Ratio	Actual Count
Walkers	5	315
Riders	3	R

$\frac{5}{3} = \frac{315}{R}$
$5R = 3(315)$
$R = \mathbf{189\ riders}$

2. $5(88) = 440$
$6(90) = 540$
$540 - 440 = \mathbf{100}$

3. $2(\$34.95) + \$0.18(300)$
$= \$69.90 + \$54.00$
$= \mathbf{\$123.90}$

4. 1 quart = 2 pints
$\$0.52 \div 2 = $ **\$0.26 per pint**
4, 12, 12, 0

5.

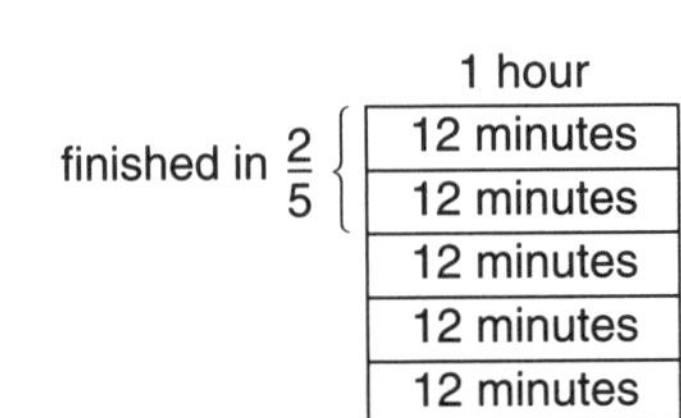

(a) **24 minutes**

(b) $\frac{2}{5} \times 100\% = \frac{200\%}{5} = \mathbf{40\%}$

6. (a) $1{,}86000 \longrightarrow \mathbf{1.86 \times 10^5}$

(b) $000004. \longrightarrow \mathbf{4 \times 10^{-5}}$

7. (a) $32.5 \longrightarrow \mathbf{32.5}$

(b) $000001.5 \longrightarrow \mathbf{0.0000015}$

8. (a) $2^{-3} = \frac{1}{2^3} = \mathbf{\frac{1}{8}}$

(b) $5^0 = \mathbf{1}$

(c) $10^{-2} = \frac{1}{10^2} = \mathbf{\frac{1}{100}}$ **or 0.01**

9. $\overset{2}{\cancel{2000}}\ \cancel{\text{milliliters}} \cdot \frac{1 \text{ liter}}{\underset{1}{\cancel{1000}}\ \cancel{\text{milliliters}}}$
= **2 liters**

10. $\frac{2}{6} = \mathbf{\frac{1}{3}}$

11. $\$330.00 \div 24 = \mathbf{\$13.75}$
24, 90, 72, 18 0, 16 0, 1 20, 1 20, 0

12.

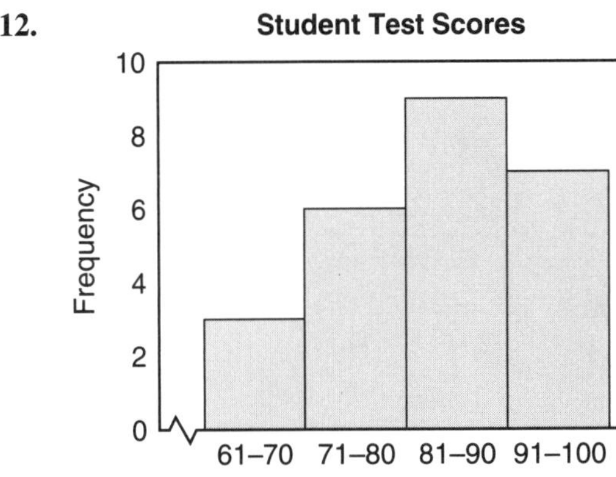

13. (a) $2.5 \times 10^{-2} = 0.025$
$2.5 \div 10^2 = \frac{2.5}{100} = 0.025$
$2.5 \times 10^{-2} \mathbf{=} 2.5 \div 10^2$

(b) $1 \times 10^{-6} = 0.000001$
one millionth $\mathbf{=} 1 \times 10^{-6}$

(c) $3^0 = 1, 2^0 = 1$
$3^0 = 2^0$

14. Perimeter = 4 yd + 3 yd + 1 yd + 1 yd + 1.5 yd + 2 yd + 1.5 yd + 4 yd = **18 yd**

15.

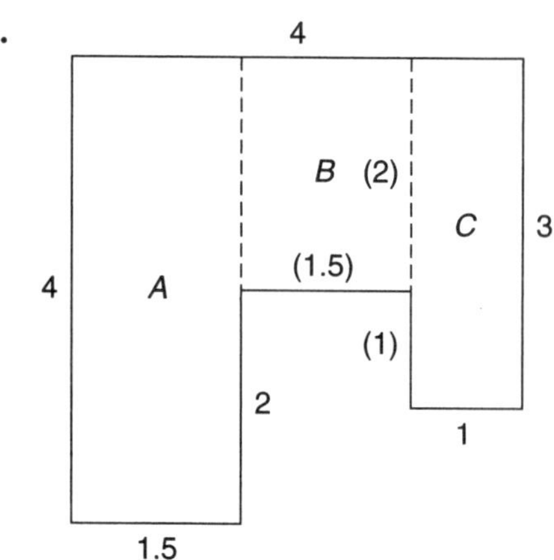

$$\begin{aligned} \text{Area } A &= (1.5\text{ yd})(4\text{ yd}) = 6\text{ yd}^2 \\ \text{Area } B &= (1.5\text{ yd})(2\text{ yd}) = 3\text{ yd}^2 \\ + \text{Area } C &= (1\text{ yd})(3\text{ yd}) = 3\text{ yd}^2 \\ \hline \text{Area of figure} &= \mathbf{12\text{ yd}^2} \end{aligned}$$

16. $4(5)(0.5) = 20(0.5) = \mathbf{10}$

17. $20.00 ÷ 4 = **$5.00**

18. $y = 3(12) + 5 = 36 + 5 = \mathbf{41}$

19. $20^2 + 10^3 - \sqrt{36}$
$= 400 + 1000 - 6 = \mathbf{1394}$

20. $48 \div 12 \div 2 + 2(3)$
$4 \div 2 + 6$
$2 + 6$
8

21.

		(12 in.)
3 yd	~~2~~ 1 ft	1 in.
− 1 yd	2 ft	3 in.

→

(3 ft)		
~~3~~ 2 yd	~~2~~ 1 ft	~~1~~ 13 in.
− 1 yd	2 ft	3 in.
		10 in.

→

~~3~~ 2 yd	~~2~~ ~~1~~ 4 ft	~~1~~ 13 in.
− 1 yd	2 ft	3 in.
1 yd	**2 ft**	**10 in.**

22.

4 gal	3 qt	1 pt	6 oz
+ 1 gal	2 qt	1 pt	5 oz
5 gal	5 qt	2 pt	11 oz

2 pt = 1 qt

1 qt	11 oz
+ 5 qt	
6 qt	11 oz

6 qt = 1 gal 2 qt

1 gal	2 qt	11 oz
+ 5 gal		
6 gal	**2 qt**	**11 oz**

23. $\overset{3}{\cancel{48}}\ \cancel{\text{oz}} \cdot \dfrac{1\text{ pt}}{\underset{1}{\cancel{16}}\ \cancel{\text{oz}}} = \mathbf{3\text{ pt}}$

24. $7 \div 1\frac{3}{4} = \frac{7}{1} \div \frac{7}{4} =$

$\dfrac{\overset{1}{\cancel{7}}}{1} \times \dfrac{4}{\underset{1}{\cancel{7}}} = 4$

$5\frac{1}{3} \cdot 4 = \frac{16}{3} \cdot \frac{4}{1} = \frac{64}{3} = \mathbf{21\frac{1}{3}}$

25.

$$\begin{aligned} 5\tfrac{1}{6} &= 5\tfrac{4}{24} \\ 3\tfrac{5}{8} &= 3\tfrac{15}{24} \\ + 2\tfrac{7}{12} &= 2\tfrac{14}{24} \\ \hline & \quad 10\tfrac{33}{24} = 11\tfrac{9}{24} = \mathbf{11\tfrac{3}{8}} \end{aligned}$$

26.

$$\begin{aligned} \tfrac{1}{20} &= \tfrac{9}{180} \\ - \tfrac{1}{36} &= \tfrac{5}{180} \\ \hline & \quad \tfrac{4}{180} = \mathbf{\tfrac{1}{45}} \end{aligned}$$

27. $4.6 \times 10^{-2} = 0.046$

$$\begin{array}{r} 0.46 \\ +\ 0.046 \\ \hline \mathbf{0.506} \end{array}$$

28.

$$\begin{array}{r} 2.300 \\ -\ 0.575 \\ \hline 1.725 \end{array} \qquad \begin{array}{r} 10.000 \\ -\ 1.725 \\ \hline \mathbf{8.275} \end{array}$$

29.
$$\begin{array}{r} 0.24 \\ \times\ 0.15 \\ \hline 1\,20 \\ 2\,4 \\ \hline \end{array}$$
$$0.03\,60 = 0.036$$
$$\begin{array}{r} 0.036 \\ \times\ \ 0.05 \\ \hline 0.00180 \end{array} = \mathbf{0.0018}$$

30. $70\overline{)0.140}$ with quotient 0.002; $2\overline{)10000}$ with quotient $\mathbf{5000}$

Lesson 58, Lesson Practice

a.

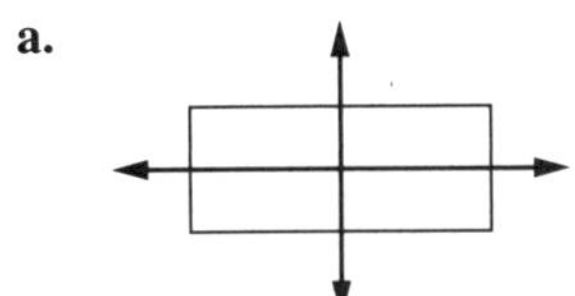

b.

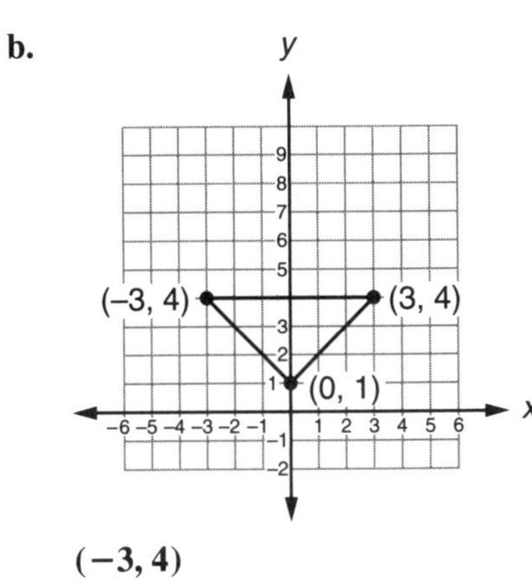

(−3, 4)

c. $7(5) = \mathbf{35}$

d. $1 + (4) = \mathbf{5}$

Lesson 58, Mixed Practice

1. 10(1.4 kilometers) = **14 kilometers**

2. 5($0.75) = **$3.75**

3.
$$17n = 340$$
$$n = \frac{340}{17}$$
$$n = 20$$
$$\begin{array}{r} 17 \\ +\ 20 \\ \hline \mathbf{37} \end{array}$$

4. (a) $\dfrac{\text{won}}{\text{lost}} = \dfrac{3}{9} = \mathbf{\dfrac{1}{3}}$

(b) $\dfrac{\text{lost}}{\text{total games}} = \dfrac{9}{12} = \mathbf{\dfrac{3}{4}}$

(c) $\dfrac{1}{4} \times 100\% = \dfrac{100\%}{4} = \mathbf{25\%}$

5. $5(120) = 600$
$$\begin{array}{r} 600 \\ 118 \\ 124 \\ +\ 142 \\ \hline 984 \end{array} = \text{total score for 8 games}$$
Average score = **123**

$$\begin{array}{r} \mathbf{123} \\ 8\overline{)984} \\ \underline{8} \\ 18 \\ \underline{16} \\ 24 \\ \underline{24} \\ 0 \end{array}$$

6.

60 questions

$\frac{3}{5}$ were multiple-choice.	12 questions
	12 questions
	12 questions
$\frac{2}{5}$ were not multiple-choice	12 questions
	12 questions

(a) **36 questions**

(b) $\dfrac{2}{5} \times 100\% = \dfrac{200\%}{5} = \mathbf{40\%}$

7. (a) $\mathbf{\overline{OA}, \overline{OB}, \overline{OC}}$

(b) $\mathbf{\overline{AC}}$ (or $\mathbf{\overline{CA}}$), $\mathbf{\overline{BC}}$ (or $\mathbf{\overline{CB}}$)

(c) **60°**

(d) **30°**

8. (a) 15000000. ⟶ **15,000,000**

(b) .00025 ⟶ **0.00025**

(c) $10^{-1} = \mathbf{\dfrac{1}{10}}$ **or 0.1**

9. 20 qt = 5 gal

10.
$$\begin{array}{r} 19.16\ldots \\ 18\overline{)345.00\ldots} \\ \underline{18} \\ 165 \\ \underline{162} \\ 3\,0 \\ \underline{1\,8} \\ 1\,20 \\ \underline{1\,08} \\ 12 \end{array}$$
19

11. **5, 0, −5**

12. (a) $6\overline{)1.000\ldots}$ quotient $0.1\overline{66}\ldots$ $\mathbf{0.1\overline{6}}$

(b) $\frac{1}{6} \times 100\% = \frac{100\%}{6} = \mathbf{16\frac{2}{3}\%}$

(c) $16\% = \frac{16}{100} = \mathbf{\frac{4}{25}}$

(d) $16\% = \frac{16}{100} = \mathbf{0.16}$

13. $2(4) = \mathbf{8}$

14. (a) $m\angle ACB = 180° - (90° + 35°)$
$= 180° - 125° = \mathbf{55°}$

(b) $\angle ACD = 180° - 55° = \mathbf{125°}$

(c) $\angle CAD = 180° - (35° + 125°)$
$= 180° - 160° = \mathbf{20°}$

15.

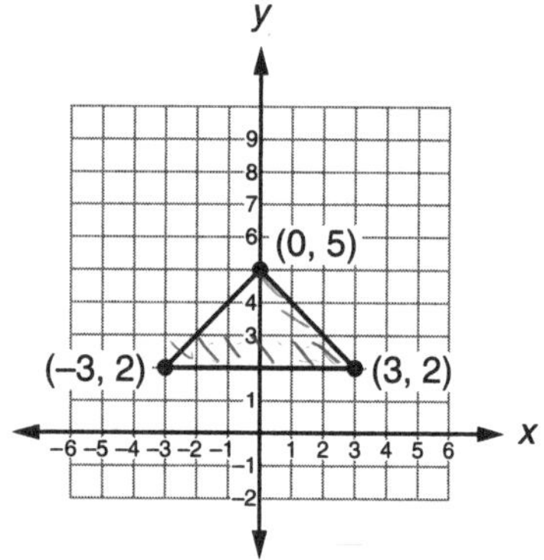

(a) **(3, 2)**

(b) $\text{Area} = \frac{(6 \text{ units})(3 \text{ units})}{2}$
$= \mathbf{9 \text{ units}^2}$

16. **5 lines**

17. (a) $\overset{7}{\cancel{210}}\ \cancel{\text{miles}} \cdot \frac{1 \text{ hr}}{\underset{2}{\cancel{60}}\ \cancel{\text{miles}}}$
$= \frac{7}{2} \text{ hr} = \mathbf{3\frac{1}{2} \text{ hr}}$

(b) $\overset{3}{\cancel{210}}\ \cancel{\text{miles}} \cdot \frac{1 \text{ hr}}{\underset{1}{\cancel{70}}\ \cancel{\text{miles}}}$
$= \mathbf{3 \text{ hr}}$

18.
$$\frac{1.5}{2} = \frac{7.5}{w}$$
$$1.5w = 2(7.5)$$
$$w = \frac{15}{1.5}$$
$$w = \mathbf{10}$$

19.
$$\begin{array}{r} 1.70 \\ -\ 0.17 \\ \hline 1.53 \end{array}$$
$y = \mathbf{1.53}$

20. $10^3 - 10^2 + 10^1 - 10^0$
$1000 - 100 + 10 - 1$
$900 + 10 - 1$
$910 - 1$
909

21. $6 + 3(2) - 4 - (5 + 3)$
$6 + 6 - 4 - 8$
$12 - 4 - 8$
$8 - 8$
0

22.

	1 gal	2 qt	1 pt
+	1 gal	2 qt	1 pt
	2 gal	4 qt	2 pt

2 pt = 1 qt
4 qt + 1 qt = 5 qt
5 qt = 1 gal 1 qt

	1 gal	1 qt
+	2 gal	
	3 gal	**1 qt**

23.

$$\begin{array}{rrr} & \overset{2}{\cancel{3}}\text{ hr} & 15\text{ min} \ (60\text{ min}) \\ 1\text{ day} & & \\ - & 8\text{ hr} & 30\text{ min} \\ \hline \end{array} \longrightarrow$$

$$\begin{array}{rrr} \overset{0}{\cancel{1}}\text{ day} & \overset{2}{\cancel{3}}\text{ hr} \ (24\text{ hr}) & \overset{75}{\cancel{15}}\text{ min} \\ - & 8\text{ hr} & 30\text{ min} \\ \hline & & 45\text{ min} \end{array} \longrightarrow$$

$$\begin{array}{rrr} \overset{0}{\cancel{1}}\text{ day} & \overset{26}{\cancel{2}}\ \cancel{3}\text{ hr} & \overset{75}{\cancel{15}}\text{ min} \\ - & 8\text{ hr} & 30\text{ min} \\ \hline & \mathbf{18\text{ hr}} & \mathbf{45\text{ min}} \end{array}$$

24. $2\ \cancel{\text{mi}} \cdot \dfrac{5280\text{ ft}}{1\ \cancel{\text{mi}}} = \mathbf{10{,}560\text{ ft}}$

25.

$$\begin{array}{rcl} 5\frac{3}{4} = 5\frac{9}{12} & \longrightarrow & 4\frac{21}{12} \\ -\ 1\frac{5}{6} = 1\frac{10}{12} & & -\ 1\frac{10}{12} \\ \hline & & 3\frac{11}{12} \end{array}$$

$$\begin{array}{rcl} 10 & \longrightarrow & 9\frac{12}{12} \\ -\ 3\frac{11}{12} & & -\ 3\frac{11}{12} \\ \hline & & \mathbf{6\frac{1}{12}} \end{array}$$

26.

$$\begin{array}{r} 2\frac{1}{5} = 2\frac{2}{10} \\ +\ 5\frac{1}{2} = 5\frac{5}{10} \\ \hline 7\frac{7}{10} \end{array}$$

$$7\frac{7}{10} \div 2\frac{1}{5} = \frac{77}{10} \div \frac{11}{5}$$

$$= \frac{\overset{7}{\cancel{77}}}{\underset{2}{\cancel{10}}} \times \frac{\overset{1}{\cancel{5}}}{\underset{1}{\cancel{11}}} = \frac{7}{2} = \mathbf{3\frac{1}{2}}$$

27. $6 \div 4\frac{1}{2} = \frac{6}{1} \div \frac{9}{2} =$

$$\frac{\overset{2}{\cancel{6}}}{1} \times \frac{2}{\underset{3}{\cancel{9}}} = \frac{4}{3}$$

$$3\frac{3}{4} \cdot \frac{4}{3} = \frac{\overset{5}{\cancel{15}}}{\underset{1}{\cancel{4}}} \cdot \frac{\overset{1}{\cancel{4}}}{\underset{1}{\cancel{3}}} = \mathbf{5}$$

28. $(6)^2 - 4(3.6)(2.5)$
$= 36 - 36 = \mathbf{0}$

29. (a) $\mathbf{2.5,\ 2,\ \frac{3}{2},\ 0,\ -\frac{1}{2},\ -1}$

(b) $\mathbf{-1, 0, 2}$

30. **Lindsey could double both numbers before dividing, forming the equivalent division problem 70 ÷ 5. She could also double both of these numbers to form 140 ÷ 10.**

Lesson 59, Lesson Practice

a.

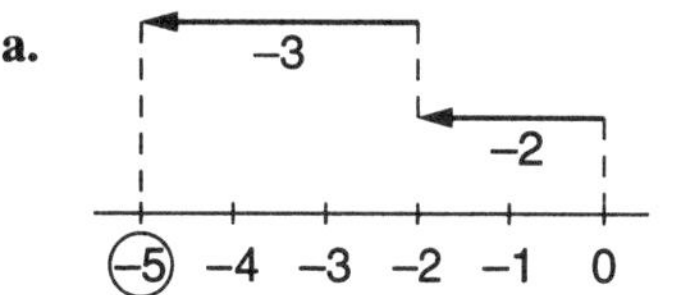

b.

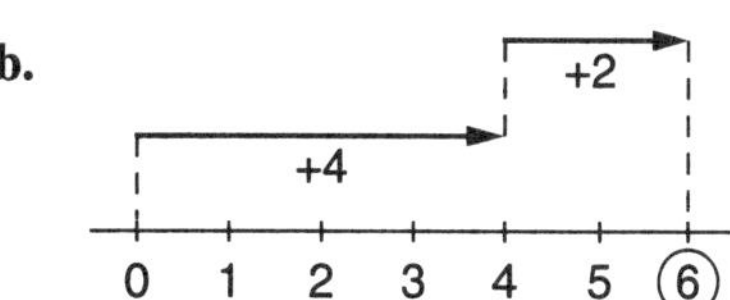

c.

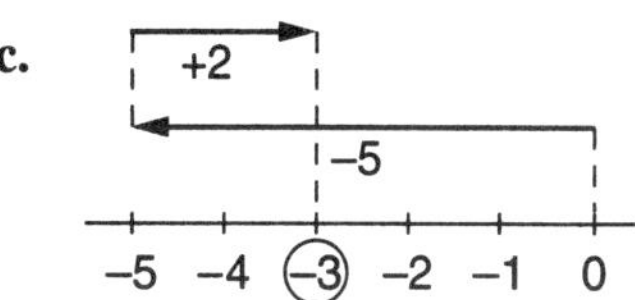

d.

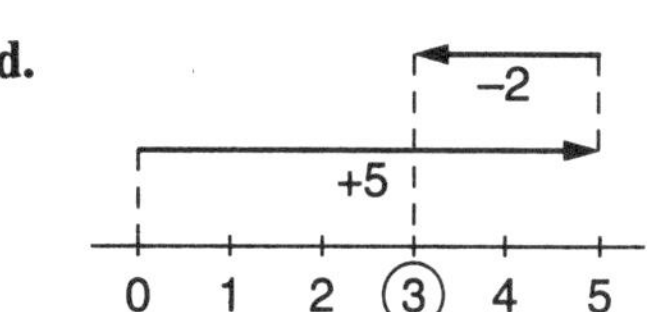

e.

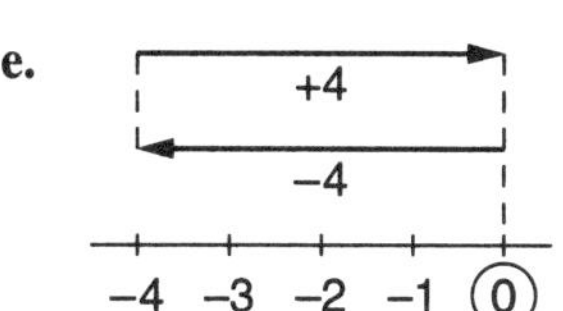

f.

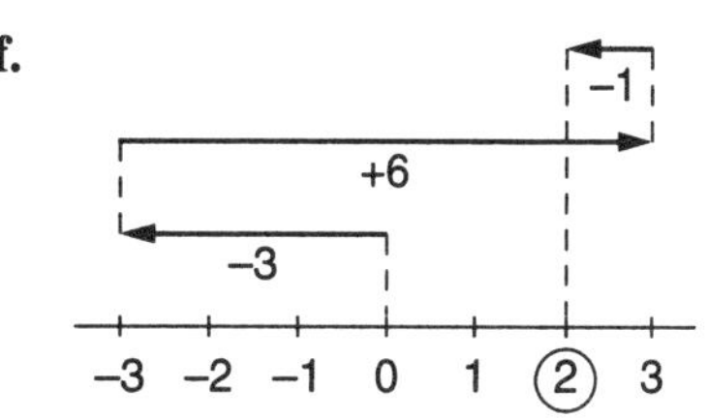

g. $|-3| + |3| = 3 + 3 = \mathbf{6}$

h. $|3 - 3| = |0| = \mathbf{0}$

i. $|5 - 3| = |2| = \mathbf{2}$

j.

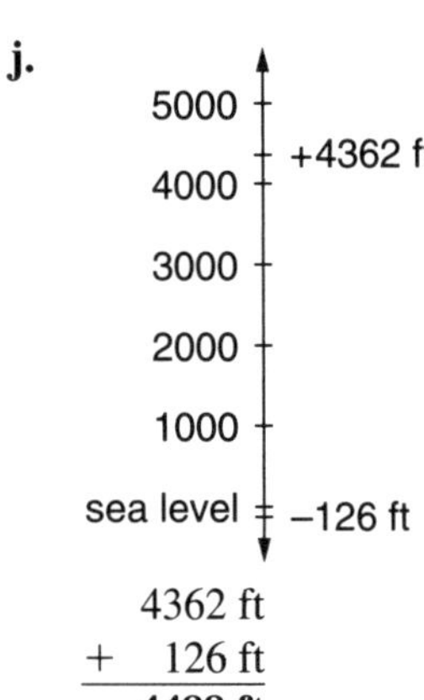

$$\begin{array}{r} 4362 \text{ ft} \\ +\ \ 126 \text{ ft} \\ \hline \mathbf{4488 \text{ ft}} \end{array}$$

k.

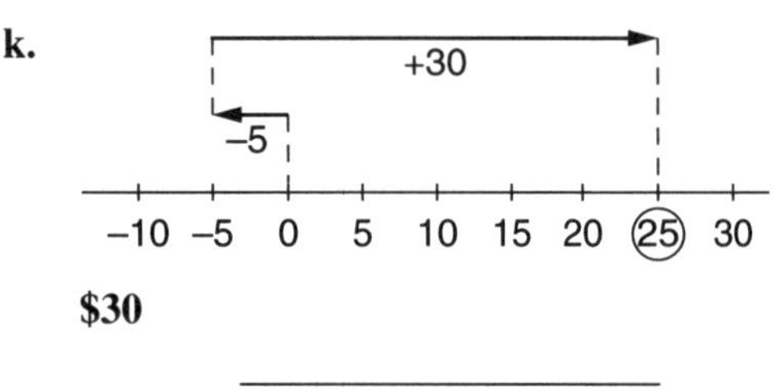

$30

Lesson 59, Mixed Practice

1. $2(\$2.35) + \$0.60(6)$
$= \$4.70 + \$3.60$
$= \mathbf{\$8.30}$

2.
$$\begin{array}{r} 90°\text{F} \\ -\ 85°\text{F} \\ \hline \mathbf{5°F} \end{array}$$

3.
$$\begin{array}{r} 82°\text{F} \\ 84°\text{F} \\ 86°\text{F} \\ 88°\text{F} \\ 84°\text{F} \\ 90°\text{F} \\ +\ 88°\text{F} \\ \hline 602°\text{F} \end{array}$$

$602°\text{F} \div 7 = \mathbf{86°F}$

4.

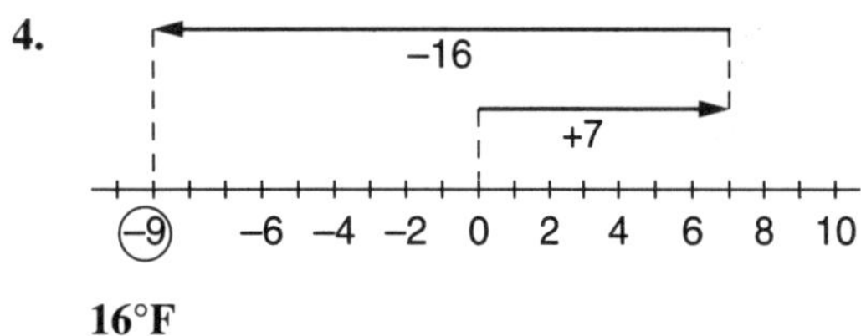

16°F

5.

	Ratio	Actual Count
Sonorous voices	7	S
Discordant voices	4	56

$\frac{7}{4} = \frac{S}{56}$
$4S = 7(56)$
$S = \mathbf{98\ voices}$

6.

20 games	
$\frac{3}{4}$ won.	5 games
	5 games
	5 games
$\frac{1}{4}$ failed to win.	5 games

(a) **15 games**

(b) $\frac{1}{4} \times 100\% = \frac{100\%}{4} = \mathbf{25\%}$

7. $|-3| = 3, |3| = 3$
$3 = 3$
$|-3| \mathbf{=} |3|$

8. (a) 4,000000000000 ⟶ $\mathbf{4 \times 10^{12}}$

(b) 3670000000, miles ⟶
3,670,000,000 miles

9. (a) .000001 meter ⟶ **0.000001 meter**

(b) 1 millimeter = 0.001 meter
1×10^{-3} meter = 0.001 meter
1 millimeter **=** 1×10^{-3} meter

10. $\overset{3}{\cancel{300}}\ \cancel{\text{mm}} \cdot \frac{1 \text{ m}}{\underset{10}{\cancel{1000}}\ \cancel{\text{mm}}} = \frac{3}{10} \text{ m} = \mathbf{0.3\ m}$

11. (a) $12\% = \frac{12}{100} = \mathbf{\frac{3}{25}}$

(b) $12\% = \frac{12}{100} = \mathbf{0.12}$

(c) $1.00\ldots \div 3 = 0.33\ldots$ $\quad \mathbf{0.\overline{3}}$

(d) $\frac{1}{3} \times 100\% = \frac{100\%}{3} = \mathbf{33\frac{1}{3}\%}$

12. (a)

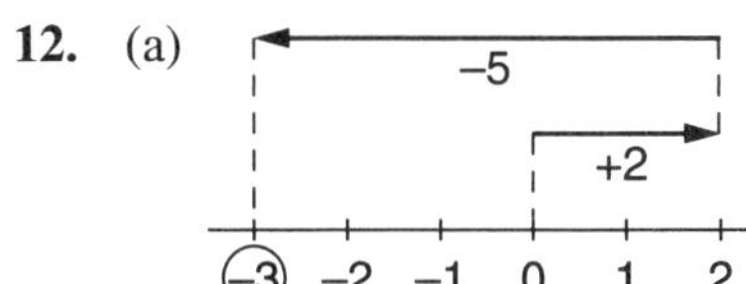

(b)

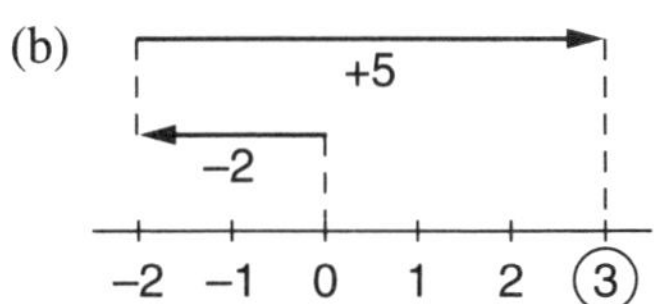

13. $8 + (12) = \mathbf{20}$

14. Perimeter = 50 mm + 60 mm + 35 mm + 15 mm + 15 mm + 25 mm + 30 mm + 20 mm = **250 mm**

15.

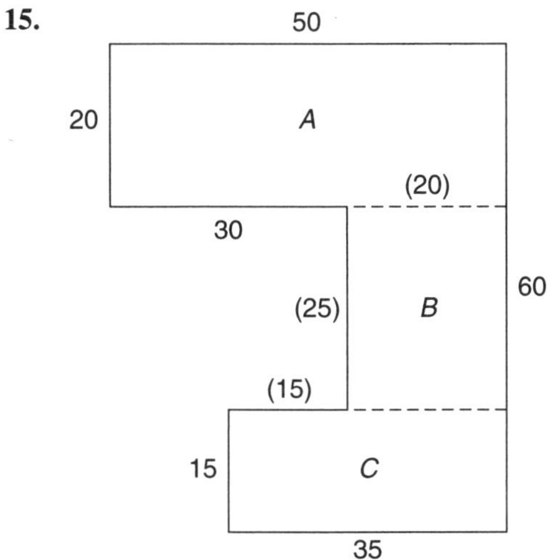

Area A = (50 mm)(20 mm) = 1000 mm^2
Area B = (20 mm)(25 mm) = 500 mm^2
+ Area C = (35 mm)(15 mm) = 525 mm^2
Area of figure = **2025 mm^2**

16. $8\overline{)4.40}$ = 0.55

$w = \mathbf{0.55}$

17. $\frac{0.8}{1} = \frac{x}{1.5}$

$1x = (0.8)(1.5)$

$x = \mathbf{1.2}$

18. $\frac{17}{30} = \frac{34}{60}$

$-\ \frac{11}{20} = \frac{33}{60}$

$n = \mathbf{\frac{1}{60}}$

19. $7\overline{)0.364}$ = 0.052

35
14
14
0

$m = \mathbf{0.052}$

20. $2^{-1} + 2^{-1} = \frac{1}{2} + \frac{1}{2}$

$= \frac{2}{2} = \mathbf{1}$

21. $\sqrt{64} - 2^3 + 4^0 = 8 - 8 + 1$

$= \mathbf{1}$

22.

	3 yd	2 ft	$7\frac{1}{2}$ in.
+	1 yd		$5\frac{1}{2}$ in.
	4 yd	2 ft	13 in.

13 in. = 1 ft 1 in.
1 ft 1 in.
2 ft
3 ft 1 in.
3 ft = 1 yd, 4 yd + 1 yd = 5 yd
5 yd 1 in.

23.

$\overset{0}{\cancel{1}}$ qt → (2 pt) 1 pt 6 oz
− 1 pt 12 oz →

$\overset{0}{\cancel{1}}$ qt $\overset{2}{\cancel{3}}$ pt → (16 oz) 6 oz
− 1 pt 12 oz →

$\overset{0}{\cancel{1}}$ qt $\overset{2}{\cancel{3}}$ pt $\overset{22}{\cancel{6}}$ oz
− 1 pt 12 oz
1 pt 10 oz

24. $2\frac{1}{2}\ \cancel{\text{hr}} \cdot \frac{50 \text{ mi}}{1\ \cancel{\text{hr}}} = \mathbf{125\ mi}$

25. $\frac{5}{9} \cdot 12 = \frac{5}{\underset{3}{\cancel{9}}} \cdot \frac{\overset{4}{\cancel{12}}}{1} = \frac{20}{3}$

$\frac{20}{3} \div 6\frac{2}{3} = \frac{20}{3} \div \frac{20}{3}$

$= \frac{\overset{1}{\cancel{20}}}{\underset{1}{\cancel{3}}} \times \frac{\overset{1}{\cancel{3}}}{\underset{1}{\cancel{20}}} = \mathbf{1}$

26. $4 - (4 - 1) = 4 - 3 = \mathbf{1}$

$$\begin{array}{r} 4 \\ -\,1\frac{1}{9} \\ \hline \end{array} \longrightarrow \begin{array}{r} 3\frac{9}{9} \\ -\,1\frac{1}{9} \\ \hline 2\frac{8}{9} \end{array}$$

$$\begin{array}{rl} 3\frac{5}{6} &= 3\frac{15}{18} \\ -\,2\frac{8}{9} &= 2\frac{16}{18} \\ \hline \end{array} \longrightarrow \begin{array}{r} 2\frac{33}{18} \\ -\,2\frac{16}{18} \\ \hline \mathbf{\frac{17}{18}} \end{array}$$

27. $(6 + 6) \div 6 = 12 \div 6 = \mathbf{2}$

$$\begin{array}{rl} 5\frac{5}{8} &= 5\frac{5}{8} \\ +\,6\frac{1}{4} &= 6\frac{2}{8} \\ \hline & 11\frac{7}{8} \end{array}$$

$$11\frac{7}{8} \div 6\frac{1}{4} = \frac{95}{8} \div \frac{25}{4}$$

$$= \frac{\overset{19}{\cancel{95}}}{\underset{2}{\cancel{8}}} \times \frac{\overset{1}{\cancel{4}}}{\underset{5}{\cancel{25}}} = \frac{19}{10} = \mathbf{1\frac{9}{10}}$$

28. $(0.1) - (0.2)(0.3)$
$= 0.1 - 0.06 = \mathbf{0.04}$

29.
$$\begin{array}{r} \$18.00 \\ \times\ \ 0.065 \\ \hline 9000 \\ 10800 \\ \hline \$1.17000 \end{array} = \mathbf{\$1.17}$$

30. $\dfrac{\text{candidate with most votes}}{\text{total votes}} = \dfrac{10}{25} = \mathbf{\dfrac{2}{5}}$

Lesson 60, Lesson Practice

a. $W_N = \mathbf{\frac{4}{5}} \times \mathbf{71}$

$W_N = \dfrac{284}{5}$

$W_N = \mathbf{56\frac{4}{5}}$

b. $\mathbf{\frac{3}{8} \times 3\frac{3}{7} = W_N}$

$\dfrac{3}{\underset{1}{\cancel{8}}} \times \dfrac{\overset{3}{\cancel{24}}}{7} = W_N$

$\dfrac{9}{7} = \mathbf{1\frac{2}{7}} = W_N$

c. $\mathbf{W_N = 0.6 \times 145}$
$W_N = \mathbf{87}$

d. $\mathbf{0.75 \times 14.4 = W_N}$
$\mathbf{10.8} = W_N$

e. $\mathbf{W_N = 0.5 \times 150}$
$W_N = \mathbf{75}$

f. $\mathbf{0.03 \times \$39 = M}$
$\mathbf{\$1.17} = M$

g. $\mathbf{W_N = 0.25 \times 64}$
$W_N = \mathbf{16}$

h. $\mathbf{0.12 \times \$250{,}000 = C}$
$\mathbf{\$30{,}000} = C$

Lesson 60, Mixed Practice

1.
$$\begin{array}{r} 7.0021 \\ -\ 5.7840 \\ \hline \mathbf{1.2181} \end{array}$$

2. $\overset{100}{\cancel{\$20}} \cdot \dfrac{1 \text{ board}}{\underset{1}{\cancel{\$0.20}}} = \mathbf{100\ boards}$

3. $\dfrac{72}{n} = 12$

$n = 6$

$72 \times 6 = \mathbf{432}$

4. (a) $\dfrac{1}{5} \times 100\% = \mathbf{20\%}$

(b) $\dfrac{\text{students who passed}}{\text{students who did not pass}} = \mathbf{\dfrac{4}{1}}$

5. $5(77 \text{ inches}) = 385 \text{ inches}$

$$\begin{array}{r} 71 \text{ inches} \\ 74 \text{ inches} \\ 78 \text{ inches} \\ +\ 78 \text{ inches} \\ \hline 301 \text{ inches} \end{array} \qquad \begin{array}{r} 385 \text{ inches} \\ -\ 301 \text{ inches} \\ \hline \textbf{84 inches} \end{array}$$

6. (a) $\mathbf{8 \times 10^{-8}}$

(b) $\mathbf{6.75 \times 10^{10}}$

7.

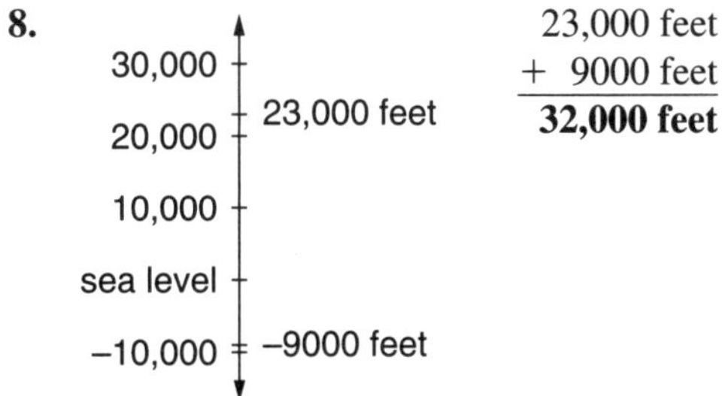

(a) **64 members**

(b) $\frac{1}{3} \times 100\% = \mathbf{33\frac{1}{3}\%}$

8.

$$\begin{array}{r} 23{,}000 \text{ feet} \\ +\ 9000 \text{ feet} \\ \hline \textbf{32,000 feet} \end{array}$$

9. $W_N = \frac{3}{4} \times 17$

$W_N = \frac{51}{4}$

$W_N = \mathbf{12\frac{3}{4}}$

10. $0.4 \times \$65 = P$

$\mathbf{\$26} = P$

11. (a) $3\overline{)1.00\ldots}$ quotient $0.33\ldots$ $\qquad \frac{1}{3} > 0.33$

(b) $|5 - 3| = |2| = 2$

$|3 - 5| = |-2| = 2$

$|5 - 3| \mathbf{=} |3 - 5|$

12. (a) $8\overline{)1.000}$ quotient $\mathbf{0.125}$

(b) $\frac{1}{8} \times 100\% = \mathbf{12\frac{1}{2}\%}$

(c) $125\% = \frac{125}{100} = \mathbf{1\frac{1}{4}}$

(d) $125\% = \frac{125}{100} = \mathbf{1.25}$

13. (a)

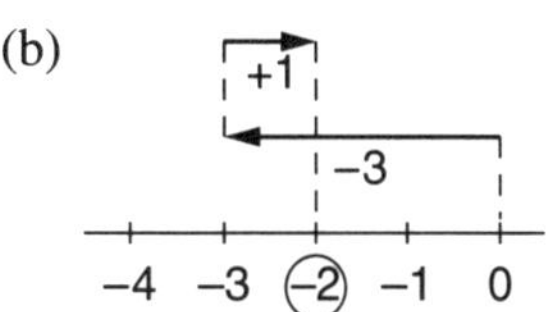

(b)

14. (a) $\mathbf{2^4 \cdot 3^2 \cdot 5^2}$

(b) $\sqrt{3600} = 60 = \mathbf{2^2 \cdot 3 \cdot 5}$

15. (a) $360° \times \frac{1}{2} = \frac{360°}{2} = \mathbf{180°}$

(b) $360° \times \frac{1}{3} = \frac{360°}{3} = \mathbf{120°}$

(c) $360° \times \frac{1}{6} = \frac{360°}{6} = \mathbf{60°}$

16. (a) $\mathbf{\Delta \textit{CDB}}$

(b) $\mathbf{\Delta \textit{CEA}}$

17. (a) $\text{Area} = \frac{(6 \text{ ft})(8 \text{ ft})}{2} = \mathbf{24 \text{ ft}^2}$

(b) $\text{Area} = \frac{(12 \text{ ft})(16 \text{ ft})}{2} = \mathbf{96 \text{ ft}^2}$

18. $\text{Area}(\Delta DEF) = \frac{(6 \text{ ft})(8 \text{ ft})}{2} = 24 \text{ ft}^2$

$96 \text{ ft}^2 - 24 \text{ ft}^2 - 24 \text{ ft}^2 = \mathbf{48 \text{ ft}^2}$

19. $$\begin{array}{r} \frac{1}{20} = \frac{3}{60} \\ + \frac{1}{30} = \frac{2}{60} \\ \hline \frac{5}{60} = \frac{1}{12} \end{array}$$

$p = \mathbf{\frac{1}{12}}$

20. $$\begin{array}{r} 0.013 \\ 9\overline{)0.117} \\ \underline{9} \\ 27 \\ \underline{27} \\ 0 \end{array}$$

$m = \mathbf{0.013}$

21. $$\begin{gathered} 3^2 + 4(3 + 2) - 2^3 \cdot 2^{-2} + \sqrt{36} \\ 9 + 4(3 + 2) - 8 \cdot \frac{1}{4} + 6 \\ 9 + 4(5) - 2 + 6 \\ 9 + 20 - 2 + 6 \\ 29 - 2 + 6 \\ 27 + 6 \\ \mathbf{33} \end{gathered}$$

22.

3 days	16 hr	48 min
+ 1 day	15 hr	54 min
4 days	31 hr	102 min

102 min = 1 hr 42 min

1 hr	42 min
+ 31 hr	
32 hr	42 min

32 hr = 1 day 8 hr

1 day	8 hr	42 min
+ 4 days		
5 days	**8 hr**	**42 min**

23. $$\begin{array}{r} 19\frac{3}{4} = 19\frac{18}{24} \\ 27\frac{7}{8} = 27\frac{21}{24} \\ + 24\frac{5}{6} = 24\frac{20}{24} \\ \hline 70\frac{59}{24} = \mathbf{72\frac{11}{24}} \end{array}$$

24. $\frac{5}{6} \cdot 4 = \frac{5}{\cancel{6}_3} \cdot \frac{\cancel{4}^2}{1} = \frac{10}{3} = 3\frac{1}{3}$

$$\begin{array}{r} 3\frac{3}{5} = 3\frac{9}{15} \\ - 3\frac{1}{3} = 3\frac{5}{15} \\ \hline \mathbf{\frac{4}{15}} \end{array}$$

25. $1\frac{1}{4} \div \frac{5}{12} = \frac{5}{4} \div \frac{5}{12}$

$= \frac{\cancel{5}^1}{\cancel{4}_1} \times \frac{\cancel{12}^3}{\cancel{5}_1} = 3$

$3 \div 24 = \frac{3}{24} = \mathbf{\frac{1}{8}}$ or **0.125**

26. $$\begin{array}{r} 0.650 \\ - 0.065 \\ \hline 0.585 \end{array} \qquad \begin{array}{r} 6.500 \\ - 0.585 \\ \hline \mathbf{5.915} \end{array}$$

27. $3 \div 0.03 = 100$
$0.3 \div 100 = \mathbf{0.003}$

28. $3.5\ \cancel{\text{centimeters}} \cdot \frac{1\ \text{meter}}{100\ \cancel{\text{centimeters}}}$

$= \frac{3.5}{100}$ meter = **0.035 meter**

29. **The first division problem can be multiplied by $\frac{100}{100}$ to form the second division problem. Since $\frac{100}{100}$ equals 1, the quotients are the same. One possibility: $\frac{\$1.50}{\$0.25} = \frac{150¢}{25¢}$**

30.

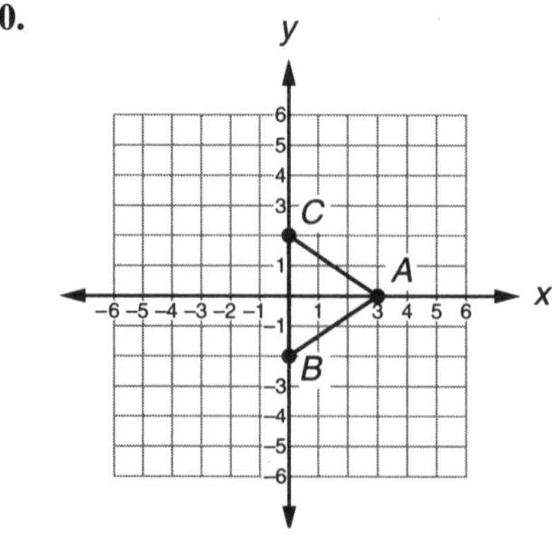

(0, 2)

Lesson 61, Lesson Practice

a. Perimeter $= 10\text{ cm} + 12\text{ cm} + 10\text{ cm} + 12\text{ cm} = \mathbf{44\text{ cm}}$

Area $= (12\text{ cm})(8\text{ cm}) = \mathbf{96\text{ cm}^2}$

b. Perimeter $= 10\text{ cm} + 13\text{ cm} + 10\text{ cm} + 13\text{ cm} = \mathbf{46\text{ cm}}$

Area $= (10\text{ cm})(12\text{ cm}) = \mathbf{120\text{ cm}^2}$

c. Perimeter $= 10\text{ cm} + 10\text{ cm} + 10\text{ cm} + 10\text{ cm} = \mathbf{43\text{ cm}}$

Area $= (10\text{ cm})(9\text{ cm}) = \mathbf{90\text{ cm}^2}$

d. $m\angle d = 180° - 75° = \mathbf{105°}$

e. $m\angle e = 180° - 105° = \mathbf{75°}$

f. $m\angle f = m\angle d = \mathbf{105°}$

g. $m\angle g = m\angle e = \mathbf{75°}$

h. $m\angle A = m\angle C = \mathbf{60°}$

i. $m\angle ADB = 180° - (90° + 60°) = 180° - 150° = \mathbf{30°}$

j. $m\angle ABC = 180° - 60° = \mathbf{120°}$

Lesson 61, Mixed Practice

1. $\frac{1}{2}$ gallon = 2 quarts = 4 pints

$4\overline{)\$1.12}$ = **\$0.28 per pint**

2.

	Ratio	Actual Count
Oatmeal	2	3 cups
Brown sugar	1	B

$$\frac{2}{1} = \frac{3\text{ cups}}{B}$$

$$2B = 1(3\text{ cups})$$

$$B = \frac{3}{2}\text{ cups} = \mathbf{1\frac{1}{2}\text{ cups}}$$

3. $3(55.0\text{ seconds}) = 165\text{ seconds}$

$54.3\text{ seconds} + 56.1\text{ seconds} + n = 165\text{ seconds}$

$n = 165\text{ seconds} - 110.4\text{ seconds}$

$n = \mathbf{54.6\text{ seconds}}$

4. $\frac{9\text{ miles}}{60\text{ minutes}} = \frac{9\text{ miles}}{1\text{ hour}} = \mathbf{9\text{ miles per hour}}$

5.
$$\begin{array}{r} 63{,}100{,}000 \\ -\ \ 7{,}060{,}000 \\ \hline 56{,}040{,}000 \end{array}$$

$56{,}040{,}000 = \mathbf{5.604 \times 10^7}$

6. (a) $\frac{7}{10} \times 100\% = \frac{700\%}{10} = \mathbf{70\%}$

(b) $\frac{\text{news area}}{\text{advertisement area}} = \mathbf{\frac{3}{7}}$

(c) $\frac{\text{advertisement area}}{\text{total area}} = \mathbf{\frac{7}{10}}$

7. (a) $\mathbf{1.05 \times 10^{-3}}$

(b) **302,000**

8. $\frac{128}{192} = \frac{\cancel{2}\cdot\cancel{2}\cdot\cancel{2}\cdot\cancel{2}\cdot\cancel{2}\cdot\cancel{2}\cdot 2}{\cancel{2}\cdot\cancel{2}\cdot\cancel{2}\cdot\cancel{2}\cdot\cancel{2}\cdot\cancel{2}\cdot 3} = \mathbf{\frac{2}{3}}$

9. $\mathbf{1760\ \cancel{\text{yards}} \cdot \frac{3\text{ feet}}{1\ \cancel{\text{yard}}} = 5280\text{ feet}}$

10. (a) **Parallelogram**

(b) **Trapezoid**

11. (a) Area $= (4\text{ m})(6\text{ m}) = \mathbf{24\text{ m}^2}$

(b) Area $= \frac{(2\text{ m})(4\text{ m})}{2} = \mathbf{4\text{ m}^2}$

(c) Area $= 24\text{ m}^2 + 4\text{ m}^2 = \mathbf{28\text{ m}^2}$

12. (a) **Obtuse angle**

(b) **Right angle**

(c) **Acute angle**

13. (a) **8**

(b) **6**

(c) **9**

(d) **2**

14. (a) Perimeter = 12 cm + 16 cm + 12 cm + 16 cm = **56 cm**

(b) Area = (16 cm)(10 cm) = **160 cm²**

(c)

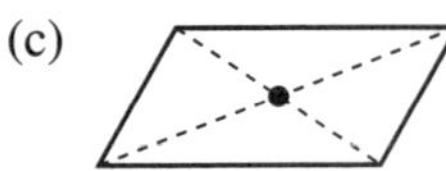

15. (a) $m\angle a = 180° - (59° + 61°) = 180° - 120° = \mathbf{60°}$

(b) $m\angle b = \mathbf{61°}$

(c) $m\angle c = \mathbf{59°}$

(d) $m\angle d = m\angle a = \mathbf{60°}$

16. $2 \cancel{\text{centimeters}} \cdot \dfrac{1 \text{ meter}}{100 \cancel{\text{centimeters}}} = \dfrac{2}{100} \text{ meter} = \mathbf{0.02 \text{ meter}}$

17.

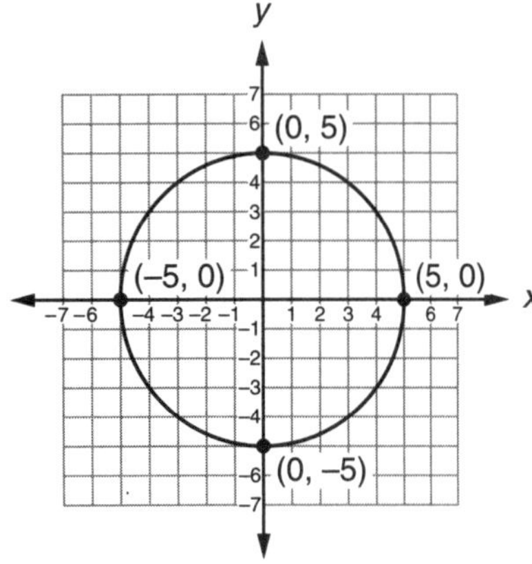

(a) **(0, 5), (0, −5)**

(b) **10 units**

18. **The scale is balanced so the 3 items on the left have a total mass of 50 g. The labeled masses total 15 g, so the cube must be 35 g because 35 g + 15 g = 50 g.**

19.

200, 180, 160, 140, 120, 100, 80, 60, 40, 20, sea level, −20, −40

+164 feet

−27 feet

$$\begin{array}{r} 164 \text{ feet} \\ +\ \ 27 \text{ feet} \\ \hline \mathbf{191 \text{ feet}} \end{array}$$

20.
$$\begin{aligned} &10 + 10 \times 10 - 10 \div 10 \\ &10 + 100 - 1 \\ &110 - 1 \\ &\mathbf{109} \end{aligned}$$

21. $2^0 - 2^{-3} = 1 - \dfrac{1}{2^3} = 1 - \dfrac{1}{8} = \dfrac{8}{8} - \dfrac{1}{8} = \mathbf{\dfrac{7}{8}}$

22. 70 cm = 0.7 m

$$\begin{array}{r} 4.5 \text{ m} \\ +\ 0.7 \text{ m} \\ \hline \mathbf{5.2 \text{ m}} \end{array}$$

23. $2.75 \cancel{L} \cdot \dfrac{1000 \text{ mL}}{1 \cancel{L}} = \mathbf{2750 \text{ mL}}$

24.
$$\begin{array}{rcl} 3\frac{1}{3} & = & 3\frac{2}{6} \\ -\ 1\frac{1}{2} & = & 1\frac{3}{6} \\ \hline \end{array} \longrightarrow \begin{array}{r} 2\frac{8}{6} \\ -\ 1\frac{3}{6} \\ \hline 1\frac{5}{6} \end{array}$$

$$\begin{array}{rcl} 5\frac{7}{8} & = & 5\frac{21}{24} \\ +\ 1\frac{5}{6} & = & 1\frac{20}{24} \\ \hline & & 6\frac{41}{24} = \mathbf{7\frac{17}{24}} \end{array}$$

25. $4\dfrac{4}{5} \cdot 1\dfrac{1}{9} \cdot 1\dfrac{7}{8}$

$= \dfrac{\overset{1}{\cancel{\overset{3}{\cancel{24}}}}}{\underset{1}{\cancel{5}}} \cdot \dfrac{10}{\underset{1}{\cancel{\underset{3}{\cancel{9}}}}} \cdot \dfrac{\overset{1}{\cancel{\overset{3}{\cancel{15}}}}}{\underset{1}{\cancel{8}}} = \mathbf{10}$

26. $3\dfrac{1}{5} \div 8 = \dfrac{16}{5} \div \dfrac{8}{1} = \dfrac{\overset{2}{\cancel{16}}}{5} \times \dfrac{1}{\underset{1}{\cancel{8}}} = \dfrac{2}{5}$

$6\dfrac{2}{3} \div \dfrac{2}{5} = \dfrac{20}{3} \div \dfrac{2}{5} = \dfrac{\overset{10}{\cancel{20}}}{3} \times \dfrac{5}{\underset{1}{\cancel{2}}} = \dfrac{50}{3}$

$= \mathbf{16\dfrac{2}{3}}$

27.
$$\begin{array}{r} 0.8 \\ +\ 0.97 \\ \hline 1.77 \end{array} \qquad \begin{array}{r} 12.00 \\ -\ \ 1.77 \\ \hline \mathbf{10.23} \end{array}$$

28.
$$\begin{array}{r} 0.05 \\ \times\ \ 2.4 \\ \hline 0.12 \end{array} \qquad \begin{array}{r} 0.005 \\ \times\ \ 0.12 \\ \hline \mathbf{0.0006} \end{array}$$

29. $4 \times 10^2 = 4 \times 100 = 400$
$0.2 \div 400 = \mathbf{0.0005}$

30. $4 \div 0.25 = 16$
$0.36 \div 16 = \mathbf{0.0225}$

Lesson 62, Lesson Practice

a. **Right triangle**

b. **Obtuse triangle**

c. **Acute triangle**

d. **Scalene triangle**

e. **Equilateral triangle**

f. **Isosceles triangle**

g. Perimeter = 3 cm + 4 cm + 4 cm = **11 cm**

h. $\angle L, \angle N, \angle M$

Lesson 62, Mixed Practice

1. 4(15 minutes) = 60 minutes
60 minutes + 10 minutes = 70 minutes
= 1 hour 10 minutes
2:40 p.m.

2.
$$\begin{array}{r} 40{,}060 \text{ miles} \\ -\ 39{,}872 \text{ miles} \\ \hline \mathbf{188 \text{ miles}} \end{array}$$

3. $\dfrac{188 \text{ miles}}{8 \text{ gallons}} = \mathbf{23.5 \text{ miles per gallon}}$

4. $24 \cdot w = 288$
$w = 12$
$24 \div 12 = \mathbf{2}$

5.

	Ratio	Actual Count
Bolsheviks	9	144
Czarists	8	C

$\dfrac{9}{8} = \dfrac{144}{C}$
$9C = 1152$
$C = \mathbf{128 \text{ czarists}}$

6.

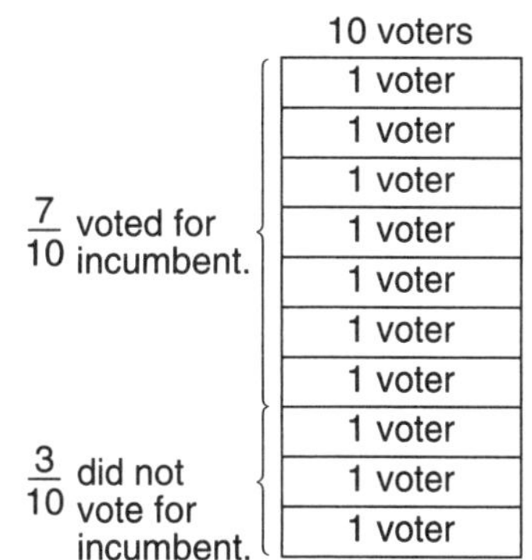

(a) $\dfrac{7}{10} \times 100\% = \dfrac{700\%}{10} = \mathbf{70\%}$

(b) $\mathbf{\dfrac{3}{10}}$

7. $\mathbf{W_N = \dfrac{5}{6} \times 3\dfrac{1}{3}}$

$W_N = \dfrac{5}{\cancel{6}_3} \times \dfrac{\cancel{10}^5}{3} = \dfrac{25}{9} = \mathbf{2\dfrac{7}{9}}$

8.
$$\begin{array}{r} \$10{,}000 \\ \times\ \ 0.085 \\ \hline 50\ 000 \\ 800\ 00 \\ \hline \$850.000 \end{array} = \$850$$
$\$10{,}000 + \$850 = \mathbf{\$10{,}850}$

9. **186,000; one hundred eighty-six thousand**

10. 1 quart $\textcircled{<}$ 1 liter

11.

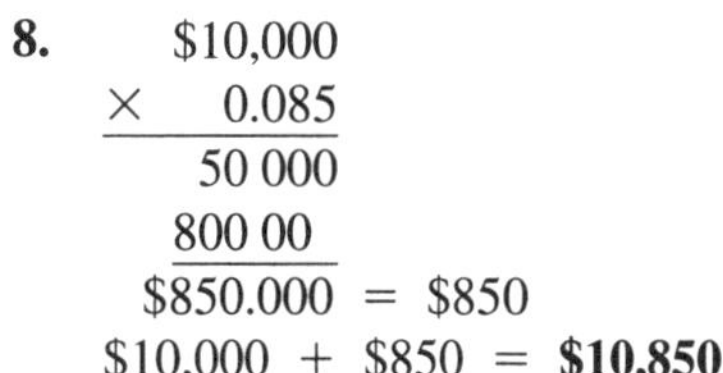

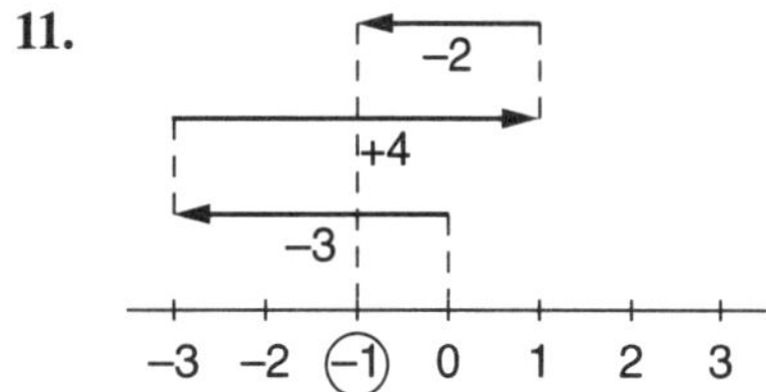

12. (a) $8\overline{)5.000}$ = **0.625**

(b) $\frac{5}{8} \times 100\% = \frac{500\%}{8} = \mathbf{62\frac{1}{2}\%}$

(c) $275\% = \frac{275}{100} = \frac{11}{4} = \mathbf{2\frac{3}{4}}$

(d) $275\% = \frac{275}{100} = \mathbf{2.75}$

13. $(12) + \frac{(12)}{(3)} - 3 =$

$12 + 4 - 3 = 16 - 3 = \mathbf{13}$

14. (a) 2^8

(b) 2^2

(c) 2^0

(d) 2^{-2}

15. (a) **ΔZWY**

(b) **ΔWYX**

(c) **ΔZWX**

16.

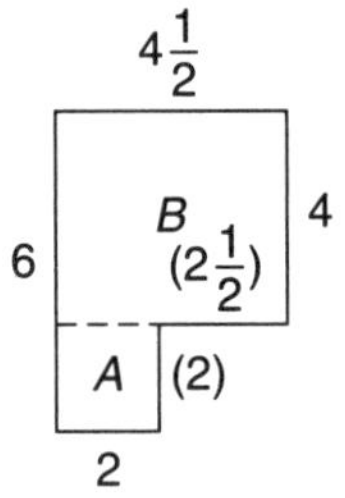

Figure: top $4\frac{1}{2}$; right 4; left 6; B $(2\frac{1}{2})$; A (2); bottom 2

(a) Perimeter $= 4\frac{1}{2}$ in. + 4 in. + $2\frac{1}{2}$ in. + 2 in. + 2 in. + 6 in. = **21 in.**

(b)
Area A = (2 in.)(2 in.) = 4 in.^{2}
+ Area B = ($4\frac{1}{2}$ in.)(4 in.) = 18 in.^{2}
Area of figure = **22 in.^{2}**

17. (a) **Isosceles triangle**

(b) $\frac{180° - 90°}{2} = \frac{90°}{2} = \mathbf{45°}$

(c) Area $= \frac{(6\text{ cm})(6\text{ cm})}{2} = \mathbf{18\text{ cm}^2}$

(d) **∠C**

18. $7\overline{)1.428}$ = **0.204**

19.
$$\frac{30}{70} = \frac{w}{\$2.10}$$
$$70w = 30(\$2.10)$$
$$w = \frac{\$63.00}{70}$$
$$w = \mathbf{\$0.90}$$

20. $5^2 + 2^5 - \sqrt{49} = 25 + 32 - 7 = \mathbf{50}$

21. $3(8) - (5)(2) + 10 \div 2$
$24 - 10 + 5$
$14 + 5$
19

22.

	1 yd	2 ft	$3\frac{3}{4}$ in.
+		2 ft	$6\frac{1}{2}$ in.
	1 yd	4 ft	$10\frac{1}{4}$ in.

4 ft = 1 yd 1 ft

	1 yd	1 ft	$10\frac{1}{4}$ in.
+	1 yd		
	2 yd	**1 ft**	**$10\frac{1}{4}$ in.**

23. 1 L = 1000 mL,
1000 mL − 50 mL = **950 mL**

24. $\frac{\overset{1}{\cancel{60}}\text{ mi}}{\cancel{1}\text{ hr}} \cdot \frac{\cancel{1}\text{ hr}}{\underset{1}{\cancel{60}}\text{ min}} = \mathbf{1\frac{mi}{min}}$

25.
$$2\frac{7}{24} = 2\frac{28}{96}$$
$$+\ 3\frac{9}{32} = 3\frac{27}{96}$$
$$\mathbf{5\frac{55}{96}}$$

26. $4\frac{1}{5} \div 1\frac{3}{4} = \frac{21}{5} \div \frac{7}{4} = \frac{\overset{3}{\cancel{21}}}{5} \times \frac{4}{\underset{1}{\cancel{7}}} = \frac{12}{5}$

$2\frac{2}{5} \div \frac{12}{5} = \frac{12}{5} \div \frac{12}{5} = \frac{\overset{1}{\cancel{12}}}{\underset{1}{\cancel{5}}} \times \frac{\overset{1}{\cancel{5}}}{\underset{1}{\cancel{12}}} = \mathbf{1}$

27. $7\frac{1}{2} \div \frac{2}{3} = \frac{15}{2} \div \frac{2}{3}$

$= \frac{15}{2} \times \frac{3}{2} = \frac{45}{4} = 11\frac{1}{4}$

$$\begin{array}{rcr} 20 & \longrightarrow & 19\frac{4}{4} \\ -\ 11\frac{1}{4} & & -\ 11\frac{1}{4} \\ \hline & & \mathbf{8\frac{3}{4}} \end{array}$$

28.

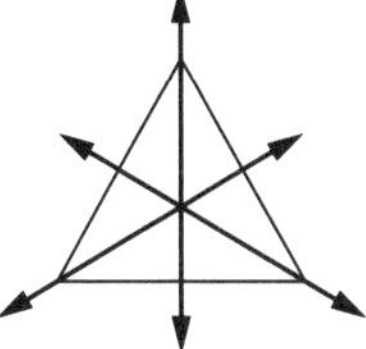

29. $|3 - 4| = |-1| = \mathbf{1}$

30.

$$\begin{array}{r} 1000 \text{ g} \\ -\ \ 250 \text{ g} \\ \hline \mathbf{750\ g} \end{array}$$

Lesson 63, Lesson Practice

a. $30 - [40 - (10 - 2)]$

$30 - [40 - (8)]$

$30 - [32]$

$\mathbf{-2}$

b. $100 - 3[2(6 - 2)]$

$100 - 3[2(4)]$

$100 - 3[8]$

$100 - 24$

$\mathbf{76}$

c. $\dfrac{10 + 9 \cdot 8 - 7}{6 \cdot 5 - 4 - 3 + 2}$

$\dfrac{10 + 72 - 7}{30 - 4 - 3 + 2}$

$\dfrac{75}{25}$

$\mathbf{3}$

d. $\dfrac{1 + 2(3 + 4) - 5}{10 - 9(8 - 7)}$

$\dfrac{1 + 14 - 5}{10 - 9}$

$\dfrac{10}{1}$

$\mathbf{10}$

e. $12 + 3(8 - |-2|)$

$12 + 3(8 - 2)$

$12 + 3(6)$

$12 + 18$

$\mathbf{30}$

Lesson 63, Mixed Practice

1. $\$6(3) + \$6(2\frac{1}{2}) = \$18 + \$15 = \mathbf{\$33}$

2. $30 \text{ min} \cdot \dfrac{70 \text{ times}}{1 \text{ min}} = 2100 \text{ times}$

$30 \text{ min} \cdot \dfrac{150 \text{ times}}{1 \text{ min}} = 4500 \text{ times}$

$$\begin{array}{r} 4500 \text{ times} \\ -\ 2100 \text{ times} \\ \hline \mathbf{2400\ times} \end{array}$$

3.

	Ratio	Actual Count
Brachiopods	2	B
Trilobites	9	720

$\dfrac{2}{9} = \dfrac{B}{720}$

$9B = 2 \cdot 720$

$B = \mathbf{160\ brachiopods}$

4. $5 \text{ days} \cdot \dfrac{18 \text{ miles}}{1 \text{ day}} = 90 \text{ miles}$

$$\begin{array}{r} 90 \text{ miles} \\ 16 \text{ miles} \\ +\ 21 \text{ miles} \\ \hline 127 \text{ miles} \end{array}$$

$$\begin{array}{r} 1017 \text{ miles} \\ -\ \ 127 \text{ miles} \\ \hline \mathbf{890\ miles} \end{array}$$

5.

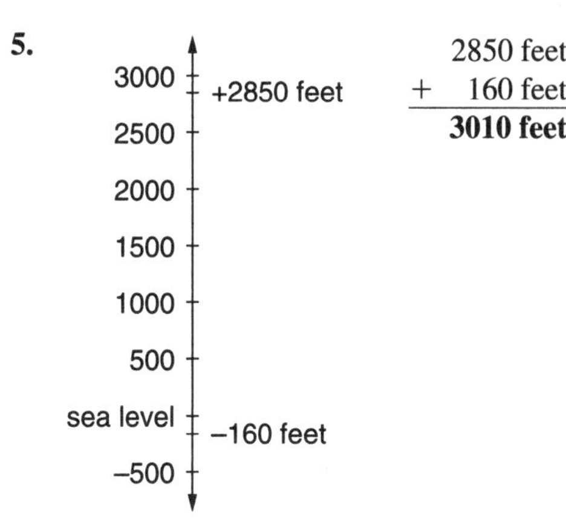

$$\begin{array}{r} 2850 \text{ feet} \\ +\ \ 160 \text{ feet} \\ \hline \mathbf{3010\ feet} \end{array}$$

6. **One hundred forty-nine million, six hundred thousand kilometers**

7.

40 cars	
$\frac{3}{10}$ were tankers.	4 cars
	4 cars
	4 cars
$\frac{7}{10}$ were not tankers.	4 cars
	4 cars
	4 cars
	4 cars
	4 cars
	4 cars
	4 cars

(a) $\mathbf{\frac{3}{10}}$

(b) $\frac{7}{10} \times 100\% = \frac{700\%}{10} = \mathbf{70\%}$

8. **Two thousandths mile per hour**

9. $\mathbf{1.5\ \cancel{km} \cdot \frac{1000\ m}{1\ \cancel{km}} = 1500\ m}$

10.

$$
\begin{array}{r}
363.3\ldots \\
12\overline{)4360.0\ldots} \\
\underline{36} \\
76 \\
\underline{72} \\
40 \\
\underline{36} \\
4\,0 \\
\underline{3\,6} \\
4
\end{array}
$$

$\mathbf{363.\overline{3}}$

11.

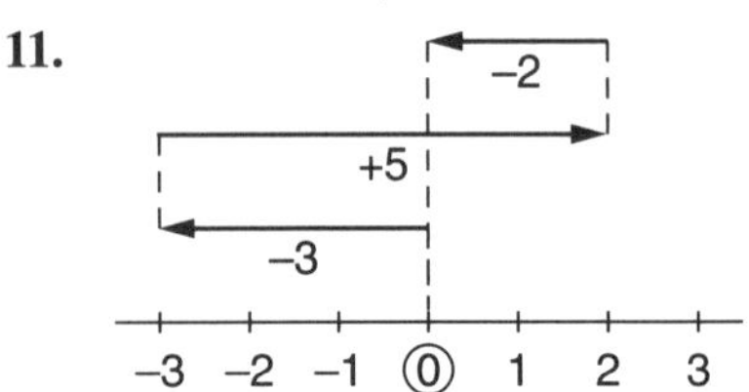

12. (a) $33\% = \mathbf{\frac{33}{100}}$

(b) $33\% = \frac{33}{100} = \mathbf{0.33}$

(c) $3\overline{)1.0}$ = $\mathbf{0.\overline{3}}$

(d) $\frac{1}{3} \times 100\% = \frac{100\%}{3} = \mathbf{33\frac{1}{3}\%}$

13. **Divide the "in" number by 3 to find the "out" number.**

14. $\frac{\text{red face card}}{\text{total cards}} = \frac{6}{52} = \mathbf{\frac{3}{26}}$

15. (a) **Isosceles triangle**

(b) Perimeter $= 5\text{ cm} + 5\text{ cm} + 5\text{ cm}$
$= \mathbf{15\ cm}$

(c) $\mathbf{\Delta ABC}$

16. (a) $m\angle BAC = \frac{180°}{3} = \mathbf{60°}$

(b) $m\angle ADB = \frac{180°}{3} = \mathbf{60°}$

(c) $m\angle BDC = 180° - 60° = \mathbf{120°}$

(d) $m\angle DBA = \frac{180°}{3} = \mathbf{60°}$

(e) $m\angle DBC = \frac{180° - 120°}{2} = \frac{60°}{2} = \mathbf{30°}$

(f) $m\angle DCB = m\angle DBC = \mathbf{30°}$

17. $\frac{\text{length of shortest side}}{\text{length of longest side}} = \frac{5}{10} = \mathbf{\frac{1}{2}}$

18.

$$
\begin{array}{rcl}
\frac{5}{18} & = & \frac{10}{36} \\
-\ \frac{1}{12} & = & \frac{3}{36} \\
\hline
 & & \mathbf{\frac{7}{36}}
\end{array}
$$

19. $2 \div 0.4 = \mathbf{5}$

20.
$$3[24 - (8 + 3 \cdot 2)] - \frac{6 + 4}{|-2|}$$
$$3[24 - (8 + 6)] - \frac{6 + 4}{2}$$
$$3[24 - (14)] - \frac{10}{2}$$
$$3[10] - 5$$
$$30 - 5$$
$$\mathbf{25}$$

21.
$$3^3 - \sqrt{3^2 + 4^2}$$
$$27 - \sqrt{9 + 16}$$
$$27 - \sqrt{25}$$
$$27 - 5$$
$$\mathbf{22}$$

22.
$$\begin{array}{rl} & \overset{0}{\cancel{1}}\text{ week } 2\text{ days } 7\text{ hr} \ \ (7\text{ days}) \\ - & 5\text{ days } 9\text{ hr} \\ \hline \end{array} \longrightarrow$$

$$\begin{array}{rl} & \overset{0}{\cancel{1}}\text{ week } \overset{8}{\cancel{9}}\!\!\!\!\overset{}{\cancel{2}}\text{ days } 7\text{ hr} \ \ (24\text{ hr}) \\ - & 5\text{ days } 9\text{ hr} \\ \hline \end{array} \longrightarrow$$

$$\begin{array}{rrrr} & \overset{0}{\cancel{1}}\text{ week} & \overset{8}{\cancel{9}}\!\!\cancel{2}\text{ days} & \overset{31}{\cancel{7}}\text{ hr} \\ - & & 5\text{ days} & 9\text{ hr} \\ \hline & & \mathbf{3\ days} & \mathbf{22\ hr} \end{array}$$

23. $\dfrac{20\text{ mi}}{1\ \cancel{\text{gal}}} \cdot \dfrac{1\ \cancel{\text{gal}}}{4\text{ qt}} = \mathbf{5\,\dfrac{mi}{qt}}$

24.
$$\begin{array}{rrl} & 4\frac{2}{3} = & 4\frac{12}{18} \\ & 3\frac{5}{6} = & 3\frac{15}{18} \\ + & 2\frac{5}{9} = & 2\frac{10}{18} \\ \hline & & 9\frac{37}{18} = \mathbf{11\frac{1}{18}} \end{array}$$

25. $12\frac{1}{2} \cdot 4\frac{4}{5} \cdot 3\frac{1}{3}$

$= \dfrac{\overset{5}{\cancel{25}}}{\underset{1}{\cancel{2}}} \cdot \dfrac{\overset{8}{\cancel{24}}}{\underset{1}{\cancel{5}}} \cdot \dfrac{\overset{5}{\cancel{10}}}{\underset{1}{\cancel{3}}} = \mathbf{200}$

26. $1\frac{2}{3} \div 3 = \frac{5}{3} \div \frac{3}{1}$

$= \frac{5}{3} \times \frac{1}{3} = \frac{5}{9}$

$$\begin{array}{rrl} & 6\frac{1}{3} = & 6\frac{3}{9} \\ - & \frac{5}{9} = & \frac{5}{9} \\ \hline \end{array} \longrightarrow \begin{array}{rr} & 5\frac{12}{9} \\ - & \frac{5}{9} \\ \hline & \mathbf{5\frac{7}{9}} \end{array}$$

27. $(3)^2 + 2(3)(4) + (4)^2$

$= 9 + 24 + 16 = \mathbf{49}$

28.

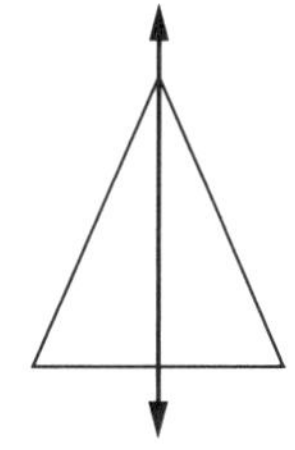

29. (a)

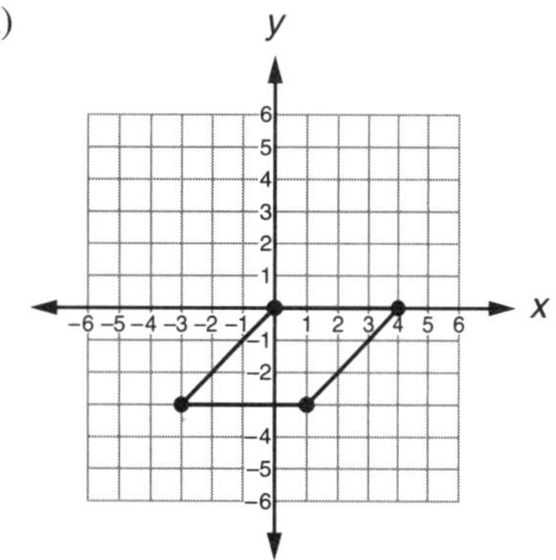

(b) Area = (4 units)(3 units)

= **12 sq. units**

(c) $\dfrac{180° - 90°}{2} = \dfrac{90°}{2} = \mathbf{45°}$

30. $\begin{array}{r} \mathbf{250\text{ g}} \\ 3\overline{)750\text{ g}} \end{array}$

Lesson 64, Lesson Practice

a. $(-56) + (+96) = \mathbf{+40}$

b. $(-28) + (-145) = \mathbf{-173}$

c. $(-5) + (+7) + (+9) + (-3)$

$(+2) + (+9) + (-3)$

$(+11) + (-3)$

$\mathbf{+8}$

d. $(-3) + (-8) + (+15)$

$(-11) + (+15)$

$\mathbf{+4}$

e. $(-12) + (-9) + (+16)$

$(-21) + (+16)$

$\mathbf{-5}$

f. $(+12) + (-18) + (+6)$

$(-6) + (+6)$

$\mathbf{0}$

g. $\left(-3\frac{5}{6}\right) + \left(+5\frac{1}{3}\right)$

$\left(-3\frac{5}{6}\right) + \left(+5\frac{2}{6}\right)$

$\left(-3\frac{5}{6}\right) + \left(+4\frac{8}{6}\right)$

$1\frac{3}{6} = \mathbf{1\frac{1}{2}}$

h. $(-1.6) + (-11.47)$
$\mathbf{-13.07}$

i. **(+\$250) + (−\$300) + (+\$525); The net result was a gain of \$475.**

Lesson 64, Mixed Practice

1.
$$\begin{array}{r} 2{,}000{,}000{,}000{,}000 \\ -\ \ 750{,}000{,}000{,}000 \\ \hline 1{,}250{,}000{,}000{,}000 \end{array}$$
$\mathbf{1.25 \times 10^{12}}$

2. $\$2.25 + \$0.15(42)$
$= \$2.25 + \$6.30 = \$8.55$
$\$10 - \$8.55 = $ **\$1.45**

3. $5(\$0.25) + 3(\$0.10) + 2(\$0.05)$
$= \$1.25 + \$0.30 + \$0.10$
$= \$1.65$

$$35\overline{)165.00}\ \ \text{quotient } 4.71$$
4 packages

4. $53 + 59 = $ **112**

5.
$$\begin{array}{r} 1.74 \\ 2.8 \\ 3.4 \\ 0.96 \\ 2 \\ +\ 1.22 \\ \hline 12.12 \end{array}$$
$12.12 \div 6 = $ **2.02**

6.

	1200 serfs
$\frac{2}{5}$ were conscripted.	240 serfs
	240 serfs
$\frac{3}{5}$ were not conscripted.	240 serfs
	240 serfs
	240 serfs

(a) **480 serfs**

(b) $\frac{3}{5} \times 100\% = \frac{300\%}{5} = \mathbf{60\%}$

7. $\mathbf{W_N = \frac{5}{9} \times 100}$

$W_N = \frac{500}{9}$

$W_N = \mathbf{55\frac{5}{9}}$

8. (a) **Sixteen million degrees Celsius**

(b) **Seven millionths meter**

9. (a) $1.6 \times 10^7 \ \textcircled{>}\ 7 \times 10^{-6}$

(b) $7 \times 10^{-6}\ \textcircled{>}\ 0$

(c) $2^{-3}\ \textcircled{<}\ 2^{-2}$

10.
$$\begin{array}{r} 16.285\ldots \\ 28\overline{)456.000\ldots} \\ \underline{28} \\ 176 \\ \underline{168} \\ 8\,0 \\ \underline{5\,6} \\ 2\,40 \\ \underline{2\,24} \\ 160 \\ \underline{140} \\ 20 \end{array}$$

(a) $\mathbf{16\frac{2}{7}}$

(b) **16.29**

(c) **16**

11. (a) $(-63) + (-14) = \mathbf{-77}$

(b) $(-16) + (+20) + (-32) = \mathbf{-28}$

12. $(-\$327) + (+\$280) = -\$47$; **a loss of \$47**

13. (a) **60°**

(b) **The chords are $\overline{AB}$ (or $\overline{BA}$), $\overline{BC}$ (or $\overline{CB}$), and $\overline{CA}$ (or $\overline{AC}$). Each chord is shorter than the diameter, which is the longest chord of a circle.**

14. $\left(\frac{2}{3}\right) + \left(\frac{2}{3}\right)\left(\frac{3}{4}\right)$

$= \frac{2}{3} + \frac{1}{2} = \frac{4}{6} + \frac{3}{6} = \frac{7}{6} = \mathbf{1\frac{1}{6}}$

15.

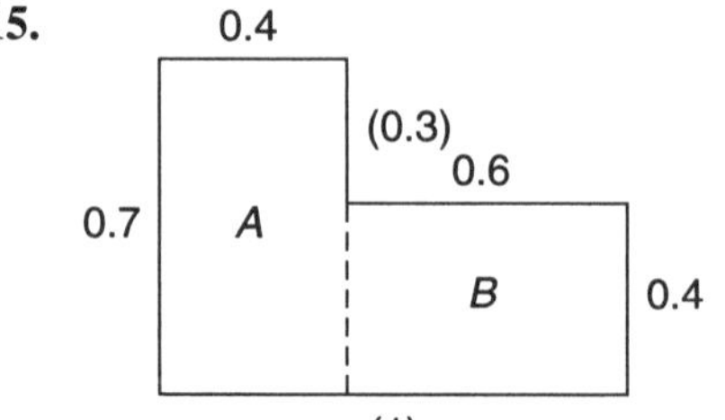

Perimeter $= 0.7\text{ m} + 0.4\text{ m} + 0.3\text{ m}$
$+ 0.6\text{ m} + 0.4\text{ m} + 1\text{ m} = \mathbf{3.4\text{ m}}$

16.
$$\begin{array}{lcl} \text{Area } A = (0.7\text{ m})(0.4\text{ m}) & = & 0.28\text{ m}^2 \\ +\ \text{Area } B = (0.6\text{ m})(0.4\text{ m}) & = & 0.24\text{ m}^2 \\ \hline \text{Area of figure} & = & \mathbf{0.52\text{ m}^2} \end{array}$$

17. $12x = 84 \qquad 12y = 48$
$x = 7 \qquad y = 4$
$7 \cdot 4 = \mathbf{28}$

18. 

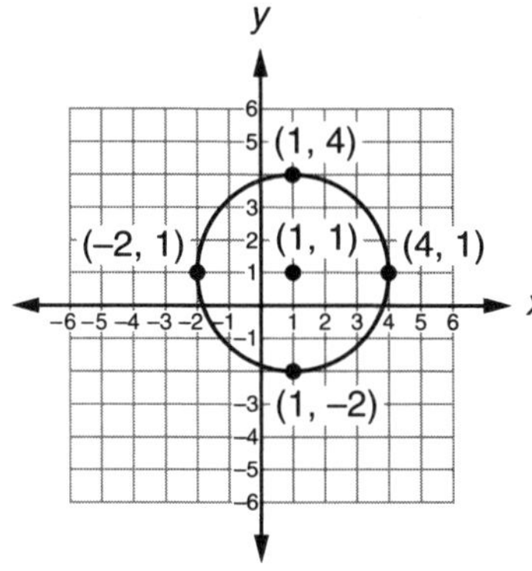

B. (−2, 1)

19. $\frac{4}{9} + \frac{2}{9} = \frac{6}{9} = \mathbf{\frac{2}{3}}$

20. $\frac{10}{25} = \mathbf{\frac{2}{5}}$ or **0.4**

21. $\frac{3^2 + 4^2}{\sqrt{3^2 + 4^2}} = \frac{9 + 16}{\sqrt{9 + 16}} = \frac{25}{\sqrt{25}} = \frac{25}{5}$
$= \mathbf{5}$

22. $6 \div 2\frac{1}{2} = \frac{6}{1} \div \frac{5}{2}$
$= \frac{6}{1} \times \frac{2}{5} = \frac{12}{5} = 2\frac{2}{5}$

$2\frac{4}{5} \div 2\frac{2}{5} = \frac{14}{5} \div \frac{12}{5}$
$= \frac{\overset{7}{\cancel{14}}}{\underset{1}{\cancel{5}}} \times \frac{\overset{1}{\cancel{5}}}{\underset{6}{\cancel{12}}} = \frac{7}{6} = \mathbf{1\frac{1}{6}}$

23. $100 - [20 + 5(4) + 3(2 + 4^0)]$
$100 - [20 + 20 + 3(2 + 1)]$
$100 - [20 + 20 + 9]$
$100 - [49]$
51

24.
$$\begin{array}{rrrrr} & 5\text{ gal} & 2\text{ qt} & 1\text{ pt} & 7\text{ oz} \\ + & 1\text{ gal} & 1\text{ qt} & 1\text{ pt} & 9\text{ oz} \\ \hline & 6\text{ gal} & 3\text{ qt} & 2\text{ pt} & 16\text{ oz} \end{array}$$
16 oz = 1 pt, 2 pt + 1 pt = 3 pt
3 pt = 1 qt 1 pt
$$\begin{array}{rrr} & 1\text{ qt} & 1\text{ pt} \\ + & 3\text{ qt} & \\ \hline & 4\text{ qt} & 1\text{ pt} \end{array}$$
4 qt = 1 gal, 6 gal + 1 gal = 7 gal, **7 gal 1 pt**

25. $\left(1\frac{1}{2}\right)^2 - \left(4 - 2\frac{1}{3}\right)$
$= \frac{9}{4} - \left(4 - 2\frac{1}{3}\right)$
$= 2\frac{1}{4} - \left(4 - 2\frac{1}{3}\right)$

$$\begin{array}{rcr} 4 & \longrightarrow & 3\frac{3}{3} \\ -\ 2\frac{1}{3} & & -\ 2\frac{1}{3} \\ \hline & & 1\frac{2}{3} \end{array}$$

$$\begin{array}{rcrcr} 2\frac{1}{4} & = & 2\frac{3}{12} & \longrightarrow & 1\frac{15}{12} \\ -\ 1\frac{2}{3} & = & 1\frac{8}{12} & & -\ 1\frac{8}{12} \\ \hline & & & & \mathbf{\frac{7}{12}} \end{array}$$

26.
$$\begin{array}{r} 0.010 \\ -\ 0.001 \\ \hline 0.009 \end{array} \qquad \begin{array}{r} 0.100 \\ -\ 0.009 \\ \hline \mathbf{0.091} \end{array}$$

27. $5.1 \div 1.5 = 3.4, 5.1 \div 3.4 = \mathbf{1.5}$

28. $5\overline{)1.0}$ = 0.2
$$\begin{array}{r} 4.375 \\ -\ 3.200 \\ \hline \mathbf{1.175} \end{array}$$

29. $\frac{\text{even primes}}{\text{total}} = \mathbf{\frac{1}{6}}$

30. a) $m\angle B = 180° - 58° = \mathbf{122°}$
b) $m\angle BCD = m\angle A = \mathbf{58°}$
c) $m\angle BCM = 180° - 58° = \mathbf{122°}$

Lesson 65, Lesson Practice

a.

	Ratio	Actual Count
Acrobats	3	*A*
Clowns	5	*C*
Total	8	72

$\frac{5}{8} = \frac{C}{72}$
$8C = 360$
$C =$ **45 clowns**

b.

	Ratio	Actual Count
Young men	8	240
Young women	9	W
Total	17	T

$$\frac{8}{17} = \frac{240}{T}$$
$$8T = 4080$$
$$T = \textbf{510 young people}$$

Lesson 65, Mixed Practice

1. (a) $\dfrac{\$2.40}{5 \text{ pounds}} = \dfrac{\$0.48}{1 \text{ pound}}$

$0.48 per pound

(b) $\$0.48 \times 8 = \mathbf{\$3.84}$

2. (a) $(0.3)(0.4) + (0.3)(0.5) = 0.12 + 0.15 = 0.27$

$0.3(0.4 + 0.5) = 0.3(0.9) = 0.27$

$\mathbf{0.27 = 0.27}$

(b) **Distributive property**

3.

	Ratio	Actual Count
Big fish	4	B
Little fish	11	L
Total	15	1320

$$\frac{4}{15} = \frac{B}{1320}$$
$$15B = 5280$$
$$B = \textbf{352 big fish}$$

4. $\dfrac{350 \text{ miles}}{15 \text{ gallons}} = 23.\overline{3}\,\dfrac{\text{miles}}{\text{gallon}}$

$\mathbf{23.\overline{3}\,\dfrac{miles}{gallon}}$

5. $\dfrac{1}{2} + \dfrac{1}{4} = \dfrac{2}{4} + \dfrac{1}{4} = \dfrac{3}{4}$

$\dfrac{3}{4} \div 2 = \dfrac{3}{4} \times \dfrac{1}{2} = \mathbf{\dfrac{3}{8}}$

6. $\mathbf{1.2 \times 10^{10}}$

7.

60 eggs
10 eggs
10 eggs
10 eggs
10 eggs
10 eggs
10 eggs

$\frac{1}{6}$ were cracked. (first 10 eggs)
$\frac{5}{6}$ were not cracked. (remaining five groups of 10 eggs)

a) **50 eggs**

b) $\dfrac{\text{cracked eggs}}{\text{uncracked eggs}} = \mathbf{\dfrac{1}{5}}$

c) $\dfrac{1}{6} \times 100\% = \mathbf{16\dfrac{2}{3}\%}$

8. a) One possibility:

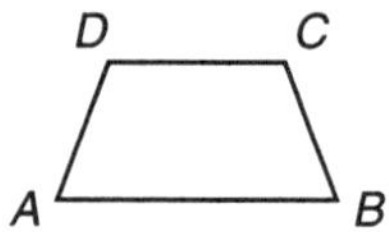

b) **Trapezoid**

9. a) $\text{Area} = \dfrac{(6 \text{ cm})(4 \text{ cm})}{2} = \mathbf{12 \text{ cm}^2}$

b) $\text{Area} = \dfrac{(6 \text{ cm})(4 \text{ cm})}{2} = \mathbf{12 \text{ cm}^2}$

c) $\text{Area} = \dfrac{(6 \text{ cm})(4 \text{ cm})}{2} = \mathbf{12 \text{ cm}^2}$

10. $0.76 + 0.88 = 1.64$

$1.64 \div 2 = \mathbf{0.82}$

11. $\mathbf{W_N = 0.75 \times 64}$

$W_N = \mathbf{48}$

12. $\mathbf{t = 0.08 \times \$7.40}$

$t = \mathbf{\$0.59}$

13. a) $(-3) + (-8) = \mathbf{-11}$

b) $(+3) + (-8) = \mathbf{-5}$

c) $(-3) + (+8) + (-5) = \mathbf{0}$

14.

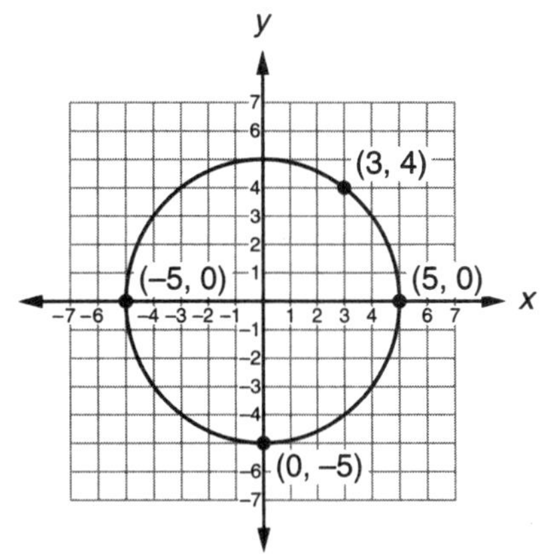

a) **(5, 0), (−5, 0)**

b) **10 units**

15. $\mathbf{0.95\ \cancel{liters} \cdot \frac{1000\ milliliters}{1\ \cancel{liter}}}$
$= \mathbf{950\ milliliters}$

16. $(5)(0.2) + 5 + \frac{5}{0.2}$
$= 1 + 5 + 25 = \mathbf{31}$

17. **27 blocks**

18. a) $\angle COD$ or $\angle DOC$

b) $\angle AOB$ or $\angle BOA$

19. $20 \times 5 = \mathbf{100}$

20. a) $m\angle A = 180° - (62° + 59°)$
$= 180° - 121° = \mathbf{59°}$

b) $\overline{AB}$ or $\overline{BA}$

c) **Isosceles triangle**

d) ***C***

21. a) **Arrange the numbers in order, and look for the middle number. Since there is an even number of scores, there are two middle numbers. So the median is the mean of the two middle numbers.**

b) $16 + 17 = 33$
$33 \div 2 = \mathbf{16.5}$

22. a) **False**

b) **True**

23.
$$\begin{array}{r} 2.20 \text{ meters} \\ -\ 2.15 \text{ meters} \\ \hline 0.05 \text{ meters} \end{array} = \mathbf{5\ centimeters}$$

24. $\frac{10^3 \cdot 10^3}{10^2} = \frac{10^6}{10^2} = \mathbf{10^4\ or\ 10{,}000}$

25.
$$\begin{array}{rrr} \overset{3}{\cancel{4}} \text{ days} & \overset{4}{\cancel{8}} \text{ hr} & 15 \text{ min} \\ -\ 1 \text{ day} & 7 \text{ hr} & 50 \text{ min} \\ \hline \end{array} \longrightarrow$$
(24 hr) (60 min)

$$\begin{array}{rrr} \overset{3}{\cancel{4}} \text{ days} & \overset{28}{\cancel{\overset{4}{\cancel{8}}}} \text{ hr} & \overset{75}{\cancel{15}} \text{ min} \\ -\ 1 \text{ day} & 7 \text{ hr} & 50 \text{ min} \\ \hline \mathbf{2\ days} & \mathbf{21\ hr} & \mathbf{25\ min} \end{array}$$

26. $4.5 \div (0.4 + 0.5) = 4.5 \div 0.9 = \mathbf{5}$

27. $\frac{3 + 0.6}{3 - 0.6} = \frac{3.6}{2.4} = \mathbf{1.5}$

28. $1\frac{1}{6} \cdot 3 = \frac{7}{\underset{2}{\cancel{6}}} \cdot \frac{\overset{1}{\cancel{3}}}{1} = \frac{7}{2} = 3\frac{1}{2}$

$4\frac{1}{5} \div 3\frac{1}{2} = \frac{21}{5} \div \frac{7}{2}$

$= \frac{\overset{3}{\cancel{21}}}{5} \times \frac{2}{\underset{1}{\cancel{7}}} = \frac{6}{5} = \mathbf{1\frac{1}{5}}$

29. $3^2 + \sqrt{4 \cdot 7 - 3}$
$= 9 + \sqrt{28 - 3}$
$= 9 + \sqrt{25} = 9 + 5 = \mathbf{14}$

30. $|-3| + 4[(5 - 2)(3 + 1)]$
$3 + 4[(3)(4)]$
$3 + 4[12]$
$3 + 48$
$\mathbf{51}$

Lesson 66, Lesson Practice

a. $C = \pi d$
$C \approx 3.14(8 \text{ in.})$
$C \approx \mathbf{25.12\ in.}$

b. $C = \pi d$
$C \approx \frac{22}{7}(42 \text{ mm})$
$C \approx \mathbf{132\ mm}$

c. $C = \pi d$
$C = \pi(4 \text{ ft})$
$C = \mathbf{4\pi \text{ ft}}$

d. $C = \pi d$
$C \approx 3.14(6 \text{ inches})$
$C \approx \mathbf{18.84 \text{ inches}}$

Lesson 66, Mixed Practice

1. $100\% - (42\% + 25\%) = \mathbf{33\%}$

$$\begin{array}{r} \$25{,}000 \\ \times \quad 0.25 \\ \hline \mathbf{\$6250} \end{array}$$

2. $10\left(1\frac{1}{4} \text{ miles}\right) = \frac{25}{2} \text{ miles} = \mathbf{12\frac{1}{2} \text{ miles}}$

3. $(1.9)(2.2) - (1.9 + 2.2) = 4.18 - 4.1$
$= \mathbf{0.08}$

4.

	Ratio	Actual Count
Dimes	5	D
Quarters	8	Q
Total	13	520

$\frac{5}{13} = \frac{D}{520}$
$13D = 2600$
$D = \mathbf{200 \text{ dimes}}$

5. $\mathbf{9 \times 10^8}$ **miles**

6.

400 acres

40 acres
40 acres
40 acres
40 acres
40 acres
40 acres
40 acres
40 acres
40 acres
40 acres

$\frac{3}{10}$ were planted with alfalfa. (first 3 rows)
$\frac{7}{10}$ were not planted with alfalfa. (remaining 7 rows)

(a) $\frac{3}{10} \times 100\% = \frac{300\%}{10} = \mathbf{30\%}$

(b) **280 acres**

7. (a) $\frac{12}{30} = \mathbf{\frac{2}{5}}$

(b) $\frac{2}{5} \times 100\% = \frac{200\%}{5} = \mathbf{40\%}$

(c) **It is more likely that the grade on a randomly selected test is not an A, because less than half the tests have A's.**

8. (a) $C = \pi d$
$C \approx 3.14(21 \text{ in.})$
$C \approx \mathbf{65.94 \text{ in.}}$

(b) $C = \pi d$
$C \approx \frac{22}{7}(21 \text{ in.})$
$C \approx \mathbf{66 \text{ in.}}$

9. (a) Area $= (14 \text{ cm})(24 \text{ cm}) = \mathbf{336 \text{ cm}^2}$

(b) Area $= \frac{(14 \text{ cm})(24 \text{ cm})}{2} = \mathbf{168 \text{ cm}^2}$

(c) Perimeter $= 25 \text{ cm} + 14 \text{ cm} + 25 \text{ cm}$
$= \mathbf{64 \text{ cm}}$

10. $\mathbf{3.25 \times 10^{10}}$

11. $\mathbf{W_N = 0.9 \times 3500}$
$W_N = \mathbf{3150}$

12. $\mathbf{W_N = \frac{5}{6} \times 2\frac{2}{5}}$

$W_N = \frac{\overset{1}{\cancel{5}}}{\underset{1}{\cancel{6}}} \times \frac{\overset{2}{\cancel{12}}}{\underset{1}{\cancel{5}}}$

$W_N = \mathbf{2}$

13. (a) $0.45 = \frac{45}{100} = \mathbf{\frac{9}{20}}$

(b) $0.45 = \frac{45}{100} = \mathbf{45\%}$

(c) $7.5\% = \frac{7.5}{100} = \mathbf{\frac{3}{40}}$

(d) $7.5\% = \frac{7.5}{100} = \mathbf{0.075}$

14. (a) $(5) + (-4) + (6) + (-1)$
$= 1 + (6) + (-1)$
$= 7 + (-1) = \mathbf{6}$

(b) $3 + (-5) + (+4) + (-2)$
$= -2 + (+4) + (-2)$
$= 2 + (-2) = \mathbf{0}$

15. $1.4\ \cancel{\text{kilograms}} \cdot \dfrac{1000\text{ grams}}{1\ \cancel{\text{kilogram}}} = \mathbf{1400\ grams}$

16. (a) $m\angle a = 180° - (90° + 35°)$
$= 180° - 125° = \mathbf{55°}$

(b) $m\angle b = m\angle a = \mathbf{55°}$

(c) $m\angle c = 180° - 55° = \mathbf{125°}$

(d) $m\angle d = m\angle b = \mathbf{55°}$

(e) $m\angle e = m\angle c = \mathbf{125°}$

17. $(3000)(500)(20) = \mathbf{30{,}000{,}000}$

18.

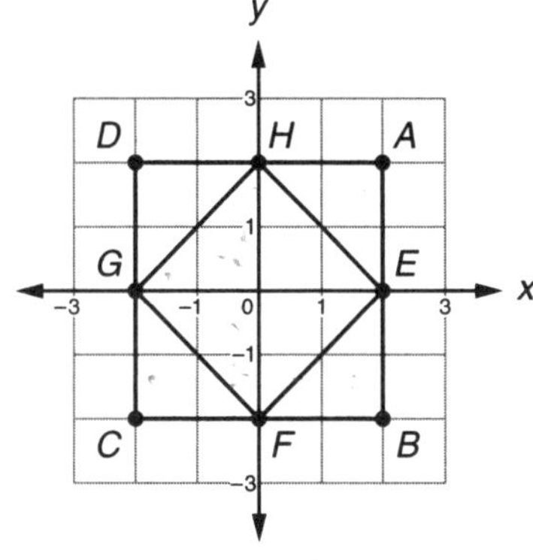

(a) Area = (4 units)(4 units) = **16 units²**

(b) **4 units**

(c) Area $= 4(1\text{ unit}^2) + 8\left(\frac{1}{2}\text{ unit}^2\right)$
$= 4\text{ units}^2 + 4\text{ units}^2 = \mathbf{8\ units^2}$

(d) $\sqrt{8}$ **units**

19. $\dfrac{0.9}{1.5} = \dfrac{12}{n}$

$0.9n = 1.5(12)$

$n = \dfrac{18}{0.9}$

$n = \mathbf{20}$

20. $\dfrac{11}{12} = \dfrac{22}{24}$

$-\dfrac{11}{24} = \dfrac{11}{24}$

$\mathbf{\dfrac{11}{24}}$

21. $2^1 - 2^0 - 2^{-1} = 2 - 1 - \dfrac{1}{2}$

$= 1 - \dfrac{1}{2} = \dfrac{2}{2} - \dfrac{1}{2} = \mathbf{\dfrac{1}{2}}$

22.
```
  4 lb   12 oz
+ 1 lb    7 oz
  5 lb   19 oz
19 oz = 1 lb 3 oz
  1 lb    3 oz
+ 5 lb
  6 lb    3 oz
```
6 lb 3 oz

23. $\dfrac{3\ \cancel{\text{ft}}}{1\text{ yd}} \cdot \dfrac{12\text{ in.}}{1\ \cancel{\text{ft}}} = \mathbf{36\ \dfrac{in.}{yd}}$

24. $16 \div (0.8 \div 0.04) = 16 \div 20 = \mathbf{0.8}$

25. $0.4[0.5 - (0.6)(0.7)]$
$0.4[0.5 - 0.42]$
$0.4[0.08]$
$\mathbf{0.032}$

26. $\dfrac{3}{8} \cdot 1\dfrac{2}{3} \cdot 4 \div 1\dfrac{2}{3}$

$= \left(\dfrac{\overset{1}{\cancel{3}}}{8} \cdot \dfrac{5}{\underset{1}{\cancel{3}}}\right) \cdot \dfrac{4}{1} \div \dfrac{5}{3}$

$= \dfrac{5}{\underset{2}{\cancel{8}}} \cdot \dfrac{\overset{1}{\cancel{4}}}{1} \div \dfrac{5}{3} = \dfrac{5}{2} \div \dfrac{5}{3}$

$= \dfrac{\overset{1}{\cancel{5}}}{2} \times \dfrac{3}{\underset{1}{\cancel{5}}} = \dfrac{3}{2} = \mathbf{1\dfrac{1}{2}}$

27. $30 - 5[4 + (3)(2) - 5]$
$30 - 5[4 + 6 - 5]$
$30 - 5[10 - 5]$
$30 - 5[5]$
$30 - 25$
$\mathbf{5}$

28. **One possibility: If a dozen flavored icicles cost $2.88, what is the price of each flavored icicle?**

29. $\dfrac{9\text{ ounces}}{2} = \mathbf{4\dfrac{1}{2}\ ounces}$

30. (a) $\overline{AB}$ **or** $\overline{BA}$**,**
$\overline{BC}$ **or** $\overline{CB}$

(b) **Isosceles triangle**

(c) **90°**

Lesson 67, Lesson Practice

a. **Triangular prism**

b. **Cone**

c. **Rectangular prism**

d. **5 faces**

e. **9 edges**

f. **6 vertices**

g.

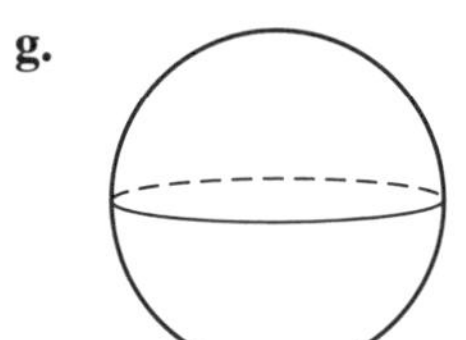

h.

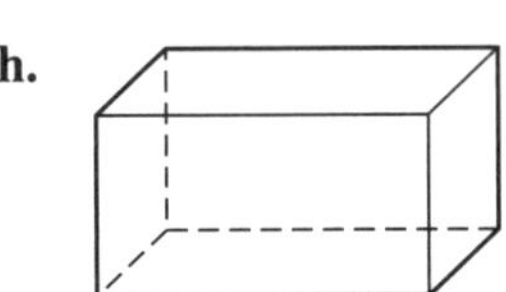

i.

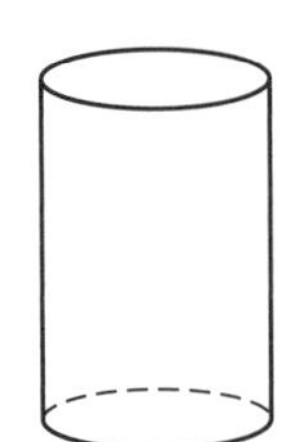

j. **Triangular prism**

k. $3 \text{ cm} \times 3 \text{ cm} = 9 \text{ cm}^2$
$6 \times 9 \text{ cm}^2 = \mathbf{54\ cm^2}$

Lesson 67, Mixed Practice

1. (a) $\dfrac{\text{red marbles}}{\text{blue marbles}} = \dfrac{20}{40} = \mathbf{\dfrac{1}{2}}$

(b) $\dfrac{\text{white marbles}}{\text{red marbles}} = \dfrac{30}{20} = \mathbf{\dfrac{3}{2}}$

(c) $\dfrac{\text{not white marbles}}{\text{total marbles}} = \dfrac{60}{90} = \mathbf{\dfrac{2}{3}}$

2. $$\left(\frac{1}{3} + \frac{1}{2}\right) - \left(\frac{1}{3} \times \frac{1}{2}\right) = \left(\frac{2}{6} + \frac{3}{6}\right) - \left(\frac{1}{6}\right) = \frac{5}{6} - \frac{1}{6} = \frac{4}{6} = \mathbf{\frac{2}{3}}$$

3. $180 \text{ pounds} - 165\frac{1}{2} \text{ pounds} = \mathbf{14\frac{1}{2}\ pounds}$

4. (a)
$$\begin{array}{r} 94 \text{ points} \\ 85 \text{ points} \\ +\ 85 \text{ points} \\ \hline 264 \text{ points} \end{array}$$

$264 \div 3 = $ **88 points**

(b) $5(92 \text{ points}) = 460 \text{ points}$
$460 \text{ points} + 264 \text{ points} = 724 \text{ points}$

$724.0 \div 8 = $ **90.5 points**

5.

	Ratio	Actual Count
Diamonds	5	D
Rubies	2	R
Total	7	210

$\dfrac{5}{7} = \dfrac{D}{210}$
$7D = 1050$
$D = $ **150 diamonds**

6.

360 dolls

$\frac{4}{5}$ were sold.

72 dolls
72 dolls
72 dolls
72 dolls
72 dolls

$\frac{1}{5}$ were not sold.

(a) **288 dolls**

(b) $\dfrac{1}{5} \times 100\% = \dfrac{100\%}{5} = \mathbf{20\%}$

7. (a) **12 edges**
(b) **6 faces**
(c) **8 vertices**

8. (a) $\text{Area} = \dfrac{(12 \text{ m})(9 \text{ m})}{2} = \mathbf{54\ m^2}$

(b) $\text{Perimeter} = 5 \text{ m} + 5 \text{ m} + 6 \text{ m} = \mathbf{16\ m}$

(c) $90° - 37° = \mathbf{53°}$

(d) **The right triangle is not symmetrical.**

9.
$$\begin{array}{r} 7.65 \\ +\ 7.83 \\ \hline 15.48 \end{array}$$

$$2\overline{)15.48}\quad \mathbf{7.74}$$

10. $\mathbf{2.5 \times 10^{-3}}$

11. $W_N = \mathbf{0.24 \times 75}$
$W_N = \mathbf{18}$

12. $W_N = \mathbf{1.2 \times 12}$
$W_N = \mathbf{14.4}$

13. (a) $(-2) + (-3) + (-4) = \mathbf{-9}$

(b) $(+2) + (-3) + (+4) = \mathbf{3}$

14. (a) $4\% = \frac{4}{100} = \mathbf{\frac{1}{25}}$

(b) $4\% = \frac{4}{100} = \mathbf{0.04}$

(c) $8\overline{)7.000}\quad \mathbf{0.875}$

(d) $\frac{7}{8} \times 100\% = \frac{700\%}{8}$

$= \mathbf{87.5\%}$ or $\mathbf{87\frac{1}{2}\%}$

15. $\overset{70}{\cancel{700}}\ \cancel{\textbf{mm}} \cdot \frac{\textbf{1 cm}}{\underset{1}{\cancel{10}}\ \cancel{\textbf{mm}}} = \textbf{70 cm}$

16. $(-\$560) + (+\$850) + (-\$280) = +\$10$
A gain of $10

17. **Multiply the "in" number by 7 to find the "out" number.** $1 \times 7 = 7$

18. (a) **7856.43**

(b) **7900**

19. $C = \pi d$
$C \approx 3.14(24 \text{ inches})$
$C \approx 75.36 \text{ inches} \approx$ **75 inches**

20. (a) $\angle A$ **and** $\angle B$

(b) $\angle B$ **and** $\angle D$

21. (a) **2(5 ft + 3 ft)**
2(8 ft)
16 ft

or

2(5 ft) + 2(3 ft)
10 ft + 6 ft
16 ft

(b) **Distributive property**

22.
$$\frac{2.5}{w} = \frac{15}{12}$$
$$15w = 2.5(12)$$
$$w = \frac{30}{15}$$
$$w = \mathbf{2}$$

23. $9 + 8\{7 \cdot 6 - 5[4 + (3 - 2 \cdot 1)]\}$
$9 + 8\{7 \cdot 6 - 5[4 + (1)]\}$
$9 + 8\{7 \cdot 6 - 5[5]\}$
$9 + 8\{7 \cdot 6 - 25\}$
$9 + 8\{42 - 25\}$
$9 + 8\{17\}$
$9 + 136$
145

24.
$$\begin{array}{rrr} \overset{0}{\cancel{1}}\text{ yd} & (3\text{ ft}) & \\ - & 1\text{ ft} & 3\text{ in.} \\ \hline \end{array} \longrightarrow$$

$$\begin{array}{rrr} \overset{0}{\cancel{1}}\text{ yd} & \overset{2}{\cancel{3}}\text{ ft} & (12\text{ in.}) \\ - & 1\text{ ft} & 3\text{ in.} \\ \hline \end{array} \longrightarrow$$

$$\begin{array}{rrr} \overset{0}{\cancel{1}}\text{ yd} & \overset{2}{\cancel{3}}\text{ ft} & 12\text{ in.} \\ - & 1\text{ ft} & 3\text{ in.} \\ \hline & \textbf{1 ft} & \textbf{9 in.} \end{array}$$

25. $6.4 - (0.6 - 0.04)$
$= 6.4 - 0.56 = \mathbf{5.84}$

26. $\frac{3 + 0.6}{3(0.6)} = \frac{3.6}{1.8} = \mathbf{2}$

27.
$$\begin{array}{rcl} 1\frac{2}{3} & = & 1\frac{8}{12} \\ +\ 3\frac{1}{4} & = & 3\frac{3}{12} \\ \hline & & 4\frac{11}{12} \end{array}$$

$$\begin{array}{rcl} 4\frac{11}{12} & = & 4\frac{11}{12} \\ -\ 1\frac{5}{6} & = & 1\frac{10}{12} \\ \hline & & \mathbf{3\frac{1}{12}} \end{array}$$

28. $\frac{3}{5} \div 3\frac{1}{5} \cdot 5\frac{1}{3} \cdot |-1|$
$$= \left(\frac{3}{5} \div \frac{16}{5}\right) \cdot \frac{16}{3} \cdot 1$$
$$= \left(\frac{3}{\cancel{5}_1} \times \frac{\cancel{5}^1}{16}\right) \cdot \frac{16}{3} \cdot 1$$
$$= \frac{\cancel{3}^1}{\cancel{16}_1} \cdot \frac{\cancel{16}^1}{\cancel{3}_1} \cdot 1 = \mathbf{1}$$

29. $3 \div 1\frac{2}{3} = \frac{3}{1} \div \frac{5}{3}$
$$= \frac{3}{1} \times \frac{3}{5} = \frac{9}{5} = 1\frac{4}{5}$$
$$3\frac{3}{4} \div 1\frac{4}{5} = \frac{15}{4} \div \frac{9}{5}$$
$$= \frac{\cancel{15}^5}{4} \times \frac{5}{\cancel{9}_3} = \frac{25}{12} = \mathbf{2\frac{1}{12}}$$

30. $5^2 - \sqrt{4^2} + 2^{-2}$
$$= 25 - 4 + \frac{1}{4} = \mathbf{21\frac{1}{4}}$$

Lesson 68, Lesson Practice

a. $(-3) - (+2)$
$(-3) + [-(+2)]$
$(-3) + [-2] = \mathbf{-5}$

b. $(-3) - (-2)$
$(-3) + [-(-2)]$
$(-3) + [2] = \mathbf{-1}$

c. $(+3) - (2)$
$(+3) + [-(+2)]$
$(+3) + [-2] = \mathbf{1}$

d. $(-3) - (+2) - (-4)$
$(-3) + [-(+2)] + [-(-4)]$
$(-3) + [-2] + [4] = \mathbf{-1}$

e. $(-8) + (-3) - (+2)$
$(-8) + (-3) + [-(+2)]$
$(-8) + (-3) + [-2] = \mathbf{-13}$

f. $(-8) - (+3) + (-2)$
$(-8) + [-(+3)] + (-2)$
$(-8) + [-3] + (-2) = \mathbf{-13}$

Lesson 68, Mixed Practice

1.
$$\begin{array}{r} 1037\text{ g} \\ -\ \ 350\text{ g} \\ \hline \mathbf{687\text{ g}} \end{array}$$

2.

	Ratio	Actual Count
Pentagons	3	12
Hexagons	5	H

$$\frac{3}{5} = \frac{12}{H}$$
$$3H = 60$$
$$H = \mathbf{20\text{ hexagons}}$$

3. $\left(\frac{1}{4} + \frac{1}{2}\right) \div \left(\frac{1}{4} \times \frac{1}{2}\right)$
$$= \left(\frac{2}{8} + \frac{4}{8}\right) \div \left(\frac{1}{8}\right)$$
$$= \frac{6}{8} \div \frac{1}{8} = \frac{6}{\cancel{8}_1} \times \frac{\cancel{8}^1}{1} = \mathbf{6}$$

4. (a) $4\overline{)\$1.24}$ = **\$0.31 per pen**

(b) 100(\$0.31) = **\$31.00**

5. (a) $\frac{60\text{ miles}}{5\text{ hours}} = 12\frac{\text{miles}}{\text{hr}}$, **12 miles per hour**

(b) $\frac{5\text{ hours}}{60\text{ miles}} = \frac{300\text{ minutes}}{60\text{ miles}}$
$$= \frac{5\text{ minutes}}{1\text{ mile}}$$, **5 minutes per mile**

6. $1000\text{ \cancel{meters}} \cdot \frac{1\text{ second}}{331\text{ \cancel{meters}}} = \frac{1000}{331}\text{ seconds}$

About 3 seconds

7. (a) **88**

(b) **84**

(c)
$$\begin{array}{r} 72 \\ 80 \\ 84 \\ 88 \\ 100 \\ 88 \\ +\ \ 76 \\ \hline 588 \end{array} \qquad \begin{array}{r} \mathbf{84} \\ 7\overline{)588} \end{array}$$

8.

$$\begin{array}{r} 8.4 \\ +\ 9.8 \\ \hline 18.2 \end{array} \qquad \begin{array}{r} \mathbf{9.1} \\ 2\overline{)18.2} \end{array}$$

9. (a) **12 cubes**

(b) **Rectangular prism**

10. (a) $C = \pi d$
$C \approx 3.14(40 \text{ cm})$
$C \approx \mathbf{125.6 \text{ cm}}$

(b) $C = \pi d$
$C = \pi(40 \text{ cm})$
$C = \mathbf{40\pi \text{ cm}}$

11.

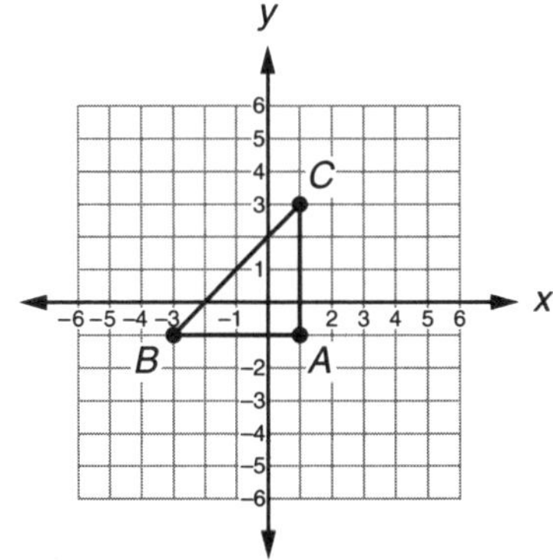

(a) **Right triangle**

(b) **Isosceles triangle**

(c) ***A***

(d) $\text{m}\angle B = \frac{90°}{2} = \mathbf{45°}$

(e) $\text{Area} = \frac{(4 \text{ units})(4 \text{ units})}{2} = \mathbf{8 \text{ sq. units}}$

12. $20{,}000 \times 30{,}000 = 600{,}000{,}000$
$= \mathbf{6 \times 10^8}$

13. $W_N = \mathbf{0.75 \times 400}$
$W_N = \mathbf{300}$

14. $W_N = \mathbf{1.5 \times 1.5}$ or $W_N = \mathbf{1\frac{1}{2} \times 1\frac{1}{2}}$
$W_N = \mathbf{2.25}$

$W_N = \frac{3}{2} \times \frac{3}{2}$

$W_N = \frac{9}{4}$

$W_N = \mathbf{2\frac{1}{4}}$

15. (a) $(-4) - (-6)$
$(-4) + [-(-6)]$
$(-4) + [6] = \mathbf{2}$

(b) $(-4) - (+6)$
$(-4) + [-(+6)]$
$(-4) + [-6] = \mathbf{-10}$

(c) $(-6) - (-4)$
$(-6) + [-(-4)]$
$(-6) + [4] = \mathbf{-2}$

(d) $(+6) - (-4)$
$(+6) + [-(-4)]$
$(+6) + [4] = \mathbf{10}$

16. $(4 \text{ in.})(4 \text{ in.}) = 16 \text{ in.}^2$
$6(16 \text{ in.}^2) = \mathbf{96 \text{ in.}^2}$

17. (a) $\begin{array}{r} \mathbf{0.12} \\ 25\overline{)3.00} \end{array}$

(b) $\frac{3}{25} \times 100\% = \frac{300\%}{25} = \mathbf{12\%}$

(c) $120\% = \frac{120}{100} = \frac{6}{5} = \mathbf{1\frac{1}{5}}$

(d) $120\% = \frac{120}{100} = \mathbf{1.2}$

18. $(4)^2 + 2(4)(5) + (5)^2 = 16 + 40 + 25$
$= \mathbf{81}$

19. (a) **Rectangular prism**

(b) **Cone**

(c) **Cylinder**

20. (a) $\text{m}\angle DCA = \frac{90°}{2} = \mathbf{45°}$

(b) $\text{m}\angle DAC = 120° - 45° = \mathbf{75°}$

(c) $\text{m}\angle CAB = \text{m}\angle DCA = \mathbf{45°}$

(d) $\text{m}\angle ABC = \text{m}\angle CDA = \mathbf{60°}$

(e) $\text{m}\angle BCA = 120° - 45° = \mathbf{75°}$

(f) $\text{m}\angle BCD = 180° - 60° = \mathbf{120°}$

21. **One possibility: How many $0.25 pens can you buy with $3.00?**

22. $\frac{4}{c} = \frac{3}{7\frac{1}{2}}$

$$3c = 4\left(7\frac{1}{2}\right)$$
$$3c = 4\left(\frac{15}{2}\right)$$
$$3c = \frac{30}{3}$$
$$c = \mathbf{10}$$

23. $\frac{(1.5)^2}{15} = \mathbf{0.15}$

24.

$$\begin{array}{r} \overset{0}{\cancel{1}}\text{ gal } (4\text{ qt}) \\ -\quad 1\text{ qt } 1\text{ pt } 1\text{ oz} \\ \hline \end{array}$$

$$\begin{array}{r} \overset{0}{\cancel{1}}\text{ gal } \overset{3}{\cancel{4}}\text{ qt } (2\text{ pt}) \\ -\quad 1\text{ qt } 1\text{ pt } 1\text{ oz} \\ \hline \end{array}$$

$$\begin{array}{r} \overset{0}{\cancel{1}}\text{ gal } \overset{3}{\cancel{4}}\text{ qt } \overset{1}{\cancel{2}}\text{ pt } (16\text{ oz}) \\ -\quad 1\text{ qt } 1\text{ pt } 1\text{ oz} \\ \hline \end{array}$$

$$\begin{array}{rrrr} \overset{0}{\cancel{1}}\text{ gal} & \overset{3}{\cancel{4}}\text{ qt} & \overset{1}{\cancel{2}}\text{ pt} & 16\text{ oz} \\ - & 1\text{ qt} & 1\text{ pt} & 1\text{ oz} \\ \hline & \mathbf{2\text{ qt}} & & \mathbf{15\text{ oz}} \end{array}$$

25. $16 \div (0.04 \div 0.8) = 16 \div 0.05 = \mathbf{320}$

26. $10 - [0.1 - (0.01)(0.1)]$

$$10 - [0.1 - 0.001]$$
$$10 - 0.099$$
$$\mathbf{9.901}$$

27. $\frac{5}{8} + \frac{2}{3} \cdot \frac{3}{4} - \frac{3}{4}$

$$= \frac{5}{8} + \frac{1}{2} - \frac{3}{4} = \frac{5}{8} + \frac{4}{8} - \frac{6}{8}$$
$$= \frac{9}{8} - \frac{6}{8} = \mathbf{\frac{3}{8}}$$

28. $4\frac{1}{2} \cdot 3\frac{3}{4} \div 1\frac{2}{3}$

$$= \left(\frac{9}{2} \cdot \frac{15}{4}\right) \div \frac{5}{3} = \frac{135}{8} \div \frac{5}{3}$$
$$= \frac{\overset{27}{\cancel{135}}}{8} \times \frac{3}{\underset{1}{\cancel{5}}} = \frac{81}{8} = \mathbf{10\frac{1}{8}}$$

29. $\sqrt{5^2 - 2^4} = \sqrt{25 - 16} = \sqrt{9} = \mathbf{3}$

30. $3 + 6[10 - (3 \cdot 4 - 5)]$

$$3 + 6[10 - (7)]$$
$$3 + 6[3]$$
$$3 + 18$$
$$\mathbf{21}$$

Lesson 69, Lesson Practice

a. $0.16 \times 10^6 = 1.6 \times 10^{-1} \times 10^6$
$= \mathbf{1.6 \times 10^5}$

b. $24 \times 10^{-7} = 2.4 \times 10^1 \times 10^{-7}$
$= \mathbf{2.4 \times 10^{-6}}$

c. $30 \times 10^5 = 3 \times 10^1 \times 10^5$
$= \mathbf{3 \times 10^6}$

d. $0.75 \times 10^{-8} = 7.5 \times 10^{-1} \times 10^{-8}$
$= \mathbf{7.5 \times 10^{-9}}$

e. $14.4 \times 10^8 = 1.44 \times 10^1 \times 10^8$
$= \mathbf{1.44 \times 10^9}$

f. $12.4 \times 10^{-5} = 1.24 \times 10^1 \times 10^{-5}$
$= \mathbf{1.24 \times 10^{-4}}$

Lesson 69, Mixed Practice

1. (a) **6.5**

(b) **6.5**

(c)

$$\begin{array}{r} 7.0 \\ 6.5 \\ 6.5 \\ 7.4 \\ 7.0 \\ 6.5 \\ +\ 6.0 \\ \hline 46.9 \end{array} \qquad 7\overline{)46.9} = \mathbf{6.7}$$

(d) $7.4 - 6.0 = \mathbf{1.4}$

2.

	Ratio	Actual Count
Won	5	15
Lost	3	L
Total	8	T

$$\frac{5}{8} = \frac{15}{T}$$
$$5T = 120$$
$$T = \mathbf{24\ games}$$

3. $\overset{5}{\cancel{10}}\ \cancel{\text{laps}} \cdot \dfrac{\overset{3}{\cancel{6}}\ \text{minutes}}{\underset{\underset{1}{\cancel{2}}}{\cancel{4}}\ \cancel{\text{laps}}} = \mathbf{15\ minutes}$

4. (a) $15 \times 10^5 = 1.5 \times 10^1 \times 10^5$
$= \mathbf{1.5 \times 10^6}$

(b) $0.15 \times 10^5 = 1.5 \times 10^{-1} \times 10^5$
$= \mathbf{1.5 \times 10^4}$

5. (a) $\dfrac{\text{do not believe in giants}}{\text{total Lilliputians}} = \mathbf{\dfrac{3}{5}}$

(b) $\dfrac{2}{5} = \dfrac{L}{60}$
$5L = 120$
$L = \mathbf{24\ Lilliputians}$

(c) $\mathbf{\dfrac{2}{5}}$

6. $C = \pi d$
$C \approx 3.14(40\text{ cm})$
$C \approx 125.6\text{ cm} \approx \mathbf{126\ cm}$

7. (a) **Sphere**

(b) **Cylinder**

(c) **Cone**

8. (a) Perimeter $= \dfrac{10}{16}\text{ in.} + \dfrac{10}{16}\text{ in.} + \dfrac{10}{16}\text{ in.}$
$= \dfrac{30}{16}\text{ in.} = \dfrac{15}{8}\text{ in.} = \mathbf{1\dfrac{7}{8}\ in.}$

(b) **60°**

(c)

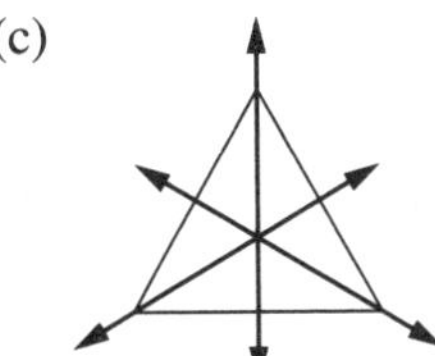

9. (a) $(-4) + (-5) - (-6)$
$(-4) + (-5) + [-(-6)]$
$(-4) + (-5) + [6]$
$\mathbf{-3}$

(b) $(-2) + (-3) - (-4) - (+5)$
$(-2) + (-3) + [-(-4)] + [-(+5)]$
$(-2) + (-3) + [4] + [-5]$
$\mathbf{-6}$

10. (a) $C = \pi d$
$C \approx 3.14(7\text{ cm})$
$C \approx \mathbf{21.98\ cm}$

(b) $C = \pi d$
$C \approx \dfrac{22}{7}(7\text{ cm})$
$C \approx \mathbf{22\ cm}$

11.

(a) Area A $= (9\text{ mm})(10\text{ mm}) = 90\text{ mm}^2$
+ Area B $= (3\text{ mm})(6\text{ mm}) = 18\text{ mm}^2$
Area of figure $= \mathbf{108\ mm^2}$

(b) Area $= \dfrac{(12\text{ mm})(10\text{ mm})}{2} = \mathbf{60\ mm^2}$

(c) $\dfrac{60}{108} = \mathbf{\dfrac{5}{9}}$

12. $\mathbf{W_N = \dfrac{1}{2} \times 200}$
$W_N = \mathbf{100}$

13. $\mathbf{W_N = 2.5 \times 4.2}$
$W_N = \mathbf{10.5}$

14. (a) $20\overline{)3.00}$ quotient **0.15**

(b) $\dfrac{3}{20} \times 100\% = \dfrac{300\%}{20} = \mathbf{15\%}$

(c) $150\% = \dfrac{150}{100} = \mathbf{1\dfrac{1}{2}}$

(d) $150\% = \dfrac{150}{100} = \mathbf{1.5}$

15. (a) $\angle \boldsymbol{TPQ}$ or $\angle \boldsymbol{QPT}$

(b) $\angle \boldsymbol{SPR}$ or $\angle \boldsymbol{RPS}$

(c) $m\angle QPT = 360° - (125° + 90°)$
$= 360° - 215° = \mathbf{145°}$

16. $(4)^2 - \sqrt{(4)} + (4)(0.5) - (4)^0$
$= 16 - 2 + 2 - 1 = \mathbf{15}$

17. **Multiply the "in" number by 2, then subtract 1 to find the "out" number.**
$4 \times 2 - 1 = 8 - 1 = \mathbf{7}$

18.
$$\begin{array}{r} 13.0909\ldots \\ 11\overline{)144.0000\ldots} \\ \underline{11} \\ 34 \\ \underline{33} \\ 1\,0 \\ \underline{0} \\ 1\,00 \\ \underline{99} \\ 10 \\ \underline{0} \\ 100 \end{array}$$

(a) $\mathbf{13.\overline{09}}$

(b) **13**

19. $1.8(20°\text{C}) + 32 = \mathbf{68°F}$

20. $(19)(2) = 38$
$7 + 31 = 38$
7 and 31

21.
$$\begin{array}{rcl} \frac{15}{16} & = & \frac{15}{16} \\ -\ \frac{5}{8} & = & \frac{10}{16} \\ \hline & & \mathbf{\frac{5}{16}} \end{array}$$

22.
$$\frac{a}{8} = \frac{3\frac{1}{2}}{2}$$
$$2a = 3\frac{1}{2}(8)$$
$$2a = \frac{7}{2}(8)$$
$$2a = 28$$
$$a = \mathbf{14}$$

23. $(4 \div 2) \cdot 3 = 2 \cdot 3 = \mathbf{6}$
$$3\frac{3}{4} \div 1\frac{2}{3} = \frac{15}{4} \div \frac{5}{3}$$
$$= \frac{\overset{3}{\cancel{15}}}{4} \times \frac{3}{\underset{1}{\cancel{5}}} = \frac{9}{4}$$
$$3 \cdot \frac{9}{4} = \frac{27}{4} = \mathbf{6\frac{3}{4}}$$

24. $4 + (5 \div 1) = 4 + 5 = \mathbf{9}$
or
$5 + (5 \div 1) = 5 + 5 = \mathbf{10}$
$$5\frac{1}{6} \div 1\frac{1}{3} = \frac{31}{6} \div \frac{4}{3}$$
$$= \frac{31}{\underset{2}{\cancel{6}}} \times \frac{\overset{1}{\cancel{3}}}{4} = \frac{31}{8} = 3\frac{7}{8}$$
$$\begin{array}{rcl} 4\frac{1}{2} & = & 4\frac{4}{8} \\ +\ 3\frac{7}{8} & = & 3\frac{7}{8} \\ \hline & & 7\frac{11}{8} = \mathbf{8\frac{3}{8}} \end{array}$$

25.
$$\begin{array}{rr} 5\text{ ft} & 7\text{ in.} \\ +\ 6\text{ ft} & 8\text{ in.} \\ \hline 11\text{ ft} & 15\text{ in.} \end{array}$$
15 in. = 1 ft 3 in.
$$\begin{array}{rr} 1\text{ ft} & 3\text{ in.} \\ +\ 11\text{ ft} & \\ \hline \mathbf{12\text{ ft}} & \mathbf{3\text{ in.}} \end{array}$$

26.
$$\frac{350\ \cancel{\text{m}}}{1\ \cancel{\text{s}}} \cdot \frac{60\ \cancel{\text{s}}}{1\text{ min}} \cdot \frac{1\text{ km}}{1000\ \cancel{\text{m}}} = \frac{21{,}000\text{ km}}{1000\text{ min}} = \mathbf{21\ \frac{km}{min}}$$

27. $6 - (0.5 \div 4) = 6 - 0.125$
$= \mathbf{5.875}$

28.
$$\begin{array}{r} \mathbf{\$100.00} \\ 75\overline{)\$7500} \end{array}$$

29.
$$\frac{432}{675} = \frac{2 \cdot 2 \cdot 2 \cdot 2 \cdot \overset{1}{\cancel{3}} \cdot \overset{1}{\cancel{3}} \cdot \overset{1}{\cancel{3}}}{\underset{1}{\cancel{3}} \cdot \underset{1}{\cancel{3}} \cdot \underset{1}{\cancel{3}} \cdot 5 \cdot 5}$$
$$= \mathbf{\frac{16}{25}}$$

30. (a) $2\frac{1}{4} = 2.25,\quad 2.25 + 0.15 = \mathbf{2.4}$

(b) $6.5 = 6\frac{1}{2}$
$$\begin{array}{rcl} 6\frac{1}{2} & = & 6\frac{3}{6} \\ +\ \frac{5}{6} & = & \frac{5}{6} \\ \hline & & 6\frac{8}{6} = 7\frac{2}{6} = \mathbf{7\frac{1}{3}} \end{array}$$

Lesson 70, Lesson Practice

a. (6 sugar cubes)(3 sugar cubes)
= 18 sugar cubes

$\frac{18 \text{ sugar cubes}}{\cancel{\text{layer}}} \times 4\ \cancel{\text{layers}} = \textbf{72 sugar cubes}$

b. (10 1-cm cubes)(10 1-cm cubes)
= 100 1-cm cubes,

$\frac{100 \text{ 1-cm cubes}}{1\ \cancel{\text{layer}}} \times 10\ \cancel{\text{layers}}$
= **1000 1-cm cubes**

c. (10 cubes)(4 cubes) = 40 cubes

$\frac{40 \text{ cubes}}{1\ \cancel{\text{layer}}} \times 6\ \cancel{\text{layers}} = 240 \text{ cubes}$

240 ft^3

d. **Answers may vary. See student work.**

Lesson 70, Mixed Practice

1. $\frac{2(38 \text{ kilometers})}{4 \text{ hours}} = \textbf{19 kilometers per hour}$

2.

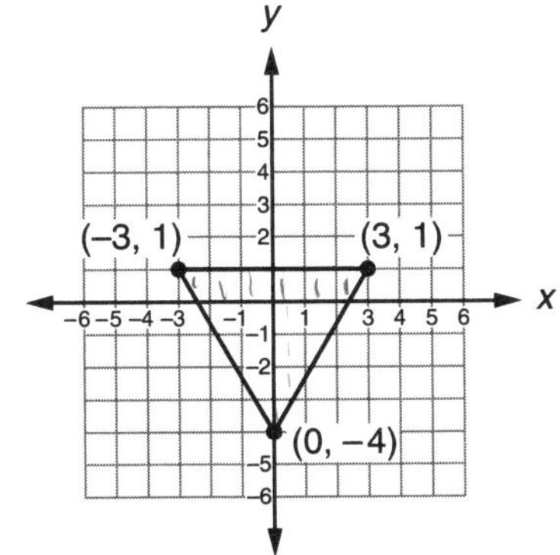

(a) **(−3, 1)**

(b) Area $= \frac{(6 \text{ units})(5 \text{ units})}{2} = \textbf{15 sq. units}$

3. **A little too large. The actual value of π is greater than 3. Dividing the circumference, 600 cm, by π results in a measurement less than 200 cm.**

4. (a) $\frac{\$1.29}{3 \text{ pounds}} = \frac{\$0.43}{1 \text{ pound}}$
\$0.43 per pound

(b) 10(\$0.43) = **\$4.30**

5. $(0.7 + 0.6) - (0.9 \times 0.8)$
$= 1.3 - 0.72 = \mathbf{0.58}$

6. (a) $\frac{3}{4}(188 \text{ hits}) = \textbf{141 hits}$

(b) $\frac{1}{4} \times 100\% = \frac{100\%}{4} = \mathbf{25\%}$

7. **$2\frac{1}{4}$-inch mark**

8. (5 1-cm cubes)(5 1-cm cubes)
= 25 1-cm cubes,

$\frac{25 \text{ 1-cm cubes}}{1\ \cancel{\text{layer}}} \times 3\ \cancel{\text{layers}}$
= **75 1-cm cubes**

9. (a) $C = \pi d$
$C = \pi(2 \text{ in.})$
$C = \mathbf{2\pi}$ **in.**

(b) $C = \pi d$
$C \approx 3.14(1 \text{ in.})$
$C \approx$ **3.14 in.**

10. (a) $12 \times 10^{-6} = 1.2 \times 10^{1} \times 10^{-6}$
$= \mathbf{1.2 \times 10^{-5}}$

(b) $0.12 \times 10^{-6} = 1.2 \times 10^{-1} \times 10^{-6}$
$= \mathbf{1.2 \times 10^{-7}}$

11.
$$\begin{array}{r} 0.74 \\ 0.83 \\ +\ 0.98 \\ \hline 2.55 \end{array} \qquad \begin{array}{r} \mathbf{0.85} \\ 3\overline{)2.55} \end{array}$$

12. $\mathbf{1.25\ \cancel{kilograms} \cdot \frac{1000\ grams}{1\ \cancel{kilogram}}}$
= **1250 grams**

13. (a) 2^9

(b) 2^3

(c) 2^{-3}

(d) 2^0

14. $\mathbf{W_N = \frac{1}{6} \times 100}$

$W_N = \frac{100}{6}$

$W_N = \mathbf{16\frac{2}{3}}$

15. (a) $14\% = \frac{14}{100} = \mathbf{\frac{7}{50}}$

(b) $14\% = \frac{14}{100} = \mathbf{0.14}$

(c) $6\overline{)5.00\ldots}$ with quotient $\mathbf{0.8\overline{3}}$

(d) $\frac{5}{6} \times 100\% = \frac{500\%}{6} = \mathbf{83\frac{1}{3}\%}$

16. (a) $(-6) - (-4) + (+2)$
$(-6) + [-(-4)] + (+2)$
$(-6) + [4] + (+2) = \mathbf{0}$

(b) $(-5) + (-2) - (-7) - (+9)$
$(-5) + (-2) + [-(-7)] + [-(+9)]$
$(-5) + (-2) + [7] + [-9]$
$\mathbf{-9}$

17. $(0.4)(0.3) - (0.4 - 0.3)$
$= 0.12 - 0.1 = \mathbf{0.02}$

18. **29,375**

19. $6 \times 8 = \mathbf{48}$

20. **Pyramid;**

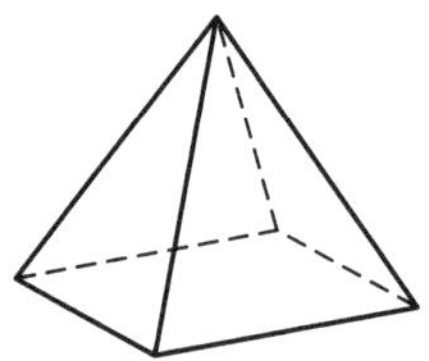

21. $2\text{ ft} \times 2\text{ ft} = 4\text{ ft}^2$,
$6(4\text{ ft}^2) = \mathbf{24\text{ ft}^2}$

22.
$$\begin{array}{r} 4.3 \\ +\ 0.8 \\ \hline \mathbf{5.1} \end{array}$$

23. $\frac{2}{d} = \frac{1.2}{1.5}$
$1.2d = 2(1.5)$
$d = \frac{3}{1.2}$
$d = \mathbf{2.5}$

24.
$$\begin{array}{rr} \overset{9}{\cancel{10}}\text{ lb} & (16\text{ oz}) \\ -\ 6\text{ lb} & 7\text{ oz} \\ \hline \end{array} \longrightarrow$$

$$\begin{array}{rr} \overset{9}{\cancel{10}}\text{ lb} & 16\text{ oz} \\ -\ 6\text{ lb} & 7\text{ oz} \\ \hline \mathbf{3\text{ lb}} & \mathbf{9\text{ oz}} \end{array}$$

25. $\frac{\$5.25}{1\ \cancel{\text{hr}}} \cdot \frac{8\ \cancel{\text{hr}}}{1\ \cancel{\text{day}}} \cdot \frac{5\ \cancel{\text{days}}}{1\text{ week}}$
$= \mathbf{\frac{\$210.00}{week}}$

26. $1\frac{2}{3} \cdot 3 = \frac{5}{\cancel{3}_1} \cdot \frac{\cancel{3}^1}{1} = 5$

$3\frac{3}{4} \div 5 = \frac{15}{4} \div \frac{5}{1}$
$= \frac{\cancel{15}^3}{4} \times \frac{1}{\cancel{5}_1} = \mathbf{\frac{3}{4}}$

27. $4\frac{1}{2} + 5\frac{1}{6} - 1\frac{1}{3}$
$= 4\frac{3}{6} + 5\frac{1}{6} - 1\frac{2}{6} = 8\frac{2}{6} = \mathbf{8\frac{1}{3}}$

28. $(0.06 \div 5) \div 0.004$
$= (0.012) \div 0.004$
$= \mathbf{3}$

29. $9\frac{1}{2} = 9.5,\quad 9.5 \times 9.2 = \mathbf{87.4}$

30. (a)
$$\begin{array}{r} \$15.00 \\ \times\ 0.06 \\ \hline \$0.9000 \end{array} = \$0.90 \qquad \begin{array}{r} \$15.00 \\ +\ \$0.90 \\ \hline \mathbf{\$15.90} \end{array}$$

(b)
$$\begin{array}{r} \$15.00 \\ \times\ 0.15 \\ \hline \mathbf{\$2.25} \end{array}$$

Lesson 71, Lesson Practice

a.

	25 students
$\frac{3}{5}$ were boys (15).	5 students
	5 students
	5 students
$\frac{2}{5}$ were girls.	5 students
	5 students

$15 \div 3 = 5$
$5 \times 5\text{ students} = $ **25 students**

b.

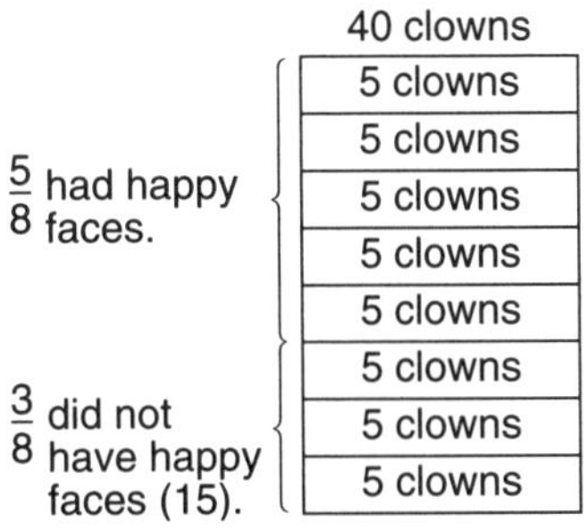

40 clowns
5 clowns
5 clowns
5 clowns
5 clowns
5 clowns
5 clowns
5 clowns
5 clowns

$\frac{5}{8}$ had happy faces.

$\frac{3}{8}$ did not have happy faces (15).

$15 \div 3 = 5$

5×8 clowns = **40 clowns**

c.

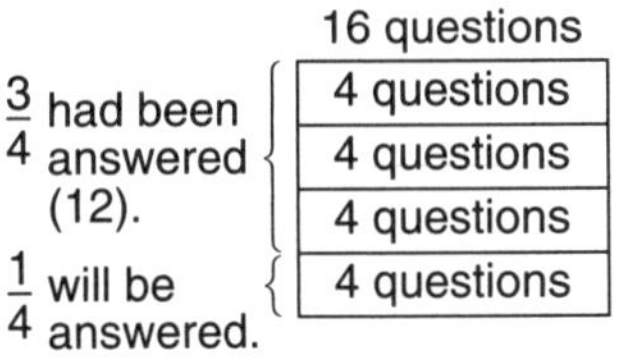

16 questions
4 questions
4 questions
4 questions
4 questions

$\frac{3}{4}$ had been answered (12).

$\frac{1}{4}$ will be answered.

$12 \div 3 = 4$

4×4 questions = **16 questions**

Lesson 71, Mixed Practice

1. 9 ~~seconds~~ $\cdot$ $\frac{331 \text{ meters}}{1 \text{ second}}$ (seconds crossed out)

= 2979 meters; **about 3 kilometers**

2.

$$\begin{array}{r} 3.33 \\ 3.45 \\ +\ 3.51 \\ \hline 10.29 \end{array} \qquad \begin{array}{r} \mathbf{3.43} \\ 3\overline{)10.29} \end{array}$$

3. 2(80 percent) + 3(90 percent)

= 430 percent

$\frac{430 \text{ percent}}{5}$ = **86 percent**

4.

$$\begin{array}{r} 20{,}000{,}000{,}000 \\ -\ \ 9{,}000{,}000{,}000 \\ \hline 11{,}000{,}000{,}000 \end{array}$$

$\mathbf{1.1 \times 10^{10}}$

5.

$$\begin{array}{r} 2 \\ 3 \\ 5 \\ 7 \\ +\ 11 \\ \hline \mathbf{28} \end{array}$$

6.

	Ratio	Actual Count
New ones	4	N
Used ones	7	U
Total	11	242

$\frac{4}{11} = \frac{N}{242}$

$11N = 968$

$N =$ **88 new ones**

7.

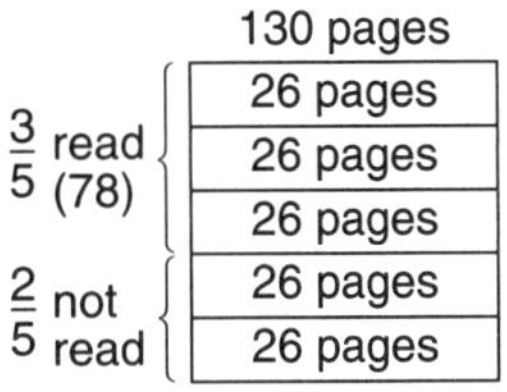

130 pages
26 pages
26 pages
26 pages
26 pages
26 pages

$\frac{3}{5}$ read (78)

$\frac{2}{5}$ not read

(a) $78 \div 3 = 26$

5×26 = **130 pages**

(b) 2×26 = **52 pages**

8. (4 1-inch cubes)(4 1-inch cubes)

= 16 1-inch cubes

$\frac{16 \text{ 1-inch cubes}}{1 \text{ layer}} \cdot 4 \text{ layers}$ (layers crossed out)

= **64 1-inch cubes**

9. $(4 \text{ in.})(4 \text{ in.}) = 16 \text{ in.}^2$

$6(16 \text{ in.}^2) = \mathbf{96 \text{ in.}^2}$

10. (a) $C \approx 3.14(28 \text{ cm})$

$C \approx$ **87.92 cm**

(b) $C \approx \frac{22}{7}(28 \text{ cm})$

$C \approx$ **88 cm**

11. (a) $\mathbf{2.5 \times 10^7}$

(b) $\mathbf{2.5 \times 10^{-5}}$

12. (a) $0.1 = \mathbf{\frac{1}{10}}$

(b) $0.1 = \frac{1}{10} = \frac{10}{100} =$ **10%**

(c) $0.5\% = \frac{0.5}{100} = \mathbf{\frac{1}{200}}$

(d) $0.5\% = \frac{0.5}{100} =$ **0.005**

13. (a) $W_N = \mathbf{0.35 \times 80}$
$W_N = \mathbf{28}$

(b) $\frac{3}{\not{4}_1} \times \not{24}^{6} = W_N$

$3(6) = W_N$

$\mathbf{18} = W_N$

14. Add 7 to the "in" number to find the "out" number. $0 + 7 = \mathbf{7}$

15.

8 vertices

16. (a) Perimeter $= 10 \text{ cm} + 12 \text{ cm} + 8 \text{ cm} + 6 \text{ cm} = \mathbf{36 \text{ cm}}$

(b) $\text{Area} = \frac{(6 \text{ cm})(8 \text{ cm})}{2} = \mathbf{24 \text{ cm}^2}$

(c) $\text{Area} = \frac{(12 \text{ cm})(8 \text{ cm})}{2} = \mathbf{48 \text{ cm}^2}$

(d) $\text{Area} = 24 \text{ cm}^2 + 48 \text{ cm}^2 = \mathbf{72 \text{ cm}^2}$

17.
$$\begin{array}{r} \$16.50 \\ \times \quad 0.15 \\ \hline \$2.475 \end{array}$$
About $2.50

18.

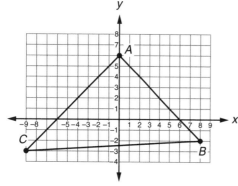

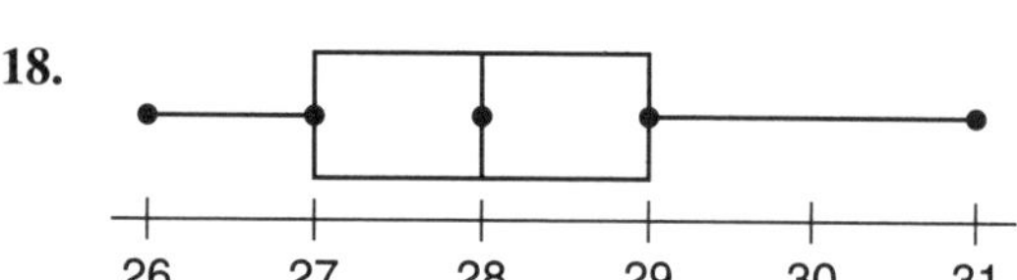

19.

$\mathbf{m\angle A = 90°}$
$\mathbf{m\angle B = 48°}$
$\mathbf{m\angle C = 42°}$

20. $(0.01) - (0.1)(0.01)$
$= 0.01 - 0.001 = \mathbf{0.009}$

21.
$$m + 5.75 = 26.4$$
$$m + 5.75 - 5.75 = 26.4 - 5.75$$
$$m = \mathbf{20.65}$$

check: $20.65 + 5.75 = 26.4$
$26.4 = 26.4$

22.
$$\frac{3}{4}x = 48$$
$$\left(\frac{\not{4}^1}{\not{3}_1}\right)\frac{\not{3}^1}{\not{4}_1}x = \left(\frac{4}{\not{3}_1}\right)\not{48}^{16}$$
$$x = \mathbf{64}$$

check: $\frac{3}{\not{4}_1}(\not{64}^{16}) = 48$

$3(16) = 48$

$48 = 48$

23. Rhombus

24.
$$\frac{4^2 + \{20 - 2[6 - (5 - 2)]\}}{\sqrt{36}}$$
$$\frac{16 + \{20 - 2[6 - (3)]\}}{6}$$
$$\frac{16 + \{20 - 2[3]\}}{6}$$
$$\frac{16 + \{20 - 6\}}{6}$$
$$\frac{16 + \{14\}}{6}$$
$$\frac{30}{6}$$
$$\mathbf{5}$$

25.
$$\begin{array}{rrr} \not{1}^{0} \text{ yd} & (\not{3}^{2} \text{ ft}) & (12 \text{ in.}) \\ - & 1 \text{ ft} & 1 \text{ in.} \\ \hline & \mathbf{1 \text{ ft}} & \mathbf{11 \text{ in.}} \end{array}$$

26. $3.5 \not{\text{hr}} \cdot \frac{60 \not{\text{min}}}{1 \not{\text{hr}}} \cdot \frac{60 \text{ s}}{1 \not{\text{min}}} = \mathbf{12{,}600 \text{ s}}$

27. $4\frac{1}{2} \cdot 2\frac{2}{3} = \frac{\not{9}^3}{\not{2}_1} \cdot \frac{\not{8}^4}{\not{3}_1} = 12$

$6\frac{2}{3} \div 12 = \frac{20}{3} \div \frac{12}{1}$

$= \frac{\not{20}^5}{3} \times \frac{1}{\not{12}_3} = \mathbf{\frac{5}{9}}$

28.

$$\begin{array}{rcl} 7\frac{1}{2} & = & 7\frac{3}{6} \\ -\ 5\frac{1}{6} & = & 5\frac{1}{6} \\ \hline & & 2\frac{2}{6} = 2\frac{1}{3} \end{array}$$

$$\begin{array}{r} 2\frac{1}{3} \\ +\ 1\frac{1}{3} \\ \hline \mathbf{3\frac{2}{3}} \end{array}$$

29. (a)

$$\begin{array}{c} (-5) + (-6) - |-7| \\ (-5) + (-6) + [-|-7|] \\ (-5) + (-6) + [-7] \\ \mathbf{-18} \end{array}$$

(b)

$$\begin{array}{c} (-15) - (-24) - (+8) \\ (-15) + [-(-24)] + [-(+8)] \\ (-15) + [24] + [-8] \\ \mathbf{1} \end{array}$$

30.

$$1.5 = 1\frac{1}{2}$$

$$\begin{array}{rcl} 2\frac{2}{3} & = & 2\frac{4}{6} \\ -\ 1\frac{1}{2} & = & 1\frac{3}{6} \\ \hline & & \mathbf{1\frac{1}{6}} \end{array}$$

LESSON 72, LESSON PRACTICE

a. **Between 4 and 6 hours**

	Case 1	Case 2
km	30	75
Hours	2	h

$$\frac{30}{2} = \frac{75}{h}$$

$$30h = 2(75)$$

$$30h = 150$$

$$h = \frac{\overset{5}{\cancel{150}}}{\underset{1}{\cancel{30}}}$$

$$h = \mathbf{5\ hours}$$

b.

$$\overset{5}{\cancel{50}}\ \cancel{\text{head}} \cdot \frac{\overset{3}{\cancel{6}}\ \text{bales}}{\underset{\underset{2}{\cancel{4}}}{\cancel{40}}\ \cancel{\text{head}}}$$

$$= \frac{15\ \text{bales}}{2} = \mathbf{7\frac{1}{2}\ bales}$$

	Case 1	Case 2
Head of cattle	40	50
Bales	6	b

$$\frac{40}{6} = \frac{50}{b}$$

$$40b = 6(50)$$

$$40b = 300$$

$$b = \frac{\overset{\overset{15}{\cancel{30}}}{\cancel{300}}}{\underset{\underset{2}{\cancel{4}}}{\cancel{40}}}$$

$$b = \frac{15}{2}\ \text{bales} = \mathbf{7\frac{1}{2}\ bales}$$

c.

	Case 1	Case 2
First number	5	9
Second number	15	n

$$\frac{5}{15} = \frac{9}{n}$$

$$5n = 15(9)$$

$$5n = 135$$

$$n = \frac{\overset{27}{\cancel{135}}}{\underset{1}{\cancel{5}}}$$

$$n = \mathbf{27}$$

LESSON 72, MIXED PRACTICE

1.

$$\begin{array}{r} 1821 \\ -\ 1769 \\ \hline \mathbf{52\ years} \end{array}$$

2.

$$4(4\ \text{points}) + 6(9\ \text{points})$$

$$= 16\ \text{points} + 54\ \text{points}$$

$$= 70\ \text{points}$$

$$\frac{70\ \text{points}}{10} = \mathbf{7\ points}$$

3.

$$\mathbf{2.5\ \cancel{liters} \cdot \frac{1000\ milliliters}{1\ \cancel{liter}}}$$

$$\mathbf{= 2500\ milliliters}$$

4. $\left(\frac{1}{2} + \frac{2}{5}\right) - \left(\frac{1}{2} \cdot \frac{2}{5}\right)$

$= \left(\frac{5}{10} + \frac{4}{10}\right) - \left(\frac{1}{5}\right)$

$= \frac{9}{10} - \frac{1}{5} = \frac{9}{10} - \frac{2}{10} = \mathbf{\frac{7}{10}}$

5.

	Ratio	Actual Count
Carnivores	2	126
Herbivores	7	H

$\frac{2}{7} = \frac{126}{H}$

$2H = 882$

$H =$ **441 herbivores**

6.

	Case 1	Case 2
Books	4	14
Pounds	9	P

$\frac{4}{9} = \frac{14}{p}$

$4p = 9(14)$

$4p = 126$

$p = \frac{\overset{63}{\cancel{126}}}{\underset{2}{\cancel{4}}}$

$p = \mathbf{31\frac{1}{2}}$ **pounds**

7. (a) $\mathbf{\frac{2}{\underset{1}{\cancel{5}}} \times \overset{12}{\cancel{60}} = W_N}$

$\mathbf{24 = W_N}$

(b) $\mathbf{M = 0.75 \times \$24}$

$\mathbf{M = \$18}$

8. $C \approx 3.14(20 \text{ in.})$

$C \approx 62.8 \text{ in.} \approx$ **63 in.**

9.

225 voters

$\frac{2}{3}$ for Kayla (150): 75 voters, 75 voters

$\frac{1}{3}$ not for Kayla: 75 voters

(a) $\frac{150 \text{ votes}}{2} = 75 \text{ votes}$

$3(75 \text{ votes}) =$ **225 votes**

(b) $1(75 \text{ votes}) =$ **75 votes**

10. $(10 \text{ ice cubes})(8 \text{ ice cubes})$

$= 80 \text{ ice cubes}$

$\frac{80 \text{ ice cubes}}{1 \cancel{\text{layer}}} \cdot 6 \cancel{\text{layers}}$

$=$ **480 ice cubes**

11. $(10 \text{ in.})(8 \text{ in.}) = 80 \text{ in.}^2$

$(6 \text{ in.})(10 \text{ in.}) = 60 \text{ in.}^2$

$(6 \text{ in.})(8 \text{ in.}) = 48 \text{ in.}^2$

$2(80 \text{ in.}^2) + 2(60 \text{ in.}^2) + 2(48 \text{ in.}^2)$

$= 160 \text{ in.}^2 + 120 \text{ in.}^2 + 96 \text{ in.}^2$

$= \mathbf{376 \text{ in.}^2}$

12. (a) $\mathbf{6 \times 10^5}$

(b) $\mathbf{6 \times 10^{-7}}$

13.

$$\begin{array}{r} 1.35 \\ 1.44 \\ +\ 1.59 \\ \hline 4.38 \end{array} \qquad 3\overline{)4.38} = \mathbf{1.46}$$

14. (a) $3\overline{)5.0} = \mathbf{0.6}$

(b) $\frac{3}{5} \times 100\% = \frac{300\%}{5} = \mathbf{60\%}$

(c) $2.5\% = \frac{2.5}{100} = \mathbf{\frac{1}{40}}$

(d) $2.5\% = \frac{2.5}{100} = \mathbf{0.025}$

15. (a) $\mathbf{2^2 \cdot 3^4 \cdot 5^2}$

(b) **90**

16. (a) Area $= (8 \text{ in.})(6 \text{ in.}) = \mathbf{48 \text{ in.}^2}$

(b) Area $= \frac{(8 \text{ in.})(6 \text{ in.})}{2} = \mathbf{24 \text{ in.}^2}$

(c) $180° - 72° = \mathbf{108°}$

17. (a) **Sphere**

(b) **Triangular prism**

(c) **Cylinder**

Only the triangular prism is a polyhedron, because it is the only figure whose faces are polygons.

18. (a) $C = \pi(60 \text{ mm})$

$C = \mathbf{60\pi \text{ mm}}$

(b) $C \approx 3.14(60 \text{ mm})$

$C \approx \mathbf{188.4 \text{ mm}}$

19. $\frac{2}{3}$ ⓢ $<$ 0.667

20. 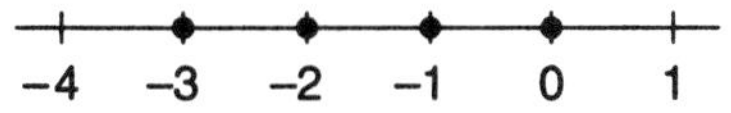

21. (a) $(5)^2 - (4)^2 = 25 - 16 = \mathbf{9}$

(b) $(5)^0 - (4)^{-1} = 1 - \frac{1}{4}$

$= \frac{4}{4} - \frac{1}{4} = \mathbf{\frac{3}{4}}$

22.

$$m - \frac{2}{3} = 1\frac{3}{4}$$

$$m - \frac{2}{3} + \frac{2}{3} = 1\frac{3}{4} + \frac{2}{3}$$

$$m = 1\frac{9}{12} + \frac{8}{12}$$

$$m = 1\frac{17}{12} = \mathbf{2\frac{5}{12}}$$

check:

$$2\frac{5}{12} - \frac{2}{3} = 1\frac{3}{4}$$

$$2\frac{5}{12} - \frac{8}{12} = 1\frac{3}{4}$$

$$1\frac{17}{12} - \frac{8}{12} = 1\frac{3}{4}$$

$$1\frac{9}{12} = 1\frac{3}{4}$$

$$1\frac{3}{4} = 1\frac{3}{4}$$

23.

$$\frac{2}{3}w = 24$$

$$\left(\frac{\cancel{3}^{1}}{\cancel{2}_{1}}\right)\frac{\cancel{2}^{1}}{\cancel{3}_{1}}w = \left(\frac{3}{\cancel{2}_{1}}\right)\cancel{24}^{12}$$

$$w = 3(12)$$

$$w = \mathbf{36}$$

check:

$$\left(\frac{2}{\cancel{3}_{1}}\right)\cancel{36}^{12} = 24$$

$$2(12) = 24$$

$$24 = 24$$

24.

$$\frac{[30 - 4(5 - 2)] + 5(3^3 - 5^2)}{\sqrt{9} + \sqrt{16}}$$

$$\frac{[30 - 12] + 5(27 - 25)}{3 + 4}$$

$$\frac{18 + 5(2)}{7}$$

$$\frac{18 + 10}{7}$$

$$\frac{28}{7}$$

$$\mathbf{4}$$

25.

$\cancel{2}^{1}$ gal	1 qt (4 qt)		→
− 1 gal	1 qt	1 pt	

$\cancel{2}^{1}$ gal	$\cancel{\cancel{1}}^{\cancel{5}\,4}$ qt	(2 pt)	→
− 1 gal	1 qt	1 pt	

$\cancel{2}^{1}$ gal	$\cancel{\cancel{1}}^{\cancel{5}\,4}$ qt	2 pt
− 1 gal	1 qt	1 pt
	3 qt	**1 pt**

26.

$$\frac{1}{\cancel{2}_{1}}\ \cancel{\text{mi}} \cdot \frac{\cancel{5280}^{\cancel{1760}\ 880}\ \cancel{\text{ft}}}{1\ \cancel{\text{mi}}} \cdot \frac{1 \text{ yd}}{\cancel{3}_{1}\ \cancel{\text{ft}}}$$

$$= \mathbf{880 \text{ yd}}$$

27.

$$4\frac{1}{2} \cdot 6\frac{2}{3} = \frac{\cancel{9}^{3}}{\cancel{2}_{1}} \cdot \frac{\cancel{20}^{10}}{\cancel{3}_{1}} = 30$$

$$\left(2\frac{1}{2}\right)^2 \div 30 = \left(\frac{5}{2}\right)^2 \div 30$$

$$= \frac{25}{4} \div \frac{30}{1} = \frac{\cancel{25}^{5}}{4} \times \frac{1}{\cancel{30}_{6}}$$

$$= \mathbf{\frac{5}{24}}$$

28.

$$5\frac{1}{6} = 5\frac{1}{6}$$

$$+\ 1\frac{1}{3} = 1\frac{2}{6}$$

$$6\frac{3}{6} = 6\frac{1}{2}$$

$$7\frac{1}{2}$$

$$-\ 6\frac{1}{2}$$

$$\mathbf{1}$$

29. (a) $(-7) + |+5| + (-9)$
$= (-7) + 5 + (-9) = \mathbf{-11}$

(b) $(16) + (-24) - (-18)$
$(16) + (-24) + [-(-18)]$
$(16) + (-24) + [18]$
$\mathbf{10}$

30. $5\frac{1}{4} = 5.25$

$$\begin{array}{r} 5.25 \\ +\ 1.9 \\ \hline \mathbf{7.15} \end{array}$$

Lesson 73, Lesson Practice

a. $(-7)(3) = \mathbf{-21}$

b. $(+4)(-8) = \mathbf{-32}$

c. $(8)(+5) = \mathbf{40}$

d. $(-8)(-3) = \mathbf{24}$

e. $\frac{25}{-5} = \mathbf{-5}$

f. $\frac{-27}{-3} = \mathbf{9}$

g. $\frac{-28}{4} = \mathbf{-7}$

h. $\frac{+30}{6} = \mathbf{5}$

i. $\frac{+45}{-3} = \mathbf{-15}$

Lesson 73, Mixed Practice

1.

	Case 1	Case 2
Packages	12	p
Minutes	5	60

$\frac{12}{5} = \frac{p}{60}$
$5p = 12(60)$
$p = \frac{720}{5}$
$p = \mathbf{144\ packages}$

2. $5(30\text{ minutes}) + 3(46\text{ minutes})$
$= 150\text{ minutes} + 138\text{ minutes}$
$= 288\text{ minutes}$

$\frac{288\text{ minutes}}{8} = \mathbf{36\ minutes}$

3. $\frac{(0.2 + 0.5)}{(0.2)(0.5)} = \frac{0.7}{0.1} = \mathbf{7}$

4. $23\ \cancel{\text{cm}} \cdot \frac{10\text{ mm}}{1\ \cancel{\text{cm}}} = \mathbf{230\ mm}$

5.

	Ratio	Actual Count
Paperback books	3	P
Hardback books	11	9240
Total	14	T

$\frac{11}{14} = \frac{9240}{T}$
$11T = 14(9240)$
$T = \frac{129{,}360}{11}$
$T = \mathbf{11{,}760\ books}$

6. (a) $\mathbf{2.4 \times 10^{-4}}$

(b) $\mathbf{2.4 \times 10^{8}}$

7.

120 questions

$\frac{1}{4}$ were true-false. { 30 questions

$\frac{3}{4}$ were not true-false. { 30 questions, 30 questions, 30 questions

(a) $4(30\text{ questions}) = \mathbf{120\ questions}$

(b) $3(30\text{ questions}) = \mathbf{90\ questions}$

8. (a) $\frac{5}{\cancel{9}_1} \times \cancel{45}^{5} = W_N$

$25 = W_N$

(b) $W_N = 0.8 \times 760$
$W_N = \mathbf{608}$

9. (a) $\frac{-36}{9} = \mathbf{-4}$

(b) $\frac{-36}{-6} = \mathbf{6}$

(c) $9(-3) = \mathbf{-27}$

(d) $(+8)(+7) = \mathbf{56}$

10. $\frac{\text{composite numbers}}{\text{total numbers}} = \mathbf{\frac{3}{8}}$

11. 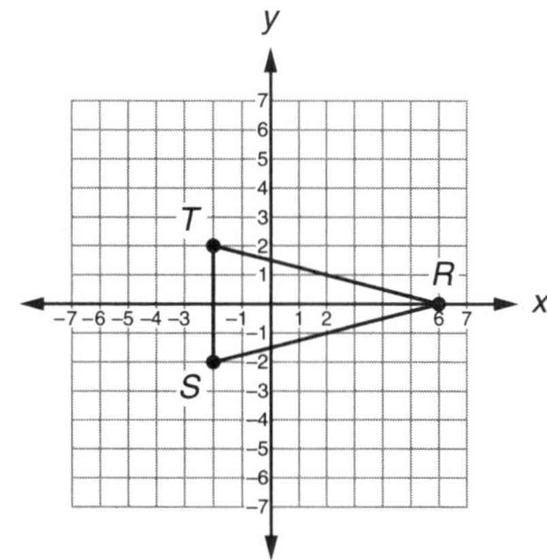

(a) **(−2, 2)**

(b) **Isosceles triangle**

(c) $m\angle S = \dfrac{180° - 28°}{2} = \mathbf{76°}$

12. **If the signs of the two factors are the same—both positive or both negative—then the product is positive. If the signs of the two factors are different, the product is negative.**

13. (4 1-ft cubes)(3 1-ft cubes)
= 12 1-ft cubes

$\dfrac{12 \text{ 1-ft cubes}}{1 \cancel{\text{layer}}} \cdot 8 \cancel{\text{layers}}$
= **96 1-ft cubes**

14. (a) $C \approx 3.14(42 \text{ m})$
$C \approx \mathbf{131.88 \text{ m}}$

(b) $C \approx \dfrac{22}{7}(42 \text{ m})$
$C \approx \mathbf{132 \text{ m}}$

15. (a) $2.5 = 2\dfrac{5}{10} = \mathbf{2\dfrac{1}{2}}$

(b) $2.5 \times 100\% = \mathbf{250\%}$

(c) $0.2\% = \dfrac{0.2}{100} = \mathbf{\dfrac{1}{500}}$

(d) $0.2\% = \dfrac{0.2}{100} = \mathbf{0.002}$

16. **Right; scalene**
$\text{Area} = \dfrac{(6 \text{ cm})(8 \text{ cm})}{2} = \mathbf{24 \text{ cm}^2}$

17. **Obtuse; scalene**
$\text{Area} = \dfrac{(4 \text{ cm})(5 \text{ cm})}{2} = \mathbf{10 \text{ cm}^2}$

18. **Acute; isosceles**
$\text{Area} = \dfrac{(6 \text{ cm})(4 \text{ cm})}{2} = \mathbf{12 \text{ cm}^2}$

19. (a) **Pyramid**
(b) **Cylinder**
(c) **Cone**

20. $\dfrac{2}{3} \times 96 = 64$

$\dfrac{5}{6} \times 84 = 70$

$64 < 70$

$\dfrac{2}{3} \text{ of } 96 \; \textcircled{<} \; \dfrac{5}{6} \text{ of } 84$

21. $\left(\dfrac{5}{6}\right)\left(\dfrac{3}{4}\right) - \left(\dfrac{5}{6} - \dfrac{3}{4}\right)$

$= \dfrac{5}{8} - \left(\dfrac{10}{12} - \dfrac{9}{12}\right) = \dfrac{5}{8} - \dfrac{1}{12}$

$= \dfrac{15}{24} - \dfrac{2}{24} = \mathbf{\dfrac{13}{24}}$

22. $\dfrac{3}{5}w = 15$

$\left(\dfrac{\overset{1}{\cancel{5}}}{\underset{1}{\cancel{3}}}\right)\left(\dfrac{\overset{1}{\cancel{3}}}{\underset{1}{\cancel{5}}}\right)w = \left(\dfrac{5}{\underset{1}{\cancel{3}}}\right)\overset{5}{\cancel{15}}$

$w = 5(5)$
$w = \mathbf{25}$

check: $\dfrac{3}{\underset{1}{\cancel{5}}}(\overset{5}{\cancel{25}}) = 15$
$3(5) = 15$
$15 = 15$

23. $b - 1.6 = (0.4)^2$
$b - 1.6 + 1.6 = (0.4)^2 + 1.6$
$b = 0.16 + 1.6$
$b = \mathbf{1.76}$

check: $1.76 - 1.6 = (0.4)^2$
$0.16 = 0.16$

24. $20w = 5.6$

$\dfrac{\overset{1}{\cancel{20}}w}{\underset{1}{\cancel{20}}} = \dfrac{5.6}{20}$

$w = \mathbf{0.28}$

check: $20(0.28) = 5.6$
$5.6 = 5.6$

25.
$$\begin{array}{rrr} 2\text{ yd} & 1\text{ ft} & 7\text{ in.} \\ +\ 1\text{ yd} & 2\text{ ft} & 8\text{ in.} \\ \hline 3\text{ yd} & 3\text{ ft} & 15\text{ in.} \end{array}$$

$15\text{ in.} = 1\text{ ft}\ \ 3\text{ in.}$

$$\begin{array}{rr} 1\text{ ft} & 3\text{ in.} \\ +\ 3\text{ ft} & \\ \hline 4\text{ ft} & 3\text{ in.} \end{array}$$

$4\text{ ft} = 1\text{ yd } 1\text{ ft}$

$$\begin{array}{rrr} 1\text{ yd} & 1\text{ ft} & 3\text{ in.} \\ +\ 3\text{ yd} & & \\ \hline \mathbf{4\ yd} & \mathbf{1\ ft} & \mathbf{3\ in.} \end{array}$$

26. $0.5\ \cancel{\text{m}} \cdot \frac{100\ \cancel{\text{cm}}}{1\ \cancel{\text{m}}} \cdot \frac{10\text{ mm}}{1\ \cancel{\text{cm}}} = \mathbf{500\ mm}$

27. $12\frac{1}{2} \cdot 4\frac{1}{5} \cdot 2\frac{2}{3} = \frac{\overset{5}{\cancel{25}}}{\underset{1}{\cancel{2}}} \cdot \frac{\overset{7}{\cancel{21}}}{\underset{1}{\cancel{5}}} \cdot \frac{\overset{4}{\cancel{8}}}{\underset{1}{\cancel{3}}} = \mathbf{140}$

28. $6\frac{2}{3} \cdot 1\frac{1}{5} = \frac{\overset{4}{\cancel{20}}}{\underset{1}{\cancel{3}}} \cdot \frac{\overset{2}{\cancel{6}}}{\underset{1}{\cancel{5}}} = 8$

$7\frac{1}{2} \div 8 = \frac{15}{2} \div \frac{8}{1} = \frac{15}{2} \times \frac{1}{8}$

$= \mathbf{\frac{15}{16}}$

29. (a) $(-8) + (-7) - (-15)$

$(-8) + (-7) + [-(-15)]$

$(-8) + (-7) + [15]$

$\mathbf{0}$

(b) $(-15) + (+11) - |+24|$

$(-15) + (+11) + [-|+24|]$

$(-15) + (+11) + [-24]$

$\mathbf{-28}$

30. $2.25 = 2\frac{1}{4}$

$2\frac{1}{4} \times 1\frac{1}{3} = \frac{\overset{3}{\cancel{9}}}{\underset{1}{\cancel{4}}} \times \frac{\overset{1}{\cancel{4}}}{\underset{1}{\cancel{3}}} = \mathbf{3}$

Lesson 74, Lesson Practice

a. $\mathbf{W_F \times 130 = 80}$

$\frac{W_F \times 130}{130} = \frac{80}{130}$

$W_F = \mathbf{\frac{8}{13}}$

b. $\mathbf{75 = W_D \times 300}$

$\frac{75}{300} = \frac{W_D \times 300}{300}$

$\mathbf{0.25} = W_D$

c. $\mathbf{80 = 0.4 \times W_N}$

$\frac{80}{0.4} = \frac{0.4 \times W_N}{0.4}$

$\mathbf{200} = W_N$

d. $\mathbf{60 = \frac{5}{6} \times W_N}$

$\frac{6}{5} \times 60 = \frac{6}{5} \times \frac{5}{6} \times W_N$

$6(12) = W_N$

$\mathbf{72} = W_N$

e. $\mathbf{60 = W_F \times 90}$

$\frac{60}{90} = \frac{W_F \times 90}{90}$

$\mathbf{\frac{2}{3}} = W_F$

f. $\mathbf{W_D \times 80 = 60}$

$\frac{W_D \times 80}{80} = \frac{60}{80}$

$W_D = \mathbf{0.75}$

g. $\mathbf{40 = 0.08 \times W_N}$

$\frac{40}{0.08} = \frac{0.08 \times W_N}{0.08}$

$\mathbf{500} = W_N$

h. $\mathbf{\frac{6}{5} \times W_N = 60}$

$\frac{5}{6} \times \frac{6}{5} \times W_N = \frac{5}{6} \times 60$

$W_N = 5(10)$

$W_N = \mathbf{50}$

Lesson 74, Mixed Practice

1. $3(28\text{ pages}) + 4(42\text{ pages})$

$= 84\text{ pages} + 168\text{ pages}$

$= 252\text{ pages}$

$\frac{252\text{ pages}}{7} = \mathbf{36\ pages}$

2. $\frac{\$1.14}{12\text{ ounces}} = \frac{\$0.095}{1\text{ ounce}}$

$\frac{\$1.28}{16\text{ ounces}} = \frac{\$0.08}{1\text{ ounce}}$

$$\begin{array}{r} \$0.095 \\ -\ \$0.08 \\ \hline \$0.015 \end{array}$$

1.5¢ per ounce

3. $4\frac{1}{2}\text{ feet} \cdot \frac{12\text{ inches}}{1\text{ foot}} = \textbf{54 inches}$

4.

	Ratio	Actual Count
Left-handed students	2	L
Right-handed students	3	18
Total	5	T

$\frac{3}{5} = \frac{18}{T}$

$3T = 90$

$T = $ **30 students**

5.

	Case 1	Case 2
Pounds	5	8
Cost	$1.40	C

$\frac{5}{\$1.40} = \frac{8}{C}$

$5C = (\$1.40)(8)$

$C = \frac{\$11.20}{5}$

$C = \textbf{\$2.24}$

6.

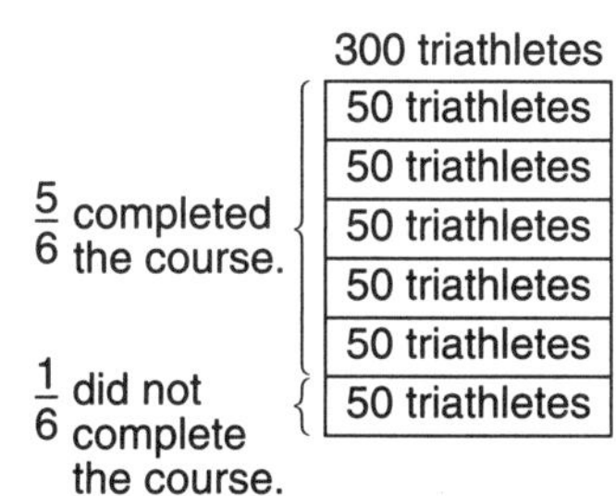

(a) **250 triathletes**

(b) $\frac{\text{completed the course}}{\text{did not complete the course}} = \mathbf{\frac{5}{1}}$

7. $\mathbf{15 = \frac{3}{8} \times W_N}$

$\frac{8}{3} \times 15 = \frac{8}{3} \times \frac{3}{8} \times W_N$

$8(5) = W_N$

$\mathbf{40} = W_N$

8. $\mathbf{70 = W_D \times 200}$

$\frac{70}{200} = \frac{W_D \times 200}{200}$

$\mathbf{0.35} = W_D$

9. $\mathbf{\frac{2}{5} \times W_N = 120}$

$\frac{5}{2} \times \frac{2}{5} \times W_N = \frac{5}{2} \times 120$

$W_N = 5(60)$

$W_N = \mathbf{300}$

10. $\mathbf{P = 0.6 \times \$180}$

$P = \textbf{\$108}$

11. $\mathbf{W_N = 0.2 \times \$35}$

$W_N = \textbf{\$7}$

12. (a) $(3\text{ in.})(3\text{ in.}) = 9\text{ in.}^2$

$\frac{9\text{ in.}^2}{1\text{ layer}} \cdot (1\text{ in.})(3\text{ layers})$

$= \mathbf{27\ in.^3}$

(b) $6(9\text{ in.}^2) = \mathbf{54\ in.^2}$

13. (a) $C \approx \frac{22}{7}(14\text{ m})$

$C \approx \mathbf{44\ m}$

(b) $C = \pi(14\text{ m})$

$C = \mathbf{14\pi\ m}$

14. (a) $3\frac{1}{2} = \mathbf{3.5}$

(b) $3\frac{1}{2} = \frac{7}{2} \times 100\% = \frac{700\%}{2} = \mathbf{350\%}$

(c) $35\% = \frac{35}{100} = \mathbf{\frac{7}{20}}$

(d) $35\% = \frac{35}{100} = \mathbf{0.35}$

15. **Multiply the "in" number by 3; then add 1 to find the "out" number.**

$5(3) + 1 = \mathbf{16}$

$25 - 1 = 24$

$24 \div 3 = \mathbf{8}$

16. $\mathbf{4.25 \times 10^8}$

17. (a) **Parallelogram**

(b) **Trapezoid**

(c) **Isosceles triangle**

18. (a) $m\angle ABC = 180° - 100° = \mathbf{80°}$

(b) $m\angle BCE = m\angle A = \mathbf{100°}$

(c) $m\angle ECD = 180° - 100° = \mathbf{80°}$

(d) $m\angle EDC = m\angle ECD = \mathbf{80°}$

(e) $m\angle DEC = 180° - (80° + 80°)$
$= 180° - 160° = \mathbf{20°}$

(f) $m\angle DEA = 20° + 80° = \mathbf{100°}$

19. **0.0103, 0.013, 0.021, 0.1023**

20.
$$\left(1\frac{1}{2} + 2\frac{2}{3}\right) - \left(1\frac{1}{2}\right)\left(2\frac{2}{3}\right)$$
$$= \left(\frac{3}{2} + \frac{8}{3}\right) - \left(\frac{3}{2}\right)\left(\frac{8}{3}\right)$$
$$= \left(\frac{3}{2} + \frac{8}{3}\right) - (4)$$
$$= \frac{9}{6} + \frac{16}{6} - \frac{24}{6}$$
$$= \frac{25}{6} - \frac{24}{6} = \mathbf{\frac{1}{6}}$$

21.
$$p + 3\frac{1}{5} = 7\frac{1}{2}$$
$$p + 3\frac{1}{5} - 3\frac{1}{5} = 7\frac{1}{2} - 3\frac{1}{5}$$
$$p = \frac{15}{2} - \frac{16}{5}$$
$$p = \frac{75}{10} - \frac{32}{10}$$
$$p = \frac{43}{10} = \mathbf{4\frac{3}{10}}$$

check:
$$4\frac{3}{10} + 3\frac{1}{5} = 7\frac{1}{2}$$
$$4\frac{3}{10} + 3\frac{2}{10} = 7\frac{1}{2}$$
$$7\frac{5}{10} = 7\frac{1}{2}$$
$$7\frac{1}{2} = 7\frac{1}{2}$$

22.
$$3n = 0.138$$
$$\frac{3n}{3} = \frac{0.138}{3}$$
$$n = \mathbf{0.046}$$

check:
$$3(0.046) = 0.138$$
$$0.138 = 0.138$$

23.
$$n - 0.36 = 4.8$$
$$n - 0.36 + 0.36 = 4.8 + 0.36$$
$$n = \mathbf{5.16}$$

check:
$$5.16 - 0.36 = 4.8$$
$$4.8 = 4.8$$

24.
$$\frac{2}{3}x = \frac{8}{9}$$
$$\left(\frac{\overset{1}{\cancel{3}}}{\underset{1}{\cancel{2}}}\right)\left(\frac{\overset{1}{\cancel{2}}}{\underset{1}{\cancel{3}}}x\right) = \left(\frac{\overset{1}{\cancel{3}}}{\underset{1}{\cancel{2}}}\right)\left(\frac{\overset{4}{\cancel{8}}}{\underset{3}{\cancel{9}}}\right)$$
$$x = \mathbf{\frac{4}{3}}$$

check:
$$\left(\frac{2}{3}\right)\left(\frac{4}{3}\right) = \frac{8}{9}$$
$$\frac{8}{9} = \frac{8}{9}$$

25.
$$\sqrt{49} + \{5[3^2 - (2^3 - \sqrt{25})] - 5^2\}$$
$$7 + \{5[9 - (8 - 5)] - 25\}$$
$$7 + \{5[9 - (3)] - 25\}$$
$$7 + \{5[6] - 25\}$$
$$7 + \{30 - 25\}$$
$$7 + \{5\}$$
$$\mathbf{12}$$

26.

(60 min) regrouped from hr: $\overset{3}{\cancel{4}}$ hr; (60 s) regrouped from min: $\overset{4}{\cancel{5}}$ min

$\overset{3}{\cancel{4}}$ hr	$\overset{4}{\cancel{5}}$ min	15 s
− 1 hr	15 min	30 s

⟶

$\overset{3}{\cancel{4}}$ hr	$\overset{64}{\cancel{\overset{4}{\cancel{5}}}}$ min	$\overset{75}{\cancel{15}}$ s
− 1 hr	15 min	30 s
2 hr	**49 min**	**45 s**

27. (a)
$$(-9) + (-11) - (+14)$$
$$(-9) + (-11) + [-(+14)]$$
$$(-9) + (-11) + [-14]$$
$$\mathbf{-34}$$

(b)
$$(26) + (-43) - |-36|$$
$$(26) + (-43) + [-|-36|]$$
$$(26) + (-43) + [-36]$$
$$\mathbf{-53}$$

28. (a) $(-3)(12) = \mathbf{-36}$

(b) $(-3)(-12) = \mathbf{36}$

(c) $\dfrac{-12}{3} = \mathbf{-4}$

(d) $\dfrac{-12}{-3} = \mathbf{4}$

29. $7.5 = 7\frac{1}{2}$

$$8\frac{1}{3} + 7\frac{1}{2} = 8\frac{2}{6} + 7\frac{3}{6} = \mathbf{15\frac{5}{6}}$$

30. **South**

Lesson 75, Lesson Practice

a.

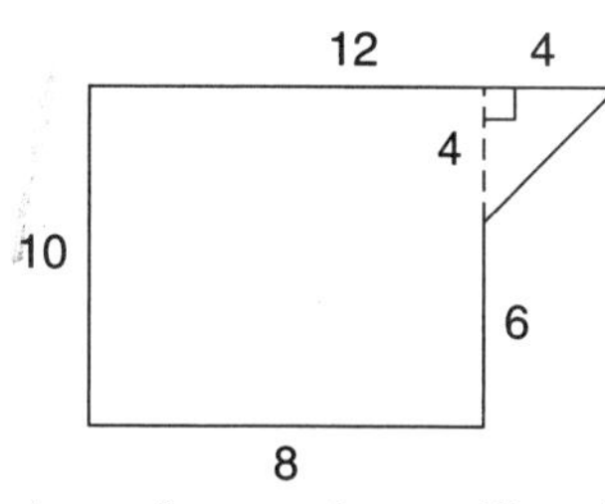

$$\begin{aligned}\text{Area of rectangle} &= (8 \text{ cm})(10 \text{ cm}) \\ &= 80 \text{ cm}^2 \\ \text{Area of triangle} &= \frac{(4 \text{ cm})(4 \text{ cm})}{2} \\ &= 8 \text{ cm}^2 \\ \text{Area of figure} &= 80 \text{ cm}^2 + 8 \text{ cm}^2 \\ &= \mathbf{88 \text{ cm}^2}\end{aligned}$$

b.

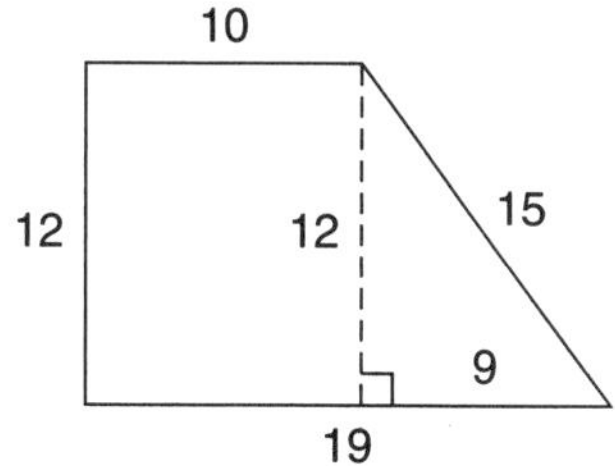

$$\begin{aligned}\text{Area of rectangle} &= (10 \text{ cm})(12 \text{ cm}) \\ &= 120 \text{ cm}^2 \\ \text{Area of triangle} &= \frac{(9 \text{ cm})(12 \text{ cm})}{2} \\ &= 54 \text{ cm}^2 \\ \text{Area of figure} &= 120 \text{ cm}^2 + 54 \text{ cm}^2 \\ &= \mathbf{174 \text{ cm}^2}\end{aligned}$$

c.

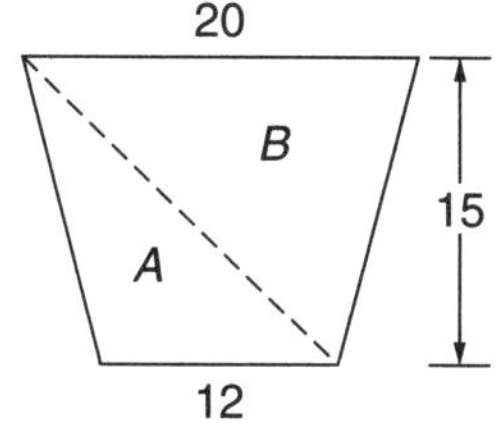

$$\begin{aligned}\text{Area of triangle } A &= \frac{(12 \text{ cm})(15 \text{ cm})}{2} \\ &= 90 \text{ cm}^2 \\ \text{Area of triangle } B &= \frac{(20 \text{ cm})(15 \text{ cm})}{2} \\ &= 150 \text{ cm}^2 \\ \text{Area of figure} &= 90 \text{ cm}^2 + 150 \text{ cm}^2 \\ &= \mathbf{240 \text{ cm}^2}\end{aligned}$$

Lesson 75, Mixed Practice

1. 5(72 seconds) + 3(80 seconds)
= 360 seconds + 240 seconds = 600 seconds

$\frac{600 \text{ seconds}}{8} = \mathbf{75 \text{ seconds}}$

2. $\frac{\$2.49}{30 \text{ ounces}} = \frac{\$0.083}{1 \text{ ounce}}$

8.3¢ per ounce

3. **1.5 kilometers**

4.

$$\begin{aligned}&\left(\frac{1}{2} + \frac{3}{5}\right) - \left(\frac{1}{2}\right)\left(\frac{3}{5}\right) \\ &= \left(\frac{5}{10} + \frac{6}{10}\right) - \left(\frac{3}{10}\right) \\ &= \frac{11}{10} - \frac{3}{10} = \frac{8}{10} \\ &= \mathbf{\frac{4}{5}}\end{aligned}$$

5.

$$\begin{aligned}\frac{3}{2} &= \frac{60 \text{ years}}{C} \\ 3C &= 2(60 \text{ years}) \\ C &= 40 \text{ years}\end{aligned}$$

$$\begin{array}{r} 60 \text{ years} \\ -\ 40 \text{ years} \\ \hline \mathbf{20 \text{ years}} \end{array}$$

6. $12.5 \times 10^{-4} \ \textcircled{=}\ 1.25 \times 10^{-3}$

7.

	Case 1	Case 2
Miles	40	100
Hours	3	h

$$\begin{aligned}\frac{40}{3} &= \frac{100}{h} \\ 40h &= 3(100) \\ h &= \frac{300}{40} \\ h &= \frac{15}{2} = \mathbf{7\frac{1}{2} \text{ hours}}\end{aligned}$$

8.

21,000 books

$\frac{2}{5}$ were checked out.
- 4200 books
- 4200 books

$\frac{3}{5}$ were not checked out.
- 4200 books
- 4200 books
- 4200 books

(a) **8400 books**

(b) **12,600 books**

9.

$$\mathbf{60 = \frac{5}{12} \times W_N}$$

$$\frac{12}{\cancel{5}_1}(\cancel{60}^{12}) = \frac{\cancel{12}^1}{\cancel{5}_1} \times \frac{\cancel{5}^1}{\cancel{12}_1} \times W_N$$

$$\mathbf{144} = W_N$$

10. $\mathbf{0.7 \times \$35.00 = M}$
$\mathbf{\$24.50} = M$

11. $\mathbf{35 = W_F \times 80}$
$$\frac{35}{80} = \frac{W_F \times 80}{80}$$
$$\mathbf{\frac{7}{16}} = W_F$$

12. $\mathbf{56 = W_D \times 70}$
$$\frac{56}{70} = \frac{W_D \times 70}{70}$$
$$\mathbf{0.8} = W_D$$

13. (a) $\frac{-120}{4} = \mathbf{-30}$

(b) $(-12)(11) = \mathbf{-132}$

(c) $\frac{-120}{-5} = \mathbf{24}$

(d) $12(+20) = \mathbf{240}$

14. $(20\text{ cm})(15\text{ cm}) = 300\text{ cm}^2$
$$\frac{300\text{ cm}^2}{1\text{ }\cancel{\text{layer}}} \cdot (1\text{ cm})(10\text{ }\cancel{\text{layers}})$$
$\mathbf{3000\text{ cm}^3}$

15. $C \approx \frac{22}{7}(11\text{ inches})$
$$C \approx \frac{242}{7}\text{ inches}$$
$$C \approx 34\frac{4}{7}\text{ inches} \approx \mathbf{34\frac{1}{2}\text{ inches}}$$

16.

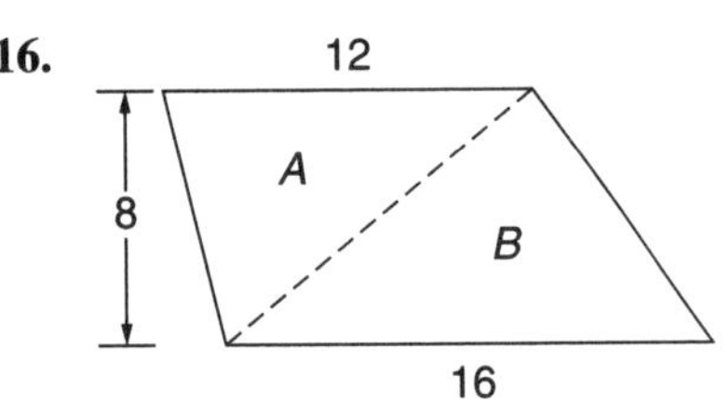

$$\text{Area of triangle } A = \frac{(12\text{ in.})(8\text{ in.})}{2} = 48\text{ in.}^2$$
$$\text{Area of triangle } B = \frac{(16\text{ in.})(8\text{ in.})}{2} = 64\text{ in.}^2$$
$$\text{Area of figure} = 48\text{ in.}^2 + 64\text{ in.}^2 = \mathbf{112\text{ in.}^2}$$

17.

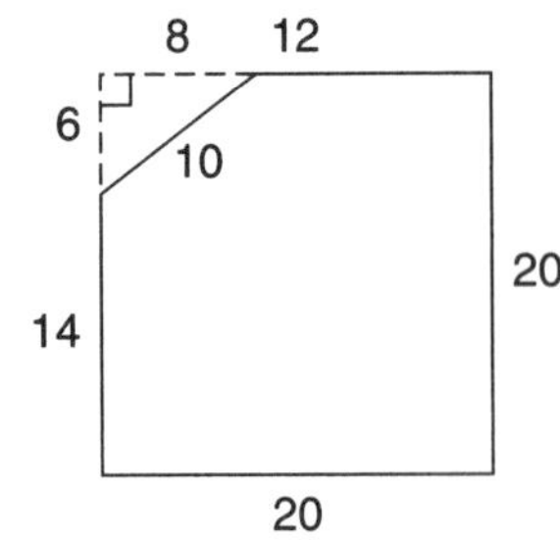

(a) **20 cm**

(b) Perimeter = 12 cm + 20 cm + 20 cm + 14 cm + 10 cm = **76 cm**

(c) $$\text{Area of rectangle} = (20\text{ cm})(20\text{ cm}) = 400\text{ cm}^2$$
$$\text{Area of triangle} = \frac{(8\text{ cm})(6\text{ cm})}{2} = 24\text{ cm}^2$$
$$\text{Area of figure} = 400\text{ cm}^2 - 24\text{ cm}^2 = \mathbf{376\text{ cm}^2}$$

18. (a) $125\% = \frac{125}{100} = \mathbf{1\frac{1}{4}}$

(b) $125\% = \frac{125}{100} = \mathbf{1.25}$

(c) $8\overline{)1.000}$ = **0.125**

(d) $\frac{1}{8} \times 100\% = \frac{100\%}{8} = \mathbf{12\frac{1}{2}\%}$ or **12.5%**

19.
$$\begin{array}{r} \$12.50 \\ \times \quad 0.20 \\ \hline \$\ 2.50 \end{array} \qquad \begin{array}{r} \$12.50 \\ +\ \$\ 2.50 \\ \hline \mathbf{\$15.00} \end{array}$$

20. $(2)^3 - (2)(0.5) - \frac{2}{0.5}$
$= 8 - 1 - 4 = \mathbf{3}$

21. $$\frac{5}{8}x = 40$$
$$\left(\frac{\cancel{8}^1}{\cancel{5}_1}\right)\frac{\cancel{5}^1}{\cancel{8}_1}x = \left(\frac{8}{\cancel{5}_1}\right)\cancel{40}^8$$
$$x = \mathbf{64}$$

check: $\frac{5}{\cancel{8}_1}(\cancel{64}^8) = 40$
$5(8) = 40$
$40 = 40$

22.
$$\begin{aligned} 1.2w &= 26.4 \\ \frac{1.2w}{1.2} &= \frac{26.4}{1.2} \\ w &= \mathbf{22} \end{aligned}$$

check:
$$\begin{aligned} 1.2(22) &= 26.4 \\ 26.4 &= 26.4 \end{aligned}$$

23.
$$\begin{aligned} y + 3.6 &= 8.47 \\ y + 3.6 - 3.6 &= 8.47 - 3.6 \\ y &= \mathbf{4.87} \end{aligned}$$

check:
$$\begin{aligned} 4.87 + 3.6 &= 8.47 \\ 8.47 &= 8.47 \end{aligned}$$

24.
$$\begin{gathered} 9^2 - [3^3 - (9 \cdot 3 - \sqrt{9})] \\ 81 - [27 - (27 - 3)] \\ 81 - [27 - (24)] \\ 81 - [3] \\ \mathbf{78} \end{gathered}$$

25.
$$\begin{array}{r} \text{2 hr } \overset{47}{\cancel{48}} \text{ min } 20 \text{ s} \rightarrow (60 \text{ s}) \\ -\ \text{1 hr } 23 \text{ min } 48 \text{ s} \\ \hline \end{array} \longrightarrow$$

$$\begin{array}{r} \text{2 hr } \overset{47}{\cancel{48}} \text{ min } \overset{80}{\cancel{20}} \text{ s} \\ -\ \text{1 hr } 23 \text{ min } 48 \text{ s} \\ \hline \textbf{1 hr 24 min 32 s} \end{array}$$

26.
$$100 \cancel{\text{yd}} \cdot \frac{3 \cancel{\text{ft}}}{1 \cancel{\text{yd}}} \cdot \frac{12 \text{ in.}}{1 \cancel{\text{ft}}}$$
$$= \mathbf{3600\ in.}$$

27.
$$\begin{aligned} 3 \div 1\frac{1}{3} &= \frac{3}{1} \div \frac{4}{3} \\ &= \frac{3}{1} \times \frac{3}{4} = \frac{9}{4} \end{aligned}$$

$$5\frac{1}{3} \cdot \frac{9}{4} = \frac{\overset{4}{\cancel{16}}}{\underset{1}{\cancel{3}}} \cdot \frac{\overset{3}{\cancel{9}}}{\underset{1}{\cancel{4}}} = \mathbf{12}$$

28.
$$\begin{aligned} & 3\frac{1}{5} + 2\frac{1}{2} - 1\frac{1}{4} \\ &= 3\frac{4}{20} + 2\frac{10}{20} - 1\frac{5}{20} \\ &= 5\frac{14}{20} - 1\frac{5}{20} = \mathbf{4\frac{9}{20}} \end{aligned}$$

29. (a)
$$\begin{gathered} (-26) + (-15) - (-40) \\ (-26) + (-15) + [-(-40)] \\ (-26) + (-15) + [40] \\ \mathbf{-1} \end{gathered}$$

(b)
$$\begin{gathered} (-5) + (-4) - (-3) - (+2) \\ (-5) + (-4) + [-(-3)] + [-(+2)] \\ (-5) + (-4) + [3] + [-2] \\ \mathbf{-8} \end{gathered}$$

30. (a) 5^7

(b) 5^3

(c) 5^0

(d) 5^{-3}

Lesson 76, Lesson Practice

a.
$$\frac{37\frac{1}{2}}{100} = \frac{\frac{75}{2}}{\frac{100}{1}}$$

$$\frac{\frac{75}{2}}{\frac{100}{1}} \cdot \frac{\frac{1}{100}}{\frac{1}{100}} = \frac{\frac{75}{200}}{1} = \frac{75}{200}$$
$$= \mathbf{\frac{3}{8}}$$

b.
$$\frac{12}{\frac{5}{6}} = \frac{\frac{12}{1}}{\frac{5}{6}}$$

$$\frac{\frac{12}{1}}{\frac{5}{6}} \cdot \frac{\frac{6}{5}}{\frac{6}{5}} = \frac{\frac{72}{5}}{1} = \frac{72}{5} = \mathbf{14\frac{2}{5}}$$

c.
$$\frac{\frac{2}{5}}{\frac{2}{3}} \cdot \frac{\frac{3}{2}}{\frac{3}{2}} = \frac{\frac{6}{10}}{1} = \frac{6}{10} = \mathbf{\frac{3}{5}}$$

d.
$$66\frac{2}{3}\% = \frac{66\frac{2}{3}}{100} = \frac{\frac{200}{3}}{\frac{100}{1}}$$

$$\frac{\frac{200}{3}}{\frac{100}{1}} \cdot \frac{\frac{1}{100}}{\frac{1}{100}} = \frac{\frac{200}{300}}{1} = \frac{200}{300} = \mathbf{\frac{2}{3}}$$

e.
$$8\frac{1}{3}\% = \frac{8\frac{1}{3}}{100} = \frac{\frac{25}{3}}{\frac{100}{1}}$$

$$\frac{\frac{25}{3}}{\frac{100}{1}} \cdot \frac{\frac{1}{100}}{\frac{1}{100}} = \frac{\frac{25}{300}}{1} = \frac{25}{300} = \mathbf{\frac{1}{12}}$$

f.
$$4\frac{1}{6}\% = \frac{4\frac{1}{6}}{100} = \frac{\frac{25}{6}}{\frac{100}{1}}$$

$$\frac{\frac{25}{6}}{\frac{100}{1}} \cdot \frac{\frac{1}{100}}{\frac{1}{100}} = \frac{\frac{25}{600}}{1} = \frac{25}{600} = \mathbf{\frac{1}{24}}$$

Lesson 76, Mixed Practice

1. $\dfrac{42 \text{ kilometers}}{1.75 \text{ hours}}$ = **24 kilometers per hour**

2.
$$\begin{array}{r} 7.9 \\ 8.3 \\ 8.1 \\ 8.1 \\ +\ 8.2 \\ \hline 40.6 \end{array} \qquad 5\overline{)40.60}\ \ \mathbf{8.12}$$

3.

	Ratio	Actual Count
Good guys	2	G
Bad guys	5	B
Total	7	35

$$\frac{2}{7} = \frac{G}{35}$$
$$7G = 35(2)$$
$$G = \frac{70}{7}$$
$$G = \mathbf{10\ guys}$$

4. $\mathbf{3.5\ \cancel{grams} \cdot \frac{1000\ milligrams}{1\ \cancel{gram}}}$
$= \mathbf{3500\ milligrams}$

5. $16\frac{2}{3}\% = \dfrac{16\frac{2}{3}}{100} = \dfrac{\frac{50}{3}}{\frac{100}{1}}$

$$\frac{\frac{50}{3}}{\frac{100}{1}} \cdot \frac{\frac{1}{100}}{\frac{1}{100}} = \frac{\frac{50}{300}}{1} = \frac{50}{300} = \mathbf{\frac{1}{6}}$$

6. **East**

7. $\dfrac{1}{\cancel{6}_1} \times \overset{24}{\cancel{144}}\text{ grams} = \mathbf{24\ grams}$

8. (a) $\sqrt{2(2)^3} = \sqrt{2^4} = 2^2 = \mathbf{4}$

(b) $(2)^{-1} \cdot (2)^{-2} = \dfrac{1}{2} \cdot \dfrac{1}{4} = \mathbf{\dfrac{1}{8}}$

9. (a) $\dfrac{-60}{-12} = \mathbf{5}$

(b) $(-8)(6) = \mathbf{-48}$

(c) $\dfrac{40}{-8} = \mathbf{-5}$

(d) $(-5)(-15) = \mathbf{75}$

10. $C = \pi(30\text{ cm})$
$C = \mathbf{30\pi\ cm}$

11.

(a) **5 faces**

(b) **8 edges**

(c) **5 vertices**

12. $\mathbf{W_N = 0.1 \times \$37.50}$
$W_N = \mathbf{\$3.75}$

13. $\mathbf{W_N = \dfrac{5}{\cancel{8}_1} \times \overset{9}{\cancel{72}}}$

$W_N = \mathbf{45}$

14. $\mathbf{25 = W_F \times 60}$
$$\frac{25}{60} = \frac{W_F \times 60}{60}$$
$$\mathbf{\frac{5}{12}} = W_F$$

15. $\mathbf{60 = W_D \times 80}$
$$\frac{60}{80} = \frac{W_D \times 80}{80}$$
$$\mathbf{0.75} = W_D$$

16. (a) $m\angle ACB = 180° - 115° = \mathbf{65°}$

(b) $m\angle ABC = m\angle ACB = \mathbf{65°}$

(c) $m\angle CAB = 180° - (65° + 65°)$
$= 180° - 130° = \mathbf{50°}$

17. (a) $6\overline{)5.00\ldots}$ quotient $0.83\ldots$ $\quad \mathbf{0.8\overline{3}}$

(b) $\dfrac{5}{6} \times 100\% = \dfrac{500\%}{6} = \mathbf{83\frac{1}{3}\%}$

(c) $0.1\% = \dfrac{0.1}{100} = \mathbf{\dfrac{1}{1000}}$

(d) $0.1\% = \dfrac{0.1}{100} = \mathbf{0.001}$

18.

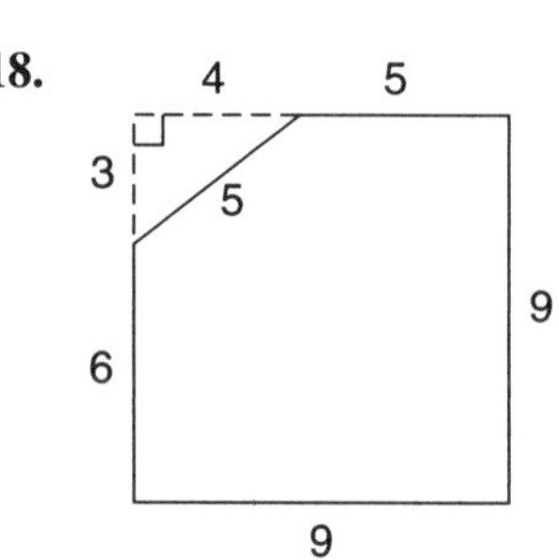

(a) Perimeter $= 5\text{ in.} + 9\text{ in.} + 9\text{ in.}$
$+ 6\text{ in.} + 5\text{ in.} = \mathbf{34\ in.}$

(b)
$$\begin{aligned}\text{Area of rectangle} &= (9\text{ in.})(9\text{ in.}) \\ &= 81\text{ in.}^2 \\ \text{Area of triangle} &= \frac{(4\text{ in.})(3\text{ in.})}{2} \\ &= 6\text{ in.}^2 \\ \text{Area of figure} &= 81\text{ in.}^2 - 6\text{ in.}^2 \\ &= \mathbf{75\text{ in.}^2}\end{aligned}$$

19. Rectangle

20.
$$\begin{array}{r} 212°\text{F} \\ +\ 32\text{ F} \\ \hline 244°\text{F} \end{array} \qquad \frac{244°\text{F}}{2} = \mathbf{122°F}$$

21.
$$\begin{aligned} x - 25 &= 96 \\ x - 25 + 25 &= 96 + 25 \\ x &= \mathbf{121} \end{aligned}$$

check:
$$\begin{aligned} 121 - 25 &= 96 \\ 96 &= 96 \end{aligned}$$

22.
$$\begin{aligned} \frac{2}{3}m &= 12 \\ \left(\frac{\cancel{3}^1}{\cancel{2}_1}\right)\frac{\cancel{2}^1}{\cancel{3}_1}m &= \left(\frac{3}{\cancel{2}_1}\right)\cancel{12}^6 \\ m &= \mathbf{18} \end{aligned}$$

check:
$$\begin{aligned} \frac{2}{\cancel{3}_1}(\cancel{18}^6) &= 12 \\ 2(6) &= 12 \\ 12 &= 12 \end{aligned}$$

23.
$$\begin{aligned} 2.5p &= 6.25 \\ \frac{2.5p}{2.5} &= \frac{6.25}{2.5} \\ p &= \mathbf{2.5} \end{aligned}$$

check:
$$\begin{aligned} (2.5)(2.5) &= 6.25 \\ 6.25 &= 6.25 \end{aligned}$$

24.
$$\begin{aligned} 10 &= f + 3\frac{1}{3} \\ 10 - 3\frac{1}{3} &= f + 3\frac{1}{3} - 3\frac{1}{3} \\ 9\frac{3}{3} - 3\frac{1}{3} &= f \\ \mathbf{6\frac{2}{3}} &= f \end{aligned}$$

check:
$$\begin{aligned} 10 &= 6\frac{2}{3} + 3\frac{1}{3} \\ 10 &= 9\frac{3}{3} \\ 10 &= 10 \end{aligned}$$

25.
$$\begin{aligned} \sqrt{13^2 - 5^2} &= \sqrt{169 - 25} \\ &= \sqrt{144} = \mathbf{12} \end{aligned}$$

26. 1 ton = 2000 lb
2000 lb − 400 lb = **1600 lb**

27.
$$\begin{aligned} &3\frac{3}{4} \times 4\frac{1}{6} \times (0.4)^2 \\ &= \frac{15}{4} \times \frac{25}{6} \times \left(\frac{4}{10}\right)^2 \\ &= \frac{\cancel{15}^5}{\cancel{4}_1} \times \frac{\cancel{25}^1}{\cancel{6}_2} \times \frac{\cancel{16}^{\cancel{4}^1}}{\cancel{100}_{\cancel{4}_1}} \\ &= \frac{5}{2} = \mathbf{2\frac{1}{2}} \end{aligned}$$

28.
$$\begin{aligned} &3\frac{1}{8} + 6.7 + 8\frac{1}{4} \\ &= 3.125 + 6.7 + 8.25 = \mathbf{18.075} \end{aligned}$$

29. (a)
$$\begin{gathered} (-3) + (-5) - (-3) - |+5| \\ (-3) + (-5) + [-(-3)] + [-|+5|] \\ (-3) + (-5) + [3] + [-5] \\ \mathbf{-10} \end{gathered}$$

(b)
$$\begin{gathered} (-73) + (-24) - (-50) \\ (-73) + (-24) + [-(-50)] \\ (-73) + (-24) + [50] \\ \mathbf{-47} \end{gathered}$$

30. The quotient is a little more than 1 because the dividend is slightly greater than the divisor.

$$\frac{\frac{5}{6}}{\frac{2}{3}} \cdot \frac{\frac{3}{2}}{\frac{3}{2}} = \frac{\frac{15}{12}}{1} = \frac{15}{12} = \frac{5}{4} = \mathbf{1\frac{1}{4}}$$

Lesson 77, Lesson Practice

a.
$$\begin{aligned} 24 &= W_P \times 40 \\ \frac{\cancel{24}^3}{\cancel{40}_5} &= \frac{W_P \times \cancel{40}^1}{\cancel{40}_1} \\ \frac{3}{5} &= W_P \end{aligned}$$

$$W_P = \frac{3}{5} \times 100\% = \mathbf{60\%}$$

b. $W_P \times 6 = 2$

$$\frac{W_P \times \overset{1}{\cancel{6}}}{\underset{1}{\cancel{6}}} = \frac{\overset{1}{\cancel{2}}}{\underset{3}{\cancel{6}}}$$

$$W_P = \frac{1}{3}$$

$$W_P = \frac{1}{3} \times 100\% = \mathbf{33\frac{1}{3}\%}$$

c. $\frac{15}{100} \times W_N = 45$

$$\frac{\overset{1}{\cancel{15}}}{\underset{1}{\cancel{100}}} \cdot \frac{\overset{1}{\cancel{100}}}{\underset{1}{\cancel{15}}} \times W_N = \overset{3}{\cancel{45}} \cdot \frac{100}{\underset{1}{\cancel{15}}}$$

$$W_N = \mathbf{300}$$

d. $W_P \times 4 = 6$

$$\frac{W_P \times 4}{4} = \frac{\overset{3}{\cancel{6}}}{\underset{2}{\cancel{4}}}$$

$$W_P = \frac{3}{2} \times 100\% = \mathbf{150\%}$$

e.

$$24 = 120\% \times W_N$$

$$24 = \frac{120}{100} \times W_N$$

$$\frac{\overset{20}{\cancel{100}}}{\underset{1}{\cancel{\cancel{\cancel{120}}}}} \times \overset{1}{\cancel{24}} = \frac{\overset{1}{\cancel{100}}}{\underset{1}{\cancel{120}}} \times \frac{\overset{1}{\cancel{120}}}{\underset{1}{\cancel{100}}} \times W_N$$

$$\mathbf{20} = W_N$$

f.

$$60 = \frac{\overset{3}{\cancel{150}}}{\underset{2}{\cancel{100}}} \times W_N$$

$$60 = \frac{\mathbf{3}}{\mathbf{2}} \times W_N$$

$$\frac{2}{\underset{1}{\cancel{3}}} \times \overset{20}{\cancel{60}} = \left(\frac{\overset{1}{\cancel{2}}}{\underset{1}{\cancel{3}}}\right)\left(\frac{\overset{1}{\cancel{3}}}{\underset{1}{\cancel{2}}}\right) \times W_N$$

$$\mathbf{40} = W_N$$

g. $W_P \times \$5.00 = \$0.35$

$$\frac{W_P \times \overset{1}{\cancel{\$5.00}}}{\underset{1}{\cancel{\$5.00}}} = \frac{\$0.35}{\$5.00}$$

$$W_P = 0.07$$

$$W_P = 0.07 \times 100\% = \mathbf{7\%}$$

Lesson 77, Mixed Practice

1.

	Ratio	Actual Count
Nickels	2	70
Pennies	5	P
Total	7	T

$$\frac{2}{7} = \frac{70}{T}$$

$$2T = 7(70)$$

$$T = \frac{490}{2}$$

$$T = \textbf{245 coins}$$

2. 0.8(50 questions) = **40 questions**

3.

$$\begin{array}{r} 80\% \\ 75\% \\ 80\% \\ 95\% \\ 80\% \\ +\ 100\% \\ \hline 510\% \end{array} \qquad 6\overline{)510\%} = \mathbf{85\%}$$

4. (a) **80%**

(b) 100% − 75% = **25%**

5. (a) **Sphere**

(b) **Cylinder**

(c) **Rectangular prism**

6.

	Case 1	Case 2
Inches	100	250
Centimeters	254	C

$$\frac{100}{254} = \frac{250}{C}$$

$$100C = (254)(250)$$

$$C = \frac{63500}{100}$$

$$C = \textbf{635 centimeters}$$

7.

30 people

$\frac{3}{5}$ agreed.	6 people
	6 people
	6 people
$\frac{2}{5}$ disagreed.	6 people
	6 people

(a) $\mathbf{\frac{2}{5}}$

(b) 12 ÷ 2 = 6, 6(5 people) = **30 people**

(c) 3(6 people) = **18 people**

(d) $\frac{\text{agreed}}{\text{disagreed}} = \frac{18}{12} = \mathbf{\frac{3}{2}}$

8. $\mathbf{40 = \frac{4}{25} \times W_N}$

$\frac{25}{\cancel{4}_1} \times \overset{10}{\cancel{40}} = \frac{\overset{1}{\cancel{25}}}{\cancel{4}_1} \times \frac{\overset{1}{\cancel{4}}}{\cancel{25}_1} \times W_N$

$\mathbf{250} = W_N$

9. $\mathbf{0.24 \times 10{,}000 = W_N}$

$\mathbf{2400} = W_N$

10. $\mathbf{0.12 \times W_N = 240}$

$\frac{\overset{1}{\cancel{0.12}} \times W_N}{\cancel{0.12}_1} = \frac{\overset{2000}{\cancel{240}}}{\cancel{0.12}_1}$

$W_N = \mathbf{2000}$

11. $\mathbf{20 = W_P \times 25}$

$\frac{\overset{4}{\cancel{20}}}{\cancel{25}_5} = \frac{W_P \times \overset{1}{\cancel{25}}}{\cancel{25}_1}$

$\frac{4}{5} = W_P$

$W_P = \frac{4}{5} \times 100\% = \mathbf{80\%}$

12. (a) $(25)(-5) = \mathbf{-125}$

(b) $(-15)(-5) = \mathbf{75}$

(c) $\frac{-250}{-5} = \mathbf{50}$

(d) $\frac{-225}{15} = \mathbf{-15}$

13. (a) $0.2 = \frac{2}{10} = \mathbf{\frac{1}{5}}$

(b) $0.2 = \frac{2}{10} = \frac{20}{100} = \mathbf{20\%}$

(c) $2\% = \frac{2}{100} = \mathbf{\frac{1}{50}}$

(d) $2\% = \frac{2}{100} = \mathbf{0.02}$

14.
$$\begin{array}{r} \$21.00 \\ \times \quad 0.075 \\ \hline \$1.575 \end{array} \longrightarrow \$1.58$$

$$\begin{array}{r} \$21.00 \\ + \ \$\ 1.58 \\ \hline \mathbf{\$22.58} \end{array}$$

15. (a) $\frac{14\frac{2}{7}}{100} = \frac{\frac{100}{7}}{\frac{100}{1}}$

$\frac{\frac{100}{7}}{\frac{100}{1}} \cdot \frac{\frac{1}{100}}{\frac{1}{100}} = \frac{\frac{100}{700}}{1} = \frac{100}{700} = \mathbf{\frac{1}{7}}$

(b) $\frac{60}{\frac{2}{3}} = \frac{\frac{60}{1}}{\frac{2}{3}}$

$\frac{\frac{60}{1}}{\frac{2}{3}} \cdot \frac{\frac{3}{2}}{\frac{3}{2}} = \frac{\frac{180}{2}}{1} = \frac{180}{2} = \mathbf{90}$

16.

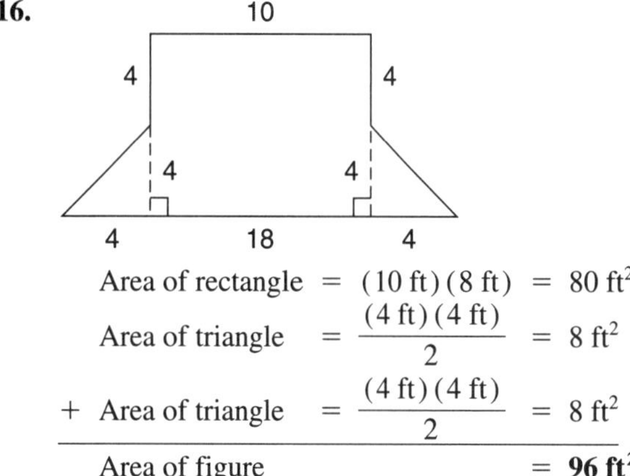

$$\begin{array}{lcll} \text{Area of rectangle} & = & (10\text{ ft})(8\text{ ft}) & = 80\text{ ft}^2 \\ \text{Area of triangle} & = & \frac{(4\text{ ft})(4\text{ ft})}{2} & = 8\text{ ft}^2 \\ + \ \text{Area of triangle} & = & \frac{(4\text{ ft})(4\text{ ft})}{2} & = 8\text{ ft}^2 \\ \hline \text{Area of figure} & & & = \mathbf{96\text{ ft}^2} \end{array}$$

17.

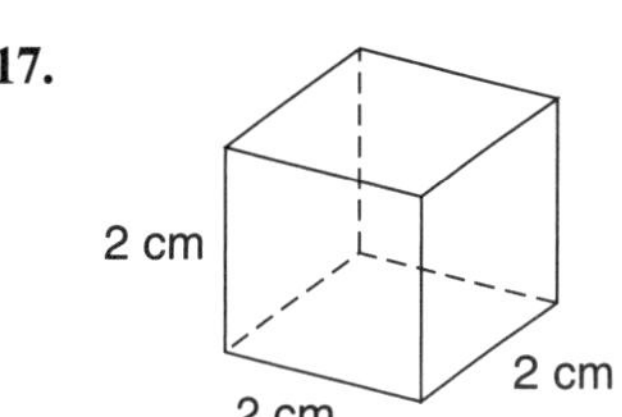

(a) $(2\text{ cm})(2\text{ cm}) = 4\text{ cm}^2$

$\frac{4\text{ cm}^2}{1\ \cancel{\text{layer}}} \cdot 1\text{ cm}(2\ \cancel{\text{layers}}) = \mathbf{8\text{ cm}^3}$

(b) **One way to find the surface area of a cube is to find the area of one face of the cube and then multiply that area by 6.**

18. $\mathbf{1.2 \times 10^{10}}$

19. (a) $C = \pi(20\text{ mm})$

$C = \mathbf{20\pi\text{ mm}}$

(b) $C \approx 3.14(20\text{ mm})$

$C \approx \mathbf{62.8\text{ mm}}$

20. $3x = 26.7$

$\frac{\overset{1}{\cancel{3}}x}{\cancel{3}_1} = \frac{\overset{8.9}{\cancel{26.7}}}{\cancel{3}_1}$

$x = \mathbf{8.9}$

check: $3(8.9) = 26.7$

$26.7 = 26.7$

21.
$$y - 3\frac{1}{3} = 7$$
$$y - 3\frac{1}{3} + 3\frac{1}{3} = 7 + 3\frac{1}{3}$$
$$y = \mathbf{10\frac{1}{3}}$$
check:
$$10\frac{1}{3} - 3\frac{1}{3} = 7$$
$$7 = 7$$

22.
$$\frac{2}{3}x = 48$$
$$\left(\frac{\cancel{3}^{1}}{\cancel{2}_{1}}\right)\left(\frac{\cancel{2}^{1}}{\cancel{3}_{1}}\right)x = \left(\frac{3}{\cancel{2}_{1}}\right)\cancel{48}^{24}$$
$$x = \mathbf{72}$$
check:
$$\frac{2}{\cancel{3}_{1}}(\cancel{72}^{24}) = 48$$
$$2(24) = 48$$
$$48 = 48$$

23. **Multiply the "in" number by 4; then add 1 to find the "out" number.**
$$3(4) + 1 = \mathbf{13}$$
$$1 - 1 = 0,\ \frac{0}{4} = \mathbf{0}$$

24.
$$5^2 - \{2^3 + 3[4^2 - (4)(\sqrt{9})]\}$$
$$25 - \{8 + 3[16 - (4)(3)]\}$$
$$25 - \{8 + 3[16 - 12]\}$$
$$25 - \{8 + 3[4]\}$$
$$25 - \{8 + 12\}$$
$$25 - 20$$
$$\mathbf{5}$$

25.

4 gal	3 qt	1 pt
+ 1 gal	2 qt	1 pt
5 gal	5 qt	2 pt

2 pt = 1 qt, 5qt + 1 qt = 6 qt
6 qt = 1 gal 2 qt

1 gal	2 qt
+ 5 gal	
6 gal	**2 qt**

26.
$$1\,\cancel{\text{ft}}^2 \cdot \frac{12\text{ in.}}{1\,\cancel{\text{ft}}} \cdot \frac{12\text{ in.}}{1\,\cancel{\text{ft}}}$$
$$= \mathbf{144\ in.^2}$$

27.
$$1\frac{1}{3} \div 3 = \frac{4}{3} \div \frac{3}{1} = \frac{4}{3} \times \frac{1}{3} = \frac{4}{9}$$
$$5\frac{1}{3} \div \frac{4}{9} = \frac{16}{3} \div \frac{4}{9} = \frac{\cancel{16}^{4}}{\cancel{3}_{1}} \times \frac{\cancel{9}^{3}}{\cancel{4}_{1}} = \mathbf{12}$$

28.
$$3\frac{1}{5} - 2\frac{1}{2} + 1\frac{1}{4} = \left(\frac{16}{5} - \frac{5}{2}\right) + \frac{5}{4}$$
$$= \left(\frac{64}{20} - \frac{50}{20}\right) + \frac{25}{20} = \frac{14}{20} + \frac{25}{20}$$
$$= \frac{39}{20} = \mathbf{1\frac{19}{20}}$$

29.
$$2.5 = 2\frac{1}{2}$$
$$3\frac{1}{3} \div 2\frac{1}{2} = \frac{10}{3} \div \frac{5}{2}$$
$$= \frac{\cancel{10}^{2}}{3} \times \frac{2}{\cancel{5}_{1}} = \frac{4}{3} = \mathbf{1\frac{1}{3}}$$

30. (a)
$$(-3) + (-4) - (+5)$$
$$(-3) + (-4) + [-(+5)]$$
$$(-3) + (-4) + [-5]$$
$$\mathbf{-12}$$

(b)
$$(-6) - (-16) - (+30)$$
$$(-6) + [-(-16)] + [-(+30)]$$
$$(-6) + [16] + [-30]$$
$$\mathbf{-20}$$

Lesson 78, Lesson Practice

a.

b.

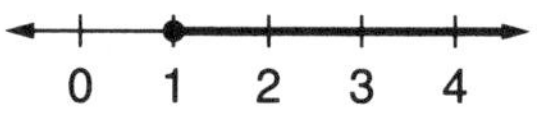

c.

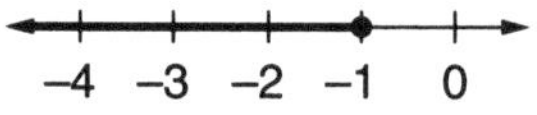

d.

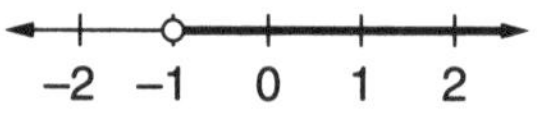

Lesson 78, Mixed Practice

1.

	Case 1	Case 2
Cartons	4	*C*
Hungry children	30	75

$$\frac{4}{30} = \frac{C}{75}$$
$$30C = 4(75)$$
$$C = \frac{300}{30}$$
$$C = \mathbf{10\ cartons}$$

2. $4(88) = 352,\ 6(90) = 540$

$$\begin{array}{r} 540 \\ -\ 352 \\ \hline 188 \end{array} \qquad 2\overline{)188} = \mathbf{94}$$

3. $\left(\frac{2}{3} + \frac{3}{4}\right) \div \left(\frac{2}{3} \times \frac{3}{4}\right)$

$$= \left(\frac{8}{12} + \frac{9}{12}\right) \div \left(\frac{1}{2}\right)$$

$$= \frac{17}{12} \div \frac{1}{2}$$

$$= \frac{17}{\cancel{12}_6} \times \frac{\cancel{2}^1}{1} = \frac{17}{6} = \mathbf{2\frac{5}{6}}$$

4.

	Ratio	Actual Count
Monocotyledons	3	M
Dicotyledons	4	84

$$\frac{3}{4} = \frac{M}{84}$$

$$4M = 3(84)$$

$$M = \frac{252}{4}$$

M = **63 monocotyledons**

5. $C \approx 3.14(21 \text{ millimeters})$

$C \approx 65.94$ millimeters

$C \approx$ **66 millimeters**

6. (a)

(b)

7. $\mathbf{1.5\ \cancel{kg} \cdot \frac{1000\ g}{1\ \cancel{kg}} = 1500\ g}$

8. $\frac{5}{\cancel{6}_1} \times \cancel{30}^5 = 25$

(a) $25 - 5 = 20$

20 more people

(b) $\frac{\text{preferred Brand } Y}{\text{preferred Brand } X} = \frac{5}{25} = \mathbf{\frac{1}{5}}$

9. $\mathbf{42 = \frac{7}{10} \times W_N}$

$$\left(\frac{10}{\cancel{7}_1}\right)\cancel{42}^6 = \left(\frac{\cancel{10}^1}{\cancel{7}_1}\right)\frac{\cancel{7}^1}{\cancel{10}_1} \times W_N$$

$$\mathbf{60} = W_N$$

10. $\mathbf{1.5 \times W_N = 600}$

$$\frac{\cancel{1.5}^1 \times W_N}{\cancel{1.5}_1} = \frac{600}{1.5}$$

$$W_N = \mathbf{400}$$

11. $\mathbf{0.4 \times 50 = W_N}$

$\mathbf{20} = W_N$

12. $\mathbf{40 = W_P \times 50}$

$$\frac{\cancel{40}^4}{\cancel{50}_5} = \frac{W_P \times \cancel{50}^1}{\cancel{50}_1}$$

$$\frac{4}{5} = W_P$$

$$W_P = \frac{4}{5} \times 100\% = \frac{400\%}{5} = \mathbf{80\%}$$

13. (a) **0.0015**

(b) $\mathbf{2.5 \times 10^7}$

14. (a) $\frac{-45}{9} = \mathbf{-5}$

(b) $\frac{-450}{15} = \mathbf{-30}$

(c) $15(-20) = \mathbf{-300}$

(d) $(-15)(-12) = \mathbf{180}$

15. (a) $50\% = \frac{50}{100} = \mathbf{\frac{1}{2}}$

(b) $50\% = \frac{50}{100} = \mathbf{0.5}$

(c) $12\overline{)1.000\ldots} = \mathbf{0.08\overline{3}}$

(d) $\frac{1}{12} \times 100\% = \frac{100\%}{12} = \mathbf{8\frac{1}{3}\%}$

16. $\frac{83\frac{1}{3}}{100} = \frac{\frac{250}{3}}{\frac{100}{1}}$

$$\frac{\frac{250}{3}}{\frac{100}{1}} \cdot \frac{\frac{1}{100}}{\frac{1}{100}} = \frac{\frac{250}{300}}{1}$$

$$= \frac{250}{300} = \mathbf{\frac{5}{6}}$$

17. 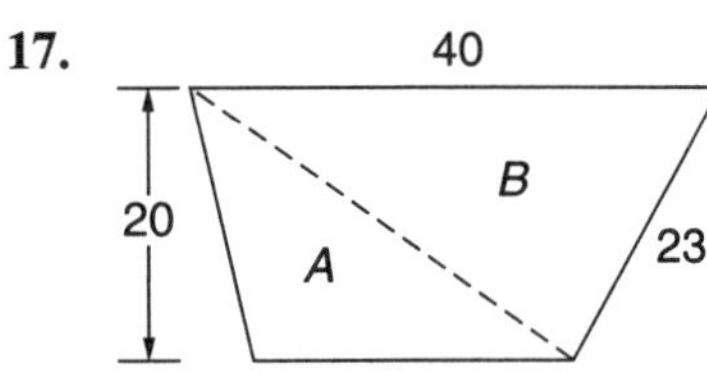

$$\text{Area of triangle } A = \frac{(24 \text{ mm})(20 \text{ mm})}{2} = 240 \text{ mm}^2$$
$$\text{Area of triangle } B = \frac{(40 \text{ mm})(20 \text{ mm})}{2} = 400 \text{ mm}^2$$
$$\text{Area of figure} = 240 \text{ mm}^2 + 400 \text{ mm}^2 = \mathbf{640\ mm^2}$$

18. 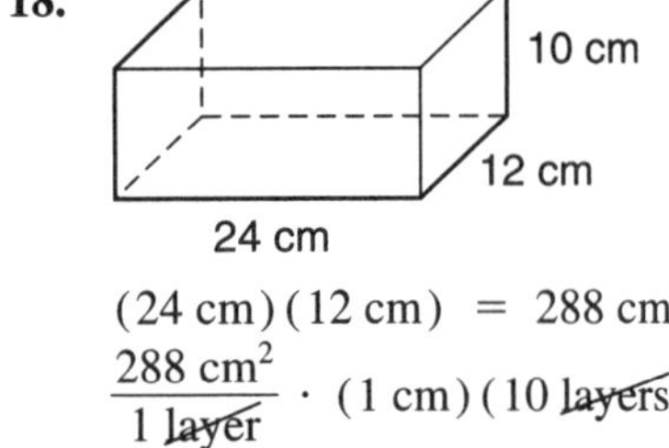

$(24 \text{ cm})(12 \text{ cm}) = 288 \text{ cm}^2$,

$$\frac{288 \text{ cm}^2}{1 \text{ layer}} \cdot (1 \text{ cm})(10 \text{ layers})$$

2880 cm³

19. **One possibility:**

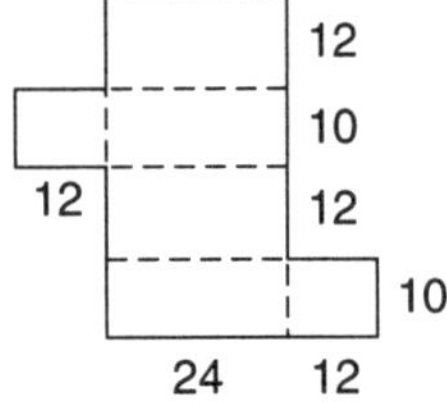

20. **Multiply the "in" number by 5, then subtract 1 to find the "out" number.**

$4(5) - 1 = \mathbf{19}$

$4 + 1 = 5,\ 5 \div 5 = \mathbf{1}$

21.
$$\begin{array}{r} \$18.50 \\ \times \quad 0.30 \\ \hline \$5.5500 \end{array} = \mathbf{\$5.55}$$

22.
$$\begin{aligned} m + 8.7 &= 10.25 \\ m + 8.7 - 8.7 &= 10.25 - 8.7 \\ m &= \mathbf{1.55} \end{aligned}$$

check:
$$\begin{aligned} 1.55 + 8.7 &= 10.25 \\ 10.25 &= 10.25 \end{aligned}$$

23.
$$\begin{aligned} \frac{4}{3}w &= 36 \\ \left(\frac{\overset{1}{\cancel{3}}}{\underset{1}{\cancel{4}}}\right)\frac{\overset{1}{\cancel{4}}}{\underset{1}{\cancel{3}}}w &= \left(\frac{3}{\underset{1}{\cancel{4}}}\right)\overset{9}{\cancel{36}} \\ w &= \mathbf{27} \end{aligned}$$

check:
$$\begin{aligned} \left(\frac{4}{\underset{1}{\cancel{3}}}\right)\overset{9}{\cancel{27}} &= 36 \\ (4)9 &= 36 \\ 36 &= 36 \end{aligned}$$

24.
$$\begin{aligned} 0.7y &= 48.3 \\ \frac{0.7y}{0.7} &= \frac{48.3}{0.7} \\ y &= \mathbf{69} \end{aligned}$$

check:
$$\begin{aligned} 0.7(69) &= 48.3 \\ 48.3 &= 48.3 \end{aligned}$$

25.
$$\begin{gathered} \{4^2 + 10[2^3 - (3)(\sqrt{4})]\} - \sqrt{36} \\ \{16 + 10[8 - (3)(2)]\} - 6 \\ \{16 + 10[8 - 6]\} - 6 \\ \{16 + 10[2]\} - 6 \\ \{16 + 20\} - 6 \\ \{36\} - 6 \\ \mathbf{30} \end{gathered}$$

26.
$$|5 - 3| - |3 - 5| = |2| - |-2| = 2 - 2 = \mathbf{0}$$

27.
$$1 \cancel{\text{m}^2} \cdot \frac{100 \text{ cm}}{1 \cancel{\text{m}}} \cdot \frac{100 \text{ cm}}{1 \cancel{\text{m}}} = \mathbf{10{,}000\ cm^2}$$

28.
$$7\frac{1}{2} \cdot 3 \cdot \left(\frac{2}{3}\right)^2 =$$
$$\frac{\overset{5}{\cancel{15}}}{\underset{1}{\cancel{2}}} \cdot \frac{\overset{1}{\cancel{3}}}{1} \cdot \frac{\overset{2}{\cancel{4}}}{\underset{1}{\cancel{\underset{\cancel{3}}{\cancel{9}}}}} = \mathbf{10}$$

29.
$$\begin{aligned} &3\frac{1}{5} - \left(2\frac{1}{2} - 1\frac{1}{4}\right) \\ &= 3\frac{4}{20} - \left(2\frac{10}{20} - 1\frac{5}{20}\right) \\ &= 3\frac{4}{20} - 1\frac{5}{20} = 2\frac{24}{20} - 1\frac{5}{20} \\ &= \mathbf{1\frac{19}{20}} \end{aligned}$$

30. (a)
$$\begin{gathered} (-10) - (-8) - (+6) \\ (-10) + [-(-8)] + [-(+6)] \\ (-10) + [8] + [-6] \\ \mathbf{-8} \end{gathered}$$

(b) $(+10) + (-20) - (-30)$
$(+10) + (-20) + [-(-30)]$
$(+10) + (-20) + [30]$
20

Lesson 79, Lesson Practice

a. x (>) y

b. m (=) n

c. **Insufficient information**

d. **Insufficient information: (Both x and y could be zero, or y could be greater.)**

Lesson 79, Mixed Practice

1. 4(33.5 students) = 134 students

$5\overline{)134.0}$ = **26.8 students**

2. $\frac{315 \text{ kilometers}}{35 \text{ liters}} = \mathbf{9 \frac{kilometers}{liter}}$

3.

	Ratio	Actual Count
Winners	7	W
Losers	5	L
Total	12	1260

$\frac{7}{12} = \frac{W}{1260}$

$12W = 7(1260)$

$W = \frac{8820}{12}$

$W = 735$ winners

$\frac{5}{12} = \frac{L}{1260}$

$12L = 5(1260)$

$L = \frac{6300}{12}$

$L = 525$ losers

$735 - 525 = \mathbf{210}$ **more winners**

4. (a) $\mathbf{3.75 \times 10^{-5}}$

(b) $\mathbf{3.75 \times 10^{7}}$

5. **Insufficient information; (x < y if both are positive; x > y if both are negative)**

6. (a)

(b)

7.

	Case 1	Case 2
Inches	4	12
Hours	3	h

$\frac{4}{3} = \frac{12}{h}$

$4h = 3(12)$

$h = \frac{36}{4}$

$h =$ **9 hours**

8.

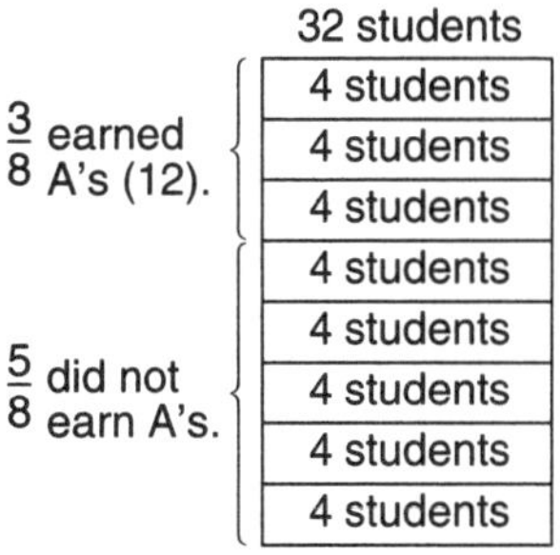

(a) $\frac{12 \text{ students}}{3} = 4$ students

5(4 students) = **20 students**

(b) $\frac{5}{8} \times 100\% = \frac{500\%}{8} = \mathbf{62\frac{1}{2}\%}$

9. $\mathbf{35 = 0.7 \times W_N}$

$\frac{35}{0.7} = \frac{0.7 \times W_N}{0.7}$

$\mathbf{50} = W_N$

10. $\mathbf{W_P \times 20 = 17}$

$\frac{W_P \times 20}{20} = \frac{17}{20}$

$W_P = \frac{17}{20}$

$W_P = \frac{17}{20} \times 100\% = \frac{1700\%}{20} = \mathbf{85\%}$

11. $\mathbf{W_P \times 20 = 25}$

$\frac{W_P \times 20}{20} = \frac{\overset{5}{\cancel{25}}}{\underset{4}{\cancel{20}}}$

$W_P = \frac{5}{4}$

$W_P = \frac{5}{4} \times 100\% = \frac{500\%}{4} = \mathbf{125\%}$

12. $$\mathbf{360 = \frac{3}{4} \times W_N}$$

$$\left(\frac{4}{\cancel{3}_1}\right)\overset{120}{\cancel{360}} = \left(\frac{\overset{1}{\cancel{4}}}{\cancel{3}_1}\right)\frac{\overset{1}{\cancel{3}}}{\cancel{4}_1} \times W_N$$

$$(4)120 = W_N$$

$$\mathbf{480} = W_N$$

13. (a) $\frac{144}{-8} = \mathbf{-18}$

(b) $\frac{-144}{+6} = \mathbf{-24}$

(c) $-12(12) = \mathbf{-144}$

(d) $-16(-9) = \mathbf{144}$

14. (a) $25\overline{)1.00}$ with quotient $\mathbf{0.04}$

(b) $\frac{1}{25} \times 100\% = \frac{100\%}{25} = \mathbf{4\%}$

(c) $8\% = \frac{8}{100} = \mathbf{\frac{2}{25}}$

(d) $8\% = \frac{8}{100} = \mathbf{0.08}$

15.

$$\begin{array}{r} \$4500 \\ \times \quad 0.05 \\ \hline \$225.00 \end{array} = \mathbf{\$225}$$

16. $$\frac{62\frac{1}{2}}{100} = \frac{\frac{125}{2}}{\frac{100}{1}}$$

$$\frac{\frac{125}{2}}{\frac{100}{1}} \cdot \frac{\frac{1}{100}}{\frac{1}{100}} = \frac{\frac{125}{200}}{1}$$

$$= \frac{125}{200} = \mathbf{\frac{5}{8}}$$

17.

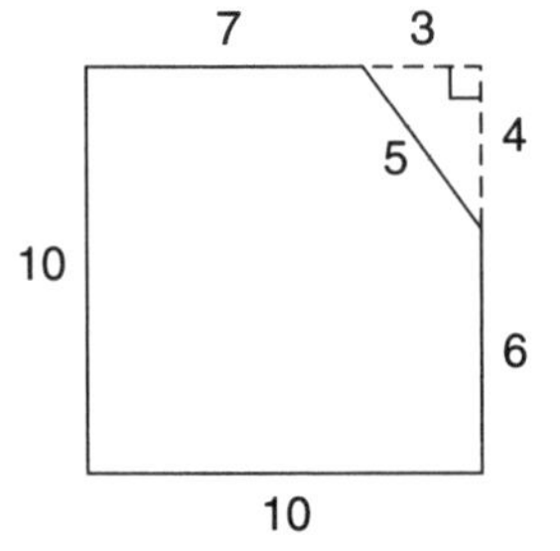

7 3 4 5 10 6 10

(a) Perimeter $= 10 \text{ in.} + 7 \text{ in.} + 5 \text{ in.} + 6 \text{ in.} + 10 \text{ in.} = \mathbf{38 \text{ in.}}$

(b) Area of square $= (10 \text{ in.})(10 \text{ in.}) = 100 \text{ in.}^2$

Area of triangle $= \frac{(3 \text{ in.})(4 \text{ in.})}{2} = 6 \text{ in.}^2$

Area of figure $= 100 \text{ in.}^2 - 6 \text{ in.}^2 = \mathbf{94 \text{ in.}^2}$

18. (a) (6 cubes)(3 cubes) = 18 cubes

$\frac{18 \text{ cubes}}{1 \text{ layer}} \cdot 4 \text{ layers} = 72 \text{ cubes}$

72 cm³

(b) $(6 \text{ cm})(3 \text{ cm}) = 18 \text{ cm}^2$

$(4 \text{ cm})(3 \text{ cm}) = 12 \text{ cm}^2$

$(6 \text{ cm})(4 \text{ cm}) = 24 \text{ cm}^2$

$2(18 \text{ cm}^2) + 2(12 \text{ cm}^2) + 2(24 \text{ cm}^2)$

$= 36 \text{ cm}^2 + 24 \text{ cm}^2 + 48 \text{ cm}^2$

$= \mathbf{108 \text{ cm}^2}$

19. (a) $C \approx 3.14(1 \text{ m})$

$C \approx \mathbf{3.14 \text{ m}}$

(b) $C = \pi(1 \text{ m})$

$C = \boldsymbol{\pi} \textbf{ m}$

20. (a) **Right; scalene**

(b) **Obtuse; isosceles**

(c) **Acute; equilateral**

21. $1.2x = 2.88$

$\frac{1.2x}{1.2} = \frac{2.88}{1.2}$

$x = \mathbf{2.4}$

check: $1.2(2.4) = 2.88$

$2.88 = 2.88$

22.
$$3\frac{1}{3} = x + \frac{5}{6}$$
$$3\frac{1}{3} - \frac{5}{6} = x + \frac{5}{6} - \frac{5}{6}$$
$$3\frac{2}{6} - \frac{5}{6} = x$$
$$2\frac{8}{6} - \frac{5}{6} = x$$
$$2\frac{3}{6} = x$$
$$\mathbf{2\frac{1}{2}} = x$$

check:
$$3\frac{1}{3} = 2\frac{1}{2} + \frac{5}{6}$$
$$3\frac{1}{3} = 2\frac{3}{6} + \frac{5}{6}$$
$$3\frac{1}{3} = 2\frac{8}{6}$$
$$3\frac{1}{3} = 3\frac{2}{6}$$
$$3\frac{1}{3} = 3\frac{1}{3}$$

23.
$$\frac{3}{2}w = \frac{9}{10}$$
$$\left(\frac{\overset{1}{\cancel{2}}}{\underset{1}{\cancel{3}}}\right)\frac{\overset{1}{\cancel{3}}}{\underset{1}{\cancel{2}}}w = \left(\frac{\overset{1}{\cancel{2}}}{\underset{1}{\cancel{3}}}\right)\frac{\overset{3}{\cancel{9}}}{\underset{5}{\cancel{10}}}$$
$$w = \mathbf{\frac{3}{5}}$$

check:
$$\left(\frac{3}{2}\right)\frac{3}{5} = \frac{9}{10}$$
$$\frac{9}{10} = \frac{9}{10}$$

24.
$$\frac{\sqrt{100} + 5[3^3 - 2(3^2 + 3)]}{5}$$
$$\frac{10 + 5[27 - 2(9 + 3)]}{5}$$
$$\frac{10 + 5[27 - 2(12)]}{5}$$
$$\frac{10 + 5[27 - 24]}{5}$$
$$\frac{10 + 5[3]}{5}$$
$$\frac{10 + 15}{5}$$
$$\frac{25}{5}$$
$$\mathbf{5}$$

25.

(60 min) (60 s)

$\overset{2}{\cancel{3}}$ hr $\overset{14}{\cancel{15}}$ min 24 s
− 2 hr 45 min 30 s →

$\overset{2}{\cancel{3}}$ hr $\overset{74}{\cancel{\overset{14}{\cancel{15}}}}$ min $\overset{84}{\cancel{24}}$ s
− 2 hr 45 min 30 s
29 min 54 s

26. $1\ \cancel{yd^2} \cdot \frac{3\text{ ft}}{1\ \cancel{yd}} \cdot \frac{3\text{ ft}}{1\ \cancel{yd}} = \mathbf{9\ ft^2}$

27.
$$7\frac{1}{2} \cdot \left(3 \div \frac{5}{9}\right) = \frac{15}{2} \cdot \left(\frac{3}{1} \div \frac{5}{9}\right)$$
$$= \frac{15}{2} \cdot \left(\frac{3}{1} \times \frac{9}{5}\right) = \frac{\overset{3}{\cancel{15}}}{2} \cdot \frac{27}{\underset{1}{\cancel{5}}}$$
$$= \frac{81}{2} = \mathbf{40\frac{1}{2}}$$

28.
$$4\frac{5}{6} + 3\frac{1}{3} + 7\frac{1}{4}$$
$$= 4\frac{10}{12} + 3\frac{4}{12} + 7\frac{3}{12}$$
$$= 14\frac{17}{12} = \mathbf{15\frac{5}{12}}$$

29. $3\frac{3}{4} = 3.75,\ 3.75 \div 1.5 = \mathbf{2.5}$

30. (a)
$$(-10) - (+20) - (-30)$$
$$(-10) + [-(+20)] + [-(-30)]$$
$$(-10) + [-20] + [30]$$
$$\mathbf{0}$$

(b)
$$(-10) - |(-20) - (+30)|$$
$$(-10) + [-|(-20) + [-(+30)]|]$$
$$(-10) + [-|(-20) + [-30]|]$$
$$(-10) + [-|-50|]$$
$$(-10) + [-(+50)]$$
$$(-10) + [-50]$$
$$\mathbf{-60}$$

Lesson 80, Lesson Practice

a. **See lesson.**

b. $\mathbf{W'(3, -4), X'(1, -4), Y'(1, -1), Z'(3, -1)}$

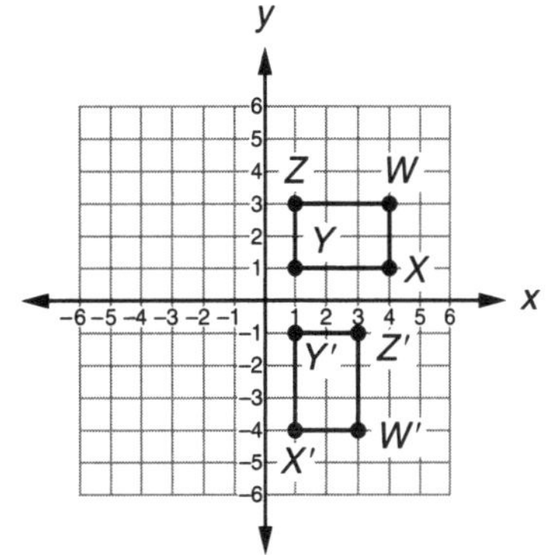

c. $\mathbf{J'(-1, -1), K'(-3, -2), L'(-1, -3)}$

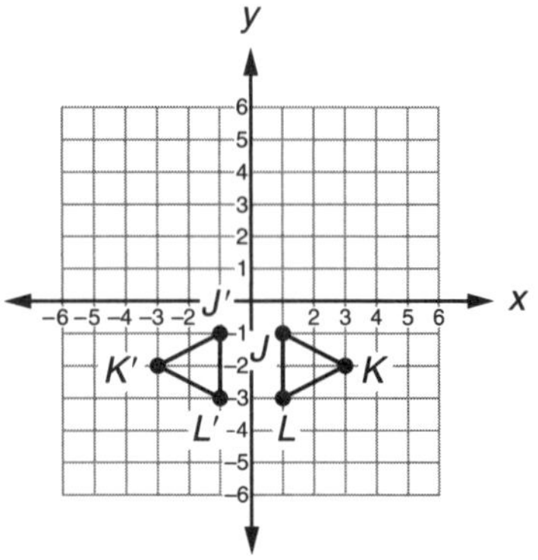

d. $\mathbf{P'(6, 0), Q'(5, -2), R'(2, -2), S'(3, 0)}$

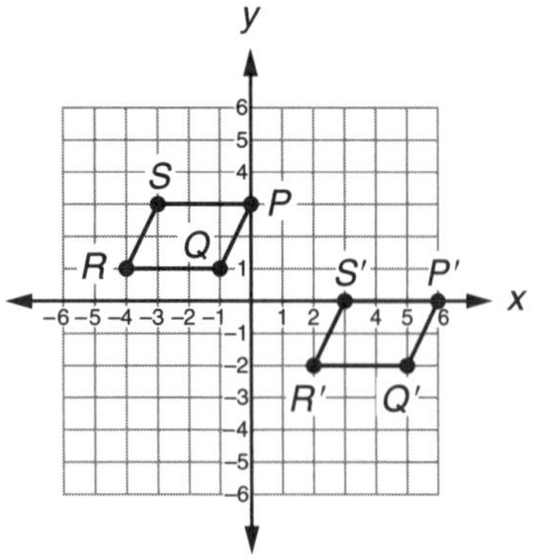

Lesson 80, Mixed Practice

1. $4(\$7.00) + 3(\$6.30)$
$= \$28.00 + \$18.90 = \$46.90$

$\begin{array}{r} \mathbf{\$6.70} \textbf{ per hour} \\ 7\overline{)\$46.90} \end{array}$

2. $(4) + [(4)^2 - (4)(3)] - 3$
$= 4 + [16 - 12] - 3$
$= 4 + [4] - 3 = 8 - 3 = \mathbf{5}$

3. **Insufficient information**

4.

	Ratio	Actual Count
Clean clothes	2	C
Dirty clothes	3	D
Total	5	30

$\frac{2}{5} = \frac{C}{30}$
$5C = 2(30)$
$C = \frac{60}{5}$
$C = \textbf{12 articles of clothing}$

5. $C \approx 3.14(30 \text{ millimeters})$
$C \approx 94.2 \text{ millimeters}$
$C \approx \textbf{94 millimeters}$

6. $1\frac{1}{2} \cancel{\text{quarts}} \cdot \frac{2 \text{ pints}}{1 \cancel{\text{quart}}} = \textbf{3 pints}$

7. (a)
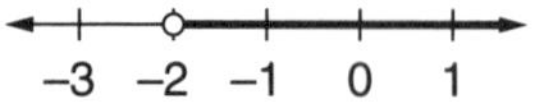

(b)
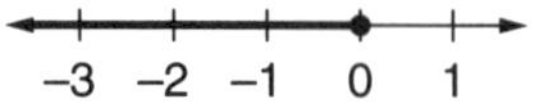

8.

	Case 1	Case 2
Minutes	25	60
Customers	400	c

$\frac{25}{400} = \frac{60}{c}$
$25c = 400(60)$
$c = \frac{24{,}000}{25}$
$c = \textbf{960 customers}$

9.
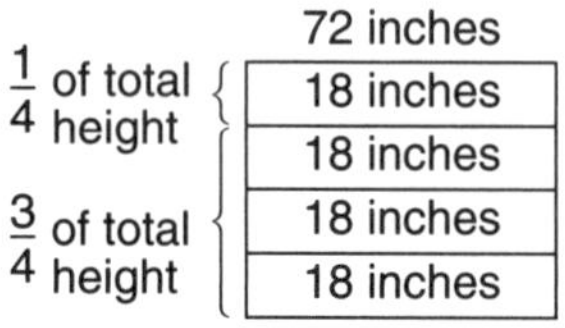

(a) $4(18 \text{ inches}) = \textbf{72 inches}$

(b) $\overset{6}{\cancel{72}} \cancel{\text{inches}} \cdot \frac{1 \text{ foot}}{\underset{1}{\cancel{12}} \cancel{\text{inches}}}$
$= \textbf{6 feet}$

10. $\mathbf{600 = \frac{5}{9} \times W_N}$

$\frac{9}{\cancel{5}}(\overset{120}{\cancel{600}}) = \left(\frac{\overset{1}{\cancel{9}}}{\underset{1}{\cancel{5}}}\right)\frac{\overset{1}{\cancel{5}}}{\underset{1}{\cancel{9}}} \times W_N$
$9(120) = W_N$
$\mathbf{1080} = W_N$

11. $\mathbf{280 = W_P \times 400}$

$\frac{\overset{7}{\cancel{280}}}{\underset{10}{\cancel{400}}} = \frac{W_P \times \overset{1}{\cancel{400}}}{\underset{1}{\cancel{400}}}$
$\frac{7}{10} = W_P$
$W_P = \frac{7}{10} \times 100\% = \frac{700\%}{10} = \mathbf{70\%}$

12. $\mathbf{W_N = 0.04 \times 400}$
$W_N = \mathbf{16}$

13. $\mathbf{60 = 0.6 \times W_N}$

$$\frac{60}{0.6} = \frac{\overset{1}{\cancel{0.6}} \times W_N}{\underset{1}{\cancel{0.6}}}$$

$$\mathbf{100} = W_N$$

14. (a) $\dfrac{600}{-15} = \mathbf{-40}$

(b) $\dfrac{-600}{-12} = \mathbf{50}$

(c) $20(-30) = \mathbf{-600}$

(d) $+15(40) = \mathbf{600}$

15.
$$\begin{array}{r} \$850 \\ \times\ 0.06 \\ \hline \$51.00 \end{array} = \mathbf{\$51}$$

16. (a) $0.3 = \mathbf{\dfrac{3}{10}}$

(b) $0.3 = \dfrac{3}{10} = \dfrac{30}{100} = \mathbf{30\%}$

(c) $12\overline{)5.000\ldots}$ $\quad \mathbf{0.41\overline{6}}$

(d) $\dfrac{5}{12} \times 100\% = \dfrac{500\%}{12} = \mathbf{41\dfrac{2}{3}\%}$

17. (a) $\mathbf{3 \times 10^7}$

(b) $\mathbf{3 \times 10^{-5}}$

18.

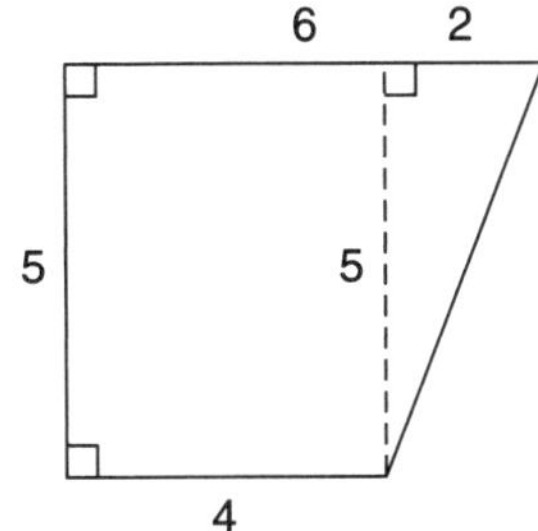

$$\begin{array}{lcccl} & \text{Area of rectangle} & = & (4\text{ m})(5\text{ m}) & = 20\text{ m}^2 \\ + & \text{Area of triangle} & = & \dfrac{(2\text{ m})(5\text{ m})}{2} & = 5\text{ m}^2 \\ \hline & \text{Area of figure} & & & = \mathbf{25\ m^2} \end{array}$$

19. (a) $(5\text{ in.})(5\text{ in.}) = 25\text{ in.}^2$

$(5\text{ in.})(25\text{ in.}^2) = \mathbf{125\ in.^3}$

(b) $6(25\text{ in.}^2) = \mathbf{150\ in.^2}$

20. $\dfrac{\text{green marbles}}{\text{total marbles}} = \dfrac{40}{100} = \mathbf{\dfrac{2}{5}}$

21. $17a = 408$

$$\frac{\overset{1}{\cancel{17}}a}{\underset{1}{\cancel{17}}} = \frac{\overset{24}{\cancel{408}}}{\underset{1}{\cancel{17}}}$$

$a = \mathbf{24}$

check: $17(24) = 408$

$408 = 408$

22. $\dfrac{3}{8}m = 48$

$$\left(\frac{\overset{1}{\cancel{8}}}{\underset{1}{\cancel{3}}}\right)\frac{\overset{1}{\cancel{3}}}{\underset{1}{\cancel{8}}}m = \left(\frac{8}{\cancel{3}}\right)\overset{16}{\cancel{48}}$$

$m = (8)16$

$m = \mathbf{128}$

check: $\dfrac{3}{\underset{1}{\cancel{8}}}(\overset{16}{\cancel{128}}) = 48$

$3(16) = 48$

$48 = 48$

23. $1.4 = x - 0.41$

$1.4 + 0.41 = x - 0.41 + 0.41$

$\mathbf{1.81} = x$

check: $1.4 = 1.81 - 0.41$

$1.4 = 1.4$

24.
$$\frac{2^3 + 4 \cdot 5 - 2 \cdot 3^2}{\sqrt{25} \cdot \sqrt{4}}$$
$$\frac{8 + 4 \cdot 5 - 2 \cdot 9}{5 \cdot 2}$$
$$\frac{8 + 20 - 2 \cdot 9}{10}$$
$$\frac{8 + 20 - 18}{10}$$
$$\frac{28 - 18}{10}$$
$$\frac{10}{10}$$
$$\mathbf{1}$$

25. $7\dfrac{1}{7} \times 1.4 = 7\dfrac{1}{7} \times 1\dfrac{4}{10}$

$$= \frac{\overset{5}{\cancel{50}}}{\underset{1}{\cancel{7}}} \times \frac{\overset{2}{\cancel{14}}}{\underset{1}{\cancel{10}}} = \mathbf{10}$$

26.

$$\begin{array}{rr} \overset{9}{\cancel{10}}\text{ lb} & 6\text{ oz} \\ -\ 7\text{ lb} & 11\text{ oz} \\ \hline \end{array} \xrightarrow{} \quad (16\text{ oz})$$

$$\begin{array}{rr} \overset{9}{\cancel{10}}\text{ lb} & \overset{22}{\cancel{6}}\text{ oz} \\ -\ 7\text{ lb} & 11\text{ oz} \\ \hline \mathbf{2\ lb} & \mathbf{11\ oz} \end{array}$$

27. $1\ \cancel{\text{cm}^2} \cdot \dfrac{10\text{ mm}}{1\ \cancel{\text{cm}}} \cdot \dfrac{10\text{ mm}}{1\ \cancel{\text{cm}}} = \mathbf{100\ mm^2}$

28. $$\overset{1}{\cancel{3}} \cdot \frac{5}{\underset{3}{\cancel{9}}} = \frac{5}{3}$$

$$7\frac{1}{2} \div \frac{5}{3} = \frac{15}{2} \div \frac{5}{3}$$

$$= \frac{\overset{3}{\cancel{15}}}{2} \times \frac{3}{\underset{1}{\cancel{5}}} = \frac{9}{2} = \mathbf{4\frac{1}{2}}$$

29. $$2^{-4} + 4^{-2} = \frac{1}{2^4} + \frac{1}{4^2}$$

$$= \frac{1}{16} + \frac{1}{16} = \frac{2}{16} = \mathbf{\frac{1}{8}}$$

30.

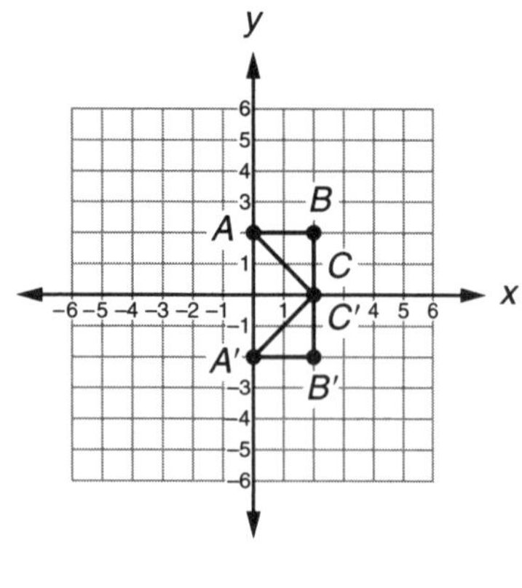

Lesson 81, Lesson Practice

a. Estimate: $\frac{21}{70} = \frac{3}{10} = 30\%$

$100\% - 30\% = \mathbf{70\%}$

	Percent	Actual Count
Planted with alfalfa	P_P	21
Not planted with alfalfa	P_N	49
Total	100	70

$$\frac{P_N}{100} = \frac{49}{70}$$

$$70P_N = 4900$$

$$P_N = \mathbf{70\%}$$

b. Estimate: $60 \times 3 =$ **180 pages**

	Percent	Actual Count
Pages read	40	120
Pages left to read	60	P
Total	100	T

$$\frac{40}{60} = \frac{120}{P}$$

$$40P = 7200$$

$$P = \textbf{180 pages}$$

c. Estimate: $\frac{26}{30} = \frac{13}{15} \approx \mathbf{87\%}$

	Percent	Actual Count
Missed	P_M	4
Correct	P_C	26
Total	100	30

$$\frac{P_C}{100} = \frac{26}{30}$$

$$30P_C = 2600$$

$$P_C = \mathbf{86\frac{2}{3}\%}$$

Lesson 81, Mixed Practice

1.

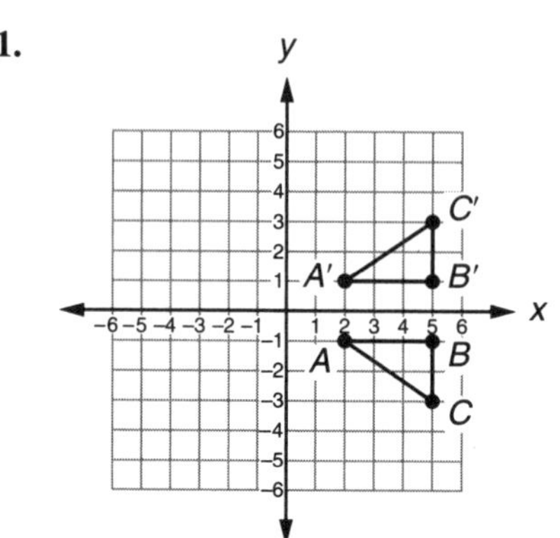

$\mathbf{A'(2, 1), B'(5, 1), C'(5, 3)}$

2. (a)

$$\begin{array}{r} 70 \\ 85 \\ 80 \\ 85 \\ 90 \\ 80 \\ 85 \\ 80 \\ 90 \\ 95 \\ 85 \\ 90 \\ 100 \\ 85 \\ + \quad 90 \\ \hline 1290 \end{array} \qquad \begin{array}{r} \mathbf{86} \\ 15\overline{)1290} \end{array}$$

(b) **85**

3. (a) **85**

(b) $100 - 70 = \mathbf{30}$

4.
$$\begin{array}{rr} \overset{5}{\not 6}\text{ ft} \longrightarrow & \overset{(12\text{ in.})}{1\text{ in.}} \longrightarrow \\ -\ 5\text{ ft} & 6\frac{1}{2}\text{ in.} \\ \hline \end{array}$$

$$\begin{array}{rr} \overset{5}{\not 6}\text{ ft} & \overset{13}{\not 1}\text{ in.} \\ -\ 5\text{ ft} & 6\frac{1}{2}\text{ in.} \\ \hline & \mathbf{6\frac{1}{2}\text{ inches}} \end{array}$$

5.

	Case 1	Case 2
Pencils	5	12
Price	75¢	p

$$\frac{5}{\$0.75} = \frac{12}{p}$$
$$5p = \$9.00$$
$$p = \mathbf{\$1.80}$$

6. (a) $x < 4$

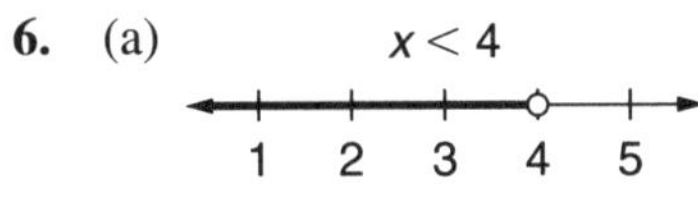

(b) $x \geq -2$

–3 –2 –1 0 1

7.

60 questions

$\frac{4}{5}$ answered correctly (48).
- 12 questions
- 12 questions
- 12 questions
- 12 questions

$\frac{1}{5}$ answered incorrectly.
- 12 questions

(a) $48 \div 4 = 12$
$5(12\text{ questions}) = \mathbf{60\text{ questions}}$

(b) $\dfrac{\text{correct answers}}{\text{incorrect answers}} = \dfrac{48}{12} = \mathbf{\dfrac{4}{1}}$

8. $3\frac{3}{4} \div 2 = \frac{15}{4} \times \frac{1}{2}$
$= \frac{15}{8} = \mathbf{1\frac{7}{8}\text{ inches}}$

9.

	Ratio	Actual Count
Gleeps	9	G
Bobbles	5	B
Total	14	2800

$$\frac{9}{14} = \frac{G}{2800}$$
$$14G = 25{,}200$$
$$G = \mathbf{1800\text{ gleeps}}$$

10. $(9)^2 + \sqrt{9} = 81 + 3 = \mathbf{84}$

11. **Insufficient information ($m < n$ if both are positive; $m > n$ if both are negative)**

12. (a) $2\frac{1}{4} = 2\frac{25}{100} = \mathbf{2.25}$

(b) $2.25 \times 100\% = \mathbf{225\%}$

(c) $2\frac{1}{4}\% = \dfrac{2\frac{1}{4}}{100} = \dfrac{\frac{9}{4}}{100} \cdot \dfrac{\frac{1}{100}}{\frac{1}{100}} = \mathbf{\dfrac{9}{400}}$

(d) $2\frac{1}{4}\% = 2.25\% = \mathbf{0.0225}$

13. $\mathbf{p = 0.4 \times \$12}$
$p = \mathbf{\$4.80}$

14. $\mathbf{0.5 \times W_N = 0.4}$
$$\frac{0.5 \times W_N}{0.5} = \frac{0.4}{0.5}$$
$W_N = \mathbf{0.8}$

15. $\dfrac{16\frac{2}{3}}{100} = \dfrac{\frac{50}{3}}{\frac{100}{1}}$

$\dfrac{\frac{50}{3}}{\frac{100}{1}} \cdot \dfrac{\frac{1}{100}}{\frac{1}{100}} = \dfrac{\frac{50}{300}}{1} = \dfrac{50}{300}$

$= \mathbf{\dfrac{1}{6}}$

16.

	Percent	Actual Count
Correct	P_C	21
Incorrect	P_I	4
Total	100	25

$$\frac{P_C}{100} = \frac{21}{25}$$
$$25P_C = 2100$$
$$P_C = \mathbf{84\%}$$

17.

	Percent	Actual Count
Left fallow	20	F
Not left fallow	80	N
Total	100	4000

$$\frac{80}{100} = \frac{N}{4000}$$
$$100N = 320{,}000$$
$$N = \mathbf{3200\text{ acres}}$$

18. (a) **Angles *ABC* and *CBD* are supplementary (total 180°), so m∠*CBD* = 40°.**

(b) **Angles *CBD* and *DBE* are complementary (total 90°), so m∠*DBE* = 50°.**

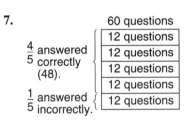

(c) **Angles DBE and EBA are supplementary (total 180°), so m$\angle EBA$ = 130°.**

(d) **360°**

19. $$\frac{3000}{6300} = \frac{\overset{1}{\cancel{2}} \cdot \overset{1}{\cancel{2}} \cdot 2 \cdot \overset{1}{\cancel{3}} \cdot \overset{1}{\cancel{5}} \cdot \overset{1}{\cancel{5}} \cdot 5}{\underset{1}{\cancel{2}} \cdot \underset{1}{\cancel{2}} \cdot \underset{1}{\cancel{3}} \cdot 3 \cdot \underset{1}{\cancel{5}} \cdot \underset{1}{\cancel{5}} \cdot 7}$$

$$= \mathbf{\frac{10}{21}}$$

20. (a)

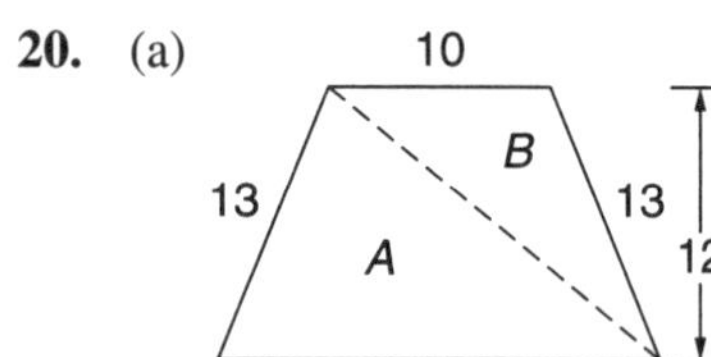

$$\text{Area of triangle } A = \frac{(20 \text{ in.})(12 \text{ in.})}{2}$$
$$= 120 \text{ in.}^2$$
$$\text{Area of triangle } B = \frac{(10 \text{ in.})(12 \text{ in.})}{2}$$
$$= 60 \text{ in.}^2$$
$$\text{Area of figure} = 120 \text{ in.}^2 + 60 \text{ in.}^2$$
$$= \mathbf{180 \text{ in.}^2}$$

(b)

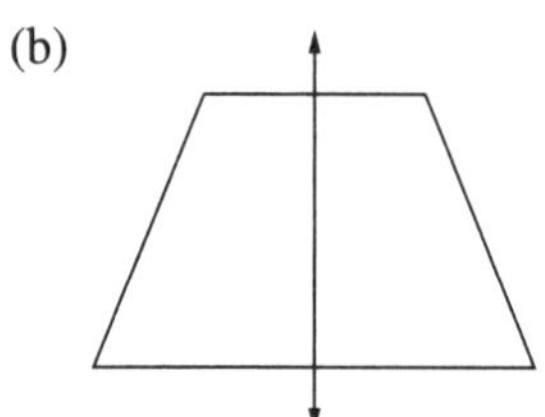

21. Double the "in" number, then subtract 1 to find the "out" number.

$4 \cdot 2 - 1 = \mathbf{7}$

$-1 + 1 = 0, 0/2 = \mathbf{0}$

22. (a) $\mathbf{5.6 \times 10^8}$

(b) $\mathbf{5.6 \times 10^{-6}}$

23. $$5x = 16.5$$
$$\frac{5x}{5} = \frac{16.5}{5}$$
$$x = \mathbf{3.3}$$

check: $$5(3.3) = 16.5$$
$$16.5 = 16.5$$

24. $$3\frac{1}{2} + a = 5\frac{3}{8}$$
$$3\frac{1}{2} - 3\frac{1}{2} + a = 5\frac{3}{8} - 3\frac{1}{2}$$
$$a = 5\frac{3}{8} - 3\frac{4}{8}$$
$$a = 4\frac{11}{8} - 3\frac{4}{8}$$
$$a = \mathbf{1\frac{7}{8}}$$

check: $$3\frac{1}{2} + 1\frac{7}{8} = 5\frac{3}{8}$$
$$3\frac{4}{8} + 1\frac{7}{8} = 5\frac{3}{8}$$
$$4\frac{11}{8} = 5\frac{3}{8}$$
$$5\frac{3}{8} = 5\frac{3}{8}$$

25. $3^2 + 5[6 - (10 - 2^3)]$

$9 + 5[6 - (10 - 8)]$

$9 + 5[6 - 2]$

$9 + 5[4]$

$9 + 20$

$\mathbf{29}$

26. $\sqrt{2^2 \cdot 3^4 \cdot 5^2} = 2 \cdot 3^2 \cdot 5$

$= 2 \cdot 9 \cdot 5 = \mathbf{90}$

27. $2\frac{2}{3} \times 4\frac{1}{2} \div 6$

$$= \left(\frac{\overset{4}{\cancel{8}}}{\underset{1}{\cancel{3}}} \times \frac{\overset{3}{\cancel{9}}}{\underset{1}{\cancel{2}}}\right) \div 6 = 12 \div 6 = \mathbf{2} \text{ or } \mathbf{\frac{2}{1}}$$

28. $(3.5)^2 - (5 - 3.4)$

$= (12.25) - (1.6) = \mathbf{10.65}$

29. (a) **108**

(b) **−75**

(c) **−20**

(d) **−5**

30. (a) $(-3) + |-4| - (-5)$

$(-3) + (4) + [-(-5)]$

$(-3) + (4) + [5]$

$\mathbf{6}$

(b) $(-18) - (+20) + (-7)$

$(-18) + [-(+20)] + (-7)$

$(-18) + [-20] + [-7]$

$\mathbf{-45}$

Lesson 82, Lesson Practice

a. $A = \pi r^2$
$A \approx 3.14(36\text{ ft}^2)$
$A \approx \mathbf{113\text{ ft}^2}$

b. $A = \pi r^2$
$A \approx 3.14(16\text{ cm}^2)$
$A \approx \mathbf{50.24\text{ cm}^2}$

c. $A = \pi r^2$
$A = \pi(16\text{ cm}^2)$
$A = \mathbf{16\pi\text{ cm}^2}$

d. $A = \pi r^2$
$A \approx \frac{22}{7}(16\text{ cm})^2$
$A \approx \frac{352}{7}\text{ cm}^2$
$A \approx \mathbf{50\frac{2}{7}\text{ cm}^2}$

Lesson 82, Mixed Practice

1. $(2\text{ ft})(4\text{ ft}) = 8\text{ ft}^2$
$\frac{8\text{ ft}^2}{1\text{ layer}}(1\text{ ft})(2.5\text{ layers})$ (layer and layers crossed out)
$= \mathbf{20\text{ ft}^3}$

2.
$6'3'' = 75''$
$6'5'' = 77''$
$5'11'' = 71''$
$6'2'' = 74''$
$+\ 6'1'' = 73''$
$370''$

$370'' \div 5 = 74''$
$74'' = \mathbf{6'\,2''}$

3.

	Ratio	Actual Count
Students	20	S
Teachers	1	48

$\frac{20}{1} = \frac{S}{48}$
$S = \mathbf{960\text{ students}}$

4. $2.54\text{ centimeters} \cdot \frac{1\text{ meter}}{100\text{ centimeters}}$ (centimeters crossed out)
$= \mathbf{0.0254\text{ meter}}$

5. (a) Number line from −5 to −1: shaded to the left with an open circle at −2.

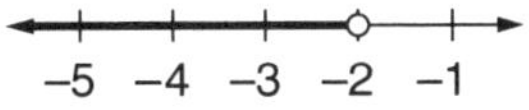

(b) Number line from −1 to 3: closed circle at 0, shaded to the right.

6.

	Case 1	Case 2
Beats	225	b
Minutes	3	5

$\frac{225}{3} = \frac{b}{5}$
$3b = 1125$
$b = \mathbf{375\text{ times}}$

7.

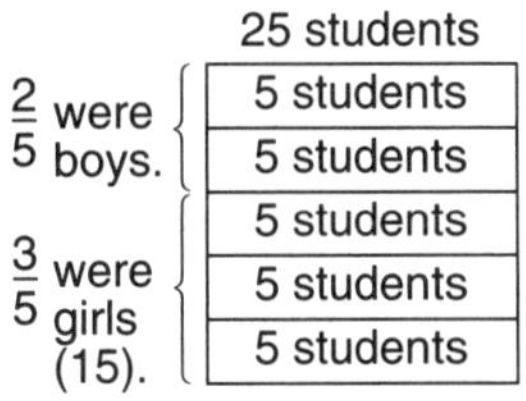

	25 students
$\frac{2}{5}$ were boys.	5 students
	5 students
$\frac{3}{5}$ were girls (15).	5 students
	5 students
	5 students

(a) $15 \div 3 = 5$
$5(5\text{ students}) = \mathbf{25\text{ students}}$

(b) $\frac{\text{girls}}{\text{boys}} = \frac{15}{10} = \mathbf{\frac{3}{2}}$

8. $x^2 - y^2 = 5^2 - 3^2 = 25 - 9 = 16$
$(x + y)(x - y) = (5 + 3)(5 - 3)$
$= (8)(2) = 16,\ 16 = 16$
$x^2 - y^2 \ \textcircled{=}\ (x + y)(x - y)$

9. Percent unshaded: $25\% + 23\% = \mathbf{48\%}$
Percent shaded: $100\% - 48\% = \mathbf{52\%}$

10. $a\ \textcircled{<}\ b$

11. (a) $C \approx 3.14\,(14\text{ cm})$
$C \approx \mathbf{43.96\text{ cm}}$

(b) $C \approx \frac{22}{7}(14\text{ cm})$ (7 and 14 cancelled to 1 and 2)
$C \approx \mathbf{44\text{ cm}}$

12. (a) $A = \pi r^2$
$A \approx 3.14\,(49\text{ cm}^2)$
$A \approx \mathbf{153.86\text{ cm}^2}$

(b) $A = \pi r^2$
$A \approx \frac{22}{7}(49\text{ cm}^2)$ (7 and 49 cancelled to 1 and 7)
$A \approx \mathbf{154\text{ cm}^2}$

13. (a) $1.6 = 1\frac{6}{10} = \mathbf{1\frac{3}{5}}$

(b) $1.6 \times 100\% = \mathbf{160\%}$

(c) $1.6\% = \frac{1.6}{100} \cdot \frac{10}{10} = \frac{16}{1000} = \mathbf{\frac{2}{125}}$

(d) $1.6\% = \mathbf{0.016}$

14. $\mathbf{M = 0.064 \times \$25}$
$M = \mathbf{\$1.60}$

15. (a) $\mathbf{1.2 \times 10^6}$

(b) $\mathbf{1.2 \times 10^{-4}}$

16.

	Percent	Actual Count
Correctly described	64	*C*
Incorrectly described	36	63
Total	100	*T*

$$\frac{64}{36} = \frac{C}{63}$$
$$36C = 4032$$
$$C = \mathbf{112\ students}$$

17.

	Percent	Actual Count
Pages read	60	180
Pages left to read	40	*P*
Total	100	*T*

$$\frac{60}{40} = \frac{180}{P}$$
$$60P = 7200$$
$$P = \mathbf{120\ pages}$$

18.

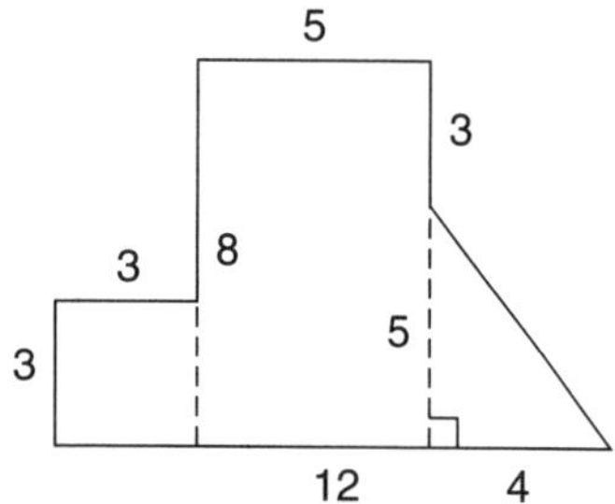

Area of rectangle = (5 in.)(8 in.) = 40 in.^{2}
Area of square = (3 in.)(3 in.) = 9 in.^{2}
+ Area of triangle = $\frac{(5\text{ in.})(4\text{ in.})}{2}$ = 10 in.^{2}

Area of figure = **59 in.^{2}**

19.

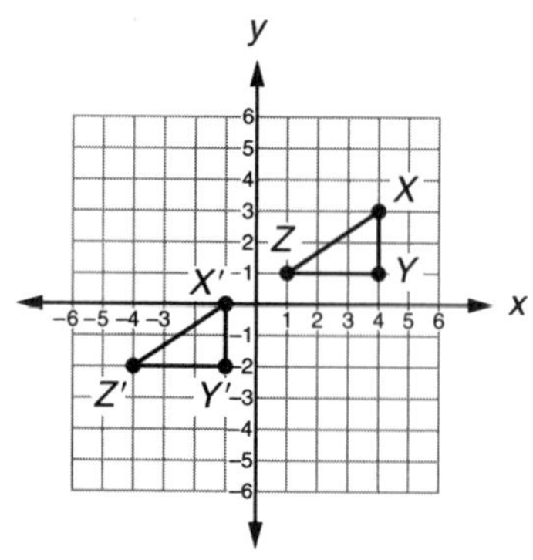

$\mathbf{X'(-1, 0), Y'(-1, -2), Z'(-4, -2)}$

20. $$\frac{240}{816} = \frac{\cancel{2}\cdot\cancel{2}\cdot\cancel{2}\cdot\cancel{2}\cdot\cancel{3}\cdot 5}{\cancel{2}\cdot\cancel{2}\cdot\cancel{2}\cdot\cancel{2}\cdot\cancel{3}\cdot 17} = \mathbf{\frac{5}{17}}$$

21. (a) **3 chords**

(b) **6 chords**

(c) **60°**

(d) **120°**

22. $\mathbf{1 \times 10^8}$

23. $$\frac{3}{4}x = 36$$
$$\left(\frac{\cancel{4}}{\cancel{3}}\right)\frac{\cancel{3}}{\cancel{4}}x = \left(\frac{4}{\cancel{3}}\right)\overset{12}{\cancel{36}}$$
$$x = \mathbf{48}$$

check: $$\frac{3}{\cancel{4}}(\overset{12}{\cancel{48}}) = 36$$
$$3(12) = 36$$
$$36 = 36$$

24. $$3.2 + a = 3.46$$
$$3.2 - 3.2 + a = 3.46 - 3.2$$
$$a = \mathbf{0.26}$$

check: $$3.2 + 0.26 = 3.46$$
$$3.46 = 3.46$$

25. $$\frac{\sqrt{3^2 + 4^2}}{5} = \frac{\sqrt{9 + 16}}{5} = \frac{\sqrt{25}}{5} = \frac{5}{5} = \mathbf{1}$$

26. $(8 - 3)^2 - (3 - 8)^2$
$= (5)^2 - (-5)^2 = 25 - 25 = \mathbf{0}$

27. $3.5 \div (7 \div 0.2)$
$= 3.5 \div 35 = \mathbf{0.1}$

28. $4\frac{1}{2} + 2\frac{2}{3} - 3$

$= 4\frac{3}{6} + 2\frac{4}{6} - 2\frac{6}{6}$

$= 6\frac{7}{6} - 2\frac{6}{6} = \mathbf{4\frac{1}{6}}$

29. (a) $\mathbf{-6}$

(b) **24**

30. (a)
$(-3) + (-4) - (-2)$
$(-3) + (-4) + [-(-2)]$
$(-3) + (-4) + [2]$
$\mathbf{-5}$

(b)
$(-20) + (+30) - |-40|$
$(-20) + (+30) + [-|-40|]$
$(-20) + (+30) + [-40]$
$\mathbf{-30}$

Lesson 83, Lesson Practice

a. $(4.2 \times 1.4) \times (10^6 \times 10^3)$
$= \mathbf{5.88 \times 10^9}$

b. $(5 \times 3) \times (10^5 \times 10^7) = 15 \times 10^{12}$
$= \mathbf{1.5 \times 10^{13}}$

c. $(4 \times 2.1) \times (10^{-3} \times 10^{-7})$
$= \mathbf{8.4 \times 10^{-10}}$

d. $(6 \times 7) \times (10^{-2} \times 10^{-5}) = 42 \times 10^{-7}$
$= \mathbf{4.2 \times 10^{-6}}$

Lesson 83, Mixed Practice

1. $\frac{\$1.12}{16 \text{ ounces}} = \frac{\$0.07}{1 \text{ ounce}}$

$\frac{\$1.32}{24 \text{ ounces}} = \frac{\$0.055}{1 \text{ ounce}}$

$\$0.070$
$-\ \$0.055$
$0.015 more per ounce

2.

	Ratio	Actual Count
Good apples	5	*G*
Bad apples	2	*B*
Total	7	70

$\frac{5}{7} = \frac{G}{70}$

$7G = 350$

$G = \mathbf{50 \text{ apples}}$

3. $15(82) + 5(90) = 1230 + 450 = 1680$

$20\overline{)1680}$ = **84**

4. $\$6(2.5) = \mathbf{\$15}$

5. $24 \cancel{\text{shillings}} \cdot \frac{12 \text{ pence}}{1 \cancel{\text{shilling}}} = \mathbf{288 \text{ pence}}$

6.

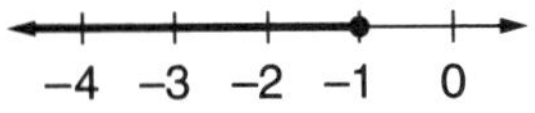

7.

	Case 1	Case 2
First number	5	20
Second number	12	*n*

$\frac{5}{12} = \frac{20}{n}$

$5n = 240$

$n = \mathbf{48}$

8. $4(1.5) + 5 = 6 + 5 = \mathbf{11}$

9. $\frac{30 \text{ points}}{5} = 6 \text{ points}$

$4(6 \text{ points}) = \mathbf{24 \text{ points}}$

10. $x(x + y) \ \textcircled{=}\ x^2 + xy$

11. (a) $C = \pi(28 \text{ cm})$
$C = \mathbf{28\pi} \text{ cm}$

(b) $C \approx \frac{22}{\cancel{7}_{1}}(\cancel{28}^{4} \text{ cm})$
$C \approx \mathbf{88 \text{ cm}}$

12. (a) $A = \pi r^2$
$A = \pi(196 \text{ cm}^2)$
$A = \mathbf{196\pi \text{ cm}^2}$

(b) $A = \pi r^2$
$A \approx \frac{22}{\cancel{7}_{1}}(\cancel{196}^{28} \text{ cm}^2)$
$A \approx \mathbf{616 \text{ cm}^2}$

13. (a) $(10 \text{ cm})(10 \text{ cm}) = 100 \text{ cm}^2$
$(100 \text{ cm}^2)(10 \text{ cm}) = \mathbf{1000 \text{ cm}^3}$

(b) $6(100 \text{ cm}^2) = \mathbf{600 \text{ cm}^2}$

14. (a) $250\% = \frac{250}{100} = 2\frac{50}{100} = \mathbf{2\frac{1}{2}}$

(b) $250\% = \frac{250}{100} = \mathbf{2.5}$

(c) $12\overline{)7.0000}$ = 0.5833 . . . = $\mathbf{0.58\overline{3}}$

$$\begin{array}{r} 0.5833\ldots \\ 12\overline{)7.0000} \\ \underline{6\,0} \\ 1\,00 \\ \underline{96} \\ 40 \\ \underline{36} \\ 40 \\ \underline{36} \\ 4 \end{array}$$

(d) $\frac{7}{12} \times 100\% = \frac{700\%}{12} = \mathbf{58\frac{1}{3}\%}$

$$\begin{array}{r} 58\frac{4}{12} = 58\frac{1}{3}\% \\ 12\overline{)700} \\ \underline{60} \\ 100 \\ \underline{96} \\ 4 \end{array}$$

15.

$$\begin{array}{r} \$8.50 \\ \times\ 0.065 \\ \hline \$0.5525 \end{array} \longrightarrow \mathbf{\$0.55}$$

16.

	Percent	Actual Count
Commercial time	P_C	12
Other	P_O	48
Total	100	60

$$\frac{P_C}{100} = \frac{12}{60}$$
$$60P_C = 1200$$
$$P_C = \mathbf{20\%}$$

17.

	Percent	Actual Count
Steam-powered	30	S
Not steam-powered	70	42
Total	100	T

$$\frac{70}{100} = \frac{42}{T}$$
$$70T = 4200$$
$$T = \mathbf{60\ boats}$$

18. $\frac{420}{630} = \frac{\mathbf{2 \cdot \cancel{2}^{1} \cdot \cancel{3}^{1} \cdot \cancel{5}^{1} \cdot \cancel{7}^{1}}}{\mathbf{\cancel{2}_{1} \cdot 3 \cdot \cancel{3}_{1} \cdot \cancel{5}_{1} \cdot \cancel{7}_{1}}}$

$= \mathbf{\frac{2}{3}}$

19.

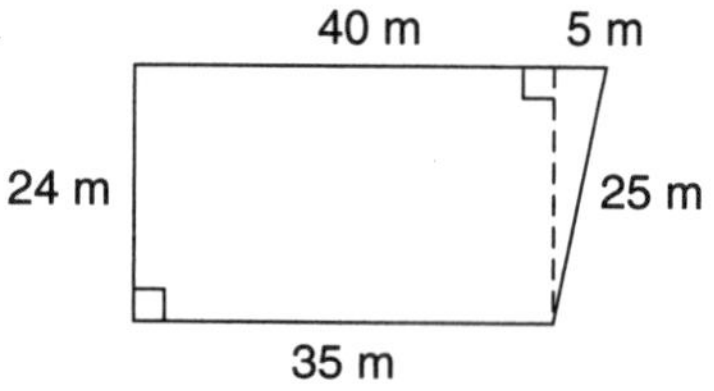

$$\begin{aligned} \text{Area of rectangle} &= (35\text{ m})(24\text{ m}) \\ &= 840\text{ m}^2 \\ \text{Area of triangle} &= \frac{(24\text{ m})(5\text{ m})}{2} \\ &= 60\text{ m}^2 \\ \text{Area of figure} &= 840\text{ m}^2 + 60\text{ m}^2 \\ &= \mathbf{900\ m^2} \end{aligned}$$

20. (a) $m\angle ECD = 180° - (90° + 54°)$
$= 180° - 144° = \mathbf{36°}$

(b) $m\angle ECB = 180° - 36° = \mathbf{144°}$

(c) $m\angle ACB = m\angle ECD = \mathbf{36°}$

(d) $m\angle BAC = \frac{180° - 36°}{2} = \frac{144°}{2} = \mathbf{72°}$

21. Multiply the "in" number by 2; then add 1 to find the "out" number.

$21 - 1 = 20, \frac{20}{2} = \mathbf{10}$

$-5(2) + 1 = -10 + 1 = \mathbf{-9}$

22. (a) $(3 \times 6) \times (10^4 \times 10^5) = 18 \times 10^9$
$= \mathbf{1.8 \times 10^{10}}$

(b) $(1.2 \times 4) \times (10^{-3} \times 10^{-6})$
$= \mathbf{4.8 \times 10^{-9}}$

23.

$$\begin{aligned} b - 1\frac{2}{3} &= 4\frac{1}{2} \\ b - 1\frac{2}{3} + 1\frac{2}{3} &= 4\frac{1}{2} + 1\frac{2}{3} \\ b &= 4\frac{3}{6} + 1\frac{4}{6} \\ b &= 5\frac{7}{6} \\ b &= \mathbf{6\frac{1}{6}} \end{aligned}$$

check:

$$\begin{aligned} 6\frac{1}{6} - 1\frac{2}{3} &= 4\frac{1}{2} \\ 6\frac{1}{6} - 1\frac{4}{6} &= 4\frac{1}{2} \\ 5\frac{7}{6} - 1\frac{4}{6} &= 4\frac{1}{2} \\ 4\frac{3}{6} &= 4\frac{1}{2} \\ 4\frac{1}{2} &= 4\frac{1}{2} \end{aligned}$$

24. $0.4y = 1.44$

$$\frac{0.4y}{0.4} = \frac{1.44}{0.4}$$

$$y = \mathbf{3.6}$$

check: $0.4(3.6) = 1.44$

$1.44 = 1.44$

25. $2^3 + 2^2 + 2^1 + 2^0 + 2^{-1}$

$$= 8 + 4 + 2 + 1 + \frac{1}{2} = \mathbf{15\frac{1}{2}}$$

26. $\frac{6}{10} \times 3\frac{1}{3} \div 2$

$$= \left(\frac{6}{10} \times \frac{10}{3}\right) \div 2 = 2 \div 2 = \mathbf{1}$$

27. (a) **4**

(b) **−60**

28.

$$\frac{5}{24} = \frac{25}{120}$$

$$-\frac{7}{60} = \frac{14}{120}$$

$$\mathbf{\frac{11}{120}}$$

29. (a) $(-3) + (-4) - (-5)$

$(-3) + (-4) + [-(-5)]$

$(-3) + (-4) + [5]$

$\mathbf{-2}$

(b) $(-15) - (+14) + (+10)$

$(-15) + [-(+14)] + (+10)$

$(-15) + [-14] + (+10)$

$\mathbf{-19}$

30.

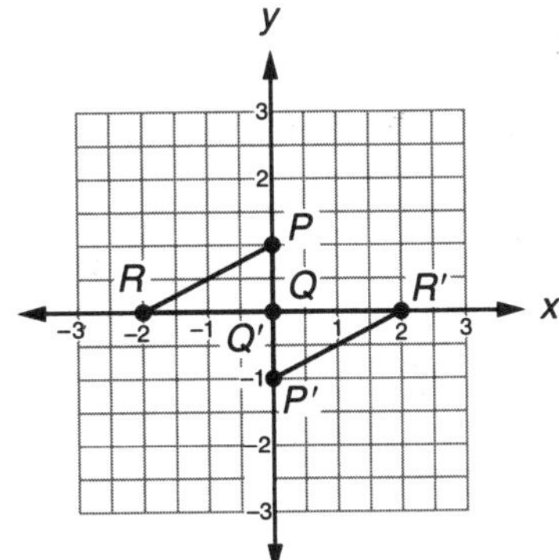

$\mathbf{P'(0, -1), Q'(0, 0), R'(2, 0)}$

Lesson 84, Lesson Practice

a. **Binomial**

b. **Trinomial**

c. **Monomial**

d. **Binomial**

e. $3a + 2a^2 - a + a^2$

$2a^2 + a^2 + 3a - a$

$\mathbf{3a^2 + 2a}$

f. $5xy - x + xy - 2x$

$5xy + xy - x - 2x$

$\mathbf{6xy - 3x}$

g. $3 + x^2 + x - 5 + 2x^2$

$x^2 + 2x^2 + x + 3 - 5$

$\mathbf{3x^2 + x - 2}$

h. $3\pi + 1.4 - \pi + 2.8$

$3\pi - \pi + 1.4 + 2.8$

$\mathbf{2\pi + 4.2}$

Lesson 84, Mixed Practice

1. **18°F**

2. $2xy + xy - 3x + x$

$\mathbf{3xy - 2x}$

3. (a) 79°F − 68°F = **11°F**

(b) **Thursday**

(c)

68°F
72°F
70°F
76°F
+ 79°F
365°F

$5\overline{)365°F}$ = 73°F

73°F − 70°F = **3°F**

4. (a)

90
90
100
95
95
85
100
100
80
+ 100
935

$10\overline{)935.0}$ = **93.5**

(b) **95**

(c) **100**

(d) $100 - 80 = \mathbf{20}$

5.

	Ratio	Actual Count
Rowboats	3	R
Sailboats	7	S
Total	10	210

$$\frac{7}{10} = \frac{S}{210}$$
$$10S = 1470$$
$$S = \textbf{147 sailboats}$$

6. **2nd**

7. $\frac{\$1.40}{4} = \frac{c}{10}$
$$4c = \$14$$
$$c = \mathbf{\$3.50}$$

8. $36 \div 3 = 12$
$5(12 \text{ members}) = \textbf{60 members}$

9. (a) $(5)^2 - 2(5) + 1 = 25 - 10 + 1$
$= \mathbf{16}$

(b) $(5 - 1)^2 = (4)^2 = \mathbf{16}$

10. $f \circleddash g$ (equals sign circled: $f = g$)

11. (a) $C \approx 3.14(6 \text{ in.})$
$C \approx \textbf{18.84 in.}$

(b) $A = \pi r^2$
$A \approx 3.14(9 \text{ in.}^2)$
$A \approx \textbf{28.26 in.}^2$

12. $\textbf{4.8 } \cancel{\textbf{meters}} \cdot \frac{\textbf{100 centimeters}}{\textbf{1 } \cancel{\textbf{meter}}}$
$= \textbf{480 centimeters}$

13.

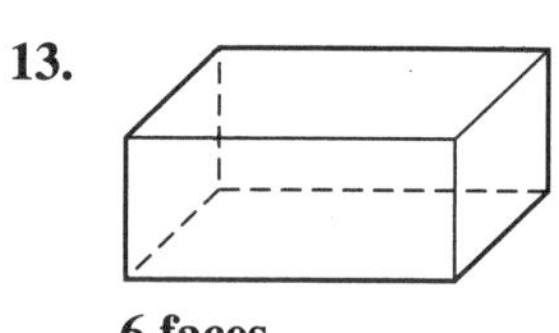

6 faces

14. (a) $1\frac{4}{5} = 1\frac{8}{10} = \mathbf{1.8}$

(b) $1.8 \times 100\% = \mathbf{180\%}$

(c) $1.8\% = \frac{1.8}{100} \cdot \frac{10}{10} = \frac{18}{1000} = \mathbf{\frac{9}{500}}$

(d) $1.8\% = \mathbf{0.018}$

15. $\mathbf{p = 0.3 \times \$18.00}$
$p = \mathbf{\$5.40}$

16. $\frac{12\frac{1}{2}}{100} = \frac{\frac{25}{2}}{\frac{100}{1}}$

$$\frac{\frac{25}{2}}{\frac{100}{1}} \cdot \frac{\frac{1}{100}}{\frac{1}{100}} = \frac{\frac{25}{200}}{1} = \frac{25}{200}$$
$$= \mathbf{\frac{1}{8}}$$

17.

	Percent	Actual Count
Flew the coop	40	36
Stayed	60	S
Total	100	T

$$\frac{40}{100} = \frac{36}{T}$$
$$40T = 3600$$
$$T = \textbf{90 pigeons}$$

18.

	Percent	Actual Count
3 feet tall or less	60	L
More than 3 feet tall	40	M
Total	100	300

$$\frac{40}{100} = \frac{M}{300}$$
$$100M = 12{,}000$$
$$M = \textbf{120 saplings}$$

19.

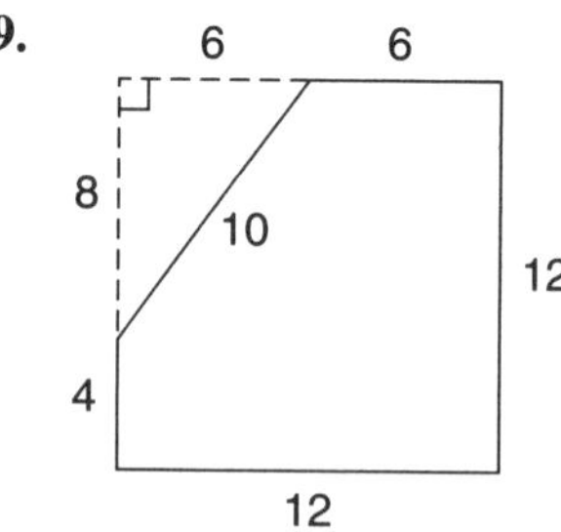

(a) Perimeter $= 12 \text{ in.} + 12 \text{ in.} + 4 \text{ in.}$
$+ 10 \text{ in.} + 6 \text{ in.}$
$= \textbf{44 in.}$

(b) Area of square $= (12 \text{ in.})(12 \text{ in.})$
$= 144 \text{ in.}^2$

Area of triangle $= \frac{(6 \text{ in.})(8 \text{ in.})}{2}$
$= 24 \text{ in.}^2$

Area of figure $= 144 \text{ in.}^2 - 24 \text{ in.}^2$
$= \textbf{120 in.}^2$

20. (a) $\frac{60°}{360°}$ $\mathbf{\frac{1}{6}}$

(b) $\frac{45°}{360°}$ $\mathbf{\frac{1}{8}}$

(c) $\frac{75°}{360°}$ $\mathbf{\frac{5}{24}}$

21. To find a term in the sequence, double the preceding term and add 1.

Note: **Other rule descriptions are possible, including "The value of the nth term is $2^n - 1$." Discuss various rules proposed by students.**

$31 \times 2 + 1 = \mathbf{63}$
$63 \times 2 + 1 = \mathbf{127}$
$127 \times 2 + 1 = \mathbf{255}$

22. (a) $(1.5 \times 3) \times (10^{-3} \times 10^6)$
$= \mathbf{4.5 \times 10^3}$

(b) $(3 \times 5) \times (10^4 \times 10^5) = 15 \times 10^9$
$= \mathbf{1.5 \times 10^{10}}$

23. (a) $\mathbf{10^6}$

(b) $\mathbf{10^{-4}}$

24.
$$b - 4.75 = 5.2$$
$$b - 4.75 + 4.75 = 5.2 + 4.75$$
$$b = \mathbf{9.95}$$
check:
$$9.95 - 4.75 = 5.2$$
$$5.2 = 5.2$$

25.
$$\frac{2}{3}y = 36$$
$$\left(\frac{\cancel{3}^{1}}{\cancel{2}_{1}}\right)\frac{\cancel{2}^{1}}{\cancel{3}_{1}}y = \left(\frac{3}{\cancel{2}_{1}}\right)\cancel{36}^{18}$$
$$y = \mathbf{54}$$
check:
$$\frac{2}{\cancel{3}_{1}}(\cancel{54}^{18}) = 36$$
$$2(18) = 36$$
$$36 = 36$$

26. $\sqrt{5^2 - 4^2} + 2^3$
$= \sqrt{25 - 16} + 8 = \sqrt{9} + 8$
$= 3 + 8 = \mathbf{11}$

27. 1 m = 1000 mm
1000 mm − 45 mm = **955 mm**

28. $0.9 \div 2.25 \times 24 = 0.4 \times 24 = \mathbf{9.6}$

29. (a) **4**

(b) **−30**

30. (a)
$$(+30) - (-50) - (+20)$$
$$(+30) + [-(-50)] + [-(+20)]$$
$$(+30) + [50] + [-20]$$
$$\mathbf{60}$$

(b)
$$(-3) - (-4) - (5)$$
$$(-3) + [-(-4)] + [-(5)]$$
$$(-3) + [4] + [-5]$$
$$\mathbf{-4}$$

LESSON 85, LESSON PRACTICE

a.
$$(-3) + (-3)(-3) - \frac{(-3)}{(+3)}$$
$$(-3) + 9 - (-1)$$
$$(-3) + 9 + [-(-1)]$$
$$(-3) + 9 + [1]$$
$$\mathbf{7}$$

b.
$$(-3) - [(-4) - (-5)(-6)]$$
$$(-3) - [(-4) - (+30)]$$
$$(-3) - [-34]$$
$$(-3) + 34$$
$$\mathbf{31}$$

c.
$$(-2)[(-3) - (-4)(-5)]$$
$$(-2)[(-3) - (+20)]$$
$$(-2)[-23]$$
$$\mathbf{46}$$

d.
$$(-5) - (-5)(-5) + |-5|$$
$$(-5) - (+25) + 5$$
$$(-5) + [-(+25)] + 5$$
$$(-5) + [-25] + 5$$
$$\mathbf{-25}$$

e.
$y = 3(3) - 1$
$y = 9 - 1$
$y = \mathbf{8}$;
$y = 3(1) - 1$
$y = 3 - 1$
$y = \mathbf{2}$;
$y = 3(0) - 1$
$y = 0 - 1$
$y = \mathbf{-1}$

f.
$$y = \frac{1}{2}x;$$
$$y = \frac{1}{2}(6)$$
$$y = \mathbf{3};$$
$$y = \frac{1}{2}(0)$$
$$y = \mathbf{0};$$
$$4 = \frac{1}{2}x$$
$$\left(\frac{2}{1}\right)4 = \left(\frac{2}{1}\right)\left(\frac{1}{2}\right)x$$
$$\mathbf{8} = x$$

g.
$$y = 8 - x$$
$$y = 8 - 7$$
$$y = \mathbf{1};$$
$$y = 8 - 1$$
$$y = \mathbf{7};$$
$$y = 8 - 4$$
$$y = \mathbf{4}$$

h. $y = x^2$

x	y
1	**1**
2	**4**
3	**9**

Lesson 85, Mixed Practice

1. (a) 70 + 80 + 90 + 80 + 70 + 90 + 75 + 95 + 100 + 90 = 840

$$840 \div 10 = \mathbf{84}$$

(b) **85**

(c) **90**

(d) **30**

2.

	Ratio	Actual Count
Won	3	*W*
Lost	1	*L*
Total	4	24

$$\frac{1}{4} = \frac{L}{24}$$
$$4L = 24$$
$$L = \mathbf{6\ games}$$

3.

	Ratio	Actual Count
Dandelions	11	*D*
Marigolds	4	44

$$\frac{11}{4} = \frac{D}{44}$$
$$4D = 484$$
$$D = \mathbf{121\ dandelions}$$

4.

	Case 1	Case 2
Miles	2	*m*
Seconds	10	60

$$\frac{2}{10} = \frac{m}{60}$$
$$10m = 120$$
$$m = \mathbf{12\ miles}$$

5. **0.98 ~~liter~~ · $\frac{\text{1000 milliliters}}{\text{1 ~~liter~~}}$ = 980 milliliters**

6.

7.

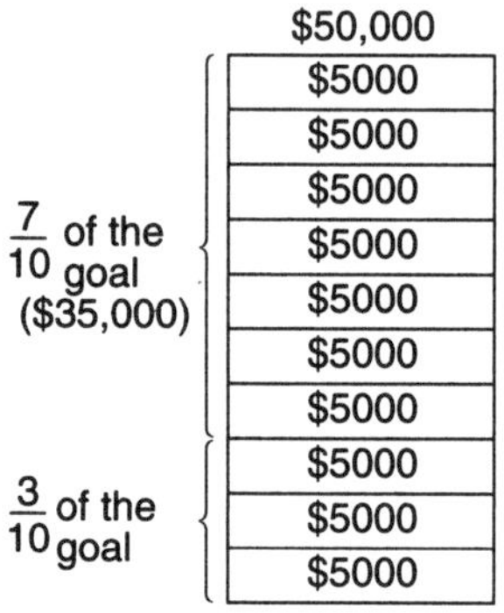

(a)
$$\frac{\$35{,}000}{7} = \$5000$$
$$10 \times \$5000 = \mathbf{\$50{,}000}$$

(b) **30%**

8. **Insufficient information**

9. (a)
$$C \approx 3.14(8\text{ m})$$
$$C \approx \mathbf{25.12\ m}$$

(b)
$$A = \pi r^2$$
$$A \approx 3.14(16\text{ m}^2)$$
$$A \approx \mathbf{50.24\ m^2}$$

10.
$$1 - \frac{8}{20} - \frac{5}{20} = \mathbf{\frac{7}{20}}$$

11.

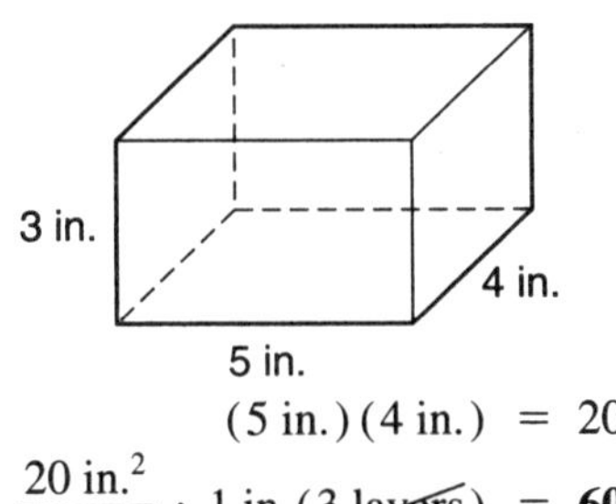

$$(5 \text{ in.})(4 \text{ in.}) = 20 \text{ in.}^2$$

$$\frac{20 \text{ in.}^2}{1 \text{ layer}} \cdot 1 \text{ in.}(3 \text{ layers}) = \mathbf{60 \text{ in.}^3}$$

12. One possibility:

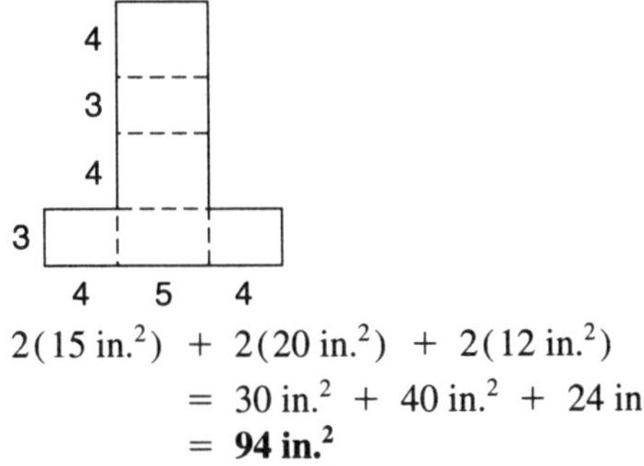

$$2(15 \text{ in.}^2) + 2(20 \text{ in.}^2) + 2(12 \text{ in.}^2)$$
$$= 30 \text{ in.}^2 + 40 \text{ in.}^2 + 24 \text{ in.}^2$$
$$= \mathbf{94 \text{ in.}^2}$$

13. (a) $\frac{1}{40} \cdot \frac{25}{25} = \frac{25}{1000} = 0.025$

(b) $\frac{1}{40} \times 100\% = \frac{100\%}{40} = \mathbf{2\frac{1}{2}\%}$

$$40\overline{)100} = 2\tfrac{20}{40} = 2\tfrac{1}{2}\%$$
$$\underline{80}$$
$$20$$

(c) $0.25\% = \frac{0.25}{100} \cdot \frac{100}{100} = \frac{25}{10{,}000} = \mathbf{\frac{1}{400}}$

(d) $0.25\% = \mathbf{0.0025}$

14.

$$\begin{array}{r} \$180{,}000 \\ \times \quad 0.06 \\ \hline \mathbf{\$10{,}800} \end{array}$$

15. (a) $\mathbf{2^3 \cdot 3^2 \cdot 5 \cdot 7^2}$

(b) **The exponents of the prime factors of 17,640 are not all even numbers.**

16.

$$\frac{8\frac{1}{3}}{100} = \frac{\frac{25}{3}}{\frac{100}{1}}$$

$$\frac{\frac{25}{3}}{\frac{100}{1}} \cdot \frac{\frac{1}{100}}{\frac{1}{100}} = \frac{\frac{25}{300}}{1} = \frac{25}{300}$$

$$= \mathbf{\frac{1}{12}}$$

17.

	Percent	Actual Count
Correct	P_C	38
Incorrect	P_I	2
Total	100	40

$$\frac{P_C}{100} = \frac{38}{40}$$
$$40P_C = 3800$$
$$P_C = \mathbf{95\%}$$

18.

	Percent	Actual Count
Happy faces	35	H
Not happy faces	65	91
Total	100	T

$$\frac{65}{100} = \frac{91}{T}$$
$$65T = 9100$$
$$T = \mathbf{140 \text{ children}}$$

19.

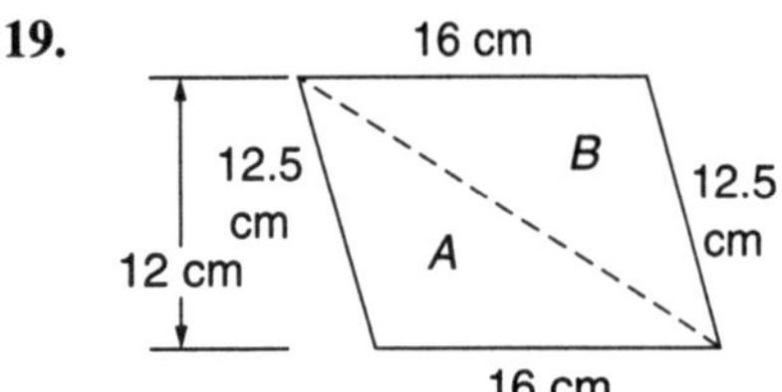

(a) **Parallelogram**

(b) Perimeter = 12.5 cm + 16 cm + 12.5 cm + 16 cm = **57 cm**

(c) Area = (12 cm)(16 cm) = **192 cm²**

(d)

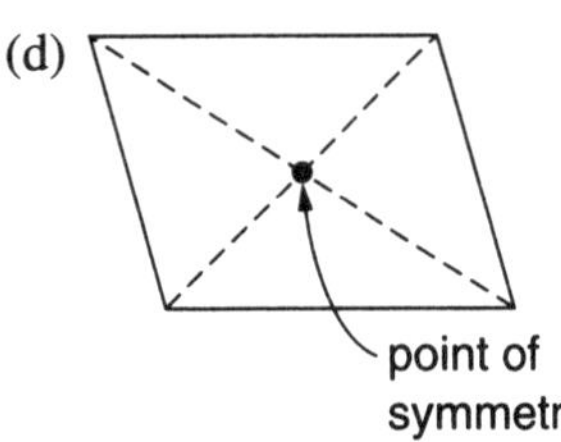

20. (a) $m\angle TOS = \mathbf{90°}$

(b) $m\angle QOT = \mathbf{180°}$

(c) $m\angle QOR = \frac{90°}{3} = \mathbf{30°}$

(d) $m\angle TOR = 90° + 60° = \mathbf{150°}$

21.

$y = 2(5) - 1$
$y = 10 - 1$
$y = \mathbf{9;}$
$y = 2(3) - 1$
$y = 6 - 1$
$y = \mathbf{5;}$
$y = 2(1) - 1$
$y = 2 - 1$
$y = \mathbf{1}$

22. $30 \times 10^5 = (5 \times 10^{-3})(6 \times 10^8)$
$= (5 \times 10^8)(6 \times 10^{-3})$

23. $13.2 = 1.2w$
$\frac{13.2}{1.2} = \frac{1.2w}{1.2}$
$\mathbf{11} = w$

check: $13.2 = 1.2(11)$
$13.2 = 13.2$

24. $c + \frac{5}{6} = 1\frac{1}{4}$
$c + \frac{5}{6} - \frac{5}{6} = 1\frac{1}{4} - \frac{5}{6}$
$c = 1\frac{3}{12} - \frac{10}{12}$
$c = \frac{15}{12} - \frac{10}{12}$
$c = \mathbf{\frac{5}{12}}$

check: $\frac{5}{12} + \frac{5}{6} = 1\frac{1}{4}$
$\frac{5}{12} + \frac{10}{12} = 1\frac{1}{4}$
$\frac{15}{12} = 1\frac{1}{4}$
$1\frac{3}{12} = 1\frac{1}{4}$
$1\frac{1}{4} = 1\frac{1}{4}$

25. $3\{20 - [6^2 - 3(10 - 4)]\}$
$3\{20 - [36 - 3(6)]\}$
$3\{20 - [36 - 18]\}$
$3\{20 - [18]\}$
$3\{2\}$
6

26.
(60 min) (60 s)
2 14
~~3~~ hr ~~15~~ min 25 s
− 2 hr 45 min 30 s

2 74 85
~~3~~ hr ~~15~~ ~~14~~ min ~~25~~ s
− 2 hr 45 min 30 s
29 min 55 s

27. $1 + 0.2 + 0.25 = \mathbf{1.45}$

28. (a) $(-2) + (-2)(+2) - \frac{(-2)}{(-2)}$
$(-2) + (-4) - 1$
$(-2) + (-4) + [-(1)]$
$(-2) - (-4) + (-1)$
$\mathbf{-7}$

(b) $(-3) - [(-2) - (+4)(-5)]$
$(-3) - [(-2) - (-20)]$
$(-3) - [(-2) + 20]$
$(-3) - [18]$
$(-3) + [-(18)]$
$(-3) + (-18)$
$\mathbf{-21}$

29. $x^2 + 6x - 2x - 12$
$\mathbf{x^2 + 4x - 12}$

30. (a) $\mathbf{D(1, -1)}$

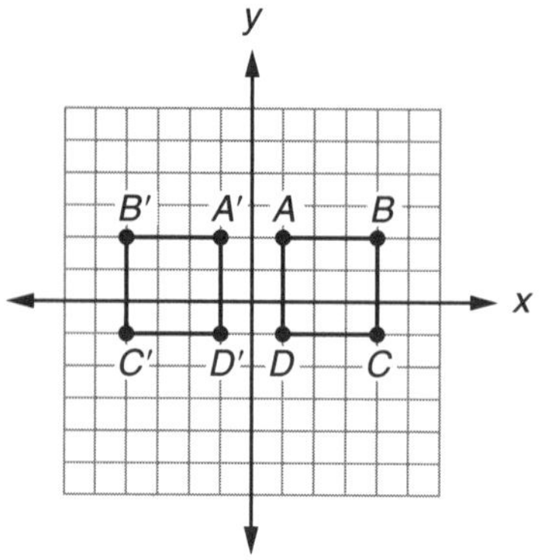

(b) $\mathbf{A'(-1, 2), B'(-4, 2),}$
$\mathbf{C'(-4, -1), D'(-1, -1)}$

Lesson 86, Lesson Practice

a.

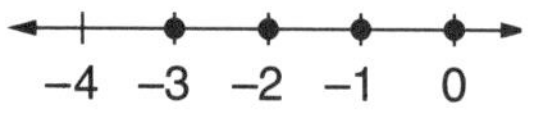

b.

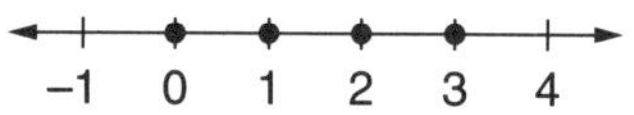

c. **False**

d. **True**

Lesson 86, Mixed Practice

1. $\frac{\$28.50}{3 \text{ ounces}} = \frac{\$9.50}{1 \text{ ounce}}$
$\frac{\$4.96}{8 \text{ ounces}} = \frac{\$0.62}{1 \text{ ounce}}$
$9.50
− $0.62
$8.88 more per ounce

2.

	Ratio	Actual Count
Rookies	2	R
Veterans	7	V
Total	9	252

$$\frac{2}{9} = \frac{R}{252}$$
$$9R = 504$$
$$R = \mathbf{56\ rookies}$$

3. (a) **213 lb**

(b) **213 lb**

(c)
$$\begin{array}{r} 197 \\ 213 \\ 246 \\ 205 \\ 238 \\ 213 \\ +\ 207 \\ \hline 1519 \end{array}$$
$$7\overline{)1519} = \mathbf{217\ lb}$$

(d) **49 lb**

4. $12 \text{ bushels} \cdot \dfrac{4 \text{ pecks}}{1 \text{ bushel}} = \mathbf{48\ pecks}$

5. $\dfrac{468 \text{ miles}}{9 \text{ hours}} = \mathbf{52\ miles\ per\ hour}$

6.

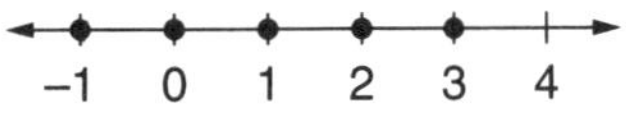

7.

	Case 1	Case 2
First number	9	n
Second number	6	30

$$\frac{9}{6} = \frac{n}{30}$$
$$6n = 270$$
$$n = \mathbf{45}$$

8. (a) $1800 \div 10 = 180$
$9(180 \text{ students}) = \mathbf{1620\ students}$

(b) $\dfrac{1}{10} \times 100\% = \mathbf{10\%}$

9. $\sqrt{(5)^2 - 4(1)(4)}$
$= \sqrt{25 - 16} = \sqrt{9} = \mathbf{3}$

10. **Insufficient information**

11. (a) $C = \pi(24 \text{ in.})$
$C = \mathbf{24\pi\ in.}$

(b) $A = \pi r^2$
$A = \pi(144 \text{ in.}^2)$
$A = \mathbf{144\pi\ in.^2}$

12. (a) $\mathbf{10^5}$

(b) $\mathbf{10^{-3}}$

13.

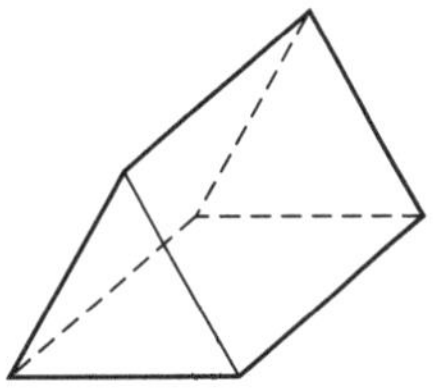

(a) **5 faces**

(b) **9 edges**

(c) **6 vertices**

14. (a) $0.9 = \mathbf{\dfrac{9}{10}}$

(b) **0.9 = 90%**

(c) $\dfrac{11}{12} = \mathbf{0.91\overline{6}}$

$$\begin{array}{r} 0.9166 \\ 12\overline{)11.0000}\ldots \\ \underline{10\ 8} \\ 20 \\ \underline{12} \\ 80 \\ \underline{72} \\ 80 \\ \underline{72} \\ 8 \end{array} = \mathbf{0.91\overline{6}}$$

(d) $\dfrac{11}{12} \times 100\% = \dfrac{1100\%}{12} = \mathbf{91\frac{2}{3}\%}$

$$\begin{array}{r} 91\frac{8}{12} \\ 12\overline{)1100} \\ \underline{108} \\ 20 \\ \underline{12} \\ 8 \end{array} = \mathbf{91\tfrac{2}{3}\%}$$

15. **North**

16.

	Percent	Actual Count
Sale price	60	\$24
Regular price	100	R

$$\frac{60}{100} = \frac{\$24}{R}$$
$$60R = \$2400$$
$$R = \mathbf{\$40}$$

17.

	Percent	Actual Count
Sprouted seeds	75	48
Unsprouted seeds	25	U
Total	100	T

$$\frac{75}{25} = \frac{48}{U}$$
$$75U = 1200$$
$$U = \textbf{16 seeds}$$

18. $\mathbf{30 = W_P \times 20}$

$$\frac{30}{20} = \frac{W_P \times 20}{20}$$
$$\frac{3}{2} = W_P$$
$$W_P = \frac{3}{2} \times 100\% = \mathbf{150\%}$$

19.

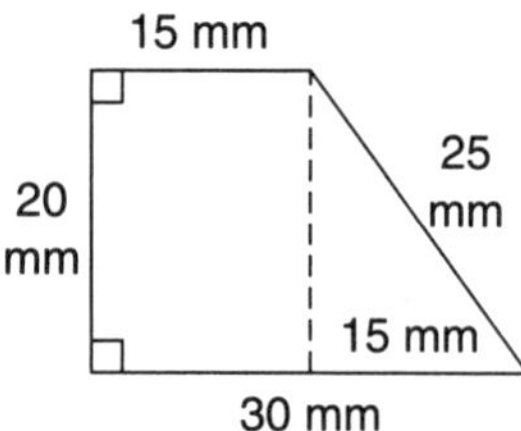

(a) **Trapezoid**

(b) Perimeter = 15 mm + 25 mm + 30 mm + 20 mm = **90 mm**

(c) Area of rectangle = (15 mm)(20 mm)
= 300 mm^2

Area of triangle = $\frac{(15 \text{ mm})(20 \text{ mm})}{2}$
= 150 mm^2

Area of figure = 300 mm^2 + 150 mm^2
= **450 mm^2**

20. (a) **120°**

(b) **165°**

(c) 165° − 30° = **135°**

21.
$$y = 3(4) + 1$$
$$y = 12 + 1$$
$$y = \mathbf{13;}$$
$$y = 3(7) + 1$$
$$y = 21 + 1$$
$$y = \mathbf{22;}$$
$$y = 3(0) + 1$$
$$y = 0 + 1$$
$$y = \mathbf{1}$$

22. (a) $(1.2 \times 1.2) \times (10^5 \times 10^{-8})$
$= \mathbf{1.44 \times 10^{-3}}$

(b) $(6 \times 7) \times (10^{-3} \times 10^{-4})$
$= 42 \times 10^{-7}$
$= \mathbf{4.2 \times 10^{-6}}$

23.
$$56 = \frac{7}{8}w$$
$$\left(\frac{\overset{}{8}}{\underset{1}{\cancel{7}}}\right)\overset{8}{\cancel{56}} = \left(\frac{\overset{1}{\cancel{8}}}{\underset{1}{\cancel{7}}}\right)\frac{\overset{1}{\cancel{7}}}{\underset{1}{\cancel{8}}}w$$
$$\mathbf{64} = w$$

check:
$$56 = \frac{7}{\underset{1}{\cancel{8}}}(\overset{8}{\cancel{64}})$$
$$56 = 7(8)$$
$$56 = 56$$

24.
$$4.8 + c = 7.34$$
$$4.8 - 4.8 + c = 7.34 - 4.8$$
$$c = \mathbf{2.54}$$

check:
$$4.8 + 2.54 = 7.34$$
$$7.34 = 7.34$$

25.
$$\sqrt{10^2 - 6^2} - \sqrt{10^2 - 8^2}$$
$$\sqrt{100 - 36} - \sqrt{100 - 64}$$
$$\sqrt{64} - \sqrt{36}$$
$$8 - 6$$
$$\mathbf{2}$$

26.

	lb	oz
	5 lb	9 oz
+	4 lb	7 oz
	9 lb	16 oz

16 oz = 1 lb

1 lb + 9 lb = **10 lb**

27. $1.4 \div 3.5 \times 1000$
$= 0.4 \times 1000 = \mathbf{400}$

28. (a) $(-4)(-5) - (-4)(+3)$
$+20 - (-12)$
$20 + [-(-12)]$
$+20 + 12$
$\mathbf{32}$

(b) $(-2)[(-3) - (-4)(+5)]$
$(-2)[(-3) - (-20)]$
$(-2)[(-3) + (20)]$
$(-2)[+17]$
$\mathbf{-34}$

29. $x^2 + 3xy + 2x^2 - xy$
$x^2 + 2x^2 + 3xy - xy$
$\mathbf{3x^2 + 2xy}$

30. $\mathbf{3 \cdot 3 \cdot x \cdot y \cdot y}$

Lesson 87, Lesson Practice

a. $(-3x)(-2xy)$
$= (-3) \cdot x \cdot (-2) \cdot x \cdot y$
$= (-3)(-2) \cdot x \cdot x \cdot y$
$= \mathbf{6x^2y}$

b. $3x^2(xy^3)$
$= (3) \cdot x \cdot x \cdot x \cdot y \cdot y \cdot y$
$= \mathbf{3x^3y^3}$

c. $(2a^2b)(-3ab^2)$
$= (2) \cdot a \cdot a \cdot b \cdot (-3) \cdot a \cdot b \cdot b$
$= (2)(-3) \cdot a \cdot a \cdot a \cdot b \cdot b \cdot b$
$= \mathbf{-6a^3b^3}$

d. $(-5x^2y)(-4x)$
$= (-5) \cdot x \cdot x \cdot y \cdot (-4) \cdot x$
$= (-5)(-4) \cdot x \cdot x \cdot x \cdot y$
$= \mathbf{20x^3y}$

e. $(-xy^2)(xy)(2y)$
$= (-1) \cdot x \cdot y \cdot y \cdot x \cdot y \cdot (2) \cdot y$
$= (-1)(2) \cdot x \cdot x \cdot y \cdot y \cdot y \cdot y$
$= \mathbf{-2x^2y^4}$

f. $(-3m)(-2mn)(m^2n)$
$= (-3) \cdot m \cdot (-2) \cdot m \cdot n \cdot m \cdot m \cdot n$
$= (-3)(-2) \cdot m \cdot m \cdot m \cdot m \cdot n \cdot n$
$= \mathbf{6m^4n^2}$

g. $(4wy)(3wx)(-w^2)(x^2y)$
$= (4) \cdot w \cdot y \cdot (3) \cdot w \cdot x \cdot (-1)$
$\cdot w \cdot w \cdot x \cdot x \cdot y$
$= (4)(3)(-1) \cdot w \cdot w \cdot w \cdot w$
$\cdot x \cdot x \cdot x \cdot y \cdot y$
$= \mathbf{-12w^4x^3y^2}$

h. $5d(-2df)(-3d^2fg)$
$= (5) \cdot d \cdot (-2) \cdot d \cdot f \cdot (-3) \cdot d \cdot d \cdot f \cdot g$
$= (5)(-2)(-3) \cdot d \cdot d \cdot d \cdot d \cdot f \cdot f \cdot g$
$= \mathbf{30d^4f^2g}$

Lesson 87, Mixed Practice

1. $2.5\ \text{~~hours~~} \cdot \dfrac{450 \text{ miles}}{1 \text{ ~~hour~~}}$
$= \mathbf{1125\ miles}$

2. **12.5 ~~centimeters~~** $\cdot$ $\dfrac{\textbf{1 meter}}{\textbf{100 ~~centimeters~~}}$
$=$ **0.125 meter**

3.

	Ratio	Actual Count
Girls	4	240
Boys	3	180
Total	7	420

$\dfrac{\text{boys}}{\text{girls}} = \mathbf{\dfrac{3}{4}}$

4.
18′ 3″ = 219″
17′10″ = 214″
+ 17′11″ = 215″
648″

$3\overline{)648''}$ = 216″

216″ = **18′**

5. $\dfrac{468 \text{ miles}}{18 \text{ gallons}} =$ **26 miles per gallon**

6.
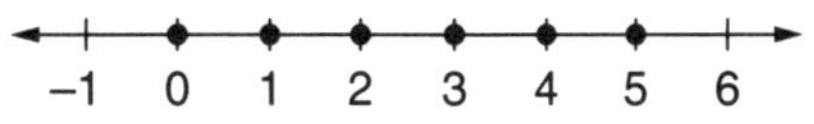

7.

	Case 1	Case 2
Yards	100	1500
Feet	36	f

$\dfrac{100}{36} = \dfrac{1500}{f}$
$100f = 54{,}000$
$f = \mathbf{540\ feet}$

8. (a) $m\angle a = 180° - 105° = \mathbf{75°}$

(b) $m\angle b = 180° - 75° = \mathbf{105°}$

(c) $m\angle c = 180° - 105° = \mathbf{75°}$

(d) $m\angle d = m\angle a = \mathbf{75°}$

(e) $m\angle e = m\angle b = \mathbf{105°}$

9. $y = 3(-4) - 1$
$y = -12 - 1$
$y = \mathbf{-13}$

10. (a) $C \approx \frac{22}{\cancel{7}_1}(\cancel{140}^{20}\text{ mm})$
$C \approx \mathbf{440\ mm}$

(b) $A = \pi r^2$
$A \approx \frac{22}{\cancel{7}_1}(\cancel{4900}^{700}\text{ mm}^2)$
$A \approx \mathbf{15{,}400\ mm^2}$

11.

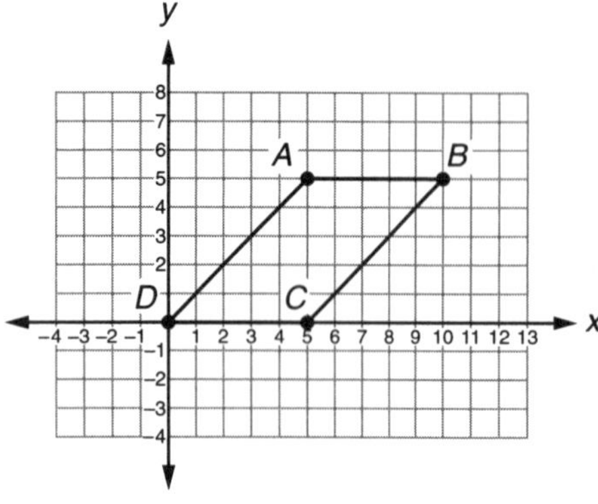

(a) Area = (5 units)(5 units)
= **25 units²**

(b) $m\angle A = \mathbf{135°}$
$m\angle B = \mathbf{45°}$
$m\angle C = \mathbf{135°}$
$m\angle D = \mathbf{45°}$

12. Bottom Rectangular prism: (6 cubes) (3 cubes)
= 18 cubes

$\frac{18\text{ cubes}}{1\text{ }\cancel{\text{layer}}} \cdot 2\ \cancel{\text{layers}} = 36\text{ cubes}$

36 in.³

Top Rectangular prism: (2 cubes) (3 cubes)
= 6 cubes

$\frac{6\text{ cubes}}{1\text{ }\cancel{\text{layer}}} \cdot 2\ \cancel{\text{layers}} = 12\text{ cubes, }12\text{ in.}^3$

$36\text{ in.}^3 + 12\text{ in.}^3 = \mathbf{48\ in.^3}$

13. (a) $12\frac{1}{2}\% = \frac{12\frac{1}{2}}{100} = \frac{\frac{25}{2}}{100}$

$= \frac{\frac{1}{100}}{\frac{1}{100}} = \frac{25}{200} = \mathbf{\frac{1}{8}}$

(b) $12\frac{1}{2}\% = 12.5\% = \mathbf{0.125}$

(c) $\frac{7}{8} = \mathbf{0.875}$

$$\begin{array}{r} \mathbf{0.875} \\ 8\overline{)7.000} \\ \underline{6\,4} \\ 60 \\ \underline{56} \\ 40 \\ \underline{40} \\ 0 \end{array}$$

(d) $\frac{7}{8} \times 100\% = \frac{700\%}{8} = \mathbf{87\frac{1}{2}\%}$

$$\begin{array}{r} 87\,\frac{4}{8} = \mathbf{87\frac{1}{2}\%} \\ 8\overline{)700} \\ \underline{64} \\ 60 \\ \underline{56} \\ 4 \end{array}$$

14. $\mathbf{W_N = \frac{1}{4} \times 4}$
$W_N = \mathbf{1}$

15.

	Percent	Actual Count
Sale price	80	\$24
Regular price	100	P

$\frac{80}{100} = \frac{\$24}{P}$
$80P = \$2400$
$P = \mathbf{\$30}$

16.

	Percent	Actual Count
Meters ran	60	M
Meters left	40	2000
Total	100	T

$\frac{40}{100} = \frac{2000}{T}$
$40T = 200{,}000$
$T = \mathbf{5000\ meters}$

17. $\mathbf{100 = W_P \times 80}$

$\frac{100}{80} = \frac{W_P \times 80}{80}$

$\frac{5}{4} = W_P$

$W_P = \frac{5}{4} \times 100\% = \mathbf{125\%}$

18.

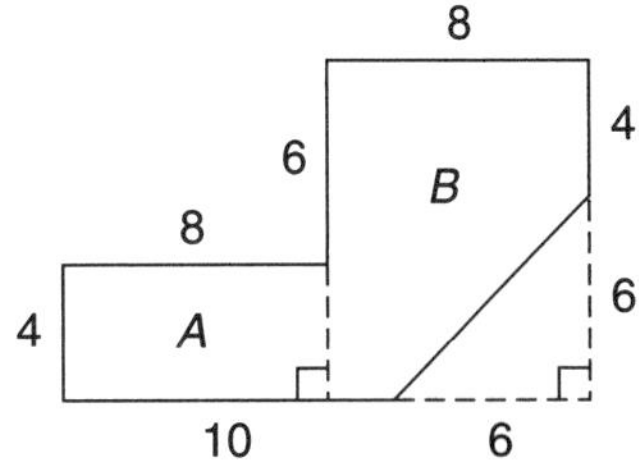

$$\begin{aligned}\text{Area of rectangle } A &= (4\text{ cm})(8\text{ cm}) \\ &= 32\text{ cm}^2 \\ \text{Area of rectangle } B &= (8\text{ cm})(10\text{ cm}) \\ &= 80\text{ cm}^2 \\ \text{Area of } A + B &= 32\text{ cm}^2 + 80\text{ cm}^2 \\ &= 112\text{ cm}^2 \\ \text{Area of triangle} &= \frac{(6\text{ cm})(6\text{ cm})}{2} \\ &= 18\text{ cm}^2 \\ 112\text{ cm}^2 - 18\text{ cm}^2 &= \mathbf{94\text{ cm}^2}\end{aligned}$$

19. (a) $m\angle AOB = \frac{90°}{3} = \mathbf{30°}$

(b) $m\angle AOC = 30° + 30° = \mathbf{60°}$

(c) $m\angle EOC = 90° + 30° = \mathbf{120°}$

(d) $\angle \boldsymbol{COA}$ or $\angle \boldsymbol{AOC}$

20.

$$\frac{66\frac{2}{3}}{100} = \frac{\frac{200}{3}}{\frac{100}{1}}$$

$$\frac{\frac{200}{3}}{\frac{100}{1}} \cdot \frac{\frac{1}{100}}{\frac{1}{100}} = \frac{\frac{200}{300}}{1} = \frac{200}{300} = \mathbf{\frac{2}{3}}$$

21.

$$y = \frac{24}{3}$$
$$y = \mathbf{8;}$$
$$y = \frac{24}{4}$$
$$y = \mathbf{6;}$$
$$y = \frac{24}{12}$$
$$y = \mathbf{2}$$

22. (a) $(4 \times 2.1) \times (10^{-5} \times 10^{-7}) = \mathbf{8.4 \times 10^{-12}}$

(b) $(4 \times 6) \times (10^5 \times 10^7) = 24 \times (10^{12}) = \mathbf{2.4 \times 10^{13}}$

23.

$$\begin{aligned} d - 8.47 &= 9.1 \\ d - 8.47 + 8.47 &= 9.1 + 8.47 \\ d &= \mathbf{17.57}\end{aligned}$$

check: $17.57 - 8.47 = 9.1$
$9.1 = 9.1$

24.

$$\begin{aligned} 0.25m &= 3.6 \\ \frac{0.25m}{0.25} &= \frac{3.6}{0.25} \\ m &= \mathbf{14.4}\end{aligned}$$

check: $0.25(14.4) = 3.6$
$3.6 = 3.6$

25.

$$\frac{3 + 5.2 - 1}{4 - 3 + 2}$$
$$\frac{8.2 - 1}{1 + 2}$$
$$\frac{7.2}{3}$$
$$\mathbf{2.4}$$

26. 1 kg = 1000 g, 1000 g − 75 g = **925 g**

27. $3.7 + 2.625 + 15 = \mathbf{21.325}$

28. (a)
$$(-5) - (-2)[(-3) - (+4)]$$
$$(-5) - (-2)[-7]$$
$$(-5) - (+14)$$
$$(-5) + [-(+14)]$$
$$(-5) + [-14]$$
$$\mathbf{-19}$$

(b)
$$\frac{(-3) + (-3)(+4)}{(+3) + (-4)}$$
$$\frac{(-3) + (-12)}{-1}$$
$$\frac{-15}{-1}$$
$$\mathbf{15}$$

29. (a) $(3x)(4y)$
$= (3) \cdot x \cdot (4) \cdot y$
$= (3)(4) \cdot x \cdot y = \mathbf{12xy}$

(b) $(6m)(-4m^2n)(-mnp)$
$= (6) \cdot m \cdot (-4) \cdot m \cdot m \cdot n \cdot (-1) \cdot m \cdot n \cdot p$
$= (6)(-4)(-1) \cdot m \cdot m \cdot m \cdot m \cdot n \cdot n \cdot p$
$= \mathbf{24m^4n^2p}$

30.
$$3ab + a - ab - 2ab + a$$
$$3ab - ab - 2ab + a + a$$
$$\mathbf{2a}$$

Lesson 88, Lesson Practice

a. $5\ \cancel{\text{yd}} \cdot \frac{3\ \cancel{\text{ft}}}{1\ \cancel{\text{yd}}} \cdot \frac{12\ \text{in.}}{1\ \cancel{\text{ft}}} = \mathbf{180\ in.}$

b. $1\frac{1}{2}\ \cancel{\text{hr}} \cdot \frac{60\ \cancel{\text{min}}}{1\ \cancel{\text{hr}}} \cdot \frac{60\ \text{s}}{1\ \cancel{\text{min}}}$
$= \mathbf{5400\ s}$

c. $15\ \cancel{\text{yd}^2} \cdot \frac{3\ \text{ft}}{1\ \cancel{\text{yd}}} \cdot \frac{3\ \text{ft}}{1\ \cancel{\text{yd}}}$
$= \mathbf{135\ ft^2}$

d. $20\ \cancel{\text{cm}^2} \cdot \frac{10\ \text{mm}}{1\ \cancel{\text{cm}}} \cdot \frac{10\ \text{mm}}{1\ \cancel{\text{cm}}}$
$= \mathbf{2000\ mm^2}$

Lesson 88, Mixed Practice

1. $\$6(3.25) = \mathbf{\$19.50}$

2. $4(93) = 372$
$10(84) = 840$
$840 - 372 = 468$
$6\overline{)468}$ = **78**

3. $6\ \cancel{\text{ft}^2} \cdot \frac{12\ \text{in.}}{1\ \cancel{\text{ft}}} \cdot \frac{12\ \text{in.}}{1\ \cancel{\text{ft}}} = \mathbf{864\ in.^2}$

4.

	Ratio	Actual Count
Woodwinds	3	15
Brass instruments	2	B

$\frac{3}{2} = \frac{15}{B}$
$3B = 30$
$B = $ **10 brass instruments**

5. 

6.

	Case 1	Case 2
Artichokes	8	36
Price	$2	p

$\frac{8}{\$2} = \frac{36}{p}$
$8p = \$72$
$p = \mathbf{\$9}$

7. 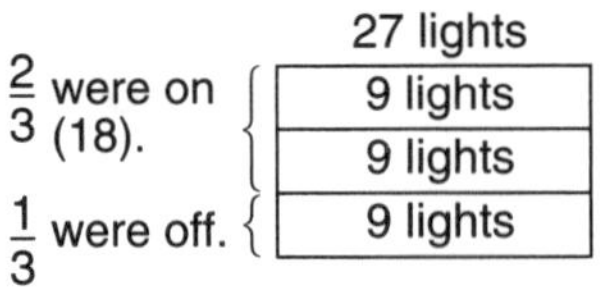

(a) $18 \div 2 = 9,\ 1(9\ \text{lights}) = $ **9 lights**

(b) $\frac{2}{3} \times 100\% = \mathbf{66\frac{2}{3}\%}$

8. $(5) - [(3) - (5 - 3)]$
$= 5 - [3 - 2] = 5 - [1] = \mathbf{4}$

9. $x \textcircled{<} y$

10. (a) $C = \pi(60\ \text{ft})$
$C \approx 3.14(60\ \text{ft})$
$C \approx \mathbf{188.4\ ft}$

(b) $A = \pi r^2$
$A \approx 3.14(900\ \text{ft}^2)$
$A \approx \mathbf{2826\ ft^2}$

11. $1 - \left(\frac{4}{12} + \frac{5}{12}\right) = \frac{3}{12} = \frac{1}{4}$

$\frac{1}{4} \times 100\% = \mathbf{25\%}$

12. 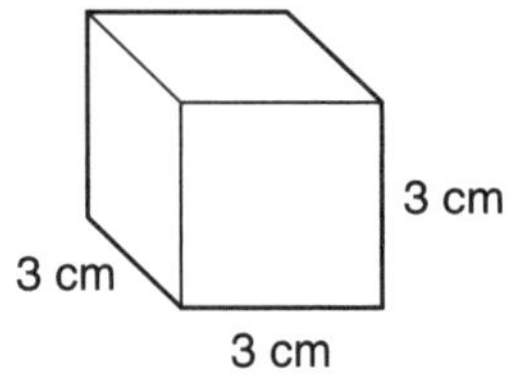

(a) $(3\ \text{cm})(3\ \text{cm}) = 9\ \text{cm}^2$
$\frac{9\ \text{cm}^2}{1\ \cancel{\text{layer}}} \cdot (1\ \text{cm})(3\ \cancel{\text{layers}}) = \mathbf{27\ cm^3}$

(b) $6(9\ \text{cm}^2) = \mathbf{54\ cm^2}$

13. $2x + 3y - 5 + x - y - 1$
$2x + x + 3y - y - 5 - 1$
$\mathbf{3x + 2y - 6}$

14. $x^2 + 2x - x - 2$
$\mathbf{x^2 + x - 2}$

15. (a) $0.125 = \frac{125}{100} = \mathbf{\frac{1}{8}}$

(b) $0.125 \times 100\% = 12.5\%$ or $\mathbf{12\frac{1}{2}\%}$

(c) $\frac{3}{8} = \mathbf{0.375}$

$$\begin{array}{r} \mathbf{0.375} \\ 8\overline{)3.000} \\ \underline{2\,4} \\ 60 \\ \underline{56} \\ 40 \\ \underline{40} \\ 0 \end{array}$$

(d) $\frac{3}{8} \times 100\% = \frac{300\%}{8} = \mathbf{37\frac{1}{2}\%}$

$$\begin{array}{r} 37\frac{4}{8} = \mathbf{37\frac{1}{2}\%} \\ 8\overline{)300} \\ \underline{24} \\ 60 \\ \underline{56} \\ 4 \end{array}$$

16. $\frac{60}{1\frac{1}{4}} = \frac{\frac{60}{1}}{\frac{5}{4}}$

$\frac{\frac{60}{1}}{\frac{5}{4}} \cdot \frac{\frac{4}{5}}{\frac{4}{5}} = \frac{\frac{240}{5}}{1} = \frac{240}{5}$

$= \mathbf{48}$

17.

	Percent	Actual Count
Sale price	P_S	\$18
Regular price	100	\$24

$\frac{P_S}{100} = \frac{\$18}{\$24}$

$24P_S = 1800$

$P_S = \mathbf{75\%}$

18.

	Percent	Actual Count
With seats	30	375
Without seats	70	W
Total	100	T

$\frac{30}{70} = \frac{375}{W}$

$30W = 26{,}250$

$W = \mathbf{875}$

19. $\mathbf{24 = \frac{1}{4} \times W_N}$

$\left(\frac{4}{1}\right)24 = \left(\frac{\cancel{4}^1}{\cancel{1}_1}\right)\left(\frac{\cancel{1}^1}{\cancel{4}_1}\right) \times W_N$

$\mathbf{96} = W_N$

20.

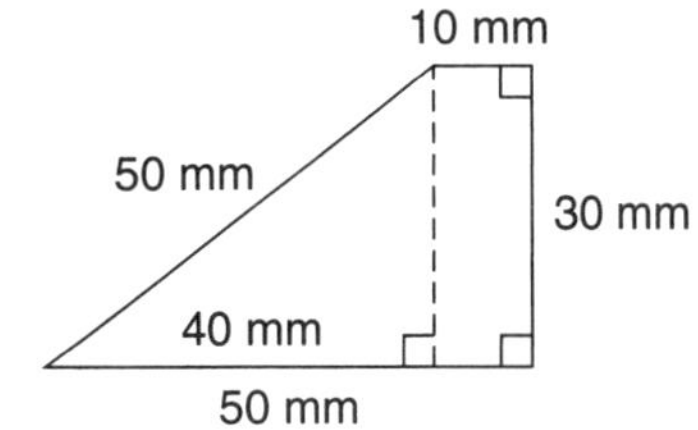

(a) **Trapezoid**

(b) Perimeter = 10 mm + 30 mm + 50 mm + 50 mm = **140 mm**

(c) Area of rectangle = (10 mm)(30 mm) = 300 mm^2

Area of triangle = $\frac{(40 \text{ mm})(30 \text{ mm})}{2}$ = 600 mm^2

Area of figure = 300 mm^2 + 600 mm^2 = **900 mm^2**

21. $y = (10) - 5$

$y = \mathbf{5;}$

$y = (7) - 5$

$y = \mathbf{2;}$

$y = (5) - 5$

$y = \mathbf{0}$

22. (a) $(9 \times 4) \times (10^{-6} \times 10^{-8})$
$= 36 \times (10^{-14})$
$= \mathbf{3.6 \times 10^{-13}}$

(b) $(9 \times 4) \times (10^{6} \times 10^{8})$
$= 36 \times (10^{14})$
$= \mathbf{3.6 \times 10^{15}}$

23. $8\frac{5}{6} = d - 5\frac{1}{2}$

$8\frac{5}{6} + 5\frac{1}{2} = d - 5\frac{1}{2} + 5\frac{1}{2}$

$8\frac{5}{6} + 5\frac{3}{6} = d$

$13\frac{8}{6} = d$

$14\frac{2}{6} = d$

$\mathbf{14\frac{1}{3}} = d$

check: $8\frac{5}{6} = 14\frac{1}{3} - 5\frac{1}{2}$

$8\frac{5}{6} = 14\frac{2}{6} - 5\frac{3}{6}$

$8\frac{5}{6} = 13\frac{8}{6} - 5\frac{3}{6}$

$8\frac{5}{6} = 8\frac{5}{6}$

24. $\frac{5}{6}m = 90$

$\left(\frac{6}{5}\right)\frac{5}{6}m = \left(\frac{6}{5}\right)90$

$m = \mathbf{108}$

check: $\frac{5}{6}(108) = 90$

$90 = 90$

25.

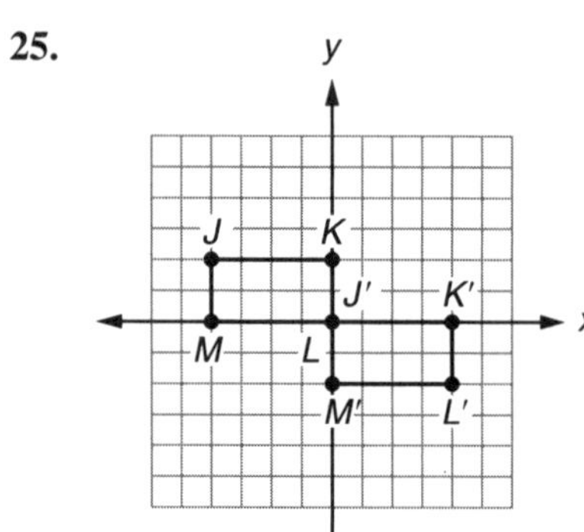

(a) $\boldsymbol{M(-4, 0)}$

(b) $\boldsymbol{J'(0, 0), K'(4, 0),}$
$\boldsymbol{L'(4, -2), M'(0, -2)}$

26. **D.** $\mathbf{4^2 + 4}$

27. $\frac{2}{3}(0.12) = 0.08$

$0.5(0.08) = \mathbf{0.04}$

28. $6\{5 \cdot 4 - 3[6 - (3 - 1)]\}$

$6\{20 - 3[6 - 2]\}$

$6\{20 - 3[4]\}$

$6\{20 - 12\}$

$6\{8\}$

$\mathbf{48}$

29. (a) $\frac{(-3)(-4) - (-3)}{(-3) - (+4)(+3)}$

$\frac{12 - (-3)}{-3 - (12)}$

$\frac{12 + 3}{-3 - 12}$

$\frac{15}{-15}$

$\mathbf{-1}$

(b) $(+5) + (-2)[(+3) - (-4)]$

$(+5) + (-2)[+3 + (+4)]$

$(+5) + (-2)[7]$

$(+5) + (-14)$

$\mathbf{-9}$

30. (a) $(-2x)(-3x)$

$= (-2) \cdot x \cdot (-3) \cdot (x)$

$= (-2)(-3) \cdot x \cdot x = \mathbf{6x^2}$

(b) $(ab)(2a^2b)(-3a)$

$= a \cdot b \cdot (2) \cdot a \cdot a \cdot b \cdot (-3) \cdot a$

$= (2)(-3) \cdot a \cdot a \cdot a \cdot a \cdot b \cdot b$

$= \mathbf{-6a^4b^2}$

Lesson 89, Lesson Practice

a. **For answers, see solutions to examples 1–4.**

b. **One possibility**:

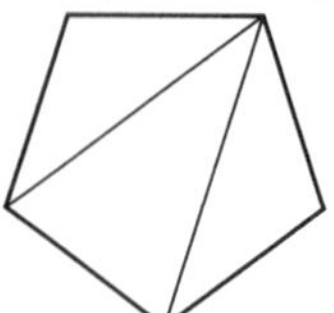

2 diagonals

c. **3 triangles**

d. $3 \times 180° = \mathbf{540°}$

e. $\frac{540°}{5} = \mathbf{108°}$

f. $\frac{360°}{5} = \mathbf{72°}$

g. $108° + 72° = \mathbf{180°}$

Lesson 89, Mixed Practice

1.

	Case 1	Case 2
Feet	440	5280
Seconds	10	s

$\frac{440}{10} = \frac{5280}{s}$

$440s = 52{,}800$

$s =$ **120 seconds** or **2 minutes**

2.

	Ratio	Actual Count
Lions	3	18
Tigers	2	T

$\frac{3}{2} = \frac{18}{T}$

$3T = 36$

$T = 12$ tigers

	Ratio	Actual Count
Tigers	3	12
Bears	4	B

$$\frac{3}{4} = \frac{12}{B}$$
$$3B = 48$$
$$B = \textbf{16 bears}$$

3. $$(30\text{ cm})(15\text{ cm}) = 450\text{ cm}^2$$
$$\frac{450\text{ cm}^2}{1\ \cancel{\text{layer}}} \cdot (1\text{ cm}) \cdot 12\ \cancel{\text{layers}} = \textbf{5400 cm}^3$$

4. $\frac{24}{61} = 0.393442\ldots$ **0.393**

5. $\overset{2}{\cancel{18}}\ \cancel{\text{ft}^2} \cdot \frac{1\text{ yd}}{\underset{1}{\cancel{3}}\ \cancel{\text{ft}}} \cdot \frac{1\text{ yd}}{\underset{1}{\cancel{3}}\ \cancel{\text{ft}}} =$ **2 square yards**

6.

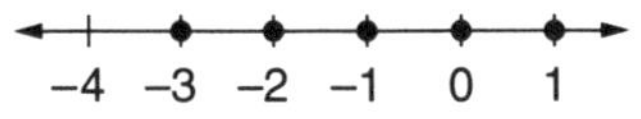

7.

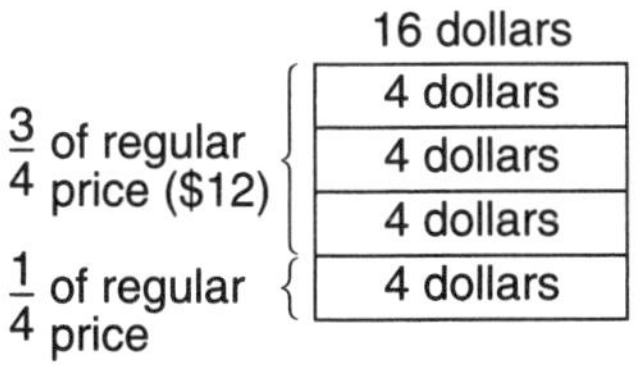

(a) $\$12 \div 3 = \$4$
$(\$4)(4) =$ **$16**

(b) $\frac{3}{4} \times 100\% =$ **75%**

8. (a) $m\angle a = 180° - (90° + 35°) =$ **55°**

(b) $m\angle b = 180° - 55° =$ **125°**

(c) $m\angle c = m\angle a =$ **55°**

(d) $m\angle d = 180° - (55° + 70°) =$ **55°**

9. (a) $C \approx \frac{22}{\underset{1}{\cancel{7}}}(\overset{6}{\cancel{42}}\text{in.})$
$C \approx$ **132 in.**

(b) $A = \pi r^2$
$A \approx \frac{22}{\underset{1}{\cancel{7}}}(\overset{63}{\cancel{441}}\text{ in.}^2)$
$A \approx$ **1386 in.²**

10. $$\frac{91\frac{2}{3}}{100} = \frac{\frac{275}{3}}{\frac{100}{1}}$$
$$\frac{\frac{275}{3}}{\frac{100}{1}} \cdot \frac{\frac{1}{100}}{\frac{1}{100}} = \frac{\frac{275}{300}}{1} = \frac{275}{300}$$
$$= \mathbf{\frac{11}{12}}$$

11. $$\frac{(10)(5) + (10)}{(10) + (5)} = \frac{50 + 10}{15}$$
$$= \frac{60}{15} = \mathbf{4}$$

12. $0.25 \bigcirc 0.5$
$a^2 \; \textcircled{<} \; a$

13. (a) $\frac{7}{8} =$ **0.875**

$$\begin{array}{r} 0.875 \\ 8\overline{)7.000} \\ \underline{6\,4} \\ 60 \\ \underline{56} \\ 40 \\ \underline{40} \\ 0 \end{array}$$

(b) $\frac{7}{8} \times 100\% = \frac{700\%}{8} = \mathbf{87\frac{1}{2}\%}$

$$\begin{array}{r} 87\frac{4}{8} \\ 8\overline{)700} \\ \underline{64} \\ 60 \\ \underline{56} \\ 4 \end{array} = 87\tfrac{1}{2}\%$$

(c) $875\% = \frac{875}{100} = 8\frac{75}{100} = \mathbf{8\frac{3}{4}}$

(d) $875\% =$ **8.75**

14. (a) **4:00, 8:00**

(b) **120°**

15.

	Percent	Actual Count
Ordered a hambuger	45	H
Other customers	55	C
Total	100	3000

$$\frac{45}{100} = \frac{H}{3000}$$
$$100H = 135{,}000$$
$$H = \textbf{1350 customers}$$

16.

	Percent	Actual Count
Sale price	75	\$24
Regular price	100	R

$$\frac{75}{100} = \frac{\$24}{R}$$
$$75R = \$2400$$
$$R = \$32$$
$$\$32 - \$24 = \mathbf{\$8}$$

17.
$$\mathbf{20 = W_P \times 200}$$
$$\frac{20}{200} = \frac{W_P \times 200}{200}$$
$$\frac{1}{10} = W_P$$
$$W_P = \frac{1}{10} \times 100\% = \mathbf{10\%}$$

18. (a)

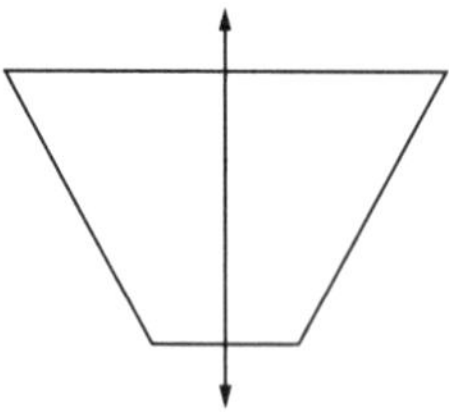

(b)

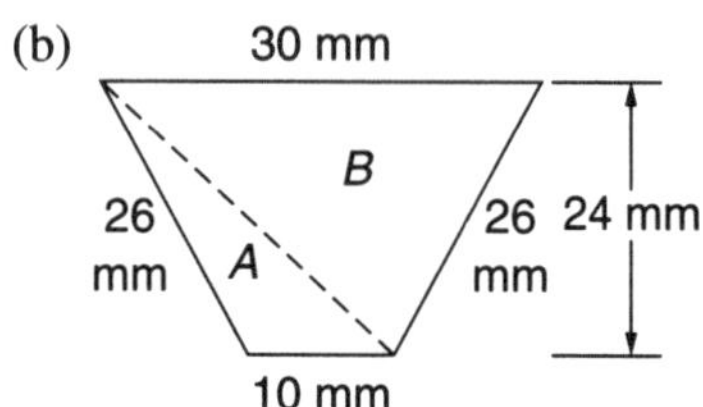

$$\text{Area of triangle } A = \frac{(10\text{ mm})(24\text{ mm})}{2}$$
$$= 120\text{ mm}^2$$
$$\text{Area of triangle } B = \frac{(30\text{ mm})(24\text{ mm})}{2}$$
$$= 360\text{ mm}^2$$
$$\text{Area of figure} = 120\text{ mm}^2 + 360\text{ mm}^2$$
$$= \mathbf{480\text{ mm}^2}$$

19. $\frac{360°}{3} = \mathbf{120°}$

20.
$$y = \frac{1}{3}(12)$$
$$y = \mathbf{4;}$$
$$y = \frac{1}{3}(9)$$
$$y = \mathbf{3;}$$
$$6 = \frac{1}{3}x$$
$$\left(\frac{3}{1}\right)6 = \left(\frac{3}{1}\right)\frac{1}{3}x$$
$$\mathbf{18} = x$$

21.
$$(1.25 \times 8) \times (10^{-3} \times 10^{-5})$$
$$= 10 \times 10^{-8}$$
$$= \mathbf{1 \times 10^{-7}}$$

22. (a)

10 cm 10 cm

4 cm

$$\text{Perimeter} = 10\text{ cm} + 10\text{ cm} + 4\text{ cm}$$
$$= \mathbf{24\text{ cm}}$$

(b) **There can only be one answer. A triangle with side lengths of 4 cm, 4 cm, and 10 cm cannot exist.**

23.
$$\frac{4}{9}p = 72$$
$$\left(\frac{\overset{1}{\cancel{9}}}{\underset{1}{\cancel{4}}}\right)\frac{\overset{1}{\cancel{4}}}{\underset{1}{\cancel{9}}}p = \left(\frac{9}{\underset{1}{\cancel{4}}}\right)\overset{18}{\cancel{72}}$$
$$p = \mathbf{162}$$

check:
$$\frac{4}{\underset{1}{\cancel{9}}}(\overset{18}{\cancel{162}}) = 72$$
$$4(18) = 72$$
$$72 = 72$$

24.
$$12.3 = 4.56 + f$$
$$12.3 - 4.56 = 4.56 - 4.56 + f$$
$$\mathbf{7.74} = f$$

check:
$$12.3 = 4.56 + 7.74$$
$$12.3 = 12.3$$

25.
$$2x + 3y - 4 + x - 3y - 1$$
$$2x + x + 3y - 3y - 4 - 1$$
$$\mathbf{3x - 5}$$

26.
$$\frac{9 \cdot 8 - 7 \cdot 6}{6 \cdot 5}$$
$$\frac{72 - 42}{30}$$
$$\frac{30}{30}$$
$$\mathbf{1}$$

27.
$$3\frac{2}{10} \times \frac{1}{4^2} \times 10^2$$
$$3\frac{2}{10} \times \frac{1}{16} \times 100$$
$$= \frac{\overset{2}{\cancel{32}}}{\underset{1}{\cancel{10}}} \times \frac{1}{\underset{1}{\cancel{16}}} \times \frac{\overset{10}{\cancel{100}}}{1} = \mathbf{20}$$

28. $4.75 + \frac{3}{4} = 4\frac{3}{4} + \frac{3}{4}$
$= 4\frac{6}{4} = 5\frac{2}{4} = 5\frac{1}{2}$

$13\frac{1}{3} - 5\frac{1}{2} = 13\frac{2}{6} - 5\frac{3}{6}$
$= 12\frac{8}{6} - 5\frac{3}{6} = \mathbf{7\frac{5}{6}}$

29. (a) $\frac{(+3) + (-4)(-6)}{(-3) + (-4) - (-6)}$

$\frac{(+3) + (24)}{-7 - (-6)}$

$\frac{27}{-1}$

$\mathbf{-27}$

(b) $(-5) - (+6)(-2) + (-2)(-3)(-1)$
$(-5) - (-12) + (-6)$
$(-5) + (+12) + (-6)$
1

30. (a) $(3x^2)(2x)$
$= (3) \cdot x \cdot x \cdot (2) \cdot x$
$= (3)(2) \cdot x \cdot x \cdot x$
$= \mathbf{6x^3}$

(b) $(-2ab)(-3b^2)(-a)$
$= (-2) \cdot a \cdot b \cdot (-3) \cdot b \cdot b \cdot (-1) \cdot a$
$= (-2)(-3)(-1) \cdot a \cdot a \cdot b \cdot b \cdot b$
$= \mathbf{-6a^2b^3}$

Lesson 90, Lesson Practice

a. $1\frac{1}{8}x = 36$

$\frac{9}{8}x = 36$

$\left(\frac{8}{9}\right)\left(\frac{9}{8}x\right) = \left(\frac{8}{9}\right) \cdot 36$

$x = \mathbf{32}$

b. $3\frac{1}{2}a = 490$

$\frac{7}{2}a = 490$

$\left(\frac{2}{7}\right)\left(\frac{7}{2}a\right) = \left(\frac{2}{7}\right)490$

$a = \mathbf{140}$

c. $2\frac{3}{4}w = 6\frac{3}{5}$

$\frac{11}{4}w = \frac{33}{5}$

$\left(\frac{4}{11}\right)\left(\frac{11}{4}w\right) = \left(\frac{4}{11}\right)\left(\frac{33}{5}\right)$

$w = \mathbf{\frac{12}{5}}$

d. $2\frac{2}{3}y = 1\frac{4}{5}$

$\frac{8}{3}y = \frac{9}{5}$

$\left(\frac{3}{8}\right)\left(\frac{8}{3}y\right) = \left(\frac{3}{8}\right)\left(\frac{9}{5}\right)$

$y = \mathbf{\frac{27}{40}}$

e. $-3x = 0.45$

$\frac{-3x}{-3} = \frac{0.45}{-3}$

$x = \mathbf{-0.15}$

f. $-\frac{3}{4}m = \frac{2}{3}$

$\left(-\frac{4}{3}\right)\left(-\frac{3}{4}m\right) = \left(-\frac{4}{3}\right)\left(\frac{2}{3}\right)$

$m = \mathbf{-\frac{8}{9}}$

g. $-10y = -1.6$

$\frac{-10y}{-10} = \frac{-1.6}{-10}$

$y = \mathbf{0.16}$

h. $-2\frac{1}{2}w = 3\frac{1}{3}$

$-\frac{5}{2}w = \frac{10}{3}$

$\left(-\frac{2}{5}\right)\left(-\frac{5}{2}w\right) = \left(-\frac{2}{5}\right)\left(\frac{10}{3}\right)$

$w = \mathbf{-\frac{4}{3}}$

Lesson 90, Mixed Practice

1. $(0.8 + 0.9) - (0.8)(0.9)$
$= 1.7 - 0.72 = 0.98$
Ninety-eight hundredths

2. (a)

$$\begin{array}{r} 8 \\ 6 \\ 9 \\ 10 \\ 8 \\ 7 \\ 9 \\ 10 \\ 8 \\ 10 \\ 9 \\ +\ 8 \\ \hline 102 \end{array} \qquad 12\overline{)102.0} = \mathbf{8.5}$$

(b) **8.5**

(c) **8**

(d) $2\frac{2}{3}y = 1\frac{4}{5}$

$\frac{8}{3}y = \frac{9}{5}$

$\left(\frac{3}{8}\right)\left(\frac{8}{3}y\right) = \left(\frac{3}{8}\right)\left(\frac{9}{5}\right)$

$\mathbf{y = \frac{27}{40}}$

3. $\frac{\$1.20}{24 \text{ ounces}} = \frac{\$0.05}{1 \text{ ounce}}$

$\frac{\$1.44}{32 \text{ ounces}} = \frac{\$0.045}{1 \text{ ounce}}$

$$\begin{array}{r} \$0.050 \\ -\ \$0.045 \\ \hline \$0.005 \end{array}$$

0.5¢ more per ounce

4. (a) $\frac{360°}{10} = \mathbf{36°}$

(b) $180° - 36° = \mathbf{144°}$

5. $x^2 + 2xy + y^2 + x^2 - y^2$

$x^2 + x^2 + 2xy + y^2 - y^2$

$\mathbf{2x^2 + 2xy}$

6.

	Percent	Actual Count
Sale price	90	\$36
Regular price	100	R

$\frac{90}{100} = \frac{\$36}{R}$

$90R = \$3600$

$R = \mathbf{\$40}$

7.

	Percent	Actual Count
Voted for Graham	75	V
Did not vote for Graham	25	D
Total	100	800

$\frac{25}{100} = \frac{D}{800}$

$100D = 20{,}000$

$D = $ **200 citizens**

8. (a) $\mathbf{24 = W_P \times 30}$

$\frac{24}{30} = \frac{W_P \times 30}{30}$

$\frac{4}{5} = W_P$

$W_P = \frac{4}{5} \times 100\% = \mathbf{80\%}$

(b) $\mathbf{30 = W_P \times 24}$

$\frac{30}{24} = \frac{W_P \times 24}{24}$

$\frac{5}{4} = W_P$

$W_P = \frac{5}{4} \times 100\% = \mathbf{125\%}$

9. $2 \cancel{\text{ft}}^2 \cdot \frac{12 \text{ in.}}{1 \cancel{\text{ft}}} \cdot \frac{12 \text{ in.}}{1 \cancel{\text{ft}}} = $ **288 square inches**

10.

	750 doctors
$\frac{2}{5}$ of doctors (300) did.	150 doctors
	150 doctors
$\frac{3}{5}$ of doctors did not.	150 doctors
	150 doctors
	150 doctors

(a) $300 \div 2 = 150$

5(150 doctors) = **750 doctors**

(b) 3(150 doctors) = **450 doctors**

11. $y = 2(4.5) + 1$

$y = 9 + 1$

$y = \mathbf{10}$

12. a ⊳ ab

13. $\frac{12 \text{ inches}}{4} = 3$ inches

(3 inches)(3 inches) = **9 square inches**

14. (a) $1.75 = 1\frac{75}{100} = \mathbf{1\frac{3}{4}}$

(b) $1.75 \times 100\% = \mathbf{175\%}$

15.
$$\begin{array}{r} \$325 \\ \times\ \ 0.06 \\ \hline \$19.50 \end{array}$$

$$\begin{array}{r} \$325 \\ +\ \$19.50 \\ \hline \mathbf{\$344.50} \end{array}$$

16. $(6 \times 8) \times (10^4 \times 10^{-7})$
$= (48 \times (10^{-3})$
$= \mathbf{4.8 \times 10^{-2}}$

17. (a) $(8 \text{ in.})(3 \text{ in.}) = 24 \text{ in.}^2$

$\frac{24 \text{ in.}^2}{1 \text{ layer}} \cdot (1 \text{ in.}) \cdot (12 \text{ layers}) = \mathbf{288 \text{ in.}^3}$

(b) $2(8 \text{ in.} \times 12 \text{ in.}) + 2(8 \text{ in.} \times 3 \text{ in.})$
$+ 2(12 \text{ in.} \times 3 \text{ in.})$
$= 192 \text{ in}^2 + 48 \text{ in.}^2 + 72 \text{ in.}^2$
$= \mathbf{312 \text{ in.}^2}$

18. (a) $C \approx 3.14(100 \text{ mm})$
$C \approx \mathbf{314 \text{ mm}}$

(b) $A = \pi r^2$
$A \approx 3.14(2500 \text{ mm}^2)$
$A \approx \mathbf{7850 \text{ mm}^2}$

19. **0**

20.

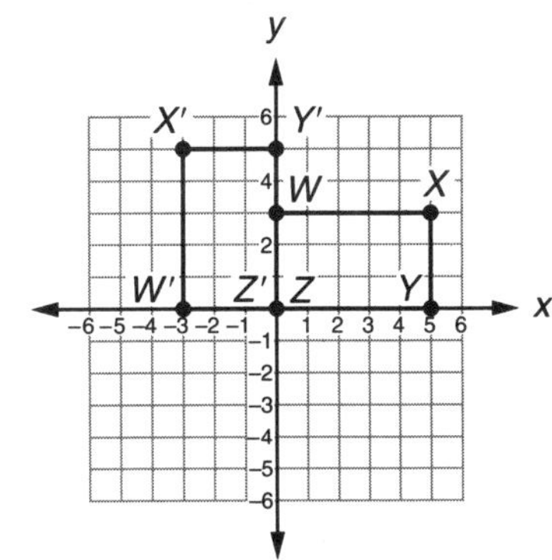

(a) ***Z* (0, 0)**

(b) ***W′* (−3, 0), *X′* (−3, 5), *Y′* (0, 5), *Z′* (0, 0)**

21. $\frac{2}{3} \times 20 = \frac{40}{3} = \mathbf{13\frac{1}{3}}$

22.

−1 0 1 2 3 4 5

23.
$x + 3.5 = 4.28$
$x + 3.5 - 3.5 = 4.28 - 3.5$
$x = \mathbf{0.78}$

24.
$2\frac{2}{3}w = 24$
$\frac{8}{3}w = 24$
$\left(\frac{\cancel{3}^{1}}{\cancel{8}_{1}}\right)\frac{\cancel{8}^{1}}{\cancel{3}_{1}}w = \left(\frac{3}{\cancel{8}_{1}}\right)\cancel{24}^{3}$
$w = \mathbf{9}$

25.
$-4y = 1.4$
$\frac{-4y}{-4} = \frac{1.4}{-4}$
$y = \mathbf{-0.35}$

26. $10^1 + 10^0 + 10^{-1}$
$= 10 + 1 + \frac{1}{10} = 11 + 0.1$
$= \mathbf{11.1}$

27. $(-2x^2)(-3xy)(-y)$
$= (-2) \cdot x \cdot x \cdot (-3) \cdot x \cdot y \cdot (-1) \cdot y$
$= (-2)(-3)(-1) \cdot x \cdot x \cdot x \cdot y \cdot y$
$= \mathbf{-6x^3y^2}$

28.
$$\begin{array}{rcl} \frac{8}{75} & = & \frac{32}{300} \\ -\ \frac{9}{100} & = & \frac{27}{300} \\ \hline & & \frac{5}{300} = \mathbf{\frac{1}{60}} \end{array}$$

29. (a) $(-3) + (-4)(-5) - (-6)$
$(-3) + (20) + (+6)$
$(-3) + (26)$
23

(b) $\frac{(-2)(-4)}{(-4) - (-2)}$
$\frac{8}{-2}$
$\mathbf{-4}$

30.
$10^2 - 5^2 = 100 - 25 = 75$
$(10 + 5)(10 - 5) = (15)(5) = 75$
$75 = 75$
$x^2 - y^2 \textcircled{=} (x + y)(x - y)$

LESSON 91, LESSON PRACTICE

a. $(3) + (3)(-2) - (-2)$
$(3) + (-6) - (-2)$
$(-3) - (-2)$
$\mathbf{-1}$

b. $-(-2) + (-5) - (-2)(-5)$
$-(-2) + (-5) - (+10)$
$(-3) - (+10)$
$\mathbf{-13}$

c. $-3 + 4 - 5 - 2$
$+4 \underbrace{- 3 - 5 - 2}$
$+4 \quad -10$
$\mathbf{-6}$

d. $-2 + 3(-4) - 5(-2)$
$-2 + (-12) - (-10)$
$-14 - (-10)$
$\mathbf{-4}$

e. $-3(-2) - 5(2) + 3(-4)$
$(+6) - (+10) + (-12)$
$\mathbf{-16}$

f. $-4(-3)(-2) - 6(-4)$
$-4(+6) - (-24)$
$(-24) - (-24)$
$\mathbf{0}$

LESSON 91, MIXED PRACTICE

1. $6(86) + 4(94) = 516 + 376$
$= 892$

$10\overline{)892.0}$ = **89.2**

2. Median $= \dfrac{7 + 9}{2} = 8$ **11 − 8 = 3**

Median $= 88 \div 8 = 11$

3. $\dfrac{130 \text{ miles}}{2.5 \text{ hours}} = $ **52 miles per hour**

4.

	Ratio	Actual Count
Laborers	3	L
Supervisors	5	S
Total	8	120

$\dfrac{3}{8} = \dfrac{L}{120}$
$8L = 360$
$L = $ **45 laborers**

5.

	Case 1	Case 2
Notebooks	3	5
Price	\$8.55	p

$\dfrac{3}{\$8.55} = \dfrac{5}{p}$
$3p = \$42.75$
$p = $ **\$14.25**

6.

	Percent	Actual Count
Sale price	90	S
Regular price	100	\$36

$\dfrac{90}{100} = \dfrac{S}{\$36}$
$100S = \$3240$
$S = $ **\$32.40**

7.

	Percent	Actual Count
People who came	80	40
Invited people	100	I

$\dfrac{80}{100} = \dfrac{40}{I}$
$80I = 4000$
$I = $ **50 people**

8. (a) $\mathbf{20 = 0.4 \times W_N}$
$\dfrac{20}{0.4} = \dfrac{0.4 \times W_N}{0.4}$
$\mathbf{50} = W_N$

(b) $\mathbf{20 = W_P \times 40}$
$\dfrac{20}{40} = \dfrac{W_P \times 40}{40}$
$\dfrac{1}{2} = W_P$
$W_P = \dfrac{1}{2} \times 100\% = $ **50%**

9. $\overset{25}{\cancel{3600}}\ \cancel{\text{in.}^2} \cdot \dfrac{1 \text{ foot}}{\underset{1}{\cancel{12}}\ \cancel{\text{in.}}} \cdot \dfrac{1 \text{ foot}}{\underset{1}{\cancel{12}}\ \cancel{\text{in.}}}$
$=$ **25 square feet**

10.

$\frac{3}{4}$ were multiple choice (60). — 80 questions: 20 questions, 20 questions, 20 questions

$\frac{1}{4}$ were not multiple choice. — 20 questions

(a) $60 \div 3 = 20$
$4(20 \text{ questions}) = $ **80 questions**

(b) **25%**

11. $(-3) - (-2) - (-3)(-2)$
$(-3) - (-2) - (+6)$
$\mathbf{-7}$

12. **Insufficient information**

13.

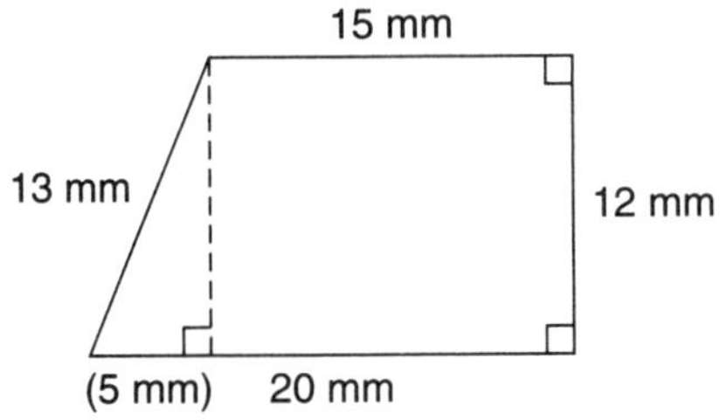

(a) **Trapezoid**

(b) Perimeter $= 15\text{ mm} + 12\text{ mm} + 20\text{ mm} + 13\text{ mm} = \mathbf{60\text{ mm}}$

(c) Area of rectangle $= (15\text{ mm})(12\text{ mm}) = 180\text{ mm}^2$
Area of triangle $= \dfrac{(5\text{ mm})(12\text{ mm})}{2} = 30\text{ mm}^2$
Area of figure $= 180\text{ mm}^2 + 30\text{ mm}^2 = \mathbf{210\text{ mm}^2}$

(d) $180° - 75° = \mathbf{105°}$

14. (a) **Associative property of addition**

(b) **Commutative property of multiplication**

(c) **Distributive property**

15.

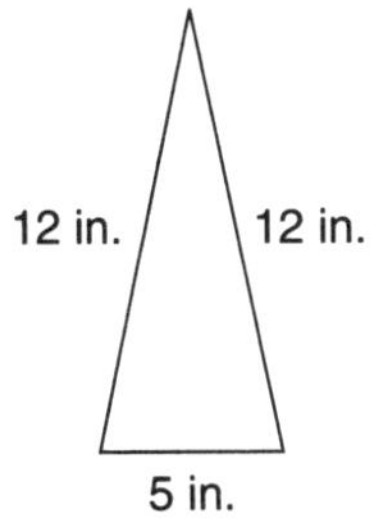

Perimeter $= 12\text{ in.} + 12\text{ in.} + 5\text{ in.} = \mathbf{29\text{ in.}}$

16. $(2.4 \times 10^{-4})(5 \times 10^{-7})$
12×10^{-11}
$(1.2 \times 10^{1}) \times 10^{-11}$
$\mathbf{1.2 \times 10^{-10}}$

17. (a) **5 faces**

(b) **8 edges**

(c) **5 vertices**

18. (a) $C \approx 3.14(8\text{ cm})$
$C \approx \mathbf{25.12\text{ cm}}$

(b) $A \approx 3.14(16\text{ cm}^2)$
$A \approx \mathbf{50.24\text{ cm}^2}$

19.

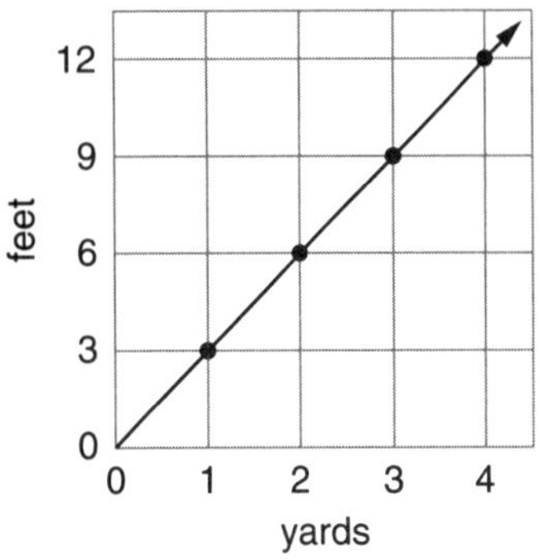

20. (a) $m\angle x = 180° - (90° + 30°) = \mathbf{60°}$

(b) $m\angle y = m\angle x = \mathbf{60°}$

(c) $m\angle A = 180° - (60° + 65°) = \mathbf{55°}$

(d) **No. The triangles do not have the same shape, nor do they have matching angles.**

21. (a) $-3x - 3 - x - 1$
$-3x - x - 3 - 1$
$\mathbf{-4x - 4}$

(b) $(-3x)(-3)(-x)(-1)$
$(-3) \cdot x \cdot (-3) \cdot (-1) \cdot x \cdot (-1)$
$(-3)(-3)(-1)(-1) \cdot x \cdot x$
$\mathbf{9x^2}$

22.

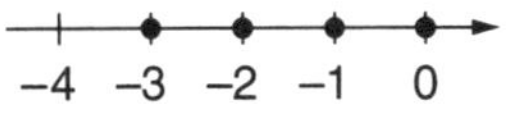

23. AB is 60 mm
BC is 40 mm
$60\text{ mm} - 40\text{ mm} = \mathbf{20\text{ mm}}$

24. $5 = y - 4.75$
$5 + 4.75 = y - 4.75 + 4.75$
$\mathbf{9.75} = y$

25. $3\frac{1}{3}y = 7\frac{1}{2}$

$\frac{10}{3}y = \frac{15}{2}$

$\left(\frac{\cancel{3}^{1}}{\cancel{10}_{1}}\right)\frac{\cancel{10}^{1}}{\cancel{3}_{1}}y = \left(\frac{3}{\cancel{10}_{2}}\right)\frac{\cancel{15}^{3}}{2}$

$y = \mathbf{\frac{9}{4}}$

26. $-9x = 414$

$$\frac{-\cancel{9}x}{-\cancel{9}} = \frac{\overset{-46}{\cancel{414}}}{\underset{1}{-\cancel{9}}}$$

$x = \mathbf{-46}$

27. $\frac{32 \text{ ft}}{1 \cancel{s}} \cdot \frac{60 \cancel{s}}{1 \text{ min}} = \mathbf{1920 \frac{ft}{min}}$

28. $5\frac{1}{3} + 2\frac{1}{2} + \frac{1}{6} = 5\frac{2}{6} + 2\frac{3}{6} + \frac{1}{6}$

$= 7\frac{6}{6} = \mathbf{8}$

29. $\frac{2.75 + 3.5}{2.5} = \frac{6.25}{2.5} = \mathbf{2.5}$

30. (a) $\frac{(-3) - (-4)(+5)}{-2}$

$\frac{(-3) - (-20)}{-2}$

$\frac{17}{-2}$

$\mathbf{-8\frac{1}{2}}$

(b) $-3(+4) - 5(+6) - 7$

$(-12) - (+30) - 7$

$\mathbf{-49}$

Lesson 92, Lesson Practice

a.

	Percent	Actual Count
Original	100	\$24.50
− Change	30	*C*
New	70	*N*

$\frac{100}{70} = \frac{\$24.50}{N}$

$100N = \$1715$

$N = \mathbf{\$17.15}$

b.

	Percent	Actual Count
Original	100	*O*
+ Change	20	*C*
New	120	60

$\frac{100}{120} = \frac{O}{60}$

$120O = 6000$

$O = \mathbf{50 \text{ students}}$

c.

	Percent	Actual Count
Original	100	*O*
− Change	20	*C*
New	80	\$120

$\frac{20}{80} = \frac{C}{\$120}$

$80C = \$2400$

$C = \mathbf{\$30}$

d.

	Percent	Actual Count
Original	100	\$15
+ Change	80	*C*
New	180	*N*

$\frac{100}{180} = \frac{\$15}{N}$

$100N = 2700$

$N = \mathbf{\$27}$

Lesson 92, Mixed Practice

1. $(7 + 11 + 13) - (2 \times 3 \times 5)$

$= 31 - 30$

$= \mathbf{1}$

2. $5(88) = 440$

$7(90) = 630$

$630 - 440 = 190$

$190 \div 2 = \mathbf{95}$

3. $\frac{2 \text{ miles}}{0.25 \text{ hour}} = \mathbf{8 \text{ miles per hour}}$

4.

	Ratio	Actual Count
Girls	9	45
Boys	7	35
Total	16	80

$\frac{35}{45} = \mathbf{\frac{7}{9}}$

5.

	Case 1	Case 2
Sparklers	24	60
Price	\$3.60	*p*

$\frac{24}{\$3.60} = \frac{60}{p}$

$24p = \$216$

$p = \mathbf{\$9.00}$

6.

	Percent	Actual Count
Original	100	340,000
+ Change	20	C
New	120	N

$$\frac{100}{120} = \frac{340{,}000}{N}$$
$$100N = 40{,}800{,}000$$
$$N = \mathbf{408{,}000}$$

7.

	Percent	Actual Count
Original	100	O
+ Change	50	C
New	150	96

$$\frac{100}{150} = \frac{O}{96}$$
$$150O = 9600$$
$$O = \textbf{64¢ per pound}$$

8. (a) $\mathbf{60 = W_P \times 75}$

$$\frac{60}{75} = \frac{W_P \times 75}{75}$$
$$\frac{12}{15} = W_P$$
$$W_P = \frac{12}{15} \times 100\% = \mathbf{80\%}$$

(b) $\mathbf{75 = W_P \times 60}$

$$\frac{75}{60} = \frac{W_P \times 60}{60}$$
$$\frac{15}{12} = W_P$$
$$W_P = \frac{15}{12} \times 100\% = \mathbf{125\%}$$

9. $100\ \cancel{\text{cm}^2} \cdot \frac{10\text{ mm}}{1\ \cancel{\text{cm}}} \cdot \frac{10\text{ mm}}{1\ \cancel{\text{cm}}}$

$= \textbf{10,000 square millimeters}$

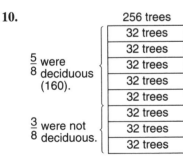

10.

256 trees

$\frac{5}{8}$ were deciduous (160).	32 trees
	32 trees
	32 trees
	32 trees
	32 trees
$\frac{3}{8}$ were not deciduous.	32 trees
	32 trees
	32 trees

(a) $160 \div 5 = 32$

$8(32\text{ trees}) = \textbf{256 trees}$

(b) $3(32\text{ trees}) = \textbf{96 trees}$

11. $y = 3(-5) - 1$

$y = -15 - 1$

$y = \mathbf{-16}$

12. $30\% \times 20 = \frac{3}{10} \times 20 = 6$

$20\% \times 30 = \frac{2}{10} \times 30 = 6$

$6 = 6$

30% of 20 ⊜ 20% of 30

13.

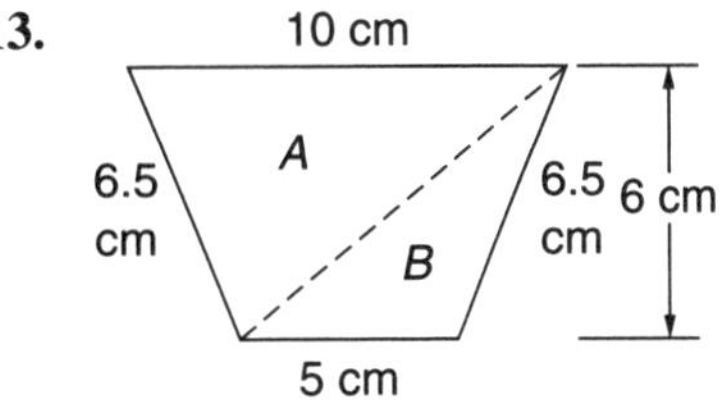

(a) Area of triangle $A = \frac{(10\text{ cm})(6\text{ cm})}{2}$

$= 30\text{ cm}^2$

Area of triangle $B = \frac{(5\text{ cm})(6\text{ cm})}{2}$

$= 15\text{ cm}^2$

Area of figure $= 30\text{ cm}^2 + 15\text{ cm}^2$

$= \mathbf{45\ cm^2}$

(b)

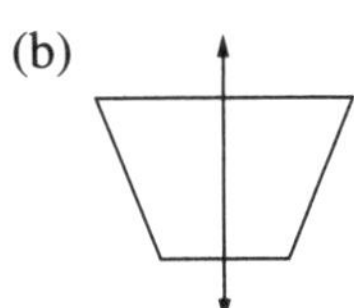

14.

	Percent	Actual Count
Original	100	\$90.00
+ Change	75	C
New	175	N

(a) $\frac{100}{175} = \frac{\$90}{N}$

$100N = \$15{,}750$

$N = \mathbf{\$157.50}$

(b)
$$\begin{array}{r} \$157.50 \\ \times\quad 0.06 \\ \hline \$9.45 \end{array} \qquad \begin{array}{r} \$157.50 \\ +\quad \$9.45 \\ \hline \mathbf{\$166.95} \end{array}$$

15. $(8 \times 10^{-5})(3 \times 10^{12})$

24×10^7

$(2.4 \times 10^1) \times 10^7$

$\mathbf{2.4 \times 10^8}$

16. (a) $\mathbf{2.\overline{3}}$

(b) $\mathbf{233\frac{1}{3}\%}$

(c) $\mathbf{\frac{1}{30}}$

(d) $\mathbf{0.0\overline{3}}$

17. $\mathbf{\frac{3}{51} = \frac{1}{17}}$

18. $W_N = 2.5 \times 60$
$W_N = \mathbf{150}$

19. (a) **2**

(b) **3**

20. $C \approx 3.14(24 \text{ inches})$
$C \approx 75.36 \text{ inches}$
$C \approx$ **75 inches**

21. $y = 2(0) + 1$
$y = 0 + 1$
$y = \mathbf{1;}$
$y = 2(3) + 1$
$y = 6 + 1$
$y = \mathbf{7;}$
$y = 2(-2) + 1$
$y = -4 + 1$
$y = \mathbf{-3}$

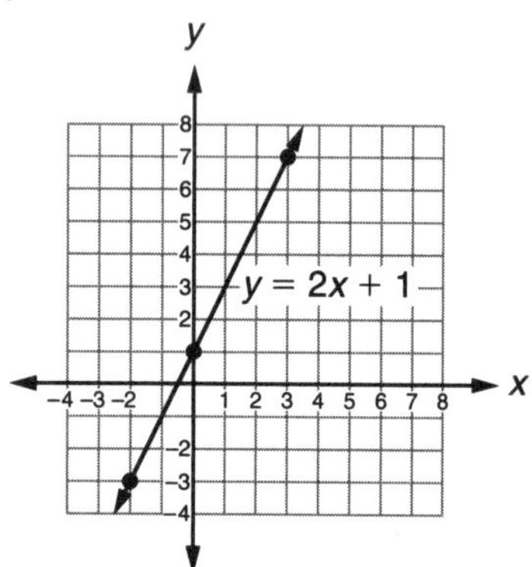

22. $180° \div 9 = 20°$
$4(20°) = \mathbf{80°}$

23. (a) $x + y + 3 + x - y - 1$
$x + x + y - y + 3 - 1$
$\mathbf{2x + 2}$

(b) $(3x)(2x) + (3x)(2)$
$[(3) \cdot x \cdot (2) \cdot x] + [(3) \cdot x \cdot (2)]$
$[(3)(2) \cdot x \cdot x] + [(3)(2) \cdot x]$
$\mathbf{6x^2 + 6x}$

24. **One possibility:**

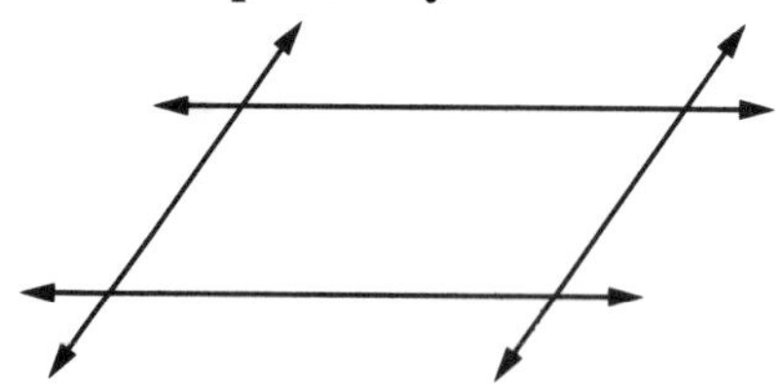

Parallelogram

25.
$$3\frac{1}{7}x = 66$$
$$\frac{22}{7}x = 66$$
$$\left(\frac{\cancel{7}^{1}}{\cancel{22}_{1}}\right)\frac{\cancel{22}^{1}}{\cancel{7}_{1}}x = \left(\frac{7}{\cancel{22}}\right)\cancel{66}^{3}$$
$$x = \mathbf{21}$$

26.
$$w - 0.15 = 4.9$$
$$w - 0.15 + 0.15 = 4.9 + 0.15$$
$$w = \mathbf{5.05}$$

27.
$$-8y = 600$$
$$\frac{-8y}{-8} = \frac{\cancel{600}^{-75}}{\cancel{-8}_{1}}$$
$$y = \mathbf{-75}$$

28. $(2 \cdot 3)^2 - 2(3^2)$
$= (6)^2 - 2(9) = 36 - 18 = \mathbf{18}$

29. $5 - \left(3\frac{1}{3} - 1\frac{1}{2}\right)$
$= 4\frac{6}{6} - \left(3\frac{2}{6} - 1\frac{3}{6}\right)$
$= 4\frac{6}{6} - \left(2\frac{8}{6} - 1\frac{3}{6}\right)$
$= 4\frac{6}{6} - 1\frac{5}{6} = \mathbf{3\frac{1}{6}}$

30. (a) $\frac{(-8)(-6)(-5)}{(-4)(-3)(-2)}$
$\frac{(48)(-5)}{(12)(-2)}$
$\frac{-240}{-24}$
10

(b) $-6 - 5(-4) - 3(-2)(-1)$
$-6 - (-20) - 3(2)$
$-6 - (-20) - (6)$
8

Lesson 93, Lesson Practice

a.
$$\begin{aligned} 8x - 15 &= 185 \\ 8x - 15 + 15 &= 185 + 15 \\ 8x &= 200 \\ \frac{8x}{8} &= \frac{200}{8} \\ x &= \mathbf{25} \end{aligned}$$

b.
$$\begin{aligned} 0.2y + 1.5 &= 3.7 \\ 0.2y + 1.5 - 1.5 &= 3.7 - 1.5 \\ 0.2y &= 2.2 \\ \frac{0.2y}{0.2} &= \frac{2.2}{0.2} \\ y &= \mathbf{11} \end{aligned}$$

c.
$$\begin{aligned} \frac{3}{4}m - \frac{1}{3} &= \frac{1}{2} \\ \frac{3}{4}m - \frac{1}{3} + \frac{1}{3} &= \frac{1}{2} + \frac{1}{3} \\ \frac{3}{4}m &= \frac{5}{6} \\ \left(\frac{4}{3}\right)\frac{3}{4}m &= \left(\frac{4}{3}\right)\frac{5}{6} \\ m &= \frac{20}{18} \\ m &= \mathbf{\frac{10}{9}} \end{aligned}$$

d.
$$\begin{aligned} 1\frac{1}{2}n + 3\frac{1}{2} &= 14 \\ 1\frac{1}{2}n + 3\frac{1}{2} - 3\frac{1}{2} &= 14 - 3\frac{1}{2} \\ 1\frac{1}{2}n &= 14 - 3\frac{1}{2} \\ 1\frac{1}{2}n &= 10\frac{1}{2} \\ \left(\frac{2}{3}\right)\frac{3}{2}n &= \left(\frac{2}{3}\right)\frac{21}{2} \\ n &= \frac{42}{6} \\ n &= \mathbf{7} \end{aligned}$$

e.
$$\begin{aligned} -6p + 36 &= 12 \\ -6p + 36 - 36 &= 12 - 36 \\ -6p &= -24 \\ \frac{-6p}{-6} &= \frac{-24}{-6} \\ p &= \mathbf{4} \end{aligned}$$

f.
$$\begin{aligned} 38 &= 4w - 26 \\ 38 + 26 &= 4w - 26 + 26 \\ 64 &= 4w \\ \mathbf{16} &= w \end{aligned}$$

g.
$$\begin{aligned} -\frac{5}{3}m + 15 &= 60 \\ -\frac{5}{3}m + 15 - 15 &= 60 - 15 \\ -\frac{5}{3}m &= 45 \\ \left(-\frac{3}{5}\right)\left(-\frac{5}{3}m\right) &= \left(-\frac{3}{5}\right)45 \\ m &= \mathbf{-27} \end{aligned}$$

h.
$$\begin{aligned} 4.5 &= 0.6d - 6.3 \\ 4.5 + 6.3 &= 0.6d - 6.3 + 6.3 \\ 10.8 &= 0.6d \\ \frac{10.8}{0.6} &= \frac{0.6d}{0.6} \\ \mathbf{18} &= d \end{aligned}$$

i.
$$\begin{aligned} 2x + 5 &\geq 1 \\ 2x + 5 - 5 &\geq 1 - 5 \\ 2x &\geq -4 \\ \frac{2x}{2} &\geq \frac{-4}{2} \\ \mathbf{x} &\geq \mathbf{-2} \end{aligned}$$

$x \geq -2$

−3 −2 −1 0 1

j.
$$\begin{aligned} 2x - 5 &< 1 \\ 2x - 5 + 5 &< 1 + 5 \\ 2x &< 6 \\ \frac{2x}{2} &< \frac{6}{2} \\ \mathbf{x} &< \mathbf{3} \end{aligned}$$

$x < 3$

0 1 2 3 4

Lesson 93, Mixed Practice

1. $\frac{60 \text{ kilometers}}{2.5 \text{ hours}} =$ **24 kilometers per hour**

2. (a) 3 + 9 + 7 + 5 + 10 + 4 + 5 + 8 + 5 + 4 + 8 + 40 = 108

$108 \div 12 = \mathbf{9}$

(b) $40 - 3 = \mathbf{37}$

3.

	Ratio	Actual Count
Red marbles	7	R
Blue marbles	5	B
Total	12	600

(a)
$$\frac{5}{12} = \frac{B}{600}$$
$$12B = 3000$$
$$B = \mathbf{250\ marbles}$$

(b) $\mathbf{\frac{5}{12}}$

4.

	Case 1	Case 2
Pterodactyls	500	p
Minutes	20	90

$$\frac{500}{20} = \frac{p}{90}$$
$$20p = 45{,}000$$
$$p = \mathbf{2250\ plastic\ pterodactyls}$$

5. (a)

	Percent	Actual Count
Original	100	\$24
− Change	25	C
New	75	N

$$\frac{100}{75} = \frac{\$24}{N}$$
$$100N = \$1800$$
$$N = \mathbf{\$18}$$

(b)

	Percent	Actual Count
Original	100	O
− Change	25	C
New	75	\$24

$$\frac{100}{75} = \frac{O}{\$24}$$
$$75O = \$2400$$
$$O = \mathbf{\$32}$$

6.
$$(-3x^2)(2xy)(-x)(3y^2)$$
$$(-3)\cdot x\cdot x\cdot(2)\cdot x\cdot y\cdot(-1)\cdot x\cdot(3)\cdot y\cdot y$$
$$(-3)(2)(-1)(3)\cdot x\cdot x\cdot x\cdot x\cdot y\cdot y\cdot y$$
$$\mathbf{18x^4y^3}$$

7. $\mathbf{\frac{2}{50} = \frac{1}{25}}$

8. $7\ \text{days}\cdot\frac{24\ \text{hours}}{1\ \text{day}}\cdot\frac{60\ \text{minutes}}{1\ \text{hour}}$ (days and hours cancelled)
$= \mathbf{10{,}080\ minutes}$

9.

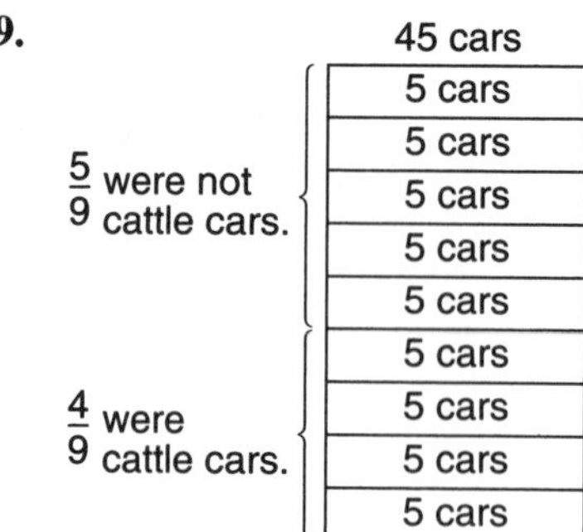

(a) **20 cattle cars**

(b) $\mathbf{55\frac{5}{9}\%}$

10. $\frac{1}{3}$ (>) 33%

11.
$$(-3)(-1) - (-3) - (-1)$$
$$(3) - (-3) - (-1)$$
$$\mathbf{7}$$

12.

```
  $7.95        $11.20        $11.20
  $0.90     ×   0.05      +   $0.56
  $2.35        $0.56         $11.76
 $11.20
```


13.

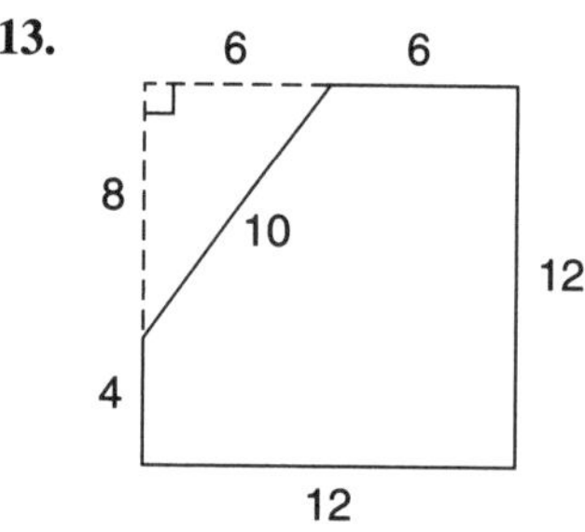

(a) Perimeter = 6 in. + 12 in. + 12 in. + 4 in. + 10 in. = **44 in.**

(b)
Area of square = (12 in.)(12 in.)
= 144 in.^{2}

Area of triangle = $\frac{(6\text{ in.})(8\text{ in.})}{2}$
= 24 in.^{2}

Area of figure = 144 in.^{2} − 24 in.^{2}
= **120 in.^{2}**

14. (a) $\mathbf{\frac{2}{25}}$

(b) **8%**

(c) $\mathbf{\frac{1}{12}}$

(d) $\mathbf{0.08\overline{3}}$

15.

	Percent	Actual Count
Original	100	$3.60
+ Change	120	C
New	220	N

$$\frac{100}{220} = \frac{\$3.60}{N}$$
$$100N = \$792$$
$$N = \mathbf{\$7.92}$$

16. $(8 \times 10^{-3})(6 \times 10^{7})$
$$48 \times 10^{4}$$
$$(4.8 \times 10^{1})10^{4}$$
$$\mathbf{4.8 \times 10^{5}}$$

17. (a) $(10 \text{ cm})(10 \text{ cm})(10 \text{ cm})$
$= \mathbf{1000\ cm^3}$

(b) $6(100 \text{ cm}^2) = \mathbf{600\ cm^2}$

18. (a) $A \approx 3.14(100 \text{ cm}^2)$
$A \approx \mathbf{314\ cm^2}$

(b) $C \approx 3.14(20 \text{ cm})$
$C \approx \mathbf{62.8\ cm}$

19. $-x + 2x^2 - 1 + x - x^2$
$$2x^2 - x^2 - x + x - 1$$
$$\mathbf{x^2 - 1}$$

20. $y = 2(1) + 3$
$y = 2 + 3$
$y = \mathbf{5;}$
$y = 2(0) + 3$
$y = 0 + 3$
$y = \mathbf{3;}$
$y = 2(-2) + 3$
$y = -4 + 3$
$y = \mathbf{-1}$

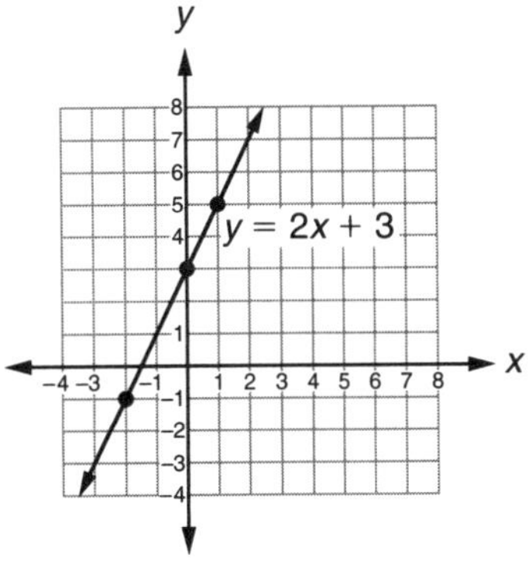

21. $60 = \mathbf{\frac{3}{8}} \times W_N$
$$\frac{8}{3} \cdot 60 = \left(\frac{8}{3}\right)\frac{3}{8} \times W_N$$
$$\mathbf{160} = W_N$$

22. $2x - 5 > -1$
$$2x - 5 + 5 > -1 + 5$$
$$2x > 4$$
$$\frac{2x}{2} > \frac{4}{2}$$
$$\mathbf{x > 2}$$

$x > 2$

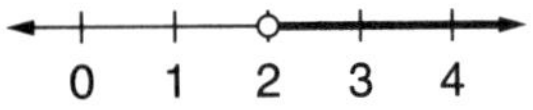

23. (a) $m\angle x = 180° - (90° + 50°)$
$= \mathbf{40°}$
$m\angle y = m\angle x = \mathbf{40°}$
$m\angle z = 180° - (90° + 40°)$
$= \mathbf{50°}$

(b) **Yes. The triangles have the same shape. Their corresponding angles are congruent.**

24.
$$\begin{array}{r} 0.42 \\ +\ 0.45 \\ \hline \mathbf{0.87} \end{array}$$

25. $3x + 2 = 9$
$$3x + 2 - 2 = 9 - 2$$
$$3x = 7$$
$$\frac{3x}{3} = \frac{7}{3}$$
$$x = \mathbf{\frac{7}{3}}$$

26. $\frac{2}{3}w + 4 = 14$
$$\frac{2}{3}w + 4 - 4 = 14 - 4$$
$$\frac{2}{3}w = 10$$
$$\left(\frac{3}{2}\right)\frac{2}{3}w = \left(\frac{3}{2}\right)10$$
$$w = \mathbf{15}$$

27. $0.2y - 1 = 7$
$$0.2y - 1 + 1 = 7 + 1$$
$$0.2y = 8$$
$$\frac{0.2y}{0.2} = \frac{8}{0.2}$$
$$y = \mathbf{40}$$

28. $-\frac{2}{3}m = -6$
$$\left(-\frac{3}{2}\right)\left(-\frac{2}{3}m\right) = \left(-\frac{3}{2}\right)(-6)$$
$$m = \mathbf{9}$$

29. $3(2^3 + \sqrt{16}) - 4^0 - 8 \cdot 2^{-3}$

$$3(8 + 4) - 1 - 8 \cdot \frac{1}{8}$$
$$3(12) - 1 - 1$$
$$36 - 2$$
$$\mathbf{34}$$

30. (a) $\dfrac{(-9)(+6)(-5)}{(-4) - (-1)}$

$$\frac{(-54)(-5)}{-3}$$
$$\frac{270}{-3}$$
$$\mathbf{-90}$$

(b) $-3(4) + 2(3) - 1$

$$(-12) + (6) - 1$$
$$\mathbf{-7}$$

Lesson 94, Lesson Practice

a.

$$p(4, 5) = \frac{1}{6} \cdot \frac{1}{6} = \frac{1}{36}$$
$$p(3, 6) = \frac{1}{6} \cdot \frac{1}{6} = \frac{1}{36}$$
$$p(5, 4) = \frac{1}{6} \cdot \frac{1}{6} = \frac{1}{36}$$
$$p(6, 3) = \frac{1}{6} \cdot \frac{1}{6} = \frac{1}{36}$$
$$\frac{1}{36} + \frac{1}{36} + \frac{1}{36} + \frac{1}{36} = \mathbf{\frac{4}{36} = \frac{1}{9}}$$

b.

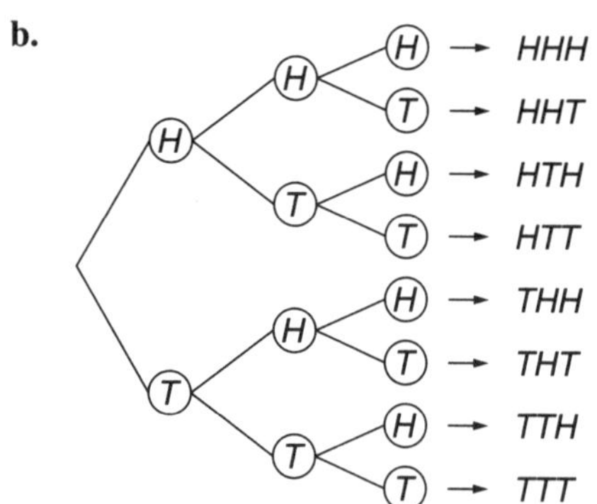

c. $\mathbf{\frac{1}{3} \cdot \frac{1}{4} = \frac{1}{12}}$

d.

Second Draw (rows: First Draw)

First Draw	Red	White	Blue
Red	R, R	R, W	R, B
White	W, R	W, W	W, B
Blue	B, R	B, W	B, B

e.

Second Draw (rows: First Draw)

First Draw	Red	White	Blue
Red		R, W	R, B
White	W, R		W, B
Blue	B, R	B, W	

f. **Independent; dependent**

Lesson 94, Mixed Practice

1.
$$\begin{array}{r} 21{,}000{,}000{,}000 \\ -\ 9{,}800{,}000{,}000 \\ \hline 11{,}200{,}000{,}000 \end{array}$$

$\mathbf{1.12 \times 10^{10}}$

2. $\dfrac{96 \text{ miles} + 240 \text{ miles}}{2 \text{ hours} + 4 \text{ hours}}$

$$= \frac{336 \text{ miles}}{6 \text{ hours}} = \textbf{56 miles per hour}$$

3. $\dfrac{\$8.40}{10 \text{ pounds}} = \dfrac{\$0.84}{1 \text{ pound}}$

$$\frac{\$10.50}{15 \text{ pounds}} = \frac{\$0.70}{1 \text{ pound}}$$

$$\begin{array}{r} \$0.84 \\ -\ \$0.70 \\ \hline \end{array}$$

10-pound box; $0.14 per pound more

4. $\dfrac{6}{12} = \mathbf{\dfrac{1}{2}}$

5.

	Ratio	Actual Count
Won	3	12
Lost	2	L
Total	5	T

$$\frac{3}{5} = \frac{12}{T}$$
$$3T = 5(12)$$
$$3T = 60$$
$$T = \textbf{20 games}$$

6.

	Case 1	Case 2
First number	24	42
Second number	36	n

$$\frac{24}{36} = \frac{42}{n}$$
$$24n = 1512$$
$$n = \mathbf{63}$$

7. $100\% - 20\% = \mathbf{80\%}$

8.

	Percent	Actual Count
Original	100	O
− Change	20	C
New	80	$20

$$\frac{100}{80} = \frac{O}{\$20}$$
$$80O = \$2000$$
$$O = \mathbf{\$25}$$

9. (a) $12 \text{ ft} \cdot \frac{12 \text{ inches}}{1 \text{ ft}} \cdot \frac{12 \text{ inches}}{1 \text{ ft}}$
= **1728 square inches**

(b) $1 \text{ km} \cdot \frac{1000 \text{ m}}{1 \text{ km}} \cdot \frac{1000 \text{ mm}}{1 \text{ m}}$
= **1,000,000 millimeters**

10.

300 male serfs

$\frac{2}{5}$ were conscripted (120).
- 60 male serfs
- 60 male serfs

$\frac{3}{5}$ were not conscripted.
- 60 male serfs
- 60 male serfs
- 60 male serfs

(a) $120 \div 2 = 60$
5(60 male serfs) = **300 male serfs**

(b) 3(60 male serfs) = **180 male serfs**

11. (a) **0**

(b) $p(1, 1) = \frac{1}{6} \cdot \frac{1}{6} = \mathbf{\frac{1}{36}}$

(c) $p(1, 2) = \frac{1}{6} \cdot \frac{1}{6} = \frac{1}{36}$

$p(2, 1) = \frac{1}{6} \cdot \frac{1}{6} = \frac{1}{36}$

$\frac{1}{36} + \frac{1}{36} = \mathbf{\frac{2}{36} = \frac{1}{18}}$

12. $y = 4(-2) - 3$
$y = -8 - 3$
$y = \mathbf{-11}$

13. $\frac{4 \text{ yards}}{4} = 1 \text{ yard} = 3 \text{ feet}$
(3 feet)(3 feet)
= **9 square feet**

14. (a)
$$\begin{array}{r} \$14{,}500 \\ \times \quad 0.065 \\ \hline \mathbf{\$942.50} \end{array}$$

(b)
$$\begin{array}{r} \$14{,}500 \\ + \quad 942.50 \\ \hline \mathbf{\$15{,}442.50} \end{array}$$

(c)
$$\begin{array}{r} \$14{,}500 \\ \times \quad 0.02 \\ \hline \mathbf{\$290} \end{array}$$

15. (a) $\mathbf{\frac{2}{3}}$

(b) $\mathbf{0.\overline{6}}$

(c) **1.75**

(d) **175%**

16. (a) $2 \times \$7.50 = \mathbf{\$15.00}$

(b) $\frac{100}{300} = \frac{\$7.50}{P}$
$P = \mathbf{\$22.50}$

17. $(2 \times 10^8)(8 \times 10^2)$
16×10^{10}
$(1.6 \times 10^1) \times 10^{10}$
$\mathbf{1.6 \times 10^{11}}$

18. (8 cubes)(6 cubes)(2 cubes)
= **96 cubes**

19. Area of square = (14 in.)(14 in.)
= 196 in.^{2}

Area of circle $\approx \frac{22}{7}$ (49 in.^{2})
$\approx$ 154 in.^{2}

$$\begin{array}{r} 196 \text{ in.}^2 \\ - \ 154 \text{ in.}^2 \\ \hline \mathbf{42 \text{ in.}^2} \end{array}$$

20.
$$\begin{array}{r} 65.4545\ldots \\ 0.11\overline{)7.200000} \\ \underline{6\,6} \\ 60 \\ \underline{55} \\ 50 \\ \underline{44} \\ 60 \\ \underline{55} \\ 50 \\ \underline{44} \\ 60 \\ \underline{55} \\ 5 \end{array}$$

$\mathbf{65.4545\ldots = 65.\overline{45}}$

21.
$$y = 3(3) - 2$$
$$y = 9 - 2$$
$$y = \mathbf{7};$$
$$y = 3(0) - 2$$
$$y = 0 - 2$$
$$y = \mathbf{-2};$$
$$y = 3(-1) - 2$$
$$y = -3 - 2$$
$$y = \mathbf{-5}$$

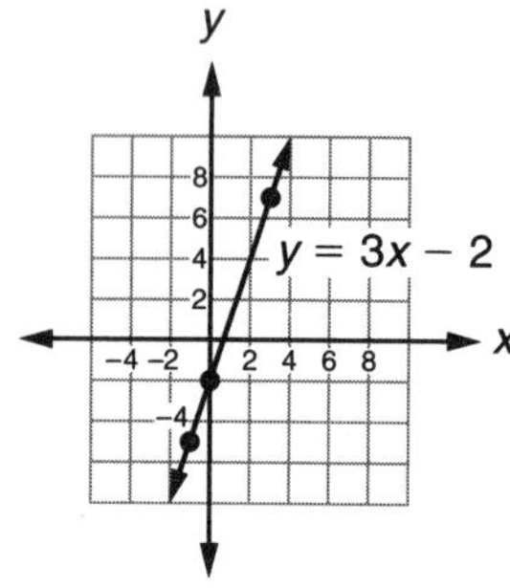

22.
$$2x - 5 < -1$$
$$2x - 5 + 5 < -1 + 5$$
$$2x < 4$$
$$\frac{2x}{2} < \frac{4}{2}$$
$$\mathbf{x < 2}$$

x < 2

−1 0 1 2 3

23. (a) $m\angle AOB = \frac{90°}{3} = \mathbf{30°}$

(b) $m\angle EOC = 90° + 45° = \mathbf{135°}$

24. AB is $1\frac{3}{4}$ in.

BC is $1\frac{1}{2}$ in.

$$1\frac{3}{4}\text{ in.} \longrightarrow 1\frac{3}{4}\text{ in.}$$
$$-1\frac{1}{2}\text{ in.} \longrightarrow -1\frac{2}{4}\text{ in.}$$
$$\mathbf{\frac{1}{4}\text{ in.}}$$

25.
$$1.2p + 4 = 28$$
$$1.2p + 4 - 4 = 28 - 4$$
$$1.2p = 24$$
$$\frac{1.2p}{1.2} = \frac{24}{1.2}$$
$$p = \mathbf{20}$$

26.
$$-6\frac{2}{3}m = 1\frac{1}{9}$$
$$-\frac{20}{3}m = \frac{10}{9}$$
$$\left(-\frac{3}{20}\right)\left(-\frac{20}{3}m\right) = \left(-\frac{3}{20}\right)\left(\frac{10}{9}\right)$$
$$m = \mathbf{-\frac{1}{6}}$$

27. (a) $6x^2 + 3x - 2x - 1$

$\mathbf{6x^2 + x - 1}$

(b)
$$(5x)(3x) - (5x)(-4)$$
$$[(5) \cdot x \cdot (3) \cdot x] - [(5) \cdot x \cdot (-4)]$$
$$[(5)(3) \cdot x \cdot x] - [(5)(-4) \cdot x]$$
$$15x^2 - (-20x)$$
$$\mathbf{15x^2 + 20x}$$

28. (a)
$$\frac{-8 - (-6) - (4)}{-3}$$
$$\frac{-8 + 6 - 4}{-3}$$
$$\frac{-6}{-3}$$
$$\mathbf{2}$$

(b)
$$-5(-4) - 3(-2) - 1$$
$$20 - (-6) - 1$$
$$\mathbf{25}$$

29.
$$(-2)^2 - 4(-1)(3)$$
$$4 - 4(-3)$$
$$4 - (-12)$$
$$\mathbf{16}$$

30. $\mathbf{Q_H D_H}$
$\mathbf{Q_H D_T}$
$\mathbf{Q_T D_H}$
$\mathbf{Q_T D_T}$

LESSON 95, LESSON PRACTICE

a. Area of base $= \frac{(8\text{ cm})(6\text{ cm})}{2} = 24\text{ cm}^2$

Volume $= (24\text{ cm}^2)(12\text{ cm}) = \mathbf{288\text{ cm}^3}$

b. Area of base $= \frac{(10\text{ cm})(6\text{ cm})}{2}$

$= 30\text{ cm}^2$

Volume $= (30\text{ cm}^2)(12\text{ cm}) = \mathbf{360\text{ cm}^3}$

c. Area of base $= \pi(3\text{ cm})^2 = 9\pi\text{ cm}^2$

Volume $= (9\pi\text{ cm}^2)(10\text{ cm}) = \mathbf{90\pi\text{ cm}^3}$

d. $$\begin{aligned}\text{Area of base} &= (7\text{ cm})(2\text{ cm}) \\ &+ (3\text{ cm})(3\text{ cm}) \\ &= 14\text{ cm}^2 + 9\text{ cm}^2 = 23\text{ cm}^3 \\ \text{Volume} &= (23\text{ cm}^2)(10\text{ cm}) = \mathbf{230\text{ cm}^3}\end{aligned}$$

e. $$\begin{aligned}\text{Area of base} &= \pi(1\text{ cm})^2 = \pi\text{ cm}^2 \\ \text{Volume} &= (\pi\text{ cm}^2)(10\text{ cm}) = \mathbf{10\pi\text{ cm}^3}\end{aligned}$$

Lesson 95, Mixed Practice

1. $$\begin{aligned}&\$1.40 + 40(\$0.35) \\ &= \$1.40 + \$14.00 = \$15.40\end{aligned}$$
$$\frac{\$15.40}{4\text{ miles}} = \mathbf{\$3.85\text{ per mile}}$$

2.

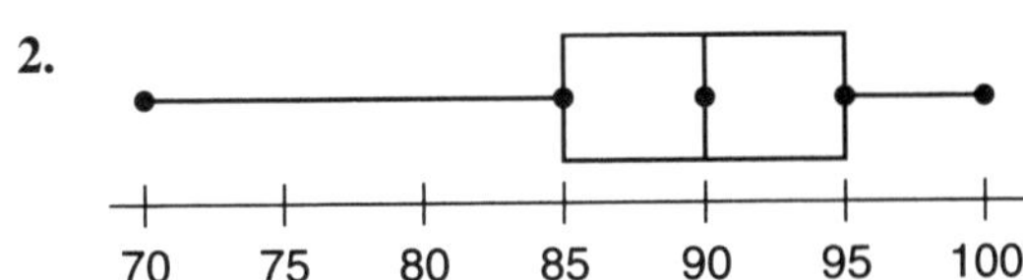

3.

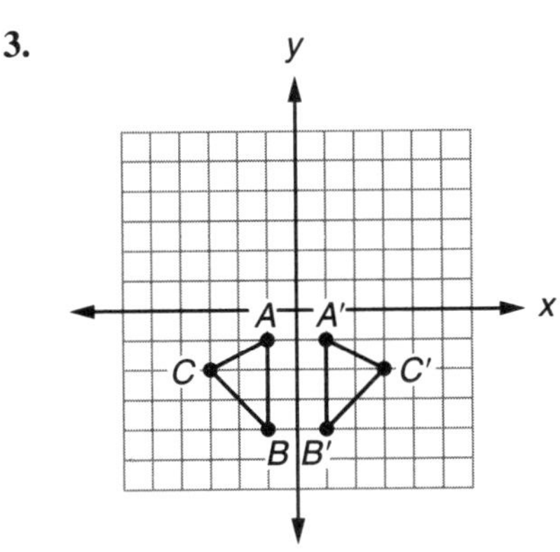

***A′*(1, −1), *B′*(1, −4), *C′*(3, −2)**

4. $\$6\left(4\frac{1}{3}\right) = \$6\left(\frac{13}{3}\right) = \mathbf{\$26}$

5. $$\begin{aligned}\text{Area of rectangle} &= (12)(8) = 96 \\ \text{Area of triangle} &= \frac{(6)(8)}{2} = 24\end{aligned}$$
$$\frac{24}{96} = \frac{1}{4} = \frac{\text{shaded area}}{\text{total area}}$$
$$\frac{\text{unshaded area}}{\text{total area}} = \frac{3}{4}$$
$$\frac{\text{shaded area}}{\text{unshaded area}} = \mathbf{\frac{1}{3}}$$

6. $$\begin{aligned}1\text{ ton} &= 2000\text{ pounds} \\ \frac{600}{\$7.20} &= \frac{2000}{p} \\ 600p &= \$14{,}400 \\ p &= \mathbf{\$24.00}\end{aligned}$$

7.

	Percent	Actual Count
Original	100	*O*
+ Change	30	*C*
New	130	\$3.90

$$\begin{aligned}\frac{100}{130} &= \frac{O}{\$3.90} \\ 130O &= \$390 \\ O &= \mathbf{\$3\text{ per unit}}\end{aligned}$$

8.

	Percent	Actual Count
Original	100	\$3.90
+ Change	30	*C*
New	130	*N*

$$\begin{aligned}\frac{100}{130} &= \frac{\$3.90}{N} \\ 100N &= \$507 \\ N &= \mathbf{\$5.07}\end{aligned}$$

9. $\overset{10}{\cancel{1000}}\ \cancel{\text{mm}^2} \cdot \frac{1\text{ cm}}{\cancel{10}\ \cancel{\text{mm}}} \cdot \frac{1\text{ cm}}{\cancel{10}\ \cancel{\text{mm}}}$
$= \mathbf{10\text{ cm}^2}$

10.

150 Lilliputians

$\frac{3}{5}$ believed.	30 Lilliputians
	30 Lilliputians
	30 Lilliputians
$\frac{2}{5}$ did not believe (60).	30 Lilliputians
	30 Lilliputians

(a) $60 \div 2 = 30$
5(30 Lilliputians) = **150 Lilliputians**

(b) 3(30 Lilliputians) = **90 Lilliputians**

11. **Insufficient information**

12. $$\begin{aligned}&(-2)[(-2) + (-3)] \\ &-2[-5] \\ &\mathbf{10}\end{aligned}$$

13. (a) $$\begin{aligned}p(1, 6) &= \frac{1}{6}\cdot\frac{1}{6} = \frac{1}{36} \\ p(3, 4) &= \frac{1}{6}\cdot\frac{1}{6} = \frac{1}{36} \\ p(6, 1) &= \frac{1}{6}\cdot\frac{1}{6} = \frac{1}{36} \\ p(4, 3) &= \frac{1}{6}\cdot\frac{1}{6} = \frac{1}{36} \\ p(2, 5) &= \frac{1}{6}\cdot\frac{1}{6} = \frac{1}{36} \\ p(5, 2) &= \frac{1}{6}\cdot\frac{1}{6} = \frac{1}{36}\end{aligned}$$
$$\frac{1}{36} + \frac{1}{36} + \frac{1}{36} + \frac{1}{36} + \frac{1}{36} + \frac{1}{36}$$
$$= \mathbf{\frac{6}{36} = \frac{1}{6}}$$

(b) $p(1, 1 \text{ or } 2 \text{ or } 3 \text{ or } 4 \text{ or } 5) = \frac{1}{6} \cdot \frac{5}{6} = \frac{5}{36}$

$p(2, 1 \text{ or } 2 \text{ or } 3 \text{ or } 4) = \frac{1}{6} \cdot \frac{4}{6} = \frac{4}{36}$

$p(3, 1 \text{ or } 2 \text{ or } 3) = \frac{1}{6} \cdot \frac{3}{6} = \frac{3}{36}$

$p(4, 1 \text{ or } 2) = \frac{1}{6} \cdot \frac{2}{6} = \frac{2}{36}$

$p(5, 1) = \frac{1}{6} \cdot \frac{1}{6} = \frac{1}{36}$

$$\frac{5}{36} + \frac{4}{36} + \frac{3}{36} + \frac{2}{36} + \frac{1}{36}$$
$$= \mathbf{\frac{15}{36}} = \mathbf{\frac{5}{12}}$$

14. Area of base $= \frac{(30 \text{ mm})(40 \text{ mm})}{2}$
$= 600 \text{ mm}^2$
Volume $= (600 \text{ mm}^2)(50 \text{ mm})$
$= \mathbf{30{,}000 \text{ mm}^3}$

15. Area of base $\approx 3.14(9 \text{ cm}^2)$
$\approx 28.26 \text{ cm}^2$
Volume $\approx (28.26 \text{ cm}^2)(10 \text{ cm})$
$\approx \mathbf{282.6 \text{ cm}^3}$

16. $3(\$1.25) + 2(\$0.95) + \$1.30$
$= \$3.75 + \$1.90 + \$1.30 = \$6.95$

$$\begin{array}{r} \$6.95 \\ \times\ 0.06 \\ \hline \$0.417 \end{array} \longrightarrow \$0.42 \qquad \begin{array}{r} \$6.95 \\ +\ \$0.42 \\ \hline \mathbf{\$7.37} \end{array}$$

17.

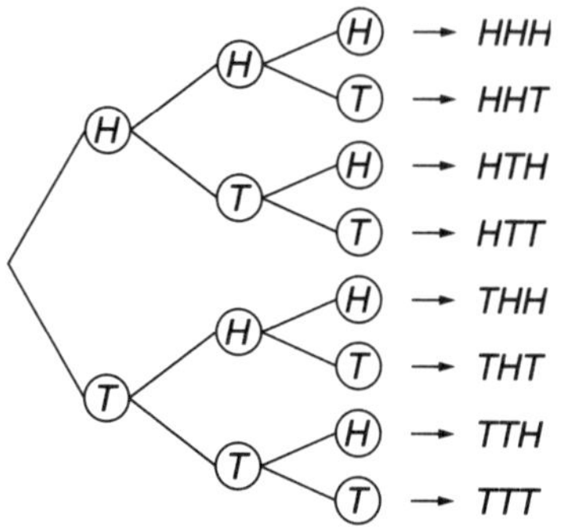

18. (a) $(-2xy)(-2x)(x^2y)$
$(-2) \cdot x \cdot y \cdot (-2) \cdot x \cdot x \cdot x \cdot y$
$(-2)(-2) \cdot x \cdot x \cdot x \cdot x \cdot y \cdot y$
$\mathbf{4x^4y^2}$

(b) $6x - 4y + 3 - 6x - 5y - 8$
$6x - 6x - 4y - 5y + 3 - 8$
$\mathbf{-9y - 5}$

19. $(8 \times 10^{-6})(4 \times 10^4)$
32×10^{-2}
$(3.2 \times 10^1) \times 10^{-2}$
$\mathbf{3.2 \times 10^{-1}}$

20. (a) $y = \frac{1}{2}(6) + 1$
$y = 3 + 1$
$y = \mathbf{4;}$
$y = \frac{1}{2}(4) + 1$
$y = 2 + 1$
$y = \mathbf{3;}$
$y = \frac{1}{2}(-2) + 1$
$y = -1 + 1$
$y = \mathbf{0}$

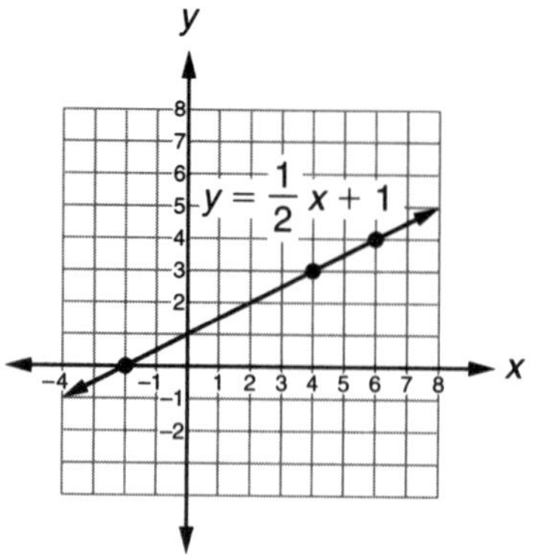

(b) **(0, 1)**

21. (a) $m\angle x = 180° - (90° + 55°) = \mathbf{35°}$
(b) $m\angle y = 180° - (90° + 35°) = \mathbf{55°}$
(c) $m\angle A = 180° - (110° + 55°)$
$= \mathbf{15°}$

22.

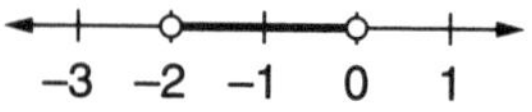

23. $(1.52 + 1.56) \div 2 = \mathbf{1.54}$

24.
$-5w + 11 = 51$
$-5w + 11 - 11 = 51 - 11$
$-5w = 40$
$\frac{-5w}{-5} = \frac{40}{-5}$
$w = \mathbf{-8}$

25.
$\frac{4}{3}x - 2 = 14$
$\frac{4}{3}x - 2 + 2 = 14 + 2$
$\frac{4}{3}x = 16$
$\left(\frac{3}{4}\right)\frac{4}{3}x = \left(\frac{3}{4}\right)16$
$x = \mathbf{12}$

26.
$$0.9x + 1.2 \leq 3$$
$$0.9x + 1.2 - 1.2 \leq 3 - 1.2$$
$$0.9x \leq 1.8$$
$$\frac{0.9x}{0.9} \leq \frac{1.8}{0.9}$$
$$x \leq \mathbf{2}$$

$x \leq 2$

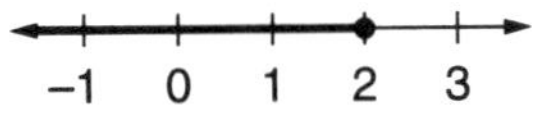

27.
$$\frac{10^3 \cdot 10^2}{10^5} - 10^{-1}$$
$$= \frac{10^5}{10^5} - \frac{1}{10}$$
$$= 1 - \frac{1}{10} = \frac{10}{10} - \frac{1}{10} = \mathbf{\frac{9}{10}} \text{ or } \mathbf{0.9}$$

28.
$$\sqrt{1^3 + 2^3} + (1 + 2)^3$$
$$= \sqrt{1 + 8} + (3)^3 = \sqrt{9} + 27$$
$$= 3 + 27 = \mathbf{30}$$

29.
$$5 - 2\frac{2}{3}\left(1\frac{3}{4}\right) = 5 - \frac{8}{3}\left(\frac{7}{4}\right)$$
$$= 5 - \frac{14}{3} = 4\frac{3}{3} - 4\frac{2}{3} = \mathbf{\frac{1}{3}}$$

30. (a)
$$\frac{(-10) + (-8) - (-6)}{(-2)(+3)}$$
$$\frac{-18 - (-6)}{-6}$$
$$\frac{-12}{-6}$$
$$\mathbf{2}$$

(b)
$$-8 + 3(-2) - 6$$
$$-8 + (-6) - 6$$
$$\mathbf{-20}$$

Lesson 96, Lesson Practice

a. $4 \times 6° = \mathbf{24°}$

b. $20 \times 6° = \mathbf{120°}$

c. $7 \times 6° = \mathbf{42°}$

d. **See student work; 55°**

e. **See student work; 15°**

f. **See student work; 45°**

g. **See student work; 145°**

h. $x(x - y)$
$\mathbf{x^2 - xy}$

i. $-3(2x - 1)$
$\mathbf{-6x + 3}$

j. $-x(x - 2)$
$\mathbf{-x^2 + 2x}$

k. $-2(4 - 3x)$
$\mathbf{-8 + 6x}$

l. $x^2 + 2x - 3(x + 2)$
$x^2 + 2x - 3x - 6$
$\mathbf{x^2 - x - 6}$

m. $x^2 - 2x - 3(x - 2)$
$x^2 - 2x - 3x + 6$
$\mathbf{x^2 - 5x + 6}$

Lesson 96, Mixed Practice

1. $3(\$280) + 5(\$240)$
$= \$840 + \$1200 = \$2040$

$$8\overline{)\$2040}$$ **\$255 per ton**

2.
$$\frac{9^2}{\sqrt{9}} = \frac{81}{3} = \mathbf{27}$$

3.
$$\frac{2000 \text{ miles}}{25 \text{ miles per gallon}} = 80 \text{ gallons}$$
$$\frac{80 \text{ gallons}}{16 \text{ gallons per tank}} = \mathbf{5 \text{ tanks}}$$

4.
$$\frac{\text{vertices}}{\text{edges}} = \mathbf{\frac{2}{3}}$$

5.

	Case 1	Case 2
Dollars	12	d
Yuan	100	475

$$\frac{12}{100} = \frac{d}{475}$$
$$100d = 5700$$
$$d = \textbf{57 dollars}$$

6.

	Percent	Actual Count
Original	100	O
− Change	20	C
New	80	60

$$\frac{100}{80} = \frac{O}{60}$$
$$80O = 6000$$
$$O = \mathbf{75}$$

7.

	Percent	Actual Count
Original	100	120
+ Change	25	C
New	125	N

$$\frac{100}{125} = \frac{120}{N}$$
$$100N = 15{,}000$$
$$N = \textbf{150 customers per day}$$

8. (a) $\mathbf{60 = W_P \times 50}$

$$\frac{60}{50} = \frac{W_P \times 50}{50}$$
$$\frac{6}{5} = W_P$$
$$W_P = \frac{6}{5} \times 100\% = \mathbf{120\%}$$

(b) $\mathbf{50 = W_P \times 60}$

$$\frac{50}{60} = \frac{W_P \times 60}{60}$$
$$\frac{5}{6} = W_P$$
$$W_P = \frac{5}{6} \times 100\% = \mathbf{83\frac{1}{3}\%}$$

9. $1.2\ \cancel{m^2} \cdot \dfrac{100\text{ cm}}{1\ \cancel{m}} \cdot \dfrac{100\text{ cm}}{1\ \cancel{m}}$

$$= \mathbf{12{,}000\ cm^2}$$

10. (a) **Angles: $\angle A$ and $\angle E$, $\angle B$ and $\angle D$, $\angle ACB$ and $\angle ECD$ (or $\angle BCA$ and $\angle DCE$)**
Sides: $\overline{AB}$ and $\overline{ED}$ (or $\overline{BA}$ and $\overline{DE}$), $\overline{BC}$ and $\overline{DC}$ (or $\overline{CB}$ and $\overline{CD}$), $\overline{AC}$ and $\overline{EC}$ (or $\overline{CA}$ and $\overline{CE}$)

(b) $m\angle ECD = 90° - 53° = \mathbf{37°}$

11. $x + y \ \textcircled{>}\ x - y$

12. $(-2)[(-4) + (-3)]$
$$-2[-7]$$
$$\mathbf{14}$$

13. 1 yard = 36 inches
Area = (9 inches)(9 inches)
= **81 square inches**

14. (a) $p(3, 3) = \frac{1}{4} \cdot \frac{1}{4} = \mathbf{\frac{1}{16}}$

(b) $p(1, 1, 1, 1) = \frac{2}{4} \cdot \frac{2}{4} \cdot \frac{2}{4} \cdot \frac{2}{4}$
$$= \frac{16}{256} = \mathbf{\frac{1}{16}}$$

15. (a) Area of base = (3 cm)(3 cm)
$= 9\text{ cm}^2$
Volume = $(9\text{ cm}^2)(3\text{ cm}) = \mathbf{27\ cm^3}$

(b) Area of base = $\dfrac{(4\text{ cm})(6\text{ cm})}{2}$
$= 12\text{ cm}^2$
Volume = $(12\text{ cm}^2)(5\text{ cm}) = \mathbf{60\ cm^3}$

16.

$$\begin{array}{r} \$14.50 \\ \times \quad 20 \\ \hline \$290 \end{array} \qquad \begin{array}{r} \$290 \\ \times\ 0.07 \\ \hline \$20.30 \end{array} \qquad \begin{array}{r} \$290 \\ +\ \$20.30 \\ \hline \mathbf{\$310.30} \end{array}$$

17. (a) $\mathbf{\frac{3}{80}}$

(b) **0.0375**

18.

	Percent	Actual Count
Original	100	\$24
− Change	$33\frac{1}{3}$	C
New	$66\frac{2}{3}$	N

(a) $\dfrac{100}{33\frac{1}{3}} = \dfrac{\$24}{C}$

$$100C = \$24\left(33\frac{1}{3}\right)$$
$$100C = \frac{\$2400}{3}$$
$$C = \mathbf{\$8}$$

(b)
$$\begin{array}{r} \$24 \\ -\ \$8 \\ \hline \mathbf{\$16} \end{array}$$

19. $24 \times 10^{-5} = \mathbf{2.4 \times 10^{-4}}$

20. (a) $C = \pi(12 \text{ m})$
$C = \mathbf{12\pi \text{ m}}$

(b) $A = \pi(36 \text{ m}^2)$
$A = \mathbf{36\pi \text{ m}^2}$

21. (a) $15 \times 6° = \mathbf{90°}$

(b) $25 \times 6° = \mathbf{150°}$

(c) $8 \times 6° = \mathbf{48°}$

22. (a) $\frac{360°}{8} = \mathbf{45°}$

(b) $180° - 45° = \mathbf{135°}$

23. $\mathbf{Q'(8, -4), R'(4, 0), S'(0, -4), T'(4, -8)}$

24.
$$0.8x + 1.5 < 4.7$$
$$0.8x + 1.5 - 1.5 < 4.7 - 1.5$$
$$0.8x < 3.2$$
$$\frac{0.8x}{0.8} < \frac{3.2}{0.8}$$
$$\mathbf{x < 4}$$

$x < 4$

−1 0 1 2 3 4 5

25.
$$2\frac{1}{2}x - 7 = 13$$
$$2\frac{1}{2}x - 7 + 7 = 13 + 7$$
$$2\frac{1}{2}x = 20$$
$$\left(\frac{2}{5}\right)\frac{5}{2}x = \left(\frac{2}{5}\right)20$$
$$x = \mathbf{8}$$

26.
$$-3x + 8 = -10$$
$$-3x + 8 - 8 = -10 - 8$$
$$-3x = -18$$
$$\frac{-3x}{-3} = \frac{-18}{-3}$$
$$x = \mathbf{6}$$

27. (a) $-3(x - 4)$
$\mathbf{-3x + 12}$

(b) $x(x + y)$
$\mathbf{x^2 + xy}$

28. (a)
$$\frac{(-4) - (-8)(-3)(-2)}{-2}$$
$$\frac{(-4) - (24)(-2)}{-2}$$
$$\frac{(-4) - (-48)}{-2}$$
$$\frac{44}{-2}$$
$$\mathbf{-22}$$

(b) $(-3)^2 + 3^2 = 9 + 9 = \mathbf{18}$

29. (a) $(-4ab^2)(-3b^2c)(5a)$
$(-4) \cdot a \cdot b \cdot b \cdot (-3) \cdot b \cdot b \cdot c \cdot (5) \cdot a$
$(-4)(-3)(5) \cdot a \cdot a \cdot b \cdot b \cdot b \cdot b \cdot c$
$\mathbf{60\,a^2b^4c}$

(b) $a^2 + ab - ab - b^2$
$\mathbf{a^2 - b^2}$

30. **A, A; A, B; A, C; B, A; B, B; B, C; C, A; C, B; C, C**

LESSON 97, LESSON PRACTICE

a. **Corresponding angles: ∠*W* and ∠*R*; ∠*Y* and ∠*Q*; ∠*X* and ∠*P***
Corresponding sides: $\overline{YW}$ and $\overline{QR}$; $\overline{WX}$ and $\overline{RP}$; $\overline{XY}$ and $\overline{PQ}$

b. **See student work.**

c.
$$\frac{6}{9} = \frac{x}{12}$$
$$9x = 72$$
$$x = \mathbf{8}$$

d. **See student work.**

e.
$$\frac{6}{9} = \frac{12}{y}$$
$$6y = 108$$
$$y = \mathbf{18}$$

f.
$$\frac{H_T}{6 \text{ ft}} = \frac{18 \text{ ft}}{9 \text{ ft}}$$
$$9 \text{ ft} \cdot H_T = 18 \text{ ft} \cdot 6 \text{ ft}$$
$$H_T = \frac{\overset{6}{\cancel{18}} \text{ ft} \cdot \overset{2}{\cancel{6}} \cancel{\text{ft}}}{\underset{\underset{1}{\cancel{3}}}{\cancel{9}} \cancel{\text{ft}}}$$
$$H_T = \mathbf{12 \text{ ft}}$$

g. **About 11 ft**

LESSON 97, MIXED PRACTICE

1. $\$8.95 \times 0.06 = \$0.537 \longrightarrow \$0.54$

   $\$8.95 + \$0.54 = \$9.49$

   $\$10.00 - \$9.49 = \mathbf{\$0.51}$

2. $2{,}000{,}000{,}000{,}000 - 300{,}000{,}000{,}000 = 1{,}700{,}000{,}000{,}000$ **1.7×10^{12}**

3. (a) **90**

   (b) **90**

   (c) **20**

4.

	Case 1	Case 2
Miles	24	*m*
Minutes	60	5

$$\frac{24}{60} = \frac{m}{5}$$
$$60m = 120$$
$$m = \mathbf{2\ miles}$$

5.

	Case 1	Case 2
Yards	3520	*y*
Minutes	5	8

$$\frac{3520}{5} = \frac{y}{8}$$
$$5y = 28{,}160$$
$$y = \mathbf{5632\ yards}$$

6. **Translation of 5 units to the right**

7. 1 yard = 36 inches

$$\frac{3}{4} \times 36 \text{ inches} = \mathbf{27\ inches}$$

8.

	Ratio	Actual Count
Leeks	5	*L*
Radishes	7	420

$$\frac{5}{7} = \frac{L}{420}$$
$$7L = 2100$$
$$L = \mathbf{300\ leeks}$$

9. $$\mathbf{40 = 2.5 \times W_N}$$
$$\frac{40}{2.5} = \frac{2.5 \times W_N}{2.5}$$
$$\mathbf{16} = W_N$$

10. $$\mathbf{40 = W_P \times 60}$$
$$\frac{40}{60} = \frac{W_P \times 60}{60}$$
$$\frac{2}{3} = W_P$$
$$W_P = \frac{2}{3} \times 100\% = \mathbf{66\frac{2}{3}\%}$$

11. $$W_D = 0.4 \times 6$$
$$W_D = \mathbf{2.4}$$

12.

	Percent	Actual Count
Original	100	*O*
+ Change	10	*C*
New	110	$17,600

$$\frac{100}{110} = \frac{O}{\$17{,}600}$$
$$110O = \$1{,}760{,}000$$
$$O = \mathbf{\$16{,}000}$$

13. $$\frac{1.78 + 2.04}{2} = \mathbf{1.91}$$

14. (a) $\mathbf{3\frac{1}{4}}$

   (b) **325%**

   (c) $\mathbf{0.1\overline{6}}$

   (d) $\mathbf{16\frac{2}{3}\%}$

15. $x + y$ ⓧ $x - y$ → $x + y < x - y$ (circled <)

16. $(5.4 \times 6) \times (10^8 \times 10^{-4})$
$= 32.4 \times 10^4 = \mathbf{3.24 \times 10^5}$

17. (a) $C \approx 3.14(20 \text{ mm})$
$C \approx \mathbf{62.8 \text{ mm}}$

(b) $A \approx 3.14(100 \text{ mm}^2)$
$A \approx \mathbf{314 \text{ mm}^2}$

18.

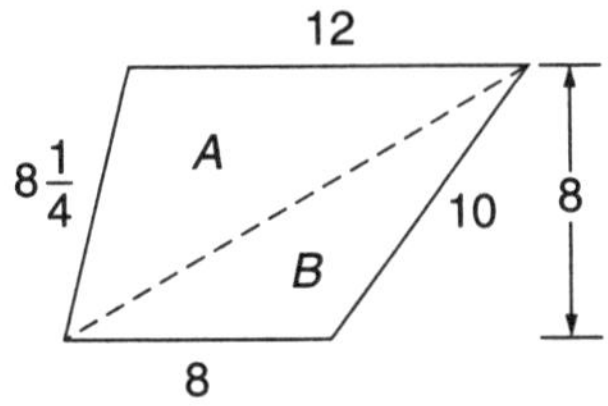

$$\text{Area of triangle } A = \frac{(12 \text{ ft})(8 \text{ ft})}{2} = 48 \text{ ft}^2$$
$$+ \text{ Area of triangle } B = \frac{(8 \text{ ft})(8 \text{ ft})}{2} = 32 \text{ ft}^2$$
$$\text{Area of figure} = \mathbf{80 \text{ ft}^2}$$

19. (a) Area of base $= \dfrac{(1 \text{ m})(2 \text{ m})}{2} = 1 \text{ m}^2$
Volume $= (1 \text{ m}^2)(2 \text{ m}) = \mathbf{2 \text{ m}^3}$

(b) Area of base $= \pi (1 \text{ m}^2) = \pi \text{ m}^2$
Volume $= (\pi \text{ m}^2)(1 \text{ m}) = \boldsymbol{\pi} \mathbf{m^3}$

20. (a) $m\angle X = 180° - (120° + 25°)$
$= \mathbf{35°}$

(b) $m\angle Y = 180° - (90° + 35°) = \mathbf{55°}$

(c) $m\angle A = 180° - (60° + 55°)$
$= \mathbf{65°}$

21. $\dfrac{x}{12 \text{ cm}} = \dfrac{10 \not{\text{cm}}}{15 \not{\text{cm}}}$
$15 \cdot x = 120 \text{ cm}$
$x = \mathbf{8 \text{ cm}}$

22. **See student diagrams.**
$\dfrac{H_P}{3 \text{ ft}} = \dfrac{72 \text{ ft}}{4 \text{ ft}}$
$4 \text{ ft} \times H_P = 3 \text{ ft} \times 72 \text{ ft}$
$H_P = \dfrac{3 \text{ ft} \times \overset{18}{\not{72}} \not{\text{ft}}}{\underset{1}{\not{4}} \not{\text{ft}}}$
$H_P = \mathbf{54 \text{ ft}}$

23. $\dfrac{(40{,}000)(600)}{80} = \mathbf{300{,}000}$

24.
$1.2m + 0.12 = 12$
$1.2m + 0.12 - 0.12 = 12 - 0.12$
$1.2m = 11.88$
$\dfrac{1.2m}{1.2} = \dfrac{11.88}{1.2}$
$m = \mathbf{9.9}$

25.
$1\frac{3}{4}y - 2 = 12$
$1\frac{3}{4}y - 2 + 2 = 12 + 2$
$1\frac{3}{4}y = 14$
$\left(\dfrac{\overset{1}{\not{4}}}{\underset{1}{\not{7}}}\right)\dfrac{\overset{1}{\not{7}}}{\underset{1}{\not{4}}}y = \left(\dfrac{4}{\underset{1}{\not{7}}}\right)\overset{2}{\not{14}}$
$y = \mathbf{8}$

26. $3x - y + 8 + x + y - 2$
$3x + x - y + y + 8 - 2$
$\mathbf{4x + 6}$

27. (a) $3(x - y)$
$\mathbf{3x - 3y}$

(b) $x(y - 3)$
$\mathbf{xy - 3x}$

28. $4\frac{1}{2} \div 1\frac{1}{8} = \dfrac{\overset{1}{\not{9}}}{\underset{1}{\not{2}}} \times \dfrac{\overset{4}{\not{8}}}{\underset{1}{\not{9}}} = 4$

$3\frac{1}{3} \div 4 = \dfrac{10}{3} \times \dfrac{1}{4} = \dfrac{10}{12} = \mathbf{\dfrac{5}{6}}$

29. $\dfrac{(-2) - (+3) + (-4)(-3)}{(-2) + (+3) - (+4)}$

$\dfrac{(-2) - (+3) + (+12)}{(-2) + (+3) - (+4)}$

$\dfrac{(-5) + (12)}{(1) - (+4)}$

$\dfrac{7}{-3}$

$\mathbf{-2\frac{1}{3}}$

30. **A, B**
A, C
B, A
B, C
C, A
C, B

Lesson 98, Lesson Practice

a. $\dfrac{6 \cdot \overset{2}{\cancel{24}}}{\underset{1}{\cancel{12}}} = \textbf{12 feet}$

b. $\dfrac{54}{\underset{3}{\cancel{36}}} \cdot \overset{1}{\cancel{12}} = \textbf{18 inches}$

c. $5 \times 3 = 15$
$7 \times 3 = \mathbf{21}$

d. $3 \times 7 = 21$
$42 \div 7 = \mathbf{6}$

e. $10f = 25$
$f = \dfrac{25}{10}$
$f = \mathbf{2.5}$

f. $(2.5)^2 = \mathbf{6.25}$

g.

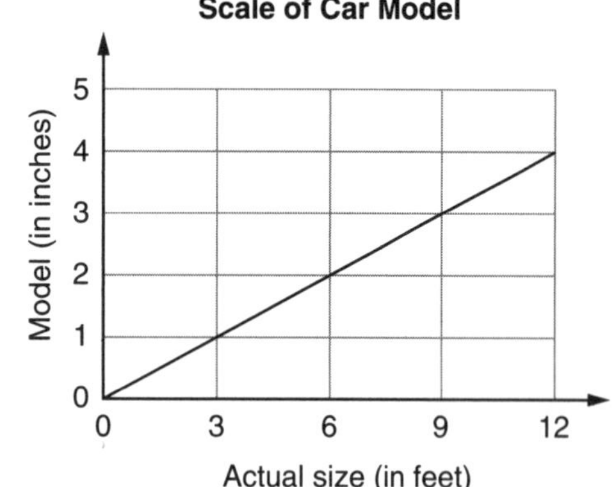

h. **C. 9 ft**

Lesson 98, Mixed Practice

1. (a) $p(2, 6) = \dfrac{1}{6} \cdot \dfrac{1}{6} = \dfrac{1}{36}$

$p(3, 5 \text{ or } 6) = \dfrac{1}{6} \cdot \dfrac{2}{6} = \dfrac{2}{36}$

$p(4, 4 \text{ or } 5 \text{ or } 6) = \dfrac{1}{6} \cdot \dfrac{3}{6} = \dfrac{3}{36}$

$p(5, 3 \text{ or } 4 \text{ or } 5 \text{ or } 6) = \dfrac{1}{6} \cdot \dfrac{4}{6} = \dfrac{4}{36}$

$p(6, 2 \text{ or } 3 \text{ or } 4 \text{ or } 5 \text{ or } 6) = \dfrac{1}{6} \cdot \dfrac{5}{6} = \dfrac{5}{36}$

$\mathbf{\dfrac{15}{36} = \dfrac{5}{12}}$

(b) **0**

2.

	Percent	Actual Count
Original	100	\$45
− Change	20	*C*
New	80	*N*

$\dfrac{100}{80} = \dfrac{\$45}{N}$
$100N = \$3600$
$N = \mathbf{\$36}$

3.

	Case 1	Case 2
Dollars	5	*d*
Kroner	40	100

$\dfrac{5}{40} = \dfrac{d}{100}$
$40d = 500$
$d = \mathbf{\$12.50}$

4.

	Percent	Actual Count
Original	100	*O*
+ Change	25	20
New	125	*N*

$\dfrac{25}{125} = \dfrac{20}{N}$
$25N = 2500$
$N = \textbf{100 students}$

5. $(3x)(x) - (x)(2x)$
$[(3) \cdot x \cdot x] - [x \cdot (2) \cdot x]$
$[(3) \cdot x \cdot x] - [(2) \cdot x \cdot x]$
$3x^2 - 2x^2$
$\mathbf{x^2}$

6. $\dfrac{6(10) + 9(15)}{15}$

$= \dfrac{60 + 135}{15} =$ **13 points per game**

7. (a)
$$\begin{array}{r} 44{,}010 \text{ miles} \\ -\ 43{,}764 \text{ miles} \\ \hline 246 \text{ miles} \end{array}$$

$\dfrac{246 \text{ miles}}{12 \text{ gallons}} =$ **20.5 miles per gallon**

(b) $\dfrac{246 \text{ miles}}{5 \text{ hours}} =$ **49.2 miles per hour**

8. $\mathbf{\dfrac{3}{5} \times W_N = 60}$

$$\left(\frac{\overset{1}{\cancel{5}}}{\underset{1}{\cancel{3}}}\right)\left(\frac{\overset{1}{\cancel{3}}}{\underset{1}{\cancel{5}}} \times W_N\right) = \left(\frac{5}{\underset{1}{\cancel{3}}}\right)\overset{20}{\cancel{60}}$$

$W_N =$ **100**

9.

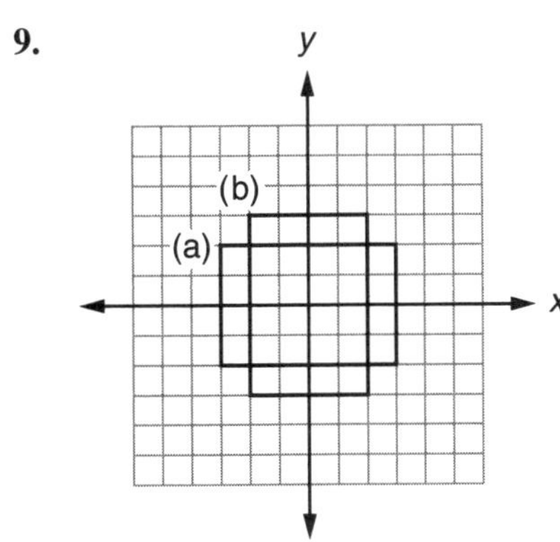

(a) **(3, −2)**

(b) **(2, 3), (2, −3), (−2, −3), (−2, 3)**

10. $\dfrac{2}{6} = \mathbf{\dfrac{1}{3}}$

11. $a = 9, \quad 9^2 =$ **81**

12. $\mathbf{40 = W_P \times 250}$

$\dfrac{40}{250} = \dfrac{W_P \times 250}{250}$

$\dfrac{4}{25} = W_P$

$W_P = \dfrac{4}{25} \times 100\% =$ **16%**

13. $\mathbf{0.4 \times W_N = 60}$

$\dfrac{0.4 \times W_N}{0.4} = \dfrac{60}{0.4}$

$W_N =$ **150**

14.

	Percent	Actual Count
Original	100	\$40
+ Change	60	C
New	160	N

$\dfrac{100}{160} = \dfrac{\$40}{N}$

$100N = \$6400$

$N =$ **\$64**

15. $2\frac{1}{8} - 1\frac{3}{8} = \frac{17}{8} - \frac{11}{8} = \frac{6}{8} = \mathbf{\frac{3}{4}}$ **inch**

16.

0 1 2 3 4

17. (a) $\mathbf{\dfrac{7}{500}}$

(b) **0.014**

18. $(1.4 \times 10^{-6})(5 \times 10^{4})$

$\mathbf{7.0 \times 10^{-2}}$

19. $y = -2(3)$

$y =$ **−6;**

$y = -2(0)$

$y =$ **0;**

$y = -2(-2)$

$y =$ **4**

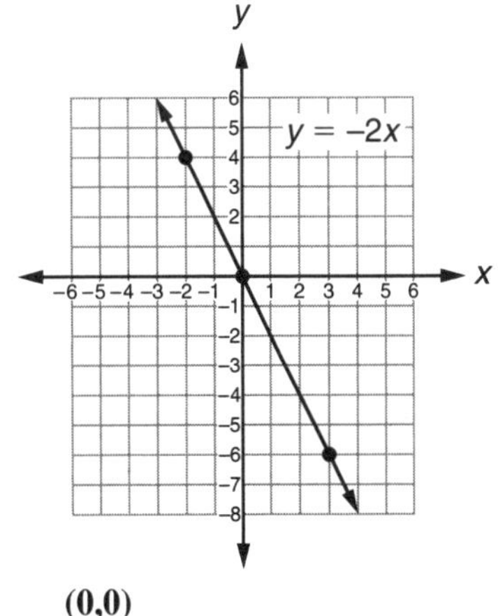

(0,0)

20. (a) $C \approx 3.14(2 \text{ ft})$

$C \approx$ **6.28 ft**

(b) $A \approx 3.14(1 \text{ ft}^2)$

$A \approx$ $\mathbf{3.14 \text{ ft}^2}$

21. **See student work; 40°.**

22.
$$\frac{x}{30} = \frac{20}{50}$$
$$50x = 600$$
$$\mathbf{x = 12\text{ in.}}$$
$$\frac{y}{16} = \frac{50}{20}$$
$$20y = 800$$
$$\mathbf{y = 40\text{ in.}}$$
$$\textbf{Area} = \frac{(16\text{ in.})(12\text{ in.})}{2} = \mathbf{96\text{ in.}^2}$$

23.
$$20f = 50$$
$$f = \frac{50}{20}$$
$$f = \mathbf{2.5}$$

24.
$$-\frac{3}{5}m + 8 = 20$$
$$-\frac{3}{5}m + 8 - 8 = 20 - 8$$
$$-\frac{3}{5}m = 12$$
$$\left(-\frac{\overset{1}{\cancel{5}}}{\underset{1}{\cancel{3}}}\right)\left(-\frac{\overset{1}{\cancel{3}}}{\underset{1}{\cancel{5}}}m\right) = \left(-\frac{5}{\underset{1}{\cancel{3}}}\right)\cancel{12}^{4}$$
$$m = \mathbf{-20}$$

25.
$$0.3x - 2.7 = 9$$
$$0.3x - 2.7 + 2.7 = 9 + 2.7$$
$$0.3x = 11.7$$
$$\frac{0.3x}{0.3} = \frac{11.7}{0.3}$$
$$x = \mathbf{39}$$

26.
$$\sqrt{5^3 - 5^2} = \sqrt{125 - 25} = \sqrt{100}$$
$$= \mathbf{10}$$

27.

$\overset{0}{\cancel{1}}$ gal → (4 qt) $\overset{0}{\cancel{1}}$ qt → (2 pt)
− 1 qt 1 pt →

$\overset{0}{\cancel{1}}$ gal $\overset{4}{\overset{0}{\cancel{1}}}$ qt 2 pt
− 1 qt 1 pt
3 qt 1 pt

28.
$$(0.25)(1.25 - 1.2)$$
$$= (0.25)(0.05) = \mathbf{0.0125}$$

29.
$$7\frac{1}{3} - \left(1\frac{3}{4} \div 3\frac{1}{2}\right)$$
$$= 7\frac{1}{3} - \left(\frac{7}{4} \div \frac{7}{2}\right) = 7\frac{1}{3} - \left(\frac{\overset{1}{\cancel{7}}}{\underset{2}{\cancel{4}}} \times \frac{\overset{1}{\cancel{2}}}{\underset{1}{\cancel{7}}}\right)$$
$$= 7\frac{1}{3} - \frac{1}{2} = 7\frac{2}{6} - \frac{3}{6} = 6\frac{8}{6} - \frac{3}{6}$$
$$= \mathbf{6\frac{5}{6}}$$

30.
$$\frac{(-2)(3) - (3)(-4)}{(-2)(-3) - (4)}$$
$$\frac{(-6) - (-12)}{(6) - (4)}$$
$$\frac{6}{2}$$
$$\mathbf{3}$$

LESSON 99, LESSON PRACTICE

a.

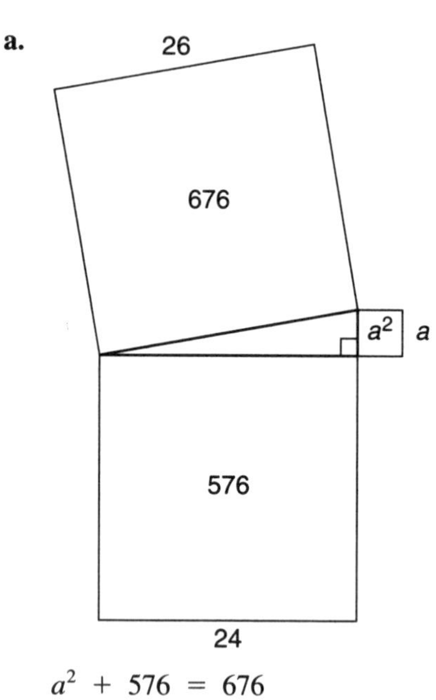

$$a^2 + 576 = 676$$
$$a^2 = 100$$
$$a = \mathbf{10}$$

b.

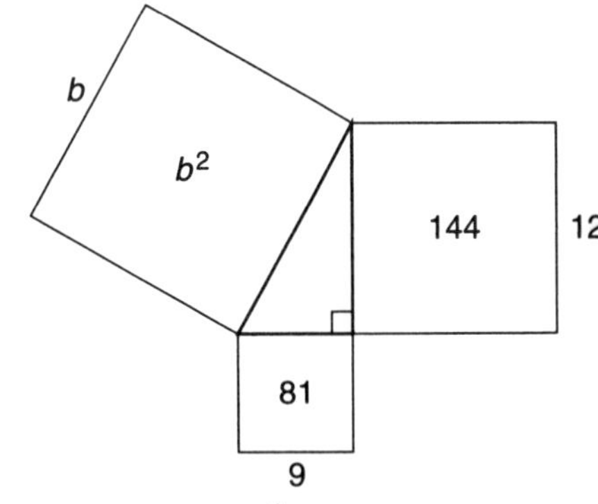

$$\begin{aligned} 81 + 144 &= b^2 \\ 225 &= b^2 \\ \mathbf{15} &= b \end{aligned}$$

c.

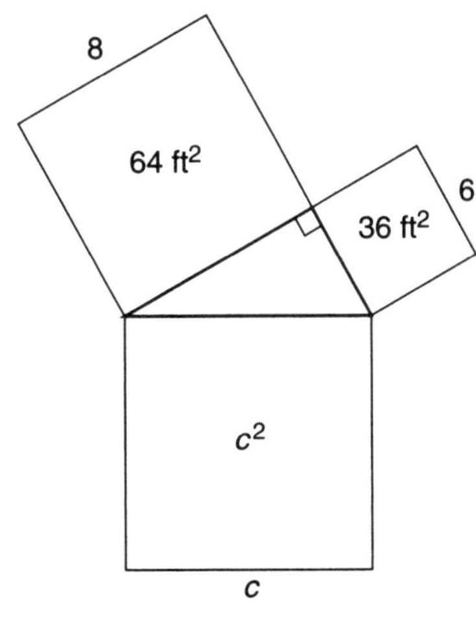

$$\begin{aligned} 64\text{ ft}^2 + 36\text{ ft}^2 &= c^2 \\ 100 &= c^2 \\ 10 &= c \\ \text{Perimeter} &= 8\text{ ft} + 6\text{ ft} + 10\text{ ft} \\ &= \mathbf{24\ ft} \end{aligned}$$

Lesson 99, Mixed Practice

1.

$$\begin{array}{r} \$15.00 \\ \times \quad 0.15 \\ \hline \mathbf{\$2.25} \end{array}$$

2.

$$\begin{array}{r} 0.0\,0\,2\,\overset{4}{\cancel{5}}{}^{1}0\,0 \\ -\ 0.0\,0\,0\,0\,2\,0 \\ \hline 0.0\,0\,2\,4\,8\,0 \end{array} \qquad \mathbf{2.48 \times 10^{-3}}$$

3. (a) $\dfrac{4(30) + 7(31) + 29}{12} = \mathbf{30.5\ days}$

(b) **31 days**

(c) **31 days**

(d) **2 days**

4. 2 pounds = 32 ounces

$$\frac{\$2.72}{32\text{ ounces}} = \frac{\$0.085}{1\text{ ounce}}$$

$$\frac{\$3.60}{48\text{ ounces}} = \frac{\$0.075}{1\text{ ounce}}$$

$$\begin{array}{r} \$0.085 \\ -\ \$0.075 \\ \hline \$0.01 \end{array}$$

1¢ more per ounce

5.

	Case 1	Case 2
Pounds	80	300
Price	\$96	p

$$\begin{aligned} \frac{80}{\$96} &= \frac{300}{p} \\ 80p &= \$28{,}800 \\ p &= \mathbf{\$360} \end{aligned}$$

6.

	Ratio	Actual Count
Stalactites	9	C
Stalagmites	5	G
Total	14	1260

$$\begin{aligned} \frac{5}{14} &= \frac{G}{1260} \\ 14G &= 6300 \\ G &= \mathbf{450\ stalagmites} \end{aligned}$$

7. $\dfrac{5}{\underset{1}{\cancel{8}}}(\overset{2}{\cancel{16}}\text{ ounces}) = \mathbf{10\ ounces}$

8. (a) $\mathbf{0.1 \times W_N = 20}$

$$\begin{aligned} \frac{0.1 \times W_N}{0.1} &= \frac{20}{0.1} \\ W_N &= \mathbf{200} \end{aligned}$$

(b) $\mathbf{20 = W_P \times 60}$

$$\begin{aligned} \frac{20}{60} &= \frac{W_P \times 60}{60} \\ \frac{1}{3} &= W_P \\ W_P &= \frac{1}{3} \times 100\% = \mathbf{33\frac{1}{3}\%} \end{aligned}$$

9. (a) **Right triangle**

(b) **Equilateral triangle**

(c) **Isosceles triangle**

10.

	Percent	Actual Count
Original	100	\$3.40
− Change	20	C
New	80	N

$$\frac{100}{80} = \frac{\$3.40}{N}$$
$$100N = \$272$$
$$N = \mathbf{\$2.72}$$

11. $100\% - 20\% = \mathbf{80\%}$

12. $\text{Area} = \dfrac{(6 \text{ units})(3 \text{ units})}{2} = \mathbf{9 \text{ units}^2}$

13.

	Scale	Measure
Model	1	8
Object	60	m

$$\frac{1}{60} = \frac{8}{m}$$
$$m = \mathbf{480 \text{ inches}}$$
$$\overset{40}{\cancel{480}}\ \cancel{\text{inches}} \cdot \frac{1 \text{ foot}}{\cancel{12}\ \cancel{\text{inches}}} = \mathbf{40 \text{ feet}}$$

14. (a) $\mathbf{1.\overline{3}}$

(b) $\mathbf{133\frac{1}{3}\%}$

(c) $\mathbf{\dfrac{1}{75}}$

(d) $\mathbf{0.01\overline{3}}$

15. (a) $(ax^2)(-2ax)(-a^2)$
$a \cdot x \cdot x \cdot (-2) \cdot a \cdot x \cdot (-1) \cdot a \cdot a$
$(-2)(-1) \cdot a \cdot a \cdot a \cdot a \cdot x \cdot x \cdot x$
$\mathbf{2a^4x^3}$

(b) $\dfrac{1}{2}\pi + \dfrac{2}{3}\pi - \pi = \dfrac{3}{6}\pi + \dfrac{4}{6}\pi - \dfrac{6}{6}\pi$
$= \dfrac{7}{6}\pi - \dfrac{6}{6}\pi = \mathbf{\dfrac{1}{6}\pi}$

16. $(8.1 \times 9) \times (10^{-6} \times 10^{10}) = 72.9 \times 10^4$
$= \mathbf{7.29 \times 10^5}$

17. $\sqrt{(15)^2 - (12)^2} = \sqrt{225 - 144}$
$= \sqrt{81} = \mathbf{9}$

18. $5^2 + c^2 = 13^2$
$25 + c^2 = 169$
$c^2 = 169 - 25$
$c^2 = 144$
$c = \mathbf{12}$

19. Area of base $\approx 3.14(100 \text{ cm}^2)$
$\approx 314 \text{ cm}^2$
Volume $\approx (314 \text{ cm}^2)(10 \text{ cm}) = \mathbf{3140 \text{ cm}^3}$

20. (a) $m\angle X = 180° - 138° = \mathbf{42°}$

(b) $m\angle Y = 180° - (100° + 42°) = \mathbf{38°}$

(c) $m\angle Z = 180° - (90° + 38°) = \mathbf{52°}$

21. (a) $\dfrac{x}{6} = \dfrac{12}{8}$
$8x = 72$
$x = \mathbf{9 \text{ inches}}$

(b) $6f = 9$
$f = \dfrac{9}{6}$
$f = \mathbf{1.5}$

(c) $(1.5)(1.5) = \mathbf{2.25 \text{ times}}$

22. $\dfrac{(40{,}000)(400)}{80} = \mathbf{200{,}000}$

23.
$4n + 1.64 = 2$
$4n + 1.64 - 1.64 = 2 - 1.64$
$4n = 0.36$
$\dfrac{4n}{4} = \dfrac{0.36}{4}$
$n = \mathbf{0.09}$

24.
$3\dfrac{1}{3}x - 1 = 49$
$3\dfrac{1}{3}x - 1 + 1 = 49 + 1$
$3\dfrac{1}{3}x = 50$
$\left(\dfrac{3}{10}\right)\left(\dfrac{10}{3}x\right) = \left(\dfrac{3}{10}\right)50$
$x = \mathbf{15}$

25. $\dfrac{17}{25} = \dfrac{m}{75}$
$25m = 1275$
$m = \mathbf{51}$

26. $3^3 + 4^2 - \sqrt{225}$
$= 27 + 16 - 15 = \mathbf{28}$

27. $\sqrt{225} - 15^0 + 10^{-1} = 15 - 1 + \dfrac{1}{10}$
$= 14 + \dfrac{1}{10} = \mathbf{14\dfrac{1}{10}}$ or $\mathbf{14.1}$

28. $\left(3\frac{1}{3}\right)\left(\frac{3}{4}\right)\left(\frac{40}{1}\right)$

$= \left(\frac{10}{\cancel{3}_1}\right)\left(\frac{\cancel{3}^1}{\cancel{4}_1}\right)\left(\frac{\cancel{40}^{10}}{1}\right) = \mathbf{100}$

29. $\dfrac{-12 - (6)(-3)}{(-12) - (-6) + (3)}$

$\dfrac{-12 - (-18)}{(-6) + 3}$

$\dfrac{6}{-3}$

$\mathbf{-2}$

30. $3(x - 2) = 3(x) - 3(2) = \mathbf{3x - 6}$

Lesson 100, Lesson Practice

a. **2 and 3**

b. **8 and 9**

c. **26 and 27**

d. $x^2 = 1^2 + 1^2$
$x^2 = 1 + 1$
$x^2 = 2$
$x = \mathbf{\sqrt{2}}$

e. $2^2 = 1^2 + y^2$
$4 = 1 + y^2$
$3 = y^2$
$\mathbf{\sqrt{3}} = y$

f.

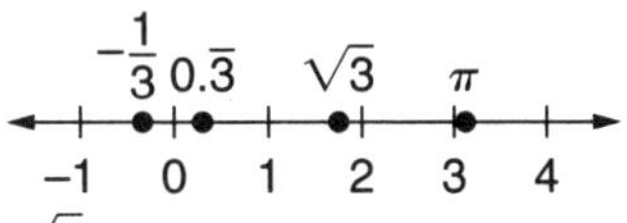

$\mathbf{\sqrt{3}, \pi}$

Lesson 100, Mixed Practice

1. $2.5(\$2.60) + 2(\$1.49)$
$= \$6.50 + \$2.98 = \$9.48$

$\$20.00 - \$9.48 = \mathbf{\$10.52}$

2. (a) $p(6) = \frac{1}{5}$

$p(4) = \frac{1}{5}$

$\frac{1}{5} + \frac{1}{5} = \mathbf{\frac{2}{5}}$

(b) $p(3, 3 \text{ or } 5 \text{ or } 7) = \frac{1}{5} \cdot \frac{3}{5} = \frac{3}{25}$

$p(5, 3 \text{ or } 5 \text{ or } 7) = \frac{1}{5} \cdot \frac{3}{5} = \frac{3}{25}$

$p(7, 3 \text{ or } 5 \text{ or } 7) = \frac{1}{5} \cdot \frac{3}{5} = \frac{3}{25}$

$\frac{3}{25} + \frac{3}{25} + \frac{3}{25} = \mathbf{\frac{9}{25}}$

3. Average $= (1 + 2 + 3 + 4 + 5 + 6 + 7 + 8 + 9 + 10) \div 10$
$= \frac{55}{10} = \mathbf{5.5}$

4. $375 \cancel{\text{miles}} \cdot \frac{1 \text{ hour}}{50 \cancel{\text{miles}}} = \mathbf{7\frac{1}{2} \text{ hours}}$

5.

	Case 1	Case 2
Kilometers	300	500
Hours	4	*h*

$\frac{300}{4} = \frac{500}{h}$
$300h = 2000$
$h = 6\frac{2}{3}$ hours

$6\frac{2}{3}$ hours $=$ **6 hours 40 minutes**

6.

	Ratio	Actual Count
Winners	1	*W*
Losers	15	*L*
Total	16	800

$\frac{1}{16} = \frac{W}{800}$
$16W = 800$
$W = $ **50 winners**

7.

	Percent	Actual Count
Original	100	*O*
– Change	30	*C*
New	70	350

$\frac{100}{70} = \frac{O}{350}$
$70O = 35{,}000$
$O = \mathbf{500}$

8.
$$\frac{3}{4} \cdot n = 36$$
$$\left(\frac{\overset{1}{\cancel{4}}}{\underset{1}{\cancel{3}}}\right)\left(\frac{\overset{1}{\cancel{3}}}{\underset{1}{\cancel{4}}}n\right) = \left(\frac{4}{\underset{1}{\cancel{3}}}\right)\overset{12}{\cancel{36}}$$
$$n = 48$$
$$\frac{1}{\underset{1}{\cancel{2}}} \cdot \overset{24}{\cancel{48}} = \mathbf{24}$$

9. (a) $\mathbf{300 = 0.06 \times W_N}$
$$\frac{300}{0.06} = \frac{0.06 \times W_N}{0.06}$$
$$\mathbf{5000} = W_N$$

(b) $\mathbf{20 = W_P \times 10}$
$$\frac{20}{10} = \frac{W_P \times 10}{10}$$
$$2 = W_P$$
$$W_P = 2 \times 100\% = \mathbf{200\%}$$

10.

$40.00	$40.00
× 0.065	+ $2.60
$2.60	**$42.60**

11.
$$x(x + 3) = x(x) + x(3)$$
$$= \mathbf{x^2 + 3x}$$

12.

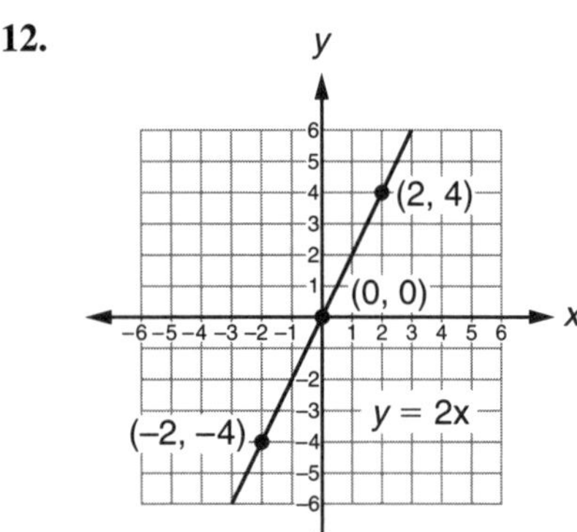

Another point from the 3rd quadrant could be (−1, −2) or (−3, −6).

13. (a) $\mathbf{2\frac{1}{2}}$ **inches**

(b) $120f = 5$
$$f = \frac{5}{120}$$
$$f = \mathbf{\frac{1}{24}}$$

(c) **14 feet**

14. (a) $2f = 6$
$$f = \frac{6}{2}$$
$$f = \mathbf{3}$$

(b) $(3)(3) =$ **9 times**

(c) $3^3 =$ **27 times**

15. **Insufficient information**

16. (a) $\mathbf{\frac{18}{25}}$

(b) **0.72**

17.
$$(4.5 \times 6) \times (10^6 \times 10^3) = 27 \times 10^9$$
$$= \mathbf{2.7 \times 10^{10}}$$

18. (a) $6^2 = 36, 7^2 = 49$
6 and 7

(b) $4^2 = 16, 5^2 = 25$
4 and 5

19. (a) $C \approx \frac{22}{\underset{1}{\cancel{7}}}(\overset{2}{\cancel{14}} \text{ in.})$
$C \approx$ **44 in.**

(b) $A \approx \frac{22}{\underset{1}{\cancel{7}}}(\overset{7}{\cancel{49}} \text{ in.}^2)$
$A \approx$ **154 in.²**

20.
$$15^2 + a^2 = 17^2$$
$$225 + a^2 = 289$$
$$a^2 = 289 - 225$$
$$a^2 = 64$$
$$a = \mathbf{8\ cm}$$

21.
$$\text{Area of base} = \frac{(3\text{ cm})(4\text{ cm})}{2}$$
$$= 6\text{ cm}^2$$
$$\text{Volume} = (6\text{ cm}^2)(6\text{ cm}) = \mathbf{36\ cm^3}$$

22.
$$\text{Area of base} \approx 3.14(4\text{ cm}^2)$$
$$\approx 12.56\text{ cm}^2$$
$$\text{Volume} \approx (12.56\text{ cm}^2)(10\text{ cm})$$
$$\approx \mathbf{125.6\ cm^3}$$

23.
$$m\angle a = 180° - 48° = \mathbf{132°}$$
$$m\angle b = 180° - 132° = \mathbf{48°}$$
$$m\angle c = 180° - (90° + 48°) = \mathbf{42°}$$

24.
$$-4\frac{1}{2}x + 8^0 = 4^3$$
$$-4\frac{1}{2}x + 1 - 1 = 64 - 1$$
$$-4\frac{1}{2}x = 63$$
$$\left(-\frac{2}{9}\right)\left(-\frac{9}{2}x\right) = \left(-\frac{2}{9}\right)63$$
$$x = \mathbf{-14}$$

25.
$$\frac{15}{w} = \frac{45}{3.3}$$
$$(45)w = 15(3.3)$$
$$\frac{45w}{45} = \frac{49.5}{45}$$
$$w = \mathbf{1.1}$$

26. $\sqrt{6^2 + 8^2} = \sqrt{36 + 64} = \sqrt{100} = \mathbf{10}$

27.
$$3\frac{1}{3}\left(7\frac{2}{10} \div \frac{3}{5}\right) = 3\frac{1}{3}\left(\frac{\cancelto{12}{\cancel{72}}}{\cancelto{1}{\cancel{10}}} \times \frac{\cancelto{1}{5}}{\cancelto{1}{3}}\right)$$
$$= 3\frac{1}{3}(12) = \frac{10}{\cancelto{1}{3}}(\cancelto{4}{12}) = \mathbf{40}$$

28. $8\frac{5}{6} - 2\frac{1}{2} - 1\frac{1}{3}$
$$= 8\frac{5}{6} - 2\frac{3}{6} - 1\frac{2}{6} = 6\frac{2}{6} - 1\frac{2}{6}$$
$$= \mathbf{5}$$

29.
$$\frac{|-18| - (2)(-3)}{(-3) + (-2) - (-4)}$$
$$\frac{18 - (-6)}{(-5) - (-4)}$$
$$\frac{24}{-1}$$
$$\mathbf{-24}$$

30.

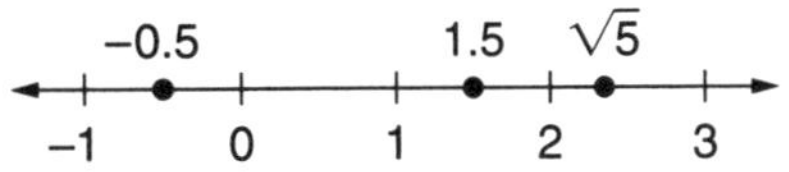

LESSON 101, LESSON PRACTICE

a.
$$\mathbf{3x + 6 = 30}$$
$$3x = 24$$
$$x = \frac{24}{3}$$
$$x = \mathbf{8}$$

b.
$$\mathbf{\frac{1}{2}x - 10 = 30}$$
$$\frac{1}{2}x = 40$$
$$\left(\frac{2}{1}\right)\left(\frac{1}{2}x\right) = \left(\frac{2}{1}\right)40$$
$$x = \mathbf{80}$$

c.
$$\mathbf{3x + 2x = 90°}$$
$$5x = 90°$$
$$x = \frac{90°}{5}$$
$$x = 18°$$
$$2(18°) = \mathbf{36°}$$

d.
$$\mathbf{x + 2x + 3x = 180°}$$
$$6x = 180°$$
$$x = \frac{180°}{6}$$
$$x = \mathbf{30°}$$
$$2x = 2(30°) = \mathbf{60°}$$
$$3x = 3(30°) = \mathbf{90°}$$

LESSON 101, MIXED PRACTICE

1. (a) **11.9**

(b) **11.8 and 11.9**

(c) **0.7**

2. $6(3.75) = **$22.50**

3.

	Case 1	Case 2
Flour	3	15
Eggs	2	*e*

$$\frac{3}{2} = \frac{15}{e}$$
$$3e = 30$$
$$e = \textbf{10 eggs}$$

4.

	Case 1	Case 2
Words	48	*w*
Seconds	60	90

$$\frac{48}{60} = \frac{w}{90}$$
$$60w = 4320$$
$$w = \textbf{72 words}$$

5.

	Percent	Actual Count
Scored 100 percent	40	10
Did not score 100 percent	60	N
Total	100	T

$$\frac{40}{100} = \frac{10}{T}$$
$$40T = 1000$$
$$T = \textbf{25 students}$$

6.

	Percent	Actual Count
Original	100	\$24
− Change	40	C
New	60	N

$$\frac{100}{60} = \frac{\$24}{N}$$
$$100N = \$1440$$
$$N = \textbf{\$14.40}$$

7. $3(x - 4) - x$
$3x - 12 - x$
$3x - x - 12$
$\mathbf{2x - 12}$

8. $3 \text{ gallons} \cdot \frac{4 \text{ quarts}}{1 \text{ gallon}} \cdot \frac{2 \text{ pints}}{1 \text{ quart}} = \textbf{24 pints}$

9.

24 games

$\frac{5}{6}$ won (20).	4 games
	4 games
	4 games
	4 games
	4 games
$\frac{1}{6}$ lost.	4 games

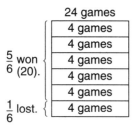

(a) $20 \div 5 = 4$, $6(4 \text{ games}) = \textbf{24 games}$

(b) $\frac{\text{won}}{\text{lost}} = \frac{20}{4} = \mathbf{\frac{5}{1}}$

10. **14 and 15**

11. $w \text{ ⓒ } m$ → $w < m$ (circled)

12.

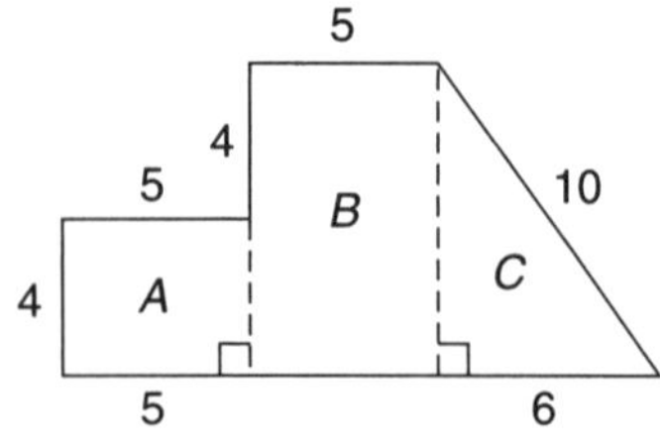

$$\begin{aligned} \text{Area } A &= (4 \text{ cm})(5 \text{ cm}) = 20 \text{ cm}^2 \\ \text{Area } B &= (5 \text{ cm})(8 \text{ cm}) = 40 \text{ cm}^2 \\ + \text{ Area } C &= \frac{(6 \text{ cm})(8 \text{ cm})}{2} = 24 \text{ cm}^2 \\ \hline \text{Area of figure} &= \mathbf{84 \text{ cm}^2} \end{aligned}$$

13. $\mathbf{6n - 3 = 45}$
$6n = 48$
$n = \mathbf{8}$

14. $(8 \times 4) \times (10^8 \times 10^{-2}) = 32 \times 10^6$
$= \mathbf{3.2 \times 10^7}$

15. (a) $\mathbf{\frac{1}{50}}$

(b) **2%**

(c) $\mathbf{\frac{1}{500}}$

(d) **0.002**

16. $y = 2(-1) + 1$
$y = -2 + 1$
$y = \mathbf{-1;}$
$y = 2(0) + 1$
$y = 0 + 1$
$y = \mathbf{1;}$
$y = 2(1) + 1$
$y = 2 + 1$
$y = \mathbf{3;}$
$y = 2(2) + 1$
$y = 4 + 1$
$y = \mathbf{5}$

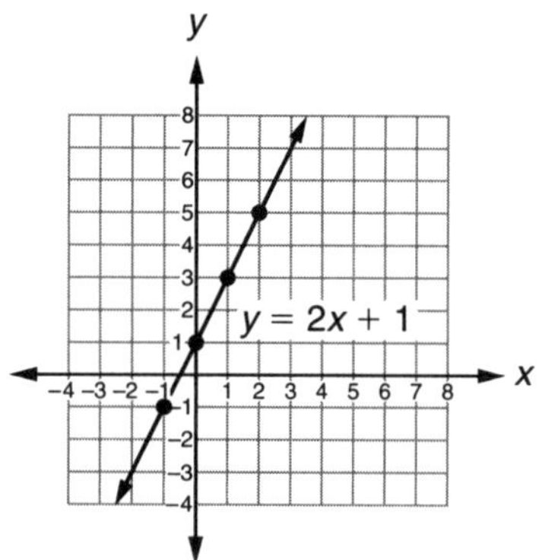

17. (a) Area of base $= (4 \text{ in.})(4 \text{ in.}) = 16 \text{ in.}^2$
Volume $= (16 \text{ in.}^2)(4 \text{ in.}) = \mathbf{64 \text{ in.}^3}$

(b) Surface area $= 6(16 \text{ in.}^2) = \mathbf{96 \text{ in.}^2}$

18. (a) $C = \pi(18 \text{ cm})$
$C = \mathbf{18\pi \text{ cm}}$

(b) $A = \pi(81 \text{ cm}^2)$
$A = \mathbf{81\pi \text{ cm}^2}$

19. **1 to 1**

20.
$$2x + x = 90°$$
$$3x = 90°$$
$$x = \frac{90°}{3}$$
$$x = \mathbf{30°}$$
$$2x = 2(30°) = \mathbf{60°}$$

21. (a)
$$9\overline{)1.2300} = 0.1366\ldots$$
$$\begin{array}{r} 9 \\ \hline 33 \\ 27 \\ \hline 60 \\ 54 \\ \hline 60 \\ 54 \\ \hline 6 \end{array}$$

$0.1366\ldots = \mathbf{0.13\overline{6}}$

(b) 0.1366 . . . rounded to three decimal places is **0.137**

22.
$$(AB)^2 = (9 \text{ cm})^2 + (12 \text{ cm})^2$$
$$(AB)^2 = 81 \text{ cm}^2 + 144 \text{ cm}^2$$
$$(AB)^2 = 225 \text{ cm}^2$$
$$AB = \mathbf{15\ cm}$$

23. (a)
$$\text{Perimeter} = 2(9 \text{ cm}) + 2(12 \text{ cm}) + 2(15 \text{ cm})$$
$$= 18 \text{ cm} + 24 \text{ cm} + 30 \text{ cm}$$
$$= \mathbf{72\ cm}$$

(b)
$$\text{Area} = \frac{(18 \text{ cm})(24 \text{ cm})}{2} = \mathbf{216\ cm^2}$$

24.
$$p(B, B) = \frac{4}{10} \cdot \frac{3}{9} = \frac{12}{90} = \mathbf{\frac{2}{15}}$$

25.
$$3\frac{1}{7}d = 88$$
$$\left(\frac{7}{22}\right)\frac{22}{7}d = \left(\frac{7}{22}\right)88$$
$$d = \mathbf{28}$$

26.
$$3x + 20 \geq 14$$
$$3x + 20 - 20 \geq 14 - 20$$
$$3x \geq -6$$
$$\frac{3x}{3} \geq \frac{-6}{3}$$
$$\mathbf{x \geq -2}$$

$x \geq -2$

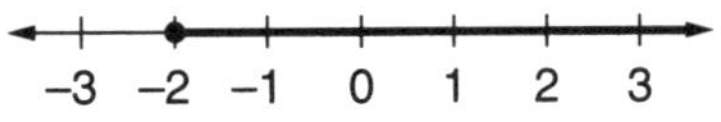

27.
$$5^2 + (3^3 - \sqrt{81})$$
$$= 25 + (27 - 9) = 25 + 18 = \mathbf{43}$$

28.
$$3x + 2(x - 1)$$
$$3x + 2x - 2$$
$$\mathbf{5x - 2}$$

29.
$$\left(4\frac{4}{9}\right)\left(2\frac{7}{10}\right)\left(1\frac{1}{3}\right) = \frac{\cancel{40}^{\,4}}{\cancel{9}_{\,1}} \cdot \frac{\cancel{27}^{\,\cancel{3}^{\,1}}}{\cancel{10}_{\,1}} \cdot \frac{4}{\cancel{3}_{\,1}} = \mathbf{16}$$

30.
$$(-2)(-3) - (-4)(-5)$$
$$(6) - (20)$$
$$\mathbf{-14}$$

Lesson 102, Lesson Practice

a. **∠*s* and ∠*u*, ∠*t* and ∠*v*, ∠*w* and ∠*y*, ∠*x* and ∠*z***

b. **∠*t* and ∠*y*, ∠*x* and ∠*u***

c. **∠*s* and ∠*z*, ∠*w* and ∠*v***

d. $\mathbf{m\angle t = m\angle v = m\angle y = 80°}$
$\mathbf{m\angle s = m\angle u = m\angle x = m\angle z = 100°}$

e.
$$3w - 10 + w = 90$$
$$4w - 10 = 90$$
$$4w - 10 + 10 = 90 + 10$$
$$4w = 100$$
$$w = \frac{100}{4}$$
$$w = \mathbf{25}$$

f.
$$x + x + 10 + 2x - 10 = 180$$
$$4x + 10 - 10 = 180$$
$$4x = 180$$
$$x = \frac{180}{4}$$
$$x = \mathbf{45}$$

g.
$$3y + 5 = y - 25$$
$$3y + 5 - y = y - 25 - y$$
$$2y + 5 = -25$$
$$2y + 5 - 5 = -25 - 5$$
$$2y = -30$$
$$y = \frac{-30}{2}$$
$$y = \mathbf{-15}$$

h.
$$\begin{aligned} 4n - 5 &= 2n + 3 \\ 4n - 5 - 2n &= 2n + 3 - 2n \\ 2n - 5 &= 3 \\ 2n - 5 + 5 &= 3 + 5 \\ 2n &= 8 \\ n &= \frac{8}{2} \\ n &= \mathbf{4} \end{aligned}$$

i.
$$\begin{aligned} 3x - 2(x - 4) &= 32 \\ 3x - 2x + 8 &= 32 \\ x + 8 &= 32 \\ x + 8 - 8 &= 32 - 8 \\ x &= \mathbf{24} \end{aligned}$$

j.
$$\begin{aligned} 3x &= 2(x - 4) \\ 3x &= 2x - 8 \\ 3x - 2x &= 2x - 8 - 2x \\ x &= \mathbf{-8} \end{aligned}$$

Lesson 102, Mixed Practice

1. (a)
$$\begin{aligned} p(1, 4) &= \frac{1}{6} \cdot \frac{1}{6} = \frac{1}{36} \\ p(4, 1) &= \frac{1}{6} \cdot \frac{1}{6} = \frac{1}{36} \\ p(2, 3) &= \frac{1}{6} \cdot \frac{1}{6} = \frac{1}{36} \\ p(3, 2) &= \frac{1}{6} \cdot \frac{1}{6} = \frac{1}{36} \end{aligned}$$
$$\frac{1}{36} + \frac{1}{36} + \frac{1}{36} + \frac{1}{36} = \mathbf{\frac{4}{36}} = \mathbf{\frac{1}{9}}$$

(b) **8 to 1**

2.
$$\begin{aligned} \mathbf{3x - 12} &= \mathbf{36} \\ 3x - 12 + 12 &= 36 + 12 \\ 3x &= 48 \\ x &= \frac{48}{3} \\ x &= \mathbf{16} \end{aligned}$$

3. (a) $\frac{360°}{10} = \mathbf{36°}$

(b) $180° - 36° = \mathbf{144°}$

4.

	Ratio	Actual Count
Youths	3	Y
Adults	7	A
Total	10	4500

$$\begin{aligned} \frac{7}{10} &= \frac{A}{4500} \\ 10A &= 31{,}500 \\ A &= \mathbf{3150\ adults} \end{aligned}$$

5.

	Case 1	Case 2
Over	2	8
Up	1	u

$$\begin{aligned} \frac{2}{1} &= \frac{8}{u} \\ 2u &= 8 \\ u &= \mathbf{4} \end{aligned}$$

6.

	Percent	Actual Count
People invited	100	40
People who came	80	P

$$\begin{aligned} \frac{100}{80} &= \frac{40}{P} \\ 100P &= 3200 \\ P &= 32 \text{ people came} \\ 40 - 32 &= \mathbf{8\ people} \end{aligned}$$

7.

	Percent	Actual Count
Sale price	60	\$24
Regular price	100	R

$$\begin{aligned} \frac{60}{100} &= \frac{\$24}{R} \\ 60R &= \$2400 \\ R &= \mathbf{\$40} \end{aligned}$$

8.
$$\begin{aligned} \mathbf{2n + 3} &= \mathbf{-13} \\ 2n + 3 - 3 &= -13 - 3 \\ 2n &= -16 \\ n &= \frac{-16}{2} \\ n &= \mathbf{-8} \end{aligned}$$

9.
$$\begin{aligned} (3x - 25) + (x + 5) &= 180° \\ 4x - 20 &= 180° \\ 4x - 20 + 20 &= 180° + 20 \\ 4x &= 200° \\ x &= \frac{200°}{4} \\ x &= 50° \end{aligned}$$
$$\mathbf{x + 5} = 50° + 5 = \mathbf{55°}$$
$$\mathbf{3x - 25} = 3(50°) - 25 = \mathbf{125°}$$

10.

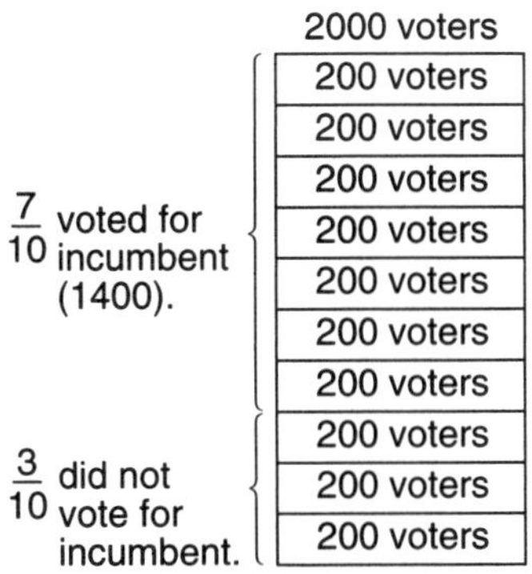

2000 voters

$\frac{7}{10}$ voted for incumbent (1400).	200 voters
	200 voters
	200 voters
	200 voters
	200 voters
	200 voters
	200 voters
$\frac{3}{10}$ did not vote for incumbent.	200 voters
	200 voters
	200 voters

(a) $1400 \div 7 = 200$
$10(200 \text{ voters}) = \mathbf{2000 \text{ voters}}$

(b) **30%**

11. $(3) + (3)(-2) - (3)(-2)$
$3 + (-6) - (-6)$
$\mathbf{3}$

12. $a \text{ Ⓛ } a - a$ (circled $<$: $a < a - a$)

13. $\dfrac{1 \text{ meter}}{4} = \dfrac{100 \text{ cm}}{4} = 25 \text{ cm}$
$(25 \text{ cm})(25 \text{ cm}) = \mathbf{625 \text{ cm}^2}$

14.
$$\begin{array}{r} \$12.95 \\ \$7.85 \\ +\ \$49.50 \\ \hline \$70.30 \end{array} \qquad \begin{array}{r} \$70.30 \\ \times\ \ 0.07 \\ \hline \$4.921 \end{array} \longrightarrow \$4.92$$
$$\begin{array}{r} \$70.30 \\ +\ \ \$4.92 \\ \hline \mathbf{\$75.22} \end{array}$$

15. $(3.5 \times 3) \times (10^5 \times 10^6) = 10.5 \times 10^{11}$
$= \mathbf{1.05 \times 10^{12}}$

16. (a) $\angle g$

(b) $\angle d$

(c) $\angle a$

(d) **70°**

17. (a) $1.25 \times 84 = W_N$
$\mathbf{105} = W_N$

(b) $1.25 \times 84 = \mathbf{105}$

18. **3 to 2**

19. Area of base $= (6 \text{ ft})(4 \text{ ft}) = 24 \text{ ft}^2$
Volume $= (24 \text{ ft}^2)(3 \text{ ft}) = \mathbf{72 \text{ ft}^3}$

20. (a) $C \approx \dfrac{22}{7}(14 \text{ m})$
$C \approx \mathbf{44 \text{ m}}$

(b) $A \approx \dfrac{22}{7}(49 \text{ m}^2)$
$A \approx \mathbf{154 \text{ m}^2}$

21. $y = 3(2)$
$y = \mathbf{6;}$
$y = 3(-1)$
$y = \mathbf{-3;}$
$y = 3(0)$
$y = \mathbf{0}$

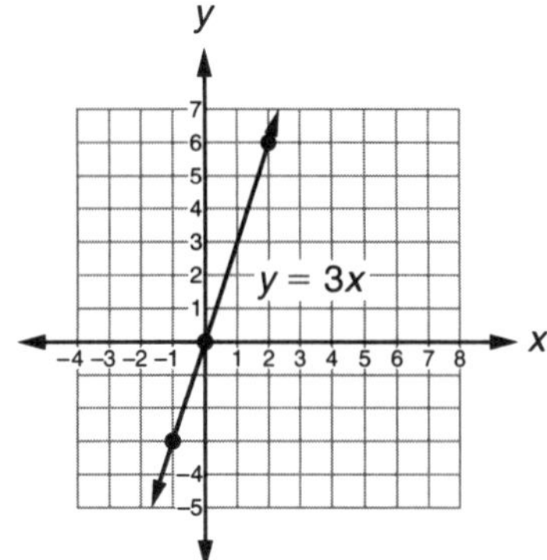

22. (a) $m\angle a = m\angle c = 180° - (90° + 34°)$
$= \mathbf{56°}$

(b) $m\angle b = 90° - 56° = \mathbf{34°}$

(c) $m\angle c = 90° - 34° = \mathbf{56°}$

23. (number line: −3, −2, −1, 0, 1; closed dot at −2, shaded to the right)

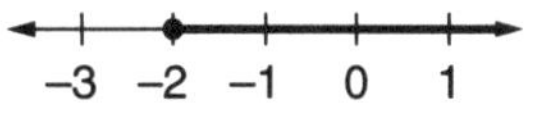

24. (number line: 0, 1, 2; points at $\frac{1}{4}$, 0.4, $\sqrt{4}$)

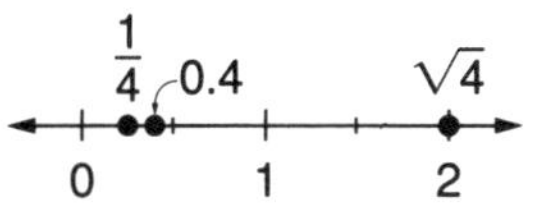

All three numbers are rational.

25. $3x + x + 3^0 = 49$
$4x + 1 = 49$
$4x + 1 - 1 = 49 - 1$
$4x = 48$
$x = \dfrac{48}{4}$
$x = \mathbf{12}$

26.
$$\begin{aligned} 3y + 2 &= y + 32 \\ 3y + 2 - y &= y + 32 - y \\ 2y + 2 &= 32 \\ 2y + 2 - 2 &= 32 - 2 \\ 2y &= 30 \\ \frac{2y}{2} &= \frac{30}{2} \\ y &= \mathbf{15} \end{aligned}$$

27.
$$\begin{aligned} x + 2(x + 3) &= 36 \\ x + 2x + 6 &= 36 \\ 3x + 6 - 6 &= 36 - 6 \\ 3x &= 30 \\ \frac{3x}{3} &= \frac{30}{3} \\ x &= \mathbf{10} \end{aligned}$$

28. (a)
$$(3x^2y)(-2x)(xy^2)$$
$$(3) \cdot x \cdot x \cdot y \cdot (-2) \cdot x \cdot x \cdot y \cdot y$$
$$\mathbf{-6x^4y^3}$$

(b)
$$-3x + 2y - x - y$$
$$-3x - x + 2y - y$$
$$\mathbf{-4x + y}$$

29. $$\left(4\frac{1}{2}\right)\left(\frac{2}{10}\right)\left(\frac{100}{1}\right) = \frac{9}{\cancel{2}_1} \cdot \frac{\cancel{2}^1}{\cancel{10}_1} \cdot \frac{\cancel{100}^{10}}{1} = \mathbf{90}$$

30.
$$\frac{(-4)(+3)}{(-2)} - (-1)$$
$$\frac{(-12)}{(-2)} + 1$$
$$6 + 1$$
$$\mathbf{7}$$

Lesson 103, Lesson Practice

a. $(-5)(-4)(-3)(-2)(-1) = \mathbf{-120}$

b. $(+5)(-4)(+3)(-2)(+1) = \mathbf{120}$

c. $(-2)^3 = (-2)(-2)(-2) = \mathbf{-8}$

d. $(-3)^4 = (-3)(-3)(-3)(-3) = \mathbf{81}$

e. $(-9)^2 = (-9)(-9) = \mathbf{81}$

f. $(-1)^5 = (-1)(-1)(-1)(-1)(-1) = \mathbf{-1}$

g. $$\frac{6a^2b^3c}{3ab} = \frac{2 \cdot \cancel{3}^1 \cdot \cancel{a}^1 \cdot a \cdot \cancel{b}^1 \cdot b \cdot b \cdot c}{\cancel{3}_1 \cdot \cancel{a}_1 \cdot \cancel{b}_1}$$
$$= \mathbf{2ab^2c}$$

h. $$\frac{8xy^3z^2}{6x^2y} = \frac{\cancel{2}^1 \cdot 2 \cdot 2 \cdot \cancel{x}^1 \cdot \cancel{y}^1 \cdot y \cdot y \cdot z \cdot z}{\cancel{2}_1 \cdot 3 \cdot \cancel{x}_1 \cdot x \cdot \cancel{y}_1}$$
$$= \mathbf{\frac{4y^2z^2}{3x}}$$

i. $$\frac{15mn^2p}{25m^2n^2} = \frac{3 \cdot \cancel{5}^1 \cdot \cancel{m}^1 \cdot \cancel{n}^1 \cdot \cancel{n}^1 \cdot p}{\cancel{5}_1 \cdot 5 \cdot \cancel{m}_1 \cdot m \cdot \cancel{n}_1 \cdot \cancel{n}_1} = \mathbf{\frac{3p}{5m}}$$

Lesson 103, Mixed Practice

1.
$$\begin{array}{r} \$25.00 \\ \times \quad 0.15 \\ \hline \mathbf{\$3.75} \end{array}$$

2. (a) **85**

(b) **90**

3.

70 75 80 85 90 95 100

4. $$\frac{1280 \text{ kilometers}}{2.5 \text{ hours}} = \textbf{512 kilometers per hour}$$

5.

	Case 1	Case 2
Dollars	\$25	d
Hours	4	7

$$\frac{\$25}{4} = \frac{d}{7}$$
$$4d = \$175$$
$$d = \mathbf{\$43.75}$$

6.

	Percent	Ratio
Lights on	40	2
Lights off	60	3

$$\frac{40}{60} = \mathbf{\frac{2}{3}}$$

7.

	Percent	Actual Count
Original	100	O
− Change	20	$25
New	80	N

$$\frac{100}{20} = \frac{O}{\$25}$$
$$20O = \$2500$$
$$O = \mathbf{\$125}$$

8.

	Percent	Actual Count
Original	100	$30
+ Change	60	C
New	160	N

$$\frac{100}{60} = \frac{\$30}{C}$$
$$100C = \$1800$$
$$C = \mathbf{\$18}$$

9. (a) 20 (54 inches) = **1080 inches**

(b) $\overset{90}{\cancel{1080}}\ \cancel{\text{inches}} \cdot \dfrac{1 \text{ foot}}{\underset{1}{\cancel{12}}\ \cancel{\text{inches}}}$ = **90 feet**

10. 20^3 = **8000 times**

11. $\frac{8}{5}$ (1000 meters) = **1600 meters**

12.

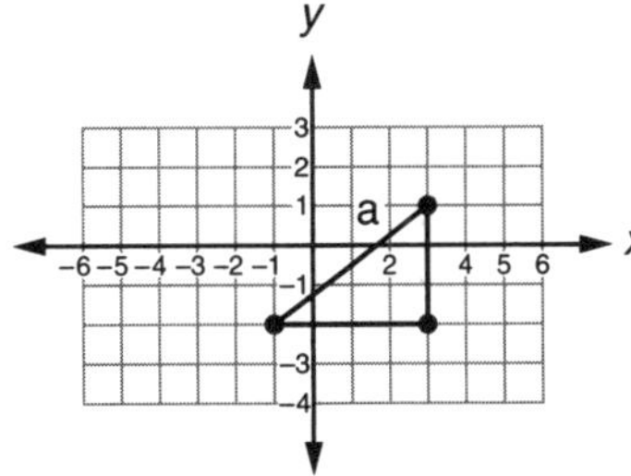

$$a^2 = (4 \text{ units})^2 + (3 \text{ units})^2$$
$$a^2 = 16 \text{ units}^2 + 9 \text{ units}^2$$
$$a^2 = 25 \text{ units}^2$$
$$a = \mathbf{5 \text{ units}}$$

13. $\frac{35}{50}$ = **70%**

14.
$$W_P \times 25 = 20$$
$$\frac{W_P \times 25}{25} = \frac{20}{25}$$
$$W_P = \frac{4}{5}$$
$$W_P = \frac{4}{5} \times 100\% = \mathbf{80\%}$$

15. (a) $\frac{120°}{360°} = \mathbf{\frac{1}{3}}$

(b) $\frac{2}{3} \times 100\% = \mathbf{66\frac{2}{3}\%}$

16. $y = \mathbf{-2;}$
$y = -0$
$y = \mathbf{0;}$
$y = -(-1)$
$y = \mathbf{1}$

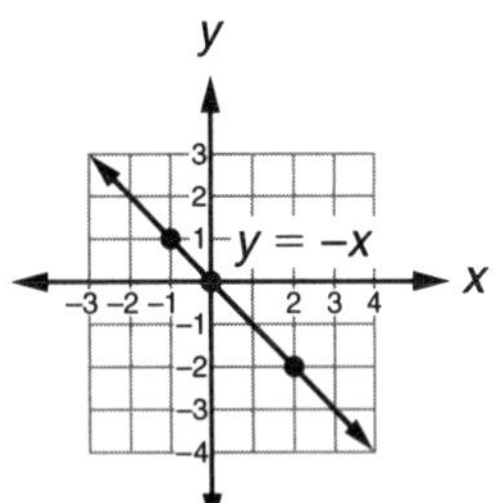

17.
$$\mathbf{2x - 3 = -7}$$
$$2x - 3 + 3 = -7 + 3$$
$$2x = -4$$
$$\frac{2x}{2} = \frac{-4}{2}$$
$$x = \mathbf{-2}$$

18. (a) m∠CAB = 90° − 36° = **54°**

(b) m∠CAD = m∠ACB = **36°**

(c) m∠ACD = m∠CAB = **54°**

19. (a) **See student work;**
$$\frac{x}{12} = \frac{12}{16}$$
$$16x = 144$$
$$x = \mathbf{9}$$

(b) $12f = 9$
$$\frac{12f}{12} = \frac{9}{12}$$
$$f = \frac{3}{4} = \mathbf{0.75}$$

20. **See student work; 50°**

21. (a) $C \approx 3.14$ (2 ft)
$C \approx$ **6.28 ft**

(b) $A \approx 3.14(1 \text{ ft}^2)$
$A \approx$ **3.14 ft²**

22. $\sqrt{144} = 12$ and $\sqrt{169} = 13$
C. $\sqrt{150}$ is between $\sqrt{144}$ and $\sqrt{169}$

23. Area of base $= \dfrac{(6 \text{ units})(3 \text{ units})}{2} = 9 \text{ units}^2$

Volume $= (9 \text{ units}^2)(6 \text{ units}) = \mathbf{54 \text{ units}^3}$

24. Area of base $\approx 3.14(9 \text{ units}^2) \approx 28.26 \text{ units}^2$

Volume $\approx (28.26 \text{ units}^2)(3 \text{ units})$

$\approx \mathbf{84.78 \text{ units}^3}$

25.
$$\begin{aligned} 3x + x - 5 &= 2(x - 2) \\ 4x - 5 &= 2x - 4 \\ 4x - 5 - 2x &= 2x - 4 - 2x \\ 2x - 5 &= -4 \\ 2x - 5 + 5 &= -4 + 5 \\ 2x &= 1 \\ \frac{2x}{2} &= \frac{1}{2} \\ x &= \mathbf{\frac{1}{2}} \end{aligned}$$

26.
$$\begin{aligned} 6\frac{2}{3}f - 5 &= 5 \\ 6\frac{2}{3}f - 5 + 5 &= 5 + 5 \\ 6\frac{2}{3}f &= 10 \\ \left(\frac{3}{20}\right)\left(\frac{20}{3}f\right) &= \left(\frac{3}{20}\right)10 \\ f &= \mathbf{\frac{3}{2}} \end{aligned}$$

27. $10\frac{1}{2} \cdot 1\frac{3}{7} \cdot 5^{-2} = \frac{\overset{3}{\cancel{21}}}{\underset{1}{\cancel{2}}} \cdot \frac{\overset{\overset{1}{\cancel{5}}}{\cancel{10}}}{\underset{1}{\cancel{7}}} \cdot \frac{1}{\underset{5}{\cancel{25}}} = \mathbf{\frac{3}{5}}$

28. $12\frac{1}{2} - 8\frac{1}{3} + 1\frac{1}{6}$

$= 12\frac{3}{6} - 8\frac{2}{6} + 1\frac{1}{6} = 5\frac{2}{6} = \mathbf{5\frac{1}{3}}$

29. (a) $\dfrac{(-3)(-2)(-1)}{-|(-3)(+2)|}$

$\dfrac{(6)(-1)}{-|(-6)|}$

$\dfrac{-6}{-(+6)}$

$\mathbf{1}$

(b) $3^2 - (-3)^2 = 9 - (9) = \mathbf{0}$

30. (a) $\dfrac{6a^3b^2c}{2abc} = \dfrac{\overset{1}{\cancel{2}} \cdot 3 \cdot \overset{1}{\cancel{a}} \cdot a \cdot a \cdot \overset{1}{\cancel{b}} \cdot b \cdot \overset{1}{\cancel{c}}}{\underset{1}{\cancel{2}} \cdot \underset{1}{\cancel{a}} \cdot \underset{1}{\cancel{b}} \cdot \underset{1}{\cancel{c}}}$

$= \mathbf{3a^2b}$

(b) $\dfrac{8x^2yz^3}{12xy^2z} = \dfrac{\overset{1}{\cancel{2}} \cdot \overset{1}{\cancel{2}} \cdot 2 \cdot \overset{1}{\cancel{x}} \cdot x \cdot \overset{1}{\cancel{y}} \cdot \overset{1}{\cancel{z}} \cdot z \cdot z}{\underset{1}{\cancel{2}} \cdot \underset{1}{\cancel{2}} \cdot 3 \cdot \underset{1}{\cancel{x}} \cdot \underset{1}{\cancel{y}} \cdot y \cdot \underset{1}{\cancel{z}}}$

$= \mathbf{\dfrac{2xz^2}{3y}}$

Lesson 104, Lesson Practice

a. $C \approx \dfrac{3.14(6 \text{ cm})}{2}$

$C \approx 9.42$ cm

Perimeter $\approx 3 \text{ cm} + 4 \text{ cm} + 9.42 \text{ cm} + 3 \text{ cm} + 10 \text{ cm} \approx \mathbf{29.42 \text{ cm}}$

b.

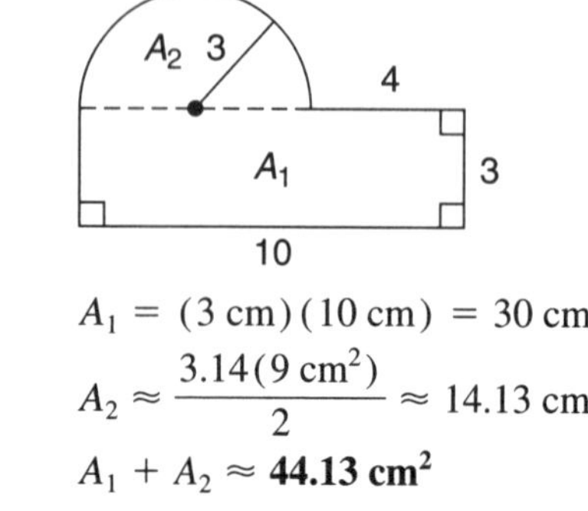

$A_1 = (3 \text{ cm})(10 \text{ cm}) = 30 \text{ cm}^2$

$A_2 \approx \dfrac{3.14(9 \text{ cm}^2)}{2} \approx 14.13 \text{ cm}^2$

$A_1 + A_2 \approx \mathbf{44.13 \text{ cm}^2}$

c. $\dfrac{45°}{360°} = \dfrac{1}{8}$

$A = \dfrac{\pi(16 \text{ cm}^2)}{8}$

$A = \dfrac{16\pi \text{ cm}^2}{8}$

$A = \mathbf{2\pi \text{ cm}^2}$

d. $C \approx \dfrac{3.14(8 \text{ cm})}{8}$

$C \approx 3.14$ cm

Perimeter $\approx 3.14 \text{ cm} + 4 \text{ cm} + 4 \text{ cm}$

$\approx \mathbf{11.14 \text{ cm}}$

Lesson 104, Mixed Practice

1.
$$\begin{array}{r} \$12.50 \\ \times \quad 0.4 \\ \hline \mathbf{\$5.00} \end{array}$$

2.
$$p(1, 1 \text{ or } 2 \text{ or } 4 \text{ or } 6) = \frac{1}{6} \cdot \frac{4}{6} = \frac{4}{36}$$
$$p(2, 1 \text{ or } 3 \text{ or } 5) = \frac{1}{6} \cdot \frac{3}{6} = \frac{3}{36}$$
$$p(3, 2 \text{ or } 4) = \frac{1}{6} \cdot \frac{2}{6} = \frac{2}{36}$$
$$p(4, 1 \text{ or } 3) = \frac{1}{6} \cdot \frac{2}{6} = \frac{2}{36}$$
$$p(5, 2 \text{ or } 6) = \frac{1}{6} \cdot \frac{2}{6} = \frac{2}{36}$$
$$p(6, 1 \text{ or } 5) = \frac{1}{6} \cdot \frac{2}{6} = \frac{2}{36}$$
$$\frac{4}{36} + \frac{3}{36} + \frac{2}{36} + \frac{2}{36} + \frac{2}{36} + \frac{2}{36}$$
$$= \mathbf{\frac{15}{36} = \frac{5}{12}}$$

3.
$$10(88) = 880$$
$$880 - 70 = 810$$
$$\frac{810}{9} = \mathbf{90}$$

4.
$$\frac{\$3.42}{36 \text{ ounces}} = \frac{\$0.095}{1 \text{ ounce}}$$
$$\frac{\$3.84}{48 \text{ ounces}} = \frac{\$0.08}{1 \text{ ounce}}$$
$$\$0.095 - \$0.08 = \$0.015$$

1.5¢ more per ounce

5.

	Case 1	Case 2
Pages	18	180
Minutes	30	m

$$\frac{18}{30} = \frac{180}{m}$$
$$18m = 5400$$
$$m = 300 \text{ minutes}$$
$$\overset{5}{\cancel{300}}\ \cancel{\text{minutes}} \cdot \frac{1 \text{ hour}}{\underset{1}{\cancel{60}}\ \cancel{\text{minutes}}} = \mathbf{5 \text{ hours}}$$

6.
$$\frac{5}{6} \times W_N = 75$$
$$\frac{6}{5}\left(\frac{5}{6} \times W_N\right) = \left(\frac{6}{5}\right)75$$
$$W_N = 90$$
$$\frac{3}{5}(90) = \mathbf{54}$$

7.

	Ratio	Actual Count
Crawfish	2	C
Tadpoles	21	1932

$$\frac{2}{21} = \frac{C}{1932}$$
$$21C = 3864$$
$$C = \mathbf{184 \text{ crawfish}}$$

8. (a)
$$\mathbf{W_P \times \$60 = \$45}$$
$$\frac{W_P \times \$60}{\$60} = \frac{\$45}{\$60}$$
$$W_P = \frac{3}{4}$$
$$W_P = \frac{3}{4} \times 100\% = \mathbf{75\%}$$

(b) $\mathbf{M = 0.45 \times \$60}$
$M = \mathbf{\$27}$

9. (a) $A = \pi(144 \text{ units}^2)$
$A = \mathbf{144\pi \text{ units}^2}$

(b) $C = \pi(24 \text{ units})$
$\mathbf{C = 24\pi \text{ units}}$

10.
$$360° - (60° + 180°) = 120°$$
$$\frac{120°}{360°} = \frac{1}{3}$$
$$A = \frac{144\pi \text{ units}^2}{3}$$
$$A = \mathbf{48\pi \text{ units}^2}$$

11. (a) $360° - 120° = \mathbf{240°}$

(b)
$$\frac{240°}{360°} = \frac{2}{3}$$
$$C = \frac{2(24\pi \text{ units})}{3}$$
$$C = \mathbf{16\pi \text{ units}}$$

12. $y = 2x - 1$

x	y
−1	−3
0	−1
1	1

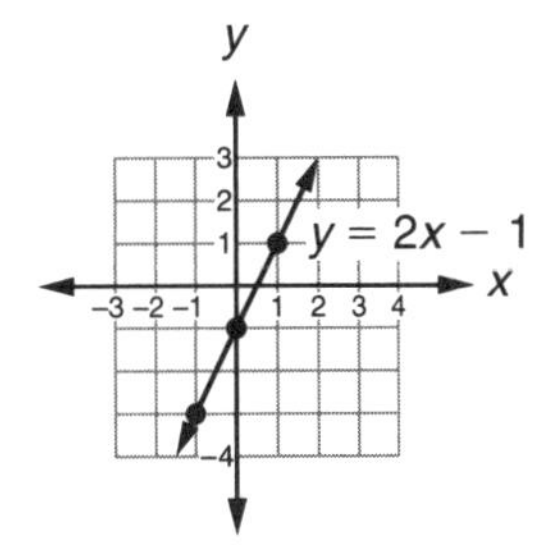

13. (a) $\mathbf{\frac{11}{500}}$

(b) **0.022**

14. (a) **75 miles**

(b) **The car traveled about 60 miles in 1 hour, so its speed was about 60 miles per hour.**

15. $ab \; \text{Ⓚ} \; a - b$ → $ab \,\textcircled{<}\, a - b$

16.
$$(3.6 \times 10^{-4})(9 \times 10^{8})$$
$$32.4 \times 10^{4}$$
$$(3.24 \times 10^{1}) \times 10^{4}$$
$$\mathbf{3.24 \times 10^{5}}$$

17.

3
A_1 3 A_2 6

$$A_1 \approx \frac{3.14(9\text{ cm}^2)}{2}$$
$$A_1 \approx 14.13\text{ cm}^2$$
$$A_2 = (3\text{ cm})(6\text{ cm}) = 18\text{ cm}^2$$
$$A_1 + A_2 \approx \mathbf{32.13\text{ cm}^2}$$

18.
$$C \approx \frac{3.14(6\text{ cm})}{2}$$
$$C \approx 9.42\text{ cm}$$
Perimeter $\approx$ 3 cm + 9.42 cm + 3 cm + 6 cm $\approx$ **21.42 cm**

19. (a)
$$\text{Area of base} = (1\text{ ft})(1\text{ ft}) = 1\text{ ft}^2$$
$$\text{Volume} = (1\text{ ft}^2)(1\text{ ft}) = 1\text{ ft}^3$$
$$1\,\cancel{\text{ft}^3} \cdot \frac{12\text{ in.}}{1\,\cancel{\text{ft}}} \cdot \frac{12\text{ in.}}{1\,\cancel{\text{ft}}} \cdot \frac{12\text{ in.}}{1\,\cancel{\text{ft}}} = \mathbf{1728\text{ in.}^3}$$

(b) $6(1\text{ ft}^2) = \mathbf{6\text{ ft}^2}$

20. $5(30°) = \mathbf{150°}$

21.
$$180° - 139° = 41°$$
$$m\angle x = 180° - (90° + 41°) = \mathbf{49°}$$

22. (a)
$$\frac{x}{13} = \frac{6}{12}$$
$$12x = 78$$
$$x = \frac{78}{12}$$
$$x = \mathbf{6\frac{1}{2}}$$

(b)
$$6f = 12$$
$$\frac{6f}{6} = \frac{12}{6}$$
$$f = \mathbf{2}$$

(c) $(2)(2) = $ **4 times**

23.
$$12^2 + y^2 = 13^2$$
$$144 + y^2 = 169$$
$$144 + y^2 - 144 = 169 - 144$$
$$y^2 = 25$$
$$y = \mathbf{5}$$

24.
$$2\frac{3}{4}w + 4 = 48$$
$$2\frac{3}{4}w + 4 - 4 = 48 - 4$$
$$2\frac{3}{4}w = 44$$
$$\left(\frac{4}{11}\right)\left(\frac{11}{4}w\right) = \left(\frac{4}{11}\right)44$$
$$w = \mathbf{16}$$

25.
$$2.4n + 1.2n - 0.12 = 7.08$$
$$3.6n - 0.12 + 0.12 = 7.08 + 0.12$$
$$3.6n = 7.2$$
$$\frac{3.6n}{3.6} = \frac{7.2}{3.6}$$
$$n = \mathbf{2}$$

26. $\sqrt{(3^2)(10^2)} = \sqrt{(9)(100)} = \sqrt{900} = \mathbf{30}$

27. (a)
$$\frac{24x^2y}{8x^3y^2} = \frac{\overset{1}{\cancel{2}} \cdot \overset{1}{\cancel{2}} \cdot \overset{1}{\cancel{2}} \cdot 3 \cdot \overset{1}{\cancel{x}} \cdot \overset{1}{\cancel{x}} \cdot \overset{1}{\cancel{y}}}{\underset{1}{\cancel{2}} \cdot \underset{1}{\cancel{2}} \cdot \underset{1}{\cancel{2}} \cdot \underset{1}{\cancel{x}} \cdot \underset{1}{\cancel{x}} \cdot x \cdot \underset{1}{\cancel{y}} \cdot y} = \mathbf{\frac{3}{xy}}$$

(b)
$$3x^2 + 2x(x - 1)$$
$$3x^2 + 2x^2 - 2x$$
$$\mathbf{5x^2 - 2x}$$

28.
$$12\frac{1}{2} - \left(8\frac{1}{3} + 1\frac{1}{6}\right)$$
$$= 12\frac{3}{6} - \left(8\frac{2}{6} + 1\frac{1}{6}\right)$$
$$= 12\frac{3}{6} - 9\frac{3}{6} = \mathbf{3}$$

29. $\left(4\frac{1}{6} \div 3\frac{3}{4}\right) \div 2.5$

$= \left(\frac{\overset{5}{\cancel{25}}}{\underset{3}{\cancel{6}}} \times \frac{\overset{2}{\cancel{4}}}{\underset{3}{\cancel{15}}}\right) \div 2\frac{1}{2} = \frac{10}{9} \div \frac{5}{2}$

$= \frac{\overset{2}{\cancel{10}}}{9} \times \frac{2}{\underset{1}{\cancel{5}}} = \mathbf{\frac{4}{9}}$

30. (a) $\frac{(-3)(4)}{-2} - \frac{(-3)(-4)}{-2}$

$\frac{(-12)}{-2} - \frac{(12)}{-2}$

$6 - (-6)$

12

(b) $\frac{(-2)^3}{(-2)^2} = \frac{\overset{1}{\cancel{(-2)}}\overset{1}{\cancel{(-2)}}(-2)}{\underset{1}{\cancel{(-2)}}\underset{1}{\cancel{(-2)}}} = \mathbf{-2}$

Lesson 105, Lesson Practice

a.

Area of rectangle	=	(10 m)(4 m)	= 40 m^2
Area of rectangle	=	(10 m)(4 m)	= 40 m^2
Area of rectangle	=	(10 m)(4 m)	= 40 m^2
Area of rectangle	=	(10 m)(4 m)	= 40 m^2
Area of square	=	(4 m)(4 m)	= 16 m^2
+ Area of square	=	(4 m)(4 m)	= 16 m^2
Total surface area			= **192 m^2**

b.

Area of triangle $= \frac{(6 \text{ in.})(8 \text{ in.})}{2}$
$= 24 \text{ in.}^2$

Area of triangle $= \frac{(6 \text{ in.})(8 \text{ in.})}{2}$
$= 24 \text{ in.}^2$

Area of rectangle = (10 in.)(10 in.)
$= 100 \text{ in.}^2$

Area of rectangle = (10 in.)(8 in.)
$= 80 \text{ in.}^2$

\+ Area of rectangle = (10 in.)(6 in.)
$= 60 \text{ in.}^2$

Total surface area $= 24 \text{ in.}^2 + 24 \text{ in.}^2 + 100 \text{ in.}^2 + 80 \text{ in.}^2 + 60 \text{ in.}^2$
$= \mathbf{288 \text{ in.}^2}$

c. Area $= \pi d \cdot$ height
Area $\approx$ (3.14)(10 cm)(4 cm)
Area $\approx$ **125.6 cm^2**

d. $A \approx 3.14(25 \text{ cm}^2) \approx 78.5 \text{ cm}^2$

Area of top	= 78.5 cm^2
Area of bottom	= 78.5 cm^2
+ Area of lateral surface	= 125.6 cm^2
Total surface area	= **282.6 cm^2**

e. $A = 4\pi r^2$
$A \approx 4(3.14)(4 \text{ cm}^2)$
$A \approx 50.24 \text{ cm}^2$
$A \approx \mathbf{50 \text{ cm}^2}$

f. **4, −4**

g. $\sqrt[3]{125} = \sqrt[3]{5 \cdot 5 \cdot 5} = \mathbf{5}$

h. $\sqrt[3]{-8} = \sqrt[3]{(-2) \cdot (-2) \cdot (-2)} = \mathbf{-2}$

Lesson 105, Mixed Practice

1.
$\overset{1}{\cancel{2}}\,\overset{9}{\cancel{0}},{}^{1}0\,0\,0,0\,0\,0,0\,0\,0$
$-\quad 9\,0\,0,0\,0\,0,0\,0\,0$
$1\,9,1\,0\,0,0\,0\,0,0\,0\,0$

1.91 × 10^{10}

2. Mean = 12.95 ÷ 5 = 2.59
Median − mean = 3.1 − 2.59 = **0.51**

3. $\sqrt{(10)^2 - (8)^2} = \sqrt{100 - 64} = \sqrt{36} = \mathbf{6}$

4. 6.5($8.50) = **$55.25**

5.

	Case 1	Case 2
Cost	$2.48	c
Kilograms	6	45

$\frac{\$2.48}{6} = \frac{c}{45}$
$6c = \$111.60$
$c = \mathbf{\$18.60}$

6.

	Percent	Actual Count
Regular price	100	$30
Sale price	75	S

(a) $\frac{100}{75} = \frac{\$30}{S}$
$100S = \$2250$
$S = \mathbf{\$22.50}$

(b) **75%**

7.

	Ratio	Actual Count
Whigs	7	W
Tories	3	T
Total	10	210

$$\frac{3}{10} = \frac{T}{210}$$
$$10T = 630$$
$$T = \mathbf{63\ Tories}$$

8.

	Percent	Actual Count
Original	100	\$60
− Change	30	C
New	70	N

$$\frac{100}{70} = \frac{\$60}{N}$$
$$100N = \$4200$$
$$N = \mathbf{\$42}$$

9. $60\ \cancel{\text{feet}} \cdot \frac{12\text{ inches}}{1\ \cancel{\text{foot}}} = 720\text{ inches}$

	Scale	Actual Count
Model	1	m
Airplane	36	720

$$\frac{1}{36} = \frac{m}{720}$$
$$36m = 720$$
$$m = \mathbf{20\ inches}$$

10. $4x + 5x = 180°$
$$9x = 180°$$
$$\frac{9x}{9} = \frac{180°}{9}$$
$$x = \mathbf{20°}$$

11. $\mathbf{W_P \times \$60 = \$3}$
$$\frac{W_P \times \$60}{\$60} = \frac{\$3}{\$60}$$
$$W_P = \frac{1}{20}$$
$$W_P = \frac{1}{20} \times 100\% = \mathbf{5\%}$$

12. $\mathbf{W_F = \frac{1}{10} \times 4}$
$$W_F = \mathbf{\frac{2}{5}}$$

13. $\mathbf{2x - 12 = 86}$
$$2x - 12 + 12 = 86 + 12$$
$$2x = 98$$
$$\frac{2x}{2} = \frac{98}{2}$$
$$x = \mathbf{49}$$

14.

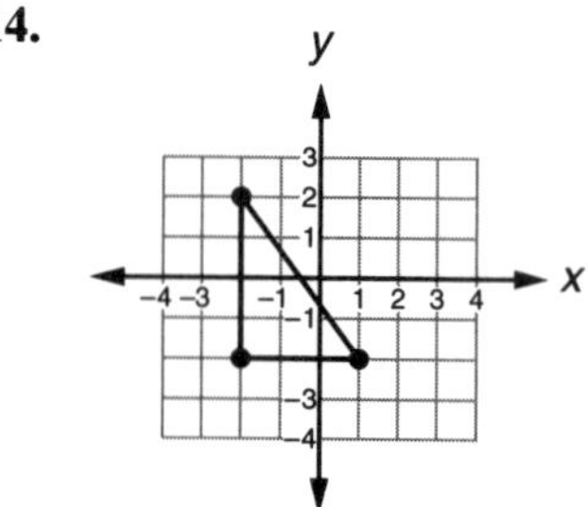

$$a^2 = (4\text{ units})^2 + (3\text{ units})^2$$
$$a^2 = 16\text{ units}^2 + 9\text{ units}^2$$
$$a^2 = 25\text{ units}^2$$
$$a = \mathbf{5\ units}$$

15. a^3 Ⓐ a^2 → $a^3 \; \textcircled{<} \; a^2$

16. $\frac{13}{52} \cdot \frac{12}{51} = \frac{156}{2652} = \mathbf{\frac{1}{17}}$

17. $A = 4\pi r^2$
$$A \approx 4(3.14)(100\text{ in.}^2)$$
$$A \approx \mathbf{1256\ in.^2}$$

18. $(8 \times 3.2) \times (10^{-4} \times 10^{-10})$
$$= 25.6 \times 10^{-14} = \mathbf{2.56 \times 10^{-13}}$$

19. $C \approx \frac{3.14(20\text{ m})}{2}$
$$C \approx 31.4\text{ m}$$
$$\text{Perimeter} \approx 31.4\text{ m} + 5\text{ m} + 30\text{ m} + 5\text{ m} + 10\text{ m} \approx \mathbf{81.4\ m}$$

20. $y = -2(3) - 1$
$y = \mathbf{-7;}$
$y = -2(-2) - 1$
$y = 4 - 1$
$y = \mathbf{3;}$
$y = -2(0) - 1$
$y = \mathbf{-1}$

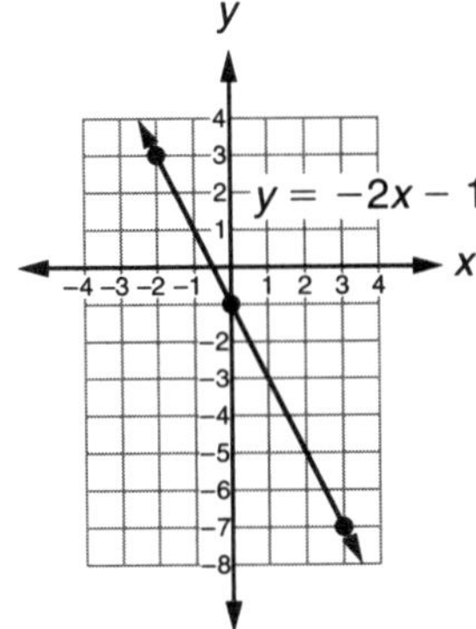

21. (a) Volume $= (5\text{ mm})(5\text{ mm})(5\text{ mm})$
$= \mathbf{125\ mm^3}$

(b) Surface area $= 6(25\text{ mm}^2) = \mathbf{150\ mm^2}$

22. Area of base $\approx 3.14(100\text{ cm}^2) \approx 314\text{ cm}^2$
Volume $\approx (314\text{ cm}^2)(10\text{ cm}) \approx \mathbf{3140\ cm^3}$

23. Lateral surface area $\approx$
$(3.14)(20\text{ cm})(10\text{ cm}) \approx 628\text{ cm}^2$

Area of top	=	314 cm^2
Area of bottom	=	314 cm^2
+ Lateral surface area	=	628 cm^2
Total surface area	=	$\mathbf{1256\ cm^2}$

24. $m\angle a = 180° - (90° + 30°) = 60°$
$m\angle y = m\angle a = 60°$
$m\angle b = 180° - (90° + 60°) = \mathbf{30°}$

25. (a) **See student work;**
$$\frac{x}{6} = \frac{8}{12}$$
$12x = 48$
$x = \mathbf{4}$

(b) $8f = 12$
$$f = \frac{12}{8}$$
$$f = \frac{3}{2}$$
$$f = 1\frac{1}{2} = \mathbf{1.5}$$

(c) $(1.5)^2 = $ **2.25 times**

26.
$$4\frac{1}{2}x + 4 = 48 - x$$
$$4\frac{1}{2}x + 4 + x = 48 - x + x$$
$$5\frac{1}{2}x + 4 = 48$$
$$5\frac{1}{2}x + 4 - 4 = 48 - 4$$
$$5\frac{1}{2}x = 44$$
$$\left(\frac{2}{11}\right)\left(\frac{11}{2}x\right) = \left(\frac{2}{11}\right)44$$
$$x = \mathbf{8}$$

27.
$$\frac{3.9}{75} = \frac{c}{25}$$
$75c = 97.5$
$$\frac{75c}{75} = \frac{97.5}{75}$$
$c = \mathbf{1.3}$

28.
$$3.2 \div \left(2\frac{1}{2} \div \frac{5}{8}\right)$$
$$= 3\frac{2}{10} \div \left(\frac{5}{2} \times \frac{8}{5}\right) = \frac{32}{10} \div \frac{4}{1}$$
$$= \frac{32}{10} \times \frac{1}{4} = \mathbf{\frac{4}{5}} \text{ or } \mathbf{0.8}$$

29. (a)
$$\frac{(2xy)(4x^2y)}{8x^2y}$$
$$= \frac{\overset{1}{\cancel{2}} \cdot \overset{1}{\cancel{x}} \cdot \overset{1}{\cancel{y}} \cdot \overset{1}{\cancel{2}} \cdot \overset{1}{\cancel{2}} \cdot \overset{1}{\cancel{x}} \cdot x \cdot y}{\underset{1}{\cancel{2}} \cdot \underset{1}{\cancel{2}} \cdot \underset{1}{\cancel{2}} \cdot \underset{1}{\cancel{x}} \cdot \underset{1}{\cancel{x}} \cdot \underset{1}{\cancel{y}}} = \mathbf{xy}$$

(b) $3(x - 3) - 3 = 3x - 9 - 3$
$= \mathbf{3x - 12}$

30. (a)
$$\frac{(-10)(-4) - (3)(-2)(-1)}{(-4) - (-2)}$$
$$\frac{(40) - (6)}{-2}$$
$$\frac{34}{-2}$$
$$\mathbf{-17}$$

(b) $(-2)^4 - (-2)^2 + \sqrt[3]{-1} + 2^0$
$= (-2)(-2)(-2)(-2) - (-2)(-2)$
$+ \sqrt[3]{(-1)(-1)(-1)} + 1$
$= (16) - (4) + (-1) + 1 = \mathbf{12}$

Lesson 106, Lesson Practice

a.
$$a + b = c$$
$$a + b - b = c - b$$
$$\mathbf{a = c - b}$$

b.
$$wx = y$$
$$\frac{wx}{x} = \frac{y}{x}$$
$$\mathbf{w = \frac{y}{x}}$$

c.
$$y - b = mx$$
$$y - b + b = mx + b$$
$$\mathbf{y = mx + b}$$

d.
$$A = bh$$
$$\frac{A}{h} = \frac{bh}{h}$$
$$\mathbf{\frac{A}{h} = b}$$

Lesson 106, Mixed Practice

1.
$$\begin{array}{r} \$1.85 \\ \$1.85 \\ \$1.85 \\ + \ \$8.95 \\ \hline \$14.50 \end{array} \qquad \begin{array}{r} \$14.50 \\ \times \ 0.06 \\ \hline \$0.87 \end{array} \qquad \begin{array}{r} \$14.50 \\ + \ \$0.87 \\ \hline \$15.37 \end{array}$$
$$\begin{array}{r} \$20.00 \\ - \ \$15.37 \\ \hline \mathbf{\$4.63} \end{array}$$

2. (a) **1 to 2**

(b) **25%**

3. $\frac{\$2.80}{16 \text{ ounces}} = \mathbf{17.5¢ \text{ per ounce}}$

4. $6(90) = 540, \ 540 - 75 = 465$
$$\frac{465}{5} = \mathbf{93}$$

5.

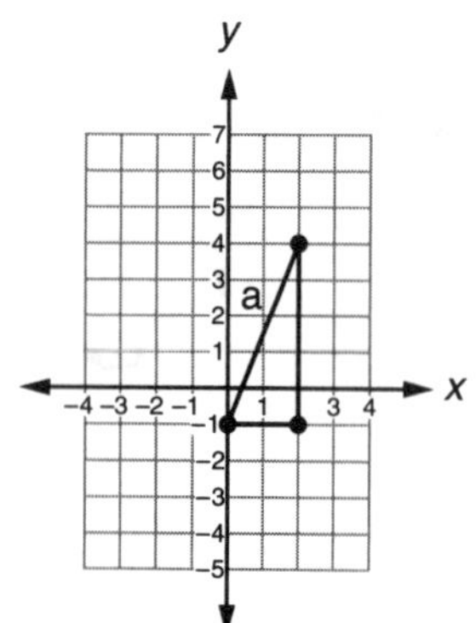

$$a^2 = (2 \text{ units})^2 + (5 \text{ units})^2$$
$$a^2 = 4 \text{ units}^2 + 25 \text{ units}^2$$
$$a^2 = 29 \text{ units}^2$$
$$a = \mathbf{\sqrt{29} \text{ units}}$$

6.

	Case 1	Case 2
Problems	3	27
Minutes	4	m

$$\frac{3}{4} = \frac{27}{m}$$
$$3m = 108$$
$$m = \mathbf{36 \text{ minutes}}$$

7.

	Ratio	Actual Count
Residents	2	R
Visitors	3	V
Total	5	60

$$\frac{3}{5} = \frac{V}{60}$$
$$5V = 180$$
$$V = \mathbf{36 \text{ visitors}}$$

8.

	Percent	Actual Count
Original	100	O
+ Change	25	C
New	125	80

$$\frac{100}{125} = \frac{O}{80}$$
$$125O = 8000$$
$$O = \mathbf{64 \text{ students}}$$

9. (a) **8 and −8**

(b) $\sqrt[3]{-64} = \sqrt[3]{(-4)(-4)(-4)} = \mathbf{-4}$

10. $\mathbf{W_N = 2.25 \times 40}$
$$W_N = \mathbf{90}$$

11. (a)

$\frac{2}{2}$ $\sqrt{2}$, $|-2|$ 2^2

0 1 2 3 4

(b) $|-2|, \frac{2}{2}, 2^2$

12.

$$66 = \frac{2}{3} \times W_N$$
$$\left(\frac{3}{2}\right)66 = \left(\frac{3}{2}\right)\frac{2}{3} \times W_N$$
$$\mathbf{99} = W_N$$

13.

$$\mathbf{0.75 \times W_N = 2.4}$$
$$\frac{0.75 \times W_N}{0.75} = \frac{2.4}{0.75}$$
$$W_N = \mathbf{3.2}$$

14. (a) $\mathbf{1\frac{1}{20}}$

(b) **1.05**

15. **See student work;**

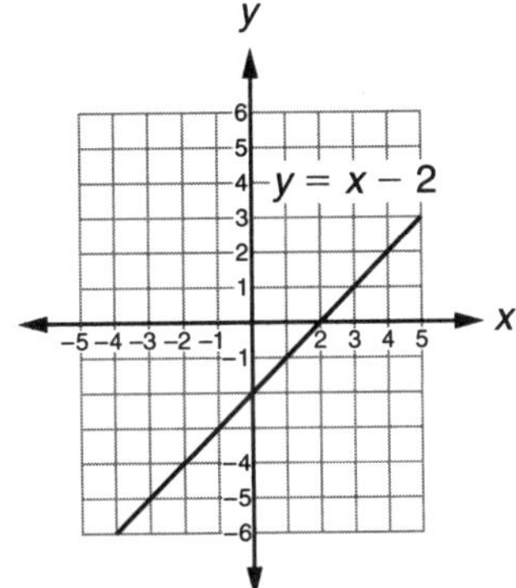

16.

$$81\overline{)6.7500} = 0.0833\ldots \rightarrow \mathbf{0.083}$$

```
     0.0833 . . .
81)6.7500
   6 48
     270
     243
      270
      243
       27
```

17.

$$(4.8 \times 6) \times (10^{-10} \times 10^{-6})$$
$$= 28.8 \times 10^{-16}$$
$$= \mathbf{2.88 \times 10^{-15}}$$

18.

$$(-3)^2 + (-5)(-3) + (6)$$
$$9 + (15) + 6$$
$$\mathbf{30}$$

19.

$$A_1 \approx \frac{(3.14)(100 \text{ mm}^2)}{2}$$
$$A_1 \approx 157 \text{ mm}^2$$
$$A_2 = (4 \text{ mm})(28 \text{ mm}) = 112 \text{ mm}^2$$
$$A_1 + A_2 \approx 157 \text{ mm}^2 + 112 \text{ mm}^2 \approx \mathbf{269 \text{ mm}^2}$$

20.

Area of triangle $= \frac{(4 \text{ cm})(3 \text{ cm})}{2} = 6 \text{ cm}^2$

Area of triangle $= \frac{(4 \text{ cm})(3 \text{ cm})}{2} = 6 \text{ cm}^2$

Area of rectangle $= (10 \text{ cm})(5 \text{ cm}) = 50 \text{ cm}^2$

Area of rectangle $= (10 \text{ cm})(4 \text{ cm}) = 40 \text{ cm}^2$

\+ Area of rectangle $= (10 \text{ cm})(3 \text{ cm}) = 30 \text{ cm}^2$

Total surface area $= \mathbf{132 \text{ cm}^2}$

21. Area of base $\approx 3.14(1 \text{ in.})^2 \approx 3.14 \text{ in.}^2$

Volume $\approx (3.14 \text{ in.}^2)(10 \text{ in.})$

$\approx \mathbf{31.4 \text{ in.}^3}$

22.

$$180° - 140° = 40°$$
$$180° - (90° + 40°) = 50°$$
$$m\angle b = 180° - (90° + 50°) = \mathbf{40°}$$

23. (a)

$$x + c = d$$
$$x + c - c = d - c$$
$$\mathbf{x = d - c}$$

(b)

$$an = b$$
$$\frac{an}{a} = \frac{b}{a}$$
$$\mathbf{n = \frac{b}{a}}$$

24.

$$6w - 2(4 + w) = w + 7$$
$$6w - 8 - 2w = w + 7$$
$$4w - 8 = w + 7$$
$$4w - 8 - w = w + 7 - w$$
$$3w - 8 = 7$$
$$3w - 8 + 8 = 7 + 8$$
$$3w = 15$$
$$\frac{3w}{3} = \frac{15}{3}$$
$$w = \mathbf{5}$$

25.
$$\begin{aligned} 6x + 8 &< 14 \\ 6x + 8 - 8 &< 14 - 8 \\ 6x &< 6 \\ \frac{6x}{6} &< \frac{6}{6} \\ \mathbf{x} &\mathbf{< 1} \end{aligned}$$

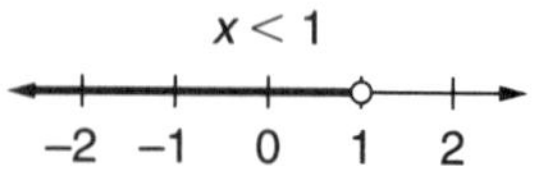

26. $37 = 3x - 5,\ 42 = 3x,\ x = \mathbf{14}$

27. $25 - [3^2 + 2(5 - 3)] = 25 - [9 + 4]$
$= 25 - 13 = \mathbf{12}$

28.
$$\frac{6x^2 + (5x)(2x)}{4x}$$
$$\frac{6x^2 + 10x^2}{4x}$$
$$\frac{16x^2}{4x}$$
$$\frac{\overset{1}{\cancel{4}} \cdot 4 \cdot \overset{1}{\cancel{x}} \cdot x}{\underset{1}{\cancel{4}} \cdot \underset{1}{\cancel{x}}} = \mathbf{4x}$$

29. $4^0 + 3^{-1} + 2^{-2}$
$$1 + \frac{1}{3} + \frac{1}{4} = \frac{12}{12} + \frac{4}{12} + \frac{3}{12} = \frac{19}{12}$$
$$= \mathbf{1\frac{7}{12}}$$

30.
$$(-3)(-2)(+4)(-1) + (-3)^2$$
$$+ \sqrt[3]{-64} - (-2)^3$$
$$(6)(+4)(-1) + (-3)(-3)$$
$$+ \sqrt[3]{(-4)(-4)(-4)} - (-2)(-2)(-2)$$
$$-24 + (9) + (-4) - (-8)$$
$$\mathbf{-11}$$

LESSON 107, LESSON PRACTICE

a. **"Yards to feet":** $\frac{\text{rise}}{\text{run}} = \frac{3}{1} = \mathbf{3}$

"Feet to yards": $\frac{\text{rise}}{\text{run}} = \mathbf{\frac{1}{3}}$

b. Graph (a): $\frac{\text{rise}}{\text{run}} = \frac{1}{1} = \mathbf{1}$

Graph (c): $\frac{\text{rise}}{\text{run}} = \frac{1}{-2} = \mathbf{-\frac{1}{2}}$

c. $\frac{\text{rise}}{\text{run}} = \mathbf{\frac{1}{3}}$

$\frac{\text{rise}}{\text{run}} = \frac{2}{-3} = \mathbf{-\frac{2}{3}}$

$\frac{\text{rise}}{\text{run}} = \mathbf{0}$

$\frac{\text{rise}}{\text{run}} = \frac{2}{-1} = \mathbf{-2}$

d. $\mathbf{\frac{1}{3};\ -\frac{2}{3};\ 0;\ -2}$

LESSON 107, MIXED PRACTICE

1. $\frac{2}{3} \times \$21 = \mathbf{\$14}$

2.
$$\begin{array}{r} \overset{0}{\cancel{1}},\overset{9}{\cancel{0}}\,\overset{9}{\cancel{0}}{}^{1}0{,}000{,}000{,}000 \\ -\quad 9\ 7\ 5{,}000{,}000{,}000 \\ \hline 2\ 5{,}000{,}000{,}000 \end{array}$$
$\mathbf{2.5 \times 10^{10}}$

3. (a) **11**

(b) **16**

4.

	Case 1	Case 2
Miles	18	m
Minutes	60	40

$$\begin{aligned} \frac{18}{60} &= \frac{m}{40} \\ 60m &= 720 \\ m &= \mathbf{12\ miles} \end{aligned}$$

5.

	Ratio	Actual Count
Earthworms	5	E
Cutworms	2	C
Total	7	140

$$\begin{aligned} \frac{5}{7} &= \frac{E}{140} \\ 7E &= 700 \\ E &= \mathbf{100\ earthworms} \end{aligned}$$

6.

	Percent	Actual Count
Original	100	\$16,550
+ Change	8	C
New	108	N

$$\begin{aligned} \frac{100}{108} &= \frac{\$16{,}550}{N} \\ 100N &= \$1{,}787{,}400 \\ N &= \mathbf{\$17{,}874} \end{aligned}$$

7.

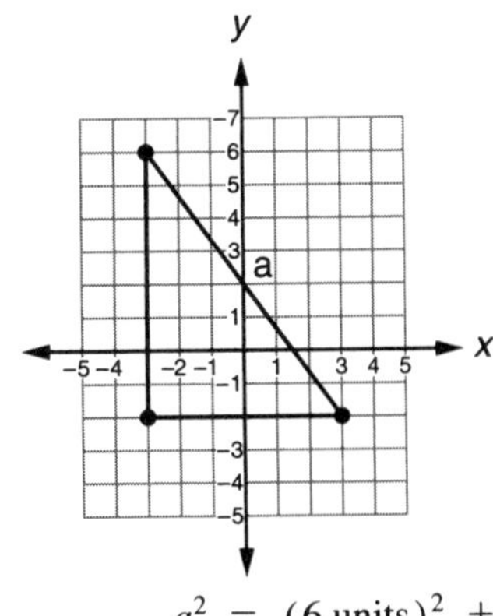

$$
\begin{aligned}
a^2 &= (6\text{ units})^2 + (8\text{ units}^2) \\
a^2 &= 36\text{ units}^2 + 64\text{ units}^2 \\
a^2 &= 100\text{ units}^2 \\
a &= 10\text{ units} \\
\text{Perimeter} &= 6\text{ units} + 8\text{ units} \\
&\quad + 10\text{ units} = \mathbf{24\ units}
\end{aligned}
$$

8. (a) $m\angle ABD = 180° - (90° + 50°) = \mathbf{40°}$

(b) $m\angle DBC = 90° - 40° = \mathbf{50°}$

(c) $m\angle BCD = 180° - (90° + 50°) = \mathbf{40°}$

(d) **All three triangles are similar.**

9.

$$
\begin{aligned}
\mathbf{60} &= \mathbf{1.25 \times W_N} \\
\frac{60}{1.25} &= \frac{1.25 \times W_N}{1.25} \\
\mathbf{48} &= W_N
\end{aligned}
$$

10.

$$
\begin{aligned}
\mathbf{60} &= \mathbf{W_P \times 25} \\
\frac{60}{25} &= \frac{W_P \times 25}{25} \\
\frac{12}{5} &= W_P \\
W_P &= \frac{12}{5} \times 100\% = \mathbf{240\%}
\end{aligned}
$$

11.

$$
\begin{aligned}
\mathbf{60} &= \mathbf{2n + 4} \\
60 - 4 &= 2n + 4 - 4 \\
56 &= 2n \\
\frac{56}{2} &= \frac{2n}{2} \\
\mathbf{28} &= n
\end{aligned}
$$

12. (a) $\dfrac{\text{not red marbles}}{\text{total marbles}} = \dfrac{\mathbf{80}}{\mathbf{100}} = \mathbf{80\%}$

(b) $p(y, y) = \dfrac{\mathbf{10}}{\mathbf{100}} \cdot \dfrac{\mathbf{9}}{\mathbf{99}} = \dfrac{90}{9900} = \dfrac{\mathbf{1}}{\mathbf{110}}$

13. (a) $\mathbf{0.8\overline{3}}$

(b) $\mathbf{83\frac{1}{3}\%}$

14. $(x - y)^2 \;\text{⊜}\; (y - x)^2$

15.

$$
\begin{aligned}
(1.8 \times 9) \times (10^{10} \times 10^{-6}) \\
&= 16.2 \times 10^4 \\
&= \mathbf{1.62 \times 10^5}
\end{aligned}
$$

16. (a) **24 and 25**

(b) $\mathbf{\sqrt{10}}$ **and** $\mathbf{-\sqrt{10}}$

17. See student work;

(a)

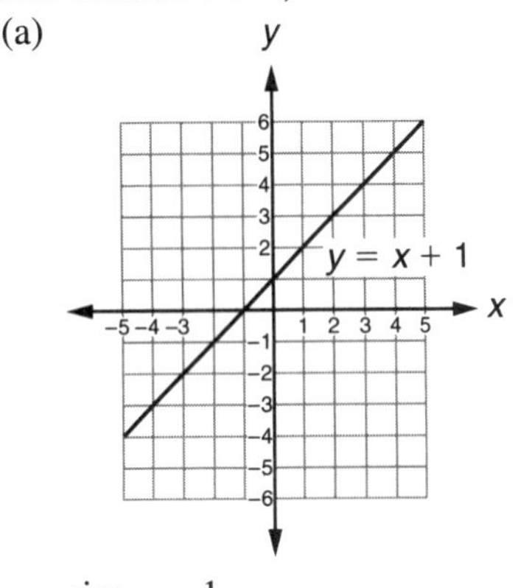

(b) $\dfrac{\text{rise}}{\text{run}} = \dfrac{1}{1} = \mathbf{1}$

18. $360° - 120° = 240°, \; \dfrac{240°}{360°} = \dfrac{2}{3}$

$$
\begin{aligned}
A &= \frac{2\pi(36\text{ cm}^2)}{3} \\
A &= \mathbf{24\pi\ cm^2}
\end{aligned}
$$

19.

Area of square	=	(4 in.)(4 in.)	= 16 in.^{2}
Area of square	=	(4 in.)(4 in.)	= 16 in.^{2}
Area of rectangle	=	(4 in.)(8 in.)	= 32 in.^{2}
Area of rectangle	=	(4 in.)(8 in.)	= 32 in.^{2}
Area of rectangle	=	(4 in.)(8 in.)	= 32 in.^{2}
+ Area of rectangle	=	(4 in.)(8 in.)	= 32 in.^{2}
Total surface area			= **160 in.^{2}**

20.

$$
\begin{aligned}
\text{Area of base} &\approx 3.14(16\text{ cm}^2) \\
&\approx 50.24\text{ cm}^2 \\
\text{Volume} &\approx (50.24\text{ cm}^2)(10\text{ cm}) \\
&\approx \mathbf{502.4\ cm^3}
\end{aligned}
$$

21.

$$
\begin{aligned}
C &\approx 3.14(8\text{ cm}) \\
C &\approx 25.12\text{ cm}
\end{aligned}
$$

Area of lateral surface	=	(25.12 cm)(10 cm)
	=	251.2 cm^2
Area of base	=	50.24 cm^2
+ Area of top	=	50.24 cm^2
Total surface area	=	**351.68 cm^2**

22. $180° - (90° + 60°) = 30°$
$90° - 30° = 60°$
$180° - (90° + 50°) = \mathbf{30°} = m\angle X$

23. $\frac{\text{rise}}{\text{run}} = \frac{2}{1} = \mathbf{2}$

24. (a)
$$x - y = z$$
$$x - y + y = z + y$$
$$\mathbf{x = z + y}$$

(b)
$$w = xy$$
$$\frac{w}{y} = \frac{xy}{y}$$
$$\mathbf{\frac{w}{y} = x}$$

25.
$$\frac{a}{21} = \frac{1.5}{7}$$
$$7a = 31.5$$
$$\frac{7a}{7} = \frac{31.5}{7}$$
$$a = \mathbf{4.5}$$

26.
$$6x + 5 = 7 + 2x$$
$$6x + 5 - 2x = 7 + 2x - 2x$$
$$4x + 5 = 7$$
$$4x + 5 - 5 = 7 - 5$$
$$4x = 2$$
$$\frac{4x}{4} = \frac{2}{4}$$
$$x = \mathbf{\frac{1}{2}}$$

27.
$$62 + 5\{20 - [4^2 + 3(2 - 1)]\}$$
$$62 + 5\{20 - [16 + 3(1)]\}$$
$$62 + 5\{20 - [19]\}$$
$$62 + 5\{1\}$$
$$62 + (5)$$
$$\mathbf{67}$$

28.
$$\frac{(6x^2y)(2xy)}{4xy^2} = \frac{\overset{1}{\cancel{2}} \cdot 3 \cdot \overset{1}{\cancel{x}} \cdot x \cdot \overset{1}{\cancel{y}} \cdot \overset{1}{\cancel{2}} \cdot x \cdot \overset{1}{\cancel{y}}}{\underset{1}{\cancel{2}} \cdot \underset{1}{\cancel{2}} \cdot \underset{1}{\cancel{x}} \cdot \underset{1}{\cancel{y}} \cdot \underset{1}{\cancel{y}}}$$
$$= \mathbf{3x^2}$$

29.
$$5\frac{1}{6} + 3\frac{1}{2} - \frac{1}{3} = 5\frac{1}{6} + 3\frac{3}{6} - \frac{2}{6}$$
$$= 8\frac{4}{6} - \frac{2}{6} = 8\frac{2}{6} = \mathbf{8\frac{1}{3}}$$

30.
$$\frac{(5)(-3)(2)(-4) + (-2)(-3)}{|-6|}$$
$$\frac{(-30)(-4) + (6)}{6}$$
$$\frac{120 + 6}{6}$$
$$\mathbf{21}$$

LESSON 108, LESSON PRACTICE

a.
$$20 = b(4)$$
$$\frac{20}{4} = b$$
$$\mathbf{5} = b$$

b.
$$20 = \frac{1}{2}(b)(4)$$
$$20 = 2b$$
$$\frac{20}{2} = b$$
$$\mathbf{10} = b$$

c.
$$F = 1.8(-40) + 32$$
$$F = \mathbf{-40}$$

LESSON 108, MIXED PRACTICE

1.
$$\begin{array}{r} \$8.35 \\ \$1.25 \\ +\ \$2.40 \\ \hline \$12.00 \end{array} \qquad \begin{array}{r} \$12.00 \\ \times\ \ 0.15 \\ \hline \mathbf{\$1.80} \end{array}$$

2.
$$\begin{array}{r} 0.000120 \\ -\ 0.000020 \\ \hline 0.000100 \end{array} \qquad \mathbf{1 \times 10^{-4}}$$

3. **4, 7, 8, 8, 8, 9, 9, 10, 12, 15**
Median = 8.5
Mode = 8

4. $p(5, 5) = \frac{4}{52} \cdot \frac{3}{51} = \mathbf{\frac{1}{221}}$

5.

	Case 1	Case 2
Dollars	\$200	d
Francs	300	240

$$\frac{\$200}{300} = \frac{d}{240}$$
$$300d = \$48{,}000$$
$$d = \mathbf{\$160}$$

6.

	Ratio	Actual Count
Red beans	5	175
Brown beans	7	B
Total	12	T

$$\frac{5}{12} = \frac{175}{T}$$
$$5T = 2100$$
$$T = \textbf{420 beans}$$

7.

	Percent	Actual Count
Original	100	\$90
− Change	35	C
New	65	N

$$\frac{100}{65} = \frac{\$90}{N}$$
$$100N = \$5850$$
$$N = \$58.50$$
$$2(\$58.50) = \textbf{\$117}$$

8. $1 \text{ ton} = 2000 \text{ pounds}$

$$\frac{3}{8}(2000 \text{ pounds}) = \textbf{750 pounds}$$

9. $\mathbf{W_N = 0.025 \times 800}$

$W_N = \mathbf{20}$

10. $\mathbf{0.1 \times W_N = \$2500}$

$$\frac{0.1 \times W_N}{0.1} = \frac{\$2500}{0.1}$$
$$W_N = \textbf{\$25,000}$$

11. $\mathbf{56 = 2x - 8}$

$$56 + 8 = 2x - 8 + 8$$
$$64 = 2x$$
$$\frac{64}{2} = \frac{2x}{2}$$
$$\mathbf{32} = x$$

12. $\dfrac{\text{rise}}{\text{run}} = \dfrac{2}{-3} = \mathbf{-\dfrac{2}{3}}$

13. (a)

	Scale	Measure
Model	1	$6/7\frac{1}{2}$
Object	24	O_1/O_2

$$\frac{1}{24} = \frac{6}{O_1} \qquad \frac{1}{24} = \frac{7.5}{O_2}$$
$$O_1 = 144 \qquad O_2 = 180$$
$$O_1 = 12 \text{ ft} \qquad O_2 = 15 \text{ ft}$$
$$12 \text{ ft} \times 15 \text{ ft} = \mathbf{180 \text{ ft}^2}$$

(b) **9 in.; We round 17 ft 9½ in. to 18 ft. Since every 2 ft is 1 in. in the floor plan, we estimate by dividing 18 by 2.**

14. $\mathbf{4x = 180°}$

$$\frac{4x}{4} = \frac{180°}{4}$$
$$\mathbf{x = 45°}$$
$$\mathbf{2x} = 2(45°) = \mathbf{90°}$$

15. $(2.8 \times 8) \times (10^5 \times 10^{-8})$

$$= 22.4 \times 10^{-3}$$
$$= \mathbf{2.24 \times 10^{-2}}$$

16. $c = 2.54(12)$

$c = \mathbf{30.48 \text{ cm}}$

17. **See student work;**

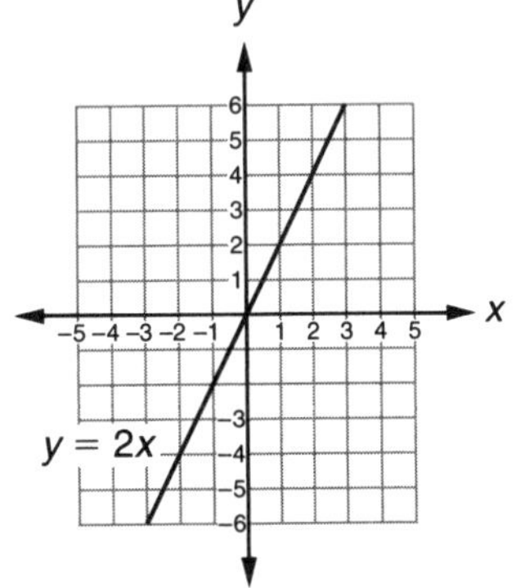

18.

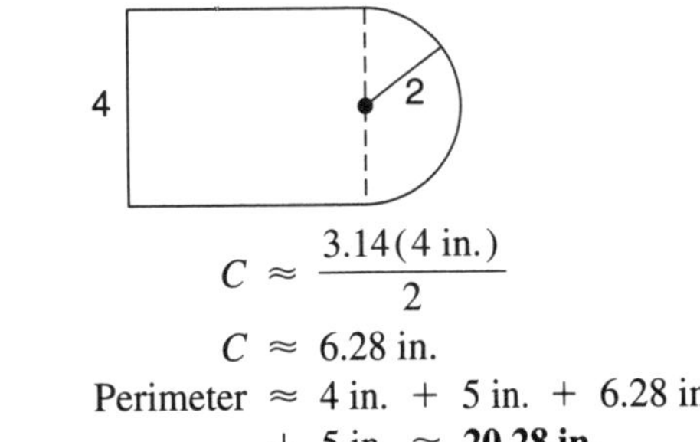

$$C \approx \frac{3.14(4 \text{ in.})}{2}$$
$$C \approx 6.28 \text{ in.}$$
$$\text{Perimeter} \approx 4 \text{ in.} + 5 \text{ in.} + 6.28 \text{ in.} + 5 \text{ in.} \approx \mathbf{20.28 \text{ in.}}$$

19. $6(100 \text{ in.}^2) = \mathbf{600 \text{ in.}^2}$

20. Area of base $\approx 3.14(25 \text{ cm}^2)$

$\approx 78.5 \text{ cm}^2$

Volume $\approx (78.5 \text{ cm}^2)(5 \text{ cm}) \approx \mathbf{392.5 \text{ cm}^3}$

21. $m\angle x = 180° - 150° = \mathbf{30°}$

22. (a) $\frac{y}{10} = \frac{9}{6}$
$6y = 90$
$y = \mathbf{15\ cm}$

(b) $6f = 9$
$f = \frac{9}{6}$
$f = 1\frac{1}{2} = \mathbf{1.5}$

(c) $(1.5)(1.5) = \mathbf{2.25\ times}$

23.
$$x^2 + (6\text{ cm})^2 = (10\text{ cm})^2$$
$$x^2 + 36\text{ cm}^2 = 100\text{ cm}^2$$
$$x^2 + 36\text{ cm}^2 - 36\text{ cm}^2 = 100\text{ cm}^2 - 36\text{ cm}^2$$
$$x^2 = 64\text{ cm}^2$$
$$x = \mathbf{8\ cm}$$

24. Surface area $= 4\pi r^2$
$\approx 4(3.14)(25\text{ in.}^2)$
$\approx \mathbf{314\ in.^2}$

25.
$$1\frac{2}{3}x = 32 - x$$
$$1\frac{2}{3}x + x = 32 - x + x$$
$$2\frac{2}{3}x = 32$$
$$\left(\frac{3}{8}\right)\left(\frac{8}{3}x\right) = \left(\frac{3}{8}\right)32$$
$$x = \mathbf{12}$$

26. $x^2 + x(x + 2)$
$x^2 + x^2 + 2x$
$\mathbf{2x^2 + 2x}$

27. $\frac{\cancel{(-2)} \cdot 2 \cdot a \cdot \cancel{x} \cdot \cancel{3} \cdot \cancel{x} \cdot y}{\cancel{(-2)} \cdot \cancel{3} \cdot \cancel{x} \cdot \cancel{x}}$
$= \mathbf{2ay}$

28. $1.1\{1.1[1.1(1000)]\}$
$1.1\{1.1[1100]\}$
$1.1\{1210\}$
1331

29. $3\frac{3}{4} \cdot 2\frac{2}{3} \div 10$
$= \frac{\overset{5}{\cancel{15}}}{\underset{1}{\cancel{4}}} \cdot \frac{\overset{2}{\cancel{8}}}{\underset{1}{\cancel{3}}} \div \frac{10}{1} = \overset{1}{\cancel{10}} \times \frac{1}{\underset{1}{\cancel{10}}} = \mathbf{1}$

30. (a) $(-6) - (7)(-4) + \sqrt[3]{125} + \frac{(-8)(-9)}{(-3)(-2)}$
$(-6) - (-28) + (5) + \frac{72}{6}$
$22 + (5) + 12$
39

(b) $(-1) + (-1)^2 + (-1)^3 + (-1)^4$
$(-1) + (1) + (-1) + (1)$
0

Lesson 109, Lesson Practice

a.
$$3x^2 - 8 = 100$$
$$3x^2 - 8 + 8 = 100 + 8$$
$$3x^2 = 108$$
$$x^2 = 36$$
$$x = \mathbf{6, -6}$$

b. $x^2 + x^2 = 12$
$2x^2 = 12$
$x^2 = 6$
$x = \mathbf{\sqrt{6}, -\sqrt{6}}$

c.
$$157 = 2(-x)^2 - 5$$
$$157 = 2x^2 - 5$$
$$157 + 5 = 2x^2 - 5 + 5$$
$$162 = 2x^2$$
$$81 = x^2$$
$$9, -9 = x$$
$$\mathbf{-9}$$

d. $7x^2 = 21$
$x^2 = 3$
$x = \sqrt{3}, -\sqrt{3}$
$\mathbf{\sqrt{3}}$

e. $\frac{w}{4} = \frac{9}{w}$
$w^2 = 36$
$w = \mathbf{6, -6}$

Lesson 109, Mixed Practice

1. $\frac{(0.2)(0.05)}{0.2 + 0.05} = \frac{0.01}{0.25} = \mathbf{0.04}$

2. (a) $\angle z$

(b) $\angle w$

(c) $\angle y$

(d)
$$\begin{aligned} 3m + m &= 180^\circ \\ 4m &= 180^\circ \\ m &= 45^\circ \\ 3m &= 3(45^\circ) = \mathbf{135^\circ} \end{aligned}$$

3.
$$\begin{aligned} 20 &= 5 + (10 \times W_D) \\ 20 - 5 &= 5 + (10 \times W_D) - 5 \\ 15 &= 10 \times W_D \\ \frac{15}{10} &= \frac{10 \times W_D}{10} \\ \mathbf{1.5} &= W_D \end{aligned}$$

4.
$$1 \cancel{\text{km}^2} \cdot \frac{1000 \text{ m}}{1 \cancel{\text{km}}} \cdot \frac{1000 \text{ m}}{1 \cancel{\text{km}}} = \mathbf{1{,}000{,}000 \text{ m}^2}$$

5.
$$\begin{aligned} 4(5) &= 20 \\ 10(5) &= 50 \\ \frac{\text{quarters}}{\text{dimes}} &= \frac{20}{50} = \mathbf{\frac{2}{5}} \end{aligned}$$

6.

	Case 1	Case 2
Meters	3000	5000
Minutes	9	m

$$\begin{aligned} \frac{3000}{9} &= \frac{5000}{m} \\ 3000m &= 45{,}000 \\ m &= \mathbf{15 \text{ minutes}} \end{aligned}$$

7.

	Percent	Actual Count
Original	100	O
+ Change	20	C
New	120	60

$$\begin{aligned} \frac{100}{120} &= \frac{O}{60} \\ 120O &= 6000 \\ O &= \mathbf{50} \end{aligned}$$

8.

	Percent	Actual Count
Original	100	\$36
− Change	25	C
New	75	N

$$\begin{aligned} \frac{100}{75} &= \frac{\$36}{N} \\ 100N &= \$2700 \\ N &= \mathbf{\$27} \end{aligned}$$

9.
$$\begin{aligned} \mathbf{60} &= \mathbf{1.5 \times W_N} \\ \frac{60}{1.5} &= \frac{1.5 \times W_N}{1.5} \\ \mathbf{40} &= W_N \end{aligned}$$

10.

702 cards

$\frac{2}{3}$ kept	234 cards
	234 cards
$\frac{1}{3}$ given away (234)	234 cards

(a) $3(234 \text{ cards}) = \mathbf{702 \text{ cards}}$

(b) $2(234 \text{ cards}) = \mathbf{468 \text{ cards}}$

11. $a - b \textcircled{>} b - a$

12.
$$\begin{aligned} p(c, c, c, c, c) &= \frac{1}{2} \cdot \frac{1}{2} \cdot \frac{1}{2} \cdot \frac{1}{2} \cdot \frac{1}{2} \\ &= \left(\frac{1}{2}\right)^5 = \mathbf{\frac{1}{32}} \end{aligned}$$

13.

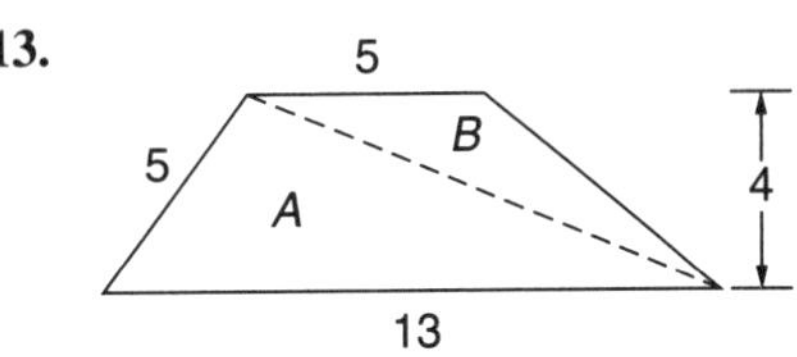

$$\begin{aligned} \text{Area of triangle } A &= \frac{(13 \text{ cm})(4 \text{ cm})}{2} = 26 \text{ cm}^2 \\ + \text{ Area of triangle } B &= \frac{(5 \text{ cm})(4 \text{ cm})}{2} = 10 \text{ cm}^2 \\ \hline \text{Area of figure} &= \mathbf{36 \text{ cm}^2} \end{aligned}$$

14.
$$\begin{aligned} \text{Area of base} &= \frac{(6 \text{ in.})(3 \text{ in.})}{2} = 9 \text{ in.}^2 \\ \text{Volume} &= (9 \text{ in.}^2)(6 \text{ in.}) = \mathbf{54 \text{ in.}^3} \end{aligned}$$

15.
$$\begin{aligned} C &\approx 3.14(6 \text{ in.}) \\ C &\approx 18.84 \text{ in.} \\ \text{Area} &\approx (18.84 \text{ in.})(3 \text{ in.}) \approx \mathbf{56.52 \text{ in.}^2} \end{aligned}$$

16. (a)
$$\begin{array}{r} \$36.00 \\ \times \ \ 0.065 \\ \hline \mathbf{\$2.34} \end{array}$$

(b)
$$\begin{array}{r} \$36.00 \\ + \ \ \$2.34 \\ \hline \mathbf{\$38.34} \end{array}$$

17. (a) $\mathbf{\frac{1}{200}}$

(b) **0.005**

18. $\dfrac{100}{166\frac{2}{3}} = \dfrac{\frac{100}{1}}{\frac{500}{3}} \cdot \dfrac{\frac{3}{500}}{\frac{3}{500}} = \dfrac{\frac{300}{500}}{1} = \dfrac{3}{5}$

$\dfrac{3}{5} = \dfrac{48}{n}$
$3n = 240$
$n = \mathbf{80}$

19. $(6 \times 10^{-8})(8 \times 10^{4})$
48×10^{-4}
$(4.8 \times 10^{1}) \times 10^{-4}$
$\mathbf{4.8 \times 10^{-3}}$

20. $y = \frac{2}{3}(6) - 1$
$y = 2(2) - 1$
$y = 4 - 1$
$y = \mathbf{3;}$
$y = \frac{2}{3}(0) - 1$
$y = 0 - 1$
$y = \mathbf{-1;}$
$y = \frac{2}{3}(-3) - 1$
$y = 2(-1) - 1$
$y = -2 - 1$
$y = \mathbf{-3}$

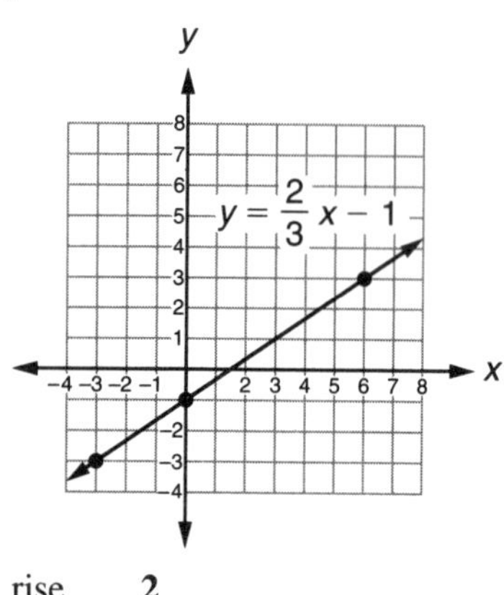

$\dfrac{\text{rise}}{\text{run}} = \mathbf{\dfrac{2}{3}}$

21.

	Ratio	Actual Count
Angle 1	7	A_1
Angle 2	8	A_2
Total	15	90°

$\dfrac{7}{15} = \dfrac{A_1}{90°}$
$15A_1 = 630°$
$A_1 = \mathbf{42°}$

22. $4x + 3x + 2x + x = 360°$
$10x = 360°$
$x = \mathbf{36°}$

23. $d^2 = (2 \text{ units})^2 + (5 \text{ units})^2$
$d^2 = 4 \text{ units}^2 + 25 \text{ units}^2$
$d^2 = 29 \text{ units}^2$
$d = \mathbf{\sqrt{29} \text{ units}}$

24. $3m^2 + 2 = 50$
$3m^2 + 2 - 2 = 50 - 2$
$3m^2 = 48$
$m^2 = 16$
$m = \mathbf{4, -4}$

25. $7(y - 2) = 4 - 2y$
$7y - 14 = 4 - 2y$
$7y - 14 + 2y = 4 - 2y + 2y$
$9y - 14 = 4$
$9y - 14 + 14 = 4 + 14$
$9y = 18$
$\dfrac{9y}{9} = \dfrac{18}{9}$
$y = \mathbf{2}$

26. $\sqrt{144} - (\sqrt{36})(\sqrt{4})$
$= 12 - (6)(2) = 12 - 12 = \mathbf{0}$

27. $x^2y + xy^2 + x(xy - y^2)$
$= x^2y + xy^2 + x^2y - xy^2$
$= \mathbf{2x^2y}$

28. $\left(1\frac{5}{9}\right)\left(1\frac{1}{2}\right) \div 2\frac{2}{3}$
$= \left(\frac{14}{9}\right)\left(\frac{3}{2}\right) \div \frac{8}{3} = \frac{7}{3} \div \frac{8}{3}$
$= \frac{7}{3} \times \frac{3}{8} = \mathbf{\frac{7}{8}}$

29. $9.5 - (4.2 - 3.4)$
$= 9.5 - 0.8 = \mathbf{8.7}$

30. (a) $\dfrac{(-18) + (-12) - (-6)(3)}{-3}$
$\dfrac{(-30) - (-18)}{-3}$
$\dfrac{-12}{-3}$
$\mathbf{4}$

(b) $\sqrt[3]{1000} - \sqrt[3]{125} = 10 - 5 = \mathbf{5}$

(c) $2^2 + 2^1 + 2^0 + 2^{-1}$
$= 4 + 2 + 1 + \frac{1}{2} = \mathbf{7\frac{1}{2}}$ or $\mathbf{7.5}$

Lesson 110, Lesson Practice

a. **\$132,528.15**

b.
$$\$6000 \times 0.08 = \$480$$
$$\frac{8}{12} \times \$480 = \$320$$
$$\$6000 + \$320 = \mathbf{\$6320}$$
$$\mathbf{\frac{8}{12}} \text{ or } \mathbf{\frac{2}{3}}$$

c. 80% of 80% of \$300
$$= 0.8 \times 0.8 \times \$300$$
$$= 0.64 \times \$300 = \mathbf{\$192}$$

Lesson 110, Mixed Practice

1. $3(\$5.95) = \$17.85$

$$\begin{array}{r} \$17.85 \\ \times \quad 0.06 \\ \hline \$1.071 \end{array} \longrightarrow \$1.07 \qquad \begin{array}{r} \$17.85 \\ + \quad \$1.07 \\ \hline \$18.92 \end{array}$$

$$\begin{array}{r} \$20.00 \\ - \ \$18.92 \\ \hline \mathbf{\$1.08} \end{array}$$

2. 90% of 75% of \$24
$$= 0.9 \times 0.75 \times \$24 = 0.675 \times \$24$$
$$= \mathbf{\$16.20}$$

3.

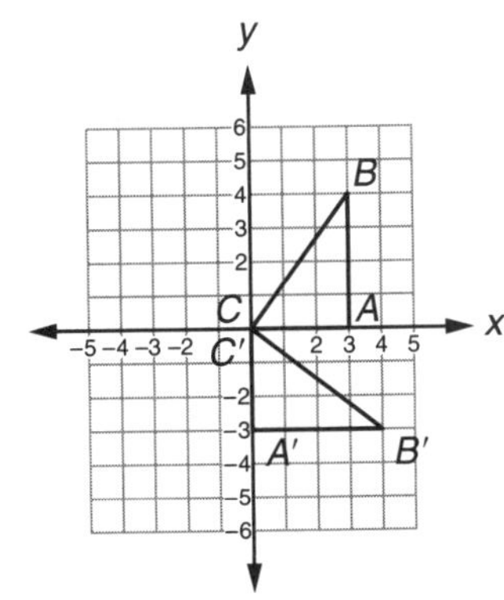

$\mathbf{A'(0, -3), B'(4, -3), C'(0, 0)}$

4.

	Case 1	Case 2
Miles	1	m
Calories	100	350

$$\frac{1}{100} = \frac{m}{350}$$
$$100m = 350$$
$$m = \mathbf{3.5 \text{ miles}}$$

5.

	Case 1	Case 2
Roses	12	30
Dollars	\$4.90	d

$$\frac{12}{\$4.90} = \frac{30}{d}$$
$$12d = \$147$$
$$d = \mathbf{\$12.25}$$

6.
$$C \approx \frac{\frac{22}{7}(7 \text{ in.})}{2}$$
$$C \approx \frac{22 \text{ in.}}{2}$$
$$C \approx 11 \text{ in.}$$
$$\text{Perimeter} \approx 11 \text{ in.} + 7 \text{ in.} + 7 \text{ in.}$$
$$+ \ 7 \text{ in.} \approx \mathbf{32 \text{ in.}}$$

7.
$$8(4) = 32$$
$$32 - (2 + 4 + 6) = \mathbf{20}$$

8. $\mathbf{150 = W_P \times 60}$
$$\frac{150}{60} = \frac{W_P \times 60}{60}$$
$$\frac{5}{2} = W_P$$
$$W_P = \frac{5}{2} \times 100\% = \mathbf{250\%}$$

9. $\mathbf{0.6 \times W_N = 150}$
$$\frac{0.6 \times W_N}{0.6} = \frac{150}{0.6}$$
$$W_N = \mathbf{250}$$

10. $\mathbf{(-x)^2 + 6 = 150}$
$$x^2 + 6 = 150$$
$$x^2 + 6 - 6 = 150 - 6$$
$$x^2 = 144$$
$$x = 12, -12$$
$$\mathbf{-12}$$

11.

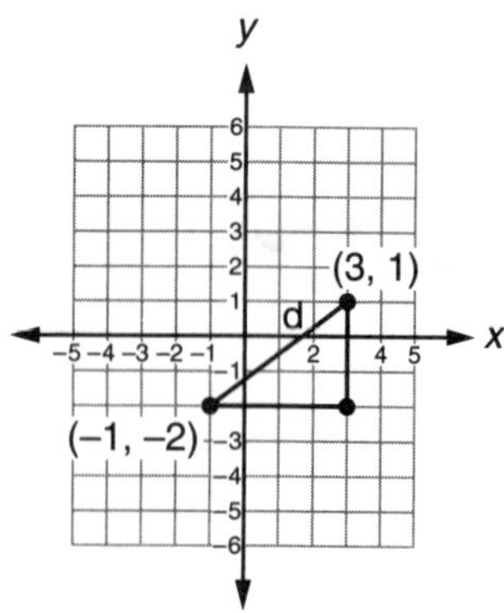

$$d^2 = (4 \text{ units})^2 + (3 \text{ units})^2$$
$$d^2 = 16 \text{ units}^2 + 9 \text{ units}^2$$
$$d^2 = 25 \text{ units}^2$$
$$d = \mathbf{5 \text{ units}}$$

12.

	Percent	Actual Count
Original	100	O
− Change	40	C
New	60	\$48

$$\frac{100}{60} = \frac{O}{\$48}$$
$$60O = \$4800$$
$$O = \mathbf{\$80}$$

13.

	Scale	Actual Size
Model	1	m
Car	36	180

$$\frac{1}{36} = \frac{m}{180}$$
$$36m = 180$$
$$m = \mathbf{5 \text{ inches}}$$

14. **8 and 9**

15. **See student work;**

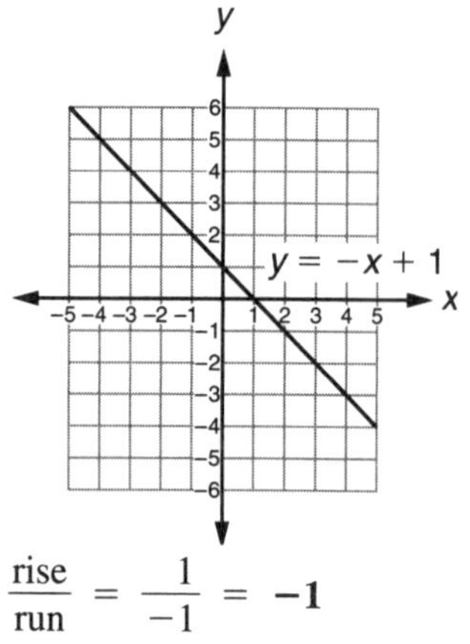

$$\frac{\text{rise}}{\text{run}} = \frac{1}{-1} = \mathbf{-1}$$

16.
$$5x + 12 \geq 2$$
$$5x + 12 - 12 \geq 2 - 12$$
$$5x \geq -10$$
$$\frac{5x}{5} \geq \frac{-10}{5}$$
$$\mathbf{x \geq -2}$$

$x \geq -2$

−3 −2 −1 0 1

17.
$$(6.3 \times 9) \times (10^7 \times 10^{-3})$$
$$= 56.7 \times 10^4$$
$$= \mathbf{5.67 \times 10^5}$$

18.
$$\frac{1}{2}y = x + 2$$
$$\left(\frac{2}{1}\right)\frac{1}{2}y = \frac{2}{1}(x + 2)$$
$$\mathbf{y = 2x + 4}$$

19.
```
    $4000
  ×  1.09
    $4360
  ×  1.09
 $4752.40
 ×   1.09
$5180.116  ⟶  $5180.12
```

\$5180.12

20. (a) **See student work;**
$$\frac{x}{8} = \frac{3}{4}$$
$$4x = 24$$
$$x = \mathbf{6 \text{ in.}}$$

(b)
$$4f = 3$$
$$f = \frac{3}{4} = \mathbf{0.75}$$

21.
$$\text{Area of base} = \frac{(16 \text{ in.})(12 \text{ in.})}{2}$$
$$= 96 \text{ in.}^2$$
$$\text{Volume} = (96 \text{ in.}^2)(10 \text{ in.}) = \mathbf{960 \text{ in.}^3}$$

22.

Area of triangle		$= 96 \text{ in.}^2$
Area of triangle		$= 96 \text{ in.}^2$
Area of rectangle	$= (10 \text{ in.})(20 \text{ in.})$	$= 200 \text{ in.}^2$
Area of rectangle	$= (10 \text{ in.})(16 \text{ in.})$	$= 160 \text{ in.}^2$
+ Area of rectangle	$= (10 \text{ in.})(12 \text{ in.})$	$= 120 \text{ in.}^2$
Total surface area		$= \mathbf{672 \text{ in.}^2}$

23.
$$m\angle x = 180° - (80° + 30°) = 70°$$
$$180° - 70° = \mathbf{110°}$$

24. $\frac{w}{2} = \frac{18}{w}$

$w^2 = 36$

$w = \mathbf{6, -6}$

25. $3\frac{1}{3}w^2 - 4 = 26$

$3\frac{1}{3}w^2 - 4 + 4 = 26 + 4$

$\frac{10}{3}w^2 = 30$

$\left(\frac{3}{10}\right)\frac{10}{3}w^2 = \left(\frac{3}{10}\right)30$

$w^2 = 9$

$w = \mathbf{3, -3}$

26. $16 - \{27 - 3[8 - (3^2 - 2^3)]\}$

$16 - \{27 - 3[8 - (9 - 8)]\}$

$16 - \{27 - 3[8 - (1)]\}$

$16 - \{27 - 3[7]\}$

$16 - \{27 - 21\}$

$16 - \{6\}$

10

27. $\frac{(6ab^2)(8ab)}{12a^2b^2}$

$= \frac{\overset{1}{\cancel{2}} \cdot \overset{1}{\cancel{3}} \cdot \overset{1}{\cancel{a}} \cdot \overset{1}{\cancel{b}} \cdot \overset{1}{\cancel{b}} \cdot \overset{1}{\cancel{2}} \cdot 2 \cdot 2 \cdot \overset{1}{\cancel{a}} \cdot b}{\underset{1}{\cancel{2}} \cdot \underset{1}{\cancel{2}} \cdot \underset{1}{\cancel{3}} \cdot \underset{1}{\cancel{a}} \cdot \underset{1}{\cancel{a}} \cdot \underset{1}{\cancel{b}} \cdot \underset{1}{\cancel{b}}}$

$= \mathbf{4b}$

28. $3\frac{1}{3} + 1\frac{1}{2} + 4\frac{5}{6}$

$= 3\frac{2}{6} + 1\frac{3}{6} + 4\frac{5}{6} = 8\frac{10}{6} = 9\frac{4}{6}$

$= \mathbf{9\frac{2}{3}}$

29. $20 \div \left(3\frac{1}{3} \div 1\frac{1}{5}\right) = 20 \div \left(\frac{\overset{5}{\cancel{10}}}{3} \times \frac{5}{\underset{3}{\cancel{6}}}\right)$

$= 20 \div \frac{25}{9} = \frac{\overset{4}{\cancel{20}}}{1} \times \frac{9}{\underset{5}{\cancel{25}}} = \frac{36}{5} = \mathbf{7\frac{1}{5}}$

30. $(-3)^2 + (-2)^3 = 9 + (-8) = \mathbf{1}$

Lesson 111, Lesson Practice

a. $2\overline{)3.6}$ = 1.8 **1.8 × 10⁶**

b. $25\overline{)75}$ = 3 $\mathbf{3 \times 10^{-6}}$

c. $3\overline{)4.5}$ = 1.5 $\mathbf{1.5 \times 10^{-4}}$

d. $15\overline{)60}$ = 4 $\mathbf{4 \times 10^{4}}$

e. $8\overline{)4.0}$ = 0.5

$0.5 \times 10^8 \longrightarrow \mathbf{5 \times 10^7}$

f. $3\overline{)1.5}$ = 0.5

$0.5 \times 10^{-8} \longrightarrow \mathbf{5 \times 10^{-9}}$

g. $6\overline{)3.6}$ = 0.6

$0.6 \times 10^{-6} \longrightarrow \mathbf{6 \times 10^{-7}}$

h. $9\overline{)1.8}$ = 0.2

$0.2 \times 10^{6} \longrightarrow \mathbf{2 \times 10^{5}}$

Lesson 111, Mixed Practice

1.
$$\begin{array}{r} 1909 \\ -\ 1859 \\ \hline 50 \end{array}$$

50 years + 1 year = **51 years (The year 1859 should be counted.)**

2. $15y = 600$

$\frac{15y}{15} = \frac{600}{15}$

$y = 40$

$40 + 15 = \mathbf{55}$

3. (a) $70\% = \frac{70}{100} = \mathbf{\frac{7}{10}}$

(b) $\frac{\text{agreed}}{\text{disagreed}} = \mathbf{\frac{3}{7}}$

4.

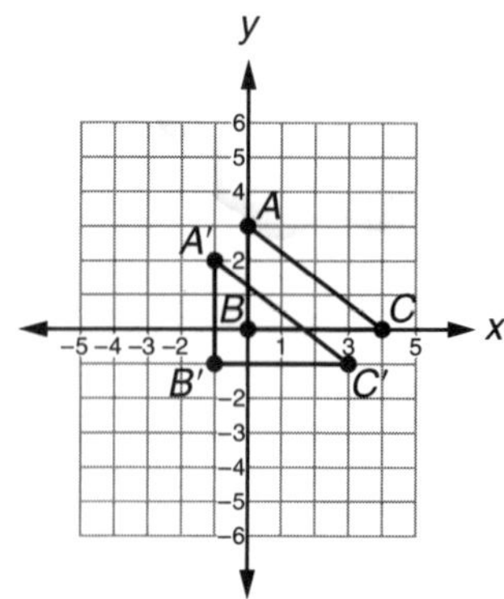

A′(−1, 2), B′(−1, −1), C′(3, −1)

5. (a) $\mathbf{2^{10}}$

(b) **32**

6. (a) $180° - 150° = \mathbf{30°}$

(b) $\dfrac{360°}{30°} = 12$, **12 sides**

(c) **Dodecagon**

7. $\dfrac{100}{60} = \dfrac{p}{\$48}$
$60p = \$4800$
$p = \mathbf{\$80}$

8. (a) $P(R, W, B) = \mathbf{\dfrac{3}{12} \cdot \dfrac{4}{11} \cdot \dfrac{5}{10} = \dfrac{1}{22}}$

(b) $P(B, W, R) = \mathbf{\dfrac{5}{12} \cdot \dfrac{4}{11} \cdot \dfrac{3}{10} = \dfrac{1}{22}}$

9. $\mathbf{2x + 6 = 36}$
$2x + 6 - 6 = 36 - 6$
$2x = 30$
$\dfrac{2x}{2} = \dfrac{30}{2}$
$x = \mathbf{15}$

10. $2x + x + x = 180°$
$4x = 180°$
$\dfrac{4x}{4} = \dfrac{180°}{4}$
$x = \mathbf{45°}$

11. $c^2 - b^2 = a^2$
$c^2 - b^2 + b^2 = a^2 + b^2$
$\mathbf{c^2 = a^2 + b^2}$

12. (a) $m\angle a = m\angle h = \mathbf{105°}$

(b) $m\angle b = 180° - 105° = \mathbf{75°}$

(c) $m\angle c = m\angle b = \mathbf{75°}$

(d) $m\angle d = m\angle a = \mathbf{105°}$

13. $F = 1.8C + 32$
$F = 1.8(17) + 32$
$F = 62.6°$
63° F

14. $\dfrac{45°}{360°} = \dfrac{1}{8}$
$A \approx \dfrac{3.14(144 \text{ in.}^2)}{8}$
$A \approx 56.52 \text{ in.}^2 \approx \mathbf{57 \text{ in.}^2}$

15. **See student work;**

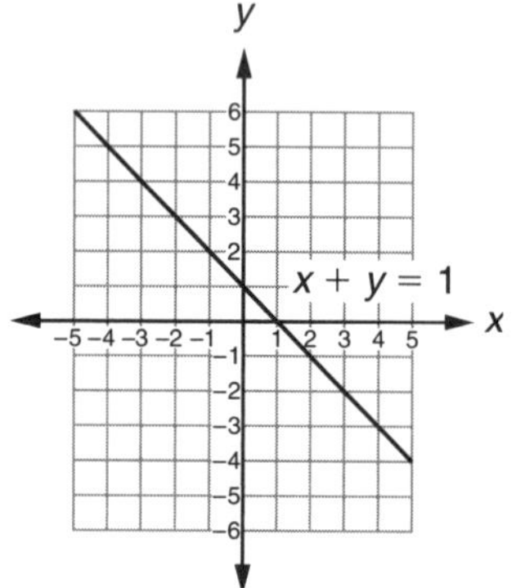

16. (a) $\dfrac{\text{rise}}{\text{run}} = \dfrac{1}{-1} = \mathbf{-1}$

(b) **(0, 1)**

17. 24 in. = 2 ft; 36 in. = 3 ft
$C \approx 3.14(2 \text{ ft})$
$C \approx 6.28 \text{ ft}$
$A \approx (6.28 \text{ ft})(3 \text{ ft})$
$A \approx \mathbf{18.84 \text{ ft}^2}$

18. Area of base $\approx 3.14(1 \text{ ft}^2)$
$\approx 3.14 \text{ ft}^2$
Volume $\approx (3.14 \text{ ft}^2)(3 \text{ ft})$
$\approx \mathbf{9.42 \text{ ft}^3}$

19. (a) $2x^2 + 1 = 19$
$2x^2 + 1 - 1 = 19 - 1$
$2x^2 = 18$
$\dfrac{2x^2}{2} = \dfrac{18}{2}$
$x^2 = 9$
$x = \mathbf{3, -3}$

(b)
$$\begin{aligned} 2x^2 - 1 &= 19 \\ 2x^2 - 1 + 1 &= 19 + 1 \\ 2x^2 &= 20 \\ \frac{2x^2}{2} &= \frac{20}{2} \\ x^2 &= 10 \\ x &= \mathbf{\sqrt{10}, -\sqrt{10}} \end{aligned}$$

20.

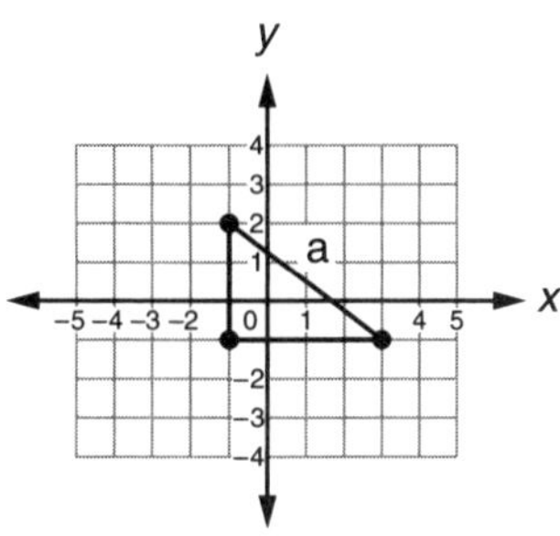

$$\begin{aligned} a^2 &= (3 \text{ units})^2 + (4 \text{ units})^2 \\ a^2 &= 9 \text{ units}^2 + 16 \text{ units}^2 \\ a^2 &= 25 \text{ units}^2 \\ a &= 5 \text{ units} \\ \text{Perimeter} &= 5 \text{ units} + 3 \text{ units} \\ &\quad + 4 \text{ units} = \mathbf{12 \text{ units}} \end{aligned}$$

21.

$$\begin{array}{r} \$5000 \\ \times \quad 1.05 \\ \hline \$5250 \\ \times \quad 1.05 \\ \hline \$5512.50 \\ \times \quad 1.05 \\ \hline \$5788.125 \\ \times \quad 1.05 \\ \hline \$6077.53125 \\ \times \quad 1.05 \\ \hline \$6381.407813 \end{array} \longrightarrow \mathbf{\$6381.41}$$

22. (a)
$$\begin{aligned} AB^2 &= (15 \text{ cm})^2 + (20 \text{ cm})^2 \\ AB^2 &= 225 \text{ cm}^2 + 400 \text{ cm}^2 \\ AB^2 &= 625 \text{ cm}^2 \\ AB &= \mathbf{25 \text{ cm}} \end{aligned}$$

(b)
$$\begin{aligned} \frac{20 \text{ cm}}{25 \text{ cm}} &= \frac{CD}{15 \text{ cm}} \\ (25 \text{ cm})CD &= 300 \text{ cm}^2 \\ CD &= \mathbf{12 \text{ cm}} \end{aligned}$$

23. (a) $6\overline{)3.6}$ with quotient 0.6 $\quad 0.6 \times 10^2 \longrightarrow \mathbf{6 \times 10^1}$

(b) $12\overline{)36}$ with quotient 3 $\quad \mathbf{3 \times 10^{-2}}$

24.
$$\begin{aligned} 180° - 140° &= 40° \\ 180° - (90° + 40°) &= 50° \\ m\angle y = 180° - 50° &= \mathbf{130°} \end{aligned}$$

25.
$$\begin{aligned} 5x + 3x &= 18 + 2x \\ 8x - 2x &= 18 + 2x - 2x \\ 6x &= 18 \\ \frac{6x}{6} &= \frac{18}{6} \\ x &= \mathbf{3} \end{aligned}$$

26.
$$\begin{aligned} \frac{3.6}{x} &= \frac{4.5}{0.06} \\ 4.5x &= 0.216 \\ \frac{4.5x}{4.5} &= \frac{0.216}{4.5} \\ x &= \mathbf{0.048} \end{aligned}$$

27. (a) $(-1)^6 + (-1)^5 = 1 + (-1) = \mathbf{0}$

(b) $(-10)^6 \div (-10)^5 = (-10)^1 = \mathbf{-10}$

28. (a)
$$\begin{aligned} &\frac{(4a^2b)(9ab^2c)}{6abc} \\ &= \frac{\overset{1}{\cancel{2}} \cdot 2 \cdot \overset{1}{\cancel{3}} \cdot 3 \cdot \overset{1}{\cancel{a}} \cdot a \cdot a \cdot \overset{1}{\cancel{b}} \cdot b \cdot b \cdot \overset{1}{\cancel{c}}}{\underset{1}{\cancel{2}} \cdot \underset{1}{\cancel{3}} \cdot \underset{1}{\cancel{a}} \cdot \underset{1}{\cancel{b}} \cdot \underset{1}{\cancel{c}}} \\ &= \mathbf{6\,a^2b^2} \end{aligned}$$

(b)
$$\begin{aligned} &x(x - c) + cx \\ &x^2 - cx + cx \\ &\mathbf{x^2} \end{aligned}$$

29.
$$\begin{aligned} &(-3) + (+2)(-4) - (-6)(-2) - (-8) \\ &(-3) + (-8) - (12) - (-8) \\ &\mathbf{-15} \end{aligned}$$

30.
$$\begin{aligned} 3\frac{1}{3} \cdot 1\frac{4}{5} &= \frac{\overset{2}{\cancel{10}}}{\underset{1}{\cancel{3}}} \cdot \frac{\overset{3}{\cancel{9}}}{\underset{1}{\cancel{5}}} = 6 \\ 6 + 1.5 &= 7.5 \\ \frac{7.5}{0.03} &= \mathbf{250} \end{aligned}$$

LESSON 112, LESSON PRACTICE

a.

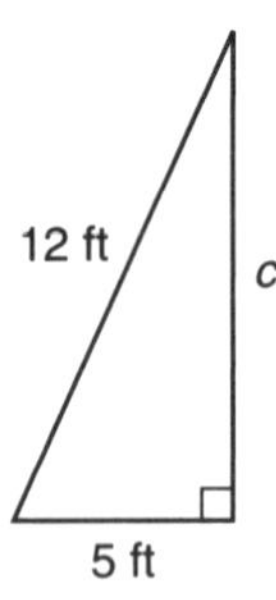

$$(5\text{ ft})^2 + c^2 = (12\text{ ft})^2$$
$$25\text{ ft}^2 + c^2 = 144\text{ ft}^2$$
$$25\text{ ft}^2 + c^2 - 25\text{ ft}^2 = 144\text{ ft}^2 - 25\text{ ft}^2$$
$$c^2 = 119\text{ ft}^2$$
$$c = \sqrt{119\text{ ft}^2} \approx 10.9\text{ ft}$$
$$c \approx \textbf{10 feet 11 inches}$$

b.
$$(AC)^2 = (400\text{ ft})^2 + (300\text{ ft})^2$$
$$(AC)^2 = 160{,}000\text{ ft}^2 + 90{,}000\text{ ft}^2$$
$$(AC)^2 = 250{,}000\text{ ft}^2$$
$$AC = 500\text{ feet}$$
$$(300\text{ feet} + 400\text{ feet}) - 500\text{ feet} = \textbf{200 feet}$$

LESSON 112, MIXED PRACTICE

1.

$$\begin{array}{r} \$3000 \\ \times\ 1.08 \\ \hline \$3240 \\ \times\ 1.08 \\ \hline \$3499.20 \\ \times\ 1.08 \\ \hline \$3799.1360 \end{array} \longrightarrow \textbf{\$3799.14}$$

2. $\sqrt{(3)^2 + (4)^2} = \sqrt{9 + 16} = \sqrt{25} = \mathbf{5}$

3. (a) **90**

(b) **95**

4. $\dfrac{840\text{ kilometers}}{10.5\text{ hours}} =$ **80 kilometers per hour**

5.

	Case 1	Case 2
Hours	6	9
Earnings	$28	*e*

$$\frac{6}{\$28} = \frac{9}{e}$$
$$6e = \$252$$
$$e = \textbf{\$42}$$

6.

	Percent	Actual Count
Original	100	*O*
− Change	25	*C*
New	75	$48

$$\frac{100}{75} = \frac{O}{\$48}$$
$$75O = \$4800$$
$$O = \textbf{\$64}$$

7.

	Percent	Actual Count
Original	100	$6
+ Change	25	*C*
New	125	*N*

$$\frac{100}{25} = \frac{\$6}{C}$$
$$100C = \$150$$
$$C = \textbf{\$1.50}$$

8. 50% of 50% of $1.00
$= (0.5)(0.5) \times \$1.00 = 0.25 \times \$1.00$
$=$ **$0.25**

9. $60\% = \dfrac{60}{100} = \dfrac{6}{10} = \dfrac{3}{5} = \dfrac{\text{boys}}{\text{total}}$

$\dfrac{\text{boys}}{\text{girls}} = \mathbf{\dfrac{3}{2}}$

10.

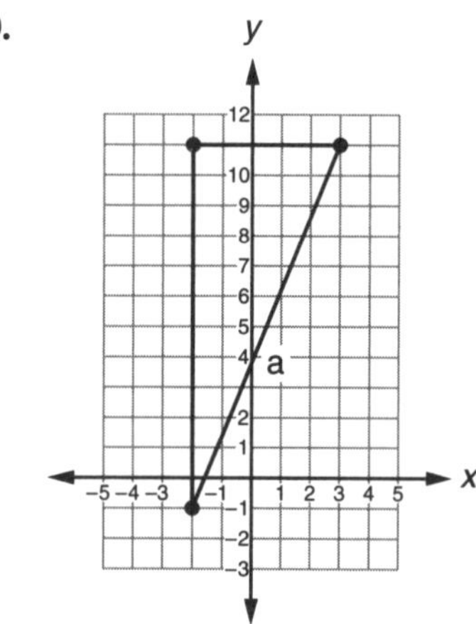

$$a^2 = (12\text{ units})^2 + (5\text{ units})^2$$
$$a^2 = 144\text{ units}^2 + 25\text{ units}^2$$
$$a^2 = 169\text{ units}^2$$
$$a = \textbf{13 units}$$

11.

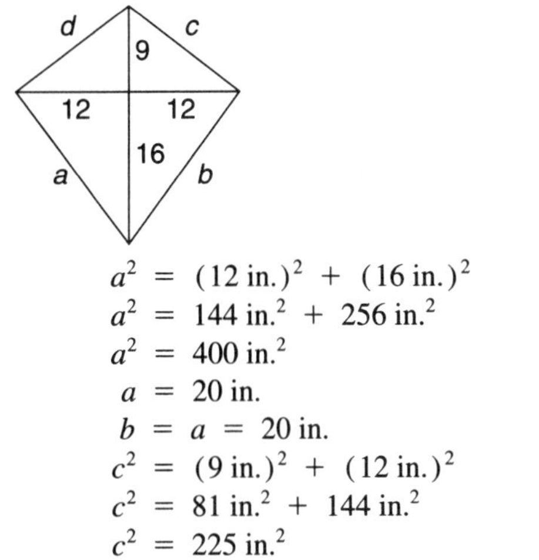

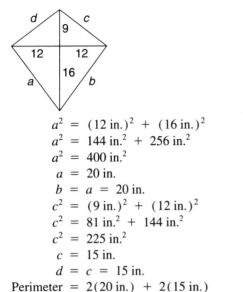

$$\begin{aligned} a^2 &= (12 \text{ in.})^2 + (16 \text{ in.})^2 \\ a^2 &= 144 \text{ in.}^2 + 256 \text{ in.}^2 \\ a^2 &= 400 \text{ in.}^2 \\ a &= 20 \text{ in.} \\ b &= a = 20 \text{ in.} \\ c^2 &= (9 \text{ in.})^2 + (12 \text{ in.})^2 \\ c^2 &= 81 \text{ in.}^2 + 144 \text{ in.}^2 \\ c^2 &= 225 \text{ in.}^2 \\ c &= 15 \text{ in.} \\ d &= c = 15 \text{ in.} \\ \text{Perimeter} &= 2(20 \text{ in.}) + 2(15 \text{ in.}) \\ &= 40 \text{ in.} + 30 \text{ in.} = \mathbf{70 \text{ inches}} \end{aligned}$$

12. $\mathbf{W_P \times 2.5 = 2}$

$$\begin{aligned} \frac{W_P \times 2.5}{2.5} &= \frac{2}{2.5} \\ W_P &= 0.8 \\ W_P &= 0.8 \times 100\% = \mathbf{80\%} \end{aligned}$$

13. $2 \times 2 \times 2 \times 2 = 16$ possible outcomes
1 favorable outcome
15 unfavorable outcomes
Odds = favorable to unfavorable
= **1 to 15**

14.

$$\begin{array}{r} \$4000 \\ \times \ \ 0.09 \\ \hline \$360 \end{array} \qquad \frac{6}{12} = \frac{1}{2}$$

$$\left(\frac{1}{2}\right)\$360 = \mathbf{\$180}$$

15. (a) **0.625**

(b) **62.5%**

16. (a) $2\overline{)5.0}$ with quotient 2.5 $\qquad \mathbf{2.5 \times 10^4}$

(b) $4\overline{)1.2}$ with quotient 0.3 $\qquad 0.3 \times 10^{-4} \longrightarrow \mathbf{3 \times 10^{-5}}$

17. $300 \not{\text{kg}} \cdot \dfrac{1000 \text{ g}}{1 \not{\text{kg}}} = \mathbf{300{,}000 \text{ g}}$

18.

$$\begin{aligned} d &= rt \\ \frac{d}{r} &= \frac{rt}{r} \\ \mathbf{\frac{d}{r}} &= \mathbf{t} \end{aligned}$$

19. **See student work;**

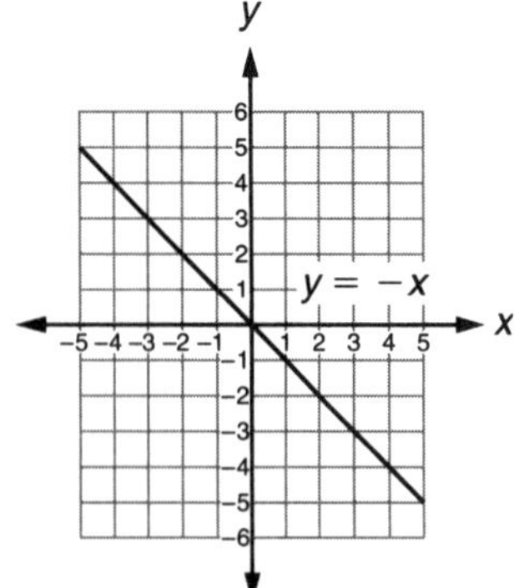

20.

$$\begin{aligned} C &\approx \frac{3.14(20 \text{ cm})}{2} \\ C &\approx 31.4 \text{ cm} \\ \text{Perimeter} &\approx 31.4 \text{ cm} + 20 \text{ cm} \\ &\quad + 20 \text{ cm} + 20 \text{ cm} \approx \mathbf{91.4 \text{ cm}} \end{aligned}$$

21.

$$\begin{aligned} \text{Area of triangle} &= \frac{(9 \text{ ft})(12 \text{ ft})}{2} = 54 \text{ ft}^2 \\ \text{Area of triangle} &= \frac{(9 \text{ ft})(12 \text{ ft})}{2} = 54 \text{ ft}^2 \\ \text{Area of rectangle} &= (10 \text{ ft})(12 \text{ ft}) = 120 \text{ ft}^2 \\ \text{Area of rectangle} &= (10 \text{ ft})(15 \text{ ft}) = 150 \text{ ft}^2 \\ + \ \text{Area of rectangle} &= (10 \text{ ft})(9 \text{ ft}) = 90 \text{ ft}^2 \\ \hline \text{Total surface area} &= \mathbf{468 \text{ ft}^2} \end{aligned}$$

22. (a) $\mathbf{2^{12} \cdot 5^{12}}$

(b) **1,000,000**

23. (a)

$$\begin{aligned} \frac{x}{9} &= \frac{8}{12} \\ 12x &= 72 \\ x &= \mathbf{6 \text{ cm}} \end{aligned}$$

(b)

$$\begin{aligned} 8f &= 12 \\ f &= \frac{12}{8} \\ f &= \frac{3}{2} = \mathbf{1.5} \end{aligned}$$

24.

$$\begin{aligned} \frac{16}{2.5} &= \frac{48}{f} \\ 16f &= 120 \\ f &= \mathbf{7.5} \end{aligned}$$

25.
$$2\frac{2}{3}x - 3 = 21$$
$$2\frac{2}{3}x - 3 + 3 = 21 + 3$$
$$2\frac{2}{3}x = 24$$
$$\left(\frac{3}{8}\right)\frac{8}{3}x = \left(\frac{3}{8}\right)24$$
$$x = \mathbf{9}$$

26.
$$10^2 - [10 - 10(10^0 - 10^{-1})]$$
$$100 - \left[10 - 10\left(1 - \frac{1}{10}\right)\right]$$
$$100 - \left[10 - 10\left(\frac{9}{10}\right)\right]$$
$$100 - [10 - 9]$$
$$100 - [1]$$
$$\mathbf{99}$$

27.
$$2\frac{3}{4} - \left(1\frac{1}{2} - \frac{1}{6}\right)$$
$$= \frac{11}{4} - \left(\frac{9}{6} - \frac{1}{6}\right) = \frac{11}{4} - \frac{8}{6}$$
$$= \frac{33}{12} - \frac{16}{12} = \frac{17}{12} = \mathbf{1\frac{5}{12}}$$

28.
$$3\frac{1}{2} \div 1\frac{2}{5} \div 3$$
$$= \left(\frac{7}{2} \times \frac{5}{7}\right) \div 3 = \frac{5}{2} \times \frac{1}{3} = \mathbf{\frac{5}{6}}$$

29.
$$|-4| - (-3)(-2)(-1) + \frac{(-5)(4)(-3)(2)}{-1}$$
$$4 - (-6) + \frac{(-20)(-6)}{-1}$$
$$4 - (-6) + \frac{120}{-1}$$
$$4 - (-6) - 120$$
$$10 + (-120)$$
$$\mathbf{-110}$$

30.
$$\text{Surface area} = 4\pi r^2$$
$$\approx 4\left(\frac{22}{7}\right)(49 \text{ cm}^2)$$
$$\approx 4(22)(7 \text{ cm}^2)$$
$$\approx 616 \text{ cm}^2$$
$$\approx \mathbf{600 \text{ cm}^2}$$

Lesson 113, Lesson Practice

a. $\mathbf{\frac{1}{3}}$

b. $\mathbf{\frac{2}{3}}$

c. $\mathbf{\frac{2}{3}}$

d. $\mathbf{\frac{1}{3}}$

e. **All of the box would be filled.** $\left(\mathbf{\frac{1}{3} + \frac{2}{3} = 1}\right)$

f.
$$\text{Volume of box} = (12 \text{ in.})(12 \text{ in.})(12 \text{ in.})$$
$$= \mathbf{1728 \text{ in.}^3}$$
$$\text{Volume of pyramid} = \frac{1}{3}(1728 \text{ in.}^3)$$
$$= \mathbf{576 \text{ in.}^3}$$

g.
$$\text{Area of base} = \pi(9 \text{ in.}^2)$$
$$= 9\pi \text{ in.}^2$$
$$\text{Volume} = \frac{1}{3}(9\pi \text{ in.}^2)(6 \text{ in.})$$
$$= \mathbf{18\pi \text{ in.}^3}$$

h.
$$\text{Volume} = \frac{4}{3}\pi(3 \text{ in.})^3$$
$$= \frac{4}{3}\pi(27 \text{ in.}^3) = \mathbf{36\pi \text{ in.}^3}$$

Lesson 113, Mixed Practice

1. 75% of 75% of $24
$$= (0.75)(0.75) \times \$24 = \mathbf{\$13.50}$$

2.
```
  0 9 9 1
  1̸0̸,0̸ 0 0,0 0 0,0 0 0
−    9 8 0,0 0 0,0 0 0
   9,0 2 0,0 0 0,0 0 0
```
$\mathbf{9.02 \times 10^9}$

3.
$$\text{Mean} = 8.45 \div 5 = 1.69$$
$$\text{Mean} - \text{median} = 1.69 - 0.75$$
$$= \mathbf{0.94}$$

4. (a) $\frac{\$24}{5 \text{ hours}} = \mathbf{\$4.80 \text{ per hour}}$

(b) $\dfrac{\$33}{6 \text{ hours}} = \mathbf{\$5.50 \text{ per hour}}$

(c)
$$\begin{array}{r} \$5.50 \\ - \ \$4.80 \\ \hline \end{array}$$
$0.70 more per hour

5.

	Case 1	Case 2
Kilograms	24	42
Cost	$31	c

$$\frac{24}{\$31} = \frac{42}{c}$$
$$24c = \$1302$$
$$c = \mathbf{\$54.25}$$

6. $\dfrac{5}{8}(1760 \text{ yards}) =$ **about 1100 yards**

7. $P(H, H) = \dfrac{13}{52} \cdot \dfrac{13}{52} = \dfrac{1}{4} \cdot \dfrac{1}{4} = \mathbf{\dfrac{1}{16}}$

8. $\mathbf{W_P \times \$30 = \$1.50}$
$$\frac{W_P \times \$30}{\$30} = \frac{\$1.50}{\$30}$$
$$W_P = 0.05$$
$$W_P = 0.05 \times 100\% = \mathbf{5\%}$$

9. $\mathbf{\dfrac{1}{2} \times W_N = 2\dfrac{1}{2}}$
$$\frac{2}{1}\left(\frac{1}{2} \times W_N\right) = \left(\frac{2}{1}\right)\frac{5}{2}$$
$$W_N = \mathbf{5}$$

10.
$$\begin{array}{r} \$5000 \\ \times \quad 1.08 \\ \hline \$5400 \\ \times \quad 1.08 \\ \hline \$5832 \\ \times \quad 1.08 \\ \hline \$6298.56 \\ - \ \$5000.00 \\ \hline \mathbf{\$1298.56} \end{array}$$

11.

	Percent	Actual Count
Original	100	$12
− Change	20	C
New	80	N

$$\frac{100}{80} = \frac{\$12}{N}$$
$$100N = \$960$$
$$N = \mathbf{\$9.60}$$

12.

	Scale	Actual Size
Model	24	6 ft = 72 in.
Figurine	1	F

$$\frac{24}{1} = \frac{72 \text{ in.}}{F}$$
$$24F = 72 \text{ in.}$$
$$F = \mathbf{3 \text{ inches}}$$

13.

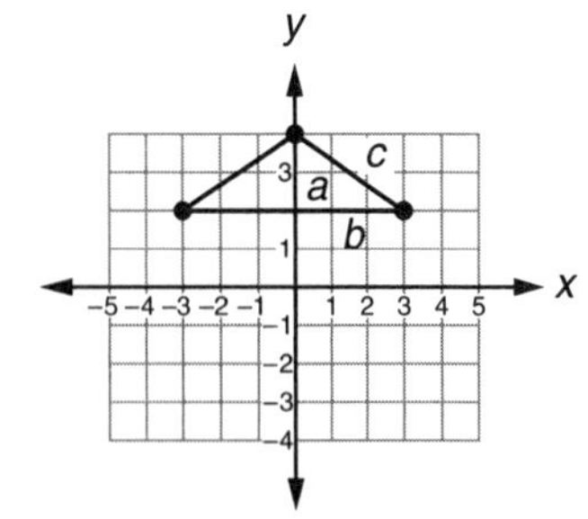

$$A = \frac{(6 \text{ units})(2 \text{ units})}{2} = \mathbf{6 \text{ units}^2}$$

14.
$$(2 \text{ units})^2 + (3 \text{ units})^2 = c^2$$
$$4 \text{ units}^2 + 9 \text{ units}^2 = c^2$$
$$13 \text{ units}^2 = c^2$$
$$\mathbf{\sqrt{13} \text{ units}} = c$$

15.
$$\text{Volume} \approx \frac{4}{3}(3)(3 \text{ cm})^3$$
$$\approx \frac{4}{3}(3)(27 \text{ cm}^3)$$
$$\approx 4(27 \text{ cm}^3)$$
$$\approx 108 \text{ cm}^3$$
$$\approx \mathbf{110 \text{ cm}^3}$$

16.
$$(6.3 \times 7) \times (10^6 \times 10^{-3})$$
$$= 44.1 \times 10^3$$
$$= \mathbf{4.41 \times 10^4}$$

17.
$$s^2 = (40 \text{ yd})^2 + (30 \text{ yd})^2$$
$$s^2 = 1600 \text{ yd}^2 + 900 \text{ yd}^2$$
$$s^2 = 2500 \text{ yd}^2$$
$$s = 50 \text{ yd}$$
$$(40 \text{ yd} + 30 \text{ yd}) - 50 \text{ yd} = \mathbf{20 \text{ yards}}$$

18. (a)

$$A = \frac{1}{2}bh$$
$$\left(\frac{2}{1}\right)A = \frac{2}{1}\left(\frac{1}{2}bh\right)$$
$$2A = bh$$
$$\frac{2A}{b} = \frac{bh}{b}$$
$$\mathbf{\frac{2A}{b} = h}$$

(b)

$$h = \frac{2(16)}{8}$$
$$h = 2(2)$$
$$h = \mathbf{4}$$

19. See student work;

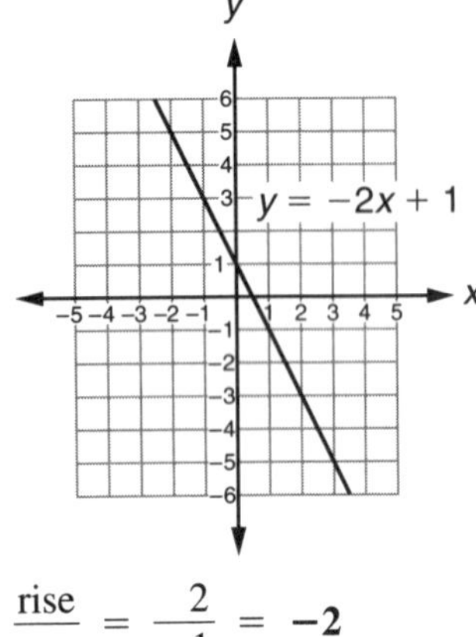

$$\frac{\text{rise}}{\text{run}} = \frac{2}{-1} = \mathbf{-2}$$

20. Area of base $= (40\text{ m})(40\text{ m}) = 1600\text{ m}^2$

Volume $= \frac{1}{3}(1600\text{ m}^2)(30\text{ m})$

$= \mathbf{16{,}000\ m^3}$

21. Area of base $\approx 3.14(100\text{ cm}^2) \approx 314\text{ cm}^2$

Volume $\approx \frac{1}{3}(314\text{ cm}^2)(60\text{ cm})$

$\approx \mathbf{6280\ cm^3}$

22. (a) $m\angle D = 180° - (90° + 30°) = \mathbf{60°}$

(b) $m\angle E = m\angle D = \mathbf{60°}$

(c) $m\angle A = m\angle C = \mathbf{30°}$

23.

$$\frac{4\text{ cm}}{6\text{ cm}} = \frac{8\text{ cm}}{CD}$$
$$(4\text{ cm})CD = 48\text{ cm}^2$$
$$CD = \mathbf{12\ cm}$$

24.

$$\frac{7.5}{d} = \frac{25}{16}$$
$$25d = 120$$
$$d = \mathbf{4.8}$$

25.

$$1\frac{3}{5}w + 17 = 49$$
$$1\frac{3}{5}w + 17 - 17 = 49 - 17$$
$$1\frac{3}{5}w = 32$$
$$\left(\frac{5}{8}\right)\frac{8}{5}w = \left(\frac{5}{8}\right)32$$
$$w = \mathbf{20}$$

26.

$$5^2 - \{4^2 - [3^2 - (2^2 - 1^2)]\}$$
$$25 - \{16 - [9 - (4 - 1)]\}$$
$$25 - \{16 - [9 - (3)]\}$$
$$25 - \{16 - [6]\}$$
$$25 - \{10\}$$
$$\mathbf{15}$$

27.

$$\frac{\overset{22}{\cancel{440}}\text{ yd}}{1\text{ min}} \cdot \frac{1\text{ min}}{\underset{\underset{1}{20}}{\cancel{60}}\text{ s}} \cdot \frac{\overset{1}{\cancel{3}}\text{ ft}}{1\text{ yd}} = \mathbf{22\ \frac{ft}{s}}$$

28.

$$1\frac{3}{4} + 2\frac{2}{3} - 3\frac{5}{6}$$
$$= 1\frac{9}{12} + 2\frac{8}{12} - 3\frac{10}{12} = \mathbf{\frac{7}{12}}$$

29.

$$\left(1\frac{3}{4}\right)\left(2\frac{2}{3}\right) \div 3\frac{5}{6}$$
$$= \left(\frac{7}{4} \cdot \frac{8}{3}\right) \div \frac{23}{6} = \frac{14}{3} \times \frac{6}{23}$$
$$= \frac{28}{23} = \mathbf{1\frac{5}{23}}$$

30.

$$(-7) + |-3| - (2)(-3) + (-4) - (-3)(-2)(-1)$$
$$(-7) + 3 - (-6) + (-4) - (-6)$$
$$-4 - (-6) + (-4) - (-6)$$
$$2 + (-4) - (-6)$$
$$-2 - (-6)$$
$$\mathbf{4}$$

Lesson 114, Lesson Practice

a.

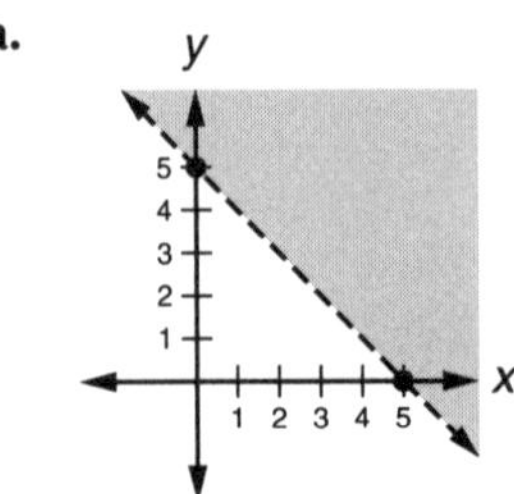

b.

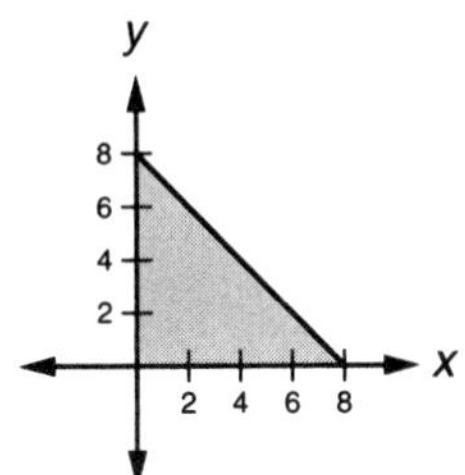

c.

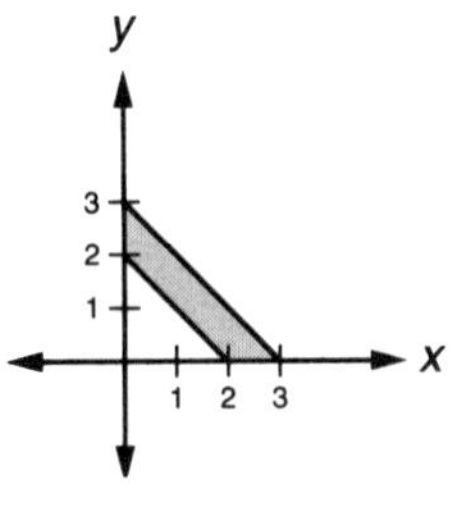

Lesson 114, Mixed Practice

1.

	Percent	Actual Count
Original	100	\$72.50
− Change	20	C
New	80	N

$$\frac{100}{80} = \frac{\$72.50}{N}$$
$$100N = \$5800$$
$$N = \$58$$

$$\begin{array}{r} \$58.00 \\ \times \quad 0.07 \\ \hline \$4.06 \end{array} \qquad \begin{array}{r} \$58.00 \\ + \quad \$4.06 \\ \hline \mathbf{\$62.06} \end{array}$$

2. $4(87) = 348,\ 6(90) = 540$

$540 - 348 = 192,\ \dfrac{192}{2} = \mathbf{96}$

3. (a) $P(B) = \dfrac{12}{27} = \mathbf{\dfrac{4}{9}}$

(b) $\mathbf{33\frac{1}{3}\%}$

(c) **7 to 2**

4. $\dfrac{\$10.80}{144 \text{ pencils}} = \dfrac{\$0.075}{1 \text{ pencil}}$

$\mathbf{7\frac{1}{2}}$**¢ per pencil**

5.

$$\begin{array}{r} \$5000 \\ \times \quad 0.08 \\ \hline \$400 \end{array}$$

$\dfrac{6}{12} = \dfrac{1}{2},\ \dfrac{\$400}{2} = \mathbf{\$200}$

6. (a) **Class Test Scores**

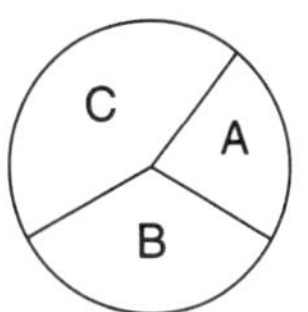

(b) $6(4 \text{ students}) = 24 \text{ students}$

$\dfrac{24 \text{ students}}{3} = 8 \text{ students}$

$24 \text{ students} - (8 \text{ students} + 6 \text{ students})$
$= \mathbf{10 \text{ students}}$

7.

	Ratio	Actual Count
Cars	5	C
Trucks	2	T
Total	7	3500

$$\frac{5}{7} = \frac{C}{3500}$$
$$7C = 17{,}500$$
$$C = \mathbf{2500 \text{ cars}}$$

8. $\text{Volume} \approx \dfrac{4}{3}(3)(2 \text{ ft})^3$

$\approx 4(8 \text{ ft}^3)$

$\approx \mathbf{32 \text{ ft}^3}$

9. $\mathbf{W_N = 1.2 \times \$240}$

$W_N = \mathbf{\$288}$

10. $\mathbf{60 = W_P \times 150}$

$$\frac{60}{150} = \frac{W_P \times 150}{150}$$
$$\frac{2}{5} = W_P$$
$$W_P = \frac{2}{5} \times 100\% = \mathbf{40\%}$$

11.

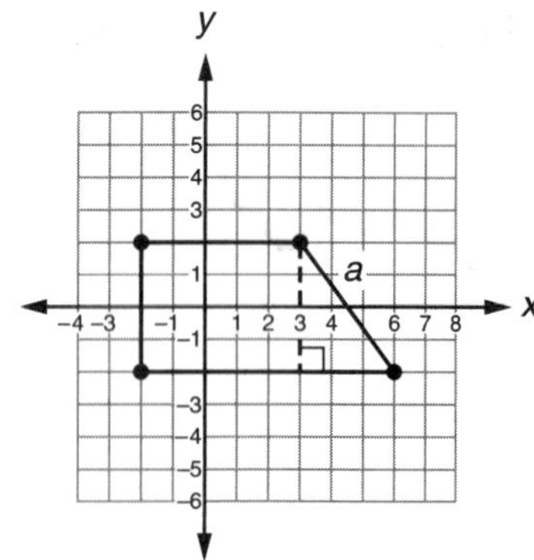

(a) Area of triangle $= \dfrac{(3 \text{ units})(4 \text{ units})}{2}$
$= 6 \text{ units}^2$
Area of rectangle $= (5 \text{ units})(4 \text{ units})$
$= 20 \text{ units}^2$
Area of figure $= 6 \text{ units}^2 + 20 \text{ units}^2$
$= \mathbf{26 \text{ units}^2}$

(b)
$$a^2 = (4 \text{ units})^2 + (3 \text{ units})^2$$
$$a^2 = 16 \text{ units}^2 + 9 \text{ units}^2$$
$$a^2 = 25 \text{ units}^2$$
$$a = 5 \text{ units}$$
Perimeter $= 5 \text{ units} + 8 \text{ units}$
$+ 4 \text{ units} + 5 \text{ units}$
$= \mathbf{22 \text{ units}}$

12. (a) $\mathbf{-6, 0.6, \sqrt{6}, 6^2}$

(b) $\mathbf{6^2, -6, 0.6}$

13. (a) **1.8**

(b) **180%**

14. (a) $2\overline{)5.0}$ = 2.5 $\quad \mathbf{2.5 \times 10^{-3}}$

(b) $5\overline{)2.0}$ = 0.4 $\quad 0.4 \times 10^3 \longrightarrow \mathbf{4 \times 10^2}$

15. $10 \times 10^{-1} = \mathbf{1}$

16. 12 ~~inches~~ $\cdot \dfrac{2.54 \text{ centimeters}}{1 \text{ ~~inch~~}}$
$= \mathbf{30.48 \text{ centimeters}}$

17. (a)
$$C = \pi d$$
$$\frac{C}{\pi} = \frac{\pi d}{\pi}$$
$$\frac{C}{\pi} = d$$

(b)
$$\frac{62.8}{3.14} \approx d$$
$$\mathbf{20} \approx d$$

18.

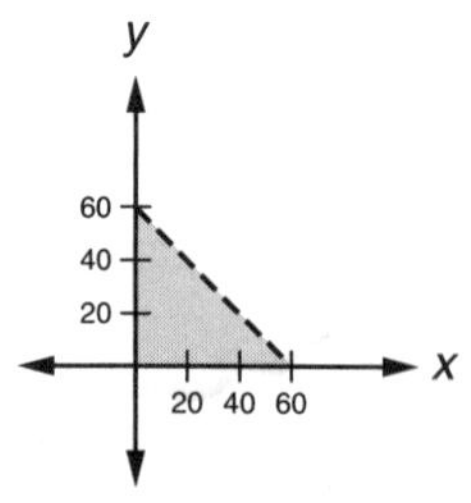

$\mathbf{x + y < 60}$

19. $C \approx \dfrac{3.14(6 \text{ cm})}{2}$
$C \approx 9.42 \text{ cm}$

$$a^2 = (6 \text{ cm})^2 + (8 \text{ cm})^2$$
$$a^2 = 36 \text{ cm}^2 + 64 \text{ cm}^2$$
$$a^2 = 100 \text{ cm}^2$$
$$a = 10 \text{ cm}$$
Perimeter $\approx 9.42 \text{ cm} + 10 \text{ cm} + 8 \text{ cm}$
$\approx \mathbf{27.42 \text{ cm}}$

20. (a) Surface area $= 6(3 \text{ ft} \times 3 \text{ ft})$
$= 6(9 \text{ ft}^2) = \mathbf{54 \text{ ft}^2}$

(b) Volume $= \dfrac{1}{3}(9 \text{ ft}^2)(3 \text{ ft}) = \mathbf{9 \text{ ft}^3}$

21. Area of base $\approx 3.14(25 \text{ m}^2)$
$\approx 78.5 \text{ m}^2$
Volume $\approx (78.5 \text{ m}^2)(3 \text{ m}) \approx \mathbf{235.5 \text{ m}^3}$

22. (a) $m\angle ACB = 180° - 130° = \mathbf{50°}$

(b) $m\angle CAB = 180° - (90° + 30°) = \mathbf{40°}$

(c) $m\angle CED = m\angle ECD$
$= 180° - 130° = 50°$
$m\angle CDE = 180° - (50° + 50°) = \mathbf{80°}$

23. Volume $= (40 \text{ cm})(10 \text{ cm})(20 \text{ cm})$
$= \mathbf{8000 \text{ cm}^3}$

24.
$$0.8m - 1.2 = 6$$
$$0.8m - 1.2 + 1.2 = 6 + 1.2$$
$$0.8m = 7.2$$
$$\frac{0.8m}{0.8} = \frac{7.2}{0.8}$$
$$m = \mathbf{9}$$

25.

$$3(x - 4) < x - 8$$
$$3x - 12 < x - 8$$
$$3x - 12 + 12 < x - 8 + 12$$
$$3x < x + 4$$
$$3x - x < x + 4 - x$$
$$2x < 4$$
$$\frac{2x}{2} < \frac{4}{2}$$
$$\mathbf{x < 2}$$

$x < 2$

−2 −1 0 1 2 3

26. $4^2 \cdot 2^{-3} \cdot 2^{-1} = \overset{1}{\cancel{16}} \cdot \frac{1}{\underset{1}{\cancel{8}}} \cdot \frac{1}{\underset{1}{\cancel{2}}} = \mathbf{1}$

27. 1 kilogram = 1000 grams
1000 grams − 50 grams = **950 grams**

28. $1\frac{2}{10}\left(3\frac{3}{4}\right) \div 4\frac{1}{2} = \left(\frac{\overset{3}{\cancel{12}}}{\underset{2}{\cancel{10}}} \cdot \frac{\overset{3}{\cancel{15}}}{\underset{1}{\cancel{4}}}\right) \div \frac{9}{2}$

$= \frac{\overset{1}{\cancel{9}}}{\underset{1}{\cancel{2}}} \cdot \frac{\overset{1}{\cancel{2}}}{\underset{1}{\cancel{9}}} = \mathbf{1}$

29. $2\frac{3}{4} - 1\frac{1}{2} - \frac{1}{6} = 2\frac{9}{12} - 1\frac{6}{12} - \frac{2}{12}$

$= \mathbf{1\frac{1}{12}}$

30.

$$(-3)(-2) - (2)(-3) - (-8) + (-2)(-3) + |-5|$$
$$(6) - (-6) - (-8) + (6) + (5)$$
$$12 - (-8) + 6 + (5)$$
$$20 + 6 + 5$$
$$\mathbf{31}$$

Lesson 115, Lesson Practice

a. **2 kg or 2000 g**

b. **3000 cm^3**

c. **1000 milliliters**

d. Volume = (25 cm)(10 cm)(8 cm)
= 2000 cm^3 = 2000 mL
= **2 liters**

Lesson 115, Mixed Practice

1.

$$\begin{array}{r} \$7000 \\ \times\ 0.08 \\ \hline \$560 \end{array}$$

$\frac{9}{12} = \frac{3}{4}, \frac{3}{4}(\$560) = \mathbf{\$420}$

2. (a) $P(H, H) = \frac{1}{2} \cdot \frac{1}{2} = \mathbf{\frac{1}{4}}$

(b) **25%**

(c) **1 to 3**

3. 4(410) = 1640
1640 miles + 600 miles = 2240 miles

$\frac{2240 \text{ miles}}{5 \text{ days}} = \mathbf{448\ \frac{mi}{day}}$

4. $\frac{\$2.16}{18 \text{ ounces}} = \frac{\$0.12}{1 \text{ ounce}}$

$\frac{\$3.36}{32 \text{ ounces}} = \frac{\$0.105}{1 \text{ ounce}}$

$$\begin{array}{r} \$0.120 \\ -\ \$0.105 \\ \hline \$0.015 \end{array}$$

$\mathbf{1\frac{1}{2}}$**¢ more per ounce**

5.

	Case 1	Case 2
Words	160	800
Minutes	5	m

$\frac{160}{5} = \frac{800}{m}$

$160m = 4000$

$m =$ **25 minutes**

6.

	Ratio	Actual Count
Guinea pigs	7	G
Rats	5	R
Total	12	120

$\frac{7}{12} = \frac{G}{120}$

$12G = 840$

$G =$ **70 guinea pigs**

7.

$$\frac{3}{4}x = 48$$
$$\left(\frac{4}{3}\right)\frac{3}{4}x = \left(\frac{4}{3}\right)48$$
$$x = 64$$
$$\frac{5}{8}(64) = \mathbf{40}$$

8.

	Percent	Actual Count
Original	100	\$1500
+ Change	40	C
New	140	N

$$\frac{100}{140} = \frac{\$1500}{N}$$

$$100N = \$210{,}000$$

$$N = \$2100$$

$$\begin{array}{r} \$2100 \\ \times \quad 0.08 \\ \hline \$168 \end{array} \qquad \begin{array}{r} \$2100 \\ + \quad \$168 \\ \hline \mathbf{\$2268} \end{array}$$

9. 80% of 75% of \$80 $= (0.8)(0.75) \times \$80$
$= \mathbf{\$48}$

10.

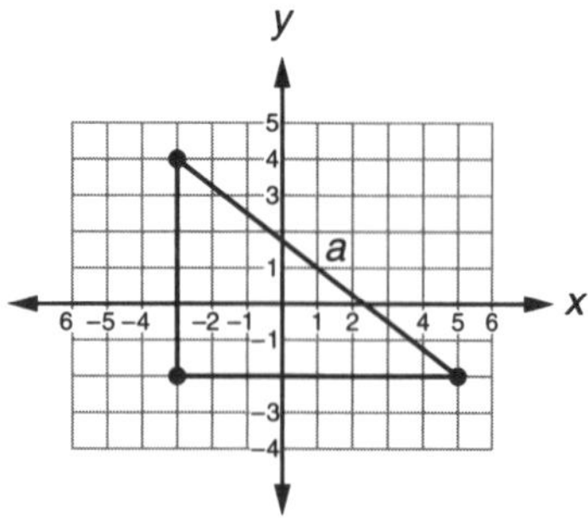

(a) Area $= \dfrac{(8 \text{ units})(6 \text{ units})}{2} = \mathbf{24 \text{ units}^2}$

(b)
$$a^2 = 64 \text{ units}^2 + 36 \text{ units}^2$$
$$a^2 = 100 \text{ units}^2$$
$$a = 10 \text{ units}$$
$$\text{Perimeter} = 10 \text{ units} + 8 \text{ units} + 6 \text{ units} = \mathbf{24 \text{ units}}$$

11. Volume $= (25 \text{ cm})(20 \text{ cm})(10 \text{ cm})$
$= 5000 \text{ cm}^3 = 5000 \text{ g} = 5 \text{ kg}$
$5 \text{ kg} + 5 \text{ kg} = \mathbf{10 \text{ kg}}$

12. (a) $\mathbf{\dfrac{7}{8}}$

(b) $\mathbf{87\dfrac{1}{2}\%}$

13. $a \div b \; \textcircled{<} \; a - b$

14. (a) $(6.4 \times 10^6)(8 \times 10^{-8})$
51.2×10^{-2}
$(5.12 \times 10^1) \times 10^{-2}$
$\mathbf{5.12 \times 10^{-1}}$

(b) $\dfrac{6.4 \times 10^6}{8 \times 10^{-8}}$

$$8\overline{)6.4} = 0.8$$

$10^6 \div 10^{-8} = 10^{14} \longleftarrow [6 - (-8) = 14]$
0.8×10^{14}
$(8 \times 10^{-1}) \times 10^{14}$
8×10^{13}

15. **36 ~~inches~~ $\cdot$ $\dfrac{\textbf{2.54 centimeters}}{\textbf{1 ~~inch~~}}$**
= 91.44 centimeters

16. (a)
$$A = \frac{1}{2}bh$$
$$\left(\frac{2}{1}\right)A = \left(\frac{2}{1}\right)\frac{1}{2}bh$$
$$2A = bh$$
$$\frac{2A}{h} = \frac{bh}{h}$$
$$\frac{2A}{h} = b$$

(b)
$$\frac{2(24)}{6} = b$$
$$\mathbf{8} = b$$

17. See student work;

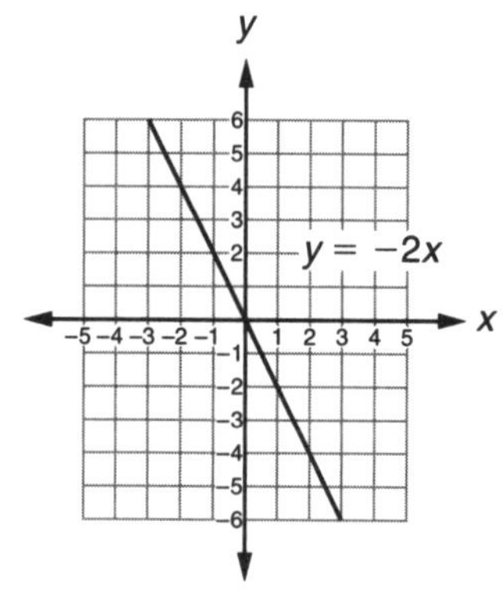

$$\frac{\text{rise}}{\text{run}} = \frac{2}{-1} = \mathbf{-2}$$

18. $A \approx \dfrac{3.14(4 \text{ mm}^2)}{2}$
$A \approx 6.28 \text{ mm}^2$

Area of square	=	(6 mm)(6 mm)
	=	36 mm²
− Area of semicircle	≈	6.28 mm²
Area of figure	≈	**29.72 mm²**

19. (a) $6(100 \text{ cm} \times 100 \text{ cm}) = 6(10{,}000 \text{ cm}^2) = \mathbf{60{,}000 \text{ cm}^2}$

(b) $\text{Volume} = (100 \text{ cm})(100 \text{ cm})(100 \text{ cm}) = \mathbf{1{,}000{,}000 \text{ cm}^3}$

(c) **1 m**

20. (a)
$$\begin{aligned}\text{Area of base} &= \pi(15 \text{ in.})^2\\ &= 225\pi \text{ in.}^2\\ \text{Volume} &= (225\pi \text{ in.}^2)(30 \text{ in.})\\ &= \mathbf{6750\pi \text{ in.}^3}\end{aligned}$$

(b)
$$\begin{aligned}\text{Volume} &= \frac{4}{3}\pi(15 \text{ in.})^3\\ &= \mathbf{4500\pi \text{ in.}^3}\end{aligned}$$

21. (a) $m\angle YXZ = 180° - (90° + 35°) = \mathbf{55°}$

(b) $m\angle WXV = 180° - (90° + 55°) = \mathbf{35°}$

(c) $m\angle WVX = 180° - (90° + 35°) = \mathbf{55°}$

22.
$$\begin{aligned}\frac{21}{14} &= \frac{12}{WV}\\ 21(WV) &= 168\\ WV &= \mathbf{8 \text{ cm}}\end{aligned}$$

23.
$$\begin{aligned}\text{Volume} &= \frac{1}{3}(6 \text{ in.} \times 6 \text{ in.} \times 6 \text{ in.})\\ &= \mathbf{72 \text{ in.}^3}\end{aligned}$$

24.
$$\begin{aligned}0.4n + 5.2 &= 12\\ 0.4n + 5.2 - 5.2 &= 12 - 5.2\\ 0.4n &= 6.8\\ \frac{0.4n}{0.4} &= \frac{6.8}{0.4}\\ n &= \mathbf{17}\end{aligned}$$

25.
$$\begin{aligned}\frac{18}{y} &= \frac{36}{28}\\ 36y &= 504\\ \frac{36y}{36} &= \frac{504}{36}\\ y &= \mathbf{14}\end{aligned}$$

26.
$$\begin{aligned}&\sqrt{5^2 - 3^2} + \sqrt{5^2 - 4^2}\\ &= \sqrt{25 - 9} + \sqrt{25 - 16} = \sqrt{16} + \sqrt{9}\\ &= 4 + 3 = \mathbf{7}\end{aligned}$$

27.

$\cancel{3}^{2}$ yd	($\cancel{3}^{2}$ ft)	(12 in.)
−	2 ft	1 in.

→

$\cancel{3}^{2}$ yd	$\cancel{3}^{2}$ ft	12 in.
−	2 ft	1 in.
2 yd		**11 in.**

28.
$$\begin{aligned}&3\frac{1}{2} \div \left(1\frac{2}{5} \div 3\right)\\ &= \frac{7}{2} \div \left(\frac{7}{5} \times \frac{1}{3}\right) = \frac{7}{2} \div \frac{7}{15}\\ &= \frac{\cancel{7}^{1}}{2} \times \frac{15}{\cancel{7}_{1}} = \frac{15}{2} = \mathbf{7\frac{1}{2}} \text{ or } \mathbf{7.5}\end{aligned}$$

29.
$$\begin{aligned}&3.5 + 2^{-2} - 2^{-3} = 3\frac{1}{2} + \frac{1}{4} - \frac{1}{8}\\ &= 3\frac{4}{8} + \frac{2}{8} - \frac{1}{8} = \mathbf{3\frac{5}{8}} \text{ or } \mathbf{3.625}\end{aligned}$$

30.
$$\begin{aligned}&\frac{(3)(-2)(4)}{(-6)(2)} + (-8) + (-4)(+5) - (2)(-3)\\ &\frac{(-6)(4)}{-12} + (-8) + (-20) - (-6)\\ &\frac{-24}{-12} + (-8) + (-20) - (-6)\\ &2 + (-8) + (-20) - (-6)\\ &-6 + (-20) - (-6)\\ &\mathbf{-20}\end{aligned}$$

Lesson 116, Lesson Practice

a. $8m^2n = \mathbf{(2)(2)(2)mmn}$

b. $12mn^2 = \mathbf{(2)(2)(3)mnn}$

c. $18x^3y^2 = \mathbf{(2)(3)(3)xxxyy}$

d.
$$\begin{aligned}&\frac{8m^2n}{4mn} + \frac{12mn^2}{4mn}\\ &2m + 3n\\ &\mathbf{4mn(2m + 3n)}\end{aligned}$$

e.
$$\begin{aligned}&\frac{8xy^2}{4xy} - \frac{4xy}{4xy}\\ &2y - 1\\ &\mathbf{4xy(2y - 1)}\end{aligned}$$

f.
$$\begin{aligned}&\frac{6a^2b^3}{3a^2b^2} + \frac{9a^3b^2}{3a^2b^2} + \frac{3a^2b^2}{3a^2b^2}\\ &2b + 3a + 1\\ &\mathbf{3a^2b^2(2b + 3a + 1)}\end{aligned}$$

Lesson 116, Mixed Practice

1. (a) $p(1,4) = \frac{1}{6} \cdot \frac{1}{6} = \frac{1}{36}$

$p(4,1) = \frac{1}{6} \cdot \frac{1}{6} = \frac{1}{36}$

$p(2,3) = \frac{1}{6} \cdot \frac{1}{6} = \frac{1}{36}$

$p(3,2) = \frac{1}{6} \cdot \frac{1}{6} = \frac{1}{36}$

$4\left(\frac{1}{36}\right) = \frac{1}{9} = 0.\overline{11}$, **0.11**

(b) **25%**

(c) **1 to 35**

2. 2^{10} bytes = **1024 bytes**

3. **The better sale seems to be the "40% of" sale, which is 60% off the regular price. Sixty percent off is better than forty percent off.**

4. (a) $\mathbf{1\frac{3}{4}}$

(b) **1.75**

(c) $\mathbf{0.08\overline{3}}$

(d) $\mathbf{8\frac{1}{3}\%}$

5.

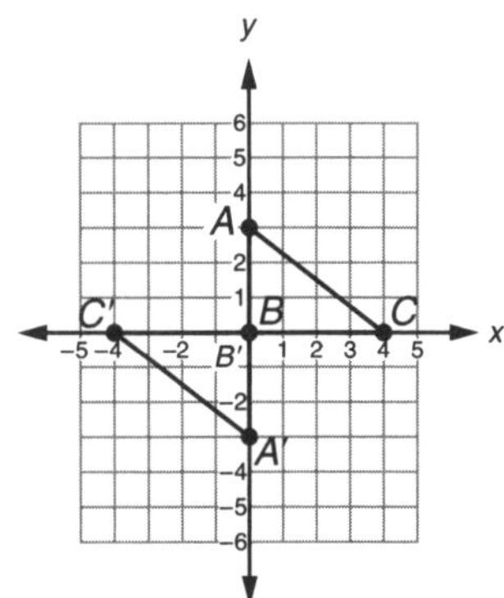

A′(0, −3), B′(0, 0), C′(−4, 0)

6. Exterior angle: $\frac{360°}{20} = \mathbf{18°}$

Interior angle: $180° - 18° = \mathbf{162°}$

7.

	Percent	Actual Count
Original	100	O
− Change	30	C
New	70	$42

$\frac{30}{70} = \frac{C}{\$42}$

$70C = \$1260$

$C = \mathbf{\$18}$

8. (a) Volume = (40 cm)(20 cm)(30 cm)

= 24,000 cm^3 = 24,000 mL

24,000 mL = **24 liters**

(b) **24 kg**

9. **24 ~~kg~~ · $\frac{2.2 \text{ lb}}{1 \text{ kg}}$ = 52.8 lb**

10.
$$\mathbf{2x - 6 = 48}$$
$$2x - 6 + 6 = 48 + 6$$
$$2x = 54$$
$$\frac{2x}{2} = \frac{54}{2}$$
$$x = \mathbf{27}$$

11.
$$(8x - 8) + (7x + 8) + (6x + 12) = 180$$
$$21x + 12 = 180$$
$$21x + 12 - 12 = 180 - 12$$
$$21x = 168$$
$$\frac{21x}{21} = \frac{168}{21}$$
$$x = 8°$$
$$7(8°) + 8 = \mathbf{64°}$$

12.
$$F = 1.8C + 32$$
$$F - 32 = 1.8C + 32 - 32$$
$$F - 32 = 1.8C$$
$$\frac{F - 32}{1.8} = \frac{1.8C}{1.8}$$
$$\mathbf{\frac{F - 32}{1.8} = C}$$

13.
$$C \approx \frac{3.14(40 \text{ in.})}{2}$$
$$C \approx 62.8 \text{ in.}$$
Perimeter ≈ 62.8 in. + 66 in. + 66 in.

≈ 194.8 in. ≈ **195 in.**

14.
$$a^2 = (15\text{ cm})^2 + (20\text{ cm})^2$$
$$a^2 = 225\text{ cm}^2 + 400\text{ cm}^2$$
$$a^2 = 625\text{ cm}^2$$
$$a = 25\text{ cm}$$

$$\text{Area of triangle} = \frac{(20\text{ cm})(15\text{ cm})}{2} = 150\text{ cm}^2$$
$$\text{Area of triangle} = \frac{(20\text{ cm})(15\text{ cm})}{2} = 150\text{ cm}^2$$
$$\text{Area of rectangle} = (20\text{ cm})(20\text{ cm}) = 400\text{ cm}^2$$
$$\text{Area of rectangle} = (15\text{ cm})(20\text{ cm}) = 300\text{ cm}^2$$
$$+\ \text{Area of rectangle} = (20\text{ cm})(25\text{ cm}) = 500\text{ cm}^2$$
$$\text{Total surface area} = \mathbf{1500\text{ cm}^2}$$

15.
$$\text{Volume} = (150\text{ cm}^2)(20\text{ cm}) = \mathbf{3000\text{ cm}^3}$$

16. (a) $\frac{\text{rise}}{\text{run}} = \frac{1}{1} = \mathbf{1;}$
(0, −2)

(b) $\frac{\text{rise}}{\text{run}} = \frac{2}{-1} = \mathbf{-2;}$
(0, 4)

17.
$$A = \frac{1}{2}(12\text{ cm} + 18\text{ cm})8\text{ cm}$$
$$= \frac{1}{2}(30\text{ cm})8\text{ cm}$$
$$= (15\text{ cm})\ 8\text{ cm}$$
$$= \mathbf{120\text{ cm}^2}$$

18.
$$3x^2 - 5 = 40$$
$$3x^2 - 5 + 5 = 40 + 5$$
$$3x^2 = 45$$
$$\frac{3x^2}{3} = \frac{45}{3}$$
$$x^2 = 15$$
$$\mathbf{x = \sqrt{15}, -\sqrt{15}}$$

19. (a) $4\overline{)8}$ with quotient 2 $\quad \mathbf{2 \times 10^{-12}}$

(b) $8\overline{)4.0}$ with quotient 0.5 $\quad 0.5 \times 10^{12} \longrightarrow \mathbf{5 \times 10^{11}}$

20. **The product is 1 because the numbers are reciprocals.**

21. (a) $9x^2y = \mathbf{(3)(3)xxy}$

(b) $\frac{10a^2b}{5ab} + \frac{15a^2b^2}{5ab} + \frac{20abc}{5ab}$
$2a + 3ab + 4c$
$\mathbf{5ab(2a + 3ab + 4c)}$

22.
$$\text{Volume} \approx \frac{4}{3}(3.14)(6\text{ in.})^3$$
$$\approx \frac{4}{3}(3.14)(216\text{ in.}^3)$$
$$\approx 904.32\text{ in.}^3$$
$$\approx \mathbf{904\text{ in.}^3}$$

23. (a) $m\angle BCD = 180° - (90° + 25°) = 180° - 115° = \mathbf{65°}$

(b) $m\angle BAC = 180° - (25° + 90°) = \mathbf{65°}$

(c) $m\angle ACD = 180° - (90° + 65°) = \mathbf{25°}$

(d) **The three triangles are similar.**

24. $\frac{BD}{BC} = \mathbf{\frac{CD}{CA}}$

25.
$$x - 15 = x + 2x + 1$$
$$x - 15 = 3x + 1$$
$$x - 15 - x = 3x + 1 - x$$
$$-15 = 2x + 1$$
$$-15 - 1 = 2x + 1 - 1$$
$$-16 = 2x$$
$$\frac{-16}{2} = \frac{2x}{2}$$
$$\mathbf{-8} = x$$

26.
$$0.12(m - 5) = 0.96$$
$$0.12m - 0.6 = 0.96$$
$$0.12m - 0.6 + 0.6 = 0.96 + 0.6$$
$$0.12m = 1.56$$
$$\frac{0.12m}{0.12} = \frac{1.56}{0.12}$$
$$m = \mathbf{13}$$

27. $a(b - c) + b(c - a)$
$ab - ac + bc - ba$
$\mathbf{-ac + bc}$ or $\mathbf{bc - ac}$

28.
$$\frac{(8x^2y)(12x^3y^2)}{(4xy)(6y^2)}$$
$$\frac{\overset{1}{\cancel{2}} \cdot \overset{1}{\cancel{2}} \cdot \overset{1}{\cancel{2}} \cdot 2 \cdot 2 \cdot \overset{1}{\cancel{3}} \cdot \overset{1}{\cancel{x}} \cdot x \cdot x \cdot x \cdot x \cdot \overset{1}{\cancel{y}} \cdot \overset{1}{\cancel{y}} \cdot \overset{1}{\cancel{y}}}{\underset{1}{\cancel{2}} \cdot \underset{1}{\cancel{2}} \cdot \underset{1}{\cancel{2}} \cdot \underset{1}{\cancel{3}} \cdot \underset{1}{\cancel{x}} \cdot \underset{1}{\cancel{y}} \cdot \underset{1}{\cancel{y}} \cdot \underset{1}{\cancel{y}}}$$
$\mathbf{4x^4}$

29. (a) $(-3)^2 + (-2)(-3) - (-2)^3$
$9 + (6) - (-8)$
$15 - (-8)$
$\mathbf{23}$

(b) $\sqrt[3]{-8} + \sqrt[3]{8} = -2 + 2 = \mathbf{0}$

30. $AD = 1.2 \text{ units} - 0.75 \text{ unit}$
$= \mathbf{0.45 \text{ unit}}$

Lesson 117, Lesson Practice

a.
$$2x + y = 3$$
$$2x + y - 2x = 3 - 2x$$
$$y = 3 - 2x$$
$$\mathbf{y = -2x + 3}$$

b.
$$y - 3 = x$$
$$y - 3 + 3 = x + 3$$
$$\mathbf{y = x + 3}$$

c.
$$2x + y - 3 = 0$$
$$2x + y - 3 + 3 = 0 + 3$$
$$2x + y = 3$$
$$2x + y - 2x = 3 - 2x$$
$$y = 3 - 2x$$
$$y = \mathbf{-2x + 3}$$

d.
$$x + y = 4 - x$$
$$x + y - x = 4 - x - x$$
$$y = 4 - 2x$$
$$\mathbf{y = -2x + 4}$$

e.

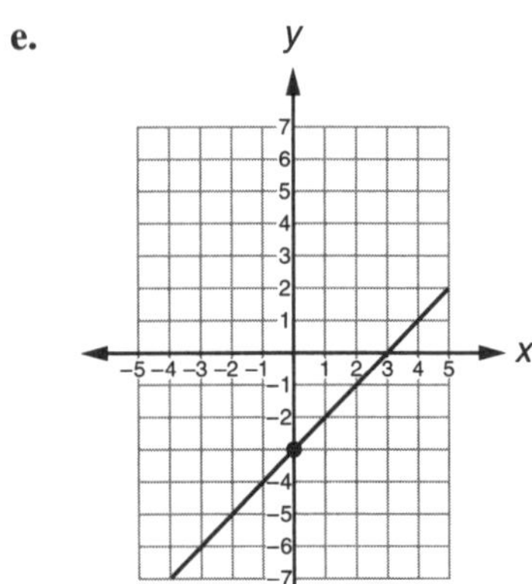

f.

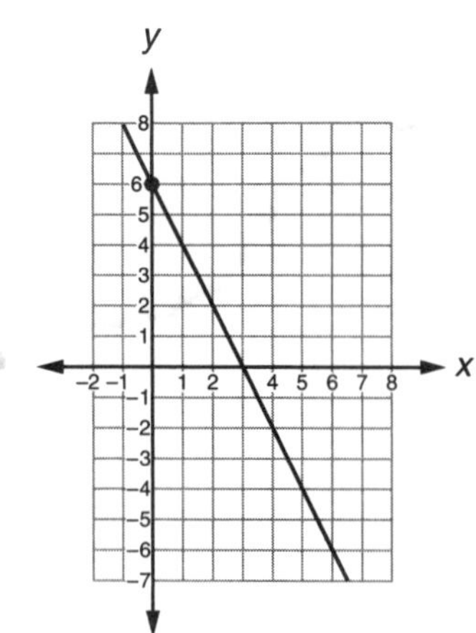

g.

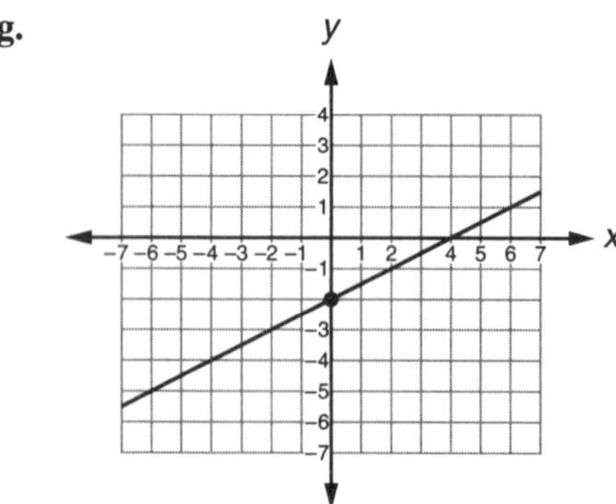

h.

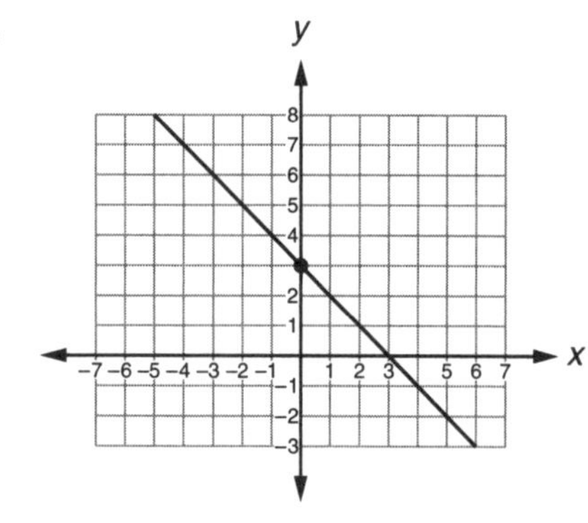

Lesson 117, Mixed Practice

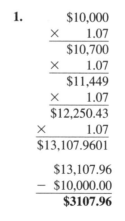

1.
$$\begin{array}{r} \$10{,}000 \\ \times \quad 1.07 \\ \hline \$10{,}700 \\ \times \quad 1.07 \\ \hline \$11{,}449 \\ \times \quad 1.07 \\ \hline \$12{,}250.43 \\ \times \quad 1.07 \\ \hline \$13{,}107.9601 \end{array}$$

$$\begin{array}{r} \$13{,}107.96 \\ -\ \$10{,}000.00 \\ \hline \mathbf{\$3107.96} \end{array}$$

2. (a) $\mathbf{\frac{1}{4}}$

(b) **1 to 3**

3. $4(75\%) + 6(85\%) = 810\%$

$$\frac{810\%}{10} = \mathbf{81\%}$$

4. (a) $\mathbf{1\frac{2}{5}}$

(b) **140%**

(c) $\mathbf{0.91\overline{6}}$

(d) $\mathbf{91\frac{2}{3}\%}$

5.

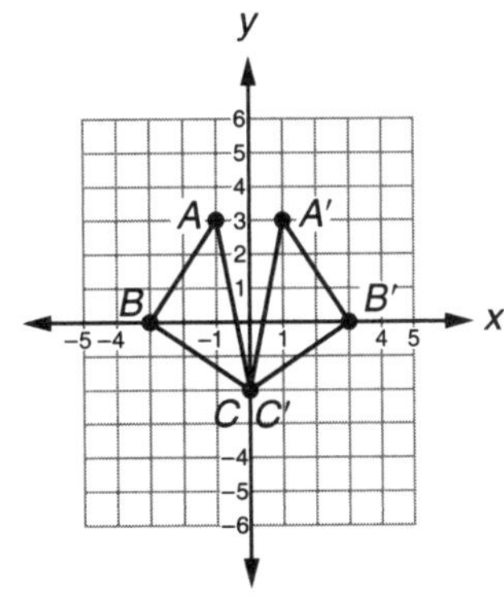

$\mathbf{A'(1, 3), B'(3, 0), C'(0, -2)}$

6. (a) $\frac{360°}{8} = \mathbf{45°}$

(b) $180° - 45° = \mathbf{135°}$

(c) **5 diagonals**

7.
$$\frac{100}{N} = \frac{1.2}{0.3}$$
$$1.2N = 30$$
$$N = \mathbf{25\%}$$

8. (a) **500 cubic centimeters**

(b) 500 mL = 500 g = **0.5 kilogram**

9. $\overset{\overset{60}{\cancel{180}}}{\cancel{540}}\text{ ft}^2 \cdot \frac{1\text{ yd}}{\underset{1}{\cancel{3}}\cancel{\text{ ft}}} \cdot \frac{1\text{ yd}}{\underset{1}{\cancel{3}}\cancel{\text{ ft}}} = \mathbf{60\ yd^2}$

10.
$$3x^2 + 6 = 81$$
$$3x^2 + 6 - 6 = 81 - 6$$
$$3x^2 = 75$$
$$\frac{3x^2}{3} = \frac{75}{3}$$
$$x^2 = 25$$
$$x = \mathbf{5, -5}$$

11.
$$(3x + 5) + (x - 5) = 180°$$
$$4x = 180°$$
$$\frac{4x}{4} = \frac{180°}{4}$$
$$x = 45°$$

$$2x + (x - 5) = 2(45°) + (45° - 5)$$
$$= 90° + 40° = 130°$$
$$m\angle y = 180 - 130° = \mathbf{50°}$$

12.
$$c^2 - a^2 = b^2$$
$$c^2 - a^2 + a^2 = b^2 + a^2$$
$$\mathbf{c^2 = b^2 + a^2} \text{ or } \mathbf{c^2 = a^2 + b^2}$$

13. (a) **0.25**

(b) $\mathbf{33\frac{1}{3}\%}$

(c) **1 to 5**

14.

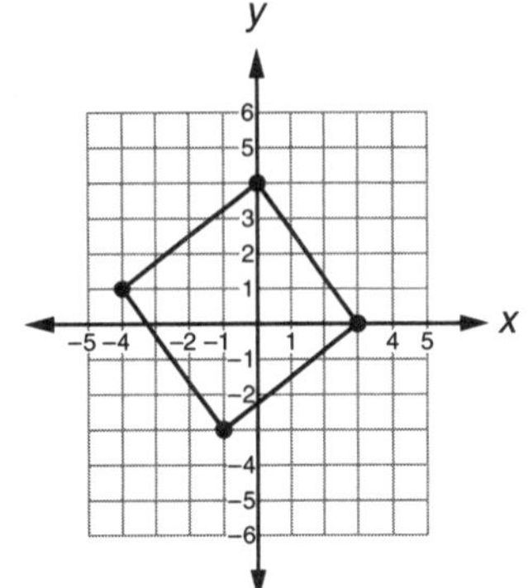

(a) **5 units**

(b) Perimeter = 4(5 units) = **20 units**

(c) Area = (5 units)(5 units) = **25 units²**

15. (a)
$$\text{Area of base} = \pi(3\text{ in.})^2$$
$$= 9\pi\text{ in.}^2$$
$$\text{Volume} = (9\pi\text{ in.}^2)(8\text{ in.})$$
$$= \mathbf{72\pi\ in.^3}$$

(b) $\text{Volume} = \frac{1}{3}(72\pi\text{ in.}^3) = \mathbf{24\pi\ in.^3}$

16. (a) $V = lwh$

$$\frac{V}{lw} = \frac{lwh}{lw}$$

$$\frac{V}{lw} = h$$

(b) $h = \dfrac{\overset{10}{\cancel{6000}}\ \text{cm}^{\cancel{3}}}{(\underset{1}{\cancel{20}}\ \cancel{\text{cm}})(\underset{1}{\cancel{30}}\ \cancel{\text{cm}})} = \mathbf{10\ cm}$

17. (a) $\dfrac{\text{rise}}{\text{run}} = \dfrac{2}{1} = \mathbf{2}$

(b) **(0, 4)**

(c) $\boldsymbol{y = 2x + 4}$

18. (a)

$$y + 5 = x$$
$$y + 5 - 5 = x - 5$$
$$\boldsymbol{y = x - 5}$$

(b)

$$2x + y = 4$$
$$2x + y - 2x = 4 - 2x$$
$$\boldsymbol{y = -2x + 4}$$

19. (a) $24xy^2 = \mathbf{(2)(2)(2)(3)}xyy$

(b) $\dfrac{3x^2}{3x} + \dfrac{6xy}{3x} - \dfrac{9x}{3x}$

$x + 2y - 3$

$\boldsymbol{3x(x + 2y - 3)}$

20. (a) $(5 \times 10^3\ \text{mm})(5 \times 10^3\ \text{mm})$

$= 25 \times 10^6\ \text{mm}^2$

$= \mathbf{2.5 \times 10^7\ mm^2}$

(b) $\mathbf{25{,}000{,}000\ mm^2}$

21. $\overset{25}{\cancel{25{,}000{,}000}}\ \cancel{\text{mm}^2} \cdot \dfrac{1\ \text{m}}{\underset{1}{\cancel{1000}}\ \cancel{\text{mm}}} \cdot \dfrac{1\ \text{m}}{\underset{1}{\cancel{1000}}\ \cancel{\text{mm}}}$

$= \mathbf{25\ m^2}$

22. (a) **Side *BD***

(b) **Side *AD***

23. $\dfrac{5}{3}\ \text{in.} - \dfrac{5}{4}\ \text{in.} = \dfrac{20}{12}\ \text{in.} - \dfrac{15}{12}\ \text{in.} = \mathbf{\dfrac{5}{12}\ in.}$

24.

$$\frac{3}{4}x + 12 < 15$$
$$\frac{3}{4}x + 12 - 12 < 15 - 12$$
$$\frac{3}{4}x < 3$$
$$\left(\frac{4}{3}\right)\frac{3}{4}x < \left(\frac{4}{3}\right)3$$
$$\boldsymbol{x < 4}$$

$x < 4$

0 1 2 3 4 5

25.

$$6w - 3w + 18 = 9(w - 4)$$
$$3w + 18 = 9w - 36$$
$$3w + 18 - 18 = 9w - 36 - 18$$
$$3w = 9w - 54$$
$$3w - 9w = 9w - 54 - 9w$$
$$-6w = -54$$
$$\frac{-6w}{-6} = \frac{-54}{-6}$$
$$w = \mathbf{9}$$

26. $3x(x - 2y) + 2xy(x + 3)$

$3x^2 - 6xy + 2x^2y + 6xy$

$\boldsymbol{3x^2 + 2x^2y}$

27. $2^{-2} + 4^{-1} + \sqrt[3]{27} + (-1)^3$

$= \dfrac{1}{4} + \dfrac{1}{4} + 3 + (-1) = \dfrac{2}{4} + 2$

$= \mathbf{2\dfrac{1}{2}}$

28.

$$(-3) + (-2)[(-3)(-2) - (+4)] - (-3)(-4)$$
$$(-3) + (-2)[(6) - (+4)] - (12)$$
$$(-3) + (-2)[2] - (12)$$
$$(-3) + (-4) - (12)$$
$$\mathbf{-19}$$

29. $4\overline{)1.2}$ with quotient 0.3 $0.3 \times 10^{-9} \longrightarrow \mathbf{3 \times 10^{-10}}$

30.

$$\frac{36a^2b^3c}{12ab^2c}$$

$$\frac{\overset{1}{\cancel{2}} \cdot \overset{1}{\cancel{2}} \cdot \overset{1}{\cancel{3}} \cdot 3 \cdot \overset{1}{\cancel{a}} \cdot a \cdot \overset{1}{\cancel{b}} \cdot \overset{1}{\cancel{b}} \cdot b \cdot \overset{1}{\cancel{c}}}{\underset{1}{\cancel{2}} \cdot \underset{1}{\cancel{2}} \cdot \underset{1}{\cancel{3}} \cdot \underset{1}{\cancel{a}} \cdot \underset{1}{\cancel{b}} \cdot \underset{1}{\cancel{b}} \cdot \underset{1}{\cancel{c}}}$$

$\boldsymbol{3ab}$

Lesson 118, Lesson Practice

a. **Answers may vary. See student work.**

b. **Answers may vary. See student work.**

Lesson 118, Mixed Practice

1.

$$\frac{100}{C} = \frac{\$180{,}000}{\$9000}$$
$$\$180{,}000C = \$900{,}000$$
$$C = \mathbf{5\%}$$

2. $\dfrac{40 \text{ cm}}{100 \text{ cm}} = \dfrac{600 \text{ cm}}{l}$

$(40 \text{ cm})l = 60{,}000 \text{ cm}^2$

$l = 1500 \text{ cm}$

About 15 meters

3. **Armando can select a Pythagorean triplet like 3-4-5 to verify that he has formed a right angle. For example, he can measure and mark from a corner 3 meters along one line and 4 meters along a proposed perpendicular line. Then he can check to see whether it is 5 meters between the marks.**

4. $15 \text{ meters} \cdot \dfrac{3.28 \text{ feet}}{1 \text{ meter}} \approx 49.2 \text{ feet}$

$\approx \mathbf{49 \text{ feet}}$

5. $\dfrac{1}{120} = \dfrac{1.5}{x}$

$(1)x = (1.5)(120)$

$x = (1.5)(120)$

$x = 180 \text{ in.} = 15 \text{ ft}$

$A = (15 \text{ ft})(15 \text{ ft}) = \mathbf{225 \text{ ft}^2}$

6. (a) $\mathbf{\dfrac{1}{9}}$

(b) $\mathbf{8\dfrac{1}{3}\%}$

(c) **1 to 17**

7.

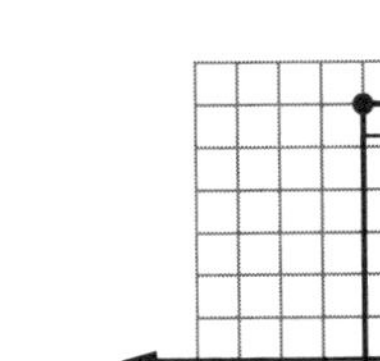

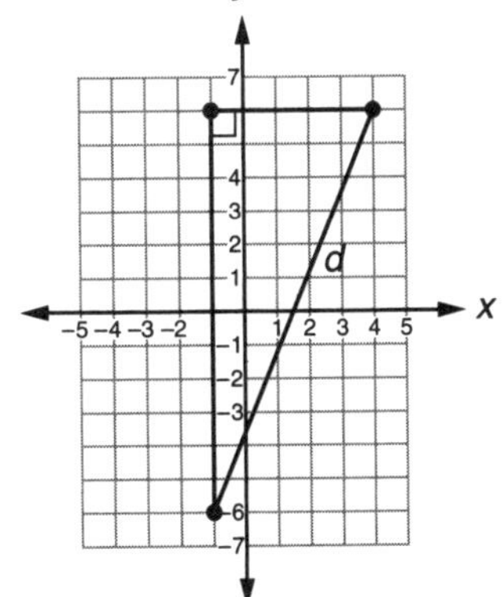

$d^2 = (12 \text{ units})^2 + (5 \text{ units})^2$

$d^2 = 144 \text{ units}^2 + 25 \text{ units}^2$

$d^2 = 169 \text{ units}^2$

$d = \mathbf{13 \text{ units}}$

8. (a) $2 \text{ L} = 2000 \text{ mL}$

$= \mathbf{2000 \text{ cubic centimeters}}$

(b) **2 kilograms**

9. $\mathbf{\dfrac{1}{2}x - \dfrac{2}{3} = \dfrac{5}{6}}$

$\dfrac{1}{2}x - \dfrac{2}{3} + \dfrac{2}{3} = \dfrac{5}{6} + \dfrac{2}{3}$

$\dfrac{1}{2}x = \dfrac{5}{6} + \dfrac{4}{6}$

$\dfrac{1}{2}x = \dfrac{9}{6}$

$\left(\dfrac{2}{1}\right)\dfrac{1}{2}x = \left(\dfrac{2}{1}\right)\left(\dfrac{9}{6}\right)$

$x = \dfrac{9}{3} = \mathbf{3}$

10. $\dfrac{200°}{2} = 100°$

$m\angle g = 180° - 100° = \mathbf{80°}$

11. $3x + y = 6$

$3x + y - 3x = 6 - 3x$

$y = 6 - 3x$

$\mathbf{y = -3x + 6}$

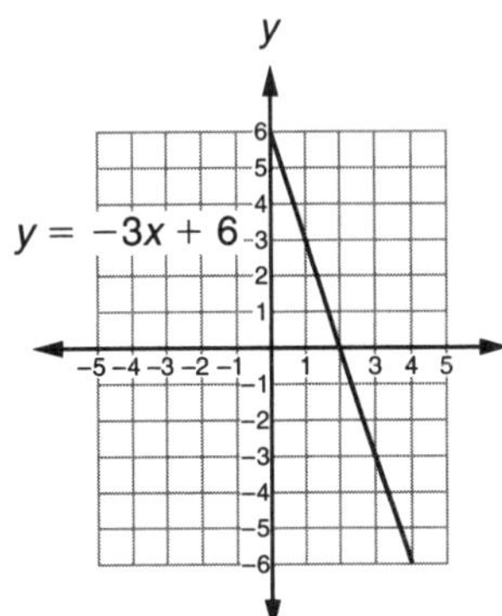

12. $(x + 30) + 3x + 2x = 180°$

$6x + 30 = 180°$

$6x + 30 - 30 = 180° - 30$

$6x = 150°$

$\dfrac{6x}{6} = \dfrac{150°}{6}$

$x = 25°$

$2x = 2(25°) = \mathbf{50°}$

13. Area of base $= (12 \text{ in.})(12 \text{ in.})$

$= 144 \text{ in.}^2$

Volume of pyramid $= \dfrac{1}{3}(144 \text{ in.}^2)(8 \text{ in.})$

$= 384 \text{ in.}^3$

Volume of cube $= (12 \text{ in.})(12 \text{ in.})(12 \text{ in.})$

$= 1728 \text{ in.}^3$

$384 \text{ in.}^3 + 1728 \text{ in.}^3 =$ **2112 cubic inches**

14. $\mathbf{AD = c - 12}$

15.
$$\frac{x}{20} = \frac{20}{25}$$
$$25x = 400$$
$$x = \mathbf{16}$$
$$y = 25 - 16$$
$$y = \mathbf{9}$$

16.
$$A \approx 4(3)(4\text{ cm})^2$$
$$\approx (12)(16\text{ cm}^2)$$
$$\approx \mathbf{192\text{ cm}^2}$$

17.
$$y - 2x + 5 = 1$$
$$y - 2x + 2x + 5 = 1 + 2x$$
$$y + 5 = 1 + 2x$$
$$y + 5 - 5 = 1 + 2x - 5$$
$$\mathbf{y = 2x - 4}$$

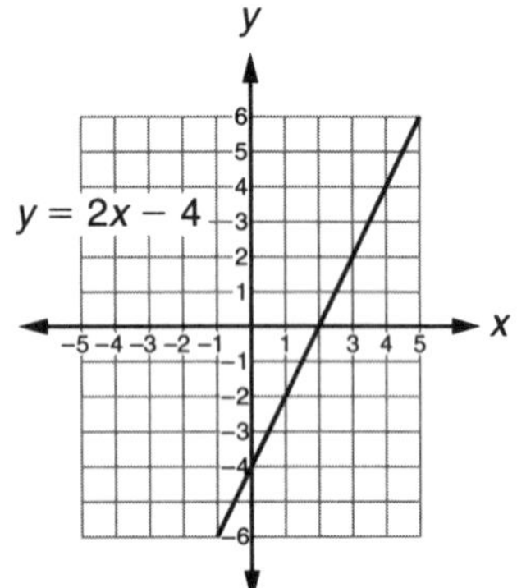

18. (a) $\frac{\text{rise}}{\text{run}} = \mathbf{\frac{1}{2}}$

(b) **−1**

(c) $\mathbf{y = \frac{1}{2}x - 1}$

19. **See student work.**

20.
$$C \approx \frac{\frac{22}{7}(7\text{ in.})}{2}$$
$$C \approx \frac{22\text{ in.}}{2}$$
$$C \approx 11\text{ in.}$$
$$\text{Perimeter} \approx 11\text{ in.} + 4\frac{1}{4}\text{ in.} + 4\frac{1}{4}\text{ in.}$$
$$+ 11\text{ in.} + 2\text{ in.} + 2\text{ in.}$$
$$\approx 26\text{ in.} + 8\frac{2}{4}\text{ in.} \approx \mathbf{34\frac{1}{2}\text{ in.}}$$

21. $\frac{1 \times 10^3}{1 \times 10^{-3}} = \mathbf{1 \times 10^6\text{ dimes}}$

22. (a)
$$\frac{x^2}{x} + \frac{x}{x}$$
$$x + 1$$
$$\mathbf{x(x + 1)}$$

(b)
$$\frac{12m^2n^3}{6mn^2} + \frac{18mn^2}{6mn^2} - \frac{24m^2n^2}{6mn^2}$$
$$2mn + 3 - 4m$$
$$\mathbf{6mn^2(2mn + 3 - 4m)}$$

23.
$$-2\frac{2}{3}w - 1\frac{1}{3} = 4$$
$$-2\frac{2}{3}w - 1\frac{1}{3} + 1\frac{1}{3} = 4 + 1\frac{1}{3}$$
$$-2\frac{2}{3}w = 5\frac{1}{3}$$
$$\left(-\frac{3}{8}\right)\left(-\frac{8}{3}w\right) = \left(-\frac{3}{8}\right)\left(\frac{16}{3}\right)$$
$$w = \mathbf{-2}$$

24.
$$5x^2 + 1 = 81$$
$$5x^2 + 1 - 1 = 81 - 1$$
$$5x^2 = 80$$
$$\frac{5x^2}{5} = \frac{80}{5}$$
$$x^2 = 16$$
$$x = \mathbf{4, -4}$$

25. $\left(\frac{1}{2}\right)^2 - 2^{-2} = \frac{1}{4} - \frac{1}{4} = \mathbf{0}$

26.
$$66\frac{2}{3}\% \text{ of } \frac{5}{6} \text{ of } 0.144$$
$$= 66\frac{2}{3}\% \text{ of } 0.12$$
$$= (0.66\overline{6})(0.12) = \mathbf{0.08} \text{ or } \mathbf{\frac{2}{25}}$$

27.
$$[-3 + (-4)(-5)] - [-4 - (-5)(-2)]$$
$$[-3 + (20)] - [-4 - (10)]$$
$$[17] - [-14]$$
$$\mathbf{31}$$

28.
$$\frac{(5x^2yz)(6xy^2z)}{10\,xyz}$$
$$\frac{\overset{1}{\cancel{2}} \cdot 3 \cdot \overset{1}{\cancel{5}} \cdot \overset{1}{\cancel{x}} \cdot x \cdot x \cdot \overset{1}{\cancel{y}} \cdot y \cdot y \cdot \overset{1}{\cancel{z}} \cdot z}{\underset{1}{\cancel{2}} \cdot \underset{1}{\cancel{5}} \cdot \underset{1}{\cancel{x}} \cdot \underset{1}{\cancel{y}} \cdot \underset{1}{\cancel{z}}}$$
$$\mathbf{3x^2y^2z}$$

29. $x(x + 2) + 2(x + 2)$
$x^2 + 2x + 2x + 4$
$\mathbf{x^2 + 4x + 4}$

30. $a^2 = (20\text{ mm})^2 + (10\text{ mm})^2$
$a^2 = 500\text{ mm}^2$
$a = \sqrt{500}\text{ mm}$
22 mm and 23 mm

Lesson 119, Lesson Practice

a. **A typical error message display is E 0. Error messages vary.**

b. **0 ÷ 0 = 7 is not a fact, because division by zero is not possible.**

c. $\mathbf{w \neq 0}$

d. $\mathbf{x \neq 1}$

e. $\mathbf{w \neq 0}$

f. $\mathbf{y \neq 3}$

g. $\mathbf{x \neq 2, -2}$

h. $\mathbf{c \neq 0}$

Lesson 119, Mixed Practice

1. $\frac{2}{50} = \frac{1}{25} = \mathbf{4\%}$

2. $\frac{100}{C} = \frac{\$20}{\$5}$
$\$20C = \$500$
$C = \mathbf{25\%}$

3. 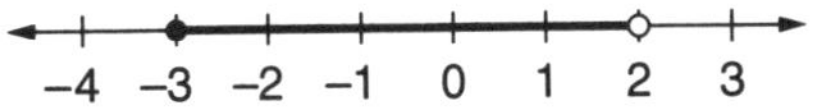 Number line from −4 to 3: closed dot at −3, open dot at 2, segment between.

4. **360°**

5. (a) $\mathbf{\frac{1}{200}}$

(b) **0.005**

(c) $\mathbf{0.\overline{8}}$

(d) $\mathbf{88\frac{8}{9}\%}$

6. (a) 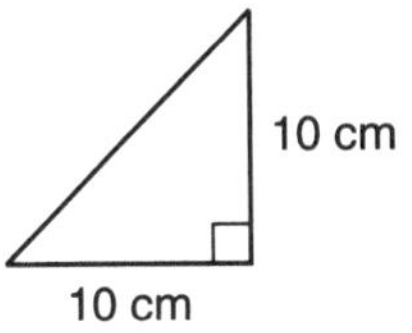 Right triangle with legs 10 cm and 10 cm.

(b) **45%**

(c) **14 cm**

7. $\frac{(6 \times 10^5)(2 \times 10^6)}{(3 \times 10^4)} = \frac{12 \times 10^{11}}{3 \times 10^4}$

$3\overline{)12}$ = 4 $\quad \mathbf{4 \times 10^7}$

8. (a) $\frac{2x^2}{x} + \frac{x}{x}$
$2x + 1$
$\mathbf{x(2x + 1)}$

(b) $\frac{3a^2b}{3a} - \frac{12a^2}{3a} + \frac{9ab^2}{3a}$
$ab - 4a + 3b^2$
$\mathbf{3a(ab - 4a + 3b^2)}$

9. Volume $= (3\text{ cm}^3) + 6(1\text{ cm}^3) + 9(1\text{ cm}^3)$
$= \mathbf{18\text{ cm}^3}$

10. Surface area $= 2(6\text{ cm}^2) + 6(3\text{ cm}^2) + 2(9\text{ cm}^2) = \mathbf{48\text{ cm}^2}$

11.
$$A = \frac{1}{2}bh$$
$$\left(\frac{2}{1}\right)A = \left(\frac{2}{1}\right)\frac{1}{2}bh$$
$$2A = bh$$
$$\frac{2A}{b} = \frac{bh}{b}$$
$$\mathbf{\frac{2A}{b} = h}$$
$$\frac{2(1.44\text{ m}^2)}{1.6\text{ m}} = h$$
$$\frac{2.88\text{ m}^2}{1.6\text{ m}} = h$$
$$\mathbf{1.8\text{ m}} = h$$

12. $\frac{\text{boys}}{\text{total}} = \frac{3}{8} \times 100\% = \mathbf{37\frac{1}{2}\%}$

13.
$$\begin{aligned} (6\text{ ft})^2 + h^2 &= (10\text{ ft})^2 \\ 36\text{ ft}^2 + h^2 &= 100\text{ ft}^2 \\ 36\text{ ft}^2 + h^2 - 36\text{ ft}^2 &= 100\text{ ft}^2 - 36\text{ ft}^2 \\ h^2 &= 64\text{ ft}^2 \\ h &= \mathbf{8\text{ ft}} \end{aligned}$$

14. (a) $\mathbf{y = 2x - 4}$

(b) $\mathbf{y = -\frac{1}{2}x + 1}$

15. **The product of the slopes is −1. The slopes are negative reciprocals.**

16.
$$\begin{array}{r} \$8000 \\ \times \quad 1.06 \\ \hline \$8480 \\ \times \quad 1.06 \\ \hline \$8988.80 \\ \times \quad 1.06 \\ \hline \$9528.1280 \\ \times \quad 1.06 \\ \hline \$10{,}099.81568 \end{array} \longrightarrow \mathbf{\$10{,}099.82}$$

17. $1250\ \cancel{\text{sq. ft}} \cdot \frac{1\text{ yd}}{3\ \cancel{\text{ft}}} \cdot \frac{1\text{ yd}}{3\ \cancel{\text{ft}}}$

$\approx$ **139 square yards**

18. (a) $\mathbf{w \neq 0}$

(b) $\mathbf{m \neq -3}$

19. $\mathbf{DA = c - x}$

20.
$$\begin{aligned} \frac{y}{20} &= \frac{15}{25} \\ 25y &= 300 \\ y &= 12\text{ in.} \\ (12\text{ in.})^2 + z^2 &= (15\text{ in.})^2 \\ 144\text{ in.}^2 + z^2 &= 225\text{ in.}^2 \\ 144\text{ in.}^2 + z^2 - 144\text{ in.}^2 & \\ &= 225\text{ in.}^2 - 144\text{ in.}^2 \\ z^2 &= 81\text{ in.}^2 \\ z &= 9\text{ in.} \\ \text{Area} &= \frac{(12\text{ in.})(9\text{ in.})}{2} = \mathbf{54\text{ in.}^2} \end{aligned}$$

21.
$$\begin{aligned} \text{Volume} &\approx \frac{4}{3}(3.14)(15\text{ cm})^3 \\ &\approx \frac{4}{3}(3.14)(3375\text{ cm}^3) \\ &\approx \mathbf{14{,}130\text{ cm}^3} \end{aligned}$$

22. **See student work.**

23.
$$\begin{aligned} \frac{2}{3}m + \frac{1}{4} &= \frac{7}{12} \\ \frac{2}{3}m + \frac{1}{4} - \frac{1}{4} &= \frac{7}{12} - \frac{1}{4} \\ \frac{2}{3}m &= \frac{7}{12} - \frac{3}{12} \\ \frac{2}{3}m &= \frac{4}{12} \\ \left(\frac{\cancel{3}^{1}}{\cancel{2}_{1}}\right)\left(\frac{\cancel{2}^{1}}{\cancel{3}_{1}}m\right) &= \left(\frac{\cancel{3}^{1}}{\cancel{2}_{1}}\right)\frac{\cancel{4}^{\cancel{2}^{1}}}{\cancel{12}_{\cancel{4}_{2}}} \\ m &= \mathbf{\frac{1}{2}} \end{aligned}$$

24.
$$\begin{aligned} 5(3 - x) &= 55 \\ 15 - 5x &= 55 \\ 15 - 5x - 15 &= 55 - 15 \\ -5x &= 40 \\ \frac{-5x}{-5} &= \frac{40}{-5} \\ x &= \mathbf{-8} \end{aligned}$$

25.
$$\begin{aligned} x + x + 12 &= 5x \\ 2x + 12 &= 5x \\ 2x + 12 - 12 &= 5x - 12 \\ 2x &= 5x - 12 \\ 2x - 5x &= 5x - 12 - 5x \\ -3x &= -12 \\ \frac{-3x}{-3} &= \frac{-12}{-3} \\ x &= \mathbf{4} \end{aligned}$$

26.
$$\begin{aligned} 10x^2 &= 100 \\ \frac{10x^2}{10} &= \frac{100}{10} \\ x^2 &= 10 \\ x &= \mathbf{\sqrt{10}, -\sqrt{10}} \end{aligned}$$

27. **300**

28.
$$\begin{aligned} &x(x + 5) - 2(x + 5) \\ &x^2 + 5x - 2x - 10 \\ &\mathbf{x^2 + 3x - 10} \end{aligned}$$

29. $\dfrac{(12xy^2z)(9x^2y^2z)}{36xyz^2}$

$$\frac{\overset{1}{\cancel{2}} \cdot \overset{1}{\cancel{2}} \cdot \overset{1}{\cancel{3}} \cdot \overset{1}{\cancel{3}} \cdot 3 \cdot \overset{1}{\cancel{x}} \cdot x \cdot x \cdot \overset{1}{\cancel{y}} \cdot y \cdot y \cdot y \cdot \overset{1}{\cancel{z}} \cdot \overset{1}{\cancel{z}}}{\underset{1}{\cancel{2}} \cdot \underset{1}{\cancel{2}} \cdot \underset{1}{\cancel{3}} \cdot \underset{1}{\cancel{3}} \cdot \underset{1}{\cancel{x}} \cdot \underset{1}{\cancel{y}} \cdot \underset{1}{\cancel{z}} \cdot \underset{1}{\cancel{z}}}$$

$\mathbf{3x^2y^3}$

30. $33\frac{1}{3}\%$ of 0.12 of $3\frac{1}{3}$

$$= \left(\frac{1}{3}\right) \times \left(\frac{\overset{4}{\cancel{12}}}{\underset{10}{\cancel{100}}} \cdot \frac{\overset{1}{\cancel{10}}}{\underset{1}{\cancel{3}}}\right)$$

$$= \frac{1}{3} \times \frac{4}{10} = \mathbf{\frac{2}{15}} \text{ or } \mathbf{0.1\overline{3}}$$

Lesson 120, Lesson Practice

a. **See student work.**

b. **See student work.**

c. **See student work.**

d. **See student work.**

Lesson 120, Mixed Practice

1. $P(\text{sum of } 7) = \frac{1}{6}$; **1 to 5**

2. $\dfrac{\$2.70}{1.08} = \mathbf{\$2.50}$

3. **Insufficient information**

4. **100°; 80°; 80°**

5. (a) $\mathbf{\dfrac{1}{1000}}$
(b) **0.001**
(c) **1.6**
(d) **160%**

6. (a)
$$\begin{aligned} a^2 + (1\text{ cm})^2 &= (2\text{ cm})^2 \\ a^2 + 1\text{ cm}^2 &= 4\text{ cm}^2 \\ a^2 + 1\text{ cm}^2 - 1\text{ cm}^2 &= 4\text{ cm}^2 - 1\text{ cm}^2 \\ a^2 &= 3\text{ cm}^2 \\ a &= \mathbf{\sqrt{3}\text{ cm}} \end{aligned}$$

(b) **1.7 cm**

7. $\dfrac{(4 \times 10^{-5})(6 \times 10^{-4})}{8 \times 10^3} = \dfrac{24 \times 10^{-9}}{8 \times 10^3}$

$8\overline{)24}$ with quotient 3 $\mathbf{3 \times 10^{-12}}$

8. (a) $\dfrac{3y^2}{y} - \dfrac{y}{y}$
$3y - 1$
$\mathbf{y(3y - 1)}$

(b) $\dfrac{6w^2}{3w} + \dfrac{9wx}{3w} - \dfrac{12w}{3w}$
$2w + 3x - 4$
$\mathbf{3w(2w + 3x - 4)}$

9. $\mathbf{\dfrac{1}{3}}$

10.
$$\begin{aligned} C &\approx (3.14)(6\text{ cm}) \\ C &\approx 18.84\text{ cm} \\ A &\approx (18.84\text{ cm})(6\text{ cm}) \\ &\approx 113.04\text{ cm}^2 \approx \mathbf{113\text{ cm}^2} \end{aligned}$$

11.
$$\begin{aligned} E &= mc^2 \\ \frac{E}{c^2} &= \frac{mc^2}{c^2} \\ \mathbf{\frac{E}{c^2}} &= \mathbf{m} \end{aligned}$$

12. $\dfrac{60}{100} = \dfrac{3}{5} = \dfrac{\text{girls}}{\text{total}}$
$\dfrac{\text{boys}}{\text{girls}} = \mathbf{\dfrac{2}{3}}$

13. line m: $\mathbf{y = -\frac{2}{3}x + 2}$

line n: $\mathbf{y = \frac{3}{2}x - 2}$

14. **The product of the slopes is −1. The slopes are negative reciprocals.**

15.
$$\left.\begin{array}{r} \$1000 \\ \times\ \ 1.2 \\ \hline \$1200 \end{array}\right\} \text{Year 1}$$
$$\left.\begin{array}{r} \times\ \ 1.2 \\ \hline \$1440 \end{array}\right\} \text{Year 2}$$
$$\left.\begin{array}{r} \times\ \ 1.2 \\ \hline \$1728 \end{array}\right\} \text{Year 3}$$
$$\left.\begin{array}{r} \times\ \ 1.2 \\ \hline \$2073.60 \end{array}\right\} \text{Year 4}$$

About 4 years

16.
$$\begin{aligned} d^2 &= (17 \text{ in.})^2 + (12 \text{ in.})^2 \\ d^2 &= 289 \text{ in.}^2 + 144 \text{ in.}^2 \\ d^2 &= 433 \text{ in.}^2 \\ d &= \sqrt{433 \text{ in.}^2} \\ d &\approx \mathbf{21 \text{ in.}} \end{aligned}$$

17. (a)
$$\begin{aligned} \text{Volume} &= (36 \text{ feet})(21 \text{ feet})\left(\frac{1}{2} \text{ feet}\right) \\ &= \mathbf{378 \text{ cubic feet}} \end{aligned}$$

(b)
$$\overset{14}{\cancel{378}} \text{ ft}^3 \cdot \frac{1 \text{ yd}}{\underset{1}{\cancel{3}} \cancel{\text{ft}}} \cdot \frac{1 \text{ yd}}{\underset{1}{\cancel{3}} \cancel{\text{ft}}} \cdot \frac{1 \text{ yd}}{\underset{1}{\cancel{3}} \cancel{\text{ft}}}$$
$$= \mathbf{14 \text{ cubic yards}}$$

18. (a) $\boldsymbol{m \neq 2}$

(b) $\boldsymbol{y \neq -5}$

19.

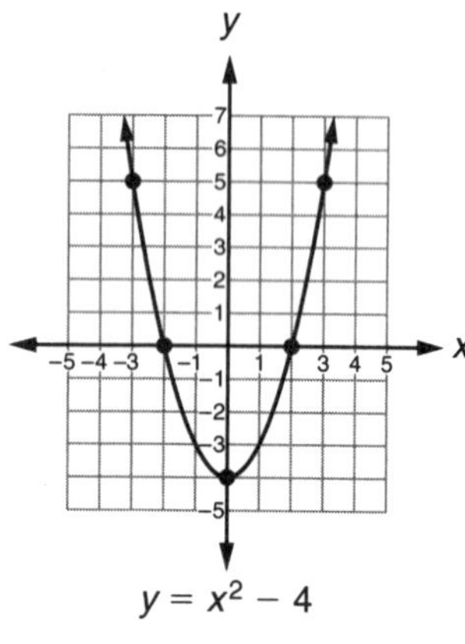

20. $\dfrac{c}{a} = \dfrac{a}{y}$

21.
$$\begin{aligned} \text{Surface area} &\approx 4(3.14)(3 \text{ in.})^2 \\ &\approx 4(3.14)(9 \text{ in.}^2) \\ &\approx 113.04 \text{ in.}^2 \\ &\approx \mathbf{113 \text{ in.}^2} \end{aligned}$$

22. 250 cubic centimeters = 250 mL = **0.25 liter**

23.
$$\begin{aligned} 15 + x &= 3x - 17 \\ 15 + x - 3x &= 3x - 17 - 3x \\ 15 - 2x &= -17 \\ 15 - 2x - 15 &= -17 - 15 \\ -2x &= -32 \\ \frac{-2x}{-2} &= \frac{-32}{-2} \\ x &= \mathbf{16} \end{aligned}$$

24.
$$\begin{aligned} 3\frac{1}{3}x - 16 &= 74 \\ 3\frac{1}{3}x - 16 + 16 &= 74 + 16 \\ 3\frac{1}{3}x &= 90 \\ \left(\frac{\overset{1}{\cancel{3}}}{\underset{1}{\cancel{10}}}\right)\left(\frac{\overset{1}{\cancel{10}}}{\underset{1}{\cancel{3}}}x\right) &= \left(\frac{3}{\underset{1}{\cancel{10}}}\right)\overset{9}{\cancel{90}} \\ x &= \mathbf{27} \end{aligned}$$

25.
$$\begin{aligned} \frac{m^2}{4} &= 9 \\ m^2 &= 36 \\ m &= \mathbf{6, -6} \end{aligned}$$

26.
$$\begin{aligned} \frac{1.2}{m} &= \frac{0.04}{8} \\ 0.04m &= 9.6 \\ \frac{0.04m}{0.04} &= \frac{9.6}{0.04} \\ m &= \mathbf{240} \end{aligned}$$

27.
$$\begin{aligned} &x(x - 5) - 2(x - 5) \\ &x^2 - 5x - 2x + 10 \\ &\mathbf{x^2 - 7x + 10} \end{aligned}$$

28.
$$\frac{(3xy)(4x^2y)(5x^2y^2)}{10x^3y^3}$$
$$\frac{\overset{1}{\cancel{2}} \cdot 2 \cdot 3 \cdot \overset{1}{\cancel{5}} \cdot \overset{1}{\cancel{x}} \cdot \overset{1}{\cancel{x}} \cdot \overset{1}{\cancel{x}} \cdot x \cdot x \cdot \overset{1}{\cancel{y}} \cdot \overset{1}{\cancel{y}} \cdot \overset{1}{\cancel{y}} \cdot y}{\underset{1}{\cancel{2}} \cdot \underset{1}{\cancel{5}} \cdot \underset{1}{\cancel{x}} \cdot \underset{1}{\cancel{x}} \cdot \underset{1}{\cancel{x}} \cdot \underset{1}{\cancel{y}} \cdot \underset{1}{\cancel{y}} \cdot \underset{1}{\cancel{y}}}$$
$$\mathbf{6x^2y}$$

29.
$$\begin{aligned} &|-8| + 3(-7) - [(-4)(-5) - 3(-2)] \\ &8 + (-21) - [(20) - (-6)] \\ &8 + (-21) - [26] \\ &\mathbf{-39} \end{aligned}$$

30.
$$\begin{aligned} \frac{7\frac{1}{2} - \frac{2}{3}(0.9)}{0.03} &= \frac{7\frac{1}{2} - \frac{\overset{1}{\cancel{2}}}{\underset{1}{\cancel{3}}}\left(\frac{\overset{3}{\cancel{9}}}{\underset{5}{\cancel{10}}}\right)}{0.03} \\ &= \frac{7\frac{1}{2} - \frac{3}{5}}{0.03} = \frac{7\frac{5}{10} - \frac{6}{10}}{0.03} \\ &= \frac{6\frac{15}{10} - \frac{6}{10}}{0.03} = \frac{6\frac{9}{10}}{0.03} \\ &= \frac{6.9}{0.03} = \mathbf{230} \end{aligned}$$